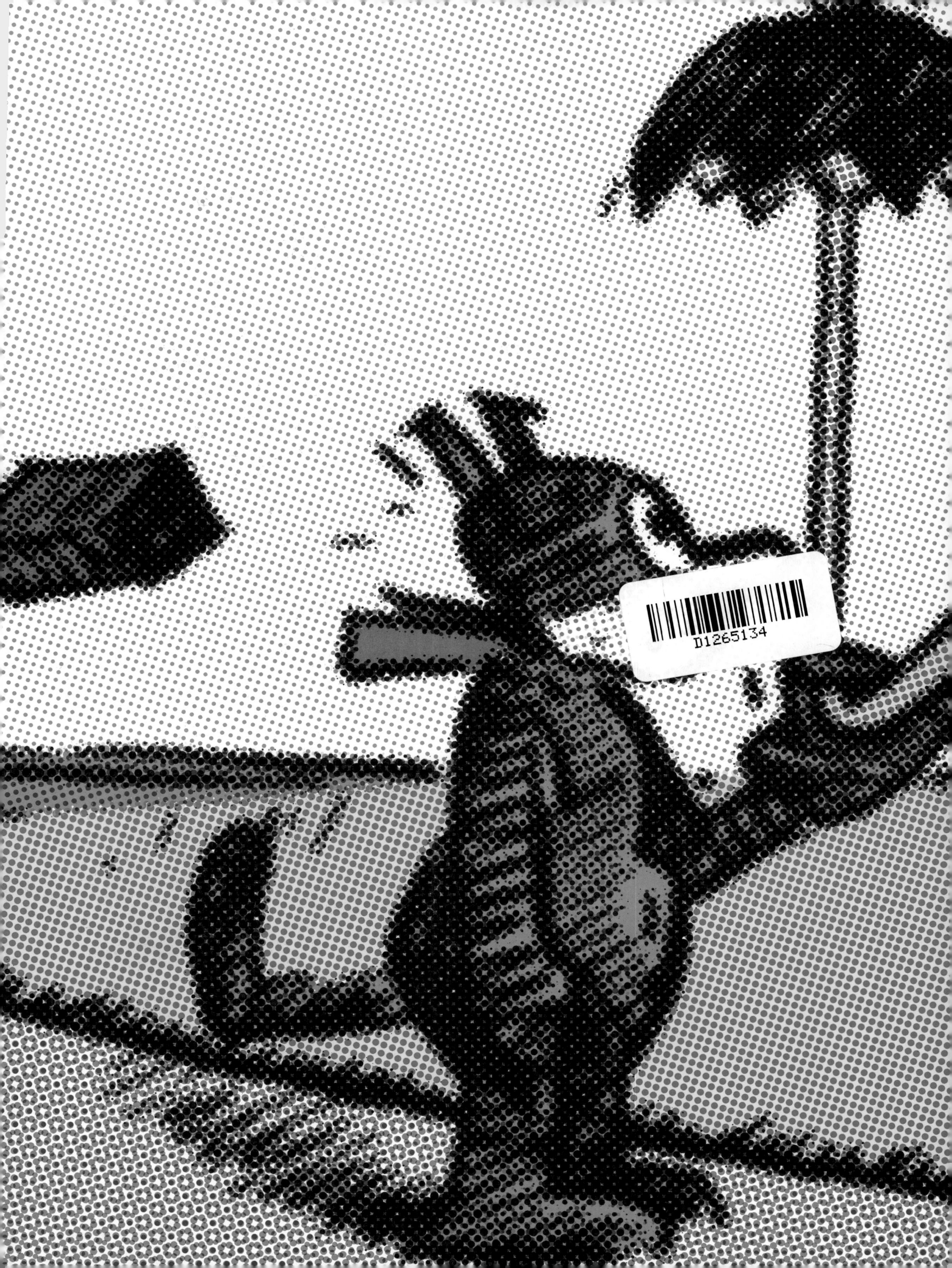

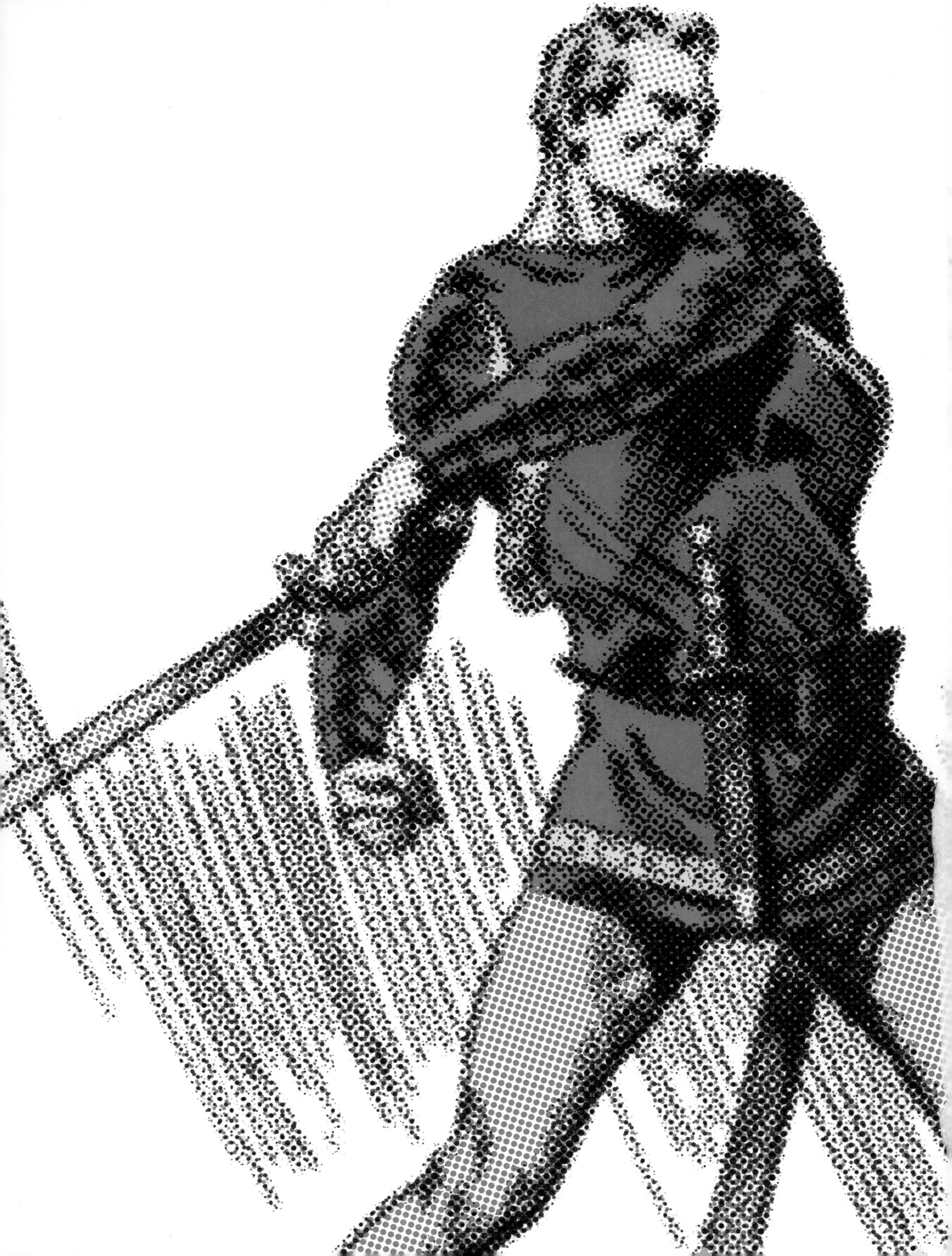

the comics
THE COMPLETE COLLECTION

BRIAN WALKER

ABRAMS COMICARTS, NEW YORK

the comics
BEFORE 1945

Thanks

To Mort, for his inspirational dedication to the art of cartooning

To Jay, for recommending me

To Eric, for his guidance and support

To Abby, Sarah, and David for their patience

Editors: Nicole Columbus, Richard Slovak
Designer: Carole Goodman/Blue Anchor Design
Production Manager: Ankur Ghosh

Cataloging-in-Publication Data is available from the Library of Congress.
ISBN: 978-0-8109-9595-6

Printed and bound in China
10 9 8 7 6 5 4 3 2

Abrams ComicArts books are available at special discounts when purchased in quantity for premiums and promotions as well as fundraising or educational use. Special editions can also be created to specification. For details, contact specialmarkets@abramsbooks.com or the address below.

THE ART OF BOOKS SINCE 1949
115 West 18th Street
New York, NY 10011
www.abramsbooks.com

contents

The Comics Before 1945

introduction 7

the turn of the century 19

the teens 67

the twenties 113

the thirties 183

the forties 287

acknowledgments 324

bibliography 324

The Comics Since 1945

introduction 338

the postwar years 349

the fifties 403

the sixties 451

the seventies 495

the eighties 551

the nineties 607

twenty-first century 659

acknowledgments 660

bibliography 660

index 666

THE TOAST MASTER—Yellow Kid original watercolor presentation piece by Richard F. Outcault. September 2, 1897.
Courtesy of Marty Goldman and the Barnum Museum

Little Rosilia McGraw: No; we won't come and play with youz, Delia Costigan. Our rejuced means may temporary necessitate our residin' in a rear tenement, but we're jist as exclusive as when we lived on the first floor front and papa had charge of the pound in the Department of Canine Captivity!

FEUDAL PRIDE IN HOGAN'S ALLEY—The first appearance of the Yellow Kid by Richard F. Outcault. June 2, 1894, Truth magazine.
Courtesy of Richard D. Olson

introduction

IT ALL BEGAN WITH THE YELLOW KID. OR DID IT? Richard Felton Outcault's bald-headed, flap-eared, buck-toothed street urchin, who made his first appearance in *Truth* magazine on June 2, 1894, is often described as "the kid who started the comics." Coulton Waugh's landmark history, *The Comics* (1947), describes a scene from a "February day of 1896" when Charles Saalburg, "foreman of the *New York World's* tint-laying Ben Day machines," used the kid's nightshirt to experiment with a faster-drying yellow ink. When Outcault's "The Great Dog Show in M'Googan Avenue" appeared in the newspaper on February 16, the bright hue made a "vivid bulls-eye in the whole big page." The Yellow Kid, as he soon became known, "caught the fancy of hundreds of thousands of readers." Waugh claimed, "A new form of communication was about to be built on this foundation." In subsequent years, this story has been repeated so many times that it is widely accepted as the official account of the birth of the art form.

The truth is, almost every aspect of Waugh's tale is a myth. The *Chicago Inter-Ocean* was the first American newspaper to install a high-speed rotary color press, in September 1892, and was publishing color comics in a small insert format by 1893. In the spring of 1894, a new weekly supplement for kids, the *Inter-Ocean Jr.,* was introduced with a regular color comic series starring *The Ting Ling Kids* by Charles Saalburg

on the cover. By 1896, Saalburg was working for the *New York World* as a cartoonist and art director—not as a press foreman. The *World,* following the lead of the *Inter-Ocean,* had purchased a four-color rotary press from R. Hoe and Company and published its first color comics on May 21, 1893. The cartoon on the cover of this supplement, by Walt McDougall, featured bright yellow hues.

In June 1893, *American Pressman* published an article, "Working Colors on Each Other," that described an inquiry from an anxious printer: "He worked his yellow first, after striking his key-form; then he put on his red and ran that off. These two colors seemed to go all right, and to 'stay put': but when he got on his blue the trouble showed itself. The impression showed up with a fatty or mottled look, especially after it had lain for some time; and the color wasn't true." The writer suggested an easy remedy for the pressman's problems: dusting the sheets with powdered magnesia would keep the inks from amalgamating. Surviving comic sections from the era provide proof that most of the problems with color printing had been worked out long before February 1896.

Roy McCardell, who was on the staff of the *New York World* in the early 1890s, claimed in his 1905 article, "Opper, Outcault and Company," that he had the original idea to publish a color comic section and suggested it to his managing editor,

Ballard Smith, in 1891. Three years later, McCardell recommended Outcault to Morrill Goddard, editor of the *Sunday World,* who was hiring artists for his new weekly comic supplement.

The first appearance of the Yellow Kid in the *New York World,* on February 17, 1895, was a black-and-white reprint of an Outcault cartoon from *Truth.* In the first color episode, on May 5, 1895, the Kid's nightshirt was blue. It was yellow on November 24, 1895, and red with black polka dots on December 15, 1895, before permanently changing back to yellow on January 5, 1896. All of these developments had taken place before Waugh's alleged pressroom incident.

In fact, Richard F. Outcault's *Hogan's Alley,* starring the Yellow Kid, did not introduce any of the important elements we now associate with newspaper comics: speech balloons, sequential narrative, recurring characters, regularly titled series, color printing, adaptation to other media, and product licensing. Speech balloons had been combined with graphic images for centuries, and sequential narrative was well established in many forms. American newspapers had been publishing cartoons since the late 1860s, and Sunday sections were printed in color before the Yellow Kid made his debut. Recurring characters, regularly titled series, and the successful merchandising of cartoon "stars" had been pioneered by other artists.

Then why is the Yellow Kid universally regarded as the poster boy for the birth of the comics? The answer lies in the long evolution of the art form and the ultimate convergence of numerous historical trends.

The first cartoonists were probably cave dwellers. Although it is tempting to imagine a dramatic scene in which a bearskin-clad creator discovered the power of pictures in a single burst of inspiration, the historical record suggests that visual storytelling evolved gradually. Egyptian hieroglyphics, Greek friezes, Roman carvings, and medieval tapestries provide evidence of this long progression.

During the Middle Ages, illuminated manuscripts combined calligraphy and illustration in extended narratives. When movable-type printing was introduced in the fifteenth century, words and images were increasingly separated, due to the different techniques used to reproduce drawings and set type. Single printed pages, known as "broadsides" or "broadsheets," were the most common medium for graphic expression; although they often contained speech balloons, they were not "comics" in the modern sense. Broadsheets initially concentrated on religious themes, but by the seventeenth and eighteenth centuries, scenes from daily life, as well as political and social satire, predominated.

The technological progress of the industrial age created an acceleration in the evolution of graphic communication. As printing and distribution methods became mechanized, periodicals and newspapers replaced broadsheets as the prime vehicles for

ARMED HEROES—British Prime Minister Henry Addington faces off against Napoleon Bonaparte in this cartoon by James Gillray. *May 18, 1803*

cartoons and illustration. Circulation climbed as literacy increased and as publishers discovered that entertainment sold better than enlightenment. It was during the nineteenth century that the comic strip took its present form.

In 1809, the English caricaturist Thomas Rowlandson introduced Dr. Syntax, a pedantic schoolmaster who appeared in a series of satirical prints in *Poetical Magazine.* When these cartoons were collected in book form, the popularity of Rowlandson's character took off. Dr. Syntax hats, coats, mugs, and plates were peddled in the shops of London. Charles Ross and Marie Duval's *Ally Sloper,* which debuted in Britain's *Judy* on August 14, 1867, and Palmer Cox's *Brownies,* which first appeared in America's *St. Nicholas* in February 1883, were later examples of popular cartoon "stars" that appeared regularly in periodicals and were merchandised successfully.

Speech balloons were still common in American political and satirical prints during the first part of the nineteenth century. This began to change with the launching of a string of successful humor magazines modeled after the British *Punch,* which began in 1841. *Yankee Doodle* (1846), *Frank Leslie's Illustrated Newspaper* (1855), *Harper's Weekly* (1857), *Wild Oats* (1870), *Puck* (1877), *Judge* (1881), and *Life* (1883) established the new standard format for "cartoons," a term introduced in 1843. The comic weeklies abandoned speech balloons in favor of a style of cartooning that placed the text below the drawings. Many of the single-panel social vignettes in these publications were conversational exchanges of the "he said, she said" variety. Although multi-panel comics and cartoons with

speech balloons could also be found in the humor magazines, it was not until the turn of the century that newspaper cartoonists "revived" these centuries-old devices.

One of the pioneers of newspaper comics, Jimmy Swinnerton, started as a sketch artist on the *San Francisco Examiner* in 1892 and created a recurring comic feature, *Little Bears,* for that paper in late 1893. In an interview published in 1934, "Swin" reminisced about the transition from magazine cartoons to newspaper comics: "In those days we swore by [cartoonist Eugene] Zimmerman and [cartoonist Frederick Burr] Opper, and the others of the grotesque school who illustrated printed jokes. It was not the fashion to have balloons showing what the characters were saying, as that was supposed to have been buried with the English [caricaturist George] Cruikshank, but along came the comic supplements, and with Dick Outcault's Yellow Kid the balloons came back and literally filled the sky."

The eighteenth-century English artist William Hogarth had explored the storytelling potential of multi-image cartoons in such popular print series as *A Harlot's Progress* (1732), but Rodolphe Töpffer is widely regarded as the father of sequential comics. In 1827, the Swiss artist, writer, and teacher produced the first of his "picture novels"—multi-panel illustrated stories with the text below the drawings. Töpffer later described his discovery in an essay on aesthetic theory: "The drawings, without their text, would have only a vague meaning; the text, without the drawings, would have no meaning at all. The combination makes up a kind of novel, all the more unique

| Mr. Oldbuck's first sight of his ladye-love. | He beholds her vanishing in the distance. |

THE ADVENTURES OF MR. OBADIAH OLDBUCK—Two panels from the earliest known American comic book, by Rodolphe Töpffer, translated from the French edition and published by Wilson and Company. September 14, 1842. Courtesy of Robert L. Beerbohm

in that it is no more like a novel than it is like anything else." Töpffer's stories were translated from the original French and reprinted in pirated editions in other countries (as there were no international copyright laws). Many scholars consider one of his graphic novels, the forty-page *Adventures of Obadiah Oldbuck,* published by Wilson and Company of New York in September 1842, to be the earliest known example of an American comic book.

The German artist Wilhelm Busch refined the art of graphic narrative in his first picture stories, published in the 1860s. *Max und Moritz,* the most famous of these *Bilderbogen,* starred two mischievous pranksters and directly influenced the American newspaper cartoonist Rudolph Dirks, who created *The Katzenjammer Kids* for William Randolph Hearst's *New York Journal* in 1897.

The first American daily newspaper to use cartoons on a regular basis was James Gordon Bennett's *New York Evening Telegram,* starting in 1867. The four-page pink sheet, which sold for two cents, showcased a large front-page political cartoon by Charles Green Bush every Friday. On March 4, 1873, a group of engravers, encouraged by advances in halftone photo-reproduction, launched the *New York Daily Graphic.* This fully illustrated newspaper featured cartoons by many of the leading artists of the day, including A. B. Frost, E. W. Kemble, and

THE BOOM IN JOURNALISM—Cartoon by Charles Green Bush.
October 25, 1883, Life magazine. Courtesy of the International Museum of Cartoon Art

Frederick B. Opper. These experiments provided the incentive for other New York City papers, including the *World* and the *Herald,* to increase their use of pictures. On September 23, 1889, unable to keep up with the competition, the *Daily Graphic* ceased publication.

After Joseph Pulitzer purchased the *New York World* in 1883, he expanded the Sunday supplement from four pages to twenty, offering a mix of sensational news, literary features, and illustrations. By 1887, the circulation of the *Sunday World* had reached 250,000. A comic supplement, modeled after successful humor magazines like *Puck* and *Judge,* was added in 1889. Many of the artists who had been working for these publications eventually found themselves drawing cartoons for the new Sunday newspaper supplements.

The newspaper business was going through a radical transformation in the latter half of the nineteenth century. Between 1870 and 1900, while the population of the United States doubled and that of city dwellers tripled, the number of English-language daily newspapers increased from 489 to 1,967. The total circulation of these publications rose, in the same period, from 2.6 million copies to 15 million. Metropolitan newspapers installed high-speed presses, subscribed to services that relayed news rapidly by telegraph, and published multiple daily editions of twenty-four to thirty-six pages. Prices dropped to as little as a penny per issue as competition became fierce.

By the mid-1890s, all of the important innovations in comic strip format and publishing were in place. Speech balloons, though temporarily out of vogue, were still familiar to most cartoonists as an effective method of incorporating dialogue into their drawings. Multi-panel cartoons with extended narrative sequences could be found in both newspapers and magazines of the time. Palmer Cox's Brownies were at the peak of their

Max und Moritz

Schnupdiwup! there goes, O Jeminy! | Schnupdiwup! da wird nach oben Schon ein Huhn heraufgehoben.

MAX UND MORITZ—Drawing from the picture story by Wilhelm Busch, first published in 1865. *Courtesy of Dover Publications*

popularity, dramatically showing how cartoon characters could be promoted and merchandised to consumers around the world. Newspaper publishers were adding color comic sections to their rapidly growing Sunday supplements. Richard F. Outcault was in the right place at the right time.

In 1890, Outcault was on the staff of *Electrical World* magazine. He also sold freelance cartoons to the comic weeklies. On June 2, 1894, a single-panel drawing by him, entitled "Feudal Pride in Hogan's Alley," appeared in *Truth* magazine. In the cartoon, a small, bald-headed boy in a nightshirt can be seen peering around the corner of "Hogan's Alley" and "Ryan's Arcade." This was the first appearance of the character who was to become the Yellow Kid. In late 1894, Outcault was hired by Morrill Goddard, editor of the *New York Sunday World*. Four more single-panel drawings featuring the curious-looking Irish slum urchin ran in *Truth* before his newspaper debut in the *New York World*, on February 17, 1895: "Fourth Ward Brownies" was a reprint of a cartoon from eight days earlier in *Truth*.

The earliest of Outcault's *Hogan's Alley* cartoons were not comic strips at all, but single-panel city scenes with cavorting slum kids. Accompanying text appeared either outside the drawings or on signs and surfaces within the compositions. The January 5, 1896, episode, "Golf—The Great Society Sport as Played in Hogan's Alley," featured the Kid (he was not officially named "Mickey Dugan" until June 7 of that year), in a yellow nightshirt, gravitating toward the center of the teeming tableau. The Kid began to speak, in the form of crude, grammatically incorrect writing pinned to his nightshirt, on April 12, 1896, in the "First Championship Game of the Hogan's Alley Baseball Team."

In the meantime, William Randolph Hearst had been stirring the pot of Park Row publishing. The son of a California silver miner who struck it rich in the Comstock Lode, Will had used the family fortune to transform the *San Francisco Examiner* into a successful West Coast version of Pulitzer's *World*. After his father died in 1891, he persuaded his mother to use a portion of the profits from the sale of their interest in the Anaconda copper mines to finance his newspaper career. Will Hearst then set his sights on New York City.

On October 10, 1895, *The Fourth Estate* (later renamed *Editor & Publisher*) announced the thirty-two-year-old's arrival from San Francisco and his purchase of the *New York Journal*: "He has money and he is not afraid of spending it. New York is the field of his ambitions and with the resources of almost unlimited capital and absolutely exhaustless courage he has entered the fight."

Hearst soon made good on the predictions about him. He dropped the price of the struggling morning paper to one cent, and in four months its circulation soared from 20,000 to 150,000. To compete, Pulitzer was forced to sell his *New*

WILLIAM RANDOLPH HEARST—*Cartoon by J. Campbell Cory. The Yellow Kid became an icon for "yellow journalism." June 8, 1898,* The Bee *magazine.* Courtesy of Mark Johnson

York World for a penny. Then, in January 1896, Hearst began raiding Pulitzer's ranks by hiring Goddard, the *Sunday World* editor, along with eleven members of Goddard's staff. Solomon Solis Carvalho resigned as the *World*'s publisher on March 19 and went to work for Hearst on March 31. The *New York Evening Journal* debuted on September 28 and soon passed a circulation mark of 175,000. By that time, the morning *Journal* was moving an average of 425,000 copies a day.

After installing a new high-speed multicolor press, Hearst acquired the services of Pulitzer's most popular cartoonist, Richard F. Outcault. With his Yellow Kid as the star attraction, the *American Humorist,* an eight-page color comic supplement in the *Sunday Journal,* debuted on October 18, 1896. Hearst sold 375,000 copies of that edition, in spite of an increase in price from three to five cents. In the meantime, Pulitzer hired George Luks to continue *Hogan's Alley* in the *World*. Although Roy McCardell reported in 1905 that "there were lawsuits for breaking of contracts and for infringement of copyright brought by both papers," there are no known court records of a legal decision regarding ownership of the Yellow Kid.

On October 25, 1896, one week after Outcault's first cartoon was published in the *Journal,* he combined sequential

THE YELLOW KID—This half-page cartoon by Richard F. Outcault was the first Yellow Kid episode to incorporate speech balloons and sequential panels.
October 25, 1896, New York Journal. Courtesy of Denis Kitchen

drawings and speech balloons for the first time. In "The Yellow Kid and His New Phonograph," dialogue could be seen emanating from Edison's invention in the form of a speech balloon. The final picture of the five-drawing composition revealed that the source of the sound was a parrot that had been concealed within the base of the device. The Yellow Kid, falling over backward, remarked, "De phonograph is a great invention— NIT! I don't tink—wait till I git dat foolish bird home I won't do a ting te him well say!" The Kid's words were contained inside a speech balloon with the tail pointing to his mouth. Newspaper readers probably chuckled and turned the page, unaware of the historic importance of this cartoon.

During the next fifteen months, Outcault repeated this multi-panel layout approximately eighteen times, in half-page cartoons done as a secondary feature to the full-page Yellow Kid episodes on the cover of the comic section. Speech balloons and multiple panels added a new dimension to Outcault's comics. When dialogue was placed within speech balloons in the drawings, the characters appeared to speak with greater immediacy than when text was placed below the illustrations. Balloons transformed two-dimensional performers into personalities with thoughts and emotions, who could speak and move simultaneously like real people. Sequential drawings created the illusion of time. The space between two successive images could represent seconds, minutes, days, or years. A progression of pictures told a story with a beginning, a middle, and an end. The combination of speech balloons and sequential

panels increased the potential for more effective character development and storytelling in comics.

Rudolph Dirks and Frederick B. Opper institutionalized Outcault's innovations. Dirks's *Katzenjammer Kids*, which debuted on December 12, 1897, was one of the first newspaper comics to use sequential panels on a regular basis, although initially the text was set in type below the pictures. Opper's *Happy Hooligan* made standard use of both panels and speech balloons soon after its debut on March 11, 1900, and it can be regarded as the first definitive modern American newspaper comic strip.

Not all comics historians agree on the significance of these developments. Doug Wheeler, an expert in nineteenth-century comics, has published numerous examples of cartoons from the late 1700s to the mid-1890s that meet the same qualifications as Outcault's historic strip. In an article announcing his discoveries, he claimed, "One of my projects has been gathering evidence that the long-held claim that the first publication of a multi-panel, sequential comic strip told entirely via word balloons or in-panel dialogue was 'The Yellow Kid and His New Phonograph' by Richard Outcault on October 25, 1896, is *wrong*." He concluded, "Our history books are flawed." Wheeler is part of a growing number of researchers into the Victorian era who argue that Outcault and the Yellow Kid should be relegated to a footnote in comics history.

The roots of this disagreement lie in the varying criteria for defining the term *comic strip*. There is no consensus among the leading comics scholars on a basic definition.

Bill Blackbeard, the founder of the San Francisco Academy of Comic Art, believes that a comic strip "may be defined as a serially published, episodic, open-ended dramatic narrative or series of linked anecdotes featuring recurrent named characters. The successive drawings regularly include ballooned dialogue that is crucial to the telling of the story."

Doug Wheeler challenges the stipulation that comic strips must contain continuing characters as "ludicrous." "Characters are story elements, the same as plot and dialogue," Wheeler maintains. "They are not the medium in which the story is told."

Pascal Lefevre and Charles Dierick, the editors of *Forging a New Medium: The Comic Strip in the Nineteenth Century,* propose that comics are a "juxtaposition of fixed (mostly drawn) pictures on a support as a communicative act." In this "prototypical definition," certain examples need not be excluded if they lack one or two of the criteria (such as speech balloons or a paper support).

Robert C. Harvey, the author of *The Art of the Funnies,* feels that definitions like this are "simply too broad to be useful as anything except a springboard to further discussion." In Harvey's view, "comics consist of pictorial narratives or expositions in which words (often lettered into the picture area within speech balloons) usually contribute to the meaning of the picture and vice versa. A pictorial narrative uses a sequence of pictures (i.e., a 'strip' of pictures); a pictorial exposition may do the same—or may not (as in single-panel cartoons—political cartoons as well as magazine-type gag cartoons)." Harvey's "visual-verbal blending" definition excludes such well-known newspaper features as *Prince Valiant* and *Tarzan,* in which the text is separate from the illustrations.

Belgian comic strip theorist Thierry Smolderen takes a unique point of view. "I'm a complete relativist about comics," claims Smolderen. "For me, there exists no absolute definition of comics: different social groups (editors, artists, readers, censors, printers, teachers, etc.) participating in the existence of the medium will forge different working definitions, by selecting and generalizing the traits that are pertinent to their way of participating in it."

All of these interpretations have merit, but the relativist approach is probably the most realistic. Cartoonists do not concern themselves with definitions. They are commercial artists and, in most cases, are hired by editors and paid by publishers. The space they work in and the audience they are entertaining are determined by the nature of the publication in which their cartoons appear. Within these boundaries, a wide range of creative expression is possible. Cartoonists make use of many tools, including speech balloons, recurring characters, and sequential narrative, and are constantly breaking rules and experimenting with the art form. Although there are cartoonists who jump from one medium to another, the parameters of

each commercial venue are distinct. Trying to impose a universal definition on this multifaceted and ever-changing graphic enterprise is virtually impossible.

Newspaper comic strips, or the "funnies," have been familiar to the American public for more than a century. They have changed considerably in size and content over the years, yet most comics still have speech balloons, panel borders, a regular cast of characters, and jokes or stories (or both). Almost all American newspapers have daily comic pages and color Sunday sections, and the most famous funnies stars, such as Little Orphan Annie, Popeye, Dick Tracy, Snoopy, and Garfield, are recognizable to readers of all ages. The Yellow Kid was the direct ancestor of these characters, and Richard F. Outcault's *Hogan's Alley* was the first successful newspaper comic feature— no more, no less.

In 1905, Roy McCardell recounted the events leading up to the Yellow Kid's debut. "The [*New York World* comic] supplement was a success from the start [May 21, 1893]," he remembered, "but it was not until a year and a half later its success became enormous. Then Outcault made his first 'hit.' Ninety-nine times out of a hundred a paper's 'hit' is accidental—caused by a picture or series of pictures that strikes the public fancy. A 'hit' is the making of the most moribund of papers; it can well be imagined how one is sought and striven for by even a successful paper. Outcault's first 'hit' was with the 'Yellow Kid.'"

As early as November 1, 1896, just a week after the "The Yellow Kid and His New Phonograph" was published, *Ev'ry Month* magazine reported, "Mr. Outcault is now having his day. His 'Yellow Kid' is familiar to a vast and applausive metropolis. His work is being bid for by the great metropolitan dailies, and at the music halls in Broadway you can see a travesty which has in it, a band of typical East Side children from the quarter which he discovered and called *Hogan's Alley.* There is a *Hogan's Alley* comedy on the road, and there are *Hogan's Alley* songs on the market. Through it all Mr. Outcault's exceedingly clever drawings depicting life in *Hogan's Alley* are appearing in a great paper every Sunday, and Mr. Outcault is making money. What else could one add to make success?"

The colorful posters that were plastered all over New York City during the height of the battle between Hearst and Pulitzer and the hundreds of products inspired by Outcault's creation were further proof that the Yellow Kid was a hit. The success of the Yellow Kid is not simply a myth created by subsequent generations of comics historians. It is a pivotal chapter in the long history of the art form.

On September 7, 1896, Outcault formally applied for copyright registration by sending a letter with a drawing of "The Yellow Dugan Kid" to the Library of Congress. Although many historians claim that Outcault obtained legal ownership

NEW YORK JOURNAL POSTER—Published at the peak of the competition between the Journal and the New York World, with art by Archie Gunn and Richard F. Outcault. *October 1896. Courtesy of Craig Koste*

of the Yellow Kid, records at the Library of Congress indicate that his request was never officially granted, due to an irregularity in the application process. Consequently, he was never able to prevent widespread exploitation of his character by other artists and manufacturers of Yellow Kid products.

The phrase "yellow journalism" is another aspect of this story that comics scholars have disputed. Roy McCardell wrote in 1905 that "the rivalry between the *World* and the *Journal* caused the papers without the attractions of Mr. Outcault's work and Mr. Luks's work to describe those papers as 'Yellow Kid journals,' and then, by dropping the monosyllable, to call them simply 'yellow journals.'" According to recent research by Mark Winchester, one of the earliest appearances of the term, used specifically to denounce the type of sensational journalism that Hearst and Pulitzer practiced, was in the *New York Times* on March 12, 1897. Bill Blackbeard argues, in his definitive history of the Yellow Kid, that the phrase can be traced to the "*Journal-Examiner* Yellow Fellow Transcontinental Bicycle Relay" sponsored by Hearst in the summer of 1896. Other writers have attempted to associate "yellow journalism" with "yellow peril" fears stemming from the First Sino-Japanese War of 1894–95, or with the "yellow-backed pamphleteering" of lurid novels in the mid-nineteenth century. Regardless of the derivation, most historians agree that the term came into wide acceptance after the sinking of the battleship *Maine*

on February 15, 1898. During the Spanish-American War, which soon followed this incident, the Yellow Kid frequently appeared as an icon of "yellow journalism" in political cartoons that were critical of the sensational and jingoistic coverage of the conflict by the New York press.

By that time, ironically, neither of the competing Yellow Kid Sunday comic features by Richard F. Outcault and George Luks was appearing any longer in the *Journal* or the *World*. Presumably, the negative association between his creation and the journalism practiced by Hearst and Pulitzer had become an embarrassment to Outcault.

In "How the Yellow Kid Was Born," published in the *New York World* on May 1, 1898, Outcault looked back on his success with little affection. "Now, it is more than six years [Outcault had his dates wrong] since my pen first traced the outlines of Mickey Dugan on paper," he recalled. "In that time I suppose I have myself made twenty thousand Yellow Kids, and when the million buttons, the innumerable toys and cigarette boxes and labels and what not are taken into consideration, some idea can be gleaned of how tired I am of him.

"I have but one request to make, and that is, when I die," Outcault concluded, "don't wear yellow crepe, don't let them put a Yellow Kid on my tombstone and don't allow the Yellow Kid himself to come to my funeral. Make him stay on the East Side, where he belongs."

A HOT POLITICAL CONVENTION IN HOGAN'S ALLEY—Original pen-and-ink Sunday page by Richard F. Outcault. July 12, 1896, New York World. Courtesy of Marty Goldman

After his death on September 25, 1928, the *Los Angeles Herald* wrote, "If the 'Yellow Kid' could come back out of the past today, he would bow his head in mourning for his creator, Richard Felton Outcault, 'father of the comic strips.'" The obituary in the *New York World* offered a more qualified eulogy: "To say the late R. F. Outcault was the inventor of the comic supplement is of course to ignore the social factors that lead up to all inventions." The controversy surrounding the origin of comics and the role of Richard F. Outcault's Yellow Kid will never die.

THE ARTWORK

The comics reproduced in this book reflect the evolution of the art form during the first half of the twentieth century. In the early years of the funnies, cartoonists experimented with many different layouts and panel arrangements, limited only by the dimensions of a newspaper page. By the 1920s, syndicates had standardized the formats for most newspaper comics, which were produced as black-and-white daily strips or panels and color Sunday pages. During the 1930s, Sunday pages were also being offered in half-page configurations.

The original drawings for both daily and Sunday features were usually done with a pen or brush and India ink on heavy illustration board, but cartoonists frequently experimented with a variety of techniques and tools to produce distinctive shading and special effects. Artists often colored a few panels of their originals as guides for the printers; eventually, however, overlays done on transparent paper replaced this method. On occasion, cartoonists also completely hand-colored their original art to give to their friends and admirers as presentation pieces.

Newspaper comics were printed much larger than they are today, but the quality of reproduction varied considerably. The color on surviving newsprint pages can be quite brilliant, although the interior pages of many early comic sections were often printed in only two colors. Comics on newsprint, in both daily and Sunday papers, can also be faded, incomplete, or out of registration. Fortunately, thousands of these newspaper sections have survived the ravages of time.

The comics on the following pages were obtained from many different sources. Original artwork from private collectors and public institutions was photographed, scanned, or photocopied to provide the sharpest images. Color photographs of black-and-white or partially colored strips often reveal pencil lines, margin notations, and deterioration of the paper. High-contrast black-and-white reproductions of pen-and-ink pieces show the strips the way they were intended to be seen. In some cases, original artwork was not available, so syndicate proofs and newspaper pages were used for source material. A select group of Sunday pages was also digitally restored by American Color, the company that currently prepares comics for all of the major syndicates, using original artwork and printed pages as color guides.

It is the author's intention to present these historical examples with the fidelity of the original artwork preserved as much as possible. For the sake of comparison, it is interesting to look at continuous tone images of the original pieces, but daily strips and panels were intended to be reproduced in high-contrast black and white. Digital color restoration of the Sunday pages corrects for the limitations of high-speed presses and cheap newsprint, but it is also important to see the Sunday funnies the way they looked to newspaper readers at the time. It is hoped that the variety of source material and the different reproduction methods used in this book will provide a comprehensive appreciation for the art of the comics during this period.

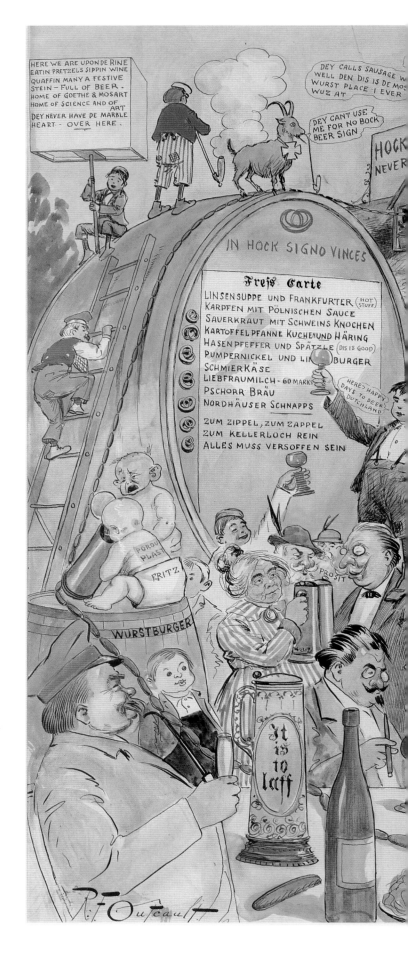

THE YELLOW KID INVADES GERMANY—Original hand-colored Sunday page by Richard F. Outcault. From January 17 to May 30, 1897, the Yellow Kid went *on a world tour.* April 4, 1897, New York Journal. *Courtesy of the International Museum of Cartoon Art*

TRAINING FOR THE FOOTBALL CHAMPIONSHIP GAME IN HOGAN'S ALLEY.

HOGAN'S ALLEY Sunday page by George B. Luks. The artist, whom Joseph Pulitzer hired as Outcault's successor, was a member of the "Ashcan School" of painters. *October 11, 1896, New York World. Courtesy of Denis Kitchen*

the turn of the century

"Stonehammer is an enterprising fellow, isn't he?"
"What's he doing now?"
"He's starting what he calls a 'newspaper.' He's going to get out a copy every year."

OUR ANTEDILUVIAN ANCESTORS cartoon by Frederick B. Opper. 1901, New York Journal. Courtesy of Editor & Publisher

IF—THE INAUGURAL DINNER AT THE WHITE HOUSE—*J. S. Pughe pictures in this lithograph what it might have looked like if William Randolph Hearst had been elected president of the United States.* June 29, 1904, Puck magazine. Courtesy of Periodyssey/Richard Samuel West Collection

T HAS BEEN CALLED THE AGE OF OPTIMISM, THE AGE OF CONFIDENCE, AND THE AGE OF INNOCENCE. THE FIRST DECADE OF THE TWENTIETH CENTURY WAS ALSO A GOLDEN AGE OF MASS ENTERTAINMENT. NICKELODEONS, NIGHTCLUBS, DANCE HALLS, MOVIE THEATERS, VAUDEVILLE HOUSES, SPORTS STADIUMS, AMUSEMENT PARKS, WORLD'S FAIR MIDWAYS, PHONOGRAPH PARLORS, AND PENNY ARCADES ATTRACTED MILLIONS OF PATRONS, EAGER TO PART WITH THEIR HARD-EARNED SPENDING MONEY.

Commercial entertainment was, for the most part, an urban enterprise. In 1900, New York City boasted more movie theaters and playhouses than any metropolis in the world and, by the end of the decade, had a combined seating capacity of more than two million. Tin Pan Alley composers, who wrote many of the songs for the stage shows, sold two billion copies of sheet music in 1910. The first nickelodeon—a small, dark room where customers watched short films projected on a screen—opened in 1905. Within three years, there were ten thousand nickelodeons drawing an estimated ten million customers a week. Professional baseball held its first World Series in 1903, and boxing, tennis, college football, golf, horse racing, and the Olympics (held in St. Louis in 1904) all thrilled American sports fans. The success of the 1893 Chicago World's Fair, which drew fourteen million visitors, was followed by

expositions in Atlanta (1895), Nashville (1897), Omaha (1898), Buffalo (1901), and St. Louis (1904). More than twenty million people, from every corner of the earth, took the trolley car ride to the Coney Island amusement parks in 1909.

Many factors contributed to this explosion in the consumption of popular culture. Although the average worker in 1910 toiled ten hours a day, six days a week, for an annual income ranging between $418 and $575, Americans had more leisure time than ever before. As the nation shifted from an agricultural to an industrial economy, labor became less skilled and more regimented. White- and blue-collar wage earners alike sought relief from their daily drudgery. Entrepreneurs and entertainers profited handsomely by providing fun seekers with a dizzying variety of ways to spend their off-hours. Telephones, phonographs, cameras, and other modern devices also made staying at home more enjoyable.

Americans were reading more. Between 1876 and 1915, illiteracy decreased from 20 percent to 6 percent. The immediate beneficiaries of this trend were magazine, book, and newspaper publishers. *The Saturday Evening Post,* which claimed weekly sales of more than two million by 1913, was the most widely read periodical in the world. *The Ladies' Home Journal, Collier's, Munsey's, McClure's,* and *Cosmopolitan* were among the many magazines that exerted a powerful influence on the social life and buying habits of the American consumer. The first "best-seller list" was published in *The Bookman* in 1895, and readers' tastes were soon being documented on a regular basis. In 1900, more than two thousand new fiction titles were issued, one-quarter of which were romance novels marketed to female readers.

Newspapers provided a daily diversion for the harried city worker. In addition to news, the metropolitan press offered sports pages, advice columns, human-interest stories, women's features, and comics. Joseph Pulitzer's *New York World* and William Randolph Hearst's *New York Journal* each passed the one million mark in circulation after the sinking of the American battleship *Maine* in Havana's harbor in 1898. The total circulation of daily newspapers throughout the United States doubled between 1892 and 1914.

The success of the Sunday newspaper was even more dramatic. *Editor & Publisher* reported on April 5, 1902, "Year by year it has grown, until today its size is formidable. The regular issues contain from 32 to 86 pages, and the specials, such as those of Christmas and Easter, from 100 to 130 pages." The comic supplement, it added, had "caught the fancy of the public, and now every illustrated Sunday newspaper has one printed in colors."

The Yellow Kid dramatically demonstrated the selling power of a popular comic character. Following Richard F. Outcault's departure from the *New York Journal* in 1898, *The Katzenjammer Kids* by Rudolph Dirks became the anchor of Hearst's flagship *American Humorist* comic section. "Katzenjammer," which means "cats' yowling" in German, was a popular colloquialism for "hangover." Dirks's pranksters, Hans and Fritz, were soon joined by the long-suffering Mama, as well as the rotund mariner, Der Captain (1902), and his trusty sidekick, Der Inspector (1905), establishing the core cast of the strip. In the first few years, Dirks rarely used speech balloons, preferring either pantomime or text beneath the panels.

Frederick B. Opper joined the Hearst staff in 1899 and was put to work drawing single-panel cartoons for the Sunday supplement. On March 11, 1900, Opper introduced his first newspaper comic feature, *Happy Hooligan,* which starred an irrepressible Irish hobo with a tin can balanced on his head. From the beginning, Opper incorporated speech balloons into his *Happy Hooligan* episodes. Cartoonists around the country were soon imitating the successful formula that Outcault, Dirks, and Opper pioneered. The unique combination of recurring characters, sequential panels, speech balloons, and bright colors eventually came to be known as the "Sunday funnies."

STOKES ADVERTISEMENT—In 1908, this comic book publisher had twenty-seven titles in print, featuring the most popular Sunday funnies stars.
Courtesy of Doug Wheeler

HAPPY HOOLIGAN—Frederick B. Opper's immortal Irish tramp. Original drawing for a **Boston Sunday American** premium. *1906. Courtesy of Richard Marschall*

Although the majority of creations introduced during the first decade featured interchangeable characters and predictable humor, some newspapers developed durable comic stars to compete with the Hearst lineup. Foxy Grandpa, Buster Brown, and Little Nemo debuted in the *New York Herald* between 1900 and 1905, the Newlyweds and their baby Snookums first appeared in the *New York World* in 1904, Hairbreadth Harry was a headliner in the *Philadelphia Press* starting in 1906, and Slim Jim became the most popular character in the World Color Printing Company stable beginning in 1910.

Newspaper chains and syndicates helped to facilitate the rapid spread of the comics. The *New York Herald* began selling its features to other papers as early as 1895. Pulitzer published the same lineup of comics in both of his newspapers, the *New York World* and the *St. Louis Post-Dispatch,* beginning in 1897. In 1900, there were eight newspaper chains, the largest being

the Scripps group of nine papers. Hearst owned six papers by 1903 and was distributing his comics to more than seventeen other clients.

Syndicates had grown steadily since the Civil War, but now, in addition to text features, they began selling color comics. The McClure Syndicate and the World Color Printing Company of St. Louis offered comic features to newspapers that were not serviced directly by the chains. The *Philadelphia North American,* the *Philadelphia Inquirer,* and the *Boston Globe* were among the many newspapers that developed their own comic talent.

In less than a decade, the Sunday funnies had grown from a local phenomenon in New York City to a nationwide mass medium. The most popular characters were familiar to millions of readers in cities across the country. By 1908, 75 percent of American Sunday newspapers were publishing comics. Three organizations—Hearst, McClure, and World Color—serviced three-quarters of this market.

With success came criticism. Religious groups had been protesting the publication of newspapers on the Christian Sabbath since the *New York Courier* issued its first Sunday edition on March 20, 1825. Seventy years later, when comics were being added to the growing Sunday supplements, these attacks continued with renewed vigor. "The Sunday newspaper is the most potent influence in our midst for the destruction of the Lord's Day as a day of rest and worship," wrote a group of Pennsylvania clergymen, known as the Sabbath Association, in July 1894. "There will ever be bigots and fanatics," responded *The Fourth Estate* in defense, "but their whole force cannot stop the progress of that engine of modern civilization—the newspaper."

A decade later, the funnies were under siege for both aesthetic and moral reasons. In June 1906, M. J. Darby, the newly elected president of the National Association of Newspaper Circulation Managers, gave an address to the organization entitled "Is the Comic Supplement a Desirable Feature?" Lamenting a decline in artistic quality, Darby said, "The crude coloring, slap-dash drawing, and very cheap and obvious funniness of the comic supplement cannot fail to debase the taste of readers and render them to a certain extent incapable of appreciating the finer forms of art."

The *Boston Herald* dropped its entire comic section in 1908, as well as its failing syndicate operation. The paper defended its decision, stating in an editorial, "The comic supplement has had its day. We discard it as we would throw aside any mechanism that has reached the end of its usefulness." The writer added, "Most discerning persons throw them aside without inspection, experience having taught them that there is no hope for improvement in these gaudy sheets." A number of prominent newspapers, including the *Milwaukee Journal,* the *Indianapolis Star,* and the *New York Tribune,* followed the lead of the *Boston Herald* and briefly discontinued their Sunday comics.

Even the father of the funnies predicted the passing of the comics. "One bunch of comic artists has been supplying all of the colored supplement pictures for the past twelve or fifteen years," wrote Outcault on January 16, 1909. "No new men in this field have appeared to startle the editors or the public. It seems only natural at the rate comics have been turned out for the last decade that the supply of ideas should become exhausted. Also the public."

Other protests, with the support of prominent religious leaders, social workers, and educators, focused on the detrimental effect that comics supposedly had on children. Maud Adams of Cincinnati, in an address to the Playground Association of America in September 1908, lamented that instead of showing proper behavior, strips like *Buster Brown* taught youngsters that "it is cunning to throw water from an upper window upon an old person and to outwit an infirm old man."

In 1909, *The Ladies' Home Journal* joined the movement, calling comics "a crime against American children." Edith Kingman Kent, chairman of the Committee for the Suppression of the Comic Supplement, warned in 1910, "The avidity with which many children seize this pernicious sheet, with its grotesque figures and vivid and crude coloring, amounts to a passion, which wise parents should regard with alarm and take steps to prevent."

In April 1911, Dr. Percival Chubb, a prominent New York educator and religious leader, presided over a meeting of the League for the Improvement of the Children's Comic Supplement. Representatives of that group and the Federation of Child Study, the International Kindergarten Union, and the Child Welfare League, as well as the president of the Academy of Design, reached a consensus that the comics needed to be reformed, not eliminated. By 1915, most of the newspapers that had dropped their color supplements had reinstated them. The crusade against comics lost its momentum. The funnies continued to grow in popularity.

There was a grain of truth in some of the criticism. Newspaper publishers promoted Sunday supplements as family entertainment. Many comic sections often included a feature designed especially for children, another primarily for adults, and several others for readers of all ages. Juvenile characters such as Little Jimmy appeared in the same pages as philanderers like Mr. Jack. Although nudity, foul language, deviant behavior, and religious comment were taboo in comics from the beginning, bad manners, sexual innuendo, and mindless violence were rampant in the early years.

Between 1900 and 1910, approximately nine million immigrants arrived on American shores, and the majority of these

SOME BITS OF AMERICAN SCENERY—*Ethnic caricatures by James Montgomery Flagg in a double-page spread.* April 1904, Life magazine

newcomers settled in the nation's largest cities. The early comics were not consciously directed toward a specific target audience, but there is little doubt that the colorful graphics appealed to immigrants, and the content of the Sunday funnies reflected this readership.

Newspaper cartoonists continued many of the traditions of slapstick and ethnic humor that had been established during the nineteenth century in minstrel shows, vaudeville acts, and comic publications. Violence, pratfalls, puns, and stereotypes were the defining characteristics of this homegrown American humor. Both on the stage and in the comics, all non-natives were fair game; Englishmen wore monocles and were uppity, pugnacious Irishmen ate corned beef and cabbage, mustached Frenchmen were overly polite and hopelessly romantic, Germans were overweight and prone to fits of temper, towheaded Swedes were naive and stubborn, and blacks ate watermelon, rolled dice, and were lazy and superstitious. Immigrants responded to these stereotypes, both positively and negatively, and recognized their fellow city dwellers in the graphic melting pot on the funnies pages.

The reformers who attacked the comics were mostly upper- and middle-class, white, native-born Americans. They were shocked by the rough-and-tumble humor of the Sunday funnies and found the characters to be vulgar, brash, and disrespectful. Immigrants and children loved the comics for the same reasons

that the ruling classes abhorred them: they celebrated anarchy, rebellion, and the triumph of the underdog.

The funnies never outgrew the bad reputation of their obstreperous youth. In 1906, the literary critic Ralph Bergengren, writing in the *Atlantic Monthly,* complained that in the comics, "Respect for property, respect for parents, for law, for decency, for truth, for beauty, for kindliness, for dignity, or for honor, are killed, without mercy." This negative attitude by self-appointed arbiters of public taste toward the "low art" of the comics has persisted ever since.

In 1905, Roy McCardell summed up the rowdy appeal of the comic supplement: "Its humor is strenuous, not to say brutal; the knock-about comedians of the old time music-halls might easily have posed for most of the pictures that the supplement has printed in its ten years of life. The characters are thrown out of windows, clubbed, kicked, knocked down and out, laid flat by trucks dropped upon them; but they turn up smilingly the next Sunday to go through the same operations in other forms."

Many of the early comics featured visual punch lines that were recycled over and over again. Maud the mule habitually gave her victims a swift kick. Everett True ended each episode by violently dispatching the source of his frustration. Scary William was forever frightened, and Willie Westinghouse Edison Smith's inventions always backfired. Cartoonists would milk these one-note gag strips for as long as they could

CLARENCE THE COP—Charles W. Kahles's popular policeman, who starred in Pulitzer's World *from 1900 to 1908, sees himself in the funnies.*
September 12, 1908. Courtesy of Bill Blackbeard

and then move on to another gimmick. Hundreds of short-lived titles, which often told readers all they needed to know about the main characters, appeared and disappeared in the formative years of the Sunday funnies.

Charles William Kahles was a prolific pioneer who created twenty-three different comic features during his thirty-three-year career. In the first decade of the century, he did strips for the McClure Syndicate as well as the *Philadelphia North American* and the *Philadelphia Press*. In 1905, he was producing eight different titles simultaneously: *Clarence the Cop, Billy Bounce, The Teasers, Mr. Buttin, Doubting Thomas, Pretending Percy, Fun in the Zoo,* and *The Terrible Twins*. His most successful creation, *Hairbreadth Harry,* was one of the first serial story strips, and it ran from October 21, 1906, to January 17, 1940. (Franklin Osborne Alexander continued it after Kahles's death on January 21, 1931.)

George Herriman, remembered today as the creator of *Krazy Kat,* was also active during this era of experimentation. Among the many short-lived features Herriman introduced before launching his first successful strip, *The Dingbat Family,* in 1910 were *Handy Andy, Tattered Tim, Professor Otto, Acrobatic Archie, Musical Mose, Major Ozone, Mr. Proones the Plunger,* and *Baron Mooch.*

Carl "Bunny" Schultze's *Foxy Grandpa,* which debuted in the *New York Herald* on January 7, 1900, was one of the most enduring of the one-note gag strips. Schultze reversed the formula of Dirks's *Katzenjammer Kids:* at the end of each Sunday page, clever Grandpa inevitably outwitted the two mischievous tykes who were trying to trick him. Schultze's feature lasted for more than eighteen years, and there were *Foxy Grandpa* plays, films, books, and toys.

Two of the most memorable strips of the era, *Buster Brown* and *Little Nemo,* also built successfully on a simple premise that was repeated in each installment. They were widely imitated, profitably merchandised, and universally praised as classic creations.

After Outcault left the *New York Journal* in 1898, he worked briefly for the *New York World* and sold freelance cartoons to *Life* and *Judge*. In 1901, he produced a feature for the *New York Herald, Pore Li'l Mose,* which starred a little black boy and his animal friends. Outcault struck gold again when he introduced *Buster Brown* in the *Herald* on May 4, 1902. A genteel version of Mickey Dugan (a.k.a. the Yellow Kid), Buster wore Little Lord Fauntleroy suits and lived in a respectable middle-class home. In each episode, this attractive and intelligent ten-year-old would initiate some form of mayhem—pulling down curtains, spilling food, breaking dishes, crashing his bicycle—with devilish naughtiness. In the end, Buster was usually spanked or otherwise punished, and he repented in the form of handwritten resolutions. The following week, he would be back to create new mischief.

BUSTER BROWN AND TIGE—The stars of Richard F. Outcault's second "hit" creation, in a special drawing for **The Bookman.** *November 1902.* Courtesy of Robert C. Harvey

The rest of the cast—Tige the bulldog, Mrs. Brown, and girlfriend Mary Jane—were modeled after Outcault's own dog, wife, and daughter.

Once again, Outcault's timing was perfect. *Buster Brown* was distributed to papers across the country, and its star became a national celebrity. Middle-class readers, who had been repelled by the urban squalor of *Hogan's Alley,* were pleasantly titillated by the polite shenanigans of Buster's suburban setting. Outcault was quick to seize on the commercial potential for marketing his character and was intent on not losing control of this creation, as he had with the Yellow Kid.

Outcault's contract with the *Herald* expired on December 31, 1905. After entertaining an offer from the *Denver Post* to draw *Buster Brown* for a yearly salary of $10,000, Outcault decided to sign with Hearst. The *Herald* continued to publish *Buster Brown,* drawn by other artists, while Outcault was producing his creation for the Hearst papers. According to *Editor & Publisher* on February 17, 1906, "as many as five papers containing *Buster Brown* pictures were recently on sale in Detroit on the same Sunday."

Outcault initiated legal action to prevent the *Herald* from releasing the competing version. The *Herald* responded by copyrighting *Buster Brown* in Washington, D.C., and, on February 6, 1906, filing a countersuit with the U.S. District Court in New York. The attorney for the *Herald* argued that because his client had invested large sums of money in promoting the feature, it was entitled to legal ownership.

Both cases were tried in the same court by the same judge. The *Herald* was awarded the right to the title, *Buster Brown,* and given clearance to continue releasing the feature. The Star Company, the Hearst-owned publisher of the *New York American* and the *Journal,* was also granted permission to produce new episodes but was not allowed to use the title.

Fortunately for Outcault, this decision applied only to control of the drawings. He had reserved the right to "dramatize" his creation and had written agreements to that effect, signed by the *Herald.* A later court case granted him all ancillary rights to the character. In the ensuing years, the Outcault Advertising Agency initiated more than thirty lawsuits against companies for illegally using *Buster Brown* artwork. There were also numerous court battles over theatrical rights. One of these stage shows earned Outcault $44,000 in royalties over a four-year period.

Buster Brown was the first comic strip character to be used as a brand name. In 1904, Outcault attended the St. Louis World's Fair and granted licenses to the Brown Shoe Company and the watch manufacturer Robert Ingersoll; they worked out a cooperative promotion, packaging shoes and watches together. Before long, Buster was endorsing a wide range of products, including textiles, dolls, toys, games, coffee, soft drinks, flour, bread, apples, suits, hosiery, and pianos.

"Buster Brown was the crucial link between comic strips and the development of a visual culture of consumption in America," explained Ian Gordon in *Comic Strips and Consumer Culture.* "Indeed 'Buster Brown' cannot be understood solely as a comic strip. All of his incarnations contributed to the makeup of his character, and each reinforced or advertised the others." In the coming years, other cartoon characters, including Popeye, Mickey Mouse, and Snoopy, would be marketed with the same synergistic techniques that Outcault pioneered with Buster Brown.

Winsor McCay's *Little Nemo in Slumberland,* which debuted in the *New York Herald* on October 15, 1905, was also based on a recurring scenario: Nemo falls asleep, dreams, and wakes up in the last panel, tumbling out of bed. From this starting point, McCay explored a world of graphic fantasy that stretched the limits of the imagination.

In 1891, McCay (who was born sometime between 1867 and 1871) started working at the Vine Street Dime Museum in Cincinnati, where he illustrated scenery, posters, and signs. This early experience in the colorful atmosphere of sideshows and carnival amusements provided inspiration for many of his later creations. After four years on the art staff of the *Cincinnati Enquirer,* McCay relocated to New York and, in 1903, was hired by James Gordon Bennett to draw cartoons for the *Telegram* and the *Herald.* Among the many features he created for these papers were *Little Sammy*

NEMO AND FRIENDS—Promotional drawing by Winsor McCay for the **Baltimore Sun, featuring the characters from LITTLE NEMO IN SLUMBERLAND.** *c. 1910*

GERTIE THE DINOSAUR—Poster advertising the release of Winsor McCay's historic animated film. *November 1914. Courtesy of Ray Winsor Moniz*

Sneeze, about a boy whose uncontrollable outbursts inevitably led to chaos, and *Hungry Henrietta,* which starred a girl with an insatiable appetite.

Although McCay never acknowledged the influence of Sigmund Freud, who had published *The Interpretation of Dreams* in 1900, a fascination with human psychology is evident in much of his work. McCay's most adult-oriented creation, *Dream of the Rarebit Fiend,* explored the obsessions of the subconscious. In each episode, after eating a rich meal of Welsh rarebit, the main character had a graphic nightmare about a deep fear, such as suffocation, weightlessness, or drowning.

Little Nemo in Slumberland was, without question, McCay's masterpiece. Between 1905 and 1911, he put on a virtuoso performance in the pages of the *New York Herald.* Majestic architecture, fanciful creatures, and evocative scenery were rendered with graphic precision. He experimented with innovative page layouts, using tall panels to suggest height and panoramas to provide breadth. Successive action sequences anticipated later experiments in film animation. His use of color took full advantage of the *Herald*'s presses, which were reputed to be the best in the business. He developed continuing story lines, chronicling Nemo's extended adventures in Befuddle Hall, Shanty Town, and across North America in an airship.

McCay was modest about his abilities. In Clare Briggs's 1926 book, *How to Draw Cartoons,* he shared with aspiring artists some of the lessons he had learned: "The greatest contributing factor to my success was an absolute craving to draw pictures all the time." "I don't think I had any more talent for drawing than other kids had, but I think it was the interest I had in drawing and the fun I had in making them that brought out what perfection I have." "The cartoonist must create, he must see in his mind a situation, maybe full of life and comedy, maybe still or dramatic or tragic."

Other cartoonists explored fantasy in the funnies, but *Little Nemo* was the most acclaimed strip in the genre. Critics of lowbrow humor praised the high artistic and moral qualities of McCay's creation, and other cartoonists were quick to imitate his successful formula. Among the many fantasy strips of the era were *Wee Willie Winkie's World* and *The Kinder-Kids* (both 1906) by Lyonel Feininger, *Nibsy, the Newsboy, in Funny Fairyland* (1906) by George McManus, *Danny Dreamer* (1907) by Clare Briggs, *The Explorigator* (1908) by Harry Grant Dart, *Mr. Twee Deedle* (1911) by Johnny Gruelle, and *Bobby Make-Believe* (1915) by Frank King.

During his long career, McCay pursued many interests. In 1906, he took his act on the road and performed "chalk talks" on the vaudeville circuit. He was a pioneer in the field of animation, and his 1914 film, *Gertie the Dinosaur,* which he cleverly incorporated into his stage show, was the first animated cartoon to feature a character with a convincing personality.

He went to work for Hearst in 1911 and was an influential political cartoonist throughout the 1920s.

McCay died of a cerebral hemorrhage on July 26, 1934. He was respected among his peers as one of the greatest cartoonists in America. "His distinction was built on unsurpassed technique, seemingly unlimited imagination, unsparing insistence on detail and inventive genius," stated one obituary.

In *The Art of the Funnies,* Robert C. Harvey summed up McCay's unique place in the history of the art form: "He was so far ahead of his time that many of his innovations were beyond the abilities of his contemporaries: what he had discovered and demonstrated about the capacities of each medium had to be rediscovered decades later by the next generation of cartoonists."

In the first years of the twentieth century, comics began to appear in daily newspapers as well as Sunday supplements. Strips and panels could be found scattered throughout the morning and evening editions, often on the sports pages. The readers of the dailies were mostly male workers, on their way to and from work. The content of many early efforts, such as *Mr. Jack, The Hall Room Boys, E. Z. Mark,* and *The Outbursts of Everett True,* reflected the tastes of this audience. Rube Goldberg, George Herriman, Jimmy Swinnerton, Gus Mager, and TAD Dorgan were among the cartoonists who paid their dues during the formative years of the funnies and went on to attain fame in the coming decades.

Bud Fisher was a sports cartoonist on the *San Francisco Chronicle* in 1907. One day he decided to try something new with his drawing. "In selecting the strip form for the picture,"

BUD FISHER—Self-caricature from The Mutt and Jeff Cartoons, the first book collection of Fisher's strip, produced by the Ball Publishing Company. 1910. *Courtesy of the International Museum of Cartoon Art*

MUTT AND JEFF WISH EVERYBODY A MERRY CHRISTMAS—*Special drawing by Bud Fisher for the* **New York American.** *1913. Courtesy of Editor & Publisher*

Fisher remembered, "I thought I would get a prominent position across the top of the page, which I did, and that pleased my vanity. I also thought the cartoon would be easy to read in this form. It was."

The strip, *Mr. A. Mutt Starts in to Play the Races,* appeared on November 15, 1907, and starred a chinless racetrack gambler. After "absorbing a little of the 'inside infor,'" Mutt placed three ten-dollar bets on "Proper," "Money Muss," and "Blondy." These were names of real horses that were running across the bay at the Emeryville racetrack. The last panel of Fisher's drawing invited readers to "See what Mr. Mutt does for himself in tomorrow's '*Chronicle.*'" It was a clever new use of the "cliffhanger," a well-known plot device popular in serialized fiction and stage melodramas of the era.

From this simple beginning, the first successful daily comic strip was born. Fisher's readers returned—day after day—to learn the results of Mutt's wagers. Many actually believed that they were legitimate tips and raced to the betting windows to put their money on the horses mentioned in the strip.

For the next few months, Mutt's daily activities revolved around gathering information for his next bet, raising money, placing wagers, and watching races, which he would lose, more often than not. After that, the whole cycle would begin again. When Mutt's horse did come in, he never held on to his winnings for long.

In 1908, Fisher's feature veered off in a new direction. In a rambling continuity, Mutt was arrested for petty thievery, tried, convicted, and sent to an insane asylum. Fisher dabbled in political commentary during the trial, using the names of real San Francisco bigwigs who were embroiled in a local corruption scandal. Somehow, during all this, Mutt still managed to place bets at the racetrack. On March 27, while in the "bughouse," Mutt met a short, bald, deluded fellow who intro-

duced himself as the famous boxing champion James Jeffries, or "Jeff" for short. Gradually the two developed a friendship, but it was not until 1910, when the first book collection, *The Mutt and Jeff Cartoons,* was published, that they officially became a team. The title of the strip remained *A. Mutt* until September 15, 1916.

The addition of Jeff raised the level of humor in Fisher's feature. Mutt's plans were now eternally doomed to failure by Jeff's ineptitude. Although Mutt would take his frustrations out on his bumbling sidekick in the form of kicks, punches, and thrown objects, Jeff never held a grudge. Together the lanky opportunist and the diminutive fall guy became a universal archetype: the mismatched pair. *Mutt and Jeff* survived for more than seventy-five years, until the strip was canceled in 1983. They remained friends to the end.

Less than a month after *A. Mutt* debuted in the *San Francisco Chronicle,* Hearst, the publisher of the *San Francisco Examiner,* hired Fisher for $45 a week, double his previous salary. With uncanny foresight Fisher wrote, "Copyright 1907, H. C. Fisher," in the last strip he submitted to the *Chronicle* and the first two he drew for the *Examiner.* He later registered the copyright in Washington, D.C. After Fisher went to work for Hearst, the *Chronicle* directed Russ Westover (who later created *Tillie the Toiler*) to draw *A. Mutt.* Fisher challenged the *Chronicle*'s right to continue his creation, and on June 7, 1908, the newspaper gave in and ceased publication of the strip. Fisher was the first cartoonist to successfully establish ownership of his creation.

In the next decade, Bud Fisher, the highest-paid cartoonist in the comics business, faced off against William Randolph Hearst, the nation's most powerful publisher, in a prolonged court battle. At stake was legal and financial control of a pen-and-ink property that Fisher had guided to success. It would be a landmark decision.

richard f. outcault

THE "FATHER OF THE NEWSPAPER COMIC STRIP" flaunted his success by sporting a natty hunter's cap, a waxed mustache, and a walking stick when he appeared in public, but he was modest about his abilities. "I am the worst artist along Park Row," he told a reporter in 1896. In a later interview, he summed up his career by claiming, "*The Yellow Kid,* my first conception, and *Buster Brown,* my last, are but mediums for the same kind of epigrammatical humor of a strain that I look on peculiarly as my own."

Richard Felton Outcault was born in Lancaster, Ohio, on January 14, 1863. His German ancestors, who arrived in America in 1720, originally spelled their name "Altgelt." Richard's father, Jesse, was a modestly successful cabinetmaker and encouraged his son's artistic interests. After attending public school, R. F. studied at McMicken College (which later became the Art Academy of Cincinnati) for three years and then found employment painting scenes on strongboxes for the Hall Safe and Lock Company.

In 1888, Edison Laboratories mounted an exhibition of electrical illumination at the Centennial Exposition of the Ohio Valley and Mid-Atlantic States in Cincinnati. Outcault was hired for the sum of $400 to provide illustrations of the display for *Electrical World* magazine, and eventually he joined the Edison company as a full-time employee, moving to its headquarters in West Orange, New Jersey. In 1889, he traveled to France as the official draftsman for the Edison exhibit at the International Exposition in Paris and studied art in the Latin Quarter.

When Outcault returned to New York in 1890, he supplemented his work for *Electrical World* by selling cartoons to *Truth, Life,* and *Judge* magazines. Some of these single-panel drawings featured scenes of tenement life, a popular subject of the era. When Joseph Pulitzer launched his new colored comic section on May 21, 1893, freelance artists like Outcault were his primary recruits, since many of the top cartoonists were already under contract to the comic weeklies. Outcault's first cartoon for the *Sunday World* was a six-panel sequence entitled "Uncle Eben's Ignorance of City Ways Prevents His Keeping an Engagement with His Wife," which appeared on September 16, 1894.

Outcault also continued to draw cartoons for *Truth,* and on February 17, 1895, the *Sunday World* reprinted one of these panels. "Fourth Ward Brownies" was the first appearance in Pulitzer's paper of the bald-headed street urchin who was to become the Yellow Kid.

Years later, Outcault described the original inspiration for his curious creation. "When I used to go about the slums on newspaper assignments," he remembered, "I would encounter

RICHARD F. OUTCAULT—Caricature by William Shields. *February 9, 1908, San Francisco Examiner*

him often, wandering out of doorways or sitting down on dirty doorsteps. I always loved the Kid. He had a sweet character and a sunny disposition, and was generous to a fault. Malice, envy or selfishness were not traits of his, and he never lost his temper."

The success of the Yellow Kid brought Outcault wealth and fame, but after less than three years he was ready to move on. He drew his last regular Yellow Kid episode for William Randolph Hearst's *New York Journal* on February 6, 1898, although his famous ragamuffin made a few guest appearances in some of his subsequent features. Outcault went back to work for Pulitzer between February 1898 and July 1900, creating a number of short-lived comics series. He then joined James Gordon Bennett's *New York Herald* and introduced *Buster Brown* on May 4, 1902.

Although Outcault was adept at rendering comedic action in his drawings, his style was more typical of the realistic illustration found in nineteenth-century humor magazines than the raucous exaggerations being pioneered in the newspaper comic sections in the first decade of the twentieth century. As the funnies evolved, Outcault's detailed cross-hatching and elegant line work began to look dated. After 1910, Outcault produced new episodes of *Buster Brown* on a semi-regular basis as he became increasingly involved in the Outcault Advertising Agency, which managed the numerous Buster Brown licensing accounts.

The last episode of *Buster Brown,* syndicated by Hearst, appeared on December 11, 1921; reprints were published until 1926. Outcault spent his retirement years traveling, lecturing, and painting, and he died at his suburban mansion in Flushing, New York, on September 25, 1928.

THE AMATEUR DIME MUSEUM IN HOGAN'S ALLEY.

HOGAN'S ALLEY Sunday page by Richard F. Outcault. The last Yellow Kid page by Outcault published in Pulitzer's paper. October 4, 1896, New York World.
Courtesy of Denis Kitchen

MCFADDEN'S ROW OF FLATS proof sheet by Richard F. Outcault. When he moved to the Journal, Outcault's version of HOGAN'S ALLEY appeared under this new title. October 25, 1896, New York Journal. Richard D. Olson Collection, The Ohio State University Cartoon Research Library. Courtesy of the Frye Art Museum, Seattle. Photo credit: Susan Dirk/Under the Light

BUSTER BROWN original hand-colored Sunday page by Richard F. Outcault. August 30, 1903, New York Herald. Courtesy of the International Museum of Cartoon Art

THE YELLOW KID HE MEETS TIGE AND MARY JANE AND BUSTER BROWN—*Original hand-colored Sunday page by Richard F. Outcault.*
July 7, 1907, American Examiner. Courtesy of the Art Wood Collection of Cartoon and Caricature, Prints and Photographs Division, Library of Congress

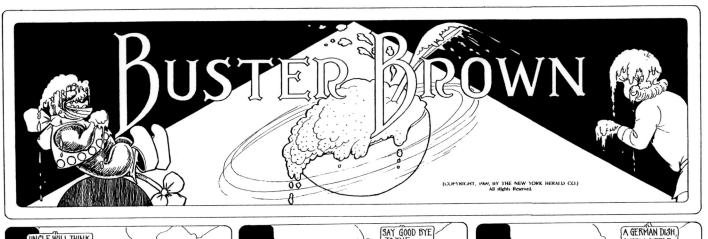

BUSTER BROWN original Sunday page. After Richard F. Outcault left the Herald to work for the Hearst newspapers in 1906, a number of artists continued his feature for that paper. This artist is unknown, although the page looks as if it may have been done by Winsor McCay, who was working for the Herald at this time. 1909, New York Herald. Courtesy of Illustration House

rudolph dirks

RUDOLPH DIRKS—Self-caricature from Comics and Their Creators. 1942

THE CREATOR of the longest-surviving feature in comics history was a newcomer to the field when he was hired by William Randolph Hearst in 1897. His immortal mischief-makers—dark-haired, bow-tied Hans and fair-haired, lace-collared Fritz—appeared in two separate, competing features for sixty-five years and still star in a weekly version syndicated by King Features.

Rudolph Dirks was born in 1877 in Heinde, Germany, and immigrated to Chicago when he was seven years old. He began selling cartoons to *Judge* and *Life* in 1894 and three years later went to work for the *New York Journal.*

According to Hearst family legend, young Willie picked up a copy of Wilhelm Busch's picture-story book *Max und Moritz* while touring Europe with his mother. Dirks himself, however, did not credit Hearst with the idea to create a comic strip based on Busch's *Bilderbogen.* On December 12, 1897, at the suggestion of his comic editor, Rudolph Block, Dirks introduced a multi-panel sequence in which three boys grappled with a gardener and his hose.

The following week, the cast had been reduced to a pair of pranksters. In the early episodes, "The Katzies" rebelled against their Mama, but in the next few years, Der Captain, a ship-wrecked sailor who acted as their surrogate father, and Der Inspector, a truant officer, became the primary victims of the boys' practical jokes.

It was obvious to readers from the beginning, by the clothing and the setting, that the Katzenjammers were German, although it was not until a few years later, when Dirks started using speech balloons on a regular basis, that the unique dialect of the characters became apparent. "Mitt dose kids, society is nix," a trademark phrase perpetually bellowed by Der Inspector, was typical of the mispronounced English spoken in the strip.

The success of Dirks's feature spawned many imitations, the foremost being *The Fineheimer Twins* by Harold Knerr, which began running in the *Philadelphia Inquirer* on February 15, 1903. When Dirks parted ways with Hearst in 1912, Knerr took over as the new artist on *The Original Katzenjammer Kids,* which was relaunched in the Hearst newspapers on November 29, 1914. In June of that same year, Pulitzer began publishing Dirks's continuation of his creation, which was retitled *The Captain and the Kids* in 1918 due to anti-German sentiment during World War I. (Knerr's feature was renamed *The Shenanigan Kids* for the same reason.)

Although he was only an adequate draftsman, Dirks pioneered the use of many comic devices that eventually became part of the art form's visual language. Parallel lines and dust clouds to indicate speed, dotted lines to represent eye contact, and sweat beads to suggest fear or nervousness were among the many forms of graphic communication that appeared regularly in the panels of *The Katzenjammer Kids.* Dirks was more of an innovator than Knerr, who drew in a polished "big-foot" style (featuring characters with oversized feet, heads, and noses) and was considered to be the more gifted of the two artistically.

In *America's Great Comic-Strip Artists,* Richard Marschall summed up this pioneer's legacy: "Dirks took the young art form's basic formula—peace, scheming, mayhem, exposure, punishment—and made it appeal to all ages and types of readers, expressed through a new vocabulary appropriate to comic strips alone. Hans and Fritz's endless explosions and chases may have seemed trivial, yet they endure. After almost a century, *The Katzenjammer Kids* can be read as a virtual 'dod-gasted' blueprint of what a comic strip is."

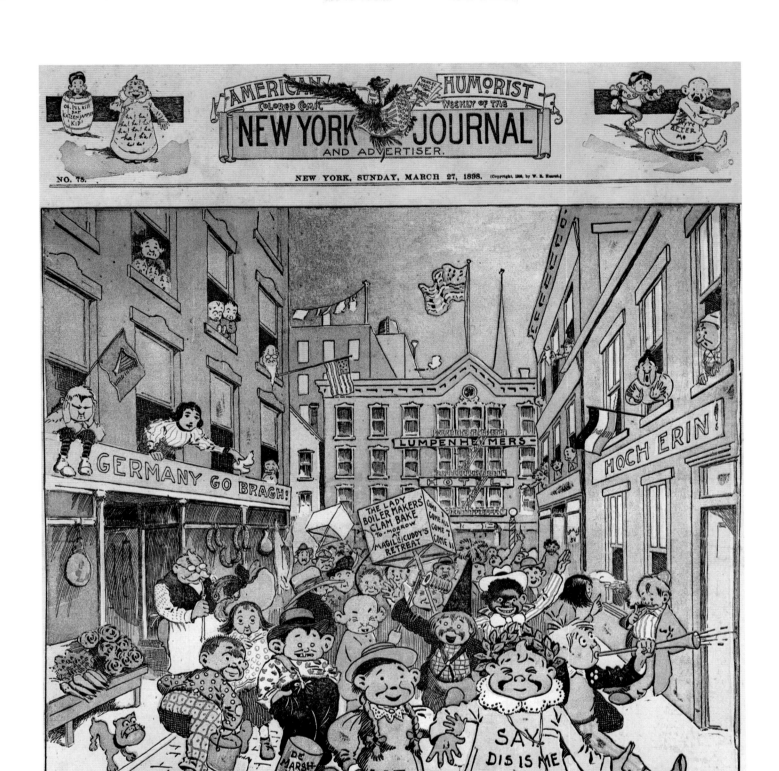

THE KATZENJAMMER KIDS Sunday page by Rudolph Dirks. This artist's Kids took over as the headliners in the Hearst comic sections after Outcault moved on. March 27, 1898, New York Journal. Courtesy of Peter Maresca

MAMA KATZENJAMMER CROSSES A BRIDGE—Sunday half-page by Rudolph Dirks. 1900, San Francisco Examiner.
Courtesy of Peter Maresca

MAMA KATZENJAMMER ISS SO STRONG! ACH,YES!—Sunday half-page by Rudolph Dirks. April 21, 1901, St. Louis Daily Globe-Democrat.
Courtesy of Mark Johnson

My! But the Katzenjammers Are Rich!

THE KATZENJAMMER KIDS original hand-colored Sunday page by Rudolph Dirks. This page was Exhibit No. 11 in the 1913 trial between the Press Publishing Company, representing Dirks, and Hearst's Star Company. Part of Dirks's breach-of-contract suit was based on his complaint that Hearst's editor, Rudolph Block, instructed him to put the Katzenjammers into high-society situations. Dirks made two or three attempts to satisfy this request before he gave up, claiming that this was not the type of humor he was comfortable doing. June 2, 1912, New York Sunday American. *Courtesy of Eugene J. Walter Jr.*

THE SHENANIGAN KIDS original hand-colored Sunday page by Harold Knerr. The Katzenjammers changed their name during World War I due to anti-German sentiment. *December 28, 1919. Courtesy of the International Museum of Cartoon Art*

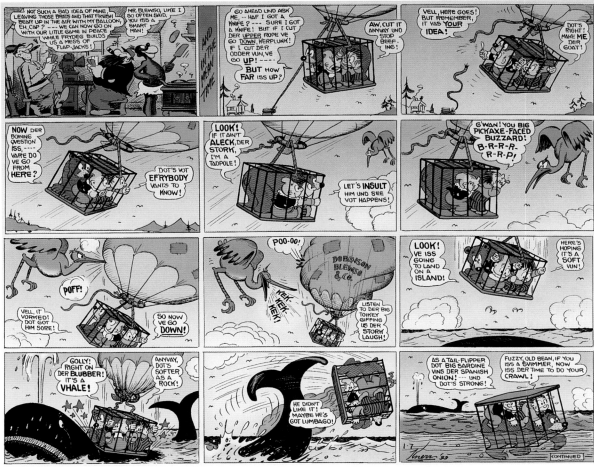

THE KATZENJAMMER KIDS original artwork with color overlays of a two-page sequence by Harold Knerr. An aviation enthusiast, Knerr frequently incorporated flying contraptions into his stories. © January 7 and 14, 1933, King Features Syndicate, Inc. Courtesy of Bruce Hamilton

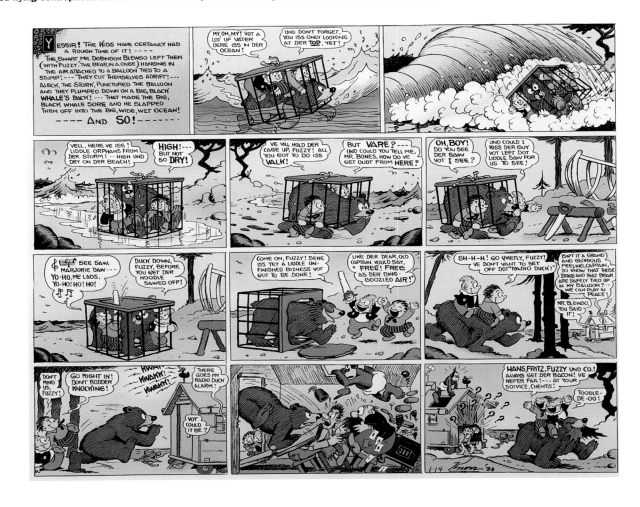

frederick b. opper

F. Opper.
AT WORK

FREDERICK B. OPPER—Caricature by T. E. Powers

THE "DEAN OF AMERICAN CARTOONISTS" was a leading artist in the humor magazines of the nineteenth century, a pioneer in the early years of the newspaper comic strip, and an influential political cartoonist for more than two decades before he retired in 1932. Five years later, when he passed away at the age of eighty, his friend Russ Westover, creator of *Tillie the Toiler,* eulogized him in a memorial radio broadcast: "Mr. Opper did with his comic characters in print what Will Rogers did on the screen and over the air—broke that tension—made people laugh and forget their troubles for awhile at least."

Frederick Burr Opper was born on January 2, 1857, in Madison, Ohio, the son of an Austrian immigrant. He dropped out of school at the age of fourteen to work for the local newspaper, and two years later he left for New York to seek his fortune as an artist. His first known published cartoon appeared in *Wild Oats* in 1876; a year later, he joined the staff of *Frank Leslie's Illustrated Newspaper.* He moved to *Puck* magazine in 1881, where he produced black-and-white cartoons and spot illustrations, as well as color lithographs, for eighteen years until he was recruited by William Randolph Hearst in 1899. The veteran cartoonist brought respectability to the press lord's "yellow journal."

In the first decade of the new century, Opper launched a string of classic newspaper comic strips in the pages of the *New York Journal* and *American,* including *Happy Hooligan* (March 11, 1900), *Our Antediluvian Ancestors* (January 20, 1901), *Alphonse and Gaston* (September 22, 1901), *And Her Name was*

Maud (June 24, 1904), and *Howson Lott* (April 25, 1909).

Opper's "trust-busting" political cartoons were also widely distributed and featured such immortal graphic icons as Willie (McKinley), Teddy (Roosevelt), Nursie (Mark Hanna), Papa (the fat-bellied Trust), and Mr. Common Man. A remarkably prolific artist, Opper illustrated books by Bill Nye, Mark Twain, Eugene Field, and Finley Peter Dunne.

An interviewer who visited the famous cartoonist at his house in New Rochelle, New York, in October 1929 observed that he worked in a modest second-floor room, which had a window that overlooked the backyard. It was equipped with a small drawing board, two bottles of India ink, and a box of crayons. A rolltop desk, a bookcase, several stuffed chairs, and a select group of drawings and photographs given to him by his fellow artists completed the Spartan surroundings.

"I have done hundreds of series in my time," Opper told the reporter. "Some of them have been popular for a time, and some haven't. You can never tell when the public's fancy is going to be tickled. All a comic artist can do is to set out to amuse and entertain whoever will look at his work. If he's got the stuff, he can do it; if he hasn't, he can't."

Opper turned from the interviewer to his drawing board and began coloring the printer's guide for his next *Happy Hooligan* strip. "Comic art is a wonderful business if the artist has the particular kind of ability it takes," he continued. "I still do enough to keep me busy but I can't work as fast as I used to."

At that time, he was turning out a Sunday page and three editorial cartoons a week. He had been a professional cartoonist for fifty-three years. Although his eyesight was failing, Fred Opper still had the right stuff.

ALPHONSE AND GASTON panel from a Sunday page by Frederick B. Opper. 1903

HAPPY HOOLIGAN original hand-colored Sunday page by Frederick B. Opper. Happy often traveled with his brothers, Gloomy Gus and Lord Montmorency.
© April 9, 1905, American-Journal-Examiner. Courtesy of Angelo Nobile

HAPPY HOOLIGAN original hand-colored Sunday page by Frederick B. Opper. Happy began his long courtship with Suzanne in 1908, which finally culminated on June 18, 1916, in their marriage. *c. 1910*, New York American. *Courtesy of Illustration House*

AND HER NAME WAS MAUD.

AND HER NAME WAS MAUD *Sunday page by Frederick B. Opper. A variation on a recurring theme, as farmer Si Slocum and Maud are upended by a motor car.* © February 27, 1921, King Features Syndicate, Inc. Courtesy of Russ Cochran

jimmy swinnerton

THE GRAND OLD MAN of cartooning is often overlooked as a pioneer of the art form. His newspaper career began before the introduction of the Sunday funnies and lasted for more than sixty years.

James Guilford Swinnerton was born in Eureka, California, on November 13, 1875, the son of a judge who was also the founder of the *Humboldt Star,* a weekly newspaper. After studying at the California Art School in San Francisco, the sixteen-year-old towhead landed a job at William Randolph Hearst's *Examiner* in 1892.

Years later, Swinnerton looked back on his early days as a newspaper cartoonist: "The artist of that date had to go to all sorts of happenings that are now covered by the staff photographers, as photographs were not yet produced successfully on news pages. A typical day was spent covering, say, a flower show or trial in the morning, a baseball game in the afternoon with, maybe, an art opening and a murder or two at night. One had to be ready to draw anything at a moment's notice. Those of us who had a comic turn in our work would try to crowd a comic drawing in whenever we could and, in so doing, our editors began to find out that a good cartoon, or comic drawing, drew more notice from readers; in that way the comic drawing in the newspaper world gradually came into its own."

The young cartoonist's talents came to the attention of his boss in 1893 when he drew a realistic illustration of Monarch, a grizzly bear Hearst had captured and put on display in San Francisco as a publicity stunt. "Swin" was asked to do a daily drawing of the state mascot, and his humorous, roly-poly version of Baby Monarch became a fixture in the paper beginning in October 1893. This continuing feature, which eventually included a full cast of little bears and human tykes, was not a comic strip as many historians have claimed, but it was one of the first examples of repeated appearances by popular characters in an American newspaper.

Little Bears became *The Journal Tigers* (inspired by the Tammany tiger, representing the Democratic Party political machine in New York) when Swinnerton went to work for the *New York Journal* in 1897. Mr. Jack, a philandering feline

JIMMY SWINNERTON—Self-caricature. April 1923, Circulation magazine

with a straw hat and cane, emerged from the pack to star in his own strip beginning in 1903. One of the little tykes also got his own Sunday page, which debuted on February 14, 1904. *Little Jimmy* was Swinnerton's most enduring creation, running almost continuously until 1958.

During his brief stay in New York City, Swinnerton went through a failed marriage, suffered a nervous breakdown, and was diagnosed with tuberculosis; the doctors gave him only two weeks to live. "If I remained much longer in New York, I would have passed on," he claimed. In the summer of 1906, Hearst put his artist friend on a train bound for Colton, California, a refuge for TB patients. Swinnerton spent the rest of his life in California and Arizona. "I arrived in pretty good condition and fell headlong, head over heels in love with the grand Arizona desert and sunsets," he remembered. "In fact I liked the place so much I forgot to die." He survived to the ripe old age of ninety-eight.

OUR TIGERS GO ABROAD—Original hand-colored Sunday page by Jimmy Swinnerton. After he came to New York in 1897, Swinnerton's LITTLE BEARS became THE JOURNAL TIGERS. *c. 1900. Courtesy of Illustration House*

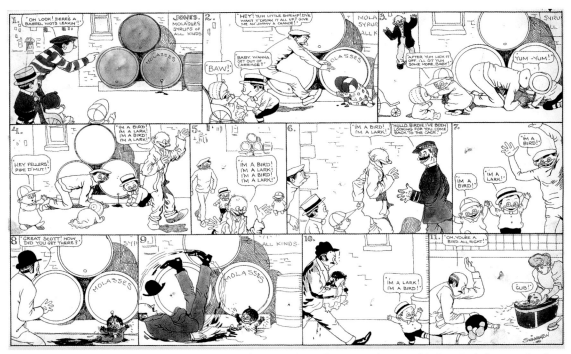

LITTLE JIMMY original Sunday half-page by Jimmy Swinnerton. Jimmy Thompson, the star of Swinnerton's long-running feature, had an innocent curiosity about the world around him and was often punished by his parents for his distractions. 1909. Courtesy of Illustration House

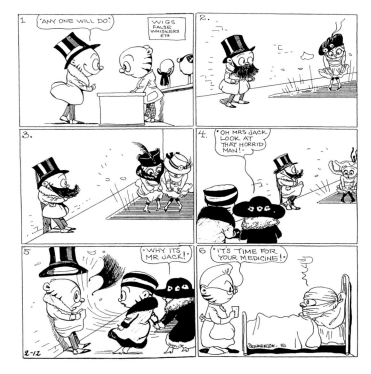

MR. JACK daily strip by Jimmy Swinnerton. 1919. Courtesy of Rob Stolzer

MR. JACK daily strip by Jimmy Swinnerton. A womanizing cat-about-town, Mr. Jack, who first appeared in the Sunday funnies in 1903, was given his own daily strip nine years later. 1914. Courtesy of Russ Cochran

PA MERELY TAKES A DIP—Original hand-colored *LITTLE JIMMY* Sunday page by Jimmy Swinnerton. *July 5, 1914. Collection of the Cartoon Art Museum, San Francisco. Photo courtesy of the Frye Art Museum, Seattle. Photo credit: Susan Dirk/Under the Light*

CARTOON PIONEERS

In addition to Outcault, Dirks, Opper, and Swinnerton, many other talented creators contributed to the development of the art form during the early years of the century. On the following pages are newspaper comics by a sampling of these innovators, some of whom also did work for the weekly humor magazines.

LATEST NEWS FROM BUGVILLE original hand-colored half-page by Gus Dirks. In 1903, Rudolph's younger brother, who was also a regular contributor to Judge *magazine, committed suicide.* c. 1902. Courtesy of Illustration House

LEANDER AND CHARLEY MEET ON THE FIELD OF HONOR—Sunday half-page by F. M. Howarth. A frequent contributor of sequential comics to the weekly humor magazines of the late nineteenth century, Howarth created LULU AND LEANDER in 1902 for the Hearst newspapers. © August 13, 1905, American-Journal-Examiner. Courtesy of Mark Johnson

FOXY GRANDPA ON THE BEACH.

BOYS—AH! HERE'S GRANDPA TAKING A SUN BATH. LET'S ROLL THE BARREL ON HIM.

BOYS—LOOK OUT, GRANDPA, SOMETHING'S COMING.

GRANDPA—HERE! WHAT'S THIS!

WHY, BOYS, IS THIS YOUR

BARREL?

WELL, THE BARREL'S ON YOU THIS TIME, BOYS.

FOXY GRANDPA Sunday half-page by Carl "Bunny" Schultze. Grandpa always outwitted his two tormentors, who were never given names.
1901, New York Herald. Courtesy of Peter Maresca

THE UPSIDE-DOWNS OF LITTLE LADY LOVEKINS AND OLD MAN MUFFAROO THE THRILLING ADVENTURE OF THE DRAGON

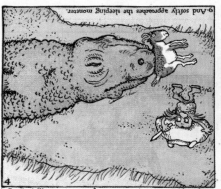

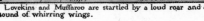

THE UPSIDE DOWNS Sunday half-page by Gustave Verbeck. This clever feature was designed to be read right side up and then turned upside down to complete the story. May 8, 1904, New York Herald. Courtesy of Peter Maresca

BILLY BOUNCE *Sunday page by Charles W. Kahles. An early Kahles creation, Billy was one of the first comic characters with superpowers.*
1905, McClure Syndicate, Inc. Courtesy of Peter Maresca

BROWNIE CLOWN OF BROWNIE TOWN Sunday page by Palmer Cox. The Brownies, who first appeared in St. Nicholas magazine in 1883, also had a short career as newspaper comics stars, beginning in 1903. October 20, 1907, Detroit News Tribune. Courtesy of Mark Johnson

SPARE RIBS AND GRAVY Sunday page by George McManus. This feature, by the creator of BRINGING UP FATHER, ran in the World *from January 28, 1912, to February 8, 1914, and revolved around the exploits of two bumbling explorers and a tribe of African natives.* c. 1912, New York World. *Courtesy of Craig Englund*

RACIAL CARICATURE

Ethnic stereotypes appeared in many of the early comics, but they gradually fell out of favor as the syndicates began marketing their features to a more diverse audience. Offensive black caricatures persisted much longer and were still relatively common in newspaper comics until World War II. Although racial stereotyping still exists today, it is no longer considered an acceptable form of graphic representation.

Certain distinguishing characteristics were common to most black caricatures. E. C. Matthews, in his 1928 instruction book, *How to Draw Funny Pictures,* advised that "the wide nose, heavy lips and fuzzy hair are all as important to a colored cartoon character as the dark complexion." Black dialect was also used to accentuate their ignorant or foolish behavior. In terms of subject matter, Matthews observed that "the cartoonist usually plays on the colored man's love of loud clothes, watermelon, chicken, crap-shooting, fear of ghosts, etc."

During the first part of the century, black characters were almost always cast in subservient roles as maids, butlers,

janitors, or stable boys. Sunshine in *Barney Google,* Mushmouth in *Moon Mullins,* Rachel in *Gasoline Alley,* and Smokey in *Joe Palooka* were typical of the black supporting players in popular strips of the 1920s and 1930s.

A comprehensive overview of newspaper comics before 1945 would be incomplete without including many of these characters. The images of black people shown here, and in subsequent chapters, must be evaluated in the historical context of the era. Important lessons can be learned by studying the visual record of racial intolerance, and hopefully these past transgressions can be avoided.

Today, cartoonists are more sensitive to their black readers and no longer rely on simplistic caricatures and clichés. Fully developed African-American characters are still a minority on the funnies pages, however. A great deal of progress needs to be made before blacks receive fair and equal treatment in the comic sections of American newspapers.

SAMBO AND HIS FUNNY NOISES Sunday page by Billy Marriner. One of the first features to star a black character, albeit a "pickaninny" with "dumb luck," Marriner's strip was syndicated from April 2, 1905, to March 21, 1915, by the McClure Syndicate. March 22, 1908, San Francisco Chronicle. Courtesy of Mark Johnson

winsor mccay

WINSOR MCCAY—Caricature by Cliff Sterrett. February 10, 1907, New York Herald

UNIVERSALLY PRAISED as the finest draftsman ever to work in the comics medium, this inspired and dedicated artist was also a pioneer in the field of film animation and an influential graphic commentator for the Hearst newspapers later in his career.

Zenas Winsor McCay was born in 1867, 1869, or 1871, according to varying accounts. A fire in his boyhood town of Spring Lake, Michigan, destroyed all of the town's records, so there is no definitive date of his birth. Winsor's parents encouraged his compulsive urge to draw, and an art teacher at the Michigan State Normal School, John Goodison, taught him important lessons in perspective, composition, and color, which he put to use throughout the rest of his life.

McCay's two most important comic strip creations, *Dream of the Rarebit Fiend* (September 10, 1904) and *Little Nemo in Slumberland* (October 15, 1905), both relied on a similar formula. Each episode would begin with a subconscious fantasy already in progress and would build to the climactic panel in which the character would awaken. Readers were conditioned by McCay's brilliant visualization techniques to instantly perceive the change between a character's internal and external point of view.

John Canemaker, McCay's biographer, eloquently described the magical charms of his masterpiece: "*Little Nemo in Slumberland* offers an extraordinary array of ravishing images that stay in the mind like remembered dreams. McCay's virtuoso draftsmanship is irresistible, as when butterflies seek shelter from the rain under an 'umbrella tree,' or the open mouth of a giant dragon becomes a traveling coach, or when a walking, talking icicle exhorts us up the cold staircase of Jack Frost's palace."

McCay's life was riddled with contradictions.

Though possessed of an imagination that bordered on the bizarre, he led a conventional middle-class existence and was often pictured at his drawing board wearing a coat, a hat, and a tie. He was relatively shy, yet he had no fear of performing on a vaudeville stage. His art was hand-drawn, but he was a pioneer in the technology of film animation. He earned a fortune during his lifetime but left very little for his family when he died.

In 1909, according to McCay, his son showed him a book of drawings that appeared to move when the pages were flipped. The child's amusement inspired him to begin experimenting with moving pictures projected on a screen. He produced four thousand drawings on rice paper, photographed each one at the Vitagraph Studio near his home in Sheepshead Bay, New York, hand-colored the 35mm frames, and incorporated the final short subject into his stage show. Between 1911 and 1921, McCay produced ten animated films.

William Randolph Hearst, who hired McCay in 1911, became disenchanted with these extracurricular activities and ordered his star cartoonist to focus exclusively on newspaper work. During the 1920s, to honor his contract, McCay cut back on public performances, film experiments, and comic strips. He turned out hundreds of detailed drawings for the Hearst papers to illustrate the editorials of Arthur Brisbane. Although some historians argue that Hearst stifled McCay's brilliant imagination, his "sermons in line" were powerful graphic statements of universal themes, which transcended Brisbane's pompous pronouncements.

"As fantasist, draftsman, observer, and reporter, satirist, innovator, and developer of new forms of communication," writes Canemaker, "McCay must be ranked among the greatest figures of twentieth-century popular art." No cartoonist has ever surpassed his achievements.

DREAM OF THE RAREBIT FIEND comic page by Winsor McCay. The artist used the pen name "Silas" on his first successful feature, which ran several days a week in the Telegram. In this episode, he gets a "big head" listening to compliments about his vaudeville stage act. *c. 1906, New York Evening Telegram (New York Herald Company). Courtesy of Craig Yoe*

DREAM OF THE RAREBIT FIEND comic page by Winsor McCay. An artist struggles with changing scenery. *1906, New York Evening Telegram (New York Herald Company).*
Courtesy of Jack Gilbert

LITTLE SAMMY SNEEZE comic page by Winsor McCay. Sammy shatters the panel borders with a powerful "kah-chow." September 24, 1905, New York Herald.
Courtesy of Ray Moniz

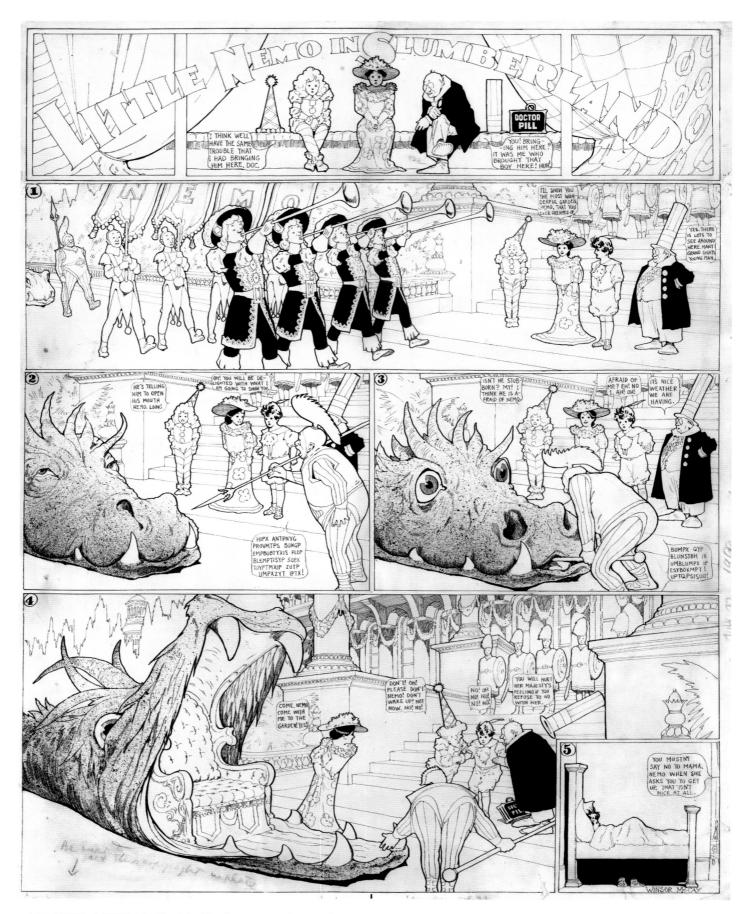

LITTLE NEMO IN SLUMBERLAND original Sunday page by Winsor McCay. This visual image of a dragon coach was adapted for McCay's **LITTLE NEMO** animated film, which was completed in 1911. July 22, 1906, New York Herald. Courtesy of Ricardo Martinez

LITTLE NEMO IN SLUMBERLAND *recolored Sunday page by Winsor McCay. This page concluded the three-part sequence with the dragon coach.*
August 5, 1906, New York Herald. Courtesy of Illustration House and American Color

FANTASY IN THE FUNNIES

The success of Winsor McCay's *Little Nemo in Slumberland* inspired other cartoonists to create comic features that explored the world of childhood dreams and imagination.

NIBSY, THE NEWSBOY, IN FUNNY FAIRYLAND Sunday page by George McManus. Nibsy is hawking Sunday editions of the "Funny Side," the New York World's comic section, in this classic episode of McManus's fantasy creation. *May 20, 1906, New York World. Courtesy of Mark Johnson*

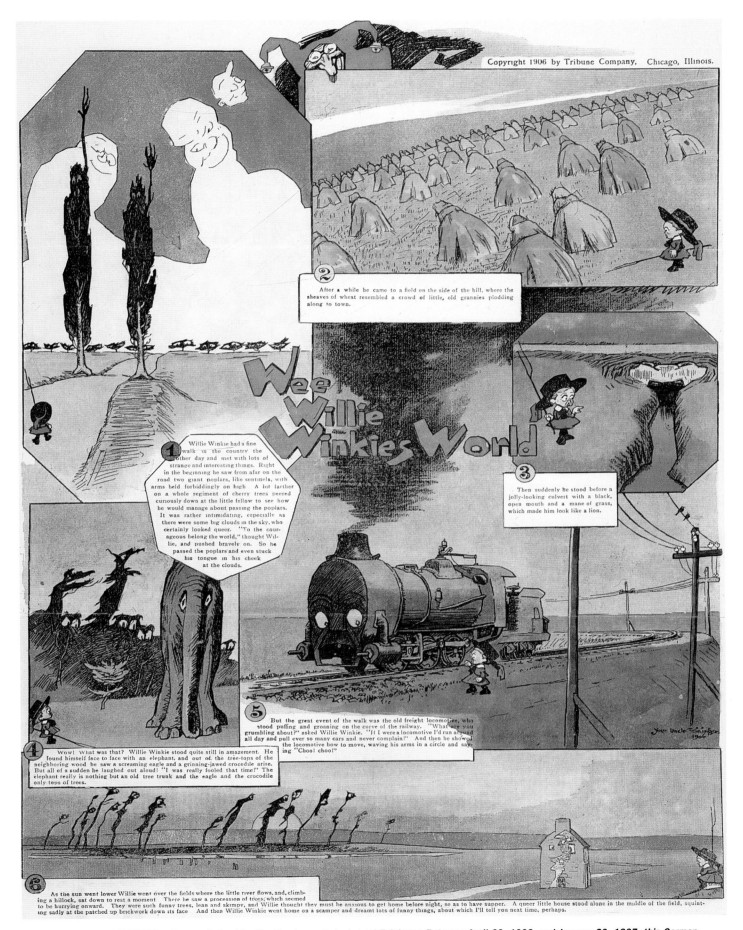

WEE WILLIE WINKIE'S WORLD color proof sheet for the Sunday page by Lyonel Feininger. Between April 29, 1906, and January 20, 1907, this German-American artist, who later became a famous painter, created two short-lived features, THE KIN-DER-KIDS and WEE WILLIE WINKIE'S WORLD, for the Tribune. *September 30, 1906, Chicago Sunday Tribune. Courtesy of Prints and Photographs Division, Library of Congress*

THE EXPLORIGATOR—Admiral Fudge Comes Back to Earth Again

THE EXPLORIGATOR Sunday page by Harry Grant Dart. A superbly illustrated page that had a brief life in the New York World from May 3 to August 9, 1908.
Courtesy of Peter Maresca

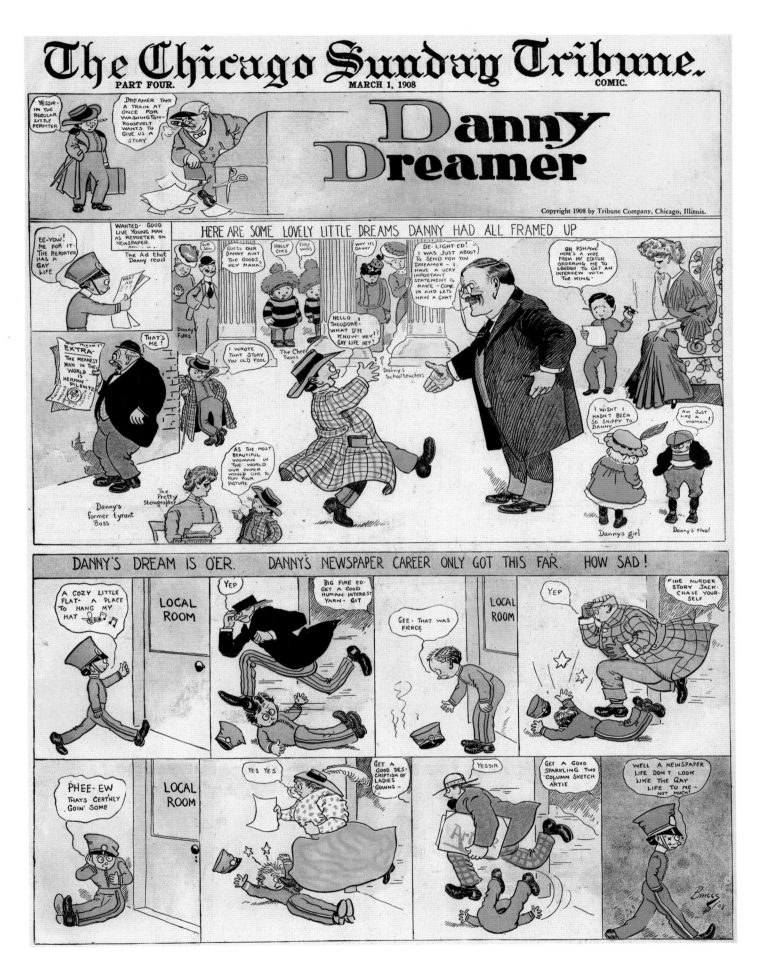

DANNY DREAMER *Sunday page by Clare Briggs. Danny meets Teddy Roosevelt in an episode of Briggs's first successful creation, which ran from December 1, 1907, to February 23, 1913, in the Tribune.* March 1, 1908, Chicago Sunday Tribune. *Courtesy of Mark Johnson*

MR. TWEE DEEDLE Sunday page by Johnny Gruelle. This charming feature followed LITTLE NEMO in the Herald and was written and illustrated by the creator of RAGGEDY ANN AND ANDY. June 28, 1914, New York Herald. Courtesy of Peter Maresca

the
teens

THE THRILL THAT COMES ONCE IN A LIFETIME daily panel by H. T. Webster. The artist looks back nostalgically on the early days of the funnies. © 1923 Press Publishing Company. Courtesy of the San Francisco Academy of Comic Art

THE CARTOONIST MAKES PEOPLE SEE THINGS!

THE CARTOONIST MAKES PEOPLE SEE THINGS—A powerful anti-German cartoon by James Montgomery Flagg. c. 1918

T HE OPTIMISM AND INNOCENCE OF THE TURN OF THE CENTURY GRADUALLY FADED BETWEEN 1910 AND 1920. A RAPID SUCCESSION OF DRAMATIC EVENTS FORCED AMERICANS TO FACE THE REALITIES OF UNREGULATED INDUSTRIALIZATION, SOCIAL INEQUALITY, AND GLOBAL CONFLICT.

The Triangle Shirtwaist Company fire on March 25, 1911, resulted in the deaths of 146 people, most of whom were immigrant seamstresses, and led directly to long-overdue labor reform laws in New York City. When the *Titanic* went down in the frigid North Atlantic on April 14–15, 1912, and 1,513 souls were lost, questions were raised about the fallibility of the vessel's designers and the much higher survival rate of its upper-class passengers. The first Model T to roll off Henry Ford's new assembly line in Highland Park, Michigan, in 1914 ushered in the modern era of mass production. In April 1914, labor unrest intensified nationwide after the Colorado state militia opened fire on striking miners, who were seeking recognition for the United Mine Workers union. The assassination of Archduke Franz Ferdinand, heir to the Austro-Hungarian throne, in Sarajevo on June 28, 1914, led directly to the disastrous "war to end all wars," which the United States entered almost three years later. D. W. Griffith's epic film *The Birth of a*

Nation opened on March 3, 1915, and sparked controversy for its sympathetic portrayal of the Ku Klux Klan. The shooting of Czar Nicholas II and his family on July 16, 1918, marked the climax of the Russian Revolution and the corresponding growth of the American socialist movement. The influenza epidemic, which started in the spring of 1918 and quickly spread across six continents, claimed more than twenty-one million victims in one year. In 1919, the United States ratified the Eighteenth Amendment, prohibiting "the manufacture, sale, or transportation of intoxicating liquors," and Congress passed the Nineteenth Amendment, stating that the "right of citizens . . . to vote shall not be denied . . . on account of sex." Eight members of the Chicago White Sox, who lost the 1919 World Series to the Cincinnati Reds, were later indicted for accepting bribes from professional gamblers to "throw" the games.

It was a time of disillusionment and uncertainty. Events were unfolding at an unprecedented pace, and Americans had an insatiable desire to keep themselves informed. Business had never been better for newspaper publishers.

In 1913, the number of daily newspapers in America reached a peak of 2,622, with a combined circulation of more than twenty-eight million. After the outbreak of World War I in 1914, metropolitan evening papers experienced a 25 percent increase in sales due to the time difference between Europe and New York; frontline dispatches were quickly added to the night editions, and the large city papers often featured five to eight pages of war news at the end of the day. As the hostilities spread, however, newsprint shortages put a halt to this growth. Paper prices rose by more than one-third between 1914 and 1917, and the total number of weekly, semiweekly, and daily publications in the United States decreased as marginal papers struggled to survive. In the postwar era of consolidation, large newspaper chains swallowed up their competitors.

The number of cities with more than one newspaper also peaked before World War I. Exclusive stories, sensational headlines, popular columnists, and powerful editorials fueled the competition between city papers. But as editors increasingly relied on the wire services—the Associated Press (AP), United Press Associations (UPA), and International News Service (INS)—for their national and international news, uniformity set in. The same reports could be found in any paper that subscribed to these services. Conversely, comics were sold on an exclusive territorial basis, so competing newspapers did not have access to the same strips and panels. Consequently, the funnies became one of the few unique features that a paper could offer to its readers. By the end of the decade, signing up one of the top strips, like *Mutt and Jeff* or *The Gumps,* could make or break a newspaper.

The syndicates that sold the most popular comic features grew in size and stature. The Newspaper Enterprise Association began servicing the Scripps chain in 1902; Joseph Pulitzer launched his Press Publishing Syndicate in 1905; and Moses Koenigsberg, a Hearst executive, established the Newspaper Feature Syndicate in 1913 and King Features two years later. Among the other organizations that joined the ranks of long-established syndicates were the George Matthew Adams Syndicate (1907), the Central Press Association (1910), Associated Newspapers (1912), the Wheeler Syndicate (1913), and the Ledger Syndicate (1918). The Chicago Tribune Syndicate, which had been distributing comics since 1901, became the Chicago Tribune–New York News Syndicate in 1919.

The syndicates gradually transformed the content of the comics. Urban, ethnic, and slapstick humor was complemented by more family-friendly fare. Although many of the creations from the first decade of the century, including *Happy Hooligan, The Katzenjammer Kids,* and *Buster Brown,* continued to be among the most popular strips, new titles released in the

FONTAINE FOX—Self-caricature by the successful syndicated cartoonist. February 11, 1928, The Saturday Evening Post. Courtesy of the International Museum of Cartoon Art

second decade provided a broader spectrum of choices for urban, suburban, and rural readers. Syndicate editors were aware of the objections raised by the anti-comics crusaders, but they were more concerned about the entertainment value of their features. Comics designed specifically for children, such as *The Teenie Weenies* (1914), *Uncle Wiggily's Adventures* (1919), and *Peter Rabbit* (1920), were launched, but the reform movement did little to change the industry.

As the syndicates became more powerful, they were able to attract the best talent. Homegrown artists who achieved local renown were quickly snapped up by the big distributors. The top cartoonists began earning huge salaries. They were also free to work where and when they wanted, as well as to entertain better offers from competing syndicates. To protect their investments, the syndicates signed artists to long-term contracts and secured the copyrights to the features they distributed.

Fontaine Fox, who had been producing a weekly panel on suburban life for the *Chicago Post* since 1908, signed a lucrative contract with the Wheeler Syndicate in 1913 to produce *Toonerville Folks.* Fox was grateful for the increased exposure and income that this arrangement made possible. "I feel toward the syndicates as Henry Ford should feel toward the man who first thought of applying the conveyor-belt system to factories and made mass production possible," Fox explained. "In drawing for many scattered newspapers, instead of one published in the city in which I lived, I had to alter the type of work I had been doing. I realized the need of identifying myself in the minds of my following with a series of characters, so as to make each cartoon's appeal as sure in San Francisco as in New York."

Will Lawler, writing in *Editor & Publisher* on February 21, 1914, summed up the role of cartoonists as circulation producers at that time: "The comic artist of today is a power in newspaperdom and in most cases is paid well, and in some handsomely, because his work when good is what attracts readers and readers make circulation. His work not only appears in the paper that pays him his salary but is syndicated in many papers throughout the United States, thus enabling the publisher to not only pay the artists good salaries but also make a profit on their labor."

In 1912, George McManus, creator of *The Newlyweds*, quit the *New York World* to work for the Hearst organization. "Mr. McManus, when approached cautiously the other evening in Louis Martin's Cafe and asked why the change, rubbed his thumb and forefinger together," observed a New York reporter. "Judging from the cracked ice he wears in his scarf, the *Journal* must have offered him a million dollars a picture. George takes his good fortune with characteristic aplomb."

According to *American Magazine*, Bud Fisher was making $78,000 a year drawing *Mutt and Jeff* in 1916; when the earnings from vaudeville lectures, animated cartoons, and novelty products were added, his annual income approached $150,000. Rube Goldberg was also reportedly making $100,000 a year from his combined *New York Mail* salary and movie royalties.

As their salaries rose and syndicates competed for their services, cartoonists became increasingly aware of their importance. Two of the top creators of this period, Rudolph Dirks and Fisher, rebelled against the control of "the Chief," William Randolph Hearst. Both disputes ended up in court.

RUDOLPH DIRKS—Early self-caricature of the legendary pioneer. June 1905, Everybody's Magazine

According to comics legend, Dirks's defection began when he decided to take an unprecedented vacation in 1912. John Dirks recounted his father's story for *Cartoonist PROfiles* in 1974:

He'd been working for 15 years on the *Katzenjammers* and he wanted a rest. When Hearst's *New York Journal*, for whom Dirks was doing the feature, heard of the cartoonist's plans, they told him to work up a year's worth of pages in advance before leaving. Dirks started on this herculean project and continued it for some months but difficulties developed. Dirks felt that his contract had been breached so he and Mrs. Dirks sailed for Europe. The *Journal* sent cables and Rudy did send some pages to them from overseas. At this point, Joseph Pulitzer's *New York World* got into the act and made vigorous efforts to get Dirks to work for them. They landed him and it was agreed between Dirks and Pulitzer that the page would be suspended until the legal aspects of his *Journal* contract were straightened out. The case went to court and became a very well-publicized affair. The final decision decreed that Rudy could draw his original characters, under a different title for the *World*, and that the *Journal* owned the original title and could produce a strip with the original characters.

LITTLE TRAGEDIES OF A NEWSPAPER OFFICE—Jimmy Murphy, creator of TOOTS AND CASPER, gets an offer that is too good to be true. December 18, 1919, Editor & Publisher

This often-retold story may not be entirely accurate. Dirks had gone on sabbaticals before and frequently took time off to paint, so the vacation could not have been the only point of contention. The cause for the break was also the result of his relationship with comic editor Rudolph Block. Many artists chafed under Block's harsh supervision, and when the *World* made Dirks a tempting financial offer, he decided to leave.

Hearst hired Harold Knerr to continue *The Katzenjammer Kids* for the *Journal* in 1914, and Dirks went on to produce an identical feature for the *World*. Dirks's version started in June 1914 and was titled *Hans und Fritz* beginning on May 23, 1915— and renamed *The Captain and the Kids* in 1918, after the United States entered the war against Germany. Including rip-offs and reprints, at one time there were five different comic strips starring mischievous twins appearing simultaneously in the nation's newspapers.

On June 13, 1914, *Editor & Publisher* ran an interview with Mama Katzenjammer about the bewildering situation she now found herself in. "I haff been to court, unt der court says Rudolph vas der varder of der kits," explained Mrs. Katzenjammer. "Den dot other mans, he say, 'Nit—I vas der vater of der kits—' unt he makes dem do stunts yust der same as Rudolph."

"Yes it must be a very distressing situation for a lady to be placed in," responded the interviewer. "Sure—it vas makin' me unt Hans unt Fritz unt der Captain vork overtime. But vat can ve do?" she sighed. "Der kits now haff two varders unt two pages efery Sountay."

Both features continued to run opposite each other, in competing newspapers, until United Feature Syndicate finally pulled the plug on *The Captain and the Kids* in 1979. King Features still distributes *The Katzenjammer Kids* to a small list of subscribers, mostly in foreign countries.

The dispute between Fisher and Hearst's Star Company lasted more than six years and culminated at the U.S. Supreme Court. In 1910, Fisher signed a five-year contract with the Star Company, publishers of the *New York American*, to draw the Mutt and Jeff strip for a salary that escalated from $200 to $300 a week. Before this contract expired in 1915, Fisher entered into a three-year agreement with John Wheeler to produce his feature exclusively for a $1,000-per-week guarantee. The Star Company responded by copyrighting the title *Mutt and Jeff* and arranging for other artists to continue the feature.

Three legal actions were then initiated. The Star Company first sought an injunction to prevent the Wheeler Syndicate from using the title and the characters. The other two suits were brought by Wheeler to prevent the Star Company from producing imitations of Fisher's creation. The judge in the original trial, as well as judges in the appeals courts, ruled in favor of Fisher in all three suits. The case ultimately

WELL, WELL! LOOK WHO'S HERE!—Caricature of Bud Fisher and his two stars published at the time he signed his new contract with the Wheeler Syndicate and began his long court battle with Hearst's Star Company. August 7, 1915, Editor & Publisher

reached the U.S. Supreme Court in November 1921. The high court refused to overrule the previous decisions of the lower courts, throwing out the appeal of the Star Company. Fisher was granted exclusive rights to reproduce his characters and legal protection from competitive imitations.

In "Confessions of a Cartoonist," published in *The Saturday Evening Post* on August 4, 1928, Fisher claimed, "I am as proud of this achievement as anything I ever did, since the whole contention of the Hearst legal forces was that they had the rights to the characters because of the popularity they had given them through publication. Our contention was that I had originated the strip on another paper where it was published before it appeared in any Hearst newspaper, and to prove it we produced the copies of the *San Francisco Chronicle* in which the drawings I had copyrighted away back in 1907 were published."

Wheeler, who started all the ruckus back in 1915, summed up Fisher's legacy in his 1961 memoir, *I've Got News for You:* "He probably did more to make the cartoon business for his more cowardly confreres than anyone else who has ever been in it." Fisher had taken on the Chief and won.

Fisher was not the only San Francisco sports cartoonist to make it big in New York. Thomas Aloysius "TAD" Dorgan

INDOOR SPORTS daily panel by TAD Dorgan. TAD, who popularized the term "hot dog" (among other expressions), makes a humorous comment on the news of the day. © December 12, 1920s, King Features Syndicate, Inc. Courtesy of the International Museum of Cartoon Art

was working at the *San Francisco Bulletin* when he attracted the attention of Arthur Brisbane, the editor of the *New York Journal,* in 1904. After coming East, TAD became the highest-paid sports cartoonist in the business. He also created three canine characters—Silk Hat Harry, a carousing dog-about-town; Curlock Holmes, a bulldog detective; and Judge Rummy, a monocled mutt—who starred in variously titled strips beginning in 1910. TAD's best-known panels were *Indoor Sports* and *Outdoor Sports,* which lampooned prizefights, ball games, and horse races, as well as office politics and home life. He also did a domestic Sunday-page feature, *For Better or Worse,* during the 1920s.

TAD is remembered today as one of the most prolific contributors to the "slanguage of America." He popularized the lingo of the speakeasies, racetracks, and smoke-filled rooms of his day and penned many of his own unique phrases, including "Yes, we have no bananas," "Half the world are squirrels and the other half are nuts," and "23-skiddoo." His description of the dachshund-like sausages being served at Coney Island in 1913 (which allegedly contained canine ingredients) as "hot dogs" has now become the accepted designation for that popular foodstuff.

Rube Goldberg replaced TAD as the sports cartoonist on the *San Francisco Bulletin* in 1905. Two years later he moved to New York and got a job at the *Evening Mail.* In addition to sports cartoons, Goldberg turned out an endless stream of clever human-interest panels, including such pun-laden classics

as *Foolish Questions, Mike and Ike—They Look Alike,* and *I'm the Guy.* One of these creations, which appeared on an irregular basis, featured *The Inventions of Professor Lucifer G. Butts.* This satirical spoof of technological progress would prove to be the cartoonist's most enduring legacy. A "Rube Goldberg device" has become the dictionary term for a wildly complicated contraption designed to accomplish the simplest of tasks.

A restless genius, Goldberg produced many comic features during his long, prolific career, including *Boob McNutt* (1915), *Bobo Baxter* (1927), *Doc Wright* (1934), *Lala Palooza* (1936), and *Rube Goldberg's Sideshow* (1938). He was also a Pulitzer Prize–winning political cartoonist, an accomplished sculptor, and one of the founders of the National Cartoonists Society.

The graphic jesters of the daily comics, much like the early pioneers of the Sunday funnies, experimented constantly. They alternated titles, casts, and situations at their whim. In addition to TAD and Rube, Gus Mager, T. E. Powers, Maurice Ketten, Harry Hershfield, Jimmy Swinnerton, and Tom McNamara were among the stars of the New York publishing world during these formative years.

The fame and fortune of American cartoonists were also fueled by the growing film industry. Newspaper comics and cinema evolved at the same time and had a close relationship in the early years. Many of the first short, live-action films borrowed sight gags familiar to readers of the funnies. A film based on Opper's *Happy Hooligan* was released by Thomas

OH! YOU VAMPIRE

WILLIAM FOX PRESENTS MUTT & JEFF IN MEETING THEDA BARA PRODUCED BY BUD FISHER DISTRIBUTED BY FOX FILM CORPORATION

MEETING THEDA BARA—Promotional poster for one of the MUTT AND JEFF animated films produced by Bud Fisher and distributed by William Fox. June 23, 1918. Courtesy of Bruce Hershenson

Krazy Kat, Silk Hat Harry, Jerry on the Job, and *Little Jimmy* had been produced.

Many of the leading cartoonists also pursued opportunities in the film business. In 1916, Goldberg was commissioned to create an animated newsreel spoof for Pathé, *The Boob Weekly,* and he reportedly earned $75,000 for his efforts. After leaving the Hearst organization, Fisher teamed up with the Barré-Bowers studio and produced a series of four-minute *Mutt and Jeff* cartoons in 1916. A year later, when he returned from military service, he set up his own operation, Bud Fisher Films Corporation, and released the studio's first series of fifteen cartoons on June 9, 1917. Fisher signed a lucrative deal with Fox to distribute his films, and fifty-two *Mutt and Jeff* cartoons were made every year until 1922. Although Fisher claimed in interviews that he personally drew all of his cartoons, he was rarely seen around the studio.

Animated adaptations of comic strip creations continued to be produced throughout the silent-film era, but Felix the Cat and Mickey Mouse were to become the major cartoon movie stars during the next two decades. These film personalities also appeared in their own newspaper comic strips.

Stories about the top-earning cartoonists, which appeared regularly in newspapers and magazines, inspired the next generation of creators. Fledgling artists, who dreamed of becoming the next Bud Fisher or Rube Goldberg, mailed in their hard-earned dollars (usually about $25 for twenty-five lessons) to the numerous cartoon correspondence schools that were established during the decade. The three most popular were the C. N. Landon, W. L. Evans, and Federal programs. Gene Byrnes (*Reg'lar Fellers*), Merrill Blosser (*Freckles and His Friends*), Edwina Dumm (*Cap Stubbs and Tippie*), Martin Branner (*Winnie Winkle*), Roy Crane (*Wash Tubbs*), and Milton Caniff (*Terry and the Pirates*) were all Landon graduates. Chester Gould (*Dick Tracy*) and Elzie Crisler Segar (*Popeye*) provided testimonials in advertisements for the W. L. Evans course as former students. Clare Briggs, Fontaine Fox, Frank King, Winsor McCay, and Sidney Smith were among the many established luminaries who served on the advisory board of the Federal School.

As the funnies were more widely distributed, new types of features began to appear. George McManus's *Bringing Up Father,* which officially began on January 2, 1913, represented an important transition in the thematic evolution of the comics. It featured ethnic caricatures, a repetitive gag formula, and an urban setting—common characteristics of strips from the first decade. But it also explored topics that were echoed in many

Edison's company in 1900, soon followed by adaptations of *Foxy Grandpa* (1902) and *The Katzenjammer Kids* (1903). Richard F. Outcault signed a contract with his old employer, Edison, for a series of eight *Buster Brown* films in 1903. One of the most notable productions of this period was Edwin S. Porter's 1906 *Dream of the Rarebit Fiend,* inspired by Winsor McCay's strip in the *New York Evening Telegram.* These were all live-action productions, however, and it was not until McCay's 1911 film of *Little Nemo in Slumberland* that the arduous task of hand-drawn animation of comic strip characters was attempted.

After McCay showed the way, animated cartoons based on popular comic strips proliferated. Emile Cohl produced thirteen *Newlywed* films between 1913 and 1914. Hearst founded the International Film Service in 1915, and by the following year, cartoons starring his funny-paper stars were screened with the Hearst Vitagraph Newsreel. By the time the studio closed in July 1918, animated adaptations of *Happy Hooligan, The Katzenjammer Kids, Bringing Up Father,*

features from the second wave of creations: family relationships and a desperate striving for social status and financial success. At the peak of its popularity, *Bringing Up Father* claimed eighty million readers in five hundred newspapers from forty-six countries and was translated into sixteen languages. McManus earned an estimated $12 million in the forty years he produced the strip.

Like many of his contemporaries, McManus experimented with numerous comic features before he hit the jackpot with his most well-known creation. Among the many short-lived titles he introduced while at the *New York World* were *Panhandle Pete* (1904), *Nibsy, the Newsboy, in Funny Fairyland* (1906), and *Spareribs and Gravy* (1912). *The Newlyweds* (1904) was the most successful feature he produced for Pulitzer's paper. Baby Snookums, who arrived in the strip on May 19, 1907, eventually stole the spotlight from the young lovebirds.

When Hearst hired him in 1912, McManus continued *The Newlyweds* under a new title, *Their Only Child,* and introduced a string of other generic family features. It was out of this revolving cycle of domestic comedies that his immortal bickering couple, Maggie and Jiggs, emerged.

The genesis of *Bringing Up Father* began in 1895 when McManus attended a performance of *The Rising Generation.* This stage production featured a nightly card game in which a former Irish laborer, played by Billy Barry, complained to his friends. He had become rich overnight and now lived on Fifth Avenue with his wife and daughter. They hoped to be accepted by their new upper-class neighbors and were mortified by his uncouth behavior. He had no desire to fit in and schemed to thwart the family's efforts to civilize him by sneaking off to play poker. McManus later adapted this plot to his new feature and milked the scenario in endlessly clever ways.

In the strip, Jiggs's wife, Maggie, and their haughty daughter, Nora, tried without success to turn him into a respectable social climber. Much to their chagrin, Jiggs's sole ambition in life was to rejoin his old working-class cronies for a plate of corned beef and cabbage and a game of cards at Dinty Moore's tavern. He would go to incredible lengths—crawling out windows, walking on ledges, hanging on wires—to achieve his goal.

McManus illustrated the costumes, interiors, and scenery in *Bringing Up Father* with a stylishly elegant line that suggested the influence of Art Deco. He was also adept at drawing hilariously caricatured secondary characters, violently hurled crockery, and voluptuously proportioned females. Zeke Zekley was McManus's assistant beginning in the mid-1930s and had a hand in the artwork for the next two decades.

In the 1920s and 1930s, McManus explored continuing plotlines that went beyond the daily domestic doings that characterized the formative years of the feature. Maggie and

GEORGE MCMANUS—Self-caricature for an article, "Jiggs, The Globe Trotter." May 1926, World Traveler magazine. Courtesy of the International Museum of Cartoon Art

Jiggs sailed off on a European tour in 1920, returned to a life of poverty after going bust in Hollywood in 1923, traveled to Japan in 1927, and, from December 1939 to July 1940, made an epic journey across the United States.

McManus, who bore a striking resemblance to his main character, told *Collier's* magazine in 1952, "I am not Jiggs. Maggie is not my wife. I have no daughter." "Yet I think I may have become Jiggs," he added. "Or, if you like, Jiggs may have become me. They say if you live long enough with a person you come to look and act as he does, and Jiggs and I have lived together for 40 years—through 85,000 drawings of the comic strip *Bringing Up Father.*" McManus passed away two years later, but Jiggs survived on the funnies pages for another four decades.

The success of *Bringing Up Father* encouraged other cartoonists and their distributors to explore the fertile field of domestic comedy. They discovered that the ethnic slang, racial stereotypes, and urban settings of the early Sunday funnies did not play as well to Middle America. The syndicates increasingly regarded their comics as marketable commodities and consciously developed them to appeal to the largest demographic.

THE GUMPS—*The main cast of Sidney Smith's popular comic strip, from a Chicago Tribune Syndicate advertisement.* February 22, 1919, Editor & Publisher

Most of the new family strips featured a combination of soon-to-be predictable character types. There was often a pretty girl, a bumbling father, an all-knowing mother, a precocious younger sibling, and a troublemaking pet. The parents dreamed of financial success and were acutely aware of their social status, while the kids pursued more frivolous activities. Story lines revolved around get-rich-quick schemes, employment opportunities, and other money-related issues.

Charles Wellington's *Pa's Son in Law* (1911), Cliff Sterrett's *Polly and Her Pals* (1912), Harry Hershfield's *Abie the Agent* (1914), Harry Tuthill's *The Bungle Family* (1918), and Jimmy Murphy's *Toots and Casper* (1918) were among the early family-oriented strips that incorporated one or more of these thematic elements. Sidney Smith's *The Gumps* (1917) was the quintessential creation in the emerging genre.

Joseph Medill Patterson, copublisher of the *Chicago Tribune*, had the idea to create a comic strip that would realistically reflect American family life, and he recruited one of the *Tribune*'s cartoonists, Sidney Smith, to produce it. The name that the Captain (as Patterson was called) chose for the new strip, *The Gumps*, which debuted on February 12, 1917, was derived from a Patterson family term used to describe pompous blowhards.

Andy Gump, the unattractive star of Smith's feature, had a long nose and no chin. His wife, Minerva, was a plain woman, and his son, Chester, was well-mannered and energetic. Andy's wealthy Uncle Bim rounded out the cast. Minerva was the brains of the family, and when the helpless Andy found himself in a jam, he would plead for his wife's assistance with a desperate cry of "Oh Min!"

The Gumps was a "talky" strip. Andy's long-winded lectures on the cost of living, taxes, and other concerns filled his speech balloons to the bursting point, and the family discussions would go on for days. In the first few years, the story lines involved fairly conventional domestic dilemmas, such as Min's overspending, Andy's New Year's Eve hangover, and predictable mother-in-law problems. Beginning in 1920, Smith's plots became more adventurous as the Gumps found themselves entwined in Bim's marital romance, Andy's political campaign, and Chester's treasure hunt. *The Gumps* evolved into what could be considered the first "soap opera strip." It was not the first feature to use continuing stories, but it was certainly the most successful one to employ the cliffhanger approach.

Patterson's instincts had been correct. The public loved *The Gumps*. The Captain seemed to sense what the average American comic strip reader wanted and knew how to give it to them. Patterson would play a pivotal role in guiding the funnies business during the next two decades.

Kid strips, which had always been popular, fit nicely into the syndicates' new marketing strategy. Wholesome humor, youthful ambition, and innocent shenanigans were just what newspaper editors and readers were looking for, and features starring juvenile protagonists proliferated. Among the many notable debuts during the decade were *Us Boys* (1912) by Tom McNamara, *Jerry on the Job* (1913) by Walter Hoban, *Bobby Make-Believe* (1915) by Frank King, *Freckles and His Friends* (1915) by Merrill Blosser, *Just Boy* (1916) by A. C. Fera, *Cap Stubbs and Tippie* (1918) by Edwina Dumm, and *Harold Teen* (1919) by Carl Ed.

Another emerging genre was the "slice-of-life" panel. John McCutcheon, who was the political cartoonist for the *Chicago Tribune* from 1903 to 1946, started the trend with occasional drawings on domestic doings in rural America. Clare Briggs, who knew McCutcheon from his years on the *Tribune* between 1907 and 1914, was influenced by his mentor and developed a panel for the *New York Tribune* in 1914 that used a rotating series of titles. *The Days of Real Sport, When a Feller Needs a Friend,* and *Ain't It a Grand and Glorious Feeling?* were among the many headings for Briggs's cartoons, which evoked nostalgia for a simpler time.

H. T. Webster, often called the "Mark Twain of the Comics," took a similar path, although his subjects were more oriented toward the suburban experience. Among Webster's most memorable titles were *The Thrill That Comes Once in a Lifetime, Life's Darkest Moments,* and *The Timid Soul,* starring Caspar Milquetoast. Fontaine Fox's *Toonerville Folks* (1908) and Clare Dwiggins's *School Days* (1909) were also outstanding newspaper panel cartoons that started during this period and focused on everyday life.

One creation that did not fit neatly into any of these categories was George Herriman's *Krazy Kat.* It has always been regarded by art critics and intellectuals as something of an anomaly on the funnies pages.

"A person with a fancy for the comic section is ordinarily prone to be ashamed of it," wrote Summerfield Baldwin in the June 1917 issue of *Cartoons* magazine. "The shame and the excuses are right and natural, save in this single instance. For to follow the adventures of Mr. Herriman's fantastic animals is a delight which no one should underestimate or fail to enjoy."

Herriman's masterpiece was based on a deceptively simple set of role reversals among his main trio of performers. Instead of chasing the mouse, Krazy Kat adores Ignatz. Instead of fleeing in fear from the cat, Ignatz attacks the lovesick feline with a brick. Instead of bullying the cat, Officer Pupp protects Krazy from Ignatz. Or, as the poet e. e. cummings put it in the introduction to a *Krazy Kat* collection published in 1946, "Dog hates mouse and worships 'cat,' mouse despises 'cat' and hates dog, 'cat' hates no one and loves mouse."

It started inauspiciously in Herriman's *The Dingbat Family* during the summer of 1910. The cat who was to become Krazy appeared as the Dingbats' pet on June 24, and on July 10 an unnamed mouse hurled a missile at the cat's skull in the lower portion of the strip. This was the beginning of a historic game of cat and mouse. Over the course of the next month, Herriman changed the name of his feature to *The Family Upstairs* and created a separate world for the cat and mouse in panels below the main action. This strip-beneath-a-strip ran regularly until October 28, 1913, when it finally became an independent daily feature. The first full-page *Krazy Kat* appeared in black-and-white on April 23, 1916, in the Hearst weekly *City Life* section. Except for a brief experiment with color, between January 7 and March 11, 1922, Herriman's page appeared only in black-and-white until it began running as a color tabloid page in 1935.

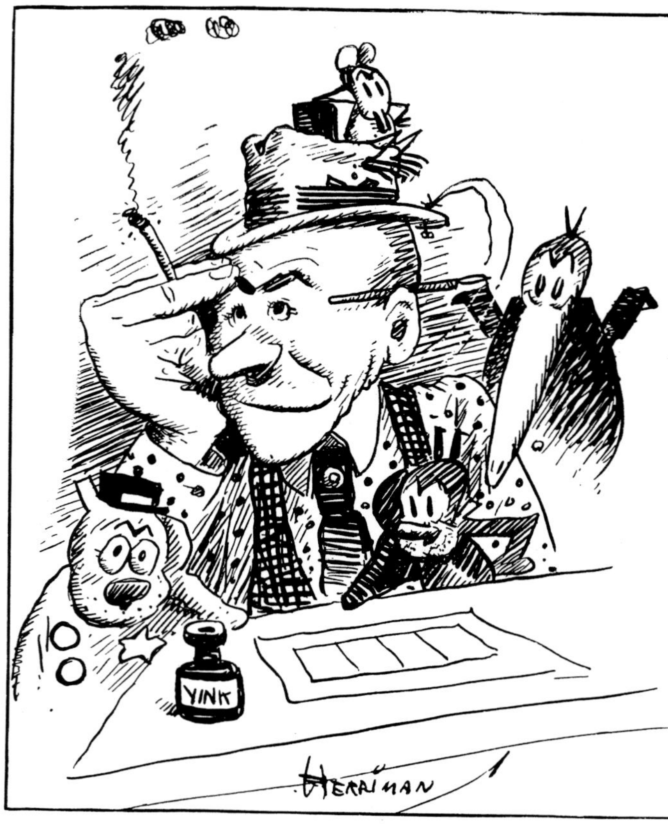
YINK
HERRIMAN

GEORGE HERRIMAN—Self-portrait of the shy cartoonist. *October 21, 1922, Judge magazine*

Hearst was Herriman's biggest fan. According to comic legend, the Chief once demanded that Herriman be given a raise. Herriman sent the money back, modestly claiming that he did not deserve extra compensation because it took so little time to produce the strip. Although *Krazy Kat* was never a financial success, Herriman was able to live comfortably—his salary was reported as $750 a week during the Depression—and he had a guaranteed lifetime contract with King Features. When Herriman died in 1944, *Krazy Kat* was appearing in only thirty-five newspapers.

The unpretentiousness of Herriman's creation left it wide open to interpretation. Many saw it as an allegory for unrequited love. Others read it is a mythic struggle between good and evil. In more recent years, some scholars have argued that because Herriman was a mulatto and Krazy Kat is black, the strip represents the artist's confusion about his own racial identity.

Herriman's message was made even more inscrutable by the fact that he never identified Krazy Kat's gender. After considering the question, Herriman explained, "I realized Krazy was something of a sprite, an elf. They have no sex. So that Kat can't be a he or a she."

The brick that Ignatz perpetually bounced off Krazy's bean has also been described symbolically. In *America's Great Comic-Strip Artists*, Richard Marschall explained, "The brick in Coconino was like the apple in Eden, an agent of both disruptive and bonding impulses."

The setting for the strip was equally significant. In *Krazy Kat: The Comic Art of George Herriman*, the authors claimed, "There can be no true understanding of George Herriman, and only a limited understanding of *Krazy Kat*, without some knowledge of the Navajo country, which includes the settlement of Kayenta as well as Monument Valley and straddles Arizona and Utah." Herriman spent many of the happiest days of his life in this part of the United States, and the cacti, mesas, buttes, and desert sky became the distinguishing characteristics of Krazy Kat's Coconino County. The constantly changing backgrounds of Herriman's pages mirrored the shifting light patterns he observed in the southwestern landscape.

Herriman was dedicated to his craft and became a master of the art form. His scratchy scribblings were remarkably expressive, and the characters moved with quirky energy, coming alive on the page. He loved to play with lines and shapes, colors and sounds, and the scenery was evocative and surreal. A graphic poet of words and images, Herriman created scripts that read like fables, and the dialogue had a syncopated rhythm that was laced with street slang, foreign accents, and clever phrasing. Each episode was an experi-ment in composition; in later years, Herriman introduced a simpler design with customized, hand-drawn logos and bold, abstract layouts.

In *The Seven Lively Arts*, published in 1924, Gilbert Seldes declared, "*Krazy Kat*, the daily comic strip of George Herriman is, to me, the most amusing and fantastic and satisfactory work of art produced in America to-day."

"Such is the work which America can pride itself on having produced," Seldes concluded in his famous essay. "It is rich with something we have too little of—fantasy. It is wise with pitying irony; it has delicacy, sensitiveness, and an unearthly beauty. The strange, unnerving, distorted trees, the language inhuman, un-animal, the events so logical, so wild, are all magic carpets and faery foam—all charged with unreality. Through them wanders Krazy, the most foolish of creatures, a gentle monster of our new mythology."

Herriman responded to Seldes in a letter that "now I've got an inflated 'mouse'—a 'kop' busting with Ego—and a 'kat' gone clean Kookoo—on my hands. . . . Gilbert being just weaklings guess they can't hold their good fortune—and I don't blame them—you said some nice things—werra—werra nice things—"

An extremely modest man, Herriman was uncomfortable with praise. He would never have accepted his place as the most universally revered cartoonist of all time. In his mind he was just drawing a comic strip about a cat, a mouse, and a dog.

KRAZY KAT, OFFICER PUPP, AND IGNATZ—Original hand-colored postcard that Herriman drew for a friend in the 1930s. *Courtesy of Jack Gilbert*

bud fisher

THE FIRST MILLIONAIRE CARTOONIST was a colorful character who traveled with Pancho Villa in Mexico, married Countess de Beaumont on a luxury liner bound for Europe, bred racehorses, and mingled in high society. He is credited with starting the first successful daily comic strip and was one of the few artists to establish ownership of his creation, in an era when syndicates controlled the rights to all of the features.

Harry Conway "Bud" Fisher was born in Chicago on April 3, 1885. He dropped out of the University of Chicago after three months and was hired as a sports cartoonist for the *San Francisco Chronicle* in 1905. It was here that he introduced his horse-racing strip, *A. Mutt,* which began running daily on November 15, 1907. Less than a month later, Fisher switched to Hearst's *San Francisco Examiner,* and then he joined the staff of the *New York American* in 1909.

Shortly before his contract with Hearst expired in 1915, he signed a lucrative deal with the Wheeler Syndicate. A prolonged court battle over the ownership of the strip ensued, and the case was not resolved until 1921. Fisher, who emerged victorious, reaped the profits from *Mutt and Jeff* newspaper sales as well as animated cartoons, stage shows, and licensed products based on the characters, and he was reportedly earning an annual salary approaching $250,000 in the early 1920s.

John Wheeler, who first met Fisher in 1913, described him as "a dapper, cocky little guy." He was also an egotistical showman who cultivated his image as a celebrity. He was often photographed in his Rolls-Royce, and he hobnobbed with celebrities and showgirls. A hard-drinking playboy, he squandered his fortune on bad investments and two failed marriages.

By the 1920s, Fisher was spending less and less time at his drawing board. He hired Ed Mack, the artist who briefly did a competing version of his strip for Hearst in 1915, as his assistant. After Mack's death in 1932, Al Smith continued to produce *Mutt and Jeff,* with only minimal input from his boss.

Tragically, Fisher spent his final years alone and forgotten. In the early 1950s, Rube Goldberg, George McManus, and Bob Dunn visited the aging cartoonist at his Park Avenue apartment. "It was like stepping back into the year 1925," remembered Dunn. "If the rest of the apartment looked shabby genteel, the bedroom looked like the corner of Skid Row and Tobacco Road. No carpeting or rug. Cigarette butts all over the parquet floor."

BUD FISHER—This caricature of the famous cartoonist shows him arriving at Saratoga carrying trophies from his victories in other horse races. *c. 1920s*

"I couldn't believe what we were seeing," he added. "The big bed had no sheet on it. Just the bare mattress. And two beaten up old pillows without pillowcases. Propped up on an elbow was the legendary creator of *Mutt and Jeff.* He hadn't shaved in at least a week."

Fisher tried to keep up professional appearances by complaining to his fellow cartoonists about getting behind with his deadlines, but they all knew he had not drawn the strip for many years. He died of cancer not long after this visit, on September 7, 1954, at the age of sixty-nine. John Wheeler summed up Fisher's demise in his 1961 autobiography, *I've Got News for You:* "He squandered his own life and was a very unhappy man." It was a tragic end for a talented artist who fought courageously for his creative independence and achieved the highest levels of success in his chosen field.

MUTT AND JEFF daily strip by Bud Fisher. Mutt takes advantage of Jeff in a game of billiards in this early example of Fisher's strip.
© 1910 H. C. Fisher. Courtesy of Jim Scancarelli

MUTT AND JEFF daily strip by Bud Fisher. Jeff is in Turkey getting the Istan-bull from three street vendors. © 1913 H. C. Fisher. Courtesy of Bruce Hamilton

MUTT AND JEFF daily strip by Bud Fisher. The boys get orders from a Prussian prince in this episode from World War I. © 1915 H. C. Fisher. Courtesy of Bruce Hamilton

MUTT AND JEFF daily strip by Bud Fisher. The famous cartoonist can't please all of his readers. © 1919 H. C. Fisher. Courtesy of Craig Yoe

MUTT AND JEFF daily strip by Bud Fisher. Although Fisher is pictured at the drawing board in panel no. 4, the strip was drawn by Ed Mack throughout the 1920s. © July 30, 1923, H. C. Fisher. Courtesy of the Cartoon Art Museum, San Francisco

MUTT AND JEFF daily strip by Bud Fisher. Mutt and Jeff shave and pose as child actors in Hollywood. © 1925 H. C. Fisher. Courtesy of Bruce Hamilton

MUTT AND JEFF daily strip by Bud Fisher. The boys try to sign up King Alfonso of Spain for their vaudeville act. © 1926 H. C. Fisher. Courtesy of Bruce Hamilton

MUTT AND JEFF daily strip by Bud Fisher. A delegation of Jeffs nominates Jeff for president. On the previous day, the Mutt convention selected Mutt as its candidate. © July 26, 1932, H. C. Fisher. Courtesy of Bruce Hamilton

MUTT AND JEFF original hand-colored Sunday page by Bud Fisher. *Jeff asks his creator for a special favor.* © November 25, 1928, H. C. Fisher. Courtesy of Jack Gilbert and the Barnum Museum

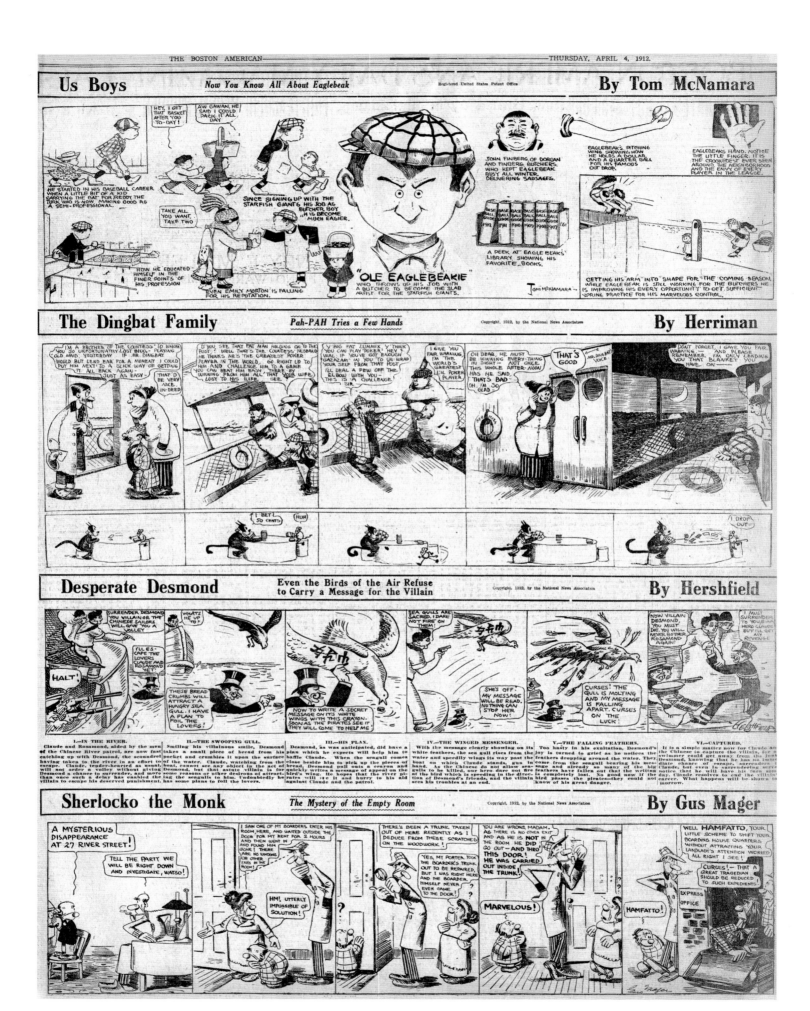

COMICS PAGE—This lineup from the Hearst-owned **Boston American** is an early example of daily strips being grouped together on the same page.
April 4, 1912. Courtesy of Mark Johnson

THE HALL ROOM BOYS comic feature by Harold Arthur McGill. This strip, which revolved around the exploits of two social pretenders, Percy and Ferdie, first appeared during the week in the New York American in 1904, before a Sunday feature was introduced in 1916 in the New York Herald. May 30, 1909. Courtesy of Richard Marschall

DAILY DOSE In the first decade of the century, newspapers published comics during the week on an irregular basis. Features would typically appear two to four days a week on the editorial and sports pages or buried amid the classified ads in the back of the afternoon editions. Between 1910 and 1915, comics that ran six days a week became more common. The Hearst papers were among the first to group these features together on the same page. Most of the daily strips were designed to appeal to city workers commuting back and forth to their jobs, so their content dealt mostly with urban and suburban themes. A sampling of some of these early creations is featured here and on the following pages.

THE OUTBURSTS OF EVERETT TRUE comic feature by A. D. Condo. One of the earliest weekday features syndicated by the Newspaper Enterprise Association, beginning on July 22, 1905, Condo's vertical-format strip starred a cranky middle-aged man with an explosive temper. c. 1920, NEA Service, Inc. Courtesy of the Art Wood Collection of Cartoon and Caricature, Prints and Photographs Division, Library of Congress

JERRY ON THE JOB daily strip by Walter Hoban. This long-running feature debuted in the New York Journal on December 29, 1913. After trying a variety of occupations, Jerry Flannigan was hired in 1915 by a railroad. The "flop" in the final panel was a signature Hoban visual device. *Courtesy of Jim Scancarelli*

AUTO OTTO daily strip by Gene Ahearn. The artist drew a strip about a devoted car enthusiast for the Newspaper Enterprise Association before creating his most successful feature, *OUR BOARDING HOUSE*, in 1921. *Courtesy of the International Museum of Cartoon Art*

FRECKLES AND HIS FRIENDS daily strip by Merrill Blosser. A graduate of the Landon School, Blosser launched his popular kid strip on September 20, 1915. Freckles grew from a ten-year-old to a teenager and outlived his creator, ending his comic career in 1973. *Courtesy of the International Museum of Cartoon Art*

HAROLD TEEN daily strip by Carl Ed. Captain Joseph Medill Patterson bought this feature for the Tribune Syndicate in 1919. Harold reached the peak of his popularity during the Roaring Twenties and continued to appear until 1959. *Courtesy of Jim Scancarelli*

DESPERATE DESMOND daily strip. 1911. Courtesy of Gary Ernest Smith

DESPERATE DESMOND portrait by Harry Hershfield.
Courtesy of Rob Stolzer

HARRY HERSHFIELD

This pioneer of daily comics launched two important features in the *New York Evening Journal* during the teens. *Desperate Desmond* (above), which debuted in 1910, was a continuity strip that burlesqued melodramas, similar to Charles W. Kahles's earlier creation, *Hairbreadth Harry*. *Abie the Agent* (right), which began in 1914, starred a middle-class Jewish businessman and ran, off and on, until 1940.

ABIE THE AGENT daily strip. 1917. Courtesy of Sandy Schechter

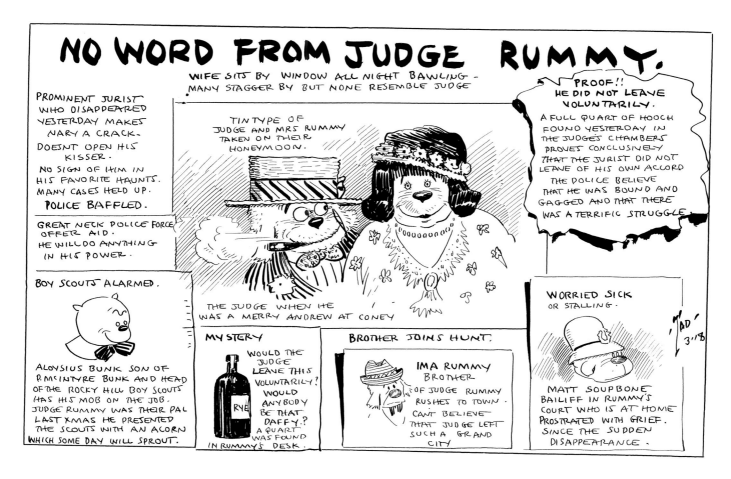

TAD DORGAN Variously titled *Judge Rummy's Court, Old Judge Rumhauser,* and *Silk Hat Harry's Divorce Suit,* Thomas Aloysius Dorgan's longest-running feature, which started around 1910 in the *New York Evening Journal,* featured a cast of carousing canines. TAD also produced a daily panel, which ran in the 1910s and 1920s in the *Evening Journal.* It alternated between scenes of professional and amateur sporting events, such as baseball, boxing, and golf, and situations set in the workplace or at home.

JUDGE RUMMY—Panel and daily strips by TAD Dorgan. *1910s. Courtesy of the International Museum of Cartoon Art (top), Rob Stolzer (middle), and Illustration House (bottom)*

OUTDOOR SPORTS daily panel by TAD Dorgan. *1920s. Courtesy of the International Museum of Cartoon Art*

INDOOR SPORTS daily panel by TAD Dorgan. *1920s. Courtesy of the San Francisco Academy of Comic Art*

PROFESSOR BUTTS GETS CAUGHT IN A REVOLVING DOOR AND BECOMES DIZZY ENOUGH TO DOPE OUT AN IDEA TO KEEP YOU FROM FORGETTING TO MAIL YOUR WIFE'S LETTER.

AS YOU WALK PAST COBBLER SHOP, HOOK(A) STRIKES SUSPENDED BOOT(B) CAUSING IT TO KICK FOOTBALL(C) THROUGH GOAL POSTS(D). FOOTBALL DROPS INTO BASKET(E) AND STRING (F) TILTS SPRINKLING CAN(G) CAUSING WATER TO SOAK COAT TAILS(H). AS COAT SHRINKS CORD(I) OPENS DOOR(J) OF CAGE ALLOWING BIRD(K) TO WALK OUT ON PERCH(L) AND GRAB WORM(M) WHICH IS ATTACHED TO STRING(N). THIS PULLS DOWN WINDOW SHADE(O) ON WHICH IS WRITTEN, "YOU SAP, MAIL THAT LETTER". A SIMPLE WAY TO AVOID ALL THIS TROUBLE IS TO MARRY A WIFE WHO CAN'T WRITE.

THE INVENTIONS OF PROFESSOR LUCIFER G. BUTTS daily panel by Rube Goldberg. c. 1910s. Courtesy of George George

RUBE GOLDBERG   The original "Rube Goldberg device" was invented by Professor Lucifer G. Butts (above), who first appeared about 1914. *I'm the Guy, Mike and Ike—They Look Alike,* and *Foolish Questions* were among the many panels Goldberg produced for the *New York Evening Mail* from 1907 to 1915, after which his work was distributed by the McNaught Syndicate.

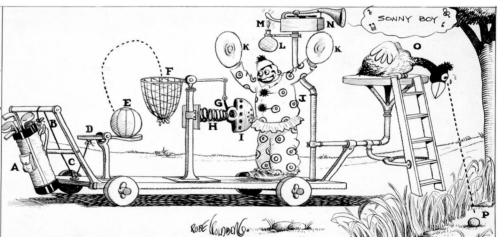

PROFESSOR BUTTS PUTS HIS HEAD IN A NUTCRACKER AND SQUEEZES OUT AN IDEA TO LOCATE LOST GOLF BALLS.

HANG GOLF BAG(A) ON HOOK(B) WHICH PULLS CORD(C) AND TILTS PADDLE(D), TOSSING BASKET BALL(E) INTO BASKET(F). WEIGHT OF BALL RELEASES HOOK(G) AND ALLOWS SPRING(H) TO PUSH HEAD-GUARD (I) INTO STOMACH OF TOY CLOWN(J) WHO CLAPS CYMBALS(K) ON RUBBER BULB(L), SQUIRTING STREAM OF WATER(M), WHICH STARTS PHONOGRAPH(N) PLAYING "SONNY BOY". SONG AWAKENS MOTHER LOVE IN SNOZZLE-BIRD(O). SHE LONGS FOR A SON AND LOOKS AROUND FOR AN EGG TO HATCH UNTIL SHE FINDS GOLF BALL(P) WHICH SHE NATURALLY MISTAKES FOR THE COVETED EGG.

IF THE SNOZZLE-BIRD WANTS A DAUGHTER HAVE THE PHONOGRAPH PLAY "RAMONA".

THE INVENTIONS OF PROFESSOR LUCIFER G. BUTTS daily panel by Rube Goldberg. c. 1910s. Courtesy of the Art Wood Collection of Cartoon and Caricature, Prints and Photographs Division, Library of Congress

THE WEEKLY MEETING OF THE TUESDAY'S LADIES CLUB and MIKE AND IKE—THEY LOOK ALIKE daily panel (with two titles running side by side) by Rube Goldberg. c. 1910s. Courtesy of the Art Wood Collection of Cartoon and Caricature, Prints and Photographs Division, Library of Congress

BOOB McNUTT *Sunday page by Rube Goldberg. The longest-running comic strip feature by Goldberg debuted in the* New York Evening Mail *on May 15, 1915, and was later distributed, until 1934, by the McNaught Syndicate.* December 15, 1918, Boston Sunday Advertiser and American. *Courtesy of Mark Johnson.*

MONK FAMILY daily strips by Gus Mager. *c. 1910s. Courtesy of Illustration House (top left), Rob Stolzer (top right), and Editor & Publisher (bottom)*

GUS MAGER After he was hired by Hearst in 1904, this self-taught artist displayed an affinity for drawing simians with monikers that defined their personalities, such as Tightwaddo the Monk, Coldfeeto the Monk, and Groucho the Monk. Mager, who was credited with giving the Marx Brothers their names, eventually came up with Sherlocko the Monk, a human sleuth who starred in a Sunday-page feature from 1910 to 1913. After that, Sherlocko became Hawkshaw the Detective and appeared in various forms until the late 1940s.

Sherlocko the Monk

By Gus Mager

The Adventure of the Vanishing Fish.

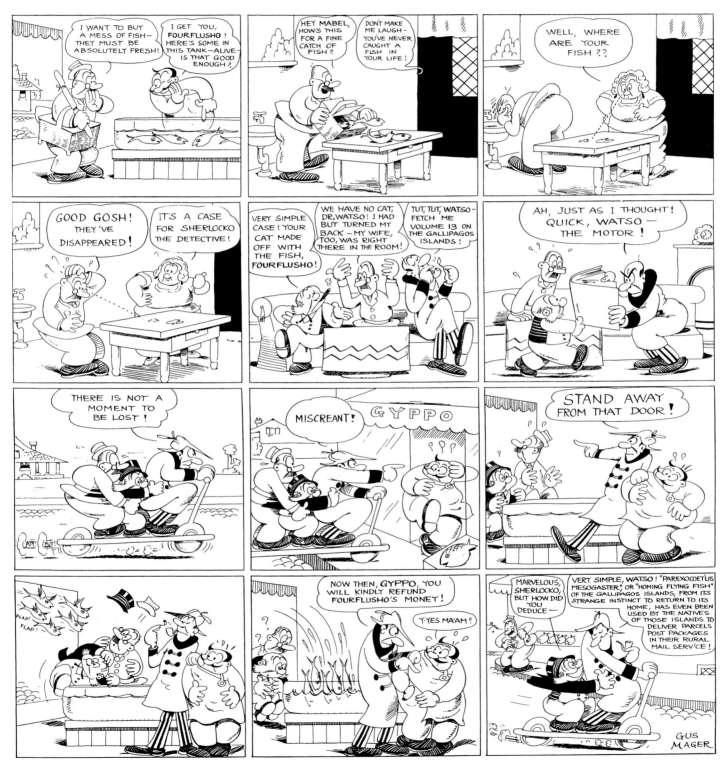

SHERLOCKO THE MONK Sunday page by Gus Mager. Sherlocko and Dr. Watso solve a typically mundane mystery.
© 1912 National News Association. Courtesy of Russ Cochran

george herriman

THE
JOE WELCH

HOW'S THE
GORDON
GANG ?

OH, YOU
LOWSE

"ORTICHOKE JOE"

GEORGE HERRIMAN—Caricature by TAD Dorgan

EARLY IN HIS CAREER, the graphic poet of the comics pages enjoyed the playful camaraderie of TAD Dorgan, Harry Hershfield, Gus Mager, and Tom McNamara in the art department of the *New York Journal* and was often seen out on the town after hours. In his later years, he lived reclusively with his daughter, thirteen stray cats, and five Scottie dogs in the hills of Hollywood. He always wore a hat, even while working at his drawing board, and was extremely modest about his artistic abilities.

George Joseph Herriman was born in New Orleans on August 22, 1880. During his lifetime, Herriman kept his background a secret. His parents were designated as "mulattos" on federal census records, and George's birth certificate listed him as "colored," although on his 1944 death certificate he is identified as "Caucasian." Herriman reportedly once told a close associate that he was "Creole" and had kinky hair because he thought he had some "Negro blood."

In light of this information, a number of contemporary writers have categorized him as "African American" and attempted to analyze his work in the context of his race. Thomas Inge, in a 1996 article, "Was Krazy Kat Black?" observed, "If Herriman thought he had 'Negro blood,' it did not seem to have much direct influence on his early art.

"People should be allowed to create their own identities beyond the traditional identifications of race and ethnicity," argued Inge. "Perhaps we should allow George Herriman that liberty."

Herriman's family moved to Los Angeles in the mid-1880s, and he grew up in a multiethnic community. At the age of

twenty, like many of his contemporaries, he hopped an eastbound freight train to see if he could break into the New York cartoon market. After selling single-panel drawings to *Judge* magazine, as well as numerous one-shot comic features to some of the fledgling syndicates, Herriman landed his first regular job as a sports cartoonist on William Randolph Hearst's *New York American* in the spring of 1904.

By August 1906, he was back in Los Angeles working for Hearst's *Los Angeles Examiner.* While at that paper, Herriman tried out more short-lived strip ideas, including *Mr. Proones the Plunger* (December 10, 1907), *Baron Mooch* (November 1, 1909), *Mary's Home from College* (December 20, 1909), and *Gooseberry Sprig* (December 23, 1909), in addition to producing daily political and sports cartoons.

Herriman was summoned back to New York, where he launched his first successful strip, *The Dingbat Family,* on June 20, 1910. It was in the panels of this feature that his famous cat and mouse were introduced. *Krazy Kat* debuted as an independent daily strip on October 28, 1913, and as a full-page feature on April 23, 1916.

Herriman also continued to experiment with other comic creations, all of which starred human characters. A mooching aristocrat, who resembled Bud Fisher's Mutt, was the star of *Baron Bean,* a daily strip that ran from January 5, 1916, to January 22, 1919. *Now Listen Mabel* (April 23 to December 18, 1919) revolved around a doomed romantic courtship, and *Us Husbands* (January 16 to December 18, 1926) featured standard domestic comedy. *Stumble Inn,* which was a daily strip from October 30, 1922, to May 12, 1923, and a color Sunday page from December 9, 1922, to January 9, 1926, took place in a boardinghouse. Herriman became the artist on the King Features gag panel *Embarrassing Moments* on April 28, 1928; introduced a regular character, Bernie Burns; and continued it until December 3, 1932. From that date until his death on April 25, 1944, he concentrated exclusively on *Krazy Kat.*

Herriman moved to California in 1922 and returned to New York only once, embarking on a cross-country trip with Tom McNamara in 1924. He lost his wife in 1934 and his first daughter five years later, and he lived with his second daughter at his Spanish-style mansion in Hollywood. He managed to continue working, in spite of arthritis and migraine headaches, right up until he died.

At the funeral, his old cartoonist friend Harry Hershfield said, "If ever there was a saint on earth, it was George Herriman." His ashes were scattered in his beloved Monument Valley.

MAJOR OZONE'S FRESH AIR CRUSADE Sunday half-page by George Herriman. One of Herriman's early syndicated features. *May 6, 1906, World Color Printing Company.* **Courtesy of Bill Blackbeard**

BARON MOOCH daily strip by George Herriman. The artist's first "dingbat" was Gooseberry Sprig, who can be seen in the far-right-hand corner of this short-lived strip. *December 14, 1909, Los Angeles Examiner. Courtesy of Art Wood*

THE FAMILY UPSTAIRS daily strip by George Herriman. Krazy Kat and Ignatz the mouse debuted in this Herriman domestic feature and eventually got their own space in panels below the main strip. *1912, New York Journal. Courtesy of Gary Ernest Smith*

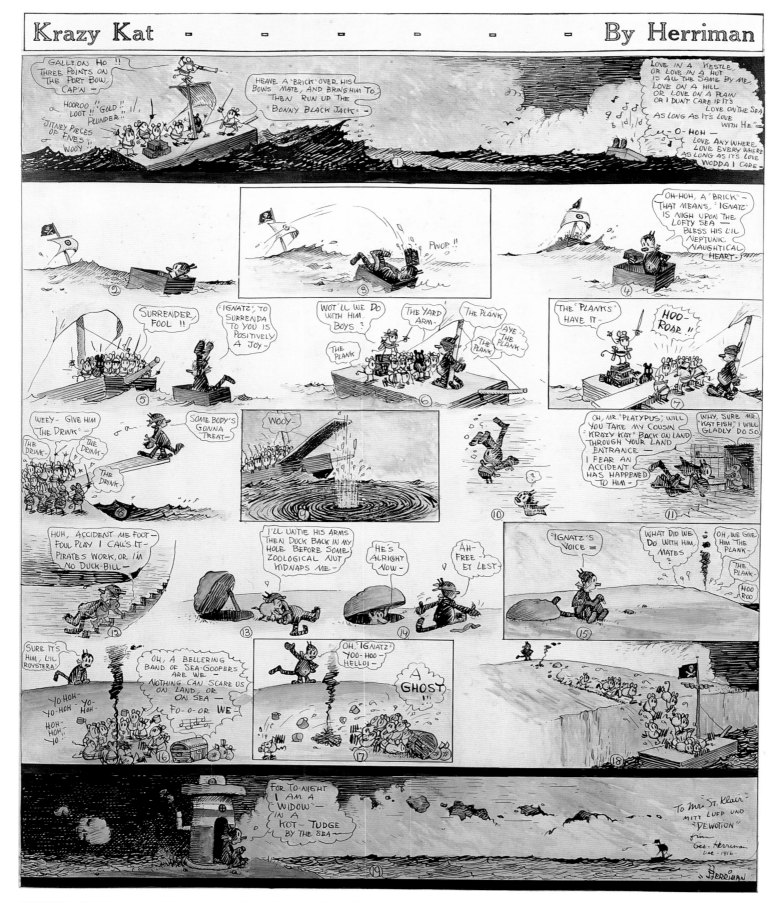

KRAZY KAT original hand-colored Sunday page by George Herriman. The artist gave this page to Rudolph Dirks's sister. *December 3, 1916. Courtesy of Jack Gilbert*

KRAZY KAT original hand-colored Sunday page by George Herriman. One of only two surviving original pages from a ten-week period in 1922 during which Herriman's feature was printed in color. It tells the story of the origins of Krazy's universe. *February 25, 1922. Courtesy of Bruce Hamilton*

KRAZY KAT *original pen-and-ink Sunday page by George Herriman. The funnies are delivered to Coconino, and the Kat puzzles over the concept of illusion versus reality.* April 16, 1922. Courtesy of Craig Yoe

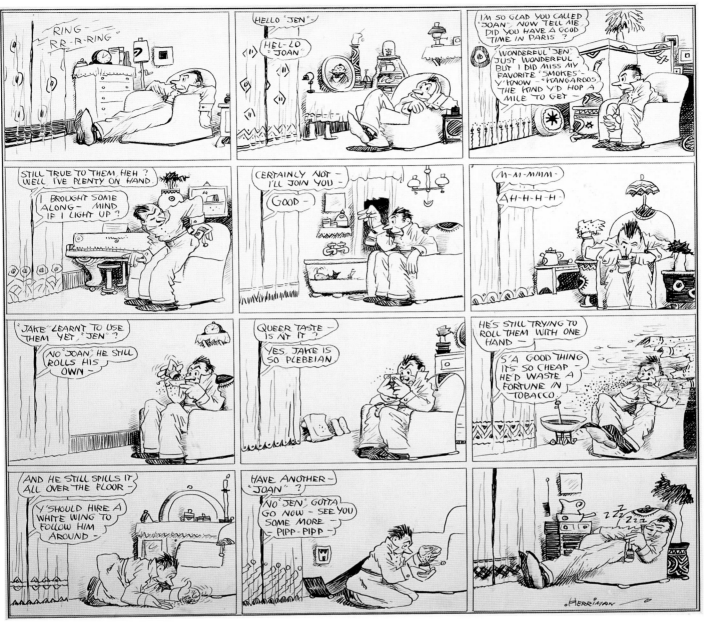

US HUSBANDS Sunday page by George Herriman. Although more conventional in theme and design than KRAZY KAT, this short-lived domestic feature still had elements of Herrimanesque inspiration. *1926. Courtesy of Jack Gilbert*

BARON BEAN daily strip by George Herriman. This aristocratic pretender starred in a daily comic strip from January 5, 1916, to January 22, 1919, syndicated by Hearst's International Feature Service. *c. 1917. Courtesy of Illustration House*

KRAZY KAT daily strip by George Herriman. *January 17, 1918. Courtesy of Jack Gilbert*

DAILY KOMICS
Although Herriman's Sunday pages receive the most praise for their innovative layouts, the daily strip, which ran from 1913 to 1944, also featured expressive art and clever writing.

KRAZY KAT hand-colored daily strip by George Herriman. *© April 19, 1922, International Feature Service, Inc. Courtesy of Jack Gilbert and the Barnum Museum*

KRAZY KAT daily strip by George Herriman. *© November 10, 1934, King Features Syndicate, Inc. Courtesy of Mort Walker*

KRAZY KAT daily strip by George Herriman. *© October 11, 1939, King Features Syndicate, Inc. Courtesy of Bruce Hamilton*

KRAZY KAT recolored Sunday page by George Herriman. This feature began appearing as a color tabloid page in the Hearst papers on June 1, 1935.
© June 11, 1939, King Features Syndicate, Inc. Courtesy of Russ Cochran and American Color

george mcmanus

GEORGE MC MANUS—*Caricature drawn by his assistant Zeke Zekley.* 1954

THE CREATOR OF THE MOST henpecked father in the funnies was a neatly dressed, corpulent fellow of Irish descent who smoked cigars and loved a good joke. He insisted that any resemblance to his lead character was purely coincidental.

George McManus was born on January 23, 1884, in St. Louis, where his father was the manager of the Grand Opera House. In his second year of high school, thirteen-year-old George Jr. was caught doodling in class by his English teacher. She sent him home with a note, complaining about the objectionable drawings. When his father saw his son's handiwork, he took the boy down to the art department of the *St. Louis Republic* and got him a job. A year later, McManus's first comic strip effort, *Alma and Oliver,* appeared in the paper. "It was a terrible mess," he later admitted.

Another tale the jovial cartoonist loved to relate involved a racing tip he received from a shoeshine boy. He took the advice and placed $100 on Hamburg Belle at 30-to-1 odds. To his surprise, the horse won the race, and he used the $3,000 payoff to buy a train ticket to New York City and start his career. The day his money ran out, he landed a job with the *New York World*. In addition to talent, the young cartoonist had the luck of the Irish.

A decade later, after a string of comic creations that included *Panhandle Pete* (February 21, 1904), *The Newlyweds* (April 10, 1904), *Nibsy, the Newsboy, in Funny Fairyland* (May 20, 1906), and *Spareribs and Gravy* (January 28, 1912), he launched his most famous feature. *Bringing Up Father*, which debuted on January 2, 1913, would make McManus a millionaire.

The life story of Jiggs was as real to him as his own anecdotal history. "He was born in Ireland, you know, and

came to this country, expecting to find the streets paved with gold," McManus told a reporter in 1926. "But they were paved with bricks and cobblestones instead. So he became a hod-carrier. Romance came into his life when he met Maggie slinging dishes in a beanery, and they were married. He threw away the hod and began to sell bricks on commission. Then he went into the brickmaking business and manufactured a brick especially designed for throwing purposes. It was much harder than the ordinary building brick and sold year around."

His rags-to-riches yarn did not end there. "Then Maggie became a social climber," McManus continued. "Wealth changed her viewpoint. Society, dukes, counts and college professors came into her life. She forgot the old crowd. But Jiggs has stuck to his clay pipe and his corned beef and cabbage. He is still as good as any other man in Dinty Moore's and willing to prove it."

There was more to the marriage than bickering and fighting, McManus pointed out: "Maggie is going to make a gentleman of Jiggs if she breaks every Ming vase in America doing it. So Maggie continues to lead her own life and Jiggs continues to lead what he can of his. Deep down in their hearts they love each other, as was demonstrated when Jiggs temporarily lost his money and had to go to work. And being Irish, they will live 'happily ever after'—at least as long as I draw them."

The story of Maggie and Jiggs was the realization of the American dream, rendered in pen-and-ink and told in daily installments. It was a reflection of George McManus's own rise to success. In the world of comics, *Bringing Up Father* is a classic example of art imitating life.

JIGGS—*Portrait by George McManus.* April 1923, *Circulation magazine*

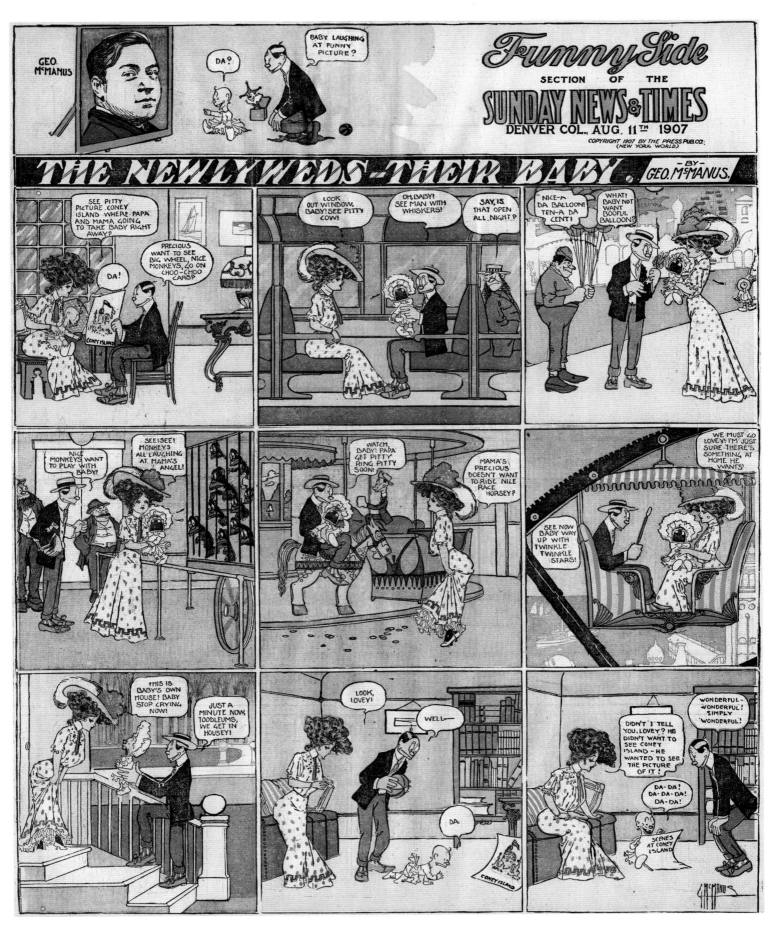

THE NEWLYWEDS—THEIR BABY Sunday page by George McManus. Snookums, who recognizes his creator at the top of this page, takes his parents on a noisy trip to Coney Island. August 11, 1907, Denver Sunday News-Times. Courtesy of Mark Johnson

BRINGING UP FATHER daily strip by George McManus. *c. 1918. Courtesy of Illustration House*

BRINGING UP FATHER daily strip by George McManus. *c. 1916. Courtesy of Sandy Schechter*

BRINGING UP FATHER daily strip by George McManus. *c. 1919. Courtesy of Craig Englund*

BRINGING UP FATHER original hand-colored Sunday page by George McManus. The Sunday version of McManus's feature debuted on April 4, 1918. This is the earliest known original example. *May 19, 1918. Courtesy of Craig Englund and Illustration House*

BRINGING UP FATHER daily strips by George McManus. Maggie and Jiggs travel to Japan in this sequence from 1927. © March 28, April 5 and 12, and May 9, 1927, International Feature Service, Inc. Courtesy of the Art Wood Collection of Cartoon and Caricature, Prints and Photographs Division, Library of Congress

BRINGING UP FATHER recolored Sunday page by George McManus. Maggie and Jiggs return to the neighborhood from their epic cross-country journey.
© July 7, 1940, King Features Syndicate, Inc. Courtesy of Russ Cochran and American Color

MAMA'S ANGEL CHILD original hand-colored Sunday page by Penny Ross. A former assistant to Richard F. Outcault, Ross created a female Buster Brown named Esther for his ornately illustrated feature, which ran from March 1, 1908, to October 17, 1920. c. 1918. Courtesy of Bill Janocha

COMICS FOR KIDS Although the anti-comics crusaders were unsuccessful in putting an end to the Sunday funnies, a number of features that appealed to children were introduced during the decade. Many of these creations starred cute kids and funny animals and provided an alternative to the more adult-oriented strips in the color comic sections.

DIMPLES original hand-colored Sunday page by Grace Drayton. Best known as the originator of the Campbell Soup Kids, Drayton created many features starring cute, dimpled tykes, including DOLLY DINGLE, which began in 1908, and DIMPLES, starting in 1914. *1913/14. Courtesy of Jack Gilbert and the Barnum Museum*

OLD DOC YAK Sunday page by Sidney Smith. Before launching *THE GUMPS* in 1917, Smith drew a humorous animal feature starring an anthropomorphic goat. It was called *BUCK NIX* when it debuted as a daily strip in 1908 and *OLD DOC YAK* after 1912. September 12, 1915, Chicago Sunday Tribune. *Courtesy of Mark Johnson*

SLIM JIM AND THE FORCE Sunday page by Stanley Armstrong. The most popular star in the World Color Printing Company's stable, Slim Jim was chased by virtually the same trio of policemen from 1910 to 1937. The feature was drawn by three different artists: George Frink (1910), Raymond Crawford Ewer (1911–14), and Stanley Armstrong (1914–37). 1920, Arizona Daily Star. Courtesy of Mark Johnson

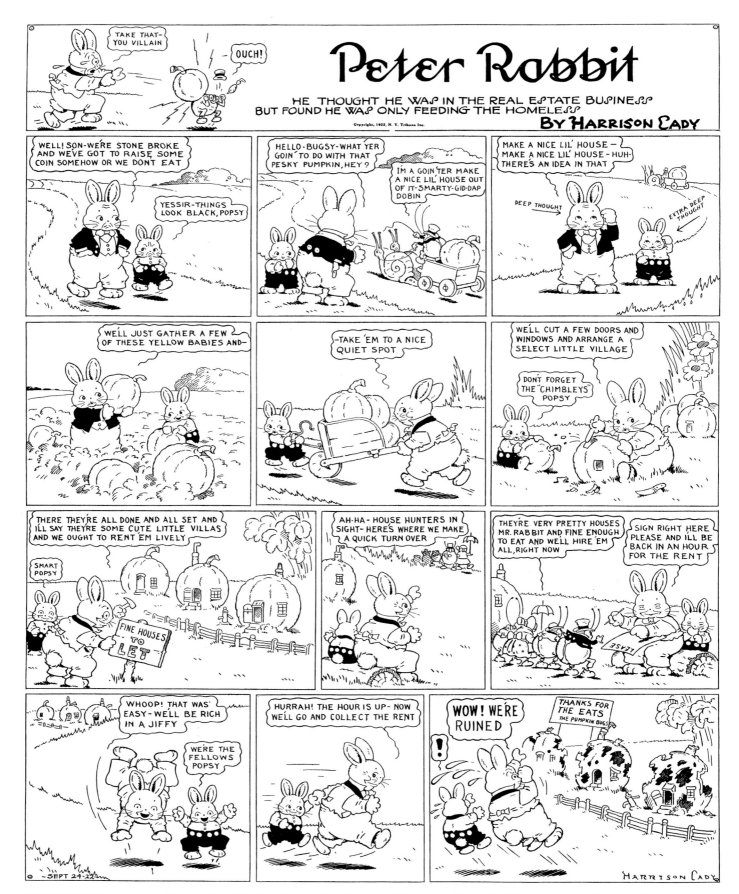

PETER RABBIT Sunday page by Harrison Cady. This funny bunny originally appeared in Thornton Burgess's children's stories, which Cady illustrated. Peter starred in a comic strip adaptation beginning in 1920. © September 24, 1922, New York Tribune, Inc. Courtesy of Bill Janocha

THE TEENIE WEENIES Sunday page by William Donahey. This band of little people, who lived in a normal-sized world, was created exclusively for the Chicago Tribune in 1914. After ten years, the full-page feature went into national syndication. *1916. Courtesy of Mark Johnson*

BOBBY MAKE-BELIEVE original Sunday page by Frank King. Before he launched GASOLINE ALLEY, Frank King drew this visually innovative boyhood fantasy strip, which ran from January 31, 1915, to December 7, 1919, in the Chicago Tribune. *c. 1918, Chicago Tribune. Courtesy of the Art Wood Collection of Cartoon and Caricature, Prints and Photographs Division, Library of Congress*

the twenties

DAYS OF REAL SPORT daily panel by Clare Briggs. The comics were useful for more than just wrapping fish. ©1927 New York Tribune, Inc. Courtesy of Editor & Publisher

MERELY MARGY *panel from a daily strip by John Held Jr.* © September 6, 1927, King Features Syndicate, Inc. Courtesy of Rob Stolzer

T**HE JAZZ AGE ROARED WITH THE SOUNDS OF PROSPERITY, PLEASURE, AND REBELLION. ANXIOUS FOR A "RETURN TO NORMALCY" AFTER THE HORRORS OF WORLD WAR I, AMERICANS TOSSED OFF THE STRICT MORAL CODES OF VICTORIAN SOCIETY AND DANCED THE CHARLESTON, DRANK BOOTLEG LIQUOR, FOLLOWED THE LATEST FADS, AND SPECULATED RECKLESSLY IN THE STOCK MARKET. POPULAR CULTURE, FUELED BY THE MASS PRODUCTION OF CONSUMER GOODS AND THE GROWING PERVASIVENESS OF THE MEDIA, UNITED THE NATION IN THE EBULLIENT PURSUIT OF GOOD TIMES.**

In 1925, President Calvin Coolidge made his famous declaration that "the business of America is business." It was a characteristic understatement by the tight-lipped chief executive. Between 1920 and 1929, the gross national product grew from $74 billion to $104.4 billion. In 1923, unemployment reached a new low of 2.4 percent. From 1913 to 1927, the buying power of a skilled laborer increased 50 percent. Americans showed their unquestioning faith in economic progress by embracing materialism and borrowing money on easy credit terms. The unshakable optimism of Wall Street investors encouraged middle-class wage earners to buy stocks on margin, paying only a fraction of the purchase price to their brokers. Volume on the New York Stock Exchange went from 227 million shares in 1920 to 920 million in 1928.

Prohibition of alcohol sales, which became law on January 16, 1920, was widely disregarded, as average citizens became common criminals by concealing illegal hooch in hip flasks. The thirteen-year "noble experiment" was a total failure, resulting in an increase in liquor consumption and the growth of organized crime. Stills, speakeasies, and rumrunners proliferated as federal agents found it easier to take bribes than arrest violators. Drinking was glamorized in movies and magazines, and a spirit of rebelliousness grew among the nation's youth.

Women voted for the first time in a national election on November 2, 1920, helping to put the handsome and affable, but incompetent, Warren Harding in the White House. Improved opportunities in the workplace made financial independence possible and encouraged more daring behavior among the fairer sex. The younger generation flaunted its newfound freedom by drinking, smoking, and swearing in public and dressing in more provocative clothing. The flapper—with her short, flimsy dress, bobbed hair, flat chest, and rolled-up silk stockings—became the icon of the Jazz Age. Youth culture flourished as shebas necked with their sheiks in the back of jalopies and shimmied to the beat of the latest hit songs.

Americans embraced a seemingly endless parade of pastimes with obsessive enthusiasm. Among the many popular fads of the era were mah-jongg, crossword puzzles, contract bridge, yo-yos, roller skating, flagpole sitting, dance marathons, and endurance races. Historic events, ranging from the first Miss America Pageant in 1921 to Charles Lindbergh's transatlantic airplane flight in 1927, grabbed headlines and captivated the nation. It was also the "Golden Age of Sport," as Babe Ruth, Jack Dempsey, Red Grange, and Bobby Jones were among the many heroes who were revered for their athletic accomplishments.

In 1926, F. Scott Fitzgerald, in describing the giddy mood of the era, wrote, "The restlessness approached hysteria. The parties were bigger. The pace was faster, the shows were broader, the buildings were higher, the morals were looser, and the liquor was cheaper; but all these benefits did not really minister to much delight. Young people wore out early—they were hard and languid at twenty-one."

Columnist Walter Lippmann summed up this trend in 1929 when he observed, "What most distinguishes the generation who have approached maturity since the debacle of idealism at the end of the War is not their rebellion against the moral code of their parents, but their disillusionment with their own rebellion. It is common for young men and women to rebel, but that they should rebel sadly and without faith in their rebellion, that they should distrust the new freedom no less than the old certainties—that is something of a novelty."

A new style of "jazz journalism" emerged during the 1920s, which mirrored the sensational tenor of the times. Although newspapers had been printed in a half-page size before, three papers, all published in New York, pioneered the modern "tabloid" format. The trend began with the *Illustrated Daily News*, which first hit the newsstands on June 26, 1919.

Inspired by the success of Alfred Hamsworth's *London Daily Mirror*, Joseph Medill Patterson, copublisher of the *Chicago Tribune*, decided to launch a tabloid paper in New York. The smaller size was easier for readers to handle traveling to work on the crowded subways, Patterson reasoned, and short articles and photographs took less time to digest. Five years later, the *Daily News* (the title was shortened during the first year), with a circulation of 750,000, was the most successful newspaper in the United States.

On June 24, 1924, William Randolph Hearst launched the *New York Daily Mirror*; three months later, Bernarr Macfadden began publication of the *Daily Graphic*. All three of these tabloid papers featured sensational headlines, lurid crime stories, and celebrity gossip, but the *Daily Graphic* outdid the competition when it came to "gutter journalism." Typical *Graphic* headlines screamed "I Know Who Killed My Brother" and "For 36 Hours I Lived Another Woman's Love Life." Fake pictures, known as "composographs," were created by superimposing speech balloons and faces on staged pictures.

By 1930, the editorial policy of the *Daily News* was changing. "The people's major interest is not in the playboy, Broadway, and divorces," Patterson told his staff, "but in how they're going to eat; and from this time forward, we'll pay attention to the struggle for existence that's just beginning." This approach proved successful and the *Daily News* continued to grow, reaching a circulation peak of 2.4 million daily readers and 4.5 million Sunday customers by 1947. The *Graphic*, which died in 1932, and the *Mirror*, which folded in 1963, never earned a profit for their publishers.

A new medium began challenging newspapers in the 1920s. One of the first independent commercial radio stations, KDKA in Pittsburgh, broadcast the results of the Harding-Cox presidential election in 1920. The number of radio households grew from 60,000 in 1922 to 13,750,000 in 1930. There were 618 stations in operation by the end of the decade.

The first newspaper-owned station was set up in the *Detroit News* building on August 20, 1920. By 1927, forty-eight newspapers owned stations, sixty-nine sponsored programs,

THE RADIO BUGGS daily strip by **Walt McDougall**. *c. 1920. Courtesy of the International Museum of Cartoon Art*

and ninety-seven provided news shows. Newspaper people were cautious about radio, however. On April 22, 1922, George Miller, editor of the *Detroit News*, claimed that "the broadcasting station never will supplant to any material extent the daily newspaper as the source of popular information."

An article in *Editor & Publisher* on February 9, 1924, pointed out the perceived shortcomings of radio among members of the newspaper fraternity: "The organized press has never shown excitement over any threatening aspect of radio, because no matter how much it may be controlled and commercialized, it possesses physical difficulties which, in general terms, makes it a poor competitor for the established newspaper. These difficulties include the impossibility of exercise of the selective process of the reader—he sits at his radio and takes what is being sent, whether he likes it or not, and he takes the full dose."

In addition to news and music, radio began to offer entertainment programs. Freeman Gosden and Charles Correll created one of the most successful shows in broadcast history when they adapted to radio their blackface vaudeville routine about a taxicab driver and his lazy partner. *Amos and Andy* debuted on Chicago's WMAQ in March 1928 and within a year was reaching forty million listeners on the NBC network. Late in 1928, an *Amos and Andy* comic strip, linked to the radio show, debuted. It was syndicated by the *Chicago Daily News*, the owner of WMAQ. By the 1930s, the crossover influence was going in the other direction, as radio programs based on the comic strips *Buck Rogers*, *Little Orphan Annie*, *Dick Tracy*, and *Terry and the Pirates* became some of the most popular programs on the airwaves.

Despite competition from radio, the newspaper business continued to thrive. The combined circulation of American newspapers reached forty million by the end of the decade, and advertising revenue totaled $860 million. *Editor & Publisher* reported in 1927 that there were eighty syndicates distributing more than two thousand different features to newspapers around the world. "Among the thousands of different types of syndicate offerings now available, the so-called 'funnies,' comic strips and cartoons, continue well in the lead as far as numbers are concerned," the magazine claimed. "Nearly 150 artists are earning their livelihood by catering to this peculiar American taste, now popular even in the Orient and South American countries."

Cartoonists' salaries increased accordingly. In 1922, Sidney Smith, creator of *The Gumps*, signed a well-publicized million-dollar contract with the Chicago Tribune–New York News Syndicate. The ten-year deal provided Smith with an annual salary of $100,000 and a new Rolls-Royce every third year. The Bell Syndicate was paying Bud Fisher a minimum of $3,000 a week for *Mutt and Jeff* in 1928, and creators of many

OLD GOLD CIGARETTES—Advertisement by Clare Briggs. *October 4, 1927.* Courtesy of Mark Johnson

of the other top features were earning between $50,000 and $100,000 a year.

The artists were also supplementing their incomes with advertising work. In 1927, more than thirty-five top cartoonists were each getting between $10 and $2,000 a drawing from advertising clients. Fontaine Fox, creator of *Toonerville Folks*, was producing cartoons for the Cooper and Brass Research Institute featuring the "Terrible-Tempered Mr. Bang," and Clare Briggs was lending his talents to a campaign for Old Gold cigarettes.

"I think that it is a big mistake for syndicate artists, whose work is being paid for as an exclusive feature by newspapers, to make an advertising drawing exactly similar in size, shape and appearance to his regular newspaper feature," admitted Fox. "If, however, the artist makes a drawing that is not exactly like his regular cartoon, but is plainly an illustration or advertisement, I do not admit any harm is done."

The syndicates distributing the work of Fox and Briggs did not see it that way, however, and in March 1928, the two artists announced that they would no longer illustrate ads for newspapers. "Mr. Fox has agreed with us," claimed Henry Snevily of the Bell Syndicate, "that to make advertising drawings in practically the same physical form as the feature cartoons and using the same characters is a bad policy, confusing to the readers." Newspaper editors, who were paying the syndicates for the exclusive right to publish these features in their market territory, had complained that competing papers could offer the same material to their readers simply by running the ads. The cartoonists were permitted to continue illustrating advertisements, but only for magazine publication.

The increasing power of the syndicates was made evident by a survey presented to the American Society of Newspaper Editors in May 1924. Although the twenty-nine editors who responded to the questionnaire admitted that most of their dealings with syndicates were positive, the overall sentiment was that they felt intimidated. "We seem all to be extravagant and cowardly in dealing with syndicates and their features," wrote one New York editor. "I am quite sure always when a feature of some merit comes to me, if I don't take it, one of my newspaper competitors will."

Among the many complaints the editors voiced in the survey were that too many features were being offered, the prices were exorbitant, unethical sales methods were often employed, the importance of features in building circulation was exaggerated, the size of exclusive territories denied them access to certain popular features, and large papers had unfair competitive advantages over smaller ones. The general consensus was in favor of home editing, using staff writers and artists, as opposed to assembling newspapers from syndicated material.

The syndicates responded to these charges in a report delivered in January 1925. They blamed newspaper editors for buying features they did not need, paying too much for the most desirable features, pressuring salesmen for unfair advantages over their competitors, driving hard bargains, breaking contracts, patronizing fly-by-night syndicates, and refusing to take risks with unproven talent.

One syndicate manager took a more compromising approach: "It seems to me that the relation between newspapers and syndicates should be one of selective cooperation. I think that syndicates do not spend enough time or thought acquainting themselves with what editors actually need in advance of trying to fill their requirements." This executive proposed that syndicates could save a lot of money by consulting newspaper editors before signing and promoting expensive talent.

Cartoonists and syndicates learned, through a long process of trial and error, what newspaper readers liked and disliked. "The comic-cartoon series has become a commodity, produced and marketed much like any other commodity, and it is just as bad business to release a comic strip with an objectionable feature as to sell complexion soap with grit in it," wrote Amram Schoenfeld in a February 1, 1930, article in *The Saturday Evening Post* entitled "The Laugh Industry."

The larger the market for comics became, the more universal the strips had to be in terms of content. Cartoonists were under increasing pressure to entertain this mass audience without offending anyone. A curious double standard developed. Newspaper readers were more sensitive about perceived transgressions in their favorite comics than they were about the same references in movies, plays, and books.

The funnies business gradually adopted a strict code of self-censorship. Among the many unwritten taboos on the comics pages were the following: Female characters should not be shown drinking, smoking, swearing, or even kissing a man who was not their spouse. Married couples were to remain eternally faithful and could never get divorced, although they were allowed to complain profusely about their relationship. A wife could physically abuse her husband, but a man could never strike a woman. Comments that might directly offend any ethnic group, nationality, religion, political persuasion, or profession were to be avoided at all costs. A long list of expletives, including "hell" and "damn," was forbidden, and comic characters were not permitted to use the Lord's name in vain. Antisocial behavior, including drunkenness, vandalism, and criminality, was not tolerated, except by villains. Readers were particularly sensitive to any activity that endangered the life of a comic strip child. References to death and disease were, in most cases, frowned upon.

There were exceptions to these rules, of course. It was acceptable for Harry Hershfield, a Jewish cartoonist, to make fun of his own people in his strip *Abie the Agent*. The same was true of George McManus, an Irishman, and his autobiographical creation, *Bringing Up Father*. Conversely, if a comic strip featured a black character in any but the most menial of roles (maids, butlers, janitors, porters, and stable boys), complaints from southern readers were inevitable.

TABOOS—Cartoonist Ken Kling used the word "diabetes" in the second panel of this WINDY RILEY comic strip, but the syndicate changed it to an imaginary disease, "haliobetis." © 1929 McNaught Syndicate, Inc. Courtesy of Robert C. Harvey

Although cartoonists often broke these taboos, they became increasingly conditioned to avoid the wrath of editors, who might cancel strips that offended readers too often. Termination meant the loss of income, and in the end, the profit motive was the bottom line.

Gilbert Seldes, in his landmark 1924 survey, *The Seven Lively Arts,* included a chapter on "The 'Vulgar' Comic Strip." Seldes put a positive spin on the challenges that cartoonists faced. "The enormous circulation [the comic strip] achieves imposes certain limitations," he wrote. "It cannot be too local, since it is syndicated throughout the country; it must avoid political and social questions because the same strip appears in papers of divergent editorial opinions; there is no room in it for acute racial caricature, although no group is immune from its mockery." Seldes concluded, "These and other restrictions have gradually made of the comic strip a changing picture of American life—and by compensation it provides us with the freest American fantasy."

During the 1920s, no individual in the comics business understood the tastes of the average newspaper reader better than Joseph Medill Patterson. As the head of the Chicago Tribune–New York News Syndicate, he launched a string of comic strips that were enormously popular during the decade. Although these features were each unique creations, they shared one important quality: readers of Patterson's strips were given a compelling reason to return each day to see what new adventures awaited the characters. They had to find out if Uncle Bim was going to marry the Widow Zander, or when Daddy Warbucks would rescue Annie, or what Winnie Winkle was wearing. They were hooked, and no day was complete without a visit with their favorite funnies friends.

Patterson and his cousin Robert McCormick became coeditors and copublishers of the *Chicago Tribune* in 1914.

Although the grandsons of the paper's founder had very different views—McCormick was a conservative and Patterson leaned toward socialism—their friendship and mutual respect fostered a cooperative relationship. For the most part, McCormick focused his attention on the business side of the operation while Patterson devoted his talents to the content of the newspaper. During World War I, Patterson enlisted as a private in the army and rose to the rank of captain in the artillery, earning him his lifelong nickname.

After returning from Europe in 1919, Patterson launched the *Illustrated Daily News* in New York, although he continued to live in Chicago until 1926. *The Gumps* ran on page 15 of the first issue, on June 26, 1919, and the comics would be an essential element of the tabloid from then on. When an eight-page color comic section was introduced on February 12, 1923, circulation jumped by sixty-five thousand.

Patterson took an active role in nurturing the syndicate's comics. He had regular meetings with his cartoonists and made crucial changes, particularly in the early developmental stages of new features. His prescient suggestions are part of comics legend. Patterson once summed up his basic formula: "Youngsters for kid appeal, a handsome guy for muscle work and love interest, a succession of pretty girls, a mysterious locale or a totally familiar one."

The Gumps was the feature that built the syndicate, and during the early 1920s the *Chicago Tribune* became known as "the Gump paper." Although Sidney Smith often took credit for the original inspiration, the strip was Patterson's brainchild from the beginning. After its debut in 1917, *The Gumps* evolved into the prototypical soap opera strip, as it chronicled the trials and tribulations of a lower-middle-class family who represented, in Patterson's view, the typical *Tribune* reader.

In 1923, the Minneapolis Board of Trade momentarily halted business so that brokers could run to the newsstands

THE GUMPS GASOLINE ALEY MOON MULLINS WINNIE WINKLE *The bread winner* HAROLD TEEN LITTLE ORPHAN ANNIE SMITTY

CAPTAIN PATTERSON'S ALL-STAR LINE-UP—The Chicago Tribune–New York News Syndicate launched a string of successful strips during the late teens and early twenties. (GASOLINE ALLEY was misspelled in the original ad.) Courtesy of Editor & Publisher

HAROLD TEEN AND LILLUMS LOVEWELL—Special drawing by Carl Ed from the Editor & Publisher series ALL IN THE DAY'S WORK. November 1, 1924. Courtesy of Editor & Publisher

to find out if Andy Gump's rich Uncle Bim had finally succumbed to the machinations of the conniving Widow Zander. When the brokenhearted Mary Gold died on April 30, 1929, there was an outpouring of sympathy as the nation mourned the pen-and-ink character as if she were flesh and blood. Smith had become a master of manipulating the emotions of his faithful fans and was famously rewarded for his efforts.

The next strip Patterson launched was Carl Ed's *The Love Life of Harold Teen,* on May 4, 1919. Harold came along just in time for the youth movement of the Roaring Twenties, sporting such fashions as toreador trousers, sloppy socks, and whoopee hats and popularizing phrases like "cute canary," "dim bulb," and "kissable kid." It provided a sanitized picture of a Jazz Age teenager, suitable for family viewing.

Winnie Winkle was not the first strip to star a working girl; that distinction belonged to A. E. Hayward's *Somebody's Stenog,* which began in 1916. When Martin Branner's creation debuted on September 20, 1920, women were about to vote for the first time in a national election and the era of emancipation was just getting into full swing. Winnie held down a job as a stenographer and supported her family—deadbeat dad Rip, well-meaning Ma, and precocious brother Perry. She managed to dress fashionably by making her own clothes and changed outfits on a daily basis. Branner's strip helped earned the *Daily News* its reputation as "the Stenographer's Gazette."

The original cast of *Gasoline Alley*—Walt Wallet, Bill, Doc, and Avery—was first shown tinkering on a flivver in the corner quadrant of Frank King's Sunday page, *The Rectangle,* on November 24, 1918. *Gasoline Alley* became a daily feature

on August 24, 1919, but a year and a half later, Patterson felt it needed more feminine appeal and told King to "get a baby in the story fast." On Valentine's Day of 1921, Walt—who was a bachelor—found an infant on his doorstep; he later named the baby Skeezix. King's creation earned the distinction of being the first strip in which the characters aged in real time. Over the course of eight decades, *Gasoline Alley* has chronicled middle-class family life in small-town America with gentle humor and quiet drama.

The next cartoonist Patterson helped to get started was Walter Berndt, a former office boy at the *New York Journal.* Following the Captain's orders, Berndt changed the name of his creation from *Bill the Office Boy,* a strip that ran for two weeks in the *New York World* in 1922, to *Smitty,* after randomly opening up a telephone book to a page of Smiths. A year after the strip was launched on November 27, 1922, Patterson directed Berndt to "put a little pathos in the *Smitty* strip" by having the boy's boss, Mr. Bailey, fire him unjustly for petty thievery. Berndt, who also became an unofficial talent scout for Patterson, took this advice well and continued to provide lighthearted suspense in the strip for the next five decades.

In 1923, the Captain was looking for a feature to compete with the roughneck appeal of King Features' *Barney Google.* He found the perfect artist to accomplish this goal in Frank Willard, a friend and former assistant of Barney's creator, Billy DeBeck. *Moon Mullins* debuted on June 19, 1923, and, after an initial period of experimentation with various locales, settled on a suburban boardinghouse, inhabited by a motley assortment of social pretenders and lowlifes. The colorful cast included Moonshine Mullins, an unrepentant con man, as well as landlady Emmy Schmaltz, the pompous Lord and Lady Plushbottom, rotund Uncle Willie, Mamie the maid, and kid brother Kayo. In characteristic fashion, Patterson named the

SMITTY—Special drawing by Walter Berndt from the Editor & Publisher series ALL IN THE DAY'S WORK. July 26, 1924. Courtesy of Editor & Publisher

lead character himself, adapting the Prohibition term for illegally distilled spirits.

The brightest new star of Patterson's stable during the 1920s was Harold Gray's Little Orphan Annie, who made her first appearance on August 5, 1924. Gray, who had worked as Sidney Smith's assistant on *The Gumps* for five years, began submitting numerous ideas for his own strip. According to syndicate legend, when the Captain saw Gray's latest effort, *Little Orphan Otto,* he exclaimed, "He looks like a pansy. Put a skirt on the kid and we'll call it *Little Orphan Annie*." Under Patterson's direction, Gray developed a unique blend of adventure, pathos, humor, and social comment. A syndicate advertisement from December 20, 1924, summed up the initial marketing pitch for *Little Orphan Annie*: "It is the comic strip Cinderella, the great child story of the ages—the story of the little girl who accepts the frowns of fortune with fortitude and the smiles of fortune with grace and kindliness."

In the first continuity, eleven-year-old Annie slugged a boy who was teasing her, displaying the feisty independence that won over the hearts of readers. Nearly two months later, she would meet a wealthy munitions manufacturer named Daddy Warbucks, and in January 1925, Annie adopted her faithful canine sidekick, Sandy. This triumvirate became the core cast of the strip. Together they faced adversity with a self-reliant determination that mirrored Harold Gray's personal philosophy.

The comic strip lineup of the Chicago Tribune–New York News Syndicate represented, in many ways, the major thematic genres of the decade. Some of these creations helped to define previously established trends, while others pioneered new ideas. Success inspired imitation in the highly competitive world of newspaper syndication.

Family strips like *The Nebbs* and *The Bungle Family* copied the proven formula of *The Gumps*. *Smitty* resembled King Features' *Jerry on the Job,* which started in 1913. King Features' *Tillie the Toiler* followed *Winnie Winkle* into the workplace. *Moon Mullins* was Patterson's answer to Hearst's *Barney Google*. *Etta Kett* spoke to the same audience as *Harold Teen*. *Ella Cinders* and *Little Annie Rooney* borrowed elements from *Little Orphan Annie*. Only *Gasoline Alley* seemed immune from the cloning process.

In assessing the historical contributions of the decade, Ron Goulart, in *The Funnies: 100 Years of American Comic Strips,* observed, "There was not, however, a Lost Generation of comic artists and the twenties produced no examples of disillusionment, nihilism or sexual revolution in the comic strip format." Cartoonist John Held Jr.'s wispy flapper, who starred in the comic strip *Merely Margy,* was widely regarded as a graphic icon of the era. But there was no voice comparable to F. Scott Fitzgerald in the comics medium.

BARNEY GOOGLE panel from a daily strip by Billy DeBeck. This pop-eyed con man broke the world's record for flagpole sitting when he hung on for twenty-one days in 1927. © June 17, 1927, King Features Syndicate, Inc. Courtesy of the San Francisco Academy of Comic Art

The frivolity of the Roaring Twenties was not entirely absent on the funnies pages, however. The excitement of baseball stadiums, racetracks, and boxing rings, the aromas of speakeasies and flophouses, and the sound of Dixieland and Tin Pan Alley were all captured by Billy DeBeck in *Barney Google*. His comic strip alter ego was the Everyman of the Jazz Age. Barney mixed "Google High Balls" in his kitchen the same month the Volstead Act was passed. He swam across the English Channel in 1926 and sat on top of a flag-pole for twenty-one days in 1927. DeBeck's rags-to-riches tales reflected the happy-go-lucky spirit of the times.

The most significant new development in the comics medium during the 1920s was the emergence of the adventure strip. Episodic continuity had been featured in newspaper comics almost from the beginning. The Yellow Kid went on an eighteen-week around-the-world tour in 1897, and Frederick B. Opper used the words "to be continued" in a three-episode sequence of *Alphonse and Gaston* in 1903. The cliffhanger approach, requiring readers to wait until the next installment to see how a story played out, was a key device employed by Charles W. Kahles in *Hairbreadth Harry* (1906) and Bud Fisher in *Mutt and Jeff* (1907). Ed Wheelan's *Midget Movies,* which first appeared with that title in 1918 and continued as *Minute Movies* in 1921, parodied narrative elements from film melodramas. "Wheelan Pictures Ink" employed a regular troupe of actors who performed western, detective, aviation, and sports scripts, anticipating the major adventure genres of the 1930s. By the 1920s, the majority of humor strips featured loosely constructed stories that could last a few days or ramble on for months.

A new breed of comic, one that added the element of physical danger to storytelling, came on the scene in the mid-1920s. Many of these strips featured juvenile heroes and exotic locales. Although Little Orphan Annie frequently found herself in dangerous situations, it was not until the 1930s that life-threatening violence—the defining characteristic of the modern adventure strip—became part of Gray's narrative blend.

Meanwhile, between February 1 and July 12, 1925, Chester Gump, the seven-year-old son of Andy and Min Gump,

BOBBY THATCHER promotional drawing by George Storm. An advertise-ment for the "original boy adventure strip" promised "detectives, fisticuffs and skullduggery at sea." © September 2, 1933, McClure Syndicate, Inc. Courtesy of Editor & Publisher

embarked on an exciting South Sea adventure in a Sunday-only continuity written by Brandon Walsh and illustrated by Stanley Link. In one of these episodes, Chester, who was aided by his faithful Chinese servant Ching Chow, fired at a native chieftain with a gun and apparently killed him (it was implied that the bullet hit its target outside of the panel border). According to comics historian Bill Blackbeard, this was "the first blood-letting in combat ever encountered in a comic strip." Over the course of the next four years, Chester would go off on two more extended adventures.

Violent gunplay was also depicted in *Phil Hardy,* a short-lived daily strip created by Jay Jerome Williams (under the pen name Edwin Alger) and George Storm in November 1925. In the opening sequence, Phil, who was shanghaied on a steamer bound for South Africa, found himself in a shoot-out between the mutinous crew and its officers. The fifteen-year-old boy was shown wielding a revolver in the bloody battle. Storm went on to launch another juvenile adventure strip, *Bobby Thatcher,* which ran for ten years beginning in 1927.

Roy Crane's *Wash Tubbs,* which debuted on April 14, 1924, was the most influential of these early adventure strips. Crane started out doing a humorous feature starring a

PHIL HARDY daily strip by George Storm. Guns were blazing in the opening sequence of Storm's first feature. © December 17, 1925, Bell Syndicate, Inc. Courtesy of the San Francisco Academy of Comic Art

WASH TUBBS daily strip by Roy Crane. Wash and Easy are shipwrecked on an island in one of their early adventures together.
© 1930 NEA Service, Inc. Courtesy of Howard Lowery

spectacled grocery clerk named Washington Tubbs III, but he quickly tired of writing daily gags about his lead character's amorous affairs and sent him off on a treasure hunt to the South Pacific. For the next five years, Crane's diminutive hero scampered around the globe, gaining and losing riches, chasing girls, and fighting his way out of jams. Violence and danger increasingly entered the story lines as Wash picked up a partner, Gozy Gallup, in 1927 and ran afoul of the roguish Bull Dawson in 1928. The transformation of Crane's creation was almost complete.

On May 6, 1929, Wash encountered a wandering soldier of fortune in the dungeons of Kandelabra, a fictitious European kingdom. Captain Easy provided the element that the rollicking adventure strip was lacking: an adult hero. The two-fisted, square-jawed adventurer showed his stuff by punching his way out of the jail. From then on, Wash and Easy were inseparable—except, of course, when the plot required otherwise.

Robert C. Harvey, in *The Art of the Funnies,* claimed, "It is impossible to overestimate the impact of this character on those who wrote and drew adventure strips in the thirties." A direct lineage can be traced from Captain Easy to Pat Ryan, the costar of Milton Caniff's *Terry and the Pirates,* as well as to Clark Kent (Superman) and Bruce Wayne (Batman) in comic books. Easy was the prototype of the flawed hero: he was just as capable of failure as triumph and had a sensitive side to his prickly personality. In 1933, Crane retitled his Sunday page *Captain Easy—Soldier of Fortune,* and he did some of his finest work in these separate continuities.

Lindbergh's daring solo flight across the Atlantic in May 1927 inspired another adventure genre: the aviation strip. *Tailspin Tommy* (July 19, 1928) by Glenn Chaffin and Hal Forrest, *Tim Tyler's Luck* (August 13, 1928) by Lyman Young, and *Skyroads* (May 27, 1929) by Lester Maitland and Dick Calkins were among the numerous creations that appeared not long after Lucky Lindy landed in Paris. All three strips initially featured young male heroes and, of course, airplanes.

In many comics histories, January 7, 1929, is recorded as the exact date when the adventure strip was born. On that day, both *Buck Rogers,* often regarded as the first science fiction strip, and *Tarzan,* one of the earliest features to be drawn in a

TARZAN special art by Hal Foster of the famous jungle hero and his simian sidekick. © 1933 United Feature Syndicate, Inc. Courtesy of Jack Gilbert

LITTLE ORPHAN ANNIE daily strip by Harold Gray. This episode appeared less than a month after the stock market crash.
© November 19, 1929, Tribune Media Services, Inc. All rights reserved. Reprinted with permission. Courtesy of the Harold Gray Collection, Boston University

realistic, illustrative style, made their debut appearance. Although the big bang theory rarely applies to developments in the comics medium, an important transition was taking place. Within a relatively short time, "blood and thunder" strips were competing for space with the previously dominant "big-foot" humor genre. This shift would be the major story in the comics industry during the next decade.

The stock market crash that began on "Black Thursday," October 24, 1929, would also have a major impact on the newspaper business. *Editor & Publisher* reported on November 2, 1929, "As the figures in the stock tables receded, the figures in [newspaper] circulation charts soared to gratifying peaks and in some instances passed World Series and national election records. In New York during the first day of the crash, newsstands resembled trading posts on the Stock Exchange floor with clamoring crowds waiting for each new edition with its heartbreaking news."

While newspaper circulation continued to remain relatively high throughout the Great Depression, advertising dropped off at an alarming rate. There was a 15 percent loss in newspaper ad revenue in 1930, 24 percent in 1931, 40 percent in 1932, and 45 percent in 1933. Although the business started to recover by the second half of the decade, many struggling publications died.

Comics continued to be among the most dependable features the newspapers had to offer to their readers in these troubled times. Cartoonists rose to the challenge and created some of the most memorable strips in comics history. The funnies helped America survive the Depression.

THE GUMPS daily strip by Sidney Smith. The original cast. © 1917. Courtesy of the San Francisco Academy of Comic Art
All The Gumps comic strips © Tribune Media Services, Inc. All rights reserved. Reprinted with permission

FAMILY LIFE Sidney Smith's continuing saga of the Gump clan debuted in 1917 and was one of the most popular features of the 1920s. Other notable creations in the emerging family strip genre were *Polly and Her Pals* (1912), *Keeping Up with the Joneses* (1913), *The Bungle Family* (1918), *Toots and Casper* (1918), *Gasoline Alley* (1919), and *The Nebbs* (1923).

THE GUMPS daily strip by Sidney Smith. Andy gets his wife's attention with his soon-to-be famous exclamation. © 1917. Courtesy of Illustration House

THE GUMPS daily strip by Sidney Smith. Golf season has arrived, but Andy has family responsibilities. © 1921. Courtesy of Bill Janocha

THE GUMPS daily strip by Sidney Smith. Andy and Uncle Bim sneak a nip in the basement and discuss marriage. © February 16, 1921. Courtesy of Rob Stolzer

THE GUMPS daily strip by Sidney Smith. Andy has a hangover on New Year's Day. © January 1, 1924. Courtesy of Rob Stolzer

THE GUMPS daily strip by Sidney Smith. Bim is returning home to Australia. © 1926. Courtesy of Jim Scancarelli

THE GUMPS daily strip by Sidney Smith. Andy ponders what to do with his newfound wealth. © 1927. Courtesy of Sandy Schechter

THE GUMPS original Sunday page by Sidney Smith. A gripping episode from Chester Gump's second adventure story, written by Brandon Walsh and illustrated by Stanley Link. © October 19, 1926. Courtesy of the Art Wood Collection of Cartoon and Caricature, Prints and Photographs Division, Library of Congress

KEEPING UP WITH THE JONESES daily strip by Pop Momand. This strip about two competing families was based on a phrase popularized in the nineteenth century. *March 11, 1929. Courtesy of Sandy Schechter*

THE BUNGLE FAMILY daily strip by Harry Tuthill. George Bungle talks to himself about the ups and downs of Wall Street investing. *October 28, 1920s. Courtesy of Rob Stolzer*

TOOTS AND CASPER daily strip by Jimmy Murphy. Inspired by the success of THE GUMPS, Murphy introduced melodrama into his domestic comedy strip in the mid-1920s. *© 1927 King Features Syndicate, Inc. Courtesy of Richard Marschall*

THE NEBBS introductory strip by Sol Hess (writer) and W. A. Carlson (artist). A successful businessman, Hess contributed ideas to Sidney Smith before starting his own family strip. *© 1923 Bell Syndicate, Inc. Courtesy of Mark Johnson*

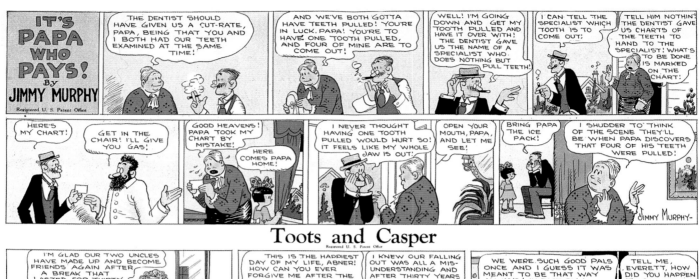

Toots and Casper

TOOTS AND CASPER and IT'S PAPA WHO PAYS! Sunday page proof by Jimmy Murphy. In January 1926, King Features Syndicate came up with a new marketing gimmick: two comics for the price of one. They directed many of their cartoonists to develop a companion feature to run at the top of their Sunday pages. Among the King "toppers" were ROSIE'S BEAU by George McManus, PARLOR, BEDROOM AND SINK by Billy DeBeck, DOT AND DASH by Cliff Sterrett, and IT'S PAPA WHO PAYS! by Jimmy Murphy. In December 1930 and January 1931, the Chicago Tribune–New York News Syndicate introduced a new batch of strips that ran at the bottom of their Sunday pages, including THAT PHONEY NICKEL by Frank King, MAW GREEN by Harold Gray, and CIGARETTE SADIE by Chester Gould. Other syndicates also offered companion features as toppers, bottomers, half-pagers, or single panels within their Sunday pages.
© May 8, 1927, King Features Syndicate, Inc. Courtesy of Richard Marschall

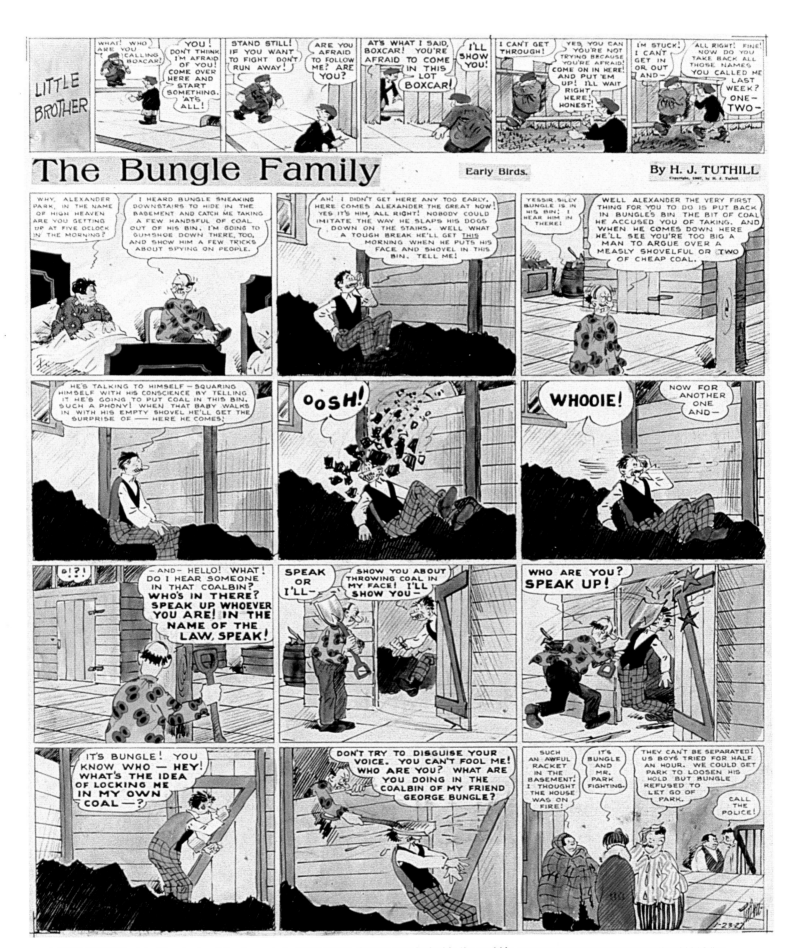

THE BUNGLE FAMILY original hand-colored Sunday page by Harry Tuthill. George gets locked in the coal bin. *January 23, 1927. Courtesy of the Sheldon Memorial Art Gallery, Howard Collection of American Popular Art*

frank king

ONE OF THE FEW STRIPS in which the characters aged at a relatively normal rate, *Gasoline Alley* is the *Our Town* of the comics pages, and the family history that has unfolded in its panels for more than eighty years reads like the Great American Novel. The creator of this epic chronicle was a gentle soul, who approached his craft with workmanlike devotion.

Frank King was born on June 11, 1883, in Cashton, Wisconsin, and his middle-class upbringing in the nearby town of Tomah provided him with a lifetime of inspiration. He landed his first job with the *Minneapolis Times* in 1901, and four years later he went to the Chicago Academy of Fine Arts. After completing his studies, he worked at Hearst's *Chicago American* and *Examiner* before ending up at the *Tribune* in 1909.

King's first successful feature for the *Chicago Tribune* was the charming fantasy strip *Bobby Make-Believe,* which debuted on January 31, 1915. He also produced a black-and-white Sunday page, *The Rectangle,* which was a collection of single-panel cartoons about life in Chicago and other miscellaneous topics.

GASOLINE ALLEY daily panel by Frank King. Walt Wallet gets some unsolicited advice on what to name his new baby. © 1921. Courtesy of Richard Marschall

All Gasoline Alley comic strips © Tribune Media Services, Inc. All rights reserved. Reprinted with permission

At the suggestion of *Tribune* copublisher Robert McCormick, King incorporated a new panel, "Sunday Morning in Gasoline Alley," into this page on November 24, 1918; it starred a group of men—Walt Wallet, Doc, Avery, and Bill—who spent their spare time tinkering with old cars. Nine months later, on August 24, 1919, *Gasoline Alley* debuted as an independent feature.

When Walt found an abandoned baby on his doorstep on Valentine's Day of 1921, the dynamics of the strip changed dramatically. In 1959, King recounted the evolution of his creation: "I had started with a popular interest: automobiles. Then I hit on an interesting human situation: Walt and Skeezix. Then I stumbled on the whole idea of growing up the characters. All these points in the progress of *Gasoline Alley* illustrate that if you mirror humanity, if people see themselves in your work, they will want to follow it, to go on seeing themselves."

King developed a clean, unembellished style for the strip that perfectly matched its wholesome tone. Throughout the 1920s and 1930s, the daily episodes traced Skeezix's growth from a baby to a teenager, as well as the cycle of romances, marriages, and births involving the rest of the cast. The Sunday pages provided a showcase for King's more ambitious efforts.

One of these flights of fantasy provided a bird's-eye view of the Wallet neighborhood, with a superimposed grid of six separate scenes. Seasonal strolls through the countryside, dream sequences, holidays, vacations, and thoughtful musings gave King the opportunity to experiment with different art techniques and visual effects.

As the characters in *Gasoline Alley* grew older and changed, they seemed to become almost human. "It is really true that my people seem to act on their own; seem to want to do certain things, almost without my planning it," King claimed. "I think that is a sign that a character has come alive. He has emerged with a personality; the original creative act is over. Now, what the strip artist does is just to cook up situations, and let the strip people react to them in their own way."

A string of talented cartoonists continued to come up with new scenarios for the folks at *Gasoline Alley.* Bill Perry took over the Sunday page in 1951, and Dick Moores assumed full-time duties on the daily strip after King died in 1969. Jim Scancarelli has written and illustrated both the daily and Sunday versions since Moores passed away in 1986. King's characters are in good hands and still have a long life in front of them.

THE RECTANGLE Sunday half-page by Frank King. The GASOLINE ALLEY gang first appeared in this Sunday-page feature that King drew from 1918 to 1920 for the Chicago Tribune. *November 23, 1919. Courtesy of Jim Scancarelli*

PATERNAL INSTINCT—Illustrations by Frank King. In 1923, Walt fought a custody battle for Skeezix. *Courtesy of Jim Scancarelli*

GASOLINE ALLEY daily strip by Frank King. The talk in the neighborhood is divided between babies and cars. *© 1921. Courtesy of Jim Scancarelli*

GASOLINE ALLEY daily strip by Frank King. Walt and his mother ponder the identity of a mysterious benefactor. © 1922. Courtesy of Jim Scancarelli

GASOLINE ALLEY daily strip by Frank King. Skeezix learns a naughty word. © 1924. Courtesy of Mort Walker

GASOLINE ALLEY daily strip by Frank King. The artist often used silhouettes to create an evocative mood in the strip. © 1925. Courtesy of the International Museum of Cartoon Art

GASOLINE ALLEY daily strip by Frank King. On June 24, 1926, Walt married Phyllis Blossom. © 1930. Courtesy of Russ Cochran

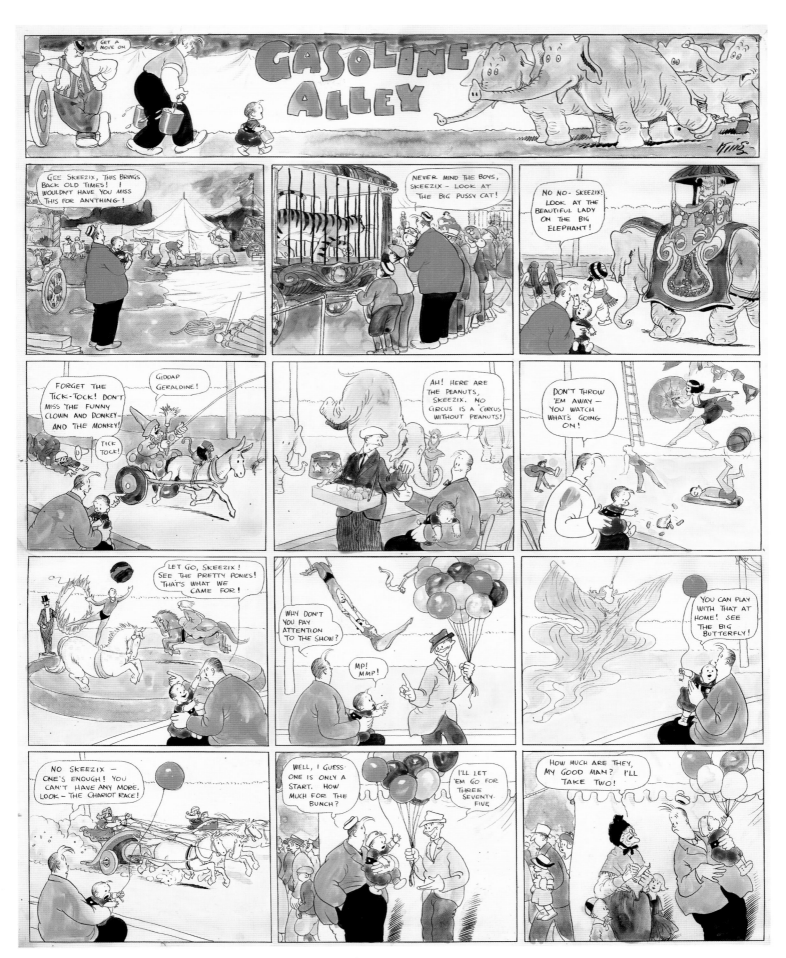

GASOLINE ALLEY original hand-colored Sunday page by Frank King. The circus comes to town. © June 11, 1922. Courtesy of Ricardo Martinez

GASOLINE ALLEY Sunday page by Frank King. The artist did many of these innovative panel-within-panel layouts in his Sunday pages. © December 24, 1931. Courtesy of Peter Maresca

GASOLINE ALLEY daily strip by Frank King. This strip was done with the scratchboard technique. © August 31, 1939. Courtesy of Jim Scancarelli

GASOLINE ALLEY daily strip by Frank King. A cast portrait. © February 10, 1942. Courtesy of Jim Scancarelli

GASOLINE ALLEY daily strip by Frank King. Skeezix gets a letter from his fiancée, Nina, while serving in the army. © June 1, 1943. Courtesy of Jim Scancarelli

GASOLINE ALLEY daily strip by Frank King. Skeezix is treated after being wounded in combat during World War II. © July 7, 1943. Courtesy of Jim Scancarelli

cliff sterrett

ONE OF THE FIRST comic strips to star an independent "new woman," *Polly and Her Pals* evolved into a graphic tour de force that captured the improvisational spirit of the Jazz Age in pen-and-ink. The creator of this classic feature is one of the most overlooked and underrated geniuses in the history of the art form.

Clifford Sterrett was born into a middle-class family of Scandinavian ancestry in Fergus Falls, Minnesota, on December 12, 1883. At the age of eighteen, he studied at the Chase Art School in Manhattan, and two years later he landed his first job in the art department of the *New York Herald*.

In 1911, Sterrett created four comic strips for the *New York Evening Telegram*: *Ventriloquial Vag, When A Man's Married, Before and After,* and *For This We Have Daughters?*. A

CLIFF STERRETT—Self-caricature from Comics and Their Creators. *1942. All Polly and Her Pals comic strips © King Features Syndicate, Inc.*

year later, when he switched over to the *New York Journal*, he adapted the latter idea and transformed it into *Positive Polly,* which debuted on December 4, 1912.

Sterrett's strip, soon renamed *Polly and Her Pals*, starred the college-aged Polly Perkins, her middle-aged parents, Paw and Maw, and the scene-stealing Kitty the cat. As the cast expanded to include a household full of quirky relatives, Paw became the central character as the eternally suffering patriarch of the clan. The gags in *Polly and Her Pals* revolved around the day-to-day trials and tribulations of this extended family group.

In the first decade of the feature, Sterrett's Sunday pages were densely packed short stories jammed with colloquial dialogue, background detail, and slapstick action. The daily strips began to display the distinctive angular design and innovative use of black-and-white that were to characterize the next phase of his artistic development.

The years between 1926 and 1935 are considered to be the high point in the evolution of Sterrett's style. He experimented with shapes, lines, and patterns to create compositions that were both geometrically balanced and playfully abstract. He

used exaggeration, distortion, and surrealism to dramatic effect. Art critics detected elements of Cubism in his work, and other cartoonists tried to incorporate "Sterrettisms"— triangular rooftops, circular flowers, checkered floors, crescent moons, and oval windows—into their strips.

The unique look of *Polly and Her Pals* has always been difficult to describe in words. Cartoonist and comic scholar Art Spiegelman made a valiant attempt in the introduction to one of the few reprint collections of the strip, published in 1990: "If comic art can be seen as a kind of picture-writing, Cliff Sterrett was its master calligrapher. His hyper-animated graceful-lined doodle-figures spout sweat drops and stars, or leave wonderful amoeba-shaped puffclouds behind them as they bounce through cheerfully dizzy and dizzying compositions at the outer edges of gravity and logic."

By the mid-1930s, Sterrett was suffering from rheumatism and had to cut back on his workload. Paul Fung took over the daily *Polly and Her Pals* strip on March 9, 1935. Sterrett continued to produce the Sunday-page episodes, with the help of assistants, until June 15, 1958. He died six years later. His legacy has yet to be fully appreciated.

POLLY AND HER PALS Sunday page by Cliff Sterrett. Although the strip was drawn in a more conventional style in the early years, some of Sterrett's trademark design elements were beginning to emerge at this stage in his artistic development. © 1917. Courtesy of Howard Lowery

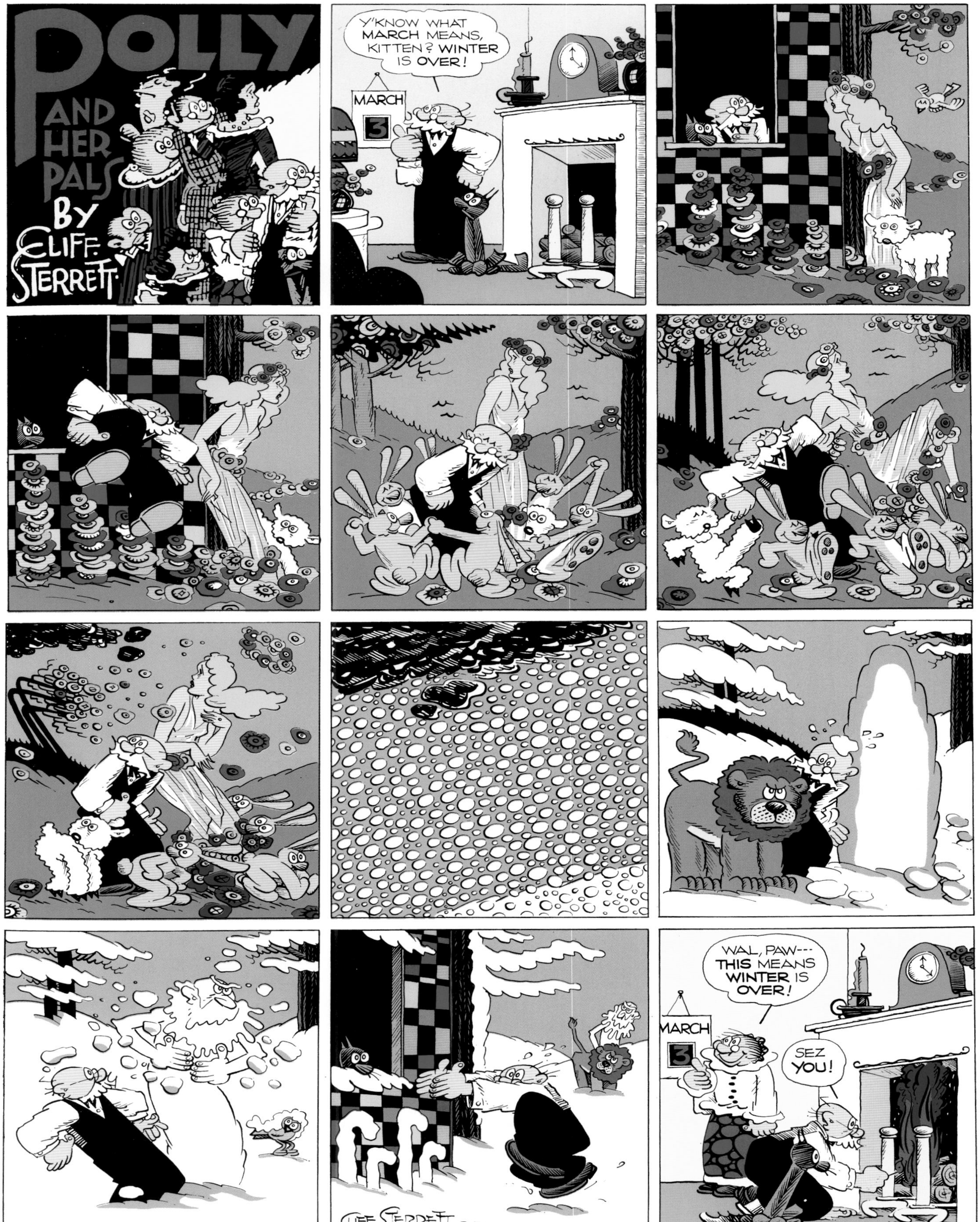
POLLY AND HER PALS BY CLIFF. STERRETT.
Y'KNOW WHAT MARCH MEANS, KITTEN? WINTER IS OVER!
MARCH
3
MARCH
3
WAL, PAW--- THIS MEANS WINTER IS OVER!
SEZ YOU!
CLIFF. STERRETT. 3.3

POLLY AND HER PALS recolored Sunday page by Cliff Sterrett. A classic episode from Sterrett's peak period. © March 3, 1935. Courtesy of Craig Yoe and American Color

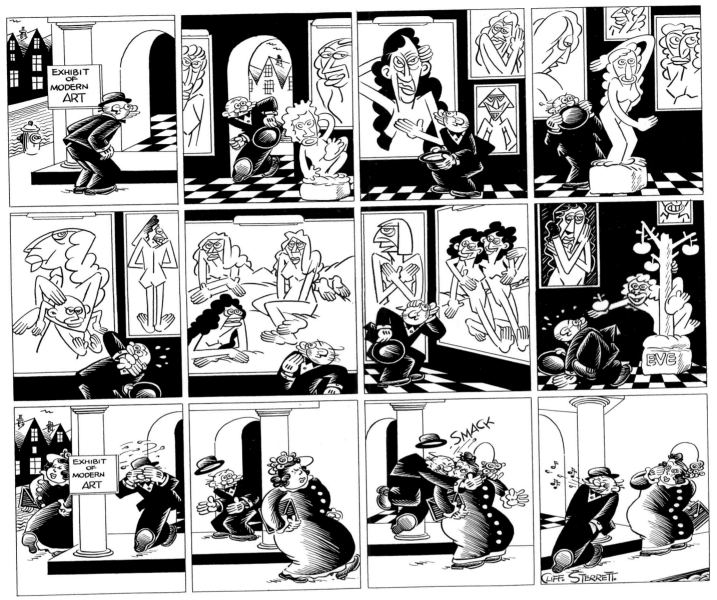

POLLY AND HER PALS *Sunday page by Cliff Sterrett. Paw's visit to an art museum gives Sterrett an opportunity to try his hand at Cubism.* © May 31, 1936.
Courtesy of the International Museum of Cartoon Art

POLLY AND HER PALS *daily strip by Cliff Sterrett. Polly's appearances became less frequent as Sterrett's strip evolved.* © 1934. Courtesy of Howard Lowery

SOMEBODY'S STENOG *daily strip by A. E. Hayward. The first successful working-girl strip debuted in 1916 and starred Cam O'Flage; her boss, Sam Smithers; and coworkers Mary Doodle and Kitty Scratch.* © January 10, 1930, Ledger Syndicate, Inc. Courtesy of Bill Janocha

THE FEMININE MYSTIQUE

During the 1920s, women exercised their new voting rights, looked for jobs outside the home, and expressed themselves more openly in public. These changes were reflected on the comics pages as strips starring female characters proliferated. Two distinct character types emerged: the working girl and the flapper. The more ambitious ones found employment in offices and dress shops, while others dabbled in acting or other short-term jobs that permitted enough changes to keep the stories interesting. Flapper fashions were popular with most of the female comic strip stars, and short skirts, long legs, bobbed hair, and lipstick became the accepted style. On the following pages is a selection of comic strips from this era featuring hardworking and attractive leading ladies.

WINNIE WINKLE THE BREADWINNER *daily strip by Martin Branner. Winnie's father, Rip, didn't have any qualms about living off his daughter's earnings.* c. 1921. © Tribune Media Services, Inc. All rights reserved. Reprinted with permission. Courtesy of All Star Auctions

TILLIE THE TOILER *daily strip by Russ Westover. The diminutive, bulb-nosed Clarence "Mac" McDougall was hopelessly in love with the leggy secretary and part-time model Tillie Jones.* © 1928 King Features Syndicate, Inc. Courtesy of Sandy Schechter

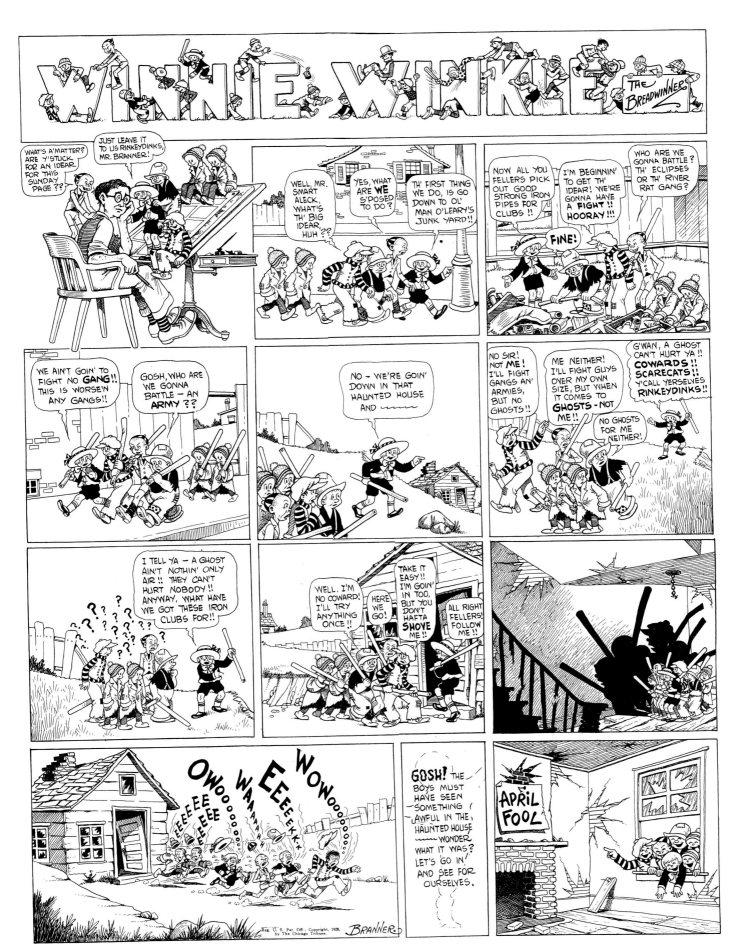

WINNIE WINKLE THE BREADWINNER Sunday page by Martin Branner, with self-caricature. Winnie's brother Perry and his gang of friends, the Rinkeydinks, took over the Sunday episodes in Branner's feature. © April 1, 1928, Tribune Media Services, Inc. All rights reserved. Reprinted with permission. Courtesy of David Applegate

BOOTS AND HER BUDDIES daily strip by Edgar (Abe) Martin. Known as "the sweetheart of the comics," Boots was an attractive blonde coed who always played by the rules. © 1930 NEA Service, Inc. Courtesy of Sandy Schechter

GUS AND GUSSIE daily strip by Jack Lait (writer) and Paul Fung (artist). Gus Donnerwetter and Gussie Abadab were aspiring actors who worked a variety of odd jobs while waiting for their big break. © May 25, 1926, King Features Syndicate, Inc. Courtesy of Sandy Schechter

ELLA CINDERS daily strip by Bill Conselman (writer) and Charlie Plumb (artist). The Cinderella of the Jazz Age, Ella was a slightly older Orphan Annie who lived a similar rags-to-riches-to-rags existence. © September 15, 1930, Metropolitan Newspaper Feature Service, Inc. Courtesy of Illustration House

ETTA KETT daily strip by Paul Robinson. This leading lady was originally designed to teach proper etiquette to young people and, as a fashion-conscious flapper, continued to set a good example by remaining eternally chaste. © August 1, 1928, Central Press Association, Inc. Courtesy of Mark Johnson

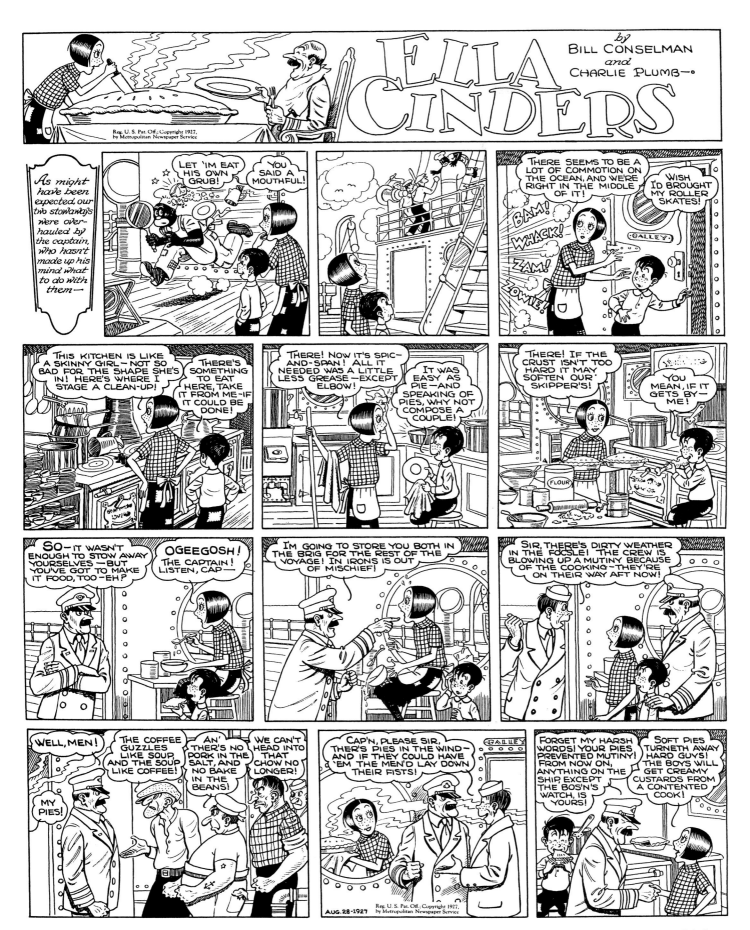

ELLA CINDERS Sunday page by Bill Conselman (writer) and Charlie Plumb (artist). Ella and her brother Blackie are stowaways on an ocean vessel during one of their out-of-luck periods. © August 28, 1927, Metropolitan Newspaper Feature Service, Inc. Courtesy of Sandy Schechter.

LADY BOUNTIFUL daily strip by Gene Carr. One of the first strips with a glamorous female lead, LADY BOUNTIFUL debuted in the New York Journal in 1902. A version was still being produced by Carr in the late 1920s. © October 18, 1928, King Features Syndicate, Inc. Courtesy of Bill Janocha

PETEY daily strip by C. A. Voight. Similar to Cliff Sterrett's Paw, Voight's Petey lived with his plump wife and pretty niece. c. 1920s, New York Tribune. Courtesy of the International Museum of Cartoon Art

FRITZI RITZ daily strip by Larry Whittington. Launched in 1922 by Whittington, FRITZI RITZ was taken over by Ernie Bushmiller in 1925.
© October 13, 1925, King Features Syndicate, Inc. Courtesy of Bill Janocha

DUMB DORA daily strip by Chic Young. This early pretty-girl strip by the creator of BLONDIE starred a brunette flapper who wasn't as dumb as her name suggested. © February 19, 1930, Newspaper Feature Service, Inc. Courtesy of the International Museum of Cartoon Art

BETTY original hand-colored Sunday page by C. A. Voight. Lester DePester, the hapless boyfriend of wealthy Betty Thompson, was always the fall guy in Voight's elegantly illustrated Sunday feature. © December 3, 1922, New York Tribune, Inc. Courtesy of Illustration House.

MERELY MARGY Sunday page by John Held Jr. Arab was Margy's main sheik. © May 25, 1930, King Features Syndicate, Inc. Courtesy of Illustration House

MERELY MARGY daily strip by John Held Jr. After making his mark as an illustrator in many of the leading magazines of the 1920s, Held created a flapper comic strip in 1927, but it did not survive long after the stock market crash. © September 6, 1927, King Features Syndicate, Inc. Courtesy of Rob Stolzer

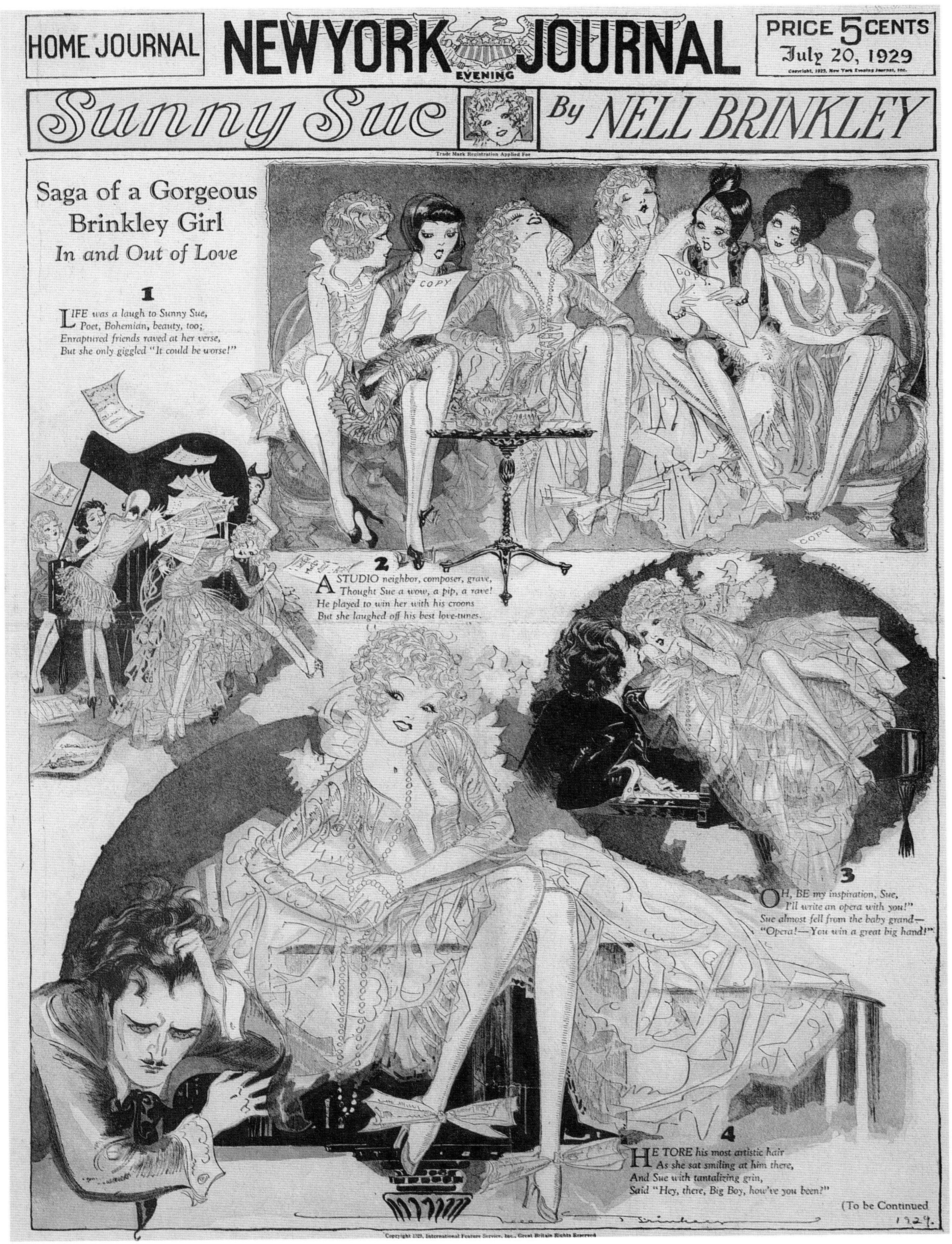
HOME JOURNAL
NEW YORK EVENING JOURNAL
PRICE 5 CENTS
July 20, 1929
Sunny Sue
By NELL BRINKLEY
Trade Mark Registration Applied For
Saga of a Gorgeous Brinkley Girl
In and Out of Love
1
LIFE was a laugh to Sunny Sue,
Poet, Bohemian, beauty, too;
Enraptured friends raved at her verse,
But she only giggled "It could be worse!"
COPY
2
A STUDIO neighbor, composer, grave,
Thought Sue a wow, a pip, a rave!
He played to win her with his croons
But she laughed off his best love-tunes.
3
OH, BE my inspiration, Sue,
I'll write an opera with you!"
Sue almost fell from the baby grand—
"Opera!—You win a great big hand!"
4
HE TORE his most artistic hair
As she sat smiling at him there,
And Sue with tantalizing grin,
Said "Hey, there, Big Boy, how've you been?"
(To be Continued
1929.

SUNNY SUE Sunday page by Nell Brinkley. The Brinkley Girl was the Gibson Girl of the Jazz Age and starred in numerous features, illustrated by Brinkley for the Hearst newspapers, from 1907 to 1937. © July 20, 1929, International Feature Service, Inc. Courtesy of the International Museum of Cartoon Art

billy debeck

THE CREATOR OF BARNEY GOOGLE, Spark Plug, and Snuffy Smith was one of the most naturally gifted cartoonists ever to work in the comics medium. He could draw gorgeous girls and goofy-looking guys and depict them in wild action and peaceful repose. He was a good letterer and a master of graphic design. Urban skylines gave his strips a sense of time and place, and mountain scenery evoked the natural beauty of Appalachia. He could be dramatic, poetic, or romantic and still be funny. As talented as he was artistically, the real secret to his success was an affinity for the common people.

William Morgan DeBeck was born on the South Side of Chicago on April 16, 1890. His parents were of French, Irish, and Welsh stock. After graduating from high school in 1908, he attended the Chicago Academy of Fine Arts and got his first job at the *Youngstown (Ohio) Telegram* in 1910. He worked briefly at the *Pittsburgh Gazette-Times* and finally landed a big-city position at the *Chicago Herald,* where he launched his first successful strip, *Married Life,* on December 9, 1915. When the *Herald* merged with the *Examiner* in May 1918, DeBeck found himself working for William Randolph Hearst.

On June 17, 1919, a new strip, *Take Barney Google, F'rinstance,* debuted in the *Chicago Herald and Examiner.* For the next three years, this henpecked, sports-loving, pop-nosed, bug-eyed character gradually diminished in height as his popularity increased. Then, on July 17, 1922, his fortunes changed. A wealthy gentleman gave Barney a sad-faced nag named Spark Plug. When the horse won the Abadaba Handicap, he became a rich man—and so did his creator.

"Spark Plug, I am happy to say, has caught on," wrote DeBeck in 1924. "All over the United States you find stuffed Spark Plugs and Spark Plug games and Spark Plug drums and Spark Plug balloons and Spark Plug tin pails. And there is a Spark Plug play on the road. The only thing that is lacking is a Spark Plug grand opera."

Throughout the rest of the 1920s and early 1930s, Barney and Spark Plug, along with Sunshine the jockey, pursued an endlessly entertaining series of humorous adventures. They entered the Comic Strip Derby, the Horseshoe Handicap, and the T-Bone Stakes. They traveled across the United States, swam the English Channel, solved a murder mystery, and joined a secret society. Barney even ran for president.

And then, on November 17, 1934, a cantankerous mountain man took aim at Barney Google in the backwoods

"*I'll say that's pretty tough!*" says Barney

BILLY DEBECK—Self-caricature. *September 1921, Circulation magazine. Courtesy of Robert Beerbohm All Barney Google comic strips © King Features Syndicate, Inc.*

of North Carolina. Snuffy Smith would eventually get equal billing in the strip, as the hillbilly and the city slicker developed a lasting friendship. The pairing brought a new source of energy and gags to the feature and helped maintain its popularity throughout the remainder of the Depression.

Billy DeBeck died of cancer on November 11, 1942, and Fred Lasswell, DeBeck's former assistant, took over the strip. *Barney Google and Snuffy Smith* had 206 clients in 1946. Forty years later, it was appearing in nearly 900 papers.

"My folks had come out of a country atmosphere, so I was very comfortable with country people," explained Lasswell. "So I started concentrating during the transition period on slowly working Barney out of there and trying to get a little more down-home feeling in the strip."

DeBeck built *Barney Google* into a solid success during his twenty-three-year tenure on the feature. Lasswell continued it for almost sixty years, until 2001 (and it is still running). He took a creation that had earned a place in comic strip history and developed it into an enduring classic.

BARNEY GOOGLE Sunday page proof by Billy DeBeck. Barney and his "sweet woman" were the stars of DeBeck's strip before Spark Plug came on the scene in 1922. This New Year's Eve episode is from the first year of the BARNEY GOOGLE Sunday page. © December 26, 1920. Courtesy of King Features Syndicate

BARNEY GOOGLE daily strip by Billy DeBeck. Barney and Spark Plug swam across the English Channel in 1926. © November 24, 1926. Courtesy of Craig Englund

BARNEY GOOGLE daily strip by Billy DeBeck. During the 1920s and early 1930s, Barney, Spark Plug, and Sunshine lived from one horse race to the next. © May 5, 1930. Courtesy of Craig Englund

BARNEY GOOGLE daily strip by Billy DeBeck. Barney dreams of his past adventures with Spark Plug. © August 20, 1931. Courtesy of Craig Englund

BARNEY GOOGLE daily strip by Billy DeBeck. Spark Plug raced against a pint-sized look-alike named Pony Boy in the International Derby in 1931. © September 8, 1931. Courtesy of Bill Janocha

BARNEY GOOGLE daily strip by Billy DeBeck. There were often "recap" strips to bring readers up to speed on DeBeck's fast-paced stories. © November 23, 1931. Courtesy of Craig Englund

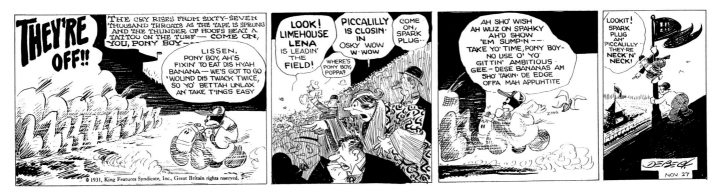

BARNEY GOOGLE daily strip by Billy DeBeck. The excitement of the racetracks was captured in this episode. © November 27, 1931. Courtesy of Craig Englund

BARNEY GOOGLE daily strip by Billy DeBeck. Sunshine, Barney's loyal jockey, was a major character in the strip from mid-1923 until Snuffy Smith stole the sidekick role in late 1934. © December 3, 1931. Courtesy of Craig Englund

BARNEY GOOGLE daily strip by Billy DeBeck. An outstanding example of DeBeck's free-flowing pen-and-ink style. © February 1, 1932. Courtesy of Craig Englund

BARNEY GOOGLE recolored Sunday page by Billy DeBeck. Barney ran for president twice: in the daily continuities in 1928 and in a Sunday-page series in 1932. © April 17, 1932. Original artwork courtesy of Howard Lowery and American Color

BARNEY GOOGLE daily strip by Billy DeBeck. A recap strip for one of DeBeck's mystery stories. © August 26, 1932. Courtesy of Sandy Schechter

BARNEY GOOGLE daily strip by Billy DeBeck. Snuffy and Lowizie (later spelled "Loweezy") made their first appearance in BARNEY GOOGLE on November 17, 1934. © December 26, 1935. Courtesy of Rob Stolzer

BARNEY GOOGLE Sunday page by Billy DeBeck. The whole population of Hootin' Holler shows up to welcome Lowizie, Snuffy, and Barney back from a trip to the city. Bunky, who first appeared in the topper feature PARLOR, BEDROOM AND SINK in 1928, became the star of his own companion strip from 1935 to 1948. © April 18, 1937. Courtesy of Peter Maresca

MOON MULLINS daily strip by Frank Willard. Moon takes a swing at boxing champion Gene Tunney. © September 19, 1927 Tribune Media Services, Inc. All rights reserved.
Reprinted with permission. Courtesy of Sandy Schechter

THE LOW LIFE

In 1924, Gilbert Seldes defended the robust vitality of what critics called the "Vulgar Comic Strip" as having "so little respect for law, order, the rights of property, the sanctity of money, the romance of marriage, and all the other foundations of American life, that if they were put into fiction the Society for the Suppression of Everything would hale them incontinently to court and our morals would be saved again." In addition to *Mutt and Jeff* and *Barney Google*, *Moon Mullins, Joe Jinks,* and *Joe and Asbestos* were among the strips that featured the exploits of con men, hustlers, and promoters in the world of racetracks, boxing rings, and saloons.

JOE JINKS daily strip by Vic Forsythe. Joe watches Dynamite Dunn fight Mysterious Mike, who turns out to be boxing champ Jack Dempsey.
© March 23, 1929, Press Publishing Company (New York World). Courtesy of Sandy Schechter

JOE AND ASBESTOS daily strip by Ken Kling. Although Kling's feature appeared in only ten newspapers, he was among the highest-earning cartoonists in the United States, with an annual salary of $100,000. His clients paid top dollar for the "hot" racing tips that were set in type and pasted into the blank spaces in the strip. © July 6, 1930, Bell Syndicate, Inc. Courtesy of Sandy Schechter

MOON MULLINS daily strip by Frank Willard. Moon's landlady, Emmy Schmaltz, disapproves of his girlfriend, Little Egypt. © March 7, 1924, Tribune Media Services, Inc.
All rights reserved. Reprinted with permission. Courtesy of the International Museum of Cartoon Art

MOON MULLINS daily strip by Frank Willard. Lord Plushbottom, shown here with the cane, married Emmy Schmaltz in 1934. © October 7, 1925 Tribune Media
Services, Inc. All rights reserved. Reprinted with permission. Courtesy of Rob Stolzer

MOON MULLINS daily strip by Frank Willard. Moon is in hot water again. © 1931 Tribune Media Services, Inc. All rights reserved. Reprinted with permission. Courtesy of Sandy Schechter

MOON MULLINS daily strip by Frank Willard. Moon's kid brother Kayo and his Uncle Willie were regulars in the strip. (Willard sent this strip to
Mort Walker, who created BEETLE BAILEY in 1950, when Walker was a young, aspiring cartoonist in the mid-1930s.) © July 24, 1933, Tribune Media
Services, Inc. All rights reserved. Reprinted with permission. Courtesy of Mort Walker

MOON MULLINS original hand-colored Sunday page by Frank Willard. The artist often featured wild slapstick and visual sight gags in his Sunday-page episodes. © 1928 Tribune Media Services, Inc. All rights reserved. Reprinted with permission. Courtesy of Gary Ernest Smith.

MOON MULLINS Sunday page by Frank Willard. Kayo plays a trick on Emmy Schmaltz.
© October 25, 1931. Tribune Media Services, Inc. All rights reserved. Reprinted with permission. Courtesy of Russ Cochran

OUR BOARDING HOUSE daily panel by Gene Ahearn. The debut appearance of Ahearn's famous blowhard, Major Hoople. © January 27, 1922, NEA Service, Inc. Courtesy of Mark Johnson

OUT OUR WAY special panel by J. R. Williams with self-caricature. In 1936, Williams had 700 daily and 242 Sunday clients, the most of any syndicated feature. © December 13, 1924, NEA Service, Inc. Courtesy of Editor & Publisher

SALESMAN SAM daily strip by George Swanson. Sam Howdy worked in J. Guzzleman's general store in Swanson's screwball strip. © May 3, 1922, NEA Service, Inc. Courtesy of Frank Pauer

PACKAGE DEAL In 1901, Robert F. Paine of the *Cleveland Press* founded the Newspaper Enterprise Association. Beginning in 1909, it distributed a selection of features to its mostly small-town clients for a package price, and the papers could choose which ones to run. On the next page is a sampling of the top strips and panels that the service offered during the 1920s.

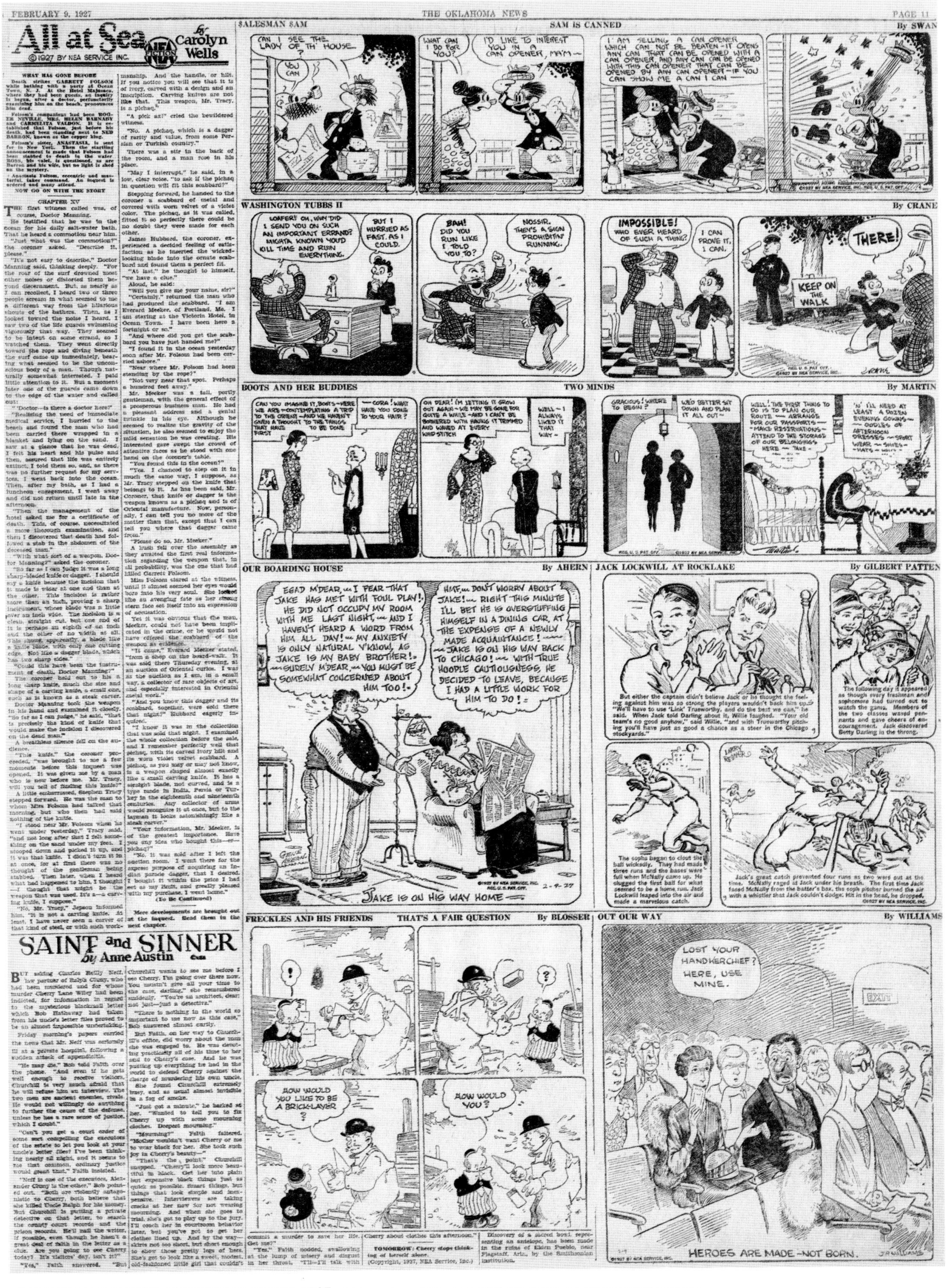

FEBRUARY 9, 1927 THE OKLAHOMA NEWS PAGE 11

All at Sea

by Carolyn Wells

©1927 BY NEA SERVICE INC.

WHAT HAS GONE BEFORE

CHAPTER XV

SAINT and SINNER

by Anne Austin

SALESMAN SAM
SAM IS CANNED
By SWAN
CAN I SEE TH' LADY OF TH' HOUSE ?
YOU CAN
WHAT CAN I DO FOR YOU?
I'D LIKE TO INTEREST YOU IN A CAN OPENER, MA'M—
I AM SELLING A CAN OPENER WHICH CAN NOT BE BEATEN—IT OPENS ANY CAN THAT CAN BE OPENED WITH A CAN OPENER, AND ANY CAN CAN BE OPENED WITH THIS CAN OPENER THAT CAN BE OPENED BY ANY CAN OPENER—IF YOU CAN SHOW ME A CAN I CAN—
WASHINGTON TUBBS II
By CRANE
LOAFER! OH, WHY DID I SEND YOU ON SUCH AN IMPORTANT ERRAND? MIGHTA KNOWN YOU'D KILL TIME AND RUIN EVERYTHING.
BUT I HURRIED AS FAST AS I COULD.
BAH! DID YOU RUN LIKE I TOLD YOU TO?
NOSSIR. THERE'S A SIGN PROHIBITIN' RUNNING.
IMPOSSIBLE! WHO EVER HEARD OF SUCH A THING?
I CAN PROVE IT, I CAN.
THERE!
KEEP ON THE WALK
BOOTS AND HER BUDDIES
TWO MINDS
By MARTIN
CAN YOU IMAGINE IT, BOOTS—HERE WE ARE—CONTEMPLATING A TRIP TO THE ORIENT—AND WE HAVEN'T GIVEN A THOUGHT TO THE THINGS THAT HAVE TO BE DONE FIRST
—CORA! WHAT HAVE YOU DONE TO YOUR HAIR?
OH DEAR! I'M LETTING IT GROW OUT AGAIN—WE MAY BE GONE FOR QUITE A WHILE—AND I CAN'T BE BOTHERED WITH HAVING IT TRIMMED AND WAVED AT EVERY WAYSTITCH
WELL—I ALWAYS LIKED IT THAT WAY—
GRACIOUS! WHERE TO BEGIN?
WE'D BETTER SIT DOWN AND PLAN IT ALL OUT—
WELL! THE FIRST THING TO DO IS TO PLAN OUR ROUTE—ARRANGE FOR OUR PASSPORTS—MAKE RESERVATIONS—ATTEND TO THE STORAGE OF OUR BELONGINGS HERE—TAKE—
'N' I'LL NEED AT LEAST A DOZEN EVENING GOWNS—OODLES OF AFTERNOON DRESSES—SPORT WEAR—SHOES—HATS—
OUR BOARDING HOUSE
By AHERN
EGAD M'DEAR,— I FEAR THAT JAKE HAS MET WITH FOUL PLAY! HE DID NOT OCCUPY MY ROOM WITH ME LAST NIGHT,— AND I HAVEN'T HEARD A WORD FROM HIM ALL DAY!— MY ANXIETY IS ONLY NATURAL Y'KNOW, AS JAKE IS MY BABY BROTHER!— — SURELY M'DEAR,— YOU MUST BE SOMEWHAT CONCERNED ABOUT HIM TOO!—
HUMF,— DON'T WORRY ABOUT JAKE!— RIGHT THIS MINUTE I'LL BET HE IS OVERSTUFFING HIMSELF IN A DINING CAR, AT THE EXPENSE OF A NEWLY MADE ACQUAINTANCE!— —JAKE IS ON HIS WAY BACK TO CHICAGO!— WITH TRUE HOOPLE CAUTIOUSNESS, HE DECIDED TO LEAVE, BECAUSE I HAD A LITTLE WORK FOR HIM TO DO!—
JAKE IS ON HIS WAY HOME
JACK LOCKWILL AT ROCKLAKE
By GILBERT PATTEN
FRECKLES AND HIS FRIENDS
THAT'S A FAIR QUESTION
By BLOSSER
HOW WOULD YOU LIKE TO BE A BRICK-LAYER?
HOW WOULD YOU?
OUT OUR WAY
By WILLIAMS
LOST YOUR HANDKERCHIEF? HERE, USE MINE.
EXIT
HEROES ARE MADE—NOT BORN.

NEWSPAPER ENTERPRISE ASSOCIATION COMICS PAGE—Oklahoma News. *© February 9, 1927, NEA Service, Inc. Courtesy of Mark Johnson*

LIFE SKETCHES
By W. E. Hill—An Artist Who Senses Spirit Of The Day

"WHAT'S WRONG WITH THE MOVIES?"

Copyright, 1922, by The Chicago Tribune

1 Outside any moving picture theatre, showing a line of movie fans waiting for the second show. "Where is Your Daughter Tonight?" a tale of the underworld—is the feature.

2 C. Hurlbutt Growl, assistant sub editor on the "Tri-monthly Review," is all of a-quiver over the condition of the movies. "What's wrong with the motion picture industry" is to be his contribution to the April "Tri-monthly," and maybe it isn't going to be full of withering phrases like "Degradation through sex appeal," "Low tone of morality" and "Sterility of Purpose." Everything's wrong with the movies, according to C. Hurlbutt. Perhaps C. H.'s latest returned scenario has something to do with it.

3 Mrs. St. John Ampico, clubwoman, and stationary advisie on committees of the Woman's Self Betterment League, is also dead sure that something is vitally wrong with the movies. Something very vital. And in her little address before the Thursday Club, Mrs. Ampico gave it as her opinion that financial ruin for the motion picture industry is inevitable unless producers can be made to realize that the American public frowns upon questionable sex films. "More educational features, daily incidents in the life of the mud lark, or the house fly for instance, that's the kind of subject our girls and boys really want to see."

4 The Right Reverend Whitely Black opines that something has got to be done, and done immediately, or the whole country will be flooded, nay inundated, with crime wave upon crime wave. And all because of the low moral tone of the motion picture of to-day. "Let us have pictures based on Bible themes," says the Right Reverend, "take the Story of Ruth and Naomi—there's material for some right minded producer!"

5 Mrs. Erda Mudie Mobrey, popular novelist, is of the opinion that the public will stay away from the movies unless the film magnates employ better scenario writers. You should have seen what they did to Mrs. Mobrey's magazine short story "Uphill, Downdale to Grandma Higgins," when it appeared on the screen. "Scarlet Hips," it was called and Mrs. Mobrey, who was present at the Monday matinee, had to be carried out kicking and screaming.

6 List to the wail of Miss Eleanor Lime Light from the speaking stage. Traveled all the way from New York to Los Angeles and back again, with nothing but a riled disposition to show for it. She didn't film as well as they hoped she would. "No place in the movies for people who can act—they want ten-year-old waitresses and nurse girls instead! That's what's the matter with the movies!"

7 And now meet Miss Tolita Cutely of Hollywood's most exclusive set and superfeature star of the Sex Playful Studios, Inc. Miss Cutely and her lady press agent are very very busy these days explaining to a breathless world what isn't the matter with the movies, and Hollywood in particular. "Tolita," explains the lady P. A. "is too busy being just a dear sweet trusting little girl to even think of all the frightful stories you read in the papers about the motion picture people. Next to her dear public, her mamma, and work, of course, she loves her dollies best. Look at this photo of Tolita tiptoeing away, after putting her Teddy bear and her Jackie Coogan doll to bed, and I know you will agree with me that here is a womanly little girl, full of sunshine and light, who has never lost her sense of values."

8 And here is a closeup of Miss Cutely in her Hollywood palace, en route to bed at 8:30 P. M., with her favorite dollies. Doesn't this change your ideas of movie people?

9 This is Adolph P. Crackwell, the film magnate, who made "Sex Playful Films" a household word. "The public," says he, via Mike Blood, his press agent, "does not want unhealthy sex plays. What the public wants and what we are striving to offer, are stories of clean universal appeal with a homely touch of human sweetness and simplicity. In fact, our next release will be a film version of Whittier's "Barefoot Boy."

10 Outside any motion picture theatre, a few weeks or months hence, snowing the customary line of fans waiting for the second show. "Paths of Shame," a screen version of Whittier's "Barefoot Boy," is the current attraction. Miss Tolita Cutely, the featured player, plays the part of the vamp who lures the Barefoot Boy to the city. "The part was especially introduced by Mr. Whittier himself, to suit Miss Cutely's rare personality," writes her P. A. Incidentally, the line of waiting fans extends around the corner, which may or may not tend to show that what's wrong with the movies is the public.

LIFE SKETCHES Sunday page by W. E. Hill. This long-running feature started as *AMONG US MORTALS* in the *New York Tribune* in 1916 and was distributed by the Chicago Tribune–New York News Syndicate beginning in 1922. Sunday Oregonian. © April 2, 1922, Chicago Tribune. Courtesy of Bill Griffith

COMMODUS
Hero of the Colesseum.
KILLED AN ELEPHANT WITH
ONE BOW SHOT —
THE ARROW PASSING COMPLETELY
THROUGH THE BODY
OF THE ELEPHANT —

Commodus
was left-handed
and red-headed

JEAN FOLEY, of Pittsburg
WROTE A LETTER OF 190 PAGES —
102,640 WORDS

GEORGE
WRIGHT
(Cincinnati
Red stockings)
1869
PLAYED 52 GAMES
HIT .518
SCORED 339 RUNS
AND MADE
59
HOMERS.

Miss
DOROTHY SMITH, of Boston
CAN TOUCH HER TOE WITH HER ELBOW

ABE THE NEWSBOY
— A San Francisco lightweight
HAS FOUGHT 906 BATTLES
— and is still fighting

RIPLEY'S BELIEVE IT OR NOT original page by Robert Ripley. This fact-based, novelty feature started as a sports cartoon in the New York Globe in *December 1918.* © 1920s. Courtesy of Bill Janocha

WHEN A FELLER NEEDS A FRIEND *daily panel by Clare Briggs. The artist often featured a small-town Tom Sawyer named "Skin-nay" in his nostalgic cartoons.* © *July 7, 1924, New York Tribune, Inc. Courtesy of Sandy Schechter*

THE TIMID SOUL *daily panel by H. T. Webster. The reticent and fussy Caspar Milquetoast was Webster's most memorable character.* © *April 13, 1936, New York Tribune, Inc. Courtesy of the International Museum of Cartoon Art*

A SLICE OF LIFE The syndicated daily panel evolved from political, sports, and humorous cartoons done by such local favorites as John McCutcheon of the *Chicago Tribune,* TAD Dorgan of the *New York Journal,* and Rube Goldberg of the *New York Evening Mail.* During the 1920s, Clare Briggs, H. T. Webster, Fontaine Fox, J. R. Williams, and Clare Dwiggins were among the artists producing nationally distributed panels that dealt with the recurrent themes of childhood, nostalgia, idle pastimes, family relationships, home life, and the workplace.

OUR SECRET AMBITIONS *daily panel by Garr Williams. The artist joined the* **Chicago Tribune** *in 1921 and took over Clare Briggs's former spot, on the front page of the second section, in 1924.* © *March 5, 1923, Chicago Tribune. Courtesy of Rob Stolzer*

MICKEY (HIMSELF) McGUIRE

TOONERVILLE FOLKS daily panel by Fontaine Fox. While working at the Chicago Post in 1908, Fox created a weekly panel that starred a group of small-town kids. When he signed a contract with the Wheeler Syndicate in 1913, he expanded the cast of the feature, which eventually was titled **TOONERVILLE FOLKS**, to include the Skipper of the Toonerville Trolley, the Powerful Katrinka, the Terrible-Tempered Mr. Bang, Aunt Eppie Hogg, and Mickey (Himself) McGuire. © 1926 Bell Syndicate, Inc. Courtesy of Sandy Schechter

THE SCHOLARS

SCHOOL DAYS daily panel by Clare Dwiggins. "Dwig" drew on his own childhood experiences for many of his creations, which included **SCHOOL DAYS** (1909), **TOM SAWYER AND HUCK FINN** (1918), and **NIPPER** (1931).
© McClure Syndicate, Inc. Courtesy of the International Museum of Cartoon Art

MOMENTS WE'D LIKE TO LIVE OVER—
FIFTH GRADE PHOTO.

OUT OUR WAY daily panel by J. R. Williams. This popular panel, which debuted on November 22, 1921, featured a rotating cast of graying mothers, slovenly kids, grizzly cowboys, and cantankerous machine-shop workers.
© October 10, 1924, NEA Service, Inc. Courtesy of Frank Pauer

DIFFICULT DECISIONS daily panel by Gluyas Williams. A regular contributor to The New Yorker from its inception in 1925, Williams also did a syndicated panel that ran under different titles from the mid-1920s to the 1940s.
© November 2, 1927, Bell Syndicate, Inc. Courtesy of the International Museum of Cartoon Art

TOONERVILLE FOLKS
BY FONTAINE FOX
McNaught Syndicate, Inc.

THE SKIPPER OF THE TOONERVILLE TROLLEY SOLVES A SERIOUS TRANSPORTATION PROBLEM

WOT TH' HEK WAS ALL THAT NOISE BACK THERE

THAT BACK PLATFORM HEZ FELL OFF AGIN AND ED WORTLE WITH IT!

YOU BETTER GO ON AND LET ME TAKE HIM IN AND FIX UP HIS HEAD

EASIEST WAY'D BE TO BACK THE CAR UP AND MAKE THE REPAIRS HERE

WHOA!

ARE YA STILL HAVIN' TROUBLE GETTIN' THE CAR STARTED WITH THAT BIG CROWD FROM THE 5.47?

WE'LL JUST LET THAT BACK PLATFORM STAY DOWN THERE FOR A SPELL

YEP, I KNOW. IT FELL OFF WHEN I WASN'T LOOKIN' AN' I AIN'T BIN ABLE T' FIND IT

YA KNOW I THINK HE KNOCKED THAT PLATFORM OFF ON PURPOSE SO HE CUD GET THE CAR STARTED EASIER

AND BE ABLE T' MAKE THE HILLS!

TOONERVILLE FOLKS Sunday page by Fontaine Fox. The TOONERVILLE FOLKS Sunday page debuted in 1918 and remained in circulation, along with the daily panel, until 1955. © McNaught Syndicate, Inc. Courtesy of Russ Cochran

SCHOOL DAYS original hand-colored Sunday page by Clare Dwiggins. The first Sunday series of Dwig's most enduring creation debuted in 1914 and was revived in 1928. © October 27, 1929, McClure Syndicate, Inc. Courtesy of Jack Gilbert and the Barnum Museum

NIPPER daily strip by Clare Dwiggins. The last major creation by this prolific artist was set in a contemporary small town and ran from 1931 to 1937. © 1930s, Public Ledger

US BOYS daily strip by Tom McNamara. One of the first of the modern kid comics, US BOYS was also the inspiration for Hal Roach's OUR GANG comedies.
© 1922 New York Evening Journal. Courtesy of Bill Janocha

CHILD STARS Everyday life, viewed through the eyes of comic strip kids, was another thematic preoccupation on the funnies pages during the 1920s. The new generation was less antisocial than the mischievous pranksters of the past, and their adventures were depicted with greater authenticity and attention to detail. Adolescents and teenagers also joined the youth movement as newspapers offered something for every age group.

REG'LAR FELLERS daily strip by Gene Byrnes. This popular feature, which began as a single panel in 1917, featured a suburban gang lead by Jimmie Dugan, the lad in the checkered cap. © December 16, 1922, Bell Syndicate, Inc. Courtesy of Rob Stolzer

SMITTY daily strip by Walter Berndt. Augustus Smith, the thirteen-year-old star of Berndt's 1922 creation, worked in Mr. Bailey's office and lived with his parents and little brother Herby. © 1923 Tribune Media Services, Inc. All rights reserved. Reprinted with permission. Courtesy of Sandy Schechter

Reg'lar Fellers
BY Gene Byrnes

MAR. 25-28-

©1928 N.Y. TRIBUNE, INC.

REG'LAR FELLERS *Sunday page by Gene Byrnes. Jimmie Dugan, Puddinhead Duffy, Baggy Scanlon, and Bump Mahoney discuss life in prison while touring their suburban neighborhood.* © March 25, 1928, New York Tribune, Inc. Courtesy of the International Museum of Cartoon Art

HAROLD TEEN original hand-colored Sunday page by Carl Ed. Harold goes for his first shave in this April Fool's Day episode.

SMITTY original daily strips by Walter Berndt. Lost dogs, office politics, and occasional vacations were typical of the lighthearted story lines during the fifty-two-year run of Berndt's feature. © April 16, 1930, January 29 and June 18, 1931, and February 2, 1932, Tribune Media Services, Inc. All rights reserved. Reprinted with permission. Courtesy of the Art Wood Collection of Cartoon and Caricature, Prints and Photographs Division, Library of Congress

harold gray

HAROLD GRAY AND LITTLE ORPHAN ANNIE—Photograph and drawing. *December 20, 1924. Courtesy of Editor & Publisher*
All Little Orphan Annie comic strips © Tribune Media Services, Inc. All rights reserved. Reprinted with permission. Courtesy of the Harold Gray Collection, Boston University (unless otherwise noted)

THE MASTER STORYTELLER of the comics, this deeply dedicated cartoonist was often criticized for using his strip to promote an agenda of conservative political beliefs. Undaunted, he never wavered from his unique personal vision, and for more than four decades he nurtured a creation that was among the top features in readership popularity.

Harold Gray was born on a farm near Kankakee, Illinois, on January 20, 1894. After graduating from Purdue University in 1917, he joined the staff of the *Chicago Tribune*. In 1920, he began assisting Sidney Smith on *The Gumps*, gaining valuable experience before launching his own strip on August 5, 1924.

Little Orphan Annie was initially modeled after Mary Pickford and, like the famous film star's characters, found herself in one predicament after another. It did not take long for Annie to establish lasting friendships, and by early 1925, she was teamed up with her loyal canine companion, Sandy, and her eternal benefactor, Daddy Warbucks. The story lines in the strip evolved from predictable melodramas in the 1920s, following the spunky waif's wandering encounters with an ever-changing cast of foster families, to extended adventure yarns in the 1930s, filled with intrigue, danger, and fantasy.

The little girl in the red dress was always the star attraction in the strip and won the devotion of newspaper readers, as well as radio, movie, and theater audiences. In Gray's eyes she was "tougher than hell, with a heart of gold and a fast left, who can take care of herself because she has to."

Critics described the style of the strip as "primitive," "awkward," and "mediocre," but Gray made the most of his admittedly limited artistic abilities. "In the beginning *Little Orphan Annie* appeared crude, but soon Gray's visuals were to transform themselves into a gallery of icons," wrote Richard Marschall in *America's Great Comic-Strip Artists.* "Indeed he was to become the comics' great expressionist, with every graphic element reflecting—even manifesting—moods, currents, and fears."

Gray made effective use of cross-hatching, and his liberally applied blacks and background shadings provided an ominous sense of foreboding. At times, Annie's famous empty eyes could be remarkably expressive; in other situations, readers saw the world through her vacant stare.

Frequently under fire for his conservative diatribes, often in the form of long monologues delivered by the characters in the strip, Gray had a philosophy that was personal and consistent. He hated pretension, intolerance, abuse of power, censorship, and governmental intervention. He fought against Franklin Delano Roosevelt's New Deal and the increasing power of the labor unions. His heroes were farmers, shopkeepers, and factory workers. At times he advocated vigilante justice and criminal behavior for the right cause. Above all, he was a champion of self-reliance.

The editorializing in the strip always remained secondary to the storytelling. Gray would set up a new situation quickly and then build suspense for weeks or months. His plots often ended with a climactic resolution. Each episode of *Little Orphan Annie* represented a day in the life of the characters, and some of the continuities stretched more than a year in length. He had a gift for finely woven yarns, laced with heartwarming pathos, dramatic tension, and moral rectitude.

In his final years before his death in 1968, Gray seemed increasingly out of step with the times, but he remained committed to his ideals until the end. Similar to his spirited orphan, he was fiercely independent and eternally optimistic—a true American original.

LITTLE ORPHAN ANNIE *original hand-colored Sunday page by Harold Gray. This early episode shows Annie with her Mary Pickford curls.*
© *January 11, 1925. Courtesy of Illustration House*

LITTLE ORPHAN ANNIE daily strip by Harold Gray. Daddy Warbucks and Annie meet for the first time. © September 27, 1924

LITTLE ORPHAN ANNIE daily strip by Harold Gray. Daddy confides his dilemma of financial success and marital failure to Annie. © October 3, 1924

LITTLE ORPHAN ANNIE daily strip by Harold Gray. A kind policeman helps Annie rescue a homeless mutt, who becomes her faithful sidekick, Sandy.
© January 21, 1925

LITTLE ORPHAN ANNIE daily strip by Harold Gray. Annie, who is living with the Silo family when a tornado destroys their farm, is reunited with Daddy.
© June 15, 1925

LITTLE ORPHAN ANNIE daily strip by Harold Gray. Mrs. Pewter fashions Annie's famous dress, which she wears from then on. © November 16, 1927

LITTLE ORPHAN ANNIE daily strip by Harold Gray. An outstanding example of Gray's authentic depiction of rural America. © July 22, 1929

LITTLE ORPHAN ANNIE daily strip by Harold Gray. After being stranded at sea, Annie is rescued by Daddy, who brings her back to civilization.
© November 13, 1930

LITTLE ORPHAN ANNIE daily strip by Harold Gray. Annie and Sandy hit the road again. © September 22, 1936. Courtesy of Rob Stolzer

LITTLE ORPHAN ANNIE Sunday page by Harold Gray. Annie and Daddy do a little Christmas shopping with their meager savings. © December 23, 1934. Courtesy of Peter Maresca

LITTLE ORPHAN ANNIE daily strip by Harold Gray. During the Depression years, Annie became increasingly involved in mystery and intrigue, as this example from the "Shanghai" sequence demonstrates. © October 31, 1938

LITTLE ORPHAN ANNIE daily strip by Harold Gray. It appears as if Annie might have walked her last road in this cliffhanger. © January 16, 1939

LITTLE ORPHAN ANNIE daily strip by Harold Gray. Punjab, Wun Wey, and the Asp became regular members of the cast in the 1930s. © May 17, 1939

LITTLE ORPHAN ANNIE daily strip by Harold Gray. Annie unwittingly helps her friend Panda blow up a German submarine, in this wartime episode. © June 6, 1942

MINUTE MOVIES two-tiered daily strip by Ed Wheelan. These comic strip serials were directed by Art Hokum and costarred the handsome Dick Dare, the lovely Hazel Dearie, the sinister Ralph McSneer, and the bumbling Fuller Phun. *November 18, c. 1928. © George Matthew Adams Syndicate, Inc. Courtesy of the Art Wood Collection of Cartoon and Caricature, Prints and Photographs Division, Library of Congress*

HAIRBREADTH HARRY daily strip by Charles W. Kahles. The artist's original HAIRBREADTH HARRY Sunday page debuted in 1906. A daily strip version was launched by the Ledger Syndicate in 1923. *© 1923 Ledger Syndicate, Inc. Courtesy of Sandy Schechter*

TO BE CONTINUED Although storytelling was an important element of the comics from the beginning, the adventure strip took its modern form in the mid-1920s. *Hairbreadth Harry* and *Minute Movies,* which started as parodies of stage and film melodramas, popularized the cliffhanger approach, while *The Gumps* and *Little Orphan Annie* raised the levels of suspense and pathos in the funnies. George Storm's juvenile adventure strips, *Phil Hardy* and *Bobby Thatcher,* added the element of danger to the mix, and by the end of the decade, Roy Crane incorporated all of these ingredients in *Wash Tubbs,* the first fully developed "blood and thunder" strip.

BOBBY THATCHER daily strip by George Storm. The illustrator on PHIL HARDY, which debuted in 1925, Storm started his own juvenile adventure strip in 1927. *© 1929 McClure Syndicate, Inc. Courtesy of Editor & Publisher*

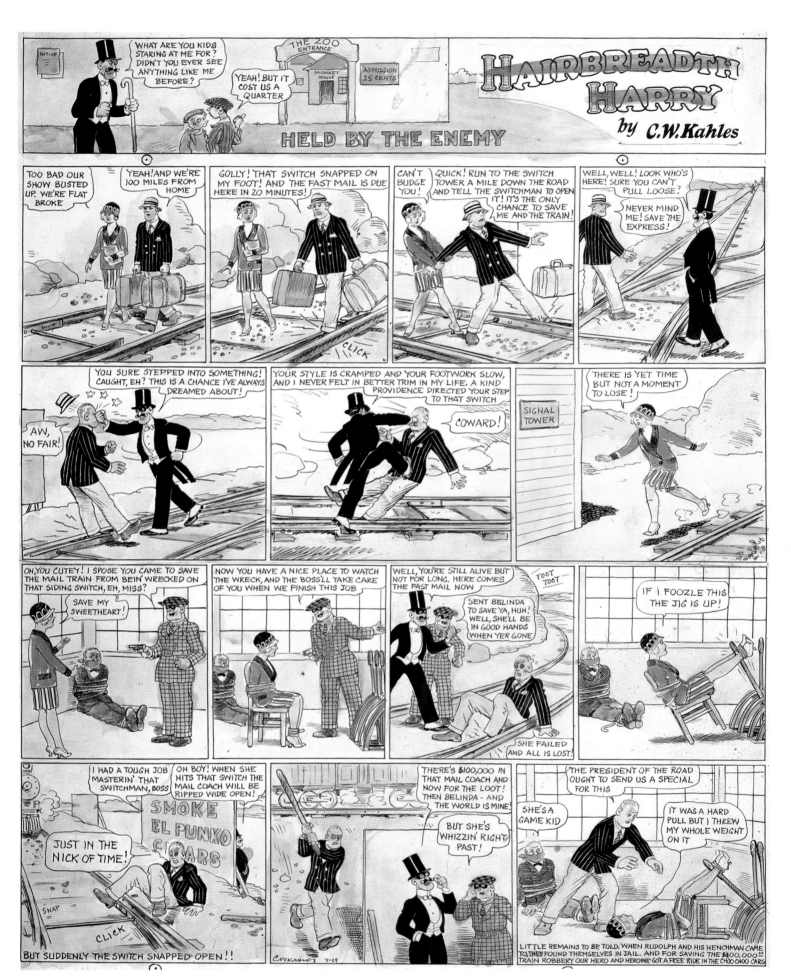

HAIRBREADTH HARRY original hand-colored Sunday page by Charles W. Kahles. A classic episode featuring the hero, Harry; the fair damsel, Belinda Blinks; and the villain, Rudolph Rassendale. © April 29, 1928, Ledger Syndicate, Inc. Courtesy of the Library of Congress. Gift of Jessie Kahles Straut.

roy crane

ROY CRANE—Self-caricature done for a 1925 Christmas card.
Courtesy of Art Wood
All Wash Tubbs and Captain Easy comic strips © NEA Service, Inc.

A MAJOR CONTRIBUTOR to the development of the adventure strip, this talented cartoonist created two classic features over the course of a career that spanned six decades. His experiments in storytelling and rendering influenced a generation of artists who expanded the horizons of the comics medium.

Royston Campbell Crane was born in Abilene, Texas, on November 22, 1901. His parents encouraged their only child's artistic interests, and when Roy was fourteen he took the C. N. Landon mail-order cartoon course. In 1920, he studied at the Chicago Academy of Fine Arts and then succumbed to youthful wanderlust, riding the rails through the Southwest and sailing to Europe on a freighter.

In 1922, he jumped ship in New York and got a job at the *New York World*, where he worked as H. T. Webster's assistant. After one false start, a panel titled *Music to the Ear*,

Crane sold a strip to his old correspondence instructor, Charles N. Landon, who also happened to be the comics editor of the Newspaper Enterprise Association.

Wash Tubbs, which starred a diminutive, skirt-chasing grocery clerk who resembled comedian Harold Lloyd, debuted on April 21, 1924. Crane soon ran out of daily jokes involving his character's preoccupations with get-rich-quick-schemes and pretty girls, so he sent him off to the South Seas on a treasure hunt. Five months into its run, *Wash Tubbs* had evolved into a picaresque adventure strip, blending continuing stories and hilarious high jinks. Over the course of the next few years, Wash picked up a sidekick, Gozy Gallup; repeatedly tangled with a brutish sea captain, Bull Dawson; and finally, in 1929, crossed paths with a handsome soldier of fortune named Captain Easy.

Although Crane had introduced dangerous villains and a dashing hero into his feature, it continued to combine thrills and laughs. "*Wash Tubbs* remained a boisterous, rollicking, fun-loving strip full of last minute dashes, free-for-all fisticuffs, galloping horse chases, pretty girls and sound effects—Bam, Pow, Boom, Sok, Lickety-whop," Robert C. Harvey wrote in *The Art of the Funnies*. "When Crane's characters ran, they ran all out—knees up to their chins. When they were knocked down in a fight, they flipped backwards, head over heels."

During the 1930s, Crane began experimenting with various shading techniques to create more atmospheric backgrounds in his strip. For a time, he used pebble board, which gave a rich texture to the drawings when a soft crayon was applied. He then switched to Craft-Tint Double Tone paper, which provided two different types of patterns when a chemical solution was painted on. Crane used these tools to render realistic jungles, deserts, oceans, and mountains. The characters who cavorted in this evocative scenery were still drawn in a conventional "big-foot" style, giving the strip a distinctive look.

Crane's next major feature, *Buz Sawyer*, which was launched by King Features on November 1, 1943, represented the final phase in his stylistic evolution. It combined fast-paced adventure stories, inspired by the dramatic events of World War II, with authentically illustrated military equipment and real locations, which Crane researched during trips around the world.

Crane continued to refine the storytelling and art in *Buz Sawyer*, with the help of talented assistants including Ralph Lane, Hank Schlensker, Ed Granberry, and Clark Haas, until he passed away in 1977. His career traced all of the major milestones in the development of the adventure strip genre, leaving other artists a well-marked trail to the uncharted territories of artistic discovery.

WASH TUBBS daily strip by Roy Crane. Wash worked in a grocery store during the first months of Crane's new feature. © 1924. Courtesy of All Star Auctions

WASH TUBBS daily strip by Roy Crane. The artist experimented with crayon pencil on pebble board to render scenery and atmosphere in this famous episode. Wash and Easy, who had just become partners, are stranded at sea. © 1930. Courtesy of the International Museum of Cartoon Art

WASH TUBBS hand-colored Sunday strip by Roy Crane. Before the CAPTAIN EASY Sunday page debuted in 1933, WASH TUBBS ran as the topper companion to J. R. Williams's OUT OUR WAY Sunday feature. © June 12, 1932. Courtesy of the Sheldon Memorial Art Gallery, Howard Collection of American Popular Art

WASH TUBBS daily strip by Roy Crane. After his introduction in 1929, Captain Easy's tough-guy persona proved to be the catalyst in the strip, as these three examples from the early 1930s demonstrate. © July 12, 1932. Courtesy of the Sheldon Memorial Art Gallery, Howard Collection of American Popular Art

WASH TUBBS daily strip by Roy Crane. © 1933. Courtesy of Rob Stolzer

WASH TUBBS daily strip by Roy Crane. © 1934. Courtesy of Russ Cochran

WASH TUBBS Sunday page panel and spot illustration by Roy Crane. The artist's patented visual storytelling technique blended humor, drama, heroics, and pretty girls. © c. 1936. Courtesy Illustration House (above) and Frank Pauer (right)

WASH TUBBS daily strip by Roy Crane. A superlative example of the special effects Crane produced using Craft-Tint Double Tone paper. © February 3, 1940. Courtesy of Frank Pauer

CAPTAIN EASY recolored Sunday page by Roy Crane. Easy had his own separate adventures in the Sunday continuities. This is the debut episode.
© July 30, 1933. Courtesy of Syracuse University and American Color

the thirties

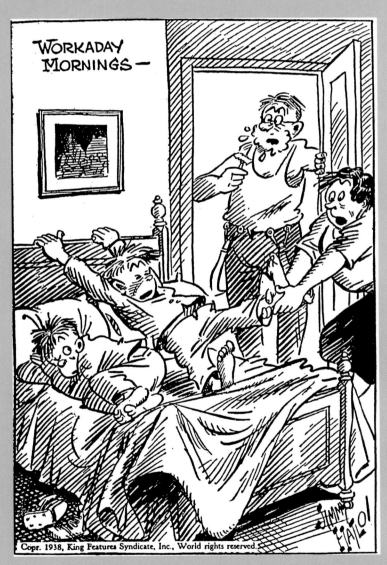

THEY'LL DO IT EVERY TIME daily panel by Jimmy Hatlo. Reading the Sunday funnies had become a weekly ritual in most American homes.
© 1938 King Features Syndicate, Inc. Courtesy of Bill Blackbeard

"It <u>would</u> storm just as I got my laundry out."

METROPOLITAN MOVIES daily panel by Denys Wortman. Mopey Dick and the Duke, the two tramps in Wortman's feature, built a ramshackle home in a shantytown during the dark days of the Depression. c. 1932. © United Feature Syndicate, Inc.

THE ROARING TWENTIES ENDED IN A PANIC. ON TUESDAY, OCTOBER 29, 1929, FIVE DAYS AFTER "BLACK THURSDAY," 16.4 MILLION SHARES WERE TRADED ON THE FLOOR OF THE NEW YORK STOCK EXCHANGE. WHEN THE BELL SOUNDED, $15 BILLION IN MARKET VALUE HAD BEEN WIPED OUT. A MONTH LATER, STOCK LOSSES HAD DOUBLED AND THREE MILLION AMERICANS WERE OUT OF WORK.

By mid-1932, the cumulative worth of Wall Street investments was 11 percent of what it had been at its peak in 1929. In the first three years after the crash, hourly wages dropped 60 percent, eighty-six thousand businesses failed, more than five thousand banks closed their doors, industrial output was cut in half, and unemployment reached fifteen million. To make matters worse, the most devastating drought in American history reduced the Great Plains to a dust bowl. On March 4, 1933, President Herbert Hoover sighed dejectedly, "We are at the end of our string. There is nothing more we can do." It was his last day in office.

The Great Depression caused catastrophic social disruption. Former bankers sold apples on street corners and stood in breadlines. Shantytowns of the dispossessed, derisively called "Hoovervilles," sprang up on the outskirts of major cities across the country. Marriage and childbirth rates declined

while crime and suicide soared. Despondent fathers, unable to find jobs, stayed at home while their wives and children looked for work. Farmers abandoned their parched land and headed west for California in a massive wave of migration. An army of World War I veterans descended on Washington, D.C., and angrily—but unsuccessfully—demanded early payment of their promised bonus for wartime service.

The new president, who took over for Hoover on that gray, chilly day in March 1933, offered hope for a better future. "The only thing we have to fear is fear itself," Franklin Delano Roosevelt assured Americans in his inaugural address. "The people of the United States have not failed. . . . They want direct, vigorous action."

FDR delivered on his promises. In the first one hundred days of the new administration, fifteen major bills were passed. The "New Deal" for the nation provided financing for farmers and home buyers, created jobs, guaranteed bank deposits, and established an "alphabet" of government agencies and initiatives (NRA, WPA, CCC, TVA) that helped get the country back on its feet. Roosevelt sold these programs to the American public via his direct "fireside chats," broadcast on network radio. He was reelected in 1936, and by 1939 the gross national product was $91 billion—a 60 percent increase in six years. The New York World's Fair of 1939, which looked toward "the World of Tomorrow," symbolized to many the end of the crisis.

"When the spirit of the people is lower than at any other time, during this Depression," Roosevelt observed in 1936, "it is a splendid thing that for just fifteen cents an American can go to a movie . . . and forget his troubles." At that time, theaters were selling more than eighty million tickets a week, as the Hollywood dream factory worked overtime to provide escapist entertainment. Movie audiences delighted in the lovable antics of Shirley Temple, the elegant footwork of Fred Astaire and Ginger Rogers, and the madcap mayhem of the Marx Brothers. *The Wizard of Oz* and *Gone With the Wind,* both released in 1939, broke box office records. Mickey Mouse, Felix the Cat, Betty Boop, and Popeye starred in both animated films and newspaper comic strips.

The 1930s were also the golden years of radio. By the end of the decade, 85 percent of the nation's households owned a receiver. The comedy of George Burns and Gracie Allen, the swing music of Benny Goodman, and the drama of *The Shadow* filled the airwaves. The opening lines of the famous theme song "Who's that little chatterbox? The one with pretty auburn locks?" signaled the start of *Adventure Time with Orphan Annie,* a popular after-school program, which aired on the NBC radio network from 1931 to 1943. In addition to uplifting moralistic tales, Annie offered her young fans premium prizes in exchange for coins wrapped in metal foil seals, obtained from jars of Ovaltine malted milk mix. Radio programs starring comic characters continued to proliferate during the decade, and one syndicate reported in 1936 that it had fourteen features being prepared for adaptation to the broadcast medium.

Newspaper comics provided cheap thrills for children of all ages. Readers could travel to the jungles of darkest Africa, the wide-open spaces of the Wild West, or the farthest reaches of outer space in the panels of their favorite features. Tarzan, Red Ryder, and Buck Rogers were among the many comic strip heroes who provided a welcome diversion for weary Americans. Direct references to the Depression were avoided, for the most part, on the funnies pages.

Comics offered more than escapism, however. In many of the humorous family features, a picture of domestic stability was portrayed, insulated from poverty, unemployment, and homelessness. Any challenge to this order usually came from within the extended cast of friends, neighbors, and relatives and was often trivial in nature. The characters would solve their problem in a clever or humorous way, and, sooner or later, things would return to normal. It was only a matter of time before another mini-crisis intruded on the harmony of the group and the cycle would begin again. The relatively untroubled life of families in the funnies must have been comforting to readers during the Depression.

Adventure strips served a similar function but accomplished it in a different way. Danger was more life-threatening in these features and posed seemingly insurmountable challenges for the protagonists. The heroes, who were male in most of the strips, would take control of the situation, often acting independently of the law, to battle the threat to the established order. In some cases, the characters required superhuman powers to defeat their enemies, and the stories were morality plays of good versus evil. The heroes rarely had to deal with the day-to-day problems of earning a living or raising a family and were always victorious in the end. These fantastic scenarios, which were a departure from the established humor formula, must have been equally reassuring to Depression readers, who felt powerless to cope with the real-life challenges they faced on a daily basis.

Newspaper circulation continued to climb during the decade, reaching a high of 41.5 million in 1937, but profits were down due to the loss of advertising revenue. Smaller papers struggled to survive and either folded or were

MAW GREEN companion feature by Harold Gray. This strip ran at the bottom of the LITTLE ORPHAN ANNIE Sunday pages during the 1930s.
© July 21, 1935, Tribune Media Services, Inc. All rights reserved. Reprinted with permission. Courtesy of Bill Blackbeard.

WILLIAM RANDOLPH HEARST—Portrait by William Downes of "the Chief" at the peak of his power. *1935. Courtesy of Editor & Publisher*

absorbed by one of the chains. *Editor & Publisher* reported that between 1924 and 1934, groups owning more than one newspaper had doubled, from 31 to 63. These organizations controlled 361 daily papers, which accounted for 37.6 percent of the total circulation.

The Hearst empire, the largest of the chains, reached its peak in 1935, with twenty-six daily and seventeen Sunday papers in nineteen cities (representing 13.6 percent of the total daily circulation and 24.2 percent of the Sunday circulation of the country), thirteen magazines, eight radio stations, two motion picture companies, four syndicates, and two wire services. The Chief, who also owned two million acres of real estate, valued at $56 million, and a vast collection of art and antiques, had an estimated personal wealth of $220 million. Financial hardship finally caught up with the organization in 1937, when many holdings, including nine daily papers and five Sunday editions, had to be liquidated to pay off debts. Hearst, who had supported FDR during his first term, withdrew his support by the mid-1930s, calling the president's economic program the "Raw Deal."

The syndicates also went through a period of growth and consolidation during the decade. United Feature Syndicate, which was founded in 1919, purchased the Metropolitan Newspaper Service on March 15, 1930, and absorbed the World Feature Service (the former syndicate department of the *New York World* newspapers) on February 28, 1931. These acquisitions added many established features to the syndicate's stable, including *Ella Cinders, Tarzan, The Captain and the Kids,* and *Fritzi Ritz.* Among the other changes in the early 1930s were the sale of Central Press Association to King Features,

the addition of comics to the roster of the Associated Press, and the merger of the North American Newspaper Alliance, the Associated Newspapers, and the Bell Syndicate into a single organization.

"These recent syndicate consolidations," claimed Monte Bourjaily, general manager of United Feature Syndicate in 1930, "are a salutary sign of the ambition to make better newspapers. The syndicate's job, as well as the newspaper's, is to inspire readers to turn off their radios to read, and to stay at home with their paper rather than to go off to the talkies."

Reader surveys were increasingly used to determine the popularity of comic strips and led directly to a new development in the field: color advertising in the Sunday funnies. Professor George Gallup, who taught at Drake, Northwestern, and Columbia universities, released his pioneering study of newspaper readership in 1930. He discovered that "more adults read the best comic strip in a newspaper on an average day than the first rate banner story." After conducting extensive interviews and analyzing the statistics, Gallup broke down his findings into categories based on gender and income. The results showed that comic strips ranked right behind the picture pages in overall popularity among his projected group of two million readers. Gallup argued that newspaper editors needed to apply scientific methods, rather than intuition, to determine varying degrees of interest among their target audience. This knowledge was also essential to the selling and placing of advertisements in the newspaper.

These findings led to the formation of Hearst Comics in 1931, a division of the company organized to develop color advertisements for the Sunday comic sections. The first successful initiative of the new group was a series for General Foods' Grape-Nuts Flakes cereal, which debuted in forty-nine papers on May 17, 1931. The comic-style ads, which starred "Egbert Energy" and "Suburban Joe," were produced by Hearst Comics and the Young & Rubicam advertising agency. General Foods reported a dramatic increase in Grape-Nuts sales as a direct result of this campaign.

John K. Jessup, a copywriter for the J. Walter Thompson agency, speculated about the future of comic advertising at a meeting on March 12, 1932. "I think advertising must admit that it will have to make use of a modified form of comic strip," explained Jessup. "Only by sponsoring a comic strip can it probably take full advantage of the strip's popularity." The leading comic section advertisers in the early 1930s were Lever Brothers (Lifebuoy, Rinso, and Lux soaps) and General Foods (Grape-Nuts, Postum, Post Toasties, Jell-O, and Minute Tapioca).

A group of 30 newspapers formed another agency, the Comic Weekly Corporation, in May 1932 to sell advertising space in their comic sections. Other organizations were soon

LITTLE ALBY advertisement for General Foods' Grape-Nuts Flakes. An early ad campaign in the Sunday comics. October 14, 1934, Omaha Bee-News. Courtesy of Mark Johnson

established, and by 1934 comic advertising was bringing in more than $9 million in additional revenue to 188 newspapers. During this period of phenomenal growth, *Puck—The Comic Weekly,* which was distributed to the seventeen Hearst Sunday papers with a combined circulation of five million, featured ads from fifty major companies, promoting seventy-five products, at a rate of $16,000 per page. By 1937, 300 newspapers were generating more than $17 million in comic section advertising revenue.

The demand for comic-style ads led to the growth of "advertising service studios," which specialized in this type of art. Thomas Johnstone, a former manager of the *New York World*'s Press Publishing Company, had one of the largest stables of artists in the business. In the mid-1930s, Johnstone's studio produced campaigns for Lux Soap, Chase and Sanborn Coffee, Nestlés Chocolate, Shell Gasoline, Ivory Soap, and Fleischmann's Yeast, and his artists earned between $100 and $1,200 per page for advertising work. King Features Syndicate set up its own service in 1937, making all of its top talents available. Fees varied according to the reputation of the artists, but their names and characters could not be used in any advertisements.

The success of comic advertising also affected the makeup of the Sunday funnies. Comic sections increased in size from four or eight pages to twelve, sixteen, twenty-four, or even thirty-two pages to accommodate advertisements. Strips were also produced in different formats to create more space. In addition to the traditional full-page size, the syndicates offered half-page and tabloid sizes. These formats allowed newspapers to double the number of comics without increasing their newsprint costs. Advertisers preferred to purchase half-page display ads to run on the same page as popular features in the half-page format.

In February 1935, *Puck—The Comic Weekly* introduced a tabloid-sized section, featuring reformatted versions of established comics as well as new creations, including *Betty Boop* by Bud Counihan, *Hejji* by Theodor Geisel (Dr. Seuss), and *The Kewpies* by Rose O'Neill. The experiment was abandoned six months later. A Hearst official explained to *Editor & Publisher* that "many of the comics, some of which had been running as long as 38 years, could not be squeezed down to the smaller size and still do justice to the art work." It would prove to be a brief respite for artistic integrity. In the coming years, the size in which comic strips were printed would continue to shrink, and it became increasingly rare for a feature to occupy a full-size newspaper page.

Fortune magazine, in an April 1933 article, "The Funny Papers," reported, "Of 2,300 U.S. dailies, only two of any importance (*New York Times* and *Boston Transcript*) see fit to exist without funnies. U.S. Funny Paper, Inc. grosses about

$6,000,000 a year. Some twenty comic-strip headliners are paid at least $1,000 a week for their labors."

Cartoonists' incomes were derived from weekly fees paid by newspapers for their creations, which ranged from $3 to $300 per paper. A modestly successful strip that appeared in 150 papers, and earned an average of $10 per paper, could bring in $1,500 a week. After the standard fifty-fifty split with the syndicate, a cartoonist in this category could earn $39,000 a year, not counting additional revenue from secondary sources.

The *Fortune* article listed Bud Fisher, Sidney Smith, and George McManus as the top earners, each with a weekly income of $1,600. A dozen other artists were also included in the list, with weekly salaries of more than $1,000 each. These estimates were actually lower than many previous figures but included only money earned directly from newspaper syndication. Licensing could increase annual earnings substantially. Clare Briggs, for example, reportedly made an additional $100,000 in 1928 for his Old Gold cigarette ads. In the depths of the Depression, these salaries were astronomical. Adjusting for inflation, $1,600 a week in 1933 would be almost $1 million a year in contemporary dollars.

Money could not prevent tragedy, however. Sidney Smith, creator of *The Gumps,* signed a new three-year contract, worth $450,000, on Saturday, October 19, 1935. After celebrating at his country home in Genoa City, Wisconsin, Smith drove a group of friends back to Chicago. As he returned to the farm early Sunday morning, Smith's small sedan collided head-on with another car, spun off the road, and crashed into a telephone pole. Smith fractured his skull and died instantly. The fifty-eight-year-old cartoonist, who was known for his fast driving, left valuable real estate holdings and personal property, as well as a $350,000 insurance policy, to his widow and two children.

Arthur Crawford, manager of the Chicago Tribune–New York News Syndicate, which distributed *The Gumps* to 350 newspapers, announced on October 26 that Stanley Link, who had worked as Smith's assistant for ten years, would continue drawing the strip, with Blair Walliser as the writer. But Link apparently was unable to agree on terms with the syndicate, and Gus Edson was named as Smith's successor. The first episode that Edson drew appeared on December 16, 1935.

In 1938, Edson remembered that "it was a grand moment" when Captain Patterson informed him he was taking over the popular feature. "But still I could not help but feel somewhat shaky at the thought of trying to fill the shoes of such a famous comic artist," he added. "I felt no differently, I suppose, than any baseball player would if called upon to pinch hit for Babe Ruth." Edson continued *The Gumps* until the syndicate finally retired the strip on October 17, 1959.

The most successful features were valuable properties, and syndicates were not inclined to end a strip when a cartoonist

POPEYE promotional drawing by E. C. Segar. **THIMBLE THEATRE STARRING POPEYE** was named the "fastest selling comic in 1936."
© November 14, 1936, King Features Syndicate, Inc. Courtesy of Editor & Publisher

died. E. C. Segar, creator of *Thimble Theatre Starring Popeye*, succumbed to leukemia on October 13, 1938, at the age of forty-three. At that time, Segar was earning $100,000 a year, the strip was appearing in five hundred newspapers, and more than six hundred licensed Popeye products were on the market. King Features quickly announced that *Popeye* would be continued. Doc Winner, a syndicate staff artist who had ghosted the feature during Segar's illness, took over initially and was succeeded in mid-1939 by the team of Tom Sims (writer) and Bela "Bill" Zaboly (illustrator).

Other long-running features, which had dwindling lists of subscribers and limited licensing programs, were terminated after the creator retired or died. *Happy Hooligan* ended on August 14, 1932, when Frederick B. Opper was finally persuaded to put down his pen. The "Dean of American Cartoonists" passed away on August 27, 1937, at the age of eighty. King Features wisely decided to discontinue *Krazy Kat* after George Herriman died on April 25, 1944.

In most cases, comics and their creators had remarkable longevity. *Editor & Publisher* reported in 1938 that there were thirty-one comics still being syndicated that had been around since before 1920. Among the durable survivors were *The Katzenjammer Kids* (1897), *Little Jimmy* (1904), *Hairbreadth Harry* (1906), *Mutt and Jeff* (1907), *Toonerville Folks* (1908), *Slim Jim* (1910), *Polly and Her Pals* (1912), *Bringing Up Father* (1913), *Krazy Kat* (1913), *Abie the Agent* (1914), *Freckles and His Friends* (1915), *The Gumps* (1917), *The Bungle Family* (1918), *Toots and Casper* (1918), *Harold Teen* (1919), *Barney Google* (1919), *Thimble Theatre* (1919), and *Gasoline Alley* (1919).

All of these features were of the traditional "funny paper" type. During the 1930s, a new genre—the adventure strip—

was beginning to challenge the humor strip in popularity. Writers, readers, and cartoonists began to debate the relative merits of the two competing styles.

In the May 1936 issue of *Forum* magazine, John Ryan vehemently attacked the new breed of comics for portraying "sadism, cannibalism, bestiality. Crude eroticism. Torturing, killing, kidnapping, monsters, madmen, creatures which are half-brute, half-human. Raw melodrama; tales of crimes and criminals; extravagant exploits in strange lands on other planets, pirate stories. . . . Vulgarity, cheap humor and cheaper wit. Sentimental stories designed for the general level of the moronic mind. Ugliness in thought and expression. All these, day after day, week after week, have become the mental food of American children young and old."

"As the mother of a couple of little boys," Mrs. A. T. Lindem wrote to the editor of the *Minneapolis Journal* in 1936, "I wish to register a protest against the unwholesomeness and dangerous influence of some of the comic strips which could more truthfully be called 'crime strips.'" Some of the criticism of the adventure genre, made by concerned parents and educators, was reminiscent of the protests voiced by anti-comics crusaders in the early years of the twentieth century.

A poll of adult comic readers, published in the April 1937 issue of *Fortune* magazine, listed the fourteen favorite strips, in order of preference, as *Little Orphan Annie, Popeye, Dick Tracy, Bringing Up Father, The Gumps, Blondie, Moon Mullins, Joe Palooka, Li'l Abner, Tillie the Toiler, Dan Dunn, Gasoline Alley, Henry,* and *Out Our Way.* Only *Dick Tracy, Joe Palooka,* and *Dan Dunn* could be called "adventure strips."

Ham Fisher, the creator of *Joe Palooka,* came to the defense of his fellow "blood and thunder" artists. "Many of the present comics are so admirably written and drawn that their appeal is more to adults than in the past," argued Fisher. "Many of them

today hold the place that another generation gave to their favorite short story writers."

The adventure strip introduced a new look to the medium. Realistically rendered characters and settings were the essential ingredients of the emerging genre. "The advent of illustrators on the comics page marked the last stage in the development of the modern comic strip," wrote Robert C. Harvey in *The Art of the Funnies.* This graphic style added another dimension to the story strip.

Hal Foster, who was an experienced commercial illustrator before he took a job as the artist on the new *Tarzan of the Apes* feature in 1929, started the trend toward realism in the comics. The drawings for the ten-week, daily newspaper "comic strip" series were done in the style of book illustrations, with text adapted from Edgar Rice Burroughs's novel set in type beneath each picture. After the initial run of the feature, from January 7 to March 16, 1929, Foster returned to his career as an advertising artist.

Tarzan was a success, and Metropolitan Newspaper Service hired Rex Maxon to replace Foster and continue the daily feature. A Sunday page was launched on March 15, 1931, and Foster was persuaded six months later to come back; he illustrated the weekly installments from September 17, 1931, to May 2, 1937.

After a year of on-the-job training, Foster began to flourish as a graphic storyteller. He experimented with close-ups, long shots, and variable panel sizes. His figures moved with power and grace. He added realistic detail to his backgrounds, costumes, and architecture and adapted a technique of contrasting black and white, known in painting as chiaroscuro, to create dramatic lighting effects. Foster's work would influence many of the artists who followed him in the adventure strip genre.

Frustrated with the quality of the *Tarzan* scripts he had to illustrate, and dissatisfied with the meager pay he received ($75 to $125 a week), Foster decided to create his own feature. As early as 1934, he drew a prototype of the historical strip he envisioned, but he tore it up because he felt it lacked authenticity. By 1936, he had finished six months of *Derek, Son of Thane.* Incredibly, United Feature Syndicate, which was then distributing *Tarzan,* turned down Foster's submission. William Randolph Hearst had admired Foster's work on *Tarzan,* and he quickly signed the artist up after his executives looked at the samples. The renamed strip, *Prince Valiant in the Days of King Arthur,* debuted in eight newspapers on February 13, 1937.

Foster's epic feature brought a new level of artistic excellence to the medium. With the freedom to write original stories and develop distinctive characters, Foster created a fantastic world of knights and maidens, adventure and romance, and made it believable with historical detail and majestic scenery.

OUT OUR WAY daily panel by J. R. Williams. "The Worry Wart" tries his hand at cartooning. © 1936 NEA Service, Inc. Courtesy of Bill Blackbeard

For more than six decades, *Prince Valiant* has provided a refined taste of classic graphic literature in the Sunday comics.

Alex Raymond also brought the talents of an illustrator to the adventure strip genre. During the early 1930s, Raymond, who was influenced by such artists as John LaGatta, Franklin Booth, and Matt Clark, worked in the King Features bullpen as a ghost artist on *Tim Tyler's Luck* and *Blondie*. He was eventually enlisted to illustrate three features that were designed to compete with *Buck Rogers, Tarzan,* and *Dick Tracy. Flash Gordon, Jungle Jim,* and *Secret Agent X-9* were all released by King Features in January 1934. Raymond left *Secret Agent X-9* in late 1935 and focused all of his creative energies on the *Flash Gordon* Sunday pages (with *Jungle Jim* as the "topper," or companion, strip). He perfected a distinctive dry brush technique to render the elegant figures of Flash Gordon and Dale Arden, and he experimented with innovative page layouts to depict the fantastic world of Mongo. Later in the decade, he switched to a more precise pen-and-ink method, which complemented the bold blacks in his balanced compositions. Although fans and students of Raymond's work differ over their preferred period of his stylistic evolution, they all agree that he was an accomplished artist and that his influence was pervasive.

Milton Caniff was another artist whose graphic innovations were to have a major impact on the field of the story strip in the 1930s. Caniff's first successful feature, *Dickie Dare,* which the Associated Press launched on July 31, 1933, began as a strip about a twelve-year-old boy who encountered such classic figures as Robin Hood, General Custer, and Captain Kidd in his imaginative fantasies. Eventually Dickie stopped daydreaming and teamed up with a real-life sidekick, Dynamite Dan Flynn, sailing the high seas in search of adventure. Caniff's juvenile story strip, which was drawn in a style similar to Lyman Young's *Tim Tyler's Luck,* attracted the attention of Captain Patterson of the Chicago Tribune–New York News Syndicate.

Patterson gave the young cartoonist a week to develop a new adventure strip and suggested an opening story line in which a young protagonist and a dashing adventurer cross paths with a lady pirate in the exotic Far East. Caniff came

TERRY AND THE PIRATES promotional drawing by Milton Caniff. This creation by Caniff had all the essential ingredients of the modern action-adventure strip. © July 17, 1937, Tribune Media Services, Inc. All rights reserved. Reprinted with permission. Courtesy of Editor & Publisher

back with a batch of samples. The Captain was impressed but decided to change the title from *Tommy Tucker* to *Terry and the Pirates*. The daily strip began on October 22, 1934, and a Sunday page was added on December 9.

Terry and the Pirates initially looked very much like *Dickie Dare*, but Caniff matured as an artist during the first year of the feature. At the time, he shared a studio in Manhattan with his old friend Noel Sickles, who was drawing *Scorchy Smith* for the Associated Press. Sickles was experimenting with a new technique, in which he boldly applied ink with a brush to create dramatic shapes and shadows. Caniff adapted this approach to his own work, blending cinematic composition, atmospheric effects, and realistic rendering with violent action, sex appeal, and dramatic suspense. Caniff was also progressing as a storyteller. The characters in *Terry and the Pirates*, in contrast to the predictable behavior of most adventure strip heroes, had multifaceted personalities, leaving readers to wonder how they would react in various situations. The plots were fast-paced and the dialogue was snappy.

Caniff became the most influential artist in the comic strip field during the 1930s, and his style was widely admired and imitated. The pioneering efforts of Hal Foster and Alex Raymond reached fruition in the work of Caniff. In the space of six years, the adventure strip had evolved into its definitive form.

The debate between the advocates of the adventure and humor genres was, for the most part, irrelevant. The comic pages during the 1930s were an eclectic mix of unique creations, many of which did not fall into either of these categories. Cartoonists experimented with endless variations on the established formulas.

Dick Tracy, which could be called an "adventure strip," featured hard-hitting action in an urban setting that closely resembled Chicago. But Chester Gould's classic detective comic, which debuted on October 4, 1931, was drawn in a style that was both realistic and uniquely expressive. The epic battle of good versus evil was symbolized by the contrast between Tracy's square-jawed profile and the hideously deformed faces of Gould's grotesque gallery of villains. Buildings, vehicles, and devices, on the other hand, were rendered with the meticulous attention to accuracy and detail of a mechanical draftsman. The success of the original cops-and-robbers comic inspired a long list of Depression-era crime strips, including *Dan Dunn, Radio Patrol, Secret Agent X-9, Red Barry,* and *Charlie Chan.*

Thimble Theatre was another creation that defied categorization. E. C. Segar's feature was originally a spoof of movie serials when it debuted on December 19, 1919. Throughout the 1920s, the strip chronicled the adventures of the Oyl clan— Nana, Cole, Olive, and Castor, along with Olive's boyfriend, Ham Gravy. Popeye first appeared on January 17, 1929, and was initially just one of the many oddball characters who made regular guest appearances in the strip. But the cantankerous sailor with the corncob pipe, bulging forearms, and squinting mug soon took over the show, as his uncompromising integrity won the allegiance of millions of newspaper readers. Segar blended humor, philosophy, violence, and surrealism in his rambling continuities, which often lasted for months. Among the many memorable pen-and-ink performers in *Thimble Theatre* were J. Wellington Wimpy, the Sea Hag, Alice the Goon, Toar, Poopdeck Pappy, Swee'pea, and Eugene the Jeep.

Blondie, which started on September 8, 1930, as a late entry in the Jazz Age pretty-girl genre, was the most successful family feature in the comics by the end of the decade. The star of the strip, Blondie Boopadoop, fell in love with Dagwood

BLONDIE *promotional drawing by Chic Young. This illustration appeared in an advertisement a week before the debut of the strip.* © *August 30, 1930, King Features Syndicate, Inc. Courtesy of Editor & Publisher*

Bumstead, a millionaire's son whose parents threatened to disinherit him after he told them of his intention to marry the flighty flapper. In protest, Dagwood went on a twenty-eight-day hunger strike in January 1933. The Bumsteads finally gave in, and one of the most memorable weddings in comic strip history took place on February 17, 1933. Dagwood gave up his family fortune and settled down to a life as the domestic Everyman, babysitting for his growing brood, crashing into the mailman, and catching hell from his boss, Mr. Dithers. Alex Raymond was Chic Young's assistant during the early 1930s and is credited with giving Blondie her sexy figure and fashionable attire. The rest of the characters were designed in a more conventional cartoon style, and, for a time, semi-realistic rendering and humorous caricature coexisted in the strip.

Al Capp's *Li'l Abner,* which debuted on August 13, 1934, was also a blend of different drawing techniques, which changed as the strip evolved. In the early episodes, Abner had a correctly proportioned physique, but over the course of time his head and feet grew in size. Daisy Mae developed a voluptuous figure, and Mammy and Pappy Yokum became shorter and more cartoon-like. Many of the other characters had exaggerated features—big noses, flappy ears, bulging eyes—attached to normal bodies. The overall effect was one of distorted naturalism, which perfectly matched Capp's savage satire of the human condition.

The personalities of the main cast were in place from the beginning. Mammy Yokum was the boss, Pappy was her straight man, Abner was the fool, and Daisy Mae was his love-struck pursuer. "While the *Li'l Abner* characters themselves are broad burlesques in the tradition of my ideals," Capp explained, "the situations in which I plunge 'em are macabre, horrible, thrilling and chilling in the new 'suspense continuity' tradition." His secret was to "throw comedy characters into melodramatic situations and to show them solving monstrous tribulations in a simple-minded way." He had discovered a unique combination of comedy and suspense, humor and adventure, and would capitalize on this successful formula for forty-three years.

The 1930s was a remarkably fertile period for comic creators. The funnies pages resembled a three-ring circus, with daredevils, clowns, jugglers, and animal acts all performing simultaneously. The syndicates released dozens of new features that exploited the full range of thematic possibilities and graphic techniques.

Joe Palooka (1930) by Ham Fisher starred a naive boxing champ and his ambitious manager, Knobby Walsh. *Mickey Mouse* (1930) by Floyd Gottfredson featured the cartoon screen star and his faithful sidekicks in rollicking adventure tales. *Alley Oop* (1933) by V. T. Hamlin, which initially had a prehistoric setting, later introduced the concept of time

travel to the comics. *Henry* (1934) by Carl Anderson and *The Little King* (1934) by Otto Soglow were performed in pantomime. *Mandrake the Magician* (1934) and *The Phantom* (1936) were both created by Lee Falk and are classics of the story strip genre. *Oaky Doaks* (1935) by R. B. Fuller provided a humorous take on knighthood. *Smokey Stover* (1935) by Bill Holman was a screwball comedy about a fireman and was jam-packed with cryptic sayings and corny puns. *Smilin' Jack* (1936) by Zack Mosley was an aviation strip created by a licensed pilot. *Nancy* (1938) by Ernie Bushmiller officially became a new feature when the spike-haired moppet usurped the starring role from her aunt Fritzi Ritz. *Red Ryder* (1938) by Fred Harmon was the most successful of the cowboy comics.

The *Superman* newspaper comic strip, which was released by the McClure Syndicate on January 16, 1939, represented

SUPERMAN promotional drawing by Wayne Boring. The Caped Crusader strikes a powerful pose in an advertisement for the comic strip.
© September 12, 1942, Superman™ and © DC Comics. All rights reserved. Used with permission.
Courtesy of Editor & Publisher

JOE PALOOKA *promotional drawing by Ham Fisher. This drawing was published not long after Great Britain declared war on Germany.*
© October 28, 1939, McNaught Syndicate, Inc. Courtesy of Editor & Publisher

another new development in the adventure genre. Booklets featuring graphic stories had been around since the mid-nineteenth century, but it was not until 1933 that the modern comic book took on its definitive form. Harry Wildenberg, an employee for Eastern Color Printing Company, came up with the idea of folding a newspaper page in half, and then again into quarters, to come up with a magazine-size booklet. Wildenberg obtained the rights from a handful of newspaper syndicates to reprint their strips and got an order from Proctor & Gamble to produce a promotional giveaway. A million copies of *The Funnies on Parade,* a thirty-two-page, full-color comic book, were published and distributed, free of charge, in the spring of 1933. When Eastern successfully experimented with selling some issues of another promotional comic book, *Famous Funnies: A Carnival of Comics,* later that year, an industry was born.

Comic book publishers soon began hiring artists to create original material for the growing market instead of reprinting newspaper comic strips. In 1936, the syndicates started releasing their own strip reprint collections in the new format. Then *Superman* debuted in *Action Comics* No. 1, dated June 1938, and the age of superheroes was under way. Within a few short years, the newsstands were overflowing with comic books starring costumed characters. Their circulation reached an all-time high in the early 1950s, when close to 1.3 billion comic books were being sold annually. At the end of the 1930s and throughout the next decade, these developments had a powerful influence on the newspaper comics business, as the syndicates

felt increasing pressure to compete with the new medium.

World events would also have a profound impact on the American comics industry. The economic hardships of the Depression led to the rise of fascist dictatorships in Germany, Italy, and Spain, and these so-called Axis powers soon formed a military alliance. Japan expanded into Manchuria in 1931 and invaded China in 1937; Italy seized Ethiopia in 1935. The Nazis took back the Rhineland in 1936, marched into Austria in 1938, and annexed Czechoslovakia in 1939. After Adolf Hitler's forces attacked Poland on September 1, 1939, Great Britain and France declared war on Germany.

It was only a matter of time until the United States would be forced to enter the global conflict. As the nation prepared for war, newspaper publishers, syndicate executives, and cartoonists looked toward an uncertain future. "We believe that the comic strips will swing more than ever to outright humor, that continuity will be lightened, that the more sorrowful aspects of some strips will be eliminated," predicted Arthur Crawford, general manager of the Chicago Tribune–New York News Syndicate, in September 1939. "Our experience has indicated that readers continue to follow the strips in time of disaster and national crisis."

Cartoonists and their characters would play an important part in the war effort. The funnies were destined to provide inspiration, education, and welcome relief to civilians on the home front and soldiers in combat. The escapism of the Depression years was coming to an end.

hal foster

THE "FATHER OF THE ADVENTURE STRIP" produced two classic creations: *Tarzan*, which debuted on January 7, 1929, and *Prince Valiant*, which began on February 13, 1937. He is credited with introducing realistic rendering, historical accuracy, and dramatic composition to the comics medium.

Harold Rudolf Foster was born in Halifax, Nova Scotia, on August 16, 1892. His father died when Harold was four years old, and his stepfather moved the family to Winnipeg, Manitoba, in 1905. As a teenager, he began teaching himself how to draw by studying the work of Edwin Austin Abbey, Howard Pyle, Arthur Rackham, and N. C. Wyeth. His first job was with the Hudson Bay Company in 1910; his many duties included illustrating women's undergarments for the mail-order catalog.

In 1919, after earning a reputation as "the best wrinkle artist in Winnipeg," Foster set out on a thousand-mile bicycle trek to Chicago. He eventually became one of the top commercial artists in the Windy City, working on accounts for Northwest Paper Company, Union Pacific Railroad, and *Popular Mechanics* magazine.

In 1927, an enterprising advertising executive, Joseph Neebe, secured the rights for a syndicated newspaper adaptation of Edgar Rice Burroughs's *Tarzan of the Apes*. Neebe was turned down by the premier illustrator of the *Tarzan* novels, J. Allen St. John, so he hired Foster instead. After the initial ten-week series was completed in 1929, Foster continued his advertising career but returned to do the *Tarzan* Sunday page starting in 1931.

Although Foster initially felt that comics were beneath his abilities, he soon found inspiration in his adopted medium and experimented with new techniques in storytelling and composition. He also became increasingly frustrated illustrating other writers' scripts. When he decided to create his own feature, he looked back in time for his subject matter.

Foster adapted the traditional romantic epic of Arthurian legend and compressed ten centuries of history into one era. "If I drew [King Arthur] as my research has shown, nobody would believe it," he explained. "I cannot draw King Arthur with a black beard, dressed in bearskins and a few odds and ends of armor that the Romans left when they went out of Britain, because that is not the image people have." Although the story is set in the fifth century, during the Roman occupation, the castles, costumes, and customs in *Prince Valiant* were more typical of the period after the Norman conquest in 1066.

The focus of the strip was primarily on sword and sorcery in the early years, but as the feature evolved, romantic and domestic drama complemented the action sequences. Prince Valiant married Aleta on February 10, 1946; his first son, Arn,

PRINCE VALIANT—Full-figure portrait by Hal Foster. *c. 1940*
All Tarzan comic strips © United Feature Syndicate, Inc.
All Prince Valiant comic strips © King Features Syndicate, Inc.

was born on August 31, 1947, followed by twin daughters in 1951 and another son in 1961. As his father got older, young Arn began taking on the more dangerous assignments. "You have to write a story the way you would compose music," Foster said. "You know, high notes and low notes. You have violence one week, and the next story will be the children and home, probably the adventure of one of the children. Then you can get into the blood and thunder again."

Foster claimed that until he went into semiretirement in 1970, he spent fifty-three hours a week on each full-page episode of *Prince Valiant*. He frequently designed spectacular panels filled with battling warriors, galloping horses, towering castles, and panoramic scenery. No other newspaper artist had the space to work in or the talent to fill it.

"It's true I've brought traditional art and illustration technique to the funnies, but it wasn't done consciously," he told interviewer Bill Crouch in 1974. "This has always been my style. Some people dissect their art in formal terms but I've never done that with my work."

He retired in 1979 and passed away three years later. A gentleman until the end, Hal Foster earned his reputation as the "Prince of Illustrators."

PRINCE VALIANT single panel from a Sunday page by Hal Foster. Val returns to his boyhood home of Thule. © 1943. Courtesy of Illustration House

TARZAN original hand-colored Sunday page by Hal Foster. A presentation piece colored by Foster and given to the family of Edgar Rice Burroughs, the creator of Tarzan, as a gift. © January 1, 1933. Courtesy of Jack Gilbert

Tarzan

by EDGAR RICE BURROUGHS

THE MIRACLE

AS TARZAN LED THE APES UP THE STAIRCASE TO ATTACK THE EGYPTIANS.........

TUTAMKEN, THE MONKEY-MAN, STOOD ALONE IN THEIR PATHWAY, SCREAMING.

BACK OF HIM WERE THE SOLDIERS WITH THEIR SPEARS READY TO REPEL THE ATTACK.

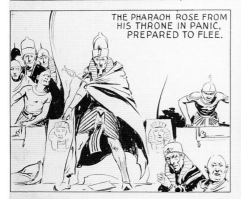

THE PHARAOH ROSE FROM HIS THRONE IN PANIC, PREPARED TO FLEE.

VON HARBEN, KNOCKED OVER IN THE ONRUSH OF THE APES, HAD FALLEN HELPLESS ON THE STAIRCASE.

BUT AS TARZAN REACHED TUTAMKEN, THE MONKEY-MAN SHOUTED IN THE LANGUAGE OF THE APES, "KAGODA!", MEANING "I SURRENDER!"

TUTAMKEN THEN RUSHED TOWARD THE THRONE, "A MIRACLE HAS HAPPENED, OH PHARAOH!" HE CRIED. "THE SOUL OF THOTH, GOD OF THE APES, HAS ENTERED INTO THIS MAN IN THE LEOPARD SKIN SO THAT HE CAN TALK THE LANGUAGE OF THE APES AND THE APES HAIL HIM AS KING! ALL EXCEPT PHARAOH, WHO IS EQUAL TO THE GODS, MUST BOW BEFORE HIM AND WORSHIP HIM!"

AS TUTAMKEN AND TARZAN ADVANCED UP THE STAIRCASE TOWARD PHARAOH'S THRONE, THE HIGH PRIEST HALTED THEM. "IF THIS MAN IS HOLY," HE SAID, "THE GODS WILL TELL US. WE WILL TAKE HIM TO THE TEMPLE".

IN THE VESTIBULE OF THE TEMPLE, THE HIGH PRIEST BURNED INCENSE BEFORE THE GREAT STATUE OF ISIS.

THEN HE LED TARZAN INTO A DARK CORRIDOR AT THE END OF WHICH A FIRE WAS BURNING IN A HUGE KETTLE.

HE SEIZED A GREAT LADLE, TOOK THE BOILING PITCH FROM THE KETTLE AND HELD IT OVER TARZAN'S HEAD. "SO WILL YOU PERISH IF YOU BETRAY THE SECRETS OF THE TEMPLE!" HE CRIED.

NEXT WEEK: THE PHARAOH'S DAUGHTER

TARZAN original Sunday page by Hal Foster. This page followed the one on the previous page. Both are from Foster's famous "Egyptian" sequence.
© January 8, 1933. Courtesy of Jack Gilbert.

Prince Valiant

IN THE DAYS OF
KING ARTHUR
BY
HAROLD R. FOSTER

SYNOPSIS: GLADLY WOULD PRINCE ARN HAVE STAYED TO DIE, FIGHTING SIDE BY SIDE WITH VAL, BUT THIS IS NO TIME FOR HEROIC GESTURES. ILENE IS STILL HELD BY THE VIKING RAIDERS. ARN SPURS ONWARD AND VAL PREPARES TO HOLD BACK THE PURSUIT.

"I WISH THE GODS HAD MADE YONDER BRAVE FOOL MY FRIEND INSTEAD OF MY SWORN ENEMY."

THE JEWELLED HILT OF THE "SINGING SWORD" FITS SNUGLY IN HIS HAND, AS VAL MARCHES RESOLUTELY TO HIS FATE

THE NORTHMEN ARE BEWILDERED AT SUCH FOOLHARDY COURAGE, SUSPECTING A TRICK— BUT ONE HUGE VIKING—

A CAPTAIN, STEPS FORWARD SAYING, "MY TWO-EDGED AXE WILL SOLVE THIS RIDDLE"— VAL'S BLADE SWISHES SOFTLY, WAITING—

BUT ERE THE AXE CAN FALL, THE "SING-ING SWORD" SHRIEKS EXULTANTLY, AS THE KEEN EDGE BITES THROUGH SHIELD AND HELMET AND A WARRIOR'S SOUL GOES WINGING TO VALHALLA.

"COME CLOSER," TAUNTS VAL, "MY BEAUTIFUL SWORD IS THIRSTY," AND HALF A HUNDRED HARDY VIKINGS CROWD FORWARD.

AGAIN AND AGAIN THE TERRIBLE SWORD RISES AND FALLS, GLEAM-ING WET IN THE SUNLIGHT, AND ABOVE THE ROAR OF THE WATERS AND THE CLASHING OF ARMS CAN BE HEARD VAL'S RING-ING BATTLE-CRY, "FOR ILENE."

= NEXT WEEK =
THE
EXECUTIONER

HAL FOSTER

71 6-19-38

PRINCE VALIANT *recolored Sunday page by Hal Foster. The "singing sword," which Prince Arn of Ord had just given to Val, was forged by the same sorcerer who made King Arthur's Excalibur.* © *June 19, 1938. Courtesy of Russ Cochran and American Color*

198   the comics

Prince Valiant

IN THE DAYS OF
KING ARTHUR
BY
HAROLD R FOSTER

SYNOPSIS: THE FRIAR UTTERS A FEW WORDS AND CLARIS IS NO LONGER A MENACE TO THE THRONE AND ALFRED BECOMES A MARRIED MAN ··· CUPID HAS MADE A SIMPERING IDIOT OF THE BOISTEROUS, TALL ROGUE WHOSE RINGING LAUGH AND CLASHING SWORD HAD KEPT THULE BUSY.

VAL IS DISGUSTED ~ A GOOD FIGHTING MAN HAS BEEN SPOILED TO MAKE JUST ANOTHER HUSBAND.

VAL RIDES HOMEWARD THROUGH A SUNNY, PEACEFUL LAND.

YES, A PEACEFUL LAND NOW ··· WHERE HEARTY YOUNG WARRIORS WEAR THEIR ARMOR ON A PEG.

FOR THE KING IS ALMOST TOO LENIENT FOR HIS TIMES AND ONLY ORDERS SUCH MURDERS AND EXECUTIONS AS ARE FOR THE PUBLIC GOOD, NEVER FOR PRIVATE PLEASURE — AND HIS PEOPLE GRUMBLE AT THE LACK OF ENTERTAINMENT.

EACH MORNING VAL TRAINS WITH THE OTHER KNIGHTS IN THE PALACE COURTYARD.

THE AFTERNOONS ARE SPENT MUCH AS HANDSOME PRINCES SPEND THEM EVERYWHERE.

VAL'S EVENINGS ARE MOST INTERESTING. SCHOLARS, POETS, TRAVELERS AND PHILOSOPHERS GATHER IN HIS ROOMS FOR DISCUSSION AND HE LEARNS MANY CURIOUS THINGS.

112 — 4-2-39

EVERY SATURDAY A GAY TOURNAMENT IS HELD AFTER WHICH THE SURVIVORS FEAST MERRILY.

IN FACT, IT IS AN IDEAL KINGDOM WHERE JUSTICE, PROSPERITY AND PEACE REIGN — AND VAL IS BORED.

NEXT WEEK
KNIGHT
ERRANT

HAL FOSTER

PRINCE VALIANT Sunday page by Hal Foster. A magnificent example of Foster's artistry featuring castles, horses, fair maidens, and jousting.
© April 2, 1939. Courtesy of Howard Lowery.

alex raymond

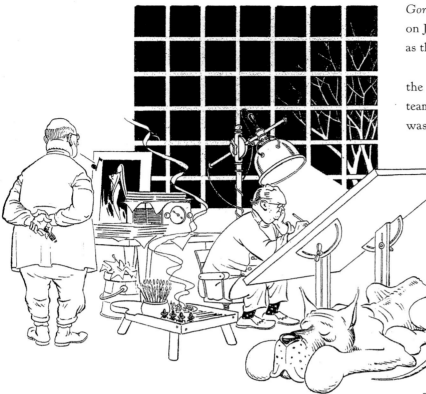

ALEX RAYMOND—Caricature by Jim Raymond from Comics and Their
Creators. 1942
All Secret Agent X-9, Jungle Jim, and Flash Gordon comic strips © King Features Syndicate, Inc.

THE ILLUSTRATOR OF FOUR MAJOR FEATURES during a relatively brief twenty-six-year career, this versatile artist left his mark on comics history. He influenced many of the top story strip creators and set a new level of artistic excellence in the field.

Alexander Gillespie Raymond was born on October 2, 1909, in the affluent suburb of New Rochelle, New York. While attending the Grand Central School of Art in Manhattan, he got a job as an order clerk at a Wall Street brokerage, but he gave up that career path after the stock market crash of 1929.

Raymond started assisting Russ Westover, a family friend and former neighbor, on *Tillie the Toiler* in late 1929 and was soon working in the King Features art department. Between 1930 and 1933, he did backgrounds and enhanced the female characters in *Blondie* for Chic Young and also ghosted *Tim Tyler's Luck* for Lyman Young, Chic's brother. During this period, Raymond's style evolved from a conventional, semi-caricatured approach, typical of the early juvenile adventure strips, to the fluid, polished look he would soon call his own.

When King Features president Joseph Connolly asked his artists to come up with strip ideas to compete with *Buck Rogers* and *Tarzan*, Raymond submitted samples for *Flash Gordon* and *Jungle Jim*. His famous double feature debuted on January 7, 1934, with *Flash* as the main attraction and *Jim* as the topper strip.

At the same time, King Features signed a contract with the popular pulp-fiction writer Dashiell Hammett and teamed him up with Raymond on *Secret Agent X-9*, which was released on January 22, 1934. This handsome detective feature, designed to compete with *Dick Tracy*, initially looked promising, with gorgeous women, violent action, and a tough-talking hero. But Hammett did not adapt well to the comic strip medium, and Raymond eventually decided to concentrate all of his efforts on his *Flash/Jim* page. By late 1935, Leslie Charteris was writing the scripts for *Secret Agent X-9* and Charles Flanders had taken over as the artist, beginning a long line of contributors to the feature, which was renamed *Secret Agent Corrigan* in 1967 and lasted until 1996.

Flash Gordon starred "a Yale graduate and renowned polo player" and his glamorous paramour, Dale Arden. The romantic adventures of these star-crossed lovers provided the recurring story line for the futuristic epic, which combined swords and horses with ray guns and spaceships in a curious hybrid of science fiction and costume drama. The melodrama unfolded on the planet Mongo, ruled by the evil Ming the Merciless.

Late in 1934, Don Moore was hired by King Features to write *Flash Gordon*. Having recently completed a four-year stint as the editorial director for *Argosy—All Story Weekly,* Moore continued to recycle tired clichés from the pulp-fiction genre for his *Flash Gordon* scripts. Raymond's artwork transcended the contrived plots and stilted dialogue, transforming the strip into a stylish adventure fantasy with mythic overtones.

Flash Gordon was one of the most popular adventure heroes of the 1930s, starring in more than 150 newspapers, a radio show, and a series of movie serials. Raymond was frequently compared to Hal Foster for his artistic accomplishments; by the early 1940s, the work of these two adventure strip masters was beginning to look remarkably similar.

Raymond enlisted in the Marines during World War II, relinquishing *Flash Gordon* to his assistant Austin Briggs. When he returned, he launched his own detective strip, *Rip Kirby,* on March 4, 1946. Ten years later, not quite forty-seven years old, Raymond died after crashing a sports car into a tree near his home in Connecticut. It was a tragic end to an illustrious career.

SECRET AGENT X-9 daily strip by Alex Raymond. Dashiell Hammett's scripts called for dangerous women, ruthless thugs, and a dashing hero, who in this episode was operating under the alias "Dexter." © June 9, 1934. Courtesy of Craig Englund

SECRET AGENT X-9 daily strip by Alex Raymond. A dramatic nighttime scene, a beautiful girl, a startling revelation, and an explosive conclusion are blended seamlessly in this outstanding example of Raymond's black-and-white artistry. © January 26, 1935. Courtesy of Bruce Hamilton

JUNGLE JIM Sunday page by Alex Raymond. Both of Raymond's weekly features were done in the tabloid format for a six-month period in 1935.
© May 26, 1935. Courtesy of Russ Cochran.

FLASH GORDON recolored Sunday page by Alex Raymond. The influence of the pulp-art genre on Raymond's style is evident in this famous episode. © June 2, 1935. Courtesy of Russ Cochran and American Color

FLASH GORDON/JUNGLE JIM Sunday page with matching topper by Alex Raymond. The artist's elegant brushwork is used to dramatic effect as Flash gradually becomes visible in an episode from the "Witch Queen" sequence. © September 8, 1935. Courtesy of Ricardo Martinez

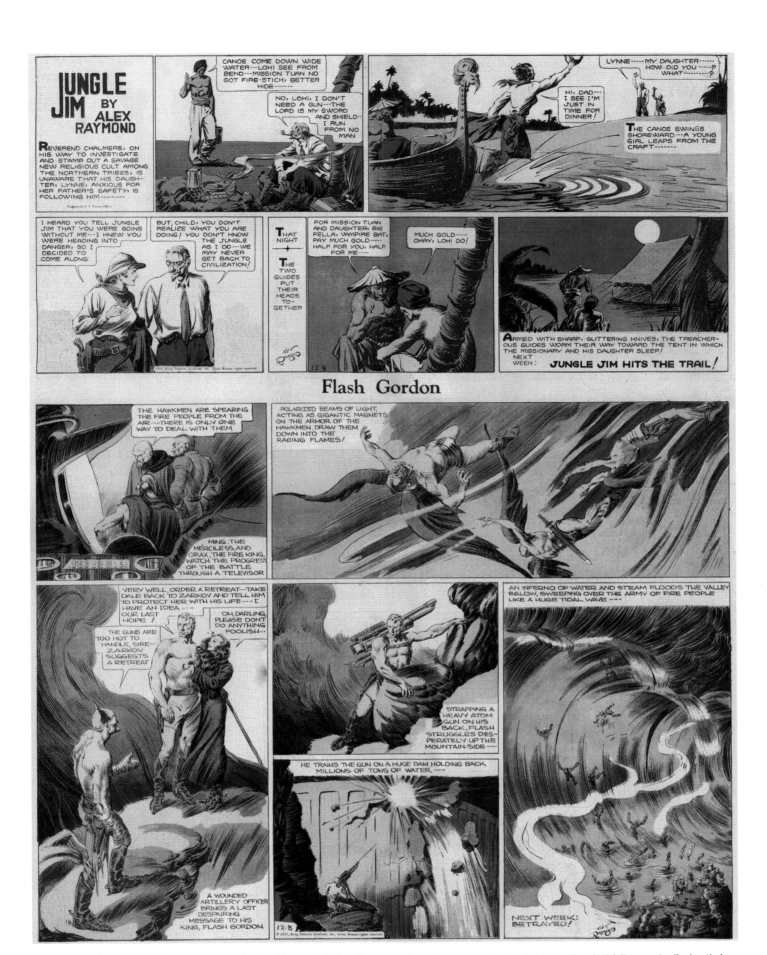

FLASH GORDON/JUNGLE JIM newspaper page by Alex Raymond. Before the paper shortages of World War II, the top artists had full pages to display their talents. © December 8, 1935. Courtesy of Peter Maresca.

FLASH GORDON Sunday page by Alex Raymond. Lost in the untamed forest of Arboria on the distant planet of Mongo, Flash and Dale are saved by a bolt of lightning. © January 31, 1937. Reproduced from a King Features proof

FLASH GORDON Sunday page by Alex Raymond. Flash crosses swords with Ming the Merciless.
© August 14, 1938. Reproduced from a King Features proof

SCORCHY SMITH daily strip by Noel Sickles. © October 18, 1935, the Associated Press. Courtesy of Art Wood

LIGHT AND SHADOW Although his career in the comics was brief, Noel Sickles is credited with introducing a revolutionary approach to realistic rendering in his work on *Scorchy Smith* from 1933 to 1936. "I did *Scorchy* on a 3-ply Strathmore sheet," Sickles explained. "The first step in inking was with a #3 Winsor-Newton brush and I'd do only the shadows in the figures and backgrounds. The outline inking was done with a 170 or 303 pen point." This "chiaroscuro technique" created a cinematic effect and had a profound influence on Sickles's studio mate, Milton Caniff, as well as many other artists who would follow in the adventure strip genre.

ADVENTURES OF PATSY daily strip by Mel Graff. The artist adopted the style of his Associated Press colleagues Caniff and Sickles for his strip, which debuted on March 11, 1935. Patsy was a female Dickie Dare. © December 2, 1935, the Associated Press

milton caniff

A TIRELESS VOLUNTEER who devoted his talents and energies to numerous organizations, including the Boy Scouts of America, the U.S. Air Force, and the National Cartoonists Society, the "Drawing Board Patriot" was the best ambassador the comics profession ever had. He was also the most influential artist in the adventure strip genre.

Milton Arthur Paul Caniff was born in Hillsboro, Ohio, on February 28, 1907. His father worked as a printer, and Milt started his lifetime association with the "inky-fingered fraternity" at the age of fourteen when the *Dayton Journal* hired him as an office boy. He also developed a passion for acting when he performed as an extra in a few Hollywood two-reel comedies during annual trips his family made to California.

Caniff attended Ohio State University from 1926 to 1930 and pursued a full schedule of extracurricular activities that included working in the art department of the *Columbus Dispatch,* acting in a local stock theater company, and drawing cartoons for the college yearbook and humor magazine. He once considered pursuing a career on the stage, but his mentor, cartoonist Billy Ireland, advised him, "Stick to the ink pots, kid, actors don't eat regularly."

After graduation, Caniff started a commercial art studio in Columbus with his friend Noel Sickles, but the Associated Press soon made him an offer to come to New York. Caniff worked at the AP from 1932 to 1934 and drew a variety of features, including a single-column, captioned cartoon, *Puffy the Pig;* a three-column panel, *The Gay Thirties*; a daily comic strip, *Dickie Dare*; and occasional spot illustrations and caricatures.

Mollie Slott, assistant manager of the Chicago Tribune–New York News Syndicate, showed some samples of *Dickie Dare* to her boss, Captain Joseph Medill Patterson, and a meeting between the powerful publisher and the young cartoonist was set up. Patterson asked Caniff to create an adventure strip for his syndicate, and the result was *Terry and the Pirates,* which debuted on October 22, 1934.

As Caniff developed his artistic and storytelling skills, the strip soared in popularity, reaching its peak during the war years. Between 1934 and 1945, he received more than ten thousand letters from his loyal readers, and in 1944 he was earning an estimated annual income of $70,000 from four hundred newspaper clients. He had also become increasingly frustrated that he did not own and control his creation. In 1945, it was revealed that Caniff was abandoning *Terry and the Pirates* after his contract with Patterson's syndicate expired at the end of 1946, to launch a new adventure strip. *Steve Canyon* debuted on January 13, 1947, and ran

MILTON CANIFF—Self-caricature from Comics and Their Creators. *1942*

until June 5, 1988, shortly after Caniff's death on April 3 of that year.

Caniff, who described himself as "an armchair Marco Polo," rarely had the opportunity to visit the exotic locales he brought to life in the panels of *Terry and the Pirates* and *Steve Canyon.* Instead he relied on an extensive "morgue" of magazines, newspaper clippings, and books filled with photographs of foreign countries, military equipment, costumes, uniforms, and numerous other items he depicted in the strip.

"Every detail must be accurate because there is always a man or woman who has been to the place you are portraying," Caniff advised aspiring cartoonists. "Remember that many people can draw well, but there are few who combine the talent with the ability to spin a gripping yarn," he continued. "Develop the two, slighting neither, and you may have the secret of a magic carpet that will send you and your readers soaring in expanses of fancy that would make the *Arabian Nights* seem like Forty Winks."

Caniff followed his own advice and created two masterpieces of comic strip storytelling in *Terry and the Pirates* and *Steve Canyon.* No cartoonist ever perfected all of the elements of the art form as well as the "Rembrandt of the Comic Strip."

The strips on this page show Caniff's evolving style from 1934 to 1937.
TERRY AND THE PIRATES introductory strip by Milton Caniff. TERRY looked very much like DICKIE DARE, in the beginning. © 1934. Courtesy of Bruce Hamilton

TERRY AND THE PIRATES daily strip (subtitled *"Show Stopper"*) by Milton Caniff. A classic Caniff cliffhanger.
© September 11, 1935. Courtesy of the Milton Caniff Collection, The Ohio State University Cartoon Research Library

TERRY AND THE PIRATES daily strip (subtitled *"The Mask Falls for the Briefest Moment"*) by Milton Caniff. The Dragon Lady reveals her true feelings for
Pat while he is sleeping. © October 24, 1936. Courtesy of Art Wood

TERRY AND THE PIRATES daily strip (subtitled *"Strip Wheeze"*) by Milton Caniff. This noncanonical strip, which was not part of any story, was probably
used for promotional purposes by newspapers. © September 7, 1937. Courtesy of the Sheldon Memorial Art Gallery, Howard Collection of American Popular Art

TERRY AND THE PIRATES daily strips by Milton Caniff. A sampling of Caniff's fully matured work, these daily episodes, starring Normandie and Burma, were painted with a blue wash to indicate where Ben Day adhesive shading was to be applied. © February 27 and June 11, 1937, and January 5 and June 8, 1938. Courtesy of the Art Wood Collection of Cartoon and Caricature, Prints and Photographs Division, Library of Congress

TERRY AND THE PIRATES Sunday page by Milton Caniff. This nighttime gun battle with Pat, Terry, and the Dragon Lady is an example of Caniff at the peak of his artistic abilities. © August 27, 1939. Courtesy of Bruce Hamilton

TERRY AND THE PIRATES *daily strip sequence by Milton Caniff. Raven Sherman, an American heiress who was providing aid to the Chinese, dies after being pushed out of the back of a truck.* © October 13, 14, 15, and 16, 1941. Courtesy of the Milton Caniff Collection, The Ohio State University Cartoon Research Library

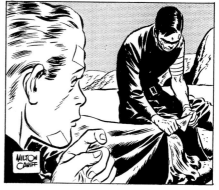

TERRY AND THE PIRATES *Sunday page by Milton Caniff. Terry and Dude Hennick say farewell to Raven in the mountains of China.*
© October 19, 1941. Courtesy of the Milton Caniff Collection, The Ohio State University Cartoon Research Library

BUCK ROGERS Sunday page by Dick Calkins (artist) and Phil Nowlan (writer). The Sunday BUCK ROGERS stories starred Buddy Deering, Wilma's teenage brother. Sunday Oregonian. © May 8, 1932, John F. Dille Company. Courtesy of Peter Maresca

BUCK ROGERS daily strip by Dick Calkins (artist) and Phil Nowlan (writer). The costars of the daily episodes were Buck Rogers and Wilma Deering.
© 1932 John F. Dille Company. Courtesy of Francisco Lopez

BLASTOFF *Buck Rogers,* which debuted on January 7, 1929, was not the first comic strip to entertain readers with adventures in outer space, but it did launch the 1930s science fiction genre. Although the artwork was crude and the dialogue was wooden, the rocket ships, ray guns, and robots in *Buck Rogers* became standard equipment in many subsequent creations. In addition to newspaper strips like *Brick Bradford* (1933) and *Flash Gordon* (1934), many of the early comic book creators also borrowed gadgets and concepts from Calkins and Nowlan's pioneering effort.

BUCK ROGERS bottom half of a Sunday page by Dick Calkins (artist) and Phil Nowlan (writer). This example is one of the few pieces of original artwork to survive from the early period of this influential strip. © 1932 John F. Dille Company. Courtesy of Francisco Lopez

THE PHANTOM Sunday page by Lee Falk (writer) and Ray Moore (artist). The origin story of "the Ghost Who Walks."
© December 29, 1940, King Features Syndicate, Inc. Courtesy of King Features Syndicate

THE PHANTOM daily strip by Lee Falk (writer) and Ray Moore (artist). The first costumed superhero in the funnies began his career on February 17, 1936. © March 25, 1937, King Features Syndicate, Inc. Courtesy of Francisco Lopez

MANDRAKE THE MAGICIAN recolored Sunday page by Lee Falk (writer) and Phil Davis (artist). Falk's magician crimefighter made his debut on **June 11, 1934.** © April 4, 1937, King Features Syndicate, Inc. Courtesy of Francisco Lopez and American Color

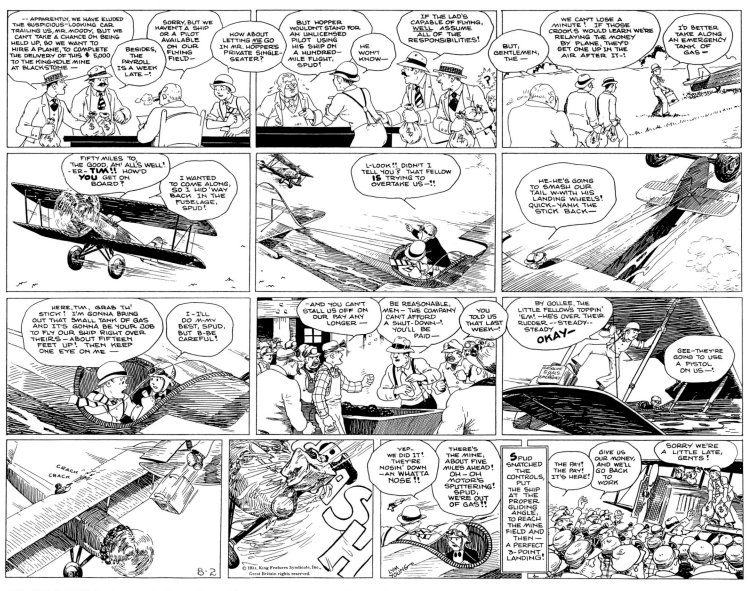

TIM TYLER'S LUCK Sunday page by Lyman Young. Tim saves the day by piloting an airplane. © August 2, 1931, King Features Syndicate, Inc. Courtesy of Francisco Lopez

FLY BOYS AND KID HEROES

Charles Lindbergh's transatlantic airplane flight in 1927 inspired a wave of aviation features, many of which starred young male daredevils. The juvenile story strip genre broadened its horizons during the 1930s to embrace exotic adventures in faraway lands, science fiction, and crimefighting.

DICKIE DARE daily strip by Milton Caniff. Dickie dreams he's fighting mutineers aboard an English vessel in Caniff's juvenile adventure strip, which debuted on July 31, 1933. © October 2, 1933, the Associated Press. Courtesy of Art Wood

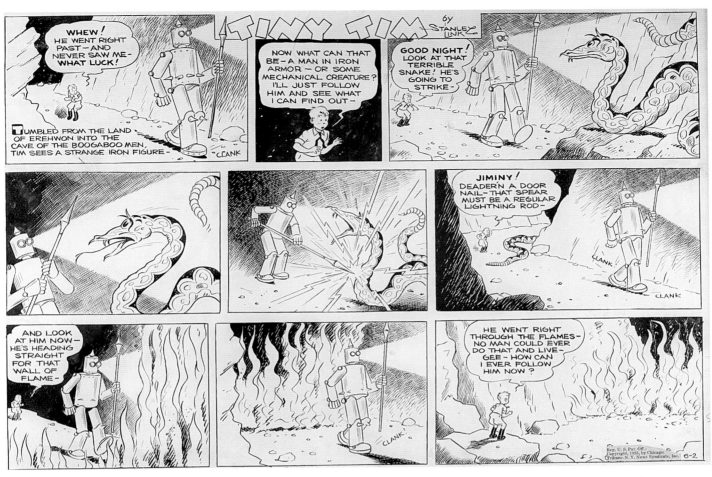

TINY TIM Sunday page by Stanley Link. Link, who ghosted many of Chester Gump's adventures in the 1920s, started his own kid strip in 1931.
© June 2, 1935, Tribune Media Services, Inc. All rights reserved. Reprinted with permission. Courtesy of All Star Auctions

MING FOO Sunday page by Brandon Walsh (writer) and Nicholas Afonsky (artist). The companion feature to *LITTLE ANNIE ROONEY* starred a juvenile hero, Joey Robbins; his Oriental sidekick, Ming Foo; and a crusty sailor, Tom Trout. © October 9, 1938, King Features Syndicate, Inc. Courtesy of King Features Syndicate

CONNIE Sunday page by Frank Godwin. Constance Courage, the star of Godwin's elegantly illustrated feature, was one of the few heroines in the adventure strip genre. © October 13, 1940, Ledger Syndicate, Inc. Courtesy of Jack Gilbert

CONNIE daily strip by Frank Godwin. CONNIE was a conventional pretty-girl strip when it debuted on November 13, 1927, but during the 1930s the stories became more fantastic. © 1935 Ledger Syndicate, Inc. Courtesy of All Star Auctions

SMILIN' JACK Sunday page by Zack Mosley. This long-running aviation strip started as a Sunday feature called ON THE WING on October 1, 1933, and ended on April 1, 1973. A licensed pilot, Mosley drew his airplanes with technical accuracy. © March 22, 1936, Tribune Media Services, Inc. All rights reserved. Reprinted with permission. Courtesy of Jim Scancarelli

SMILIN' JACK daily strips by Zack Mosley. The daily strip version of SMILIN' JACK began on June 15, 1936. Jack, who grew his trademark mustache after this episode, operated a commercial aviation business. © June 22 and September 9, 1936, Tribune Media Services, Inc. All rights reserved. Reprinted with permission. Courtesy of All Star Auctions (above) and Sandy Schechter (below)

JOE PALOOKA daily strip by Ham Fisher. Joe tries to impress Ann Howe in this early episode. © March 7, 1933, McNaught Syndicate, Inc. Courtesy of Russ Cochran

COMIC HEAVYWEIGHT One of the most successful sports features of all time was Ham Fisher's *Joe Palooka,* which debuted on April 19, 1930, and continued until November 4, 1984. In addition to the naive prizefighter, the cast included Joe's brash manager, Knobby Walsh; his wealthy girlfriend, Ann Howe; and Smokey, his personal assistant and closest friend.

The plots frequently culminated in exciting boxing bouts, but they also dealt with Joe's romantic exploits and adventures in foreign countries. Although Fisher came up with most of the stories, he was not a talented artist and employed a succession of ghosts, including Phil Boyle, Al Capp, and Mo Leff.

JOE PALOOKA daily strips by Ham Fisher. Joe defends his heavyweight title and gets a hero's welcome. © February 11 and August 20, 1938, McNaught Syndicate, Inc.
Courtesy of the Art Wood Collection of Cartoon and Caricature, Prints and Photographs Division, Library of Congress

JOE PALOOKA Sunday page by Ham Fisher. Joe was a fighter with a heart of gold and could never turn down a request to support a charitable cause.
© 1932 McNaught Syndicate, Inc. Courtesy of Peter Maresca

TAILSPIN TOMMY daily strip by Glenn Chaffin (writer) and Hal Forrest (artist). One of the first aviation strips, TAILSPIN TOMMY debuted on May 21, 1928, the year after Lindbergh's historic flight. © 1933 Bell Syndicate, Inc. Courtesy of Russ Cochran

BRICK BRADFORD daily strip by William Ritt (writer) and Clarence Gray (artist). The early episodes of Ritt's creation, which began on August 21, 1933, dealt with mythological themes, before venturing into time travel. © June 21, 1935, Central Press Association, Inc. Courtesy of Francisco Lopez

MICKEY FINN daily strip by Lank Leonard. The Irish flatfoot made his first appearance on April 6, 1936, and continued to walk the beat until December 21, 1975. In this early episode, he has not yet joined the police force. © 1936 McNaught Syndicate, Inc. Courtesy of Morris Weiss

RED RYDER daily strip by Fred Harmon. One of the most popular and enduring cowboy comics, RED RYDER was launched as a Sunday feature on November 6, 1938, and a daily strip on March 27, 1939. © May 2, 1939, NEA Service, Inc. Courtesy of Gary Ernest Smith

RED RYDER Sunday page by Fred Harmon. Red's longtime companion was Little Beaver, a ten-year-old orphaned Navajo.
© 1941 NEA Service, Inc. Courtesy of Peter Maresca

chester gould

THE "MASTER SLEUTH OF THE COMICS" provided vicarious thrills to newspaper readers who wanted to see thugs like Al Capone brought to justice. "I have always been disgusted when I read or learn of gangsters and criminals escaping their just dues under the law," claimed the creator of the square-jawed flatfoot in 1934. "And for that reason I invented in Dick Tracy a detective who could either shoot down these public enemies or put them in jail where they belong."

Chester Gould, was born in Pawnee, Oklahoma, on November 20, 1900. His father, who was a printer for the *Pawnee Courier-Dispatch,* wanted him to be a lawyer, but the boy's first love was drawing. After winning a cartoon contest sponsored by *The American Boy* magazine in 1917, Chester mailed in $20 for twenty lessons from the W. L. Evans School of Cartooning in Cleveland. He attended Oklahoma A&M University from 1919 to 1921 but graduated from Northwestern in 1923 with a degree in business.

Gould was still more interested in becoming a cartoonist, and he attended classes at the Chicago Academy of Fine Arts and worked in the art department of the *Chicago American* while finishing college at night. Determined to sell a comic strip of his own, he doggedly sent samples of his work to newspapers and syndicates, claiming to have created more than sixty different ideas between 1921 and 1931. He managed to have a few features published, including *Fillum Fables* (1924), *Radio Cats* (1924), and *The Girl Friends* (1931), but none of them caught on.

Joseph Medill Patterson of the Chicago Tribune–New York News Syndicate finally responded favorably to one of Gould's submissions. On August 13, 1931, the determined cartoonist received a telegram: "YOUR PLAINCLOTHES TRACY HAS POSSIBILITIES STOP WOULD LIKE TO SEE YOU WHEN I GO TO CHICAGO NEXT STOP PLEASE CALL TRIBUNE OFFICE MONDAY ABOUT NOON FOR AN APPOINTMENT = JM PATTERSON."

In the sample Gould had sent to Patterson, Plainclothes Tracy, a modern-day Sherlock Holmes, battled Big Boy, a thinly disguised caricature of Chicago mob boss Al Capone. Patterson changed the name of the lead character to "Dick Tracy" and suggested an opening story line in which Tracy joined the police force after his girlfriend's father was brutally shot down by robbers. Gould followed Patterson's advice and turned out two weeks of strips in two days.

Dick Tracy debuted on October 4, 1931, and the public responded immediately to the raw violence in the hard-hitting strip. Gould later recalled, "At that time, no cartoon had ever shown a detective character fighting it out face to face with

CHESTER GOULD—Self-caricature with his most famous villains. *August 14, 1944,* Life magazine. *Courtesy of the International Museum of Cartoon Art*
All Dick Tracy comic strips © Tribune Media Services, Inc. All rights reserved. Reprinted with permission

crooks via the hot lead route." Three years after its debut, *Dick Tracy* was appearing in 90 newspapers; a decade later, Gould's list had grown to 250 daily and 125 Sunday clients.

In *Dick Tracy: The Official Biography,* Jay Maeder summed up the unique appeal of Gould's creation: "His strip was defined by fast-action story lines that could kick the breath out of you, arrestingly stylized artwork that was both super-realistic and weirdly cartoonish, a famous rogues' gallery of villains, an unrelievedly grim Calvinist conscience that informed every move every one of its characters ever made—and always the pathological mayhem. The strip was a dark and perverse and vicious thing, sensationally full of blood-splashed cruelty from its first week, the single most spectacularly gruesome feature the comics had ever known; there has never been another newspaper strip so full of the batterings, shootings, knifings, drownings, torchings, crushings, gurglings, gaspings, shriekings, pleadings and bleatings that Chester Gould gleefully served up as often as he possibly could."

Gould was described in 1944 as an "affable, well-adjusted man who drinks bourbon neat, smokes nine good cigars a day and plays poker whenever he gets the chance." Although he was criticized later in his career for glorifying violence, he continued to produce his ghoulishly entertaining creation until he retired in 1977.

DICK TRACY daily strip by Chester Gould. A corrupt politician takes his own life. © December 28, 1931. Courtesy of the International Museum of Cartoon Art

DICK TRACY daily strip by Chester Gould. Tracy proposes to his girlfriend, Tess Trueheart—but he didn't marry her until Christmas Eve, 1949.
© December 30, 1931. Courtesy of Matt Masterson

DICK TRACY daily strip by Chester Gould. Junior and Dick go to visit the mother of slain gangster Giorgio Spaldoni. © May 10, 1934. Courtesy of Matt Masterson

DICK TRACY daily strip by Chester Gould. Tracy walks into a trap at Boris Arson's headquarters. © January 19, 1935. Courtesy of Matt Masterson

DICK TRACY Sunday page by Chester Gould. Dick meets his future charge, Junior, for the first time. © September 8, 1932, Detroit Free Press. Courtesy of Peter Maresca

DICK TRACY Sunday page by Chester Gould. Tracy goes after Stud Bronzen's human-smuggling operation with his bare fists.
© March 13, 1938. Courtesy of Matt Masterson

DICK TRACY daily strip by Chester Gould. Dick is lost in a blizzard trying to rescue an abducted child, Johnny Wreath. © March 23, 1943. Courtesy of Matt Masterson

DICK TRACY daily strip by Chester Gould. A dramatic chase scene with 88 Keyes, a gold-digging bandleader. © May 29, 1943. Courtesy of Matt Masterson

DICK TRACY daily strip by Chester Gould. Mrs. Pruneface tracks Tracy in the rain. © July 17, 1943. Courtesy of Matt Masterson

DICK TRACY daily strip by Chester Gould. Tracy is trapped in one of Gould's ghoulish "Near-Deathtraps." © August 10, 1943. Courtesy of Matt Masterson

DICK TRACY *daily strip by Chester Gould. The demise of Flattop Jones, a hired killer.* © May 16, 1944. Courtesy of Matt Masterson

DICK TRACY *daily strip by Chester Gould. The final appearance of Gould's most famous 1940s villain, on a slab in the city morgue.*
© May 17, 1944. Courtesy of the International Museum of Cartoon Art

DICK TRACY *daily strip by Chester Gould. Tracy fights the Brow, a notorious Axis spy.* © September 22, 1944. Courtesy of Matt Masterson

DICK TRACY *daily strip by Chester Gould. A violent shoot-out with Measles.* © February 27, 1945. Courtesy of Matt Masterson

RADIO PATROL Sunday page by Eddie Sullivan (writer) and Charlie Schmidt (artist). Sergeant Pat, Stutterin' Sam, Molly Day, and Pinky Pinkerton plan a Christmas dinner. © December 25, 1937, King Features Syndicate, Inc. Courtesy of Francisco Lopez

RADIO PATROL daily strip by Eddie Sullivan (writer) and Charlie Schmidt (artist). The success of DICK TRACY spawned many other crime strips. RADIO PATROL, the first feature to star uniformed policemen, debuted on April 16, 1934. © December 25, 1934, King Features Syndicate, Inc. Courtesy of Francisco Lopez

JIM HARDY daily strip by Dick Moores. A former assistant to Chester Gould on DICK TRACY, Moores created his own strip, which starred an ex-convict, on June 8, 1936. © July 24, 1936, United Feature Syndicate, Inc.

RED BARRY Sunday page by Will Gould. The artist, who was no relation to Chester, introduced his fast-talking, hard-hitting crimefighter to newspaper readers on *March 19, 1934.* © *May 5, 1935, King Features Syndicate, Inc. Courtesy of Francisco Lopez*

CURLEY HARPER Sunday page by Lyman Young. Curley started out as a college athlete in the companion feature to TIM TYLER'S LUCK on March 31, 1935, and eventually became an investigative reporter. © September 18, 1938, King Features Syndicate, Inc. Courtesy of Francisco Lopez

DAN DUNN daily strip by Norman Marsh. Dan, a square-jawed detective with a trench coat and fedora hat, was the most blatant rip-off of DICK TRACY.
© March 16, 1938, Publishers Syndicate. Courtesy of Russ Cochran

DAN DUNN daily strip by Norman Marsh. This strip was launched on September 25, 1933, and ended on October 3, 1943, a year and a half after its creator reenlisted in the Marines. © April 9, 1938, Publishers Syndicate. Courtesy of Bill Janocha

MICKEY FINN Sunday page by Lank Leonard. The Sunday version of Leonard's strip debuted on May 17, 1936, with NIPPIE as the topper strip.
© November 7, 1937, McNaught Syndicate, Inc. Courtesy of Jim Scancarelli

CHARLIE CHAN Sunday page by Alfred Andriola. The comic strip adaptation was
launched as a Sunday page on October 30, 1938, and continued until May 31, 1942.
© November 17, 1940, McNaught Syndicate, Inc. Courtesy of Francisco Lopez

CHARLIE CHAN—Portrait by Alfred Andriola. The Oriental
sleuth initially starred in a series of six novels by Earl
Derr Biggers, beginning in 1925. © September 10, 1938,
McNaught Syndicate, Inc. Courtesy of Editor & Publisher

CHARLIE CHAN daily strip by Alfred Andriola. The artist, a former assistant to Milton Caniff, produced his strip with the help of Charles Raab and others.
© August 18, 1939, McNaught Syndicate, Inc. Courtesy of All Star Auctions

SKYROADS *daily strip by Russell Keaton. Created by two pilots, Lieutenant Lester Maitland and Dick Calkins, in 1929, this aviation strip was drawn by Russell Keaton in the 1930s.* © 1938 John F. Dille Company. Courtesy of Bill Janocha

DON WINSLOW OF THE NAVY *daily strip by Frank V. Martinek (writer) and Leon Beroth (artist). Designed in 1934 as a recruiting tool by Martinek, a former navy intelligence officer, DON WINSLOW featured suspenseful espionage stories and authentic detail.* © February 25, 1938, Bell Syndicate, Inc. Courtesy of Bill Janocha

MYRA NORTH, SPECIAL NURSE *daily strip by Ray Thompson (writer) and Charles Coll (artist). This blonde-haired registered nurse, who began her adventures in 1936, managed to attend to her medical duties while fighting criminals and spies.* © 1937 NEA Service, Inc. Courtesy of Bill Janocha

SCORCHY SMITH *daily strip by Bert Christman. A talented artist who took over SCORCHY SMITH from Noel Sickles in 1936, Christman left the strip in 1938 to fly airplanes for the navy and was killed in combat in 1942.* © June 3, 1938, the Associated Press. Courtesy of Bill Janocha

e. c. segar

POPEYE, THE PERPETUALLY SCOWLING, grammatically challenged sea dog with superstrength, became a hero to millions of Americans during the worst days of the Depression for his stubborn integrity and no-punches-pulled approach to problem solving. The spinach-eating sailor made his first appearance in the *Thimble Theatre* comic strip after it was a decade old. Nine years later, the man who created him passed away at the height of his career.

Elzie Crisler Segar was born in the small town of Chester, Illinois, on the banks of the Mississippi River, on December 8, 1894. At the age of twelve, he went to work at the Chester Opera House, where he ran the projector, accompanied the pianist on drums, and drew with chalk on the sidewalk in front of the theater to promote the shows. In the spring of 1916, he completed the W. L. Evans correspondence course in cartooning, and soon afterward he left for Chicago to pursue his fortune.

The legendary cartoonist Richard F. Outcault helped Segar obtain employment at the *Chicago Herald,* where he was given his first strip assignment, *Charlie Chaplin's Comic Capers.* In 1917, he started his own feature, *Barry the Boob,* about a bumbling soldier in the European war. Soon after, the *Herald* went bankrupt and was taken over by William Randolph Hearst. Segar ended up working for Hearst's *Chicago American,* where he created a local interest feature entitled *Looping the Loop.* His cartoons attracted the attention of Hearst's editor, Arthur Brisbane, and he was summoned to New York, where King Features launched *Thimble Theatre* on December 19, 1919.

Initially modeled after Ed Wheelan's *Midget Movies,* Segar's strip featured a cast of pen-and-ink performers who spoofed popular films and plays. Segar soon gave up on the original premise and began weaving stories around the continuing adventures of Olive Oyl, her endlessly scheming brother Castor, and her boyfriend Harold Hamgravy (whose name was later changed to Ham Gravy). Segar's writing and drawing skills matured as his cast expanded and the plots stretched out in length; by the end of the decade, however, *Thimble Theatre* was appearing in only a few dozen newspapers.

In 1929, Castor Oyl plotted to make a fortune at a gambling casino on Dice Island with the help of Bernice the Whiffle Hen, a bird who guaranteed good luck when the three hairs on her head were rubbed. After buying a boat, Castor went down to the docks and hired a sailor, with a squint in one eye and a corncob pipe, to man the vessel. Segar initially intended for Popeye to be another incidental character in the strip, but readers responded to his feisty

E. C. SEGAR—Self-caricature from an advertisement for the W. L. Evans School of Cartooning. 1917, Cartoons magazine. Courtesy of Illustration House
All Thimble Theatre comic strips © King Features Syndicate, Inc.

personality almost immediately. As the list of newspapers subscribing to *Thimble Theatre* continued to grow, Popeye became a national celebrity, starring in a series of animated films produced by the Fleischer Studio and endorsing hundreds of products, all of which earned millions of dollars in licensing fees.

Until his death on October 13, 1938, at the age of forty-three, Segar offered up a masterful blend of comedy, fantasy, satire, and suspense in *Thimble Theatre Starring Popeye* (renamed in 1931). He introduced a string of memorable characters to play off his hero's idiosyncrasies, including the parasitic sidekick J. Wellington Wimpy (1931), archrival Bluto (who appeared only briefly in the strip during 1932), adopted "infink" Swee'pea (1933), and long-lost Poopdeck Pappy (1936).

Segar also popularized a lexicon of comic expressions in the strip. Popeye's signature sayings, "I yam what I yam an' tha's all I yam" and "Blow me down!" became classic catchphrases, as were Wimpy's "I will gladly pay you Tuesday for a hamburger today" and "Let's you and him fight." Among the many words Segar added to the popular vernacular were "jeep" and "goon."

Bud Sagendorf, who was hired as Segar's assistant a little more than a year after Popeye was introduced, described his employer as "short of stature, slight of frame, mild-mannered and somewhat introverted." During the 1930s, Segar lived in Santa Monica, California, eighteen miles away from George Herriman. According to Sagendorf, the two cartoonists, who even looked alike, never met. Although they shared a mutual professional admiration, they were each too shy to impose on the other.

THIMBLE THEATRE and THE FIVE FIFTEEN promotional drawing by E. C. Segar. More than seven years before the debut of Popeye, Segar drew the cast of his two comic features in this advertisement for the W. L. Evans School of Cartooning. © November 25, 1921. Courtesy of Bruce Hamilton

THIMBLE THEATRE STARRING POPEYE daily strip by E. C. Segar. Popeye, Olive Oyl, and Merlock Jones are on board the Blue Squid in an episode from the fourth month of the "Eighth Sea" continuity. © September 5, 1932. Courtesy of Bruce Hamilton

THIMBLE THEATRE STARRING POPEYE daily strip by E. C. Segar. Bluto, the star villain in the Fleischer Studio's animated POPEYE films, appeared only briefly in Segar's strip, during 1932. © September 22, 1932. Courtesy of Jerry Dumas

THIMBLE THEATRE STARRING POPEYE daily strip by E. C. Segar. King Blozo appears in the first day of the "Long Live the King" story, during which Segar dabbled in political commentary. © November 14, 1932. Courtesy of Bruce Hamilton

THIMBLE THEATRE Sunday page by E. C. Segar. Popeye breaks out of jail to fight Kid Jolt. One of the few existing original Sunday pages with the matching *SAPPO* topper feature. © December 21, 1930. Courtesy of Illustration House

THIMBLE THEATRE STARRING POPEYE daily strip by E. C. Segar. After being rescued by Popeye, Toar, a nine-hundred-pound prehistoric caveman, shows his appreciation with a kiss. © May 8, 1935. Courtesy of Bruce Hamilton

THIMBLE THEATRE STARRING POPEYE daily strip by E. C. Segar. Wimpy launches the good ship **Hamburger**. © June 10, 1935. Courtesy of Bruce Hamilton

THIMBLE THEATRE STARRING POPEYE daily strip by E. C. Segar. Swee'pea, who was left on Popeye's doorstep on July 28, 1933, is as fearless as his adopted father. © February 21, 1936. Courtesy of Craig Englund

THIMBLE THEATRE STARRING POPEYE daily strip by E. C. Segar. Olive asks all-knowing Eugene the Jeep some probing questions. © June 2, 1936. Courtesy of Bruce Hamilton

THIMBLE THEATRE STARRING POPEYE daily strip by E. C. Segar. Six mermaids follow Poopdeck Pappy from Barnacle Island.
© November 20, 1936. Courtesy of Bruce Hamilton

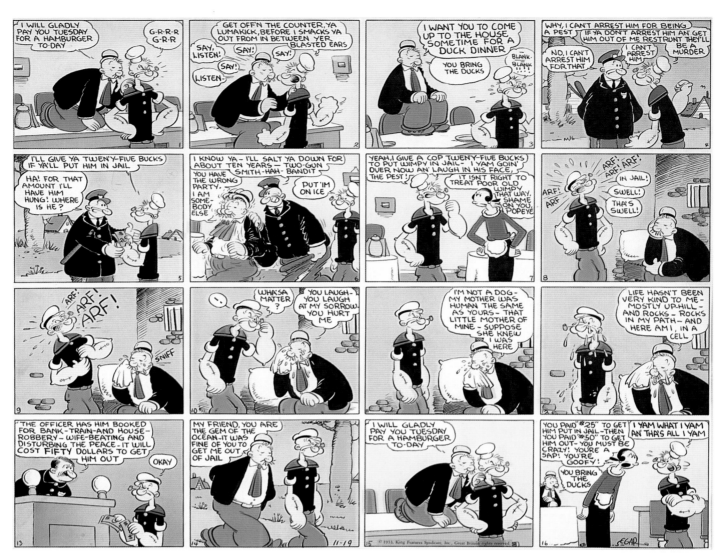

THIMBLE THEATRE STARRING POPEYE original pen-and-ink Sunday page by E. C. Segar, with color overlay. This classic Sunday page features two of Wimpy's most quotable phrases and ends with Popeye's signature saying. © November 19, 1933. Courtesy of Bruce Hamilton

THIMBLE THEATRE STARRING POPEYE daily strip by E. C. Segar. Popeye is flummoxed by the Sea Hag. © January 11, 1937. Courtesy of Bruce Hamilton

THIMBLE THEATRE STARRING POPEYE daily strip by E. C. Segar. Wimpy toots up a hamburger on the Sea Hag's magic flute. The orange stains are from rubber cement used to attach the Ben Day shading. © January 26, 1937. Courtesy of Bruce Hamilton

THIMBLE THEATRE STARRING POPEYE *recolored Sunday page by E. C. Segar. A number of newspaper editors refused to run this gruesome episode.*
© October 1, 1933. Courtesy of Bruce Hamilton and American Color

THIMBLE THEATRE STARRING POPEYE *daily strip by E. C. Segar. Popeye lectures his ninety-nine-year-old father on the virtues of dignity.* © September 18, 1937.
Courtesy of Bruce Hamilton

THIMBLE THEATRE STARRING POPEYE *daily strip by E. C. Segar. A strip from the last story Segar worked on, which he was unable to finish due to deteriorating health.* © August 15, 1938. Courtesy of Bruce Hamilton

chic young

BLONDIE BOOPADOOP AND DAGWOOD BUMSTEAD got off to a rocky start. The son of a tycoon, Dagwood was just one of Blondie's many boyfriends. After announcing his intention to marry the blonde-haired gold digger, bumbling Bumstead could not obtain his parents' approval for the proposed union. To protest, he went on a twenty-eight-day hunger strike. This episode gave the struggling feature the boost it needed. By the time the couple wed on February 17, 1933, *Blondie* was on its way to becoming the most popular comic strip in America, a position it maintained for five decades. Blondie and Dagwood's creator was no overnight success either.

Murat Bernard Young was born in Chicago on January 9, 1901, but grew up in St. Louis. After graduating from high school, he returned to his birthplace and enrolled at the Art Institute of Chicago. In 1921, he created his first comic strip, *The Affairs of Jane,* for the Newspaper Enterprise Association, but it lasted only six months. He tried another pretty-girl feature, *Beautiful Bab,* for the Bell Syndicate in 1922. That effort survived for four months. Undaunted, Young sold *Dumb Dora* to King Features in 1924. He continued this strip for six years, until the syndicate turned down his request for a bigger salary.

Blondie, Young's fourth feature with a female lead, was launched by King Features on September 8, 1930. After a modest start, sales of the strip stalled, and it was eventually canceled in Hearst's flagship paper, the *New York American.* Apparently, readers struggling with the hardships of the Depression were no longer entertained by the screwball antics of a ditzy flapper and her rich boyfriends. In desperation, Young and the syndicate decided to have Blondie fall in love with one of her suitors and get married. As a final twist, her new husband would get disinherited and the couple would be condemned to a life of middle-class drudgery.

The solution worked; sympathetic readers identified with Blondie and Dagwood's struggles, and Young's feature started to pick up new subscribers. The wedding was an event worthy of national media attention, and circulation continued to climb after Baby Dumpling (named "Alexander" after Young's assistant Alex Raymond) was born on April 15, 1934.

Within a few short years, all of the supporting players and recurring scenarios were in place. Dagwood worked at J. C. Dithers and Company while his boss's wife, Cora, went shopping with Blondie. Next-door neighbors Herb Woodley and Tootsie joined the cast, and the Bumstead family grew to include Cookie, who was born in 1941, and Daisy the dog, who had five puppies later that same year. Dagwood was forever oversleeping, crashing into the mailman, and chasing

CHIC YOUNG—Self-caricature. *c. 1945. Courtesy of the International Museum of Cartoon Art*
All Blondie comic strips © King Features Syndicate, Inc.

after his bus. He sought relief from this daily routine by snoozing on the couch, soaking in the bathtub, or raiding the icebox for the ingredients to his famous sandwich.

In 1938, Columbia Pictures produced the first of twenty-eight *Blondie* movies, starring Penny Singleton and Arthur Lake. A successful radio show and two television series followed during the next three decades. Licensed products, including books, games, greeting cards, dolls, clothing, cosmetics, and various other household items, brought in additional income.

By 1948, Young was earning an annual salary of $300,000 and *Blondie* was appearing in 1,136 daily and Sunday papers. It was the number one strip in the business.

When asked to describe his creation, the modest cartoonist mused, "It is difficult to define *Blondie* as a continuity strip, but I do use the greatest, simplest, and most interesting continuity of all, the continuity of life itself, and add a little humor, the spice of life."

"I prefer to call *Blondie* a streamlined gag strip," he added, "whose happenings are true and have occurred in almost every home. You, see I am catering to the average American family."

It took a few false starts, but Chic Young had discovered the secret to success on the funnies pages.

BLONDIE daily strip by Chic Young. Dagwood introduces Blondie to his wealthy father in the debut episode of Young's feature.
© September 8, 1930. Courtesy of Craig Englund

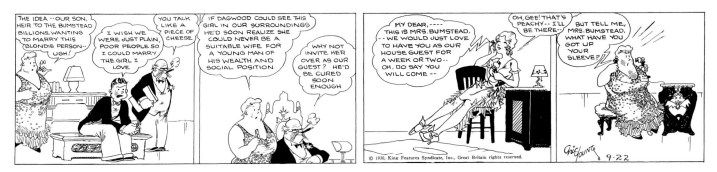

BLONDIE daily strip by Chic Young. The Bumsteads come up with a plan to show their son the folly of his marital plans. © September 22, 1930. Courtesy of Art Wood

BLONDIE daily strip by Chic Young. Mrs. Bumstead tricks Dagwood into dating other girls. © August 20, 1931. Courtesy of Craig Englund

BLONDIE daily strip by Chic Young. Blondie and Dagwood are apart on Christmas Day. © December 25, 1931. Courtesy of Craig Englund

BLONDIE daily strip by Chic Young. Dagwood was sick in bed a few days before he started his famous hunger strike. © December 31, 1932. Courtesy of David Applegate

Dagwood went on a hunger strike in January 1933 to force his parents to grant him permission to marry Blondie.
BLONDIE daily strip by Chic Young. The first episode of the twenty-eight-day protest. © January 3, 1933. Courtesy of Craig Englund

BLONDIE daily strip by Chic Young. The doctor makes a prediction. © January 5, 1933. Courtesy of Craig Englund

BLONDIE daily strip by Chic Young. A missing goldfish. © January 14, 1933. Courtesy of Craig Englund

BLONDIE daily strip by Chic Young. The end is near. © January 25, 1933. Courtesy of Craig Englund

BLONDIE daily strip by Chic Young. The Bumsteads give in, and the hunger strike is over. © January 30, 1933. Courtesy of Craig Englund

BLONDIE Sunday page by Chic Young. The entire Bumstead clan opposes Blondie and Dagwood's marriage. © *January 29, 1933. Courtesy of Craig Englund*

BLONDIE daily strip by Chic Young. The historic wedding of Blondie and Dagwood. © *February 17, 1933. Courtesy of the Library of Congress*

BLONDIE daily strip by Chic Young. Newlywed Blondie has a jealousy problem. © *May 16, 1933. Courtesy of Craig Englund*

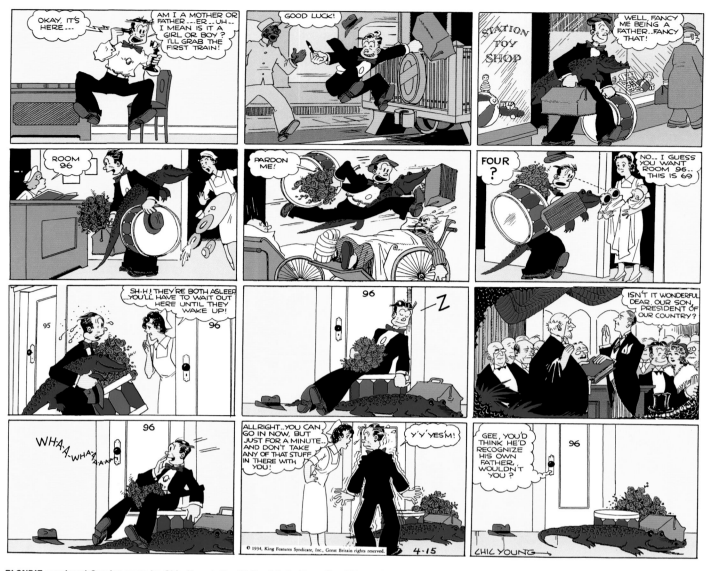

BLONDIE *recolored Sunday page by Chic Young. The birth of Baby Dumpling (Alexander).* © April 15, 1934. Courtesy of Craig Englund and American Color

BLONDIE *daily strip by Chic Young. Baby Dumpling comes home.* © April 27, 1934. Courtesy of Richard Marschall

BLONDIE *daily strip by Chic Young. Blondie and Dagwood take the baby on vacation.* © July 24, 1934. Courtesy of Craig Englund

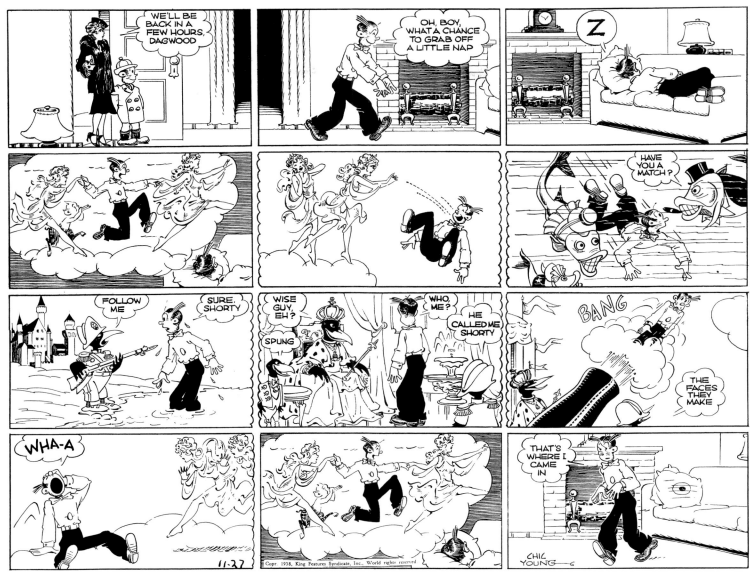

BLONDIE Sunday page by Chic Young. Dagwood has a wild dream while napping on the couch. © November 27, 1938. Courtesy of the Library of Congress

BLONDIE daily strip by Chic Young. The secret to Dagwood's sandwich is revealed. © October 9, 1944. Courtesy of the Library of Congress

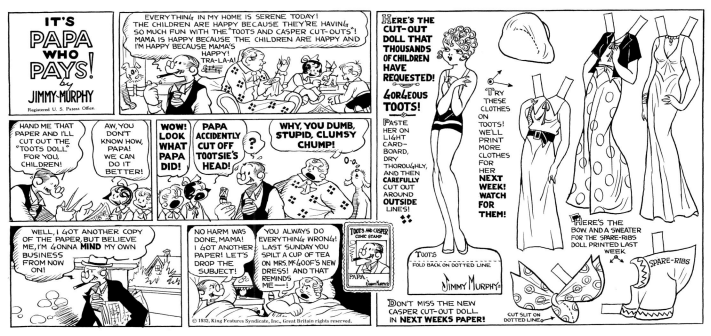

IT'S PAPA WHO PAYS! topper strip for TOOTS AND CASPER Sunday page by Jimmy Murphy. Cutout dolls were popular during the 1930s.
© 1932 King Features Syndicate, Inc. Courtesy of the International Museum of Cartoon Art

PAPER DOLLS   Pretty girls continued to grace the funnies pages during the 1930s, as the flapper look gave way to more sophisticated styles and comic strip females tried to keep up with the glamour queens of the movies. Starring roles ranged from dangerous femme fatales to demure domestic divas, complementing the working girl and college coed parts that predominated in the 1920s. A new crop of illustrators, influenced by the work of John Held Jr. and Russell Patterson, joined the ranks of newspaper comic artists.

THE VAN SWAGGERS topper strip for TILLIE THE TOILER Sunday page by Russ Westover. Readers were invited to send in fashion designs.
© 1934 King Features Syndicate, Inc. Courtesy of the International Museum of Cartoon Art

A SPORTING DECISION

© 1935, EVERYWEEK

1-13-35

A SPORTING DECISION *illustration by Ethel Hays. One of the most successful women cartoonists of the 1920s and 1930s, Hays drew a daily panel,* **FLAPPER FANNY,** *for the Newspaper Enterprise Association, as well as illustrations for the Sunday newspapers.* © *January 13, 1935, Everyweek magazine. Courtesy of the International Museum of Cartoon Art*

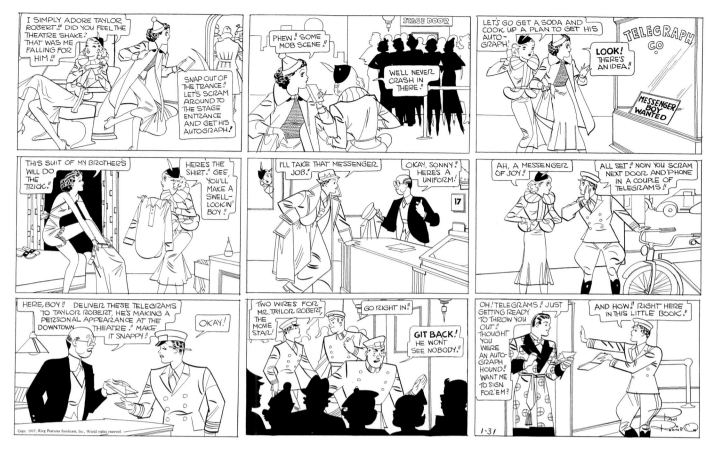

ETTA KETT Sunday page by Paul Robinson. Etta dresses in her brother's suit to get an autograph from a handsome movie star.
© January 31, 1937, King Features Syndicate, Inc. Courtesy of the International Museum of Cartoon Art

OH, DIANA daily strip by Don Flowers. Diana speaks out for women's rights. © April 15, 1936, the Associated Press. Courtesy of the International Museum of Cartoon Art

OH, DIANA daily strip by Don Flowers. The artist also did a daily panel, MODEST MAIDENS, for the Associated Press.
© May 12, 1938, the Associated Press. Courtesy of Jim Scancarelli

GAGS AND GALS Sunday page by Jefferson Machamer. He worked as an artist for *Judge* magazine in the 1920s before creating a comic strip, PETTING PATTY, in 1928 and a syndicated Sunday-page feature, GAGS AND GALS, in 1935. © April 18, 1937, King Features Syndicate, Inc. Courtesy of Richard Marschall

DUMB DORA daily strip by Bill Dwyer. Chic Young's 1925 flapper strip was taken over by Paul Fung in 1930 and Bill Dwyer in 1932 before ending in 1934. This example was ghosted by Dwyer's friend Milton Caniff. © September 6, 1932, King Features Syndicate, Inc. Courtesy of Bill Janocha

al capp

AL CAPP—Self-caricature from Comics and Their Creators. 1942
All Li'l Abner comic strips © Capp Enterprises, Inc.

Any resemblance to any actual character, living or dead, is purely accidental!

THE CREATOR OF ABNER, MAMMY AND PAPPY YOKUM, and Daisy Mae Scragg wrote in 1977, "I knew all my characters from Strip One. In forty-three years, there was never any basic change in them." *Li'l Abner*, which debuted on August 13, 1934, and continued until November 13, 1977, was syndicated to nine hundred newspapers at the peak of its popularity and inspired a Broadway musical, a feature film, an amusement park (Dogpatch U.S.A.), and a soft drink (Kickapoo Joy Juice).

Alfred Gerald Caplin (who later changed his name to Capp) was born in New Haven, Connecticut, on September 28, 1909. His parents, who were Russian Jews, struggled to support their four children, and the family moved frequently. At the age of nine, after losing his leg in a trolley car accident, Alfred decided to become a cartoonist. He took classes in figure drawing and perspective at the Pennsylvania School of Fine Arts, the Boston Museum School, and the Designers Art School but never graduated from high school.

In 1932, Capp got his first job drawing a syndicated panel, *Mister Gilfeather,* for the Associated Press in New York, but he quit after six months and went home to Boston. The following year, he returned to Manhattan, where he was hired by Ham Fisher to work on the *Joe Palooka* comic strip. When Fisher left on a six-week vacation, Capp wrote and drew a series of six Sunday pages in which Joe Palooka and his manager, Knobby Walsh, traveled to Kentucky to visit a backwoods boxer named Big Leviticus and his family. Shortly after this story ran in November 1933, Capp quit and finished

preparing twelve weeks of samples for his own hillbilly strip. In later years, Fisher would accuse his former employee of stealing his characters, but Capp had, in fact, "ghosted" the Big Leviticus sequence.

King Features liked Capp's idea but wanted him to make some changes, so he sold it to United Feature Syndicate, as it was, for less money. *Li'l Abner* debuted inauspiciously in eight papers, but the twenty-five-year-old cartoonist had a formula he knew would make the strip successful.

"My family of innocents is surrounded by a world of super-average people," Capp explained years later. "This innocence of theirs is indestructible, so that while they possess all the homely virtues in which we profess to believe, they seem ingenuous because the world around them is irritated by them, cheats them, kicks them around. They are trusting, kind, loyal, generous, and patriotic. It's a truly bewildering world in which they find themselves."

Although Capp's political leanings changed over the years, readers never had any trouble distinguishing the heroes from the villains in *Li'l Abner.* Corrupt politicians, con men, snobs, fools, and whiners were among the phonies skewered by his caustic pen. Capp's targets were selfishness, pretension, and ignorance, and his weapon was satire.

The driving force behind the strip was the attraction between Abner and Daisy Mae. The scantily clad mountain girl, who became more voluptuous as the years went by, was madly in love with the handsome hillbilly, but Abner was equally consumed with the urge to escape from her clutches. In November 1937, Capp introduced an event in which the unattached females of Dogpatch chased the available men and, according to tradition, could marry any bachelor they caught. Sadie Hawkins Day was observed annually in the strip for many years, as well as on college campuses across the country.

On March 29, 1952, Abner finally gave in to Daisy Mae's charms and married her. "Something went out of the strip with the wedding," wrote comic historian Ron Goulart, "and the domesticated Abner was not the man he had been before the fateful day when Marryin' Sam tied the knot."

Li'l Abner continued to be one of the most popular comics in America throughout the rest of the 1950s and early 1960s, but it began losing papers after Capp's political satire became increasingly vitriolic and he was convicted of sexually harassing a twenty-year-old college coed in 1972. The man who John Steinbeck claimed, in 1952, "may very possibly be the best writer in the world today" died in 1979, two years after he put down his pen. There has never been another cartoonist quite like him.

LI'L ABNER daily strip no. 1 by Al Capp. The debut appearance of Capp's lovable hillbilly. © August 13, 1934. Courtesy of Craig Englund

LI'L ABNER daily strip no. 23 by Al Capp. The country boy visits the big city in the strip's first continuity. © 1934. Courtesy of Sandy Schechter

LI'L ABNER daily strip by Al Capp. Abner tries to make Daisy Mae jealous. © February 29, 1936. Courtesy of Bill Janocha

LI'L ABNER daily strip by Al Capp. Fantastic Brown prepares for a shotgun wedding between Abner and his daughter. © March 11, 1936. Courtesy of Craig Englund

LI'L ABNER daily strip by Al Capp. After the first episode in 1937, Sadie Hawkins Day became an annual tradition. © November 20, 1937. Courtesy of Denis Kitchen

LI'L ABNER daily strip by Al Capp. Romantic misunderstandings were a perennial problem until Abner and Daisy Mae got hitched in 1952. © October 25, 1938. Courtesy of Denis Kitchen

LI'L ABNER daily strip by Al Capp. The artist used bold lettering, judicious blacks, heavy panel borders, and innovative layouts to make his strip stand out on the comics pages. © 1939. Courtesy of Denis Kitchen

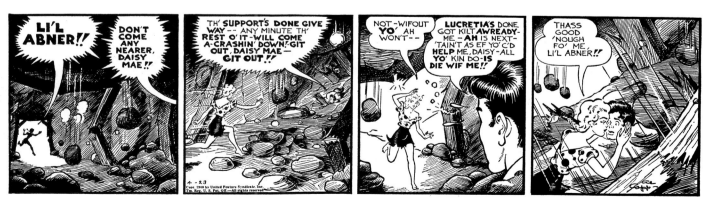

LI'L ABNER daily strip by Al Capp. Daisy Mae comes to Abner's rescue. © April 23, 1940. Courtesy of Denis Kitchen

LI'L ABNER recolored Sunday page by Al Capp. Cinder-Abner stars in a fairy-tale takeoff. The ADVICE FO' CHILLUN topper warns kids about jumping off moving vehicles. This was how Capp lost his leg. © July 10, 1938. Courtesy of Bruce Hamilton and American Color

LI'L ABNER daily strips by Al Capp. In this superhero spoof, Abner was hired to masquerade as the Flying Avenger.
© June 7 and 26, 1941. Courtesy of the Art Wood Collection of Cartoon and Caricature, Prints and Photographs Division, Library of Congress

LI'L ABNER daily strips by Al Capp. It looks as if Daisy Mae has finally caught Abner in another Sadie Hawkins Day race.
© September 25 and November 15, 1943. Courtesy of the Art Wood Collection of Cartoon and Caricature, Prints and Photographs Division, Library of Congress

LI'L ABNER Sunday page by Al Capp. FEARLESS FOSDICK by Lester Gooch was Capp's parody of Chester Gould's DICK TRACY. The indestructible detective was a regular guest in the strip for many years. © May 30, 1943. Courtesy of the Swann Collection, Prints and Photographs Division, Library of Congress

ALLEY OOP promotional drawing by V. T. Hamlin. The Sunday page debuted on September 9, 1934. © July 21, 1934, NEA Service, Inc. Courtesy of Editor & Publisher

PREHYSTERIA Vincent Hamlin's caveman comic, *Alley Oop,* was launched by the Newspaper Enterprise Association on August 7, 1933. After six years of adventures in the Stone Age land of Moo, Hamlin sent his star on a journey through time. Among the many places Oop visited were ancient Troy, Cleopatra's Egypt, and the Spanish Main. Ralph B. Fuller's *Oaky Doaks,* which took place "when knighthood was in flower," was another strip that reinterpreted history with a humorous spin.

ALLEY OOP daily strip by V. T. Hamlin. In addition to Oop, the original cast included his girlfriend Oola and sidekick Foozy, King Guzzle, Queen Umpateedle, and Dinny the stegasaurus. © 1933 NEA Service, Inc. Courtesy of Gary Ernest Smith

ALLEY OOP daily strip by V. T. Hamlin. The artist was adept at rendering both atmosphere and action with his distinctive crosshatch technique.
© April 27, 1934, NEA Service, Inc. Courtesy of Gary Ernest Smith

ALLEY OOP Sunday page by V. T. Hamlin. An amateur paleontologist, Hamlin provided scientific facts about dinosaurs in the DINNY'S FAMILY ALBUM companion feature. © November 11, 1934, NEA Service, Inc. Courtesy of Peter Maresca

ALLEY OOP Sunday page by V. T. Hamlin. A swashbuckling pirate sequence from the later time-travel period. © July 13, 1941, NEA Service, Inc. Courtesy of Gary Ernest Smith

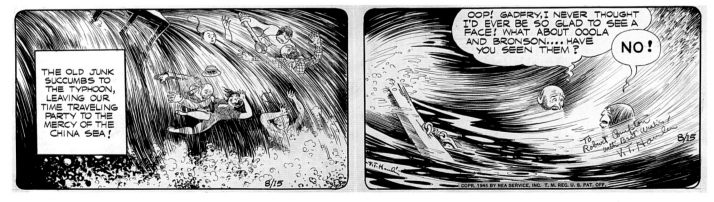

ALLEY OOP daily strip by V. T. Hamlin. Oop and friends are swept into the surging ocean by a typhoon in this example of Hamlin's fluid brushwork.
© August 15, 1945, NEA Service, Inc. Courtesy of All Star Auctions

OAKY DOAKS Sunday page by R. B. Fuller. This feature debuted as a daily strip on June 17, 1935, and as a Sunday page six years later. In this episode, the bumbling knight matches his limited wits with the evil sorceress Witch Hazel. © April 30, 1944, the Associated Press. Courtesy of the Art Wood Collection of Cartoon and Caricature, Prints and Photographs Division, Library of Congress

SMOKEY STOVER Sunday page by Bill Holman. This wacky weekly feature, which debuted on March 10, 1935, and continued until 1973, was filled with visual puns and nonsensical sayings. © August 25, 1940, Tribune Media Services, Inc. All rights reserved. Reprinted with permission. Courtesy of the International Museum of Cartoon Art

SMOKEY STOVER promotional drawing by Bill Holman. The frenetic fireman answers the alarm. © November 19, 1938, Tribune Media Services, Inc. All rights reserved. Reprinted with permission. Courtesy of Editor & Publisher

SCREWBALL STRIPS

The madcap humor of the Marx Brothers was mirrored on the funnies pages by a number of comic features during the 1930s. These creations blended slapstick chaos, wacky characters, and an abundance of puns and sight gags. Rube Goldberg paved the way for this type of comedy with his various strips and panels in the teens and twenties, and Bill Holman further refined the tradition with his 1935 Sunday feature, *Smokey Stover*. Gene Ahearn, Milt Gross, George Swanson, and Harry Hershfield were also practitioners of the screwball school of comics.

SMOKEY STOVER daily strip by Bill Holman. This feature ran as a daily strip for only a brief time during the 1930s. © December 30, 1938, Tribune Media Services, Inc. All rights reserved. Reprinted with permission. Courtesy of Jim Scancarelli

BOOB MCNUTT *Sunday page by Rube Goldberg. This weekly page included two companion features, BILL and BOOB MCNUTT'S ARK, which provided additional outlets for his prolific imagination.* © January 21, 1934, Star Company. Courtesy of the International Museum of Cartoon Art

ABIE THE AGENT Sunday page by Harry Hershfield. Abie was a car salesman when the strip started in 1914. By the 1930s, he was the boss of his own company. © August 3, 1930, International Feature Service, Inc. Courtesy of Russ Cochran

ABIE THE AGENT daily strip by Harry Hershfield. The artist lost a court battle with Hearst in 1931 and did not draw his feature for four years, until the dispute was finally resolved in 1935. © December 18, 1931, International Feature Service, Inc. Courtesy of Bill Janocha

THE SQUIRREL CAGE Sunday page (companion feature to ROOM AND BOARD) by Gene Ahearn. The bearded hitchhiker, who uttered the nonsensical phrase "Nov shmoz ka pop," is a favorite with comic trivia buffs. © December 19, 1937, King Features Syndicate, Inc. Courtesy of Sandy Schechter

OUR BOARDING HOUSE consecutive daily panels by Gene Ahearn. When Ahearn switched syndicates from the Newspaper Enterprise Association to King Features in 1936, his famous phony, Major Hoople, became Judge Puffle in the feature, renamed ROOM AND BOARD. © June 12 and 13, 1935, NEA Service, Inc.
Courtesy of the Art Wood Collection of Cartoon and Caricature, Prints and Photographs Division, Library of Congress

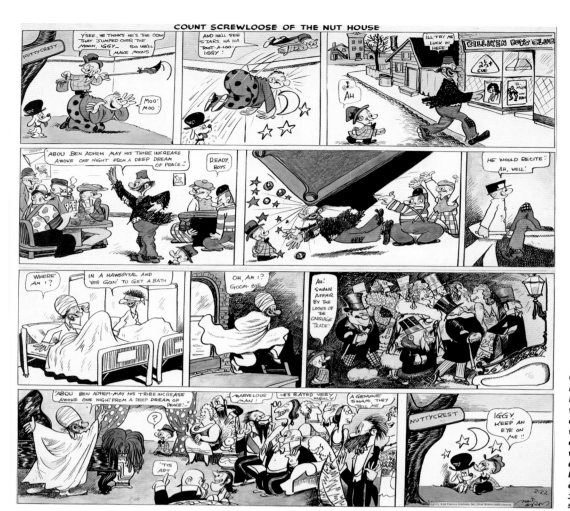

COUNT SCREWLOOSE OF THE NUT HOUSE hand-colored Sunday page by Milt Gross. The Count was a screwball with delusions of grandeur who escaped from an insane asylum on a weekly basis, only to return after encountering the lunacy of the real world. Gross's most famous feature debuted in the New York World on February 17, 1929, and was syndicated by King Features, beginning in 1930. © February 22, 1931, King Features Syndicate, Inc. Courtesy of Bill Alger

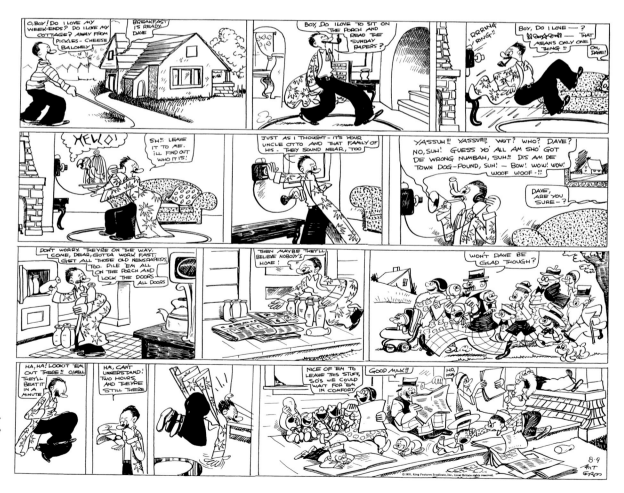

DAVE'S DELICATESSEN Sunday page by Milt Gross. The artist launched this zany feature, which shared a page with *COUNT SCREWLOOSE*, on June 7, 1931. © August 9, 1931, King Features Syndicate, Inc. Courtesy of Sandy Schechter

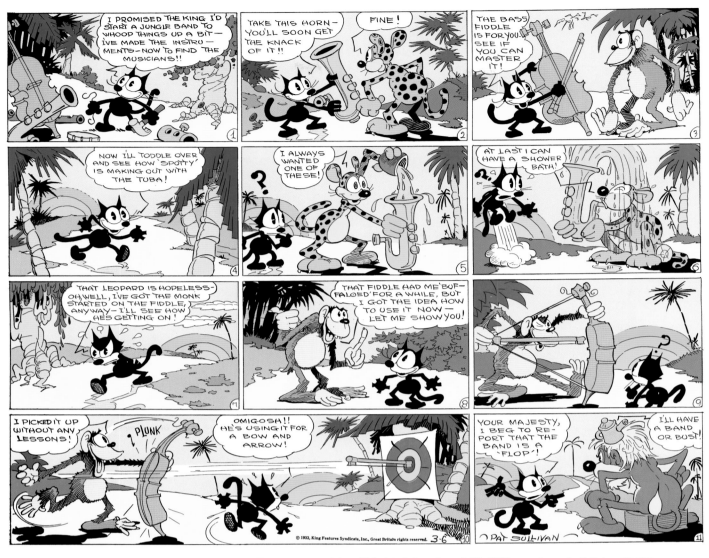

FELIX THE CAT recolored Sunday page by Pat Sullivan. The newspaper strip, which debuted on August 12, 1923, was drawn by Felix's animator, Otto Messmer, until 1955. © March 6, 1932, King Features Syndicate, Inc. Courtesy of Russ Cochran and American Color

CARTOON CROSSOVERS

Many of the top animated movie stars and newspaper comic characters were adapted to other mediums in the late 1920s and 1930s. *Felix the Cat* and *Mickey Mouse* were among the most successful comic strip spin-offs to be licensed from film studios, while Betty Boop's career as a syndicated siren was relatively short. E. C. Segar's Popeye had his own animated series during the 1930s, and a number of other pen-and-ink personalities, including the Toonerville Folks, the Katzenjammer Kids, Henry, Little Jimmy, Barney Google, and Krazy Kat, also made screen appearances.

BETTY BOOP daily strip by Bud Counihan. The boop-oop-a-doop girl starred in her own comic strip from July 23, 1934, to November 27, 1937.
© October 31, 1934, King Features Syndicate, Inc. Courtesy of the International Museum of Cartoon Art

SILLY SYMPHONY Sunday page, starring Donald Duck, by Al Taliaferro. The artist was a master at capturing Donald's manic energy.
© September 6, 1936, Disney Enterprises, Inc. Distributed by King Features Syndicate, Inc. Courtesy of Bruce Hamilton

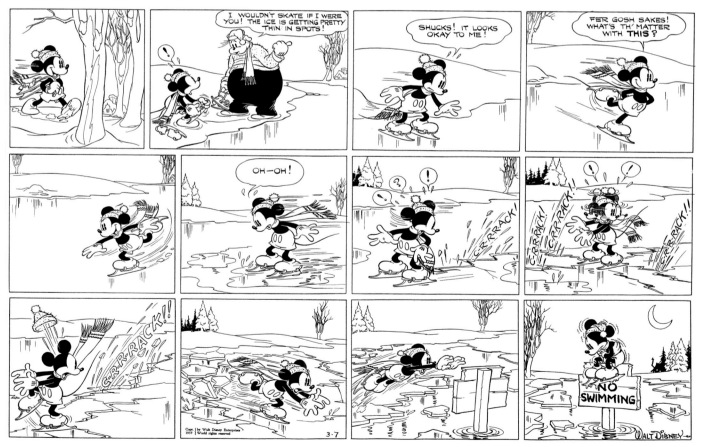

MICKEY MOUSE Sunday page penciled by Floyd Gottfredson and inked by Ted Thwaites. Mickey usually performed visual sight gags on Sunday.
© March 7, 1937, Disney Enterprises, Inc. Distributed by King Features Syndicate, Inc. Courtesy of Bruce Hamilton

MICKEY MOUSE daily strip from the "Blaggard Castle" story, penciled by Floyd Gottfredson and inked by Ted Thwaites. This episode was inspired by the animated film short **THE MAD DOCTOR.** © February 3, 1933, Disney Enterprises, Inc. Distributed by King Features Syndicate, Inc. Courtesy of Bruce Hamilton

MICKEY MOUSE daily strip, with Peg Leg Pete, penciled by Floyd Gottfredson and inked by Ted Thwaites. Mickey's nemesis made his first strip appearance in **1930.** © March 16, 1934, Disney Enterprises, Inc. Distributed by King Features Syndicate, Inc. Courtesy of Rob Stolzer

MICKEY MOUSE daily strip from the "Bad Bandit of Inferno Gulch" sequence, penciled by Floyd Gottfredson and inked by Ted Thwaites. Mickey, astride his faithful nag, Steamboat, is confronted by the masked Bat Bandit. © June 6, 1934, Disney Enterprises, Inc. Distributed by King Features Syndicate, Inc. Courtesy of Bruce Hamilton

DISNEY EVERY DAY

Mickey Mouse was less than two years old when he became the star of a comic strip on January 13, 1930. The original gags were written by Walt Disney and drawn by animator Ub Iwerks. Floyd Gottfredson, a gifted cartoonist and writer who would work on the feature for forty-five years, took over the daily strip in May 1930 and began producing extended humorous adventure stories. A *Mickey* Sunday page, also drawn by Gottfredson, debuted on January 10, 1932. Donald Duck made his first newspaper appearance, illustrated by Al Taliaferro, in the topper strip, *Silly Symphony,* on September 16, 1934, and was given his own feature beginning in 1938. Other Disney characters, including Snow White, the Three Little Pigs, and the Ugly Duckling, also made guest appearances in *Silly Symphony* during the 1930s.

MICKEY MOUSE daily strip, with color overlay, from the "Seven Ghosts" story, penciled by Floyd Gottfredson and inked by Ted Thwaites. This was the first sequence to feature Mickey, Donald, and Goofy in costarring roles. © October 8, 1936, Disney Enterprises, Inc. Distributed by King Features Syndicate, Inc. Courtesy of Bruce Hamilton

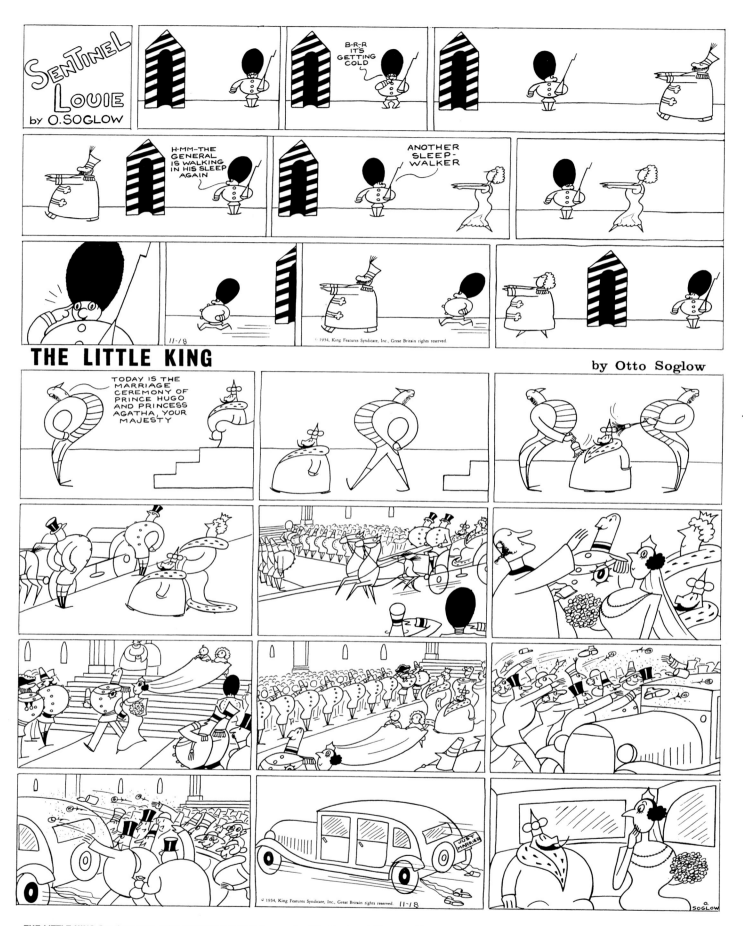

THE LITTLE KING Sunday page, with SENTINEL LOUIE topper, by Otto Soglow. This speechless monarch first appeared in the pages of The New Yorker in 1931 before making its newspaper debut in 1934. © November 18, 1934, King Features Syndicate, Inc. Courtesy of Howard Lowery

BRUTUS Sunday page by Johnny Gruelle. The creator of RAGGEDY ANN AND ANDY produced another comic strip feature, which starred a domestic every-man named Brutus Dudd, from November 17, 1929, to February 27, 1938. © August 28, 1932, New York Tribune, Inc. Courtesy of Bill Janocha

THE HOME OF RIGHT AROUND HOME—Self-portrait by Dudley Fisher. In 1935, Fisher introduced his bird's-eye-view page in the Columbus Dispatch; three years later, it went into national syndication as RIGHT AROUND HOME. *June 30, 1945, Editor & Publisher. Courtesy of Jack Gilbert*

MYRTLE consecutive daily strips by Dudley Fisher. The daughter in the RIGHT AROUND HOME family starred in her own spin-off strip beginning on *May 26, 1941.* © August 22 and 23, 1941, King Features Syndicate, Inc. Courtesy of King Features Syndicate

RIGHT AROUND HOME original hand-colored Sunday page by Dudley Fisher. The crowded compositions by Fisher gradually shifted from rural to suburban scenes and were inspired by his own Ohio neighborhood. © September 18, 1938, King Features Syndicate, Inc. Courtesy of Jack Gilbert

PETE THE TRAMP daily strip by C. D. Russell. Pete was a fixture in Judge magazine before his newspaper debut on January 10, 1932.
© January 22, 1936, King Features Syndicate, Inc. Courtesy of Sandy Schechter

APPLE MARY daily strip by Martha Orr. The artist's Depression-era grandmother, who first appeared on October 29, 1934, was later transformed by Allen Saunders and Ken Ernst into the matronly busybody Mary Worth. © December 27, 1937, Publishers Syndicate. Courtesy of the International Museum of Cartoon Art

BIG CHIEF WAHOO daily strip by Allen Saunders (writer) and Elmer Woggon (artist). Saunders's first successful creation began as a western parody in 1936 before it evolved into an adventure strip, renamed STEVE ROPER, in 1947. © January 23, 1937, Publishers Syndicate. Courtesy of Bill Janocha

ABBIE AN' SLATS daily strip by Al Capp (writer) and Raeburn Van Buren (artist). Capp's second feature, which debuted on July 12, 1937, starred a tough city kid and his spinster aunt, and it showcased the talents of Van Buren, an accomplished illustrator. © October 9, 1939, United Feature Syndicate, Inc. Courtesy of Gill Fox

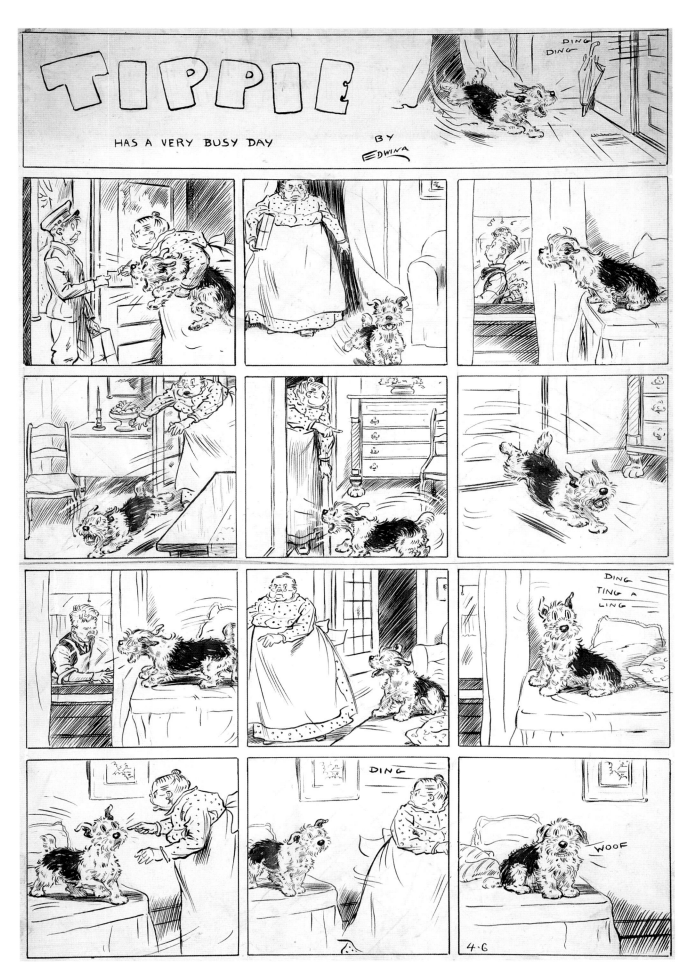

TIPPIE Sunday page by Edwina Dumm. One of the most endearing canines in the comics debuted in the daily strip CAP STUBBS in 1918 and became the star of his own Sunday page in 1934. © April 6, 1935, King Features Syndicate, Inc. Courtesy of Illustration House

NAPOLEON

By Clifford McBride

12-22-35   (c) Arthur J. LaFave

NAPOLEON Sunday page by Clifford McBride. The ungainly pooch, Napoleon, and his portly owner, Uncle Elby, first appeared in McBride's weekly gag feature during the 1920s before becoming costars of their own daily comic strip on June 6, 1932. © December 22, 1935, Arthur J. LaFave. Courtesy of Russ Cochran

THE KEWPIES Sunday page by Rose O'Neill. A pioneer in the early years of the funnies, O'Neill created her comic cupids in 1905. After gaining popularity in the leading women's magazines, THE KEWPIES was first launched as a newspaper feature in 1917 and revived as a Sunday page in 1935. © February 1, 1936, Rose O'Neill. Courtesy of Illustration House

SKIPPY Sunday page by Percy Crosby. This kid, who habitually wore the same checkered cap, shorts, and bow tie, first appeared in Life magazine in 1923 before a daily comic strip was released on June 23, 1925. The Sunday page followed on October 7, 1926. © December 29, 1935, Percy L. Crosby/King Features Syndicate, Inc. Courtesy of Mort Walker

CHILD PHILOSOPHERS

Although the younger generation of funnies folk still had a relatively carefree existence during the Depression, the problems of the real world were starting to have an effect. Certain characters, such as Little Orphan Annie and Skippy, displayed a strong instinct for survival and often engaged in extended monologues, talking to themselves or their juvenile and canine companions with adult sophistication. More inclined to face their challenges with a spunky independence, kids in the comics were starting to grow up.

SKIPPY daily strip by Percy Crosby. SKIPPY reached the peak of its popularity in the mid-1930s, but the strip declined as Crosby struggled with mental illness, and it ended on December 8, 1945. © November 13, 1937, Percy L. Crosby/King Features Syndicate, Inc. Courtesy of the International Museum of Cartoon Art

LITTLE FOLKS introductory strip by "Tack" Knight. A former assistant to Gene Byrnes on REG'LAR FELLERS, Knight produced this kid strip from 1930 to 1933. © 1930 Tribune Media Services, Inc. All rights reserved. Reprinted with permission. Courtesy of Illustration House

MUGGS AND SKEETER daily strip by Wally Bishop. Muggs was a ten-year-old boy who maintained his comic strip career for forty-seven years.
© August 18, 1931, Central Press Association, Inc. Courtesy of Russ Cochran

CAP STUBBS AND TIPPIE daily strip by Edwina Dumm. Her low-key feature, which ran for forty-eight years, was about the simple relationship between a boy and his dog. © October 16, 1933, George Matthew Adams Service, Inc. Courtesy of Frank Pauer

HENRY daily strip by Carl Anderson. The artist was sixty-seven years old when his bald-headed boy first appeared in The Saturday Evening Post in 1932. Hearst signed Anderson up two years later to do a comic strip starring the silent kid. © July 4, 1935, King Features Syndicate, Inc. Courtesy of Russ Cochran

LITTLE ANNIE ROONEY Sunday page by Brandon Walsh (writer) and Nicholas Afonsky (artist). Afonsky, who illustrated the Sunday page from 1934 to 1943, was the most gifted artist to work on this feature. © August 2, 1935, King Features Syndicate, Inc. Courtesy of the International Museum of Cartoon Art

LITTLE ANNIE ROONEY daily strip by Brandon Walsh (writer) and Darrell McClure (artist). This obvious imitation of LITTLE ORPHAN ANNIE was scripted for most of its thirty-seven-year run by Walsh, a former ghostwriter on THE GUMPS. © April 1, 1931, King Features Syndicate, Inc. Courtesy of Sandy Schechter

LITTLE ANNIE ROONEY daily strip by Brandon Walsh (writer) and Darrell McClure (artist). McClure, who took over as the artist on the LITTLE ANNIE ROONEY daily strip on October 6, 1930, and drew both versions after Afonsky died in 1943, continued the feature until April 16, 1966. © December 25, 1941, King Features Syndicate, Inc. Courtesy of the International Museum of Cartoon Art

SKEETS Sunday page by Dow Walling. The artist produced this charming Sunday feature from 1932 to 1951. © February 19, 1933, New York Tribune, Inc. Courtesy of Bill Janocha

FRITZI RITZ daily strip by Ernie Bushmiller. After only two months on the scene, Nancy was already getting the last laugh.
© October 10, 1933, United Feature Syndicate, Inc. Courtesy of Sandy Schechter

GAG GIRL Fritzi Ritz's niece was first introduced in Ernie Bushmiller's strip in August 1933. Over the course of the next five years, the spike-haired moppet gradually usurped the starring role, and in 1938, the name of the feature was officially changed to *Nancy*. By 1948, Bushmiller's brainchild was one of the top strips in the business, with 450 newspaper clients.

NANCY promotional drawing by Ernie Bushmiller. Nancy was once described as a chipmunk with a case of the mumps. *December 18, 1937, Editor & Publisher.*
© United Feature Syndicate, Inc.

NANCY daily strip by Ernie Bushmiller. The artist used his visual ingenuity to help Nancy solve problems.
© August 1, 1941, United Feature Syndicate, Inc. Courtesy of Matt Masterson

NANCY daily strip by Ernie Bushmiller. Nancy's pal Sluggo made his debut on January 24, 1938. © September 5, 1942, United Feature Syndicate, Inc. Courtesy of Gill Fox

FRITZI RITZ and NANCY matching Sunday half-pages by Ernie Bushmiller. The first FRITZI RITZ Sunday page debuted on October 6, 1929, and was joined by the PHIL FUMBLE topper strip in 1930. When Nancy got her own Sunday feature in 1938, Phil got kicked upstairs to the new FRITZI RITZ half-page.
© July 21, 1940, United Feature Syndicate, Inc. Courtesy of Howard Lowery

THE THRILL THAT COMES ONCE IN A LIFETIME daily panel by H. T. Webster. An early comic art collector is born.
© October 2, 1937, New York Tribune, Inc. Courtesy of Rob Stolzer

the
forties

"Can't you read those comics a bit louder? I'm stuck back here in
the kitchen all day and never know what's going on in the world."

THE NEIGHBORS daily panel by George Clark. This newspaper feature was done in the modern style of magazine
gag cartooning. © April 21, 1941, Tribune Media Services, Inc. All rights reserved. Reprinted with permission. Courtesy of Editor & Publisher

SNUFFY SMITH—Special drawing by Billy DeBeck. A rare political statement by the creator of BARNEY GOOGLE.
© October 12, 1940, King Features Syndicate, Inc. Courtesy of Editor & Publisher

AMERICA WATCHED AND WAITED WHILE THE WAR IN EUROPE ESCALATED. ON MAY 10, 1940, THE GERMAN ARMY LAUNCHED A BLITZKRIEG THROUGH THE NETHERLANDS, BELGIUM, AND LUXEMBOURG, AND BY JUNE IT WAS OCCUPYING FRANCE. THE GERMAN AIR FORCE BEGAN BOMBING COASTAL TOWNS ALONG THE ENGLISH CHANNEL IN JULY, AND THE LUFTWAFFE COMMENCED A MASSIVE AERIAL ASSAULT AGAINST BRITAIN'S CITIES ON AUGUST 13, 1940. ROMANIA, YUGOSLAVIA, AND GREECE ALSO FELL TO THE AXIS POWERS, AND, ON JUNE 22, 1941, THE LARGEST INVASION FORCE IN HISTORY, THREE MILLION STRONG, MARCHED INTO THE SOVIET UNION ON AN EIGHTEEN-HUNDRED-MILE FRONT.

The tide began turning against isolationists in the United States. According to a poll taken in December 1939, 67.4 percent of American citizens opposed getting involved in the conflict; six months later, 67.5 percent supported some form of aid to the European allies. On December 17, 1940, President Roosevelt introduced his "Lend-Lease" plan, which proposed the loan of supplies in exchange for future compensation. On February 4, 1941, Ohio Congressman John Vorys criticized FDR's program in a speech to the House of Representatives. "Our policy now is like that of Popeye's friend [Wimpy]—'let's you and him fight,'" declared Vorys. The Lend-Lease Act passed the House by a vote of 260 to 165 in March and immediately provided for $7 billion in food, tanks, trucks, planes, guns, ammunition, and other vital supplies, which were shipped to Britain in

1941. The "arsenal of democracy" was gearing up for America's entry into the war.

Within three days after the Japanese surprise attack on the U.S. naval base at Pearl Harbor, Hawaii, on December 7, 1941, Germany and Italy also declared war on the United States. A sleeping giant had been awakened.

In 1939, only 2 percent of the nation's industrial output was military-related. In the year after Pearl Harbor, war production quadrupled; by 1944, the defense budget accounted for 45 percent of the gross national product. The standing army, which numbered 188,000 volunteers in 1939, swelled to more than a million soldiers in the year after the Selective Training and Service Act was signed into law on September 16, 1940. Women filled positions that men left behind, and by 1943, sixteen million women had jobs outside the home.

Americans on the home front contributed to the cause in many ways. They bought $135 billion in War Bonds, grew their own food in Victory Gardens, and volunteered for civil defense duty. Children collected used metal and rubber to be recycled into armaments. Rationing of gasoline and groceries became a sacrifice that citizens learned to live with. The United Service Organizations (USO) recruited forty-five hundred actors and performers, including Bob Hope, Bing Crosby, and Duke Ellington, to put on shows for GIs around the world. Hollywood producers turned out propaganda and training movies for the military, and more than twenty-nine thousand volunteers from the film industry served in the armed forces.

Cartoonists also did their part, by creating special drawings for government agencies, making personal appearances for war veterans, and providing morale-boosting messages in their features. Popeye became the official "spokescharacter" for the U.S. Navy, in a series of recruitment ads that began appearing in newspapers in July 1941. Al Capp created a special, color Sunday-page feature for the Treasury Department in 1942: *Small Fry,* which was later renamed *Small Change,* persuaded readers to buy War Bonds and was distributed to newspapers free of charge. Little Orphan Annie's Junior Commando movement, which was inspired by a plotline in Harold Gray's strip in the summer of 1942, organized more than a hundred thousand youngsters nationwide into small local groups to round up newspapers, scrap metal, old tires, and kitchen grease to be used as raw materials for the munitions factories. A troupe of cartoonists that included Milton Caniff, Gus Edson, Ernie Bushmiller, and Rube Goldberg gave chalk talks to wounded GIs recuperating in home-front hospitals.

"The knights of the drawing board are doing their bit to help Uncle Sam speed the day of victory over the Axis," lauded *Editor & Publisher* on September 19, 1942. "The nation's syndicate cartoonists whose material appears in newspapers over the land have enlisted for the duration to aid in doing the job of keeping up the morale of the fighting men and the folks at home."

Many comic strip characters signed up for active duty. Joe Palooka was one of the first to enlist, on November 29, 1940, soon after the draft became official. His creator, Ham Fisher, was a loyal FDR supporter and had visited Fort Dix in New Jersey to gather background material prior to the episode in which Joe marched into a U.S. Army recruiting office. For the next six years, Fisher's simpleminded boxing champ served his country valiantly, although he never rose above the rank of private first class.

Milton Caniff's Terry Lee became a flight officer in the U.S. Army Air Force, and Pat Ryan rose to the rank of lieutenant in the navy. Roy Crane's Captain Easy was a captain in army intelligence. Russ Westover's Tillie the Toiler joined

TERRY LEE—*Character portrait by Milton Caniff. Terry enlisted in the Army Air Force on October 17, 1942.* © October 18, 1943, Tribune Media Services, Inc. All rights reserved. Reprinted with permission

the Women's Army Auxiliary Corps. Frank King's Skeezix served as a corporal in army ordnance. Billy DeBeck's Snuffy Smith was accepted by the army on November 13, 1940, and Barney Google enlisted in the navy in September 1941. Don Winslow of the navy and Sergeant Stony Craig of the Marines were already signed up when the war started and continued to serve in active duty.

Other comic strip stars did their part on the home front. Secret Agent X-9 tracked spies for the Federal Bureau of Investigation in Washington, D.C., and Dick Tracy did undercover work for naval intelligence. Freckles and his friends rolled bandages for the Red Cross, assisted at a military canteen, sold bonds and stamps, and volunteered for civil defense duty. Nancy and Sluggo collected scrap metal. Meanwhile, Blondie and Dagwood, Maggie and Jiggs, Andy and Min, and many of the other comic strip couples continued with business as usual on the nation's funnies pages.

Cartoonists also saw active duty. Alex Raymond turned *Flash Gordon* over to his assistant, Austin Briggs, and joined the Marines in February 1944. Zack Mosley, the creator of *Smilin' Jack,* was a submarine spotter for the Civil Air Patrol in Florida. Gus Arriola launched *Gordo* on November 24, 1941, two weeks before the attack on Pearl Harbor. He had to discontinue the strip on October 28, 1942, after he enlisted in the army. Arriola did animation work for the First Motion Picture Unit during the war and resumed the *Gordo* Sunday page on May 2, 1943, but he could not restart the daily strip until June 24, 1946. Bert Christman, who took over *Scorchy Smith* from Noel Sickles in 1936, enlisted as a navy pilot in 1938 and, after Pearl Harbor, was flying with the American Volunteer Group of aviators. His plane was shot down in Burma on January 23, 1942, and Christman was killed by machine gun fire before he could reach the ground in his parachute.

Most of the established creators remained at home for the duration, but a handful of servicemen earned their cartooning stripes overseas during the war. Bill Mauldin, who was eighteen years old when he enlisted in 1940, started drawing cartoons for the *45th Division News.* He experienced the grim realities of frontline combat in Italy and France and was wounded at Salerno in 1943. His most famous wartime series, *Up Front,* starred two weary, unshaven foot soldiers, Willie and Joe, and appeared in the *Army Times, Stars and Stripes,* and two book collections. United Feature began distributing it as a syndicated panel on April 17, 1944, and Mauldin won the Pulitzer Prize in 1945 for his uncompromising cartoons.

In one of his books, *The Brass Ring,* Mauldin claimed that he was once reproached by General George Patton. Angry about the cartoonist's honest portrayal of an infantryman's life in the foxholes and trenches, Patton bellowed at Mauldin, "You know as well as I do that you can't have an army without respect for officers. What are you trying to do, incite a goddamn mutiny?" Mauldin told Patton he was only drawing what he had observed and refused to change his approach.

After he returned home on June 15, 1945, Mauldin adapted his two dog-faced GIs to a newspaper panel, initially titled *Sweatin' It Out,* for United Feature Syndicate. "I began with these guys when they were inducted, went through training with them, saw them fight in Italy and France," Mauldin explained. "Now they're coming home pooped out and are going to have to find out how to be civilians. They might even acquire wives." The feature was criticized as being too political for a syndicated panel and ended after Mauldin's contract with United Feature expired in 1949.

George Baker worked at the Disney Studio for four years before he was drafted into the army in June 1941. After Baker's

THE SAD SACK promotional drawing by Sergeant George Baker. From an advertisement for the first syndicated release of Baker's wartime strip.
© December 2, 1944, Consolidated News Features, Inc. Courtesy of Editor & Publisher

winning entry in a cartoon contest was published in *Life* magazine, *Yank,* the new army weekly, requested regular submissions from him. "I had to devise an average soldier," Baker remembered. "The state of mind of a soldier was more authentic and real to me than his outer appearance. So therefore my character looked resigned, tired, helpless and beaten." The title Baker chose for his new feature was a shortened version of "a sad sack of s . . . ," which was military slang for a loser.

The Sad Sack premiered on June 17, 1942, and was immediately a hit with GIs. Simon and Schuster published book collections of Baker's cartoons in 1944 and 1946, and Consolidated News Features obtained the right to syndicate *The Sad Sack* to thirty newspapers for twenty-two weeks, beginning in December 1944. At the end of the war, Bell Syndicate took over the distribution, and on May 5, 1946, Sad Sack became a civilian. The newspaper Sunday page lasted until the mid-1950s, but a comic book adaptation, published by Harvey Comics from 1949 to 1982, was more successful after Sad Sack reenlisted in 1951. Fred Rhoades, a Marine veteran who drew *Gizmo & Eightball* for *Leatherneck* magazine during the war, took over the *Sad Sack* comic book in 1954.

Special publications for military personnel, ranging from large-circulation periodicals to single-page camp newsletters, proliferated during the war. In addition to world and local news, photos, editorials, letters, and pinups, most of them included cartoons. *Stars and Stripes,* a daily tabloid newspaper of eight to sixteen pages with a circulation of more than a million, featured Mauldin's *Up Front,* Baker's *The Sad Sack,* Caniff's *Male Call,* Dave Breger's *G.I. Joe,* Dick Wingert's *Hubert,* and Leonard Sansone's *The Wolf. Yank,* a twenty-four-page weekly magazine with a circulation of about 2.5 million, also printed the cartoons of Mauldin, Baker, and Breger. *Leatherneck,* a monthly produced by the Marine Corps in Washington, D.C., offered *Hashmark* by Fred Lasswell and *Gizmo & Eightball* by Fred Rhoades.

In the summer of 1942, the army set up the Camp Newspaper Service in New York to distribute features to more than three thousand GI publications. This military-run operation sent out weekly proof sheets and mats to bases around the world. Among the established features that the syndicates provided free of charge were *Gasoline Alley, Smilin' Jack, Blondie, Nancy, Li'l Abner,* and *Joe Palooka.*

Caniff, who was unable to be on active duty because of phlebitis, was determined to help boost the morale of the troops. In addition to creating special drawings for many government campaigns and making appearances at veteran hospitals, he began producing a special weekly *Terry and the Pirates* strip for the Camp Newspaper Service in October 1942. After a newspaper editor in Florida complained about a nearby military base violating the paper's territorial exclusivity in regard to *Terry* by publishing the strip in the base's newsletter, Caniff decided to develop a different weekly feature expressly for distribution to the armed services. *Male Call,* which its creator described as a "two-minute furlough," debuted on January 24, 1943, and did not include any of the characters from *Terry and the Pirates.* Instead, it starred a sexy, brunette femme fatale who had a thing for men in uniform.

"Miss Lace is probably the most delectable pen-and-ink creation of all time, the camp follower of every fighting man's dreams," Bill Mauldin remembered. "Milton Caniff produced in her a confection of femininity which put all the 'pin-ups' in the shade, and he never realized a nickel's profit from her." An estimated fifteen million GIs looked forward to her weekly appearances from 1943 to 1946.

While military publishing thrived, the war closed many foreign markets for the major newspaper syndicates. King Features, which had twenty-six overseas bureaus, was hit the hardest. After the Nazis invaded Belgium, the Netherlands, and France, American comics were banned in most newspapers in those countries. Publishers in England were forced to cancel features due to paper shortages. Currency exchange restrictions, the closing of shipping lanes, and the loss of advertising revenue further restricted business. The syndicates tried to compensate by expanding their sales efforts in South America.

Shortages of materials, including newsprint and ink, also hurt business on the home front. On February 16, 1942, the

"Here y'are, men, latest copies of 'Stars and Stripes' an' 'Yank'!"

PRIVATE BREGER panel by Lieutenant Dave Breger. The Allied invasion forces were provided with entertaining reading matter.
© c. 1944, King Features Syndicate, Inc.

Atlanta Constitution and the *Atlanta Journal* announced that they were both cutting their daily comics by half, from two pages to one, to conserve paper. "All of your favorites will remain, more than a dozen comic adventure strips and panels," the papers assured their readers, " but war has struck in the midst of these amusing people and we break the bad news this morning." *Jane Arden* and *Mary Worth's Family* were among the strips that were canceled.

The syndicates quickly responded to this threat by offering their comics in reduced sizes. On April 20, 1942, United Feature Syndicate began distributing its daily strips in a four-column width, as well as in the standard five- and six-column formats (one column is approximately two inches wide). A special committee of the American Society of Newspaper Editors (ASNE) reported on February 16, 1943, that 70 percent of the nation's daily papers were running comics in the four-column size. The committee also proposed that the legibility of the comics could be maintained by shortening the balloons and eliminating complicated art detail, and it predicted that the five- and six-column widths would be a thing of the past after the next government cut in newsprint supply.

Newspapers were also demanding a reduction in the size of color comics to half-page and one-third-page formats to conserve paper and ink. The ASNE committee proposed that the standard width of a Sunday comics page should be cut back. King Features announced in March 1943 that many of its

This is it

BUZ SAWYER promotional drawing by Roy Crane. Buz and his sidekick, Rosco Sweeney, in an advertisement for Crane's new adventure strip.
© January 1944 King Features Syndicate, Inc. Courtesy of Editor & Publisher

strips, including *Blondie, Thimble Theatre Starring Popeye, Mickey Mouse, Bringing Up Father,* and *Barney Google and Snuffy Smith,* were being offered in a one-third-page size.

Early in 1944, Fred Ferguson, president of the Newspaper Enterprise Association, looked forward to the end of the war but speculated that "even with more newsprint available, I don't see why the newspapers would want to return to a six-column comic strip. The artists have got over the hump of adjusting their work, and they've succeeded admirably in fitting into smaller spaces. As a matter of fact, with more tightly written balloons, the material has improved." Comic strips would never be restored to their prewar dimensions.

After the hostilities ended and the foreign markets were reopened, international distribution of comics became a growth industry. "We never did any promotion in the South American and European countries," claimed Mollie Slott, assistant manager of the Chicago Tribune–New York News Syndicate, "but the war and the GIs' enthusiasm for comics has opened up a big field for us there."

Cartoonists also sought new opportunities. In 1943, Roy Crane announced that he had signed a contract with King Features to create a new adventure strip. Crane's assistant, Leslie Turner, took over *Wash Tubbs/Captain Easy* in May 1943, which continued to be distributed by the Newspaper Enterprise Association. When *Buz Sawyer* debuted on

November 1, 1943, Crane's lead character was a navy pilot on the aircraft carrier *Tippecanoe.* Buz and his buddy, Rosco Sweeney, were shot down and stranded on a tropical island in their first months of duty and continued fighting on the Pacific front throughout the war. When Emperor Hirohito capitulated on August 15, 1945, Buz and Rosco had just escaped from a Japanese submarine and were on their way to participate in a bombing raid over Tokyo. Crane rushed out a special strip explaining that "the current story sequence began before the Jap surrender," and he requested the readers' patience while the continuity reached its conclusion. *Tim Tyler's Luck, Jungle Jim,* and *Superman* were among the other adventure strips that were caught in the middle of war stories when the fighting stopped.

Caniff also decided during the war to launch a new feature for a competing syndicate. In January 1945, when the story got out that he had signed a contract with Marshall Field, publisher of the *Chicago Sun* and *PM,* Caniff was still obliged to continue *Terry and the Pirates* for the Chicago Tribune–New York News Syndicate until October 1946. "I'm a lame duck," he admitted. "That makes me anxious to do the best job I can on *Terry.*" Field guaranteed Caniff $525,000 for five years and full ownership of a strip he had yet to conceive. King Features, the selling agent, claimed in an advertisement on May 19, 1945, that 162 newspapers had agreed to carry

Caniff's new creation "sight unseen." By the time *Steve Canyon* debuted on January 13, 1947, a total of 234 subscribers had been convinced that Caniff's new strip would be a winner.

As comic books gained in popularity during the late 1930s and early 1940s, newspaper syndicates searched for ways to respond to the challenge. In April 1940, the Chicago Tribune–New York News Syndicate produced a sixteen-page oblong color booklet, measuring $10\frac{1}{2}$ by $8\frac{1}{2}$ inches, that was inserted in the *Sunday Tribune* comic section. Readers got twice as many comics for their money, and sales of the *Tribune* increased by one hundred thousand issues. Early editions of that syndicate's *Sunday Comics Magazine* contained such recycled features as *Texas Slim* by Ferd Johnson and *Bobby Make-Believe* by Frank King, but eventually it added new creations, including *Streamer Kelly* by Jack Ryan, *Mr. Ex* by Bert Whitman, and *Brenda Starr, Reporter* by Dale Messick.

Victor Fox, a former accountant for Detective Comics, claimed that no matter how hard the syndicates tried to imitate the comic book format, they would not succeed unless they offered juvenile readers "thriller" stories. Fox had started his own publishing company and boasted that his monthly and bimonthly magazines had a total circulation of more than five million. The Fox Feature Syndicate also provided Sunday-page and daily strip versions of many of their comic book features, including *The Blue Beetle, The Green Mask, Spark Stevens,* and *Red Dexter.* Fox announced in May 1940 that he would be making available to newspapers a sixteen-page comic magazine that featured many of his adventure heroes; however, there is no evidence the Fox booklet was ever produced.

The Register and Tribune Syndicate of Des Moines, Iowa, jumped on the newspaper insert bandwagon on June 2, 1940. Its sixteen-page *Comic Book Section* featured three complete stories and was initially distributed to five newspapers, including the *Washington Star, Baltimore Sun,* and *Philadelphia Record.* The seven-page lead story starred a masked detective, named the Spirit, and was written and drawn by Will Eisner. The original stories for the backup strips, *Lady Luck* and *Mr. Mystic,* were also developed by Eisner but drawn by other artists.

"I decided my leading figure wouldn't be what we call a costume character," Eisner remembered in 1941. "I gave him a mask, as a sort of fillip to his personality. And he had to be on the side of the law, of course, but I believed it would be better if he worked a little outside of the law." Eisner's comic-noir character stalked the mean streets of Central City,

THE SPIRIT comic page by Will Eisner. The "splash page" was an Eisner innovation.
© January 12, 1941, and 1974 by Will Eisner

which closely resembled the gritty urban milieu of the cartoonist's New York home.

The most successful of the comic book insert features, *The Spirit* appeared as a daily strip from October 13, 1941, to March 11, 1944. The comic book version, which sold more than five million copies a week, lasted until October 5, 1952. Although the syndicates continued to introduce thriller features throughout the 1940s, strips starring costumed crime fighters were, for the most part, short-lived on the funnies pages.

In November 1945, *Editor & Publisher* hosted a luncheon at the Hotel Astor in New York City for a group of prominent women comic artists. Among the attendees were Edwina Dumm (*Cap Stubbs and Tippie*), Hilda Terry (*Teena*), Tarpe Mills (*Miss Fury*), Odin Waugh (*Dickie Dare*), Dale Messick (*Brenda Starr*), and Virginia Clark (*Oh, Diana*).

"The occasion was historic," *Editor & Publisher* claimed. Not only was it the first major gathering of female cartoonists, "but it also marked the return of women to the same proportionate position in the field as in the very early days when Kate Carew drew *The Angel Child.*"

Other female pioneers from the first decades of the funnies included Rose O'Neill (*The Kewpies*), Grace Drayton (*Dimples*),

Nell Brinkley (*The Adventures of Prudence Primm*), and Ethel Hays (*Flapper Fanny*). Although Martha Orr's *Apple Mary*, which debuted on October 29, 1934, was a modest success in the Depression years, the percentage of women cartoonists declined during the ascendancy of the adventure strip.

"No woman cartoonist has ever broken into the front lines of comic strips," claimed Amram Schoenfeld in 1930. "The newspaper cartoon is a form of art in which women do not seem to be entirely at home," he continued, "the comic strip apparently demanding a type of humor and technique which is essentially masculine."

This sexist attitude was typical in the male-dominated funnies business of the 1930s. During World War II, however, as women became essential to the workforce, opportunities also opened up in the comics industry. In fact, one of the most powerful syndicate executives at that time was Mollie Slott, assistant manager of the Chicago Tribune–New York News Syndicate.

Slott had been hired by the Tribune Syndicate in 1914 as a secretary and had risen through the ranks of the company during the 1920s. In her first seven years, she worked for six different managers, learning aspects of the business from each of them. Slott ran the office during the periods between bosses, while the search was on for a new executive to replace the previous one. She became indispensable to the running of the syndicate operation.

In 1933, Captain Patterson summoned Slott to New York from the *Tribune* offices in Chicago. She adapted well to the change and had a major influence on the selection of many new strips, including *Smilin' Jack*, *Terry and the Pirates*, and *Smokey Stover*. She also convinced Patterson to take a chance with *Brenda Starr*.

Dale Messick, who changed her name from Dalia to disguise her gender when submitting her work by mail, initially presented a strip about a woman bandit to the syndicate. Patterson, who reportedly claimed that he had once hired a woman cartoonist and was determined not to do so again, rejected Messick's idea outright. But when Slott looked at the samples, she saw potential in the young woman's work. At Slott's suggestion, Messick turned her heroine into a feisty, red-haired newspaper reporter and named her after the famous debutante Brenda Frazier. Patterson reluctantly added *Brenda Starr, Reporter* to the syndicate's lineup but refused to carry it in his flagship paper, the *New York Daily News*—and it did not appear there until after his death in 1946. The strip debuted on June 30, 1940, in the *Tribune*'s sixteen-page comic book insert as a Sunday-only feature; a daily version was added on October 22, 1945. Messick was one of the first women to succeed in the story strip genre, and she continued to produce *Brenda Starr*, with the help of a team of talented assistants, until her retirement in 1980.

On March 27, 1942, an exhibition entitled "The Comic Strip, Its Ancient and Honorable Lineage and Present Significance" opened at the American Institute of Graphic Arts in New York City. The National Arts Club hosted a dinner on April 6, honoring two dozen of the comic artists whose work was included in the display. Dr. Emanuel Winternitz from the Metropolitan Museum of Art spoke at the event, praising the comic strip as a work of art. Among the cartoonists in attendance were Milton Caniff, Billy DeBeck, H. H. Knerr, Alex Raymond, Rube Goldberg, and Harry Hershfield.

"The funnies are being taken seriously as art after all these years," reported *Editor & Publisher*. "The exhibit, and the plans for its tour of the larger cities, certainly is a tribute to the knights of the drawing board who have for years and today continue to bring happiness into the homes of the vast newspaper reading public."

Events within the comics pages also made headlines during the first half of the decade. On October 16, 1941, Raven Sherman, a major character in Milton Caniff's *Terry and the Pirates*, died after being pushed out of the back of a moving truck. Readers reacted emotionally to the loss and sent letters and telegrams, expressing both sympathy and outrage, to the syndicate's offices. Students at colleges across the country held

BRENDA STARR promotional drawing by Dale Messick. The cast of Messick's strip is introduced. October 31, 1941, San Francisco Call-Bulletin. © Tribune Media Services, Inc. All rights reserved. Reprinted with permission. Courtesy of Trina Robbins

mock funerals for the fictitious American heiress who had been using her money to supply medical aid to the Chinese.

"I am not certain how the dastardly idea to kill off Raven generated in my mind," Caniff reminisced in 1979. "Perhaps a letter from a reader which said, 'You are always having people fighting, but not one ever gets killed, or even badly hurt,' lighted the macabre spark. More likely it was simply a promotion device with which I hoped to publicize *Terry and the Pirates.*"

A publicity gimmick in another popular comic strip set off a different response from readers. Chic Young announced on April 13, 1941, that Blondie was expecting her second child, and King Features offered a $100 prize for the best name. The syndicate received 431,275 submissions. Among the many unusual names readers sent in for the baby girl were Daggy-Doo, Tad Pole, Bottle Neck, and Zephyr. Beatrice Barken of Cleveland had the winning entry: Cookie.

A strike of the New York Newspaper and Mail Deliverers in July 1945 led to a series of events that dramatically revealed how indispensable comics were to daily life in the city. The seventeen hundred union workers, who were demanding an exorbitant pension package, refused to deliver papers throughout the metropolitan area, forcing readers to stand in long lines outside the publishers' offices to pick up each day's edition.

Mayor Fiorello LaGuardia felt he had to do something to appease the masses. On Sunday, July 8, 1945, with newsreel

cameras rolling, the mayor went on the radio and read the latest installment of *Dick Tracy.* "Crash, goes the big heavy pot over Wetwash Wally's head the minute he opens the door," bellowed the mayor into the microphone, vocalizing the violent conclusion to Chester Gould's Sunday page.

As the strike dragged into its second week, LaGuardia took to the airwaves again on July 15, this time bringing readers up-to-date on developments in *Little Orphan Annie.* "Don't be a crook! That's the moral!" the mayor exclaimed, emulating the melodramatic tone of Harold Gray's closing lines.

The strike ended on the following Tuesday. After seventeen days without newspapers, readers were finally able to catch up with the story lines in their favorite comic strips. New Yorkers had survived the crisis, with the help of their charismatic leader.

In the five decades since the Yellow Kid made his first appearance, the funnies, which began as an experiment in newspaper publishing, had become an essential element of American life. Comic strip characters were everywhere. They starred in live action and animated films, stage plays and radio programs. Their adventures were retold in books and inspired hit songs. Their faces were used to sell thousands of products.

Comic strip creators did more than entertain. They made significant contributions to the folklore and language of popular culture. Terms like "jeep," "hot dog," palooka," and "dingbat" were introduced in the comics, as well as such immortal phrases as "Leapin' Lizards," "I yam what I yam," and "great balls o' fire." Sadie Hawkins Day was celebrated as a national holiday, and Superman was revered as an American hero.

The social changes of the first half of the twentieth century were also recorded in the funnies pages. As newspapers increased their circulation and the comics were adapted to other forms of entertainment, cartoon art became the visual language of the mass media. Cartoonists invented symbols and ideas that were universally recognizable to this vast audience. At the same time, they also made observations that were fresh and meaningful to their readers. As a result, the best of their work reflected what was currently humorous and of vital concern on the day it was published. In re-creating fads and fashions, technological progress, historical events, and social changes, cartoons can reveal far more than the written word alone.

The newspaper business has faced many challenges in the postwar years, but the comics remain a vital part of the entertainment industry. Cartoonists have preserved the past with their drawings and continue to enrich our cultural legacy. It is impossible to understand American history in the twentieth century without an appreciation and understanding of the newspaper comic strip.

THE COMICS GO TO WAR Many funnies characters were already in uniform before the Japanese attack on Pearl Harbor on December 7, 1941; after America retaliated, the conflict continued to have a dramatic impact on the content of the comics. Although many strip stars signed up for active duty, relatively few saw actual combat. The harsh realities of training and fighting were, for the most part, depicted in the cartoons produced specifically for the troops by GI artists such as Bill Mauldin, Dave Breger, and George Baker.

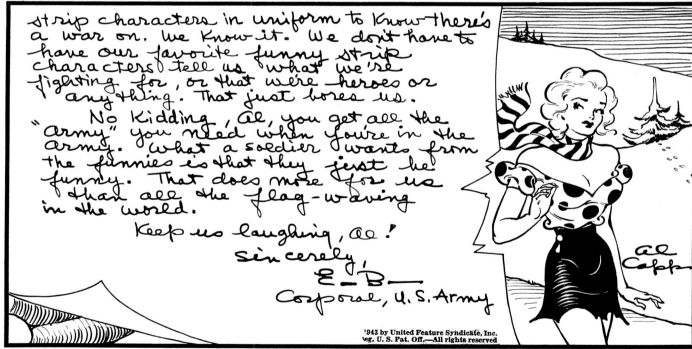

LI'L ABNER daily strip by Al Capp. A letter from an army corporal helped Capp explain to his readers why Abner was staying home.
© December 25, 1943, Capp Enterprises, Inc. Courtesy of Art Wood

BARNEY GOOGLE AND SNUFFY SMITH Sunday page by Billy DeBeck. After Snuffy joined the army, his fellow "yardbirds" came up with this catchy tune.
© October 19, 1941, King Features Syndicate, Inc. Courtesy of the International Museum of Cartoon Art

BARNEY GOOGLE AND SNUFFY SMITH daily strip by Billy DeBeck. Snuffy takes an important message from Winston Churchill.
© 1941 King Features Syndicate, Inc. Courtesy of Art Wood

JOE PALOOKA daily strip by Ham Fisher. Joe was fighting against the Nazis in Yugoslavia when he encountered a female partisan fighter in this wartime episode. © August 14, 1943, McNaught Syndicate, Inc. Courtesy of Jim Scancarelli

BARNEY BAXTER Sunday page by Frank Miller. Barney and Gus battle a Japanese fleet sailing toward the Suez Canal.
© January 3, 1943, King Features Syndicate, Inc. Courtesy of Peter Myer

BUZ SAWYER daily strip no. 15 by Roy Crane. An early example of Crane's second major comic strip creation. © 1943 King Features Syndicate, Inc. Courtesy of Jim Scancarelli

BUZ SAWYER daily strip by Roy Crane. Buz hears the news of the Japanese surrender. © August 28, 1945, King Features Syndicate, Inc. Courtesy of King Features Syndicate

BUZ SAWYER daily strips by Roy Crane. The war veteran returns home. © October 4 and 5, 1945, King Features Syndicate, Inc. Courtesy of King Features Syndicate

TILLIE THE TOILER Sunday page by Russ Westover. Tillie joined the Women's Army Auxiliary Corps before her boyfriend, Mac, signed up. © September 6, 1942, King Features Syndicate, Inc. Courtesy of the International Museum of Cartoon Art

VESTA WEST Sunday page by Ray Bailey. Vesta gets a letter from a friend who is serving with the Women's Army Auxiliary Corps.
© April 4, 1943, Tribune Media Services, Inc. All rights reserved. Reprinted with permission. Courtesy of the International Museum of Cartoon Art

TERRY AND THE PIRATES daily strip by Milton Caniff. Terry is far from home on Christmas Day.
© December 25, 1943, Tribune Media Services, Inc. All rights reserved. Reprinted with permission. Courtesy of Bruce Hamilton

DRAFTIE daily strip by Paul Fogarty (writer) and William Juhre (artist). Lem and Oinie do their part in this wartime feature.
© March 27, 1944, John F. Dille Company. Courtesy of Bill Janocha

TIM TYLER'S LUCK Sunday page by Lyman Young. Tim and his buddies were still fighting the Japanese after the war had ended.
© September 30, 1945, King Features Syndicate, Inc. Courtesy of King Features Syndicate

"Th' hell this ain't th' most important hole in th' world. I'm in it."

"Wisht somebody would tell me there's a Santa Claus."

UP FRONT daily panels by Bill Mauldin. The artist won the Pulitzer Prize for his war cartoons in 1945.
© 1944 and 1945 United Feature Syndicate, Inc.

"You'll git over it, Joe. Oncet I wuz gonna write a book exposin' th' Army after th' war, myself."

V-E Day
"Th' hell with it. I ain't standin' up till he does!"

TERRY AND THE PIRATES *daily strip by Milton Caniff. The artist drew a strip for the Camp Newspaper Service that initially starred Burma.*
© October 18, 1942, Tribune Media Services, Inc. All rights reserved. Reprinted with permission. Courtesy of the Milton Caniff Collection, The Ohio State University Cartoon Research Library

MALE CALL *daily strip by Milton Caniff. Miss Lace, who replaced Burma, received many letters from adoring GIs.* © October 10, 1943, by Milton Caniff. Courtesy of Art Wood

MALE CALL *daily strip by Milton Caniff. The female anatomy was a Caniff specialty.* © August 20, 1944, by Milton Caniff. Courtesy of the Milton Caniff Collection, The Ohio State University Cartoon Research Library

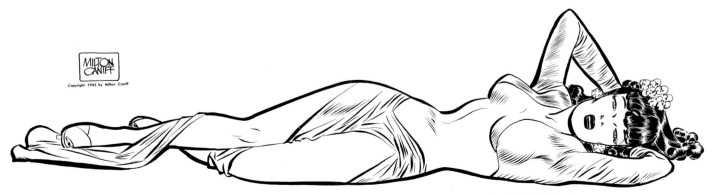

MALE CALL *daily strip by Milton Caniff. Some of Caniff's ideas, such as this one, were rejected.* © 1943 by Milton Caniff. Courtesy of the Milton Caniff Collection, The Ohio State University Cartoon Research Library

ENLISTED MAN'S RAG

THE SAD SACK cartoons by Sergeant George Baker. Two examples of Baker's popular series, which ran in Yank magazine during the war. © c. 1942, Sad Sack Inc.

SEX HYGIENE

"Stars and Stripes newspaper? I think I gotta news
item for you."

"Gee . . . ! I was always SURE I'd be dancin' with joy
when I left the Army . . . but . . . I feel kinda funny
instead . . ."

SUPERMAN daily strip by Jerry Siegel and Joe Shuster. This wartime episode was probably drawn by Wayne Boring.
© 1942 Superman™ and © DC Comics. All rights reserved. Used with permission. Courtesy of Craig Englund

HAVE YOU SEEN *Wonder Woman* ?

KING FEATURES SYNDICATE

TO THE RESCUE Costumed crimefighters and adventure heroes continued to invade the funnies pages during the war years. Superman battled the Nazis, and strips starring Batman and Wonder Woman were launched. Comic heroines joined their male counterparts as the strong-armed Rosie the Riveter became a national icon for female empowerment. Soldiers, aviators, cowboys, ape-men, and space rangers dominated the genre, and even journalists joined the ranks of adventure strip characters.

WONDER WOMAN promotional drawing for the syndicated strip written by William Moulton Marsten and illustrated by H. G. Peter. The newspaper strip lasted only a year. © April 29, 1944, Wonder Woman™ and © DC Comics. All rights reserved. Used with permission. Courtesy of Editor & Publisher

BATMAN AND ROBIN debut strip by Bob Kane. Artists on this strip, which ran for three years, included Jack Burnley and Dick Sprang.
© October 25, 1943, Batman™ and © DC Comics. All rights reserved. Used with permission

SUPERMAN recolored Sunday page by Wayne Boring. An episode of Superman's "Service for Servicemen" campaign.

BATMAN AND ROBIN recolored Sunday page by Bob Kane. The first page of the BATMAN Sunday feature.

MISS FURY *Sunday page by Tarpe Mills. Marla Drake dons her black leopard-skin costume to fight the Nazis.* © 1943 Bell Syndicate, Inc. Courtesy of Peter Maresca.

SPARKY WATTS daily strip by Gordon "Boody" Rogers. A former assistant to Zack Mosley on SMILIN' JACK, Rogers created this superhero spoof in the early 1940s. © July 31, 1940s, Frank Jay Markey Syndicate. Courtesy of Craig Yoe

THE SHADOW daily strip by Vernon Greene. A comic strip starring the mystery man popularized in pulp fiction and radio began in 1940.
© 1940s Ledger Syndicate, Inc. Courtesy of the International Museum of Cartoon Art

FLASH GORDON daily strip by Austin Briggs. Alex Raymond's assistant drew the FLASH GORDON daily strip from its debut on May 27, 1940, until June 1944.
© October 23, 1943, King Features Syndicate, Inc. Courtesy of Bill Janocha

JOHNNY HAZARD daily strip by Frank Robbins. This wartime adventure feature started on June 5, 1944, the day before D-Day.
© December 27, 1944, King Features Syndicate, Inc. Courtesy of Jim Scancarelli

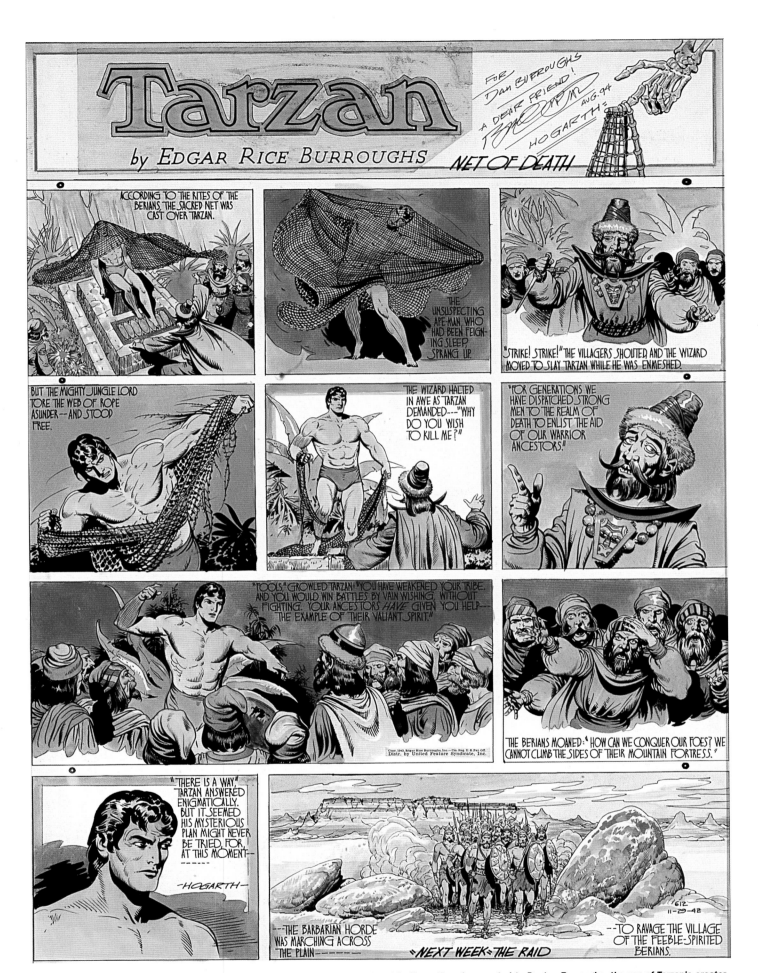

TARZAN hand-colored Sunday page by Burne Hogarth. This original was colored by Hogarth and presented to Danton Burroughs, the son of Tarzan's creator, in 1994. Hogarth illustrated the feature from 1937 to 1950, with the exception of two years between 1945 and 1947.

© November 29, 1942, United Feature Syndicate, Inc. Courtesy of Bruce Hamilton

KING OF THE ROYAL MOUNTED Sunday page by Zane Grey (writer) and Jim Gary (artist). Sergeant King was a Canadian Mountie who always got his man. He was frequently accompanied by Betty Blake and her brother Kid. © January 23, 1944, King Features Syndicate, Inc. Courtesy of King Features Syndicate

KING OF THE ROYAL MOUNTED consecutive daily strips by Zane Grey (writer) and Allen Dean (artist). This northwestern adventure strip was scripted by the famed western novelist Zane Grey. The Sunday page was launched on February 17, 1935, and a daily version followed a year later.
© March 9 and 10, 1937, King Features Syndicate, Inc. Courtesy of King Features Syndicate

BRONCHO BILL

by Harry O'Neill

WANTED

GRAY EAGLE, THE CRAFTY INDIAN CHIEF, TRAPPED THE RED WARRIOR WHO STOLE BILL'S HORSE AND THE BOYS' PLEADINGS IN BEHALF OF THE SCOUNDREL DID NOT SAVE HIM FROM PUNISHMENT

UGH! CHIEF THANKUM PALEFACE MUCH FOR GIFT OF HEAP FINE HORSES —

FAREWELL, HONORABLE GRAY EAGLE AND FAIR PRINCESS!

THERE WERE TEARS IN THE EYES OF MAID O'THE SUN, AS BILL HEADED BACK ACROSS THE BIG HORNS, FOR SHERIDAN AND HOME

A SUDDEN MOUNTAIN STORM DROVE BILL INTO THE MOUTH OF AN APPARENTLY DESERTED CAVE, AROUND WHICH THE HOWLING WIND MADE WAILING SOUNDS LIKE A HUMAN VOICE —

BILL DID NOT KNOW HIS PRESENCE HAD HALTED THE RETURN OF A DEMENTED DWELLER —

THE RAIN OVER, AS SUDDENLY AS IT STARTED, HE MOUNTED TO RESUME HIS JOURNEY, AS A BULLET WHIZZED PAST HIS EAR

SPOTTING THE MARKSMAN, BILL RETURNED THE FIRE, AIMING NOT TO KILL —

LOCOED HERMIT, I RECKON — GIDDAP, BLACKIE! LET'S GET GOING!

Copr. 1941 by United Feature Syndicate, Inc.
Tm. Reg. U. S. Pat. Off.—All rights reserved

REACHING HOME PAST HIS BIRTHDAY, THE BOY FOUND A SMALL CELEBRATION AWAITING HIM —

BILL'S NEW OUTFIT MET WITH THE HEARTY APPROVAL OF ALL

COME ON! BLACKIE'S WAITING, PROUD AS A PEACOCK, IN HIS NEW SADDLE!

AMONG MANY PRESENTS RECEIVED, NELL GAVE HIM AN ENTIRE NEW COWBOY ATTIRE —

GEE! THANKS, NELL!

HURRY AND PUT 'EM ON, UNCLE BILL — THE SHERIFF'S WAITIN' T'SEE YUH, IN TOWN

THAT'S WHY SHERIFF ROGERS WANTS TO SEE YOU — OLD MAN JAMISON MADE OFF WITH A LITTLE CHILD

GREAT SCOTT! I JUST SAW THAT MAN — I THOUGHT I HEARD A HUMAN VOICE AT THAT CAVE —

NEXT WEEK — FUR AND FEATHERS

BRONCHO BILL Sunday page by Harry O'Neill. One of the earliest western features, BRONCHO BILL debuted in 1928 as YOUNG BUFFALO BILL and was produced by O'Neill until 1950. © May 4, 1941, United Feature Syndicate, Inc. Courtesy of Jack Gilbert

FOREIGN CORRESPONDENT daily strip by Charles Raab. An acquaintance and admirer of Milton Caniff, Raab worked on *TERRY AND THE PIRATES*, *CHARLIE CHAN*, and *ADVENTURES OF PATSY* before trying to launch his own creation, *FOREIGN CORRESPONDENT*, in 1943.
c. 1943. Courtesy of the International Museum of Cartoon Art

FLYING JENNY story recap strip by Russell Keaton. This feature, which debuted in October 1939, was the first strip to star a female aviator.
© November 6, 1939, Bell Syndicate, Inc. Courtesy of Denis Kitchen

HAP HOOPER, WASHINGTON CORRESPONDENT daily strip by William Laas (writer) and Jack Sparling (artist). Hap, who made his first appearance on January 29, 1940, worked as a newspaper reporter and hunted spies during the war. © May 12, 1942, United Feature Syndicate, Inc. Courtesy of Ethan Roberts

INVISIBLE SCARLET O'NEIL daily strip by Russell Stamm. A former assistant to Chester Gould, Stamm introduced Scarlet, who had the ability to become invisible, to newspaper readers on June 3, 1940. © March 17, 1942, Chicago Times, Inc. Courtesy of Russ Cochran

BRENDA STARR Sunday half-page by Dale Messick. This lady reporter, who made her first appearance on June 30, 1940, was a fiery redhead with a short temper. © June 1, 1941, Tribune Media Services, Inc. All rights reserved. Reprinted with permission. Courtesy of Sandy Schechter

MARY WORTH Sunday page by Allen Saunders (writer) and Ken Ernst (artist). Ernst and Saunders renamed APPLE MARY in 1944, after the feature had been transformed into the prototypical modern soap opera strip. © December 17, 1944, Publishers Syndicate. Courtesy of Russ Cochran

BARNABY—The first four daily strips by Crockett Johnson. This streamlined strip, which debuted in the liberal New York tabloid PM on April 20, 1942, starred a little boy and his imaginary fairy godfather, Mr. O'Malley. It was embraced by artists, writers, and intellectuals but lasted only a decade.
© April 20, 21, 22, and 23, 1942, Field Publications

COMIC RELIEF

Launching a feature in the midst of a world war was a risky proposition, but the syndicates were still determined to develop new talent in the early 1940s. Although the serious mood of the nation was more conducive to adventure and story strips, daily laughs were also needed. A handful of creators came up with features that had little to do with the armed services but contributed to the cause by providing a welcome respite from the grim realities of the global conflict.

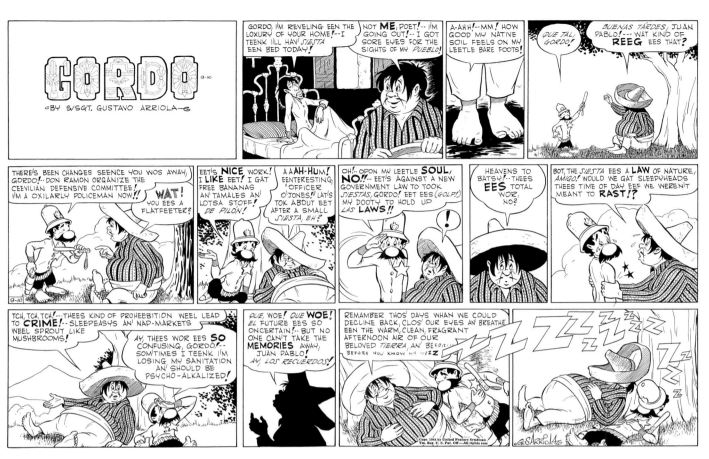

GORDO Sunday page by Gus Arriola. Gordo Lopez, who made his debut on November 24, 1941, was a fat, lazy Mexican dirt farmer from the tiny village of Del Monte. After a six-month hiatus, Arriola managed to continue his Sunday page while serving in the army during the war.
© September 10, 1944, United Feature Syndicate, Inc. Courtesy of the International Museum of Cartoon Art

BUGS BUNNY Sunday page by Roger Armstrong. The star of the Warner Bros. Studio got his own Sunday feature on January 10, 1943. A daily strip followed in 1946. © October 24, 1943, Warner Bros. Entertainment Inc. Courtesy of Russ Cochran

THEY'LL DO IT EVERY TIME daily panel by Jimmy Hatlo. This popular panel debuted in the San Francisco Call-Bulletin in 1929 and was nationally syndicated beginning on May 4, 1936.
© December 24, 1937, King Features Syndicate, Inc. Courtesy of King Features Syndicate

LITTLE IODINE daily panel by Jimmy Hatlo. A regular character in THEY'LL DO IT EVERY TIME, Hatlo's little brat became the star of her own feature on July 4, 1943. © 1943 King Features Syndicate, Inc. Courtesy of King Features Syndicate

JIMMY HATLO—Self-caricature from Comics and Their Creators. © 1942

THE FLOP FAMILY by SWAN-o

THE FLOP FAMILY daily panel by George Swanson. The creator of SALESMAN SAM and ELZA POPPIN launched a new feature, drawn in his trademark screwball style, on August 29, 1943. © September 26, 1943, King Features Syndicate, Inc. Courtesy of the International Museum of Cartoon Art

FRED LASSWELL—Self-caricature. c. 1945. Courtesy of Mark Cohen

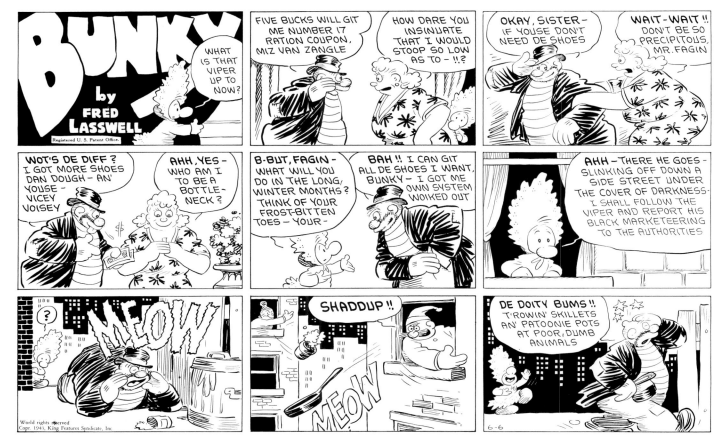

BUNKY Sunday half-page by Fred Lasswell. After Billy DeBeck died on November 11, 1942, his assistant, Fred Lasswell, took over both BARNEY GOOGLE AND SNUFFY SMITH and its companion feature, BUNKY. Wearing his baby bonnet, Bunker Hill Jr. wandered the world with his unsavory companion, Fagin, in search of adventure. © June 6, 1943, King Features Syndicate, Inc. Courtesy of Jim Scancarelli

will eisner

THE SPIRIT WAS THE STAR of a sixteen-page weekly comic magazine that was syndicated to newspapers from 1940 to 1952. The creator of this masked crime fighter was the only artist to successfully adapt the comic book format to the Sunday funnies.

Will Eisner was born in Brooklyn on March 6, 1917, the son of Jewish immigrants. He discovered comics when he worked as a newsboy on Wall Street. "To me art, being a syndicated cartoonist, represented a way out of the ghetto," Eisner remembered.

After graduating from De Witt Clinton High School in the Bronx, he attended classes at the Art Students League. He also worked in a printshop, got a night job at the *New York American,* and was the art director for *Eve* magazine, which folded shortly after he was fired.

In 1936, after selling a few of his strips to a struggling comics magazine, he teamed up with Jerry Iger and opened one of the first successful comic book art shops. With a staff that eventually reached twenty (including Bob Kane, Jack Kirby, and Lou Fine), the shop turned out fifteen comic books a month. In addition to selling their work to publishers like Quality, Fiction House, and Fox, they produced comics in a Sunday-page format for foreign clients.

In 1939, Everett "Busy" Arnold of Quality approached Eisner with an offer to design a comic book for newspaper syndication. Eisner terminated his partnership with Iger and created *The Weekly Comic Book* (also known as *The Spirit Section*), which was distributed by the Register and Tribune Syndicate and debuted on June 2, 1940. Eisner wrote and illustrated the seven-page lead feature, *The Spirit,* and developed the two backup series, *Lady Luck* and *Mr. Mystic.*

Eisner's creation became the testing ground for his experiments in page layout, atmospheric rendering, and dramatic scripting. "Surreal perspectives and lighting effects gave *The Spirit* a compelling aura of mystery," wrote Catherine Yronwode in *The Art of Will Eisner.* "This was augmented by Eisner's seemingly obsessive desire to draw water in all its forms, from rain-swept streets to fog-enshrouded, rotting wharves. The graphic close-ups of brutal violence, carefully off-set by bouts of slapstick comedy and sexual innuendo, left the reader in a constant state of emotional and aesthetic surprise."

A daily comic strip version of *The Spirit* was launched on October 13, 1941, but it was not the ideal vehicle for Eisner's talents, and it ended in 1944. "The problem is that it's such a confining operation," Eisner explained. "I couldn't be as imaginative or do all the things I wanted to do. I'm a great experimenter—I get my kicks from experimenting and breaking

WILL EISNER—Self-caricature. © *1974 by Will Eisner*

down walls—and there was no 'elbow room' in a daily strip. It was like conducting a symphony in a telephone booth."

After serving in the army from 1942 to 1945, Eisner resumed work on *The Spirit,* which other artists had continued in his absence. Between December 23, 1945, and August 12, 1951, Eisner had a hand in all of the weekly episodes and was at the peak of his creative powers. The series ended in 1952, after he turned the work over to assistants.

For the next sixteen years, Eisner operated a commercial studio that produced instructional comics for a wide range of clients, including the Department of Labor and New York Telephone. In 1978, he published *A Contract with God and Other Tenement Stories.* The four illustrated vignettes in the 192-page book were based on Eisner's experiences growing up during the Depression in the Bronx. The sixty-one-year-old cartoonist had discovered a new format—the graphic novel—to further explore the potential for personal expression in the comics medium.

THE SPIRIT—Portrait by Will Eisner. © *1974 by Will Eisner*

SELF PORTRAIT

May 3, 1942

THE SPIRIT comic page by Will Eisner. In one of the last stories he did before joining the army, Eisner pictured himself at the drawing board.
© May 3, 1942, and 1974 by Will Eisner. Courtesy of Will Eisner

THE SPIRIT splash page by Will Eisner. The artist did not want his lead character to be a costumed superhero, but he added the mask to pacify his publisher. © August 25, 1940, and 1974 by Will Eisner. Courtesy of Will Eisner

© Copyright 1974, Will Eisner

THE SPIRIT splash page by Will Eisner. "At the Prom" is one of only two known original pages to have survived from Eisner's prewar period. © December 1, 1940, 1974 by Will Eisner. Courtesy of Denis Kitchen

THE SPIRIT daily strip by Will Eisner. While Eisner served in the army from 1942 to 1945, the daily strip was drawn by Jack Cole and Lou Fine.
© December 25, 1943, and 1974 by Will Eisner. Courtesy of Art Wood

ACKNOWLEDGMENTS

The author would like to thank the following individuals and organizations for their invaluable assistance in producing this book:

Individuals: Bill Alger, Rob Andrews, David Applegate, David Astor, Ralph Bakshi, Bob Beerbohm, Ed Black, Bill Blackbeard, John Canemaker, John Carlin, Jim Carlsson, Alfredo Castelli, Russ Cochran, Bill Crouch, Jerry Dumas, Will Eisner, Craig Englund, John Fawcett, Gill Fox, Jim Gauthier, Jack Gilbert, Marty Goldman, Carole Goodman, Ian Gordon, Ron Goulart, Bruce Hamilton, R. C. Harvey, Tom Heintjes, Todd Hignite, Eric Himmel, Jud Hurd, Tom Inge, Bill Janocha, Mark Johnson, Denis Kitchen, Charlie Kochman, Francisco Lopez, Howard Lowery, Joe and Nadia Mannarino, Peter Maresca, Richard Marschall, Ricardo Martinez, Matt Masterson, Patrick McDonnell, Joe McGuckin, Peter Merolo, Peter Myer, Angelo Nobile, Richard Olson, Frank Pauer, Trina Robbins, Ethan Roberts, Jim Scancarelli, Sandy Schechter, Richard Slovak, Gary Smith, John Snyder, Art Spiegelman, David Stanford, Rob Stolzer, Mort and Catherine Walker, Neal Walker, Eugene Walters, Morris Weiss, Doug Wheeler, Jason Whiton, Malcolm Whyte, Mark Winchester, Art Wood, and Craig Yoe.

Syndicates: King Features—Jim Cavett, Mark Johnson, Jay Kennedy, Karen Moy, and Claudia Smith. Tribune Media Services—Jan Bunch and Lee Hall. United Media—Maura Peters.

Organizations and institutions: American Color—Andy Olsen. Boston University—Dr. Howard Gotlieb, Sean Noel, and J. C. Johnson. Cartoon Art Museum—Jenny Robb Dietzen and Andrew Farago. Cartoon Research Library, Ohio State University—Lucy Shelton Caswell and Marilyn Scott. Frye Art Museum—Richard West. Illustration House—Roger Reed and Walt Reed. International Museum of Cartoon Art—Stephen Charla, Alexis Faro, and Jeanne Greever. Library of Congress—Sara Duke. Periodyssey—Richard West. Syracuse University—Carolyn Davis. University of Nebraska Sheldon Memorial Art Gallery—Dan Siedell.

ARTICLES

The following comics-related periodicals were used for general research:

Cartoonews. Published six times a year from April 1975 to 1980 by Jim Ivey, Orlando.

Cartoonist PROfiles. 146 issues were published quarterly between March 1969 and June 2005 by Cartoonist PROfiles, Inc. 281 Bayberry Lane, Westport, CT 06430.

Cartoons Magazine. Published monthly from January 1912 to June 1921 by H. H. Windsor, Chicago.

Circulation. Published from 1921 to 1926 (or later) by King Features Syndicate. Only twelve different issues of this rare magazine are known to exist.

Comic Art. Published since fall 2002 (now annually) by Buenaventura Press, P.O. Box 23661, Oakland, CA 94623.

Comic Book Marketplace. Issues #1–#120 published between 1991 and 2005 by Gemstone Publishing, P.O. Box 469, West Plains, MO 65775.

Comic Buyer's Guide. Published monthly by F + W Publications, Inc. 700 E. State St., Iola, WI 54990.

The Comics Journal. Published (now monthly) since January 1977 by Fantagraphics Books, Inc., 7563 Lake City Way N.E., Seattle, WA 98115.

Editor & Publisher. Published monthly by BPI Communications, Inc. 770 Broadway, New York, NY 10003.

Hogan's Alley. Published (now annually) since autumn 1994 by Bull Moose Publishing Corp., P.O. Box 4784, Atlanta, GA 30362.

Inks. Twelve issues were published, three times a year, between February 1994 and November 1997 by the Ohio State University Press, 1070 Carmack Road, Columbus, OH 43110.

Nemo. Thirty-two issues were published between June 1983 and January 1992 by Fantagraphic Books, Inc. 7563 Lake City Way N.E., Seattle, WA 98115.

The R.F. Outcault Reader. The Official Newsletter of the R.F. Outcault Society. Published quarterly from March 1991 (vol. 1, no. 1) to December 1999 (vol. 9, no. 4). Richard Olson, editor.

The World of Comic Art. Published quarterly from June 1966 to March 1972 by World of Comic Art Publications, P.O. Box 507, Hawthorne, CA 90250.

GENERAL HISTORIES

Alder, Eric. "100 Years of Laughter." *Kansas City Star/ Charlotte Observer,* May 5, 1995.

Caniff, Milton. "Don't Laugh at the Comics." *Cosmopolitan,* November 1958.

Daviss, Bennett. "World of Funnies Is 'Warped with Fancy, Woofed with Dreams.'" *Smithsonian,* November 1987.

DeLeon, Clark. "A Century of Comics." *Philadelphia Inquirer,* April 30, 1995.

Dunn, William. "The Funnies as Fine Art." *The Detroit News Magazine,* March 22, 1981.

Feiffer, Jules (guest editor, special edition). "Comic Rave." *Civilization,* July 1998.

Folkman, David. "The Great Cartoonists of the Century." *Liberty,* winter 1973.

"Funnies Man: Ernie McGee." *Cincinnati Pictorial Enquirer,* Oct. 20, 1957.

Kelly, Walt. "The Funnies Are Relevant." *The Fort Mudge Most #75,* 2001.

Kogan, Rick. "Tales from the Strips." *Chicago Tribune,* Feb. 9, 1995.

Lewis, Boyd. "The Comics—Still Alive at 75." *Chicago Tribune,* Nov. 14, 1971.

Maltin, Leonard. "A Fond Look at the Sunday Funnies." *Diversion,* July 1982.

Marschall, Richard. "Comic Masters." *Horizon,* July 1980.

———. "100 Years of the Funnies." *American History,* October 1995.

Murray, Will (principal historian), and Kim Howard Johnson (contributing writer). "100 Years of Comics" (special edition). *Starlog Millennium 2000 Series,* 2000.

Precker, Michael. "Comic Relief." *Dallas Morning News,* April 8, 1995.

Rizzo, Frank. "AJC Comics Week." *Atlanta Journal-Constitution,* Sept. 21-27, 2003.

"75 Years of American Newspaper Comics." *The American Legion Magazine,* December 1971.

Sheridan, Martin. "Comics and Their Creators." *Literary Digest,* 1930s. Included in this series were short profiles of Gene Ahearn, Merrill Blosser, Robert M. Brinkerhoff, Gene Byrnes, Percy L. Crosby, Billy DeBeck, Bill Dwyer, Vic Forsythe, Rube Goldberg, Milt Gross, Johnny Gruelle, Edgar E. Martin, J. Carver Pusey, Otto Soglow, Cliff Sterrett, H. T. Webster, and J. R. Williams.

Updike, John. "Lost Art." *The New Yorker,* Dec. 15, 1997.

Walker, Brian. "100 Years of the Sunday Funnies: Part 1, 1895-1945." *Collectors' Showcase,* vol. 15, no. 2, April/May 1995.

NOTES

The following articles and books were quoted directly or referred to for specific facts. The listings are by chapter and subject, in order of appearance.

INTRODUCTION

The Yellow Kid: Blackbeard, Bill. "First Balloon Trip to the Rainbow: Outcault's Accidental (and Unnoticed) Invention of the Comic Strip (1896)." *Comic Buyer's Guide #1143,* Oct. 13, 1995.

Canemaker, John. "The Kid from Hogan's Alley." *The New York Times Book Review,* Dec. 17, 1995.

Dreiser, Theodore. "A Metropolitan Favorite: Something About R. F. Outcault, the 'Yellow Kid' and 'Hogan's Alley.'" *Ev'ry Month,* vol. 3, no. 2, Nov. 1, 1896.

Harvey, R. C. "The Origin of a New Species." *Cartoonist PROfiles #105,* March 1995.

Kanfer, Stefan. "From the Yellow Kid to Yellow Journalism." *Civilization,* May/June 1995.

Maeder, Jay. "Polychromous Effulgence: R.F. Outcault." *New York Daily News,* April 25, 1999.

Marschall, Richard. "Shibboleths: Exploding Myths, Looking for New Origins, Redefining Our Terms: The Advent of the Comic Strip." *The Comics Journal #68,* 1982.

McCardell, Roy L. "Opper, Outcault and Company." *Everybody's Magazine,* June 1905.

Olson, Richard D. "R.F. Outcault: The Father of the Comics." *Collectors' Showcase,* vol. 15, no. 2, April/May 1995.

———. "Richard Fenton Outcault's Yellow Kid." *Inks,* vol. 2, no. 3, November 1995.

Outcault, Richard. "How the Yellow Kid Was Born." *New York World,* May 1, 1898.

Reilly, Jim. "The Yellow Kid." *Syracuse Herald American,* April 19, 1992.

Color printing: "Working Colors on Each Other." *American Pressman,* June 1893.

Jimmy Swinnerton: "Sprightly Comics Really Middle-Aged." *Editor & Publisher,* July 21, 1934.

Early comics: Harvey, R. C. "More New Historic Beginnings for Comics." *The Comics Journal* #246, September 2002.

Paviat, Eric. "Proto-Comics: Comics Before Newspaper Strips." *Comic Buyer's Guide* #1129, July 7, 1995.

Robb, Jenny E. "The Lineage of the Newspaper Comic Strip from Hogarth to Howarth." In *Before the Yellow Kid: Precursors of the American Newspaper Comic Strip.* Columbus: The Ohio State University Libraries, 1995.

Wheeler, Doug. "Comic Strips Before the Yellow Kid." *Comic Buyer's Guide* #1525, Feb. 7, 2003.

Wheeler, Doug, Robert L. Beerbohm, and Richard D. Olson. "The Victorian Age Before the Yellow Kid: American Comics of the 19th Century." *The Official Overstreet Comic Book Price Guide* (33rd ed.). Timonium, Md.: Gemstone Publishing, 2003.

Wheeler, Doug, Robert L. Beerbohm, and Leonardo De Sa. "Topffer in America" and "The Myth of the Yellow Kid." *Comic Art* #3, summer 2003.

Hearst and Pulitzer (articles in chronological order): "W.R. Hearst Here." *The Fourth Estate,* Oct. 10, 1895.

"Money Well Spent." *The Fourth Estate,* Jan. 30, 1896.

"The Journal's Rapid Strides." *The Fourth Estate,* Oct. 22, 1896.

Collings, James L. "Personalities and Piracy in Early Syndicate Days." *Editor & Publisher,* June 27, 1959.

Turner, Hy. "This Was Park Row!" *Editor & Publisher,* June 27, 1959.

Yellow journalism: Campbell, Joseph W. *Yellow Journalism: Puncturing Myths, Defining Legacies.* Praeger, 2001.

Winchester, Mark D. "Hully Gee, It's a War!!!" *Inks,* vol. 2, no. 3, November 1995.

THE TURN OF THE CENTURY

Sunday papers (articles in chronological order): "What Americans Read." *The Fourth Estate,* April 19, 1894.

"The Sunday Newspaper" (editorial). *Editor & Publisher,* April 5, 1902.

"Brief Historical Review of American Sunday Journalism." *Editor & Publisher,* Oct. 27, 1917.

Lee, James Melvin. "Story of the First Sunday Newspapers Published in America." *Editor & Publisher,* Oct. 3, 1925.

McCaleb, Kenneth. "Every Exciting Sunday." *Editor & Publisher,* June 27, 1959.

Harvey, R. C. "Fine-Tuning the Form." *Cartoonist PROfiles* #106, June 1995.

Barker, Kenneth S. "The Comic Series of the New York Sunday Herald and the New York Sunday Tribune." *Inks,* vol. 3, no. 2, May 1996.

Beerbohm, Robert L., Doug Wheeler, and Richard D. Olson. "The Platinum Age: 1897–1938." *The Official Overstreet Comic Book Price Guide* (33rd ed.). Timonium, Md.: Gemstone Publishing, 2003.

Syndicates: Lewis, Boyd. "The Syndicates and How They Grew." *Saturday Review,* Dec. 11, 1971.

Marschall, Richard. "A History of Newspaper Syndication." In *The World Encyclopedia of Comics.* Philadelphia: Chelsea House Publishers, 1999.

Protests (articles in chronological order): "Against Sunday Papers." *The Fourth Estate,* April 5, 1894.

"War on Sunday Newspapers." *The Fourth Estate,* July 19, 1894.

"Comic Supplement." *Editor & Publisher,* June 16, 1906.

"Sunday Paper's Sins." *Editor & Publisher,* Nov. 2, 1907.

"Comic Supplement." *Editor & Publisher,* Sept. 19, 1908.

"Defense of Comics." *Editor & Publisher,* Oct. 3, 1908.

Outcault, R. F. "End of Comics: Artist Predicts Passing of the Feature Which He Made Famous." *Editor & Publisher,* Jan. 16, 1909.

"Comic Supplements: League for Their Improvement Discusses Subject at Mass Meeting." *Editor & Publisher,* April 8, 1911.

Bevona, Donald E. "First Sunday Editions Had No Place in Home." *Editor & Publisher,* June 27, 1959.

Nyberg, Amy Kiste. "Percival Chubb and the League for the Improvement of the Children's Comic Supplement." *Inks,* vol. 3, no. 3, November 1996.

Harvey, Robert C. "When Comics Were for Kids." *The Comics Journal* (special edition), winter 2002.

Buster Brown court case (articles in chronological order): "The Buster Brown Affair." *Editor & Publisher,* Dec. 9, 1905.

"Buster Is in Court." *Editor & Publisher,* Feb. 17, 1906.

"'Buster Brown' Injunction." *Editor & Publisher,* March 31, 1906.

Winchester, Mark D. "Litigation and Early Comic Strips: The Lawsuits of Outcault, Dirks and Fisher." *Inks,* vol. 2, no. 2, May 1995.

Early pioneers: Fried, Alan. "Lyonel Feininger: A Kinder, Gentler Comic Strip." *Inks,* vol. 3, no. 3, November 1996.

Gordon, Ian. "Laying the Foundation" (F. M. Howarth). *Hogan's Alley* #9, summer 2001.

Johnson, Mark. "The Two Worlds of Danny Dreamer." *Nemo* #7, June 1984.

———. "The Pioneer and Satire Strip Hairbreadth Harry." *Nemo* #14, August 1985.

———. "Hairbreadth Harry, Our Forgotten Hero." *Battle for Belinda.* Hairbreadth Harry exhibition catalog. Philadelphia: Federal Reserve Bank, 1987.

———. "The Outbursts of Everett True." *Nemo* #26, September 1987.

Lawson, Helen. "The Katzenjammers' Secret" (H. H. Knerr). *Circulation,* vol. 2, no. 9, September 1922.

Marschall, Richard. "The Explorigator: Dreamship of the Universe." *Nemo* #5, February 1984.

———. "George McManus' Pioneer Work of Fantasy: Nibsy the Newsboy." *Nemo* #9, October 1984.

———. "The Forgotten Genius: Gustave Verbeek." *Nemo* #10, December 1984.

———. "The Force Was with Him: The Escapades of Slim Jim." *Nemo* #11, May 1985.

O'Gara, Gil. "Schultze's 'Foxy Grandpa.'" *Comic Buyer's Guide,* Nov. 28, 1986.

Robbins, Trina. "Women and Children First." *Inks,* vol. 2, no. 3, November 1995.

Spiegelman, Art. "Art Every Sunday" (Lyonel Feininger). *The New York Times Book Review,* Oct. 2, 1994.

Straut, Jessie Kahles, and Phil Love. "C.W. Kahles . . . Most Neglected Genius." *Cartoonist PROfiles* #31, September 1976.

First daily strip: Fisher, Bud. "Confessions of a Cartoonist." *The Saturday Evening Post,* four-part article, July 28 and Aug. 4, 11, and 18, 1928.

Harvey, R. C. "Bud Fisher and the Daily Comic Strip." *Inks,* vol. 1, no. 1, February 1994.

Rogers, Bogart. "Hero of San Francisco." *The American Mercury,* December 1954.

Richard F. Outcault: Campbell, Gordon. "The Yellow Kid/Buster Brown." *Cartoonist PROfiles* #51, September 1981.

Hake, Ted. "Buster Brown: America's First Comic Salesman." *Collectibles Monthly,* July 1977.

Hancock, La Touche. "American Caricature and Comic Art." *The Bookman,* November 1902.

Marschall, Richard. "Buster Brown: The Bad Boy Who Made Good." Introduction to *Buster Brown.* Westport, Conn.: Hyperion Press, 1977.

Rudolph Dirks: Blackbeard, Bill. "Max, Maurice and Willie." *Nemo* #2, August 1983.

Dirks, John. "Rudolph Dirks." *Cartoonist PROfiles* #23, September 1974.

Dirks, Rudolph. "Katzenjammer Kids Creator Reveals Rise of Comics." *The Open Road,* January 1950.

Frederick B. Opper: Campbell, Gordon. "Frederick Opper." *Cartoonist PROfiles* #45, March 1980.

Clarke, Penelope. "Mr. Frederick Burr Opper." *Circulation,* vol. 2, no. 9, September 1922.

"F. Opper, Dean of Cartoonists, Dies in Retirement at 82." *Editor & Publisher,* Sept. 4, 1937.

Harvey, R. C. "Who Was Frederick Burr Opper?" *Comics Buyer's Guide* #1154, Dec. 29, 1995.

"Leading Cartoonists of America: Frederick Burr Opper." *Editor & Publisher,* July 19, 1913.

Marschall, Richard. "Opper's Immortal Tramp." Introduction to *Happy Hooligan.* Westport, Conn.: Hyperion Press, 1977.

"Opper of 'The Old Guard.'" *The Dead-Line,* vol. 1, no. 1, September 1917.

Outcault, Richard F. "Opper: Fifty Years a Funmaker." *Circulation,* vol. 5, no. 25, July 1926.

Perry, John. "F. Opper, at 72, Still Working Hard." *Editor & Publisher,* Oct. 12, 1929.

Jimmy Swinnerton: Blackbeard, Bill. "The Man Who Grew Up with the Comics." *Nemo* #22, October 1986.

Campbell, Gordon. "Swinnerton." *Cartoonist PROfiles* #59, September 1983.

"James Swinnerton Dead at 98; Pioneer Newspaper Cartoonist." *New York Times,* Sept. 7, 1974.

Monchak, Stephen J. "Swinnerton Creates New Comic for King Features." *Editor & Publisher,* July 21, 1941.

Phelps, Donald. "Jimmy and Company." *Nemo* #22, October 1986.

Yendis, Beol. "Li'l Ole Bear, M.D." *Circulation,* vol. 5, no. 24, May 1926.

Winsor McCay: Campbell, Gordon. "Winsor McCay." *Cartoonist PROfiles* #46, June 1980.

"Leading Cartoonists of America: Winsor McCay." *Editor & Publisher,* Aug. 2, 1913.

Marschall, Richard. "In His Own Words: Winsor McCay on Life, Art, Animation . . . and the Danger of Greasy Foods." *Nemo* #3, October 1983.

"McCay Leaves Herald." *Editor & Publisher,* June 1, 1911.

"Winsor McCay, Famous Cartoonist and Artist, Dies Suddenly at 63." *Editor & Publisher,* July 28, 1934.

"Winsor McCay: Sketch of the Well-Known Creator of 'Little Nemo.'" *Editor & Publisher,* Dec. 25, 1909.

THE TEENS

Comics business (articles in chronological order): "New Feature Syndicate: M. Koenigsberg Heads New Enterprise." *Editor & Publisher,* Sept. 13, 1913.

Lawler, Will. "The Value of Comics." *Editor & Publisher,* Feb. 21, 1914.

Jackson, Tom. "Katzenjammer Kids: Their Mother Tells E&P Reporter of Hardships." *Editor & Publisher,* June 13, 1914.

"Nation's Laughs Profitable to the Comic Artists." *New York Sun,* May 2, 1915.

Anderson, Isaac. "Why Is a Comic Section?" *Editor & Publisher,* Oct. 27, 1917.

"He Has Originated Hearst Comics for Twenty Years" (Rudolph Block). *Editor & Publisher,* Feb. 8, 1919.

War (articles in chronological order): "New York City Papers Decrease Size to Help Conserve News Print Supply." *Editor & Publisher,* Aug. 5, 1916.

"Two Chief Officers of the Chicago Tribune Enlisted in Nation's Fighting Forces" (Robert McCormick and J. M. Patterson). *Editor & Publisher,* Nov. 10, 1917.

"Donnelly Sees End of Sunday Comics." *Editor & Publisher,* Sept. 14, 1918.

"Premier Cartoonists Work for Liberty Loan." *Editor & Publisher,* Sept. 28, 1918.

"Fontaine Fox Tells His Wife How War Helped Cartoonists." *Editor & Publisher,* Jan. 11, 1919.

"Capt. Joseph Medill Patterson Comes Back from the War to Resume His Important Role in Journalism." *Editor & Publisher,* Feb. 22, 1919.

Animation: Jameson, Martin. "With the Cartoonists in Filmland." *Cartoons,* March 1917.

Cartoonists: "Briggs Brings Skin-nay 'Over' At Last!" *The Dead-Line,* vol. 1, no. 1, September 1917.

Campbell, Gordon. "Briggs." *Cartoonist PROfiles* #53, March 1982.

———. "Fontaine Fox." *Cartoonist PROfiles* #53, March 1982.

———. "Rube Goldberg." *Cartoonist PROfiles* #57, March 1983.

Clark, Arthur "Ted." "The World's Longest Trolley Ride." (Fontaine Fox). *Nemo* #23, December 1986.

———. "Fontaine Fox's Toonerville Trolley." *Cartoonist PROfiles* #113, March 1997.

Corbett James J. "TAD—An Appreciation." *Circulation,* vol. 2, no. 9, September 1922.

Dorgan, T. A. "The Fable of the Sap Who Listened Ahead." *Circulation,* vol. 1, no. 3, July 1921.

Dowhan, Michael W. "Peter Rabbit: Harrison Cady's Masterwork." *Cartoonist PROfiles* #59, September 1983.

"End of the Line" (Fontaine Fox). *Time,* Feb. 21, 1955.

Fox, Fontaine. "A Queer Way to Make a Living." *The Saturday Evening Post,* Feb. 11, 1928.

"Fox Longs for Old Newspaper Days." *Editor & Publisher,* Nov. 9, 1929.

Goldberg, Rube. "Seriously Speaking of Comic Artists." *Circulation,* vol. 2, no. 12, April 1923.

———. "It Happened to a Rube." *The Saturday Evening Post,* Nov. 10, 1928.

———. "Comics, New Style and Old." *The Saturday Evening Post,* Dec. 15, 1928.

"How Sid Smith Got His Own Goat." *The Dead-Line,* vol. 1, no. 1, September 1917.

Ivey, Jim. "Cartooning's Renaissance Man: The Many Comic Inventions of Rube Goldberg." *Nemo* #24, February 1987.

Johnson, Mark. "Squirrel Food" (Gene Ahearn). *Nemo* #25, April 1987.

Kramer, Hilton. "Laughter That Is Close to Tears" (Rube Goldberg). *New York Times,* Jan. 16, 1977.

Langreich, William P. "How the Comickers Regard Their Characters." *Cartoons,* two parts, April and May 1917.

"Leading Cartoonists of America" (profile series). *Editor & Publisher:* Fontaine Fox, May 3, 1913; Rube Goldberg, May 31, 1913.

"Little Tragedies of a Newspaper Office" (profile series). *Editor & Publisher:* Clare Briggs, Aug. 4, 1917; Gene Byrnes, Dec. 29, 1917; Percy Crosby, Nov. 24, 1917; Billy DeBeck, Sept. 22, 1917; Clare Dwiggins, Feb. 16, 1918; Paul Fung, Sept. 8, 1917; Jimmy Murphy, June 16, 1917, and Dec. 18, 1919; Cliff Sterrett, July 14, 1917; H. T. Webster, July 7, 1917; Garr Williams, Feb. 23, 1918.

Marschall, Richard. "The Teenie Weenies." *Nemo* #6, April 1984.

McGeehan. W. O. "The World His Stage, The Studio His Prison" (TAD). *Liberty,* 1925.

McIntire, O. O. "TAD: The Balladeer of Broadway." *Cosmopolitan,* 1926.

Medbury, John P. "The Cartoonist's Mirror" (Rube Goldberg). *Circulation,* vol. 1, no. 4, September 1921.

Mellon, Ben. "Oh Min! Call Chester—Here Comes Our Sid" (Sidney Smith). *Editor & Publisher,* Nov. 11, 1922.

"Press and Sports World Laud TAD in Final Tribute to Genius." *Editor & Publisher,* May 11, 1929.

Resnick, David. "Harry Hershfield, 85 Muses: 'Ish Kabibble!'" *Editor & Publisher,* Oct. 17, 1970.

Smith, Sherwin D. "Fontaine Fox's Toonerville Trolley." *The New York Times Book Review,* Sept. 3, 1972.

Stevens, Parke. "'Abie' with a Past" (Harry Hershfield). *Circulation,* vol. 2, no. 11, March 1923.

Walker, Brian. "A Collection of Cartoons by Thomas Aloysius Dorgan." Exhibition catalog. Port Chester, N.Y.: Museum of Cartoon Art, 1978.

Correspondence courses: Advertisements for the Cartoon School of the Chicago Academy of Fine Arts, the Federal Course in Applied Cartooning, the Landon School of Illustrating and Cartooning, and The W. L. Evans School of Cartooning. *Cartoons,* 1916 to 1918.

Marschall, Richard. "Mail-Order Success!" *Cartoonist PROfiles* #30, June 1976.

Bud Fisher (articles in chronological order): "Big 'Comics' in Court." *Editor & Publisher,* Aug. 7, 1915.

"Fisher's Right to 'Mutt and Jeff' Upheld." *Editor & Publisher*, Sept. 4, 1915.

"Cartoons Are Subject to Barter and Sale." *Editor & Publisher*, Aug. 26, 1916.

Wheeler, John N. "A Captain of Comic Industry." *The American Magazine*, 1916.

"Guarantee of Cartoon Rights in Bud Fisher Suit." *Editor & Publisher*, May 25, 1918.

"Star Company May Reproduce 'Mutt and Jeff' Cartoons." *Editor & Publisher*, June 29, 1918.

Mellon, Ben. "Press Pays Bud Fisher $200,000 Annually for Famous 'Mutt and Jeff' Comics." *Editor & Publisher*, April 17, 1919.

"Hearst-Fisher Case Again." *Editor & Publisher*, May 14, 1921.

"Uphold Artist's Right to Creations." *Editor & Publisher*, July 23, 1921.

"Fisher Owns Mutt and Jeff." *Editor & Publisher*, Nov. 19, 1921.

"Bud Fisher Makes $3000 a Week." *Editor & Publisher*, June 23, 1928.

"Bud Fisher, Comic Strip Pioneer, Dies." *Editor & Publisher*, Sept. 11, 1954.

Hurd, Jud. "Bud Fisher Scrapbooks." *Cartoonist PROfiles* #3, September 1969, and #4, December 1969.

Dunn, Bob. "Said and Dunn" (visit with Fisher). *Cartoonist PROfiles* #22, June 1974.

George McManus: Campbell, Eugene. "Jiggs at Home." *Circulation*, vol. 1, no. 4, September 1921.

Dillon, Philip R. "The Newlyweds." *Editor & Publisher*, Dec. 24, 1910.

"Gag a Day." *Time*, Dec. 10, 1945.

Hurd, Jud. "Bringing Up Father." *Cartoonist PROfiles* #44, December 1979.

Jones, Llewellyn Rees. "Jiggs, The Globe-Trotter." *World Traveler*, May 1926.

"Let George Do It—He Did." *Editor & Publisher*, July 13, 1912.

Marschall, Richard. "The Decorative Art of George McManus." *Nemo* #14, August 1985.

McManus, George. "If This Be Pessimism—." *Circulation*, vol. 2, no. 11, March 1923.

———. "Jiggs and I." *Collier's*, three-part series, Jan. 19 and 26 and Feb. 2, 1952.

Pew, Marlen. "Horse, Hard Work Won Success for McManus." *Editor & Publisher*, Nov. 16, 1935.

Schuyler, Philip. "McManus Gives a Lesson in Comic Art." *Editor & Publisher*, Sept. 27, 1924.

Staunton, Helen M. "McManus Celebrates 1/3 Century of Jiggs." *Editor & Publisher*, Dec. 1, 1945.

George Herriman: Baldwin, Summerfield. "A Genius of the Comic Page." *Cartoons*, June 1917.

Blackbeard, Bill. "The Forgotten Years of George Herriman." *Nemo* #1, June 1983.

Dorgan, T. A. "This Is About Garge Herriman." *Circulation*, vol. 2, no. 11, March 1923.

Herriman, George. "George Herriman." *The Dead-Line*, vol. 1, no. 1, September 1917.

Inge, M. Thomas. "Herriman's Coconino Baron." Introduction to *Baron Bean*. Westport, Conn.: Hyperion Press, 1977.

———. "George Herriman's Early Years." *Cartoonist PROfiles* #96, December 1992.

———. "Was Krazy Kat Black? The Racial Identity of George Herriman." *Inks*, vol. 3, no. 2, May 1996.

Laughlin, Robert. "When the Kat Went Krazy." *Hogan's Alley* #5, spring 1998.

Marschall, Richard. "The Diary of a Deluded Dandy" (Baron Bean). *Nemo* #16, December 1985.

———. "Stumble Inn." *Hogan's Alley* #4, summer 1997.

THE TWENTIES

Comics business: Barker, Kenneth. "Longtime Companions" (topper strips). *Hogan's Alley* #11, summer 2003.

Brisbane, Arthur. "Why Are Comic Pictures Necessary in Sunday Newspapers?" *Circulation*, vol. 1, no. 3, July 1921.

"Editors Paying Less for Features as Syndicate Bill Grows." *Editor & Publisher*, Jan. 19, 1929.

"In Interview Hearst Speaks Plainly of Policies of His Organization." *Editor & Publisher*, June 21, 1924.

Ivey, Jim. "When Comics Wore Toppers." *Nemo* #18, April 1986.

"'Kid' Comics Growing Up, Survey Shows." *Editor & Publisher*, May 19, 1928.

Robb, Arthur T. "30 Group Ownerships Control 150 U.S. Dailies." *Editor & Publisher*, Feb. 16, 1924.

Roche, John F. "Stock Crash Made Circulations Soar." *Editor & Publisher*, Nov. 2, 1929.

Schoenfeld, Amram. "The Laugh Industry." *The Saturday Evening Post*, Feb. 1, 1930.

Smith, Steven. "The Critic That Walked by Himself" (Gilbert Seldes). *Hogan's Alley* #6, winter 1999.

Williams, Frank H. "Studying Daily Newspaper Comics Will Help Ad Writers." *Editor & Publisher*, March 12, 1921.

Syndicates: "Concentration Trend in Syndicate Field." *Editor & Publisher*, Jan. 15, 1927.

"Editors Hotly Discuss Syndicate Methods." *Editor & Publisher*, May 3, 1924.

Schuyler, Philip. "1927 Sees Decrease in Number of Syndicates." *Editor & Publisher*, Aug. 27, 1927.

"Syndicate Men Declare Editors Are Responsible for Many Abuses in Syndicate Material." *Editor & Publisher*, Jan. 24, 1925.

Radio: Hearst, William Randolph. "Radio No Menace to Press, Says Hearst." *Editor & Publisher*, April 18, 1931.

Ormsbee, Thomas H. "Newspapers Capitalize Radio Craze in Manifold Ways." *Editor & Publisher*, April 22, 1922.

Pew, Marlen. "Radio Discussed as Press Threat or Promise." *Editor & Publisher*, Feb. 9, 1924.

Schuyler, Philip. "What of Newspapers in This Radio Age?" *Editor & Publisher*, April 23, 1927.

Advertising: "Briggs and Fox Agree to Quit Ads." *Editor & Publisher*, March 3, 1928.

Franklin, Hammond Edward. "Old Gold Using 1180 Newspapers." *Editor & Publisher*, June 8, 1930.

Schuyler, Philip. "Celebrities Keen for Advertising Copy Work." *Editor & Publisher*, Oct. 1, 1927.

Adventure strips: Blackbeard, Bill. "Easy Does It: The Gentle Introduction of Adventure into the Comics." Introduction to *The Complete Wash Tubbs & Captain Easy*. Vol. 5, *1930–1931*. New York: NBM, 1988.

Goulart, Ron. "George Storm, Pioneer of the Adventure Strip." *Nemo* #4, December 1983.

———. "To Be Continued: The Rise and Spread of Humorous Continuity Strips." In *What's So Funny? The Humor Comic Strip in America*. Salina, Kan.: Salina Art Center, 1998.

Harvey, Robert C. "The Adventure Strip Arrives . . . with Ruffles and Flourishes." *Cartoonist PROfiles* #107, September 1995.

Captain Patterson: Gilmore, Lucille Brian. "Medill's Grandsons Build on Great Tradition." *Editor & Publisher*, April 26, 1924.

Harvey, Robert C. "The Captain and the Comics." *Inks*, vol. 2, no. 3, November 1995.

Perry, John W. "N.Y. News, Now 15, Holds Grip on Masses." *Editor & Publisher*, June 30, 1934.

Schneider, Walter E. "Fabulous Rise of N.Y. Daily News Due to Capt. Patterson's Genius." *Editor & Publisher*, June 24, 1939.

Cartoonists: "All in a Day's Work" (profile series). *Editor & Publisher*, 1924: Walter Berndt, July 26; Roy Crane, Sept. 13; Percy Crosby, June 7; T. A. Dorgan, March 15; Carl Ed, Nov. 1; Milt Gross, April 26; Ethel Hays, Dec. 4; A. E. Hayward, Dec. 6; John Held Jr., Oct. 25; Charles W. Kahles, Nov. 15; Ken Kling, July 12; Frederick B. Opper, March 22; H. T. Webster, May 3; Garr Williams, March 29; J. R. Williams, Dec. 13.

Beatty, Jerome. "Interpreter of the Timid Soul" (H. T. Webster). *Reader's Digest*, April 1938.

"Bungles Bopped" (Harry Tuthill). *Time*, June 11, 1945.

Campbell, Gordon. "J.R. Williams." *Cartoonist PROfiles* #56, December 1982.

———. "Believe It or Not." *Cartoonist PROfiles* #60, December 1983.

"Clare Briggs, Cartoon Genius, Dies at 54." *Editor & Publisher,* Jan. 11, 1930.

Clark, Neil M. "Sidney Smith and His 'Gumps.'" *American Magazine,* March 1923.

Davis, Elrick. "Yes! They're from Cleveland" (J. R. Williams). *Cleveland Press,* June 5, 1935.

Erwin, Ray. "Walter Berndt Was a 'Smitty' Himself." *Editor & Publisher,* Feb. 8, 1964.

Goulart, Ron. "The Life and Times of Bunker Hill, Jr." *Nemo* #3, October 1983.

Griffith, Bill. "W.E. Hill: An Appreciation." *The Comics Journal* (special edition), summer 2002.

Heintjes, Tom. "Puttin' on the Ritz: Larry Whittington's Fritzi Ritz." *Hogan's Alley* #7, winter 2000.

Howard, Clive. "The Magnificent Roughneck" (Frank Willard). *The Saturday Evening Post,* Aug. 9, 1947.

Hurd, Jud. "The Bungle Family." *Cartoonist PROfiles* #34, June 1977.

Johnston, William. "At School Webster Ranked Lowest in His Class in Drawing." *Editor & Publisher,* March 3, 1923.

Kelly, Frank K. "America's No. 1 Suburbanite" (Gluyas Williams). *Better Homes and Gardens,* November 1947.

Knoll, Erwin. "30 Years with 'Moon'—Willard Still Has D.T.'s." *Editor & Publisher,* June 27, 1953.

Maeder, Jay. "1/8 Sure Thing—Joe and Asbestos." *New York Daily News,* May 29, 2003.

Marschall, Richard. "Gluyas Williams." *Nemo* #3, October 1983.

———. "Hairbreadth Harry Returns to Earth." *Nemo* #16, December 1985.

———. "The Bee's Knees; the Cat's Pajamas—John Held's Flapper Strips." *Nemo* #22, October 1986.

Perry, John W. "Forget the Average Reader—Webster." *Editor & Publisher,* Nov. 2, 1929.

———. "Fox Longs for Old Newspaper Days." *Editor & Publisher,* Nov. 9, 1929.

Pew, Marlen E. "Carl Ed Ends 20 Years as 'Harold Teen' Artist." *Editor & Publisher,* Jan. 21, 1939.

Phelps, Donald. "The Panel Art of J.R. Williams." *Nemo* #3, October 1983.

———. "The Bungle Family's Little Glories of Inanity." *Nemo* #5, February 1984.

———. "Boarding House Days and Arabian Nights." *Nemo* #13, July 1985.

———. "The Tenants of Moonshine." *Nemo* #14, August 1985.

Pritchett, Richard. "The Inimitable Gluyas Williams." *Yankee,* February 1976.

Rath, Jay. "Dwig—Pen-and-Ink Poet." *Nemo* #11, May 1985.

Ripley, Robert. "There Ain't No Such Animal." *The Saturday Evening Post,* Feb. 6, 1932.

Frank King: Brandenburg, George A. "King's Characters Are Now in 3rd Generation." *Editor & Publisher,* Dec. 22, 1945.

Johnson, Mark. "Frank King's Make-Believe World: The Pre-Gasoline Era." *Nemo* #12, June 1985.

King, Frank. "Home Life in the Comics." *Art Instruction Inc.,* 1959. Reprinted in *Drawn Quarterly* #3, May 2000.

"King of the Comics Strips." *Modern Maturity,* December/January 1968.

Marschall, Richard. "Gasoline Alley's Flights of Fantasy." *Nemo* #29, February 1989.

Monchak, Stephen J. "Frank King's 'Skeezix' Marks 20th Anniversary." *Editor & Publisher,* Feb. 8, 1941.

Pew, Marlen. "Readers Congratulate Author on Skeezix' Rise." *Editor & Publisher,* Sept. 24, 1938.

Phelps, Donald. "The Boys of Winter." *Hogan's Alley* #1, autumn 1994.

Cliff Sterrett: Groth, Gary. "The Comic Genius of Cliff Sterrett." *Nemo* #1, June 1983.

Karfiol, Bernard. "Polly as 'Higher' Art!" *Circulation,* vol. 5, no. 25, July 1926.

Marschall, Richard. "The Genius of Cliff Sterrett and Polly and Her Pals." Introduction to *The Complete Polly and Her Pals.* Vol. 1. Abington, Pa.: Remco Worldservice Books, 1990.

Spiegelman, Art. "Polyphonic Polly: Hot and Sweet." Introduction to *The Complete Polly and Her Pals.* Vol. 1. Abington, Pa.: Remco Worldservice Books, 1990.

Billy DeBeck: "Barney Google Man." *Newsweek,* Nov. 23, 1942.

"Barney Google's Birthday." *Newsweek,* Oct. 14, 1940.

DeBeck, Billy. "Open the Golden Gate! Spark Plug is Coming!" *Circulation,* vol. 5, no. 25, July 1926.

"DeBeck Dies." *Time,* Nov. 23, 1942.

Goulart, Ron. "Barney Google": Meet the Man Who Gave Us Spark Plug, Snuffy Smith and Lots of Laughs." *ComicScene* #4, 1988.

Monchak, Stephen J. "Billy DeBeck Marks 20th Year with King." *Editor & Publisher,* Oct. 7, 1939.

Schoenfeld, Amram. "A Portrait in Zowie." *Esquire,* November 1935.

Harold Gray: Barker, Kenneth. "The Life and Love, Friends and Foes, Trials and Triumphs of Little Orphan Annie." *Nemo* #8, August 1984.

Blackbeard, Bill. "Hot Alligator! How Little Orphan Annie Beat the Pants off the Boys at Strip Dice and MCed the First Comic Strip." *The Comics Journal* (special edition), summer 2002.

Marschall, Richard. "The Master." *Nemo* #8, August 1984.

McCracken, Harry. "Annie's Real 'Daddy.'" *Nemo* #8, August 1984.

Phelps, Donald. "Who's That Little Chatterbox?" *Nemo* #8, August 1984.

"There Are Tears and Laughter in this New Chicago Tribune Comic Strip" (advertisement). *Editor & Publisher,* Dec. 20, 1924.

Roy Crane: Crane, Roy. "Roy Crane and Buz Sawyer." *Cartoonist PROfiles* #3, September 1969.

Harvey, Robert C. "A Flourish of Trumpets: Roy Crane and the Adventure Strip." *The Comics Journal* #157, March 1993.

Hurd, Jud. "Roy Crane's Scrapbook." *Cartoonist PROfiles* #5, March 1970; #6, June 1970; #9; March 1971; #13, March 1972.

THE THIRTIES

Comics business (articles in chronological order): "United Feature Syndicate Buys Metropolitan Service from Elser." *Editor & Publisher,* March 15, 1930.

Perry, John P. "Syndicate Mergers an Aid to Dailies." *Editor & Publisher,* April 5, 1930.

"World Feature Service Taken Over by United Feature Syndicate." *Editor & Publisher,* April 11, 1930.

McAdam, Charles V. "Plop! Wham! Zowie!" *College Humor,* February 1931.

Roche, John F. "Syndicate Men Discuss Feature Trend." *Editor & Publisher,* Sept. 3, 1932.

"The Funny Papers." *Fortune,* April 1933.

Robb, Arthur. "Newspaper Groups Doubled in Decade." *Editor & Publisher,* Feb. 17, 1934.

"Comic Weekly Goes to Tabloid Size." *Editor & Publisher,* Dec. 29, 1934.

"Comic Weekly Back to Full Size." *Editor & Publisher,* May 11, 1935.

Bassett, Warren L. "Hearst Wealth Placed at $220,000,000." *Editor & Publisher,* Sept. 28, 1935.

"Syndicates Now in Their Heyday." *Editor & Publisher,* Sept. 26, 1936.

"Funny Strips: Cartoon-Drawing Is Big Business; Effects on Children Debated." *The Literary Digest,* Dec. 12, 1936.

Brown, Robert U. "Syndicate Editors Tell How to Find Comic Strip Popularity." *Editor & Publisher,* Feb. 20, 1937.

Bassett, Warren L. "W.R. Hearst Celebrates his 50th Year as a Newspaper Publisher." *Editor & Publisher,* March 6, 1937.

Monchak, Stephen J. "Readers Expected to Turn to Comic Humor for War Relief." *Editor & Publisher,* Sept. 30, 1939.

Surveys and advertising (articles in chronological order): Mann, Robert S. "Comic Section Advertising Starts: General Foods Using 49 Papers." *Editor & Publisher,* May 16, 1931.

Brandenburg, George A. "Research Shows Reader Preference." *Editor & Publisher,* Jan. 16, 1932.

"To Sell Space in 30 Comic Sections." *Editor & Publisher,* May 7, 1932.

"11 Dailies Unite to Sell Comic Space." *Editor & Publisher,* June 4, 1932.

Clemow, Bice. "Four-Color Comic Advertising Shows Amazing Growth Since 1931." *Editor & Publisher,* Feb. 9, 1935.

"Big Demand for Sunday Feature Copy" and "Sunday Sections Lead Linage Upturn." *Editor & Publisher,* March 28, 1936.

Brown, Robert U. "Comic Art for Advertisers; 'Swing Pictures' Make Debut." *Editor & Publisher,* Feb. 27, 1937.

Mann, Robert S. "Comic, Roto, Color, and Magazines Bring Linage Worth $41,000,000." *Editor & Publisher,* March 27, 1937.

Heintjes, Tom. "Funny Business." *Hogan's Alley* #10, summer 2002.

Longevity (articles in chronological order): "Sidney Smith Dies in Auto Crash." *Editor & Publisher,* Oct. 26, 1935.

"Edson Doing The Gumps." *Editor & Publisher,* Dec. 21, 1935.

Brown, Robert U. "Gus Edson Completing Successful Year as Author of 'The Gumps.'" *Editor & Publisher,* Nov. 21, 1936.

———. "31 Comics Among 62 Features Surviving Before 1920." *Editor & Publisher,* March 19, 1938.

"Segar, Creator of Popeye, Dies on Coast at 43." *Editor & Publisher,* Oct. 22, 1938.

Pew, Marlen. "Filling Sid Smith's Shoes Toughest Job, Says Edson." *Editor & Publisher,* Oct. 29, 1938.

Cartoonists: Andrae, Tom. "The Mouse's Other Master: Floyd Gottfredson's 45 Years With Mickey." *Nemo* #6, April 1984.

Andrae, Tom, Geoffry Blum, and Gary Coddington. "Of Superman and Kids with Dreams. A Rare Interview with the Creators of Superman: Jerry Siegel and Joe Shuster." *Nemo* #2, August 1983.

Andriola, Alfred. "Charlie Chan: A Mystery Strip." Sales brochure. McNaught Syndicate, 1938.

Beatty, Albert R. "Edwina and Her Dogs." *The American Kennel Gazette,* Dec. 1, 1937.

Becattini, Alberto. "A Concise History of Disney Newspaper Strips." *Comic Book Marketplace* #95, October 2002.

Berchtold, William E. "Men of Comics." *New Outlook,* May 1935.

Brown, Robert U. "Ham Fisher Signs Big Contract." *Editor & Publisher,* April 17, 1937.

———. "Carl Anderson at 73 Hits Syndicate Heights." *Editor & Publisher,* March 12, 1938.

Bumbry, Bob. "Joe Palooka Perennial Champ." *Look,* Oct. 14, 1947.

Calkins, Dick. "That Prophetable Guy, Buck Rogers." *Liberty,* 1945.

Coma, Javier. "The Costumes of Tim Tyler, The Disguises of Lyman Young." *Nemo* #15, October 1985.

Cowley, Malcolm. "The Most of John Held, Jr." *The New York Times Book Review,* Nov. 19, 1972.

Crouch, Bill. "Noel Sickles." *Cartoonist PROfiles* #29, March 1976.

Dale, Bert. "Meet Dick Calkins." *The Open Road,* December 1947.

———. "Meet Bill Holman." *The Open Road,* October 1948.

Dunn, Bob. "The Little King by Otto Soglow." *Cartoonist PROfiles* #26, June 1975.

Feiffer, Jules. "Jerry Siegel: The Minsk Theory of Krypton." *The New York Times Magazine,* Dec. 29, 1996.

"Foo!" (Bill Holman). *Newsweek,* May 22, 1961.

Hamlin, Vincent. "The Man Who Walked with Dinosaurs." *Inks,* vol. 3, no. 2, May 1996.

Harvey, Robert C. "Joe Palooka and the Most Famous Food Fight of the Funnies." *The Comics Journal* #168, May 1994.

Hay, Clayton. "Notary Sojac" (Bill Holman). *Seattle Times,* Dec. 26, 1948.

"Henry and Philbert" (Carl Anderson). *Time,* Feb. 11, 1935.

Hurd, Jud. "Lee Falk." *Cartoonist PROfiles* #27, September 1975.

Kaler, Dave. "Percy Leo Crosby." *Cartoonist PROfiles* #34, June 1977.

Kobler, John. "Up, Up and Awa-a-y! The Rise of Superman Inc." *The Saturday Evening Post,* June 21, 1941.

Marschall, Richard. "When Knights Were Bold, But More So Damsels" (Oaky Doaks). *Nemo* #20, July 1986.

———. "Joe Palooka Retains the Title." *Nemo* #22, October 1986.

———. "Ming Foo: Threats and Thrills, Fantasy and Fortune Cookies." *Nemo* #29, February 1989.

Marschall, Richard, and Bill Janocha. "Edwina at 93." *Nemo* #25, April 1987.

Monchak, Stephen J. "Zack Mosley Goes Up to Get Lowdown on Flying." *Editor & Publisher,* June 22, 1940.

Mosley, Zack. "Smilin' Jack and Zack." *AOPA Pilot,* December 1964.

"Nancy, Sluggo and Ernie." *Newsweek,* June 28, 1948.

Neal, Jim. "Zack Mosley Dies, Creator of 'Smilin' Jack.'" *Comic Buyer's Guide* #1053, Jan. 21, 1994.

Pew, Marlen. "Ernie Bushmiller Changes Name of Strip to 'Nancy.'" *Editor & Publisher,* June 11, 1938.

———. "FDR 'Saves' Joe Palooka from Foreign Legion." *Editor & Publisher,* July 2, 1938.

———. "NEA's 'Alley Oop' to Have Modern Locale." *Editor & Publisher,* April 1, 1939.

Phelps, Donald. "Wild Blue Yonder" (Zack Mosley). *Nemo* #7, June 1984.

———. "Holman's Legacy to Popular Humor." *The Comics Journal* (special edition), winter 2002.

Philips, McCandlish. "Returning from the 25th Century . . . Buck Rogers." *New York Times,* Dec. 2, 1969.

Poling, James. "Ryder of the Comic Page." *Collier's,* Aug. 14, 1948.

Powers, Grant. "Themselves All Over." *The American Legion Magazine,* July 1939.

Rath, Jay. "Silents Please! The Unspeakable Greatness of Carl Anderson's 'Henry.'" *Nemo* #26, September 1987.

Shutt, Craig. "Man of Strips" (Superman). *Hogan's Alley* #5, spring 1998.

Singer, Charles. "Joe Palooka: Cartoon Champon." *Ring, The Bible of Boxing,* December 1983.

Sprague, Andy. "Remembering Zack Mosley." *Cartoonist PROfiles* #110, June 1996.

Adventure strips: Andriola, Alfred. "The Story Strips." *Cartoonist PROfiles* #14, June 1972, and #15, September 1972.

Brown, Robert U. "Artists Ponder What's Happened to Humor in Comics." *Editor & Publisher,* March 13, 1937.

———. "Humor Tops Adventure Cartoons in Fortune's Popularity Poll." *Editor & Publisher,* March 27, 1937.

Goulart, Ron. "Leaping Tall Buildings, Falling on Faces." *Nemo* #2, August 1983.

Marschall, Richard. "The Class of '34." *Hogan's Alley* #1, autumn 1994.

Monchak, Stephen J. "Fox Sees Adventure Comics in Ascendancy." *Editor & Publisher,* Oct. 7, 1939.

Pew, Marlen. "Protest Against 'Crime Comics.'" *Editor & Publisher,* July 4, 1936.

Hal Foster: "Classic Episodes in Hal Foster's Prince Valiant." Exhibition catalog. Greenwich, Conn.: Museum of Cartoon Art, June 1975.

Crouch, Bill. "Prince Valiant by Hal Foster" (interview). *Cartoonist PROfiles* #22, June 1974.

Cuccolini, Guilio C. "Howard Pyle and the Roots of the Artistry of Hal Foster." *Hogan's Alley* #5, spring 1998.

Harvey, Robert C. "Foster's Tarzan and How it Grew." *The Comics Journal* #158, April 1993.

———. "Fostering the Adventure Strip." *Comic Book Marketplace* #89, March 2002.

Kane, Brian M. "The Making of Hal Foster, Prince of Illustrators—Father of the Adventure Strip." *Comic Book Marketplace* #89, March 2002.

Maley, Don. "Hal Foster Both Lives and Loves the Days of Camelot." *Editor & Publisher,* Jan. 25, 1969.

Monchak, Stephen J. "A Two-Fisted Artist Draws 'Prince Valiant.'" *Editor & Publisher,* April 8, 1939.

"'Prince Valiant' Hero for 25 Years." *Editor & Publisher,* Feb. 3, 1962.

Saba, Arn. "Prince Harold." *Canadian Weekend,* 1979.

———. "Drawing on History: Hal Foster's Last Interview." *The Comics Journal* #102, September 1985.

Schreiber, Fred. "The Master, Hal Foster." *Nemo* #9, October 1984.

Alex Raymond: Cuthbert, Raymond A. "Alex Raymond's Flash Gordon: The Comic Strip as Epic Fantasy." *Comic Book Marketplace* #93, August 2002.

Harvey, Robert C. "Raymond and the Right Stuff." *Comic Book Marketplace* #93, August 2002.

Monchak, Stephen J. "Credit Jules Verne for Raymond's 'Flash Gordon.'" *Editor & Publisher*, Aug. 10, 1940.

Winiewicz, Dave. "Flash Gordon: 1935 to 1936." *Comic Book Marketplace* #93, August 2002.

Milton Caniff: Bainbridge, John. "Significant Sig and the Funnies." *The New Yorker*, Jan. 8, 1944.

Caniff, Milton. "There Had to Be a Choice: 'Stick to Your Ink Pots Kid,' Said the Sage of Scioto." *The Quill*, September 1937.

———. "How to Be a Comic Artist." In *Milton Caniff: Rembrandt of the Comic Strip*. Philadelphia: David McKay, 1946.

———. "Detour Guide for an Armchair Marco Polo." King Features Syndicate publication, 1947.

"Dumas from Ohio." *Newsweek*, April 24, 1950.

Harvey, Robert C. "Of Miscellany and Milt." *The Comics Journal* #128, April 1989.

———. "Spotlighting the Art of Milton Caniff" (special issue). *Comic Book Marketplace* #96, November 2002.

Horak, Carl J. "The 60-Year Impact of 'Terry and the Pirates.'" *Comics Buyer's Guide* #1092, Oct. 21, 1994.

Marschall, Richard. "Of Stout Fellahs and Real Thrills: Milton Caniff's Early Adventure Strip, 'Dickie Dare.'" *Nemo* #15, October 1985.

Saba, Arn. "Milton Caniff: An Interview with One of the Masters of Comic Art." *The Comics Journal* #108, May 1986.

"A Salute to Milton Caniff on the Occasion of the 10th Anniversary of 'Terry and the Pirates.'" *The Magazine of Sigma Chi*, February/March 1945.

Small, Collie. "Strip Teaser in Black and White." *The Saturday Evening Post*, Aug. 10, 1946.

Staunton, Helen M. "Steve Canyon—Milton Caniff Unveils His New Strip." *Editor & Publisher*, Nov. 23, 1946.

Chester Gould: Bainbridge, John. "Chester Gould." *Life*, Aug. 14, 1944.

Brandenburg, George A. "Gould Starts 15th Year with Dick Tracy," *Editor & Publisher*, Oct. 6, 1945.

Collins, Max Allen. "Detective and Determination, Comics and Cadillacs: The Chester Gould Interview." *Nemo* #17, February 1986.

DeHaven, Tom. "Bud, Which Way to the Noble Hotel?" *Nemo* #17, February 1986.

"Dick Tracy: The Art of Chester Gould." Exhibition catalog. Port Chester, N.Y.: Museum of Cartoon Art, October 1978.

"Dick Tracy's Creator a Mild Man; Trims Hedges and Plays Violin." *Editor & Publisher*, July 7, 1934.

Phelps, Donald. "Flat Foot Floogie." *Nemo* #17, February 1986.

Walker, Brian. "Good vs. Evil in Black and White." Dick Tracy exhibition catalog. Rye Brook, N.Y.: Museum of Cartoon Art, November 1990.

Yoder, Robert M. "Dick Tracy's Boss." *The Saturday Evening Post*, Dec. 17, 1949.

E. C. Segar: Blackbeard, Bill. "Enter Popeye: The Sailor Who Saved a Sinking Ship." Introduction to *Thimble Theatre Introducing Popeye*. Westport, Conn.: Hyperion Press, 1977.

———. "E.C. Segar's Knockouts of 1925 (and Low Blows Before and After): The Unknown Thimble Theatre Period." *Nemo* #3, October 1983.

Pew, Marlen. "Segar Recovers, Renews King Features Contract." *Editor & Publisher*, June 4, 1938.

Chic Young: Alexander, Jack. "The Dagwood and Blondie Man." *The Saturday Evening Post*, April 10, 1948.

Boyesil, Ned. "Not So Dumb—Dumb Dora." *Circulation*, vol. 5, no. 24, May 1926.

Bryan, J. "His Girl Blondie." *Life*, Aug. 15, 1942.

Pew, Marlen E. "'Chic' Young Completes 8 Years with King." *Editor & Publisher*, Oct. 1, 1938.

Van Gelder, Lawrence. "Chic Young, Creator of 'Blondie,' Dead." *New York Times*, March 16, 1973.

Al Capp: Caplin, Elliott. "We Called Him Alfred . . ." *Cartoonist PROfiles* #48, December 1980.

Capp, Al. "Innocents in Peril." *The World of Li'l Abner*. New York: Ballantine Books, 1952.

———. "Why I Let Abner Marry." *Life*, March 31, 1952.

———. "My Life as an Immortal Myth." *Life*, April 30, 1965.

"Die Monstersinger." *Time*, Nov. 6, 1950.

"Li'l Abner's Mad Capp." *Newsweek*, Nov. 24, 1947.

Maloney, Russell. "Li'l Abner's Capp." *Life*, June 24, 1946.

Marschall, Richard. "Saying Something About the Status Quo" (Capp's last interview). *Nemo* #18, April 1986.

Pew, Marlen E. "Capp Completes 5 Years with United Features." *Editor & Publisher*, Aug. 6, 1938.

"Playboy Interview: Al Capp." *Playboy*, December 1966.

Safire, William. "Gasp! Sob! Li'l Abner is No More." *New York Times*, Nov. 6, 1977.

Schreiner, Dave. "The Storyteller." Introduction to *Li'l Abner*. vol. 1. Princeton, Wis.: Kitchen Sink Press, 1988.

Shenker, Israel. "Al Capp, Harbinger of the Age of Irreverence, Gives Up Cartoons but Not Irascibility." *New York Times*, Nov. 11, 1977.

———. "Al Capp, Creator of 'Li'l Abner,' Is Dead at 70." *New York Times*, Nov. 7, 1979.

Steinbeck, John. Introduction to *The World of Li'l Abner*. New York: Ballantine Books, 1952.

THE FORTIES

Comics go to war: Black, John. "'Yank,' New Army Paper, Off to Flying Start." *Editor & Publisher*, June 20, 1942.

Caniff, Milton. "Comic Strips at War." *Vogue*, July 15, 1943.

———. "The Comics." In *While You Were Gone: A Report on Wartime Life in the United States*. New York: Simon and Schuster, 1946.

Harvey, Robert C. "Cartoonists at War." *The Comics Journal* #118, December 1987.

———. "Chiaroscuro Kipling and a Bit of Lace." *The Comics Journal* #119, January 1988.

Monchak, S. J. "Popeye Assumes Navy Recruiting Assignment." *Editor & Publisher*, July 26, 1941.

———. "Syndicates Cooperating in Defense Bond Sales." *Editor & Publisher*, Jan. 31, 1942.

———. "Scorchy Smith Creator Dead." *Editor & Publisher*, Feb. 7, 1942.

———. "'Junior Commando' Idea Appeals to U.S. Youth." *Editor & Publisher*, Aug. 21, 1942.

———. "Cartoonists Important Factor in Keeping Nation's Morale." *Editor & Publisher*, Sept. 19, 1942.

———. "Sub Hunting, Drawing Are Mosley's Jobs Now." *Editor & Publisher*, April 3, 1943.

Rhode, Michael. "She May *Look* Clean But . . ." *Hogan's Alley* #8, fall 2000.

Staunton, Helen. "New Comics Furnished to GI Papers Overseas." *Editor & Publisher*, July 8, 1944.

Vaughn, Don. "War-Toons." *The Retired Officer Magazine*, June 1998.

Walker, Jerry. "Comic Artists Cheer Veterans by Chalk Talks." *Editor & Publisher*, Oct. 28, 1944.

GI cartoonists: Campbell, Gordon. "Sad Sack." *Cartoonist PROfiles* #69, March 1986.

Freeman, William M. "George Baker, Creator of Sad Sack Cartoon, Is Dead." *New York Times*, May 9, 1975.

Marschall, Richard. "The World War II Cartoonist Corps." *Nemo* #12, June 1985.

Monchak, Stephen J. "Caniff Drawing Again for Army Papers." *Editor &*
Publisher, Jan. 30, 1943.

Rovner, Samuel. "United Signs Mauldin, Army Cartoonist." *Editor &*
Publisher, April 1, 1944.

Shutt, Craig. "Sad Sack's Two Commanding Officers." *Hogan's Alley* #7, winter 2000.

Staunton, Helen M. "Mauldin's GIs Return Minus the Whiskers." *Editor &*
Publisher, June 16, 1945.

Sweeney, Jim. "World War II Show Includes Mauldin, Caniff, Combat
Artists." *The Comics Journal* #170, August 1994.

"Where Are the Cartoonists of WWII?" *American Legion Magazine,* 1951.

Comics business: Bassett, Warren L. "Dailies Are Warned Against
Hoarding" (paper shortages). *Editor & Publisher,* June 17, 1941.

Harvey, R. C. "Cushlamochree! Their Creators Abandoned Them!" *Comic*
Buyer's Guide #1225, May 9, 1997.

Monchak, Stephen J. "War Closing European Markets to Syndicates." *Editor*
& Publisher, May 11, 1940.

———. "Woman Executive Holds Sway Over Ace Syndicate Artists"
(Mollie Slott). *Editor & Publisher,* Nov. 2, 1940.

———. "Selling King Abroad Poses Many Problems." *Editor & Publisher,*
Nov. 25, 1940.

———. "Syndicates Are Big Business, With 35 Million in Annual Sales."
Editor & Publisher, Sept. 20, 1941.

———. "Syndicates Are Feeling Effects of War Economy." *Editor &*
Publisher, Feb. 15, 1942.

———. "Should Color Comics Pages Be Smaller?" *Editor & Publisher,*
May 23, 1942.

———. "Strip Standardization Proposed for Duration." *Editor & Publisher,*
Jan. 16, 1943.

Rovner, Samuel. "Syndicate Heads See Good Volume in '44." *Editor &*
Publisher, Feb. 5, 1944.

Staunton, Helen M. "Syndicate Heads See Boom Coming in Field." *Editor &*
Publisher, Jan. 27, 1945.

———. "Will Comic Strips Return to Former Size?" *Editor & Publisher,*
Feb. 10, 1945.

———. "Syndicates Strengthen Europe Bridgehead." *Editor & Publisher,*
June 2, 1945.

———. "Comics Reconvert Too, with Jap Surrender." *Editor & Publisher,*
Aug. 18, 1945.

———. "Syndicate War Years Foreshadow Expansion." *Editor & Publisher,*
Oct. 6, 1945.

Comic books: Monchak, Stephen J. "Format Change Won't Help Comics,
Fox Says." *Editor & Publisher,* May 18, 1940.

———. "Syndicates Study New Comic Book Technique." *Editor & Publisher,*
June 1, 1940.

———. "R&T Syndicate Offers 16-Page Color Comic Book." *Editor &*
Publisher, June 8, 1940.

Comics events: Maeder, Jay. "Special Delivery: LaGuardia Reads the
Funnies, July 1945." *New York Daily News,* Aug. 31, 2000.

Monchak, Stephen J. "400,000 Names Submitted for Blondie's Baby." *Editor*
& Publisher, May 10, 1941.

———. "Of Caniff's Raven Sherman." *Editor & Publisher,* Oct. 18, 1941.

———. "Art Groups Recognize The 'Funnies' as Art." *Editor & Publisher,*
April 18, 1942.

Staunton, Helen M. "Women Comic Artists Entertained by E&P." *Editor &*
Publisher, Nov. 10, 1945.

Cartoonists: Coker, Paul. "Gus Arriola Interview." *Cartoonist PROfiles* #16,
December 1972.

Feldman, Linda. "Starr Power." *Los Angeles Times,* April 26, 1999.

Frank, Ann. "Starr-Crossed: Between the Lines with Dale Messick." *Fort*
Lauderdale News/Sun-Sentinel, Nov. 25, 1979.

Hurd, Jud. "Dale Messick Interview." *Cartoonist PROfiles* #16, December 1972.

Monchak, Stephen J. "United's New Strip Has Mexican Locale" (Gordo).
Editor & Publisher, Nov. 8, 1941.

———. "Arriola Enlists, United's 'Gordo' Strip Suspended." *Editor &*
Publisher, Oct. 3, 1942.

Sujka, Sharon. "Dale Messick Hasn't Missed a Daily 'Brenda Starr' Deadline."
Editor & Publisher, Nov. 23, 1974.

Will Eisner: Eisner, Will. "The Spirit: How It Came To Be." Preface to *Will*
Eisner's The Spirit Archives. Vol. 1. New York: DC Comics, 2000.

Harvey, Robert C. "The Consummate Comic Book." Introduction to *Will*
Eisner's The Spirit Archives. Vol. 1. New York: DC Comics, 2000.

Moore, Alan. "The Pioneering Spirit." Foreword to *Will Eisner's The Spirit*
Archives. Vol. 1. New York: DC Comics, 2000.

Shutt, Craig. "Eisner's Thwarted Dreams." *Hogan's Alley* #11, 2003.

BOOKS

GENERAL HISTORIES

Appel, John J. *Cartoons and Ethnicity.* Columbus: Ohio State University
Libraries, 1992.

Becker, Stephen. *Comic Art in America.* New York: Simon and Schuster, 1959.

Berger, Arthur Asa. *The Comic-Stripped American.* Baltimore: Penguin
Books, 1973.

Blackbeard, Bill. *The Yellow Kid.* Northampton, Mass: Kitchen Sink Press, 1995.

Blackbeard, Bill, and Dale Crain, eds. *The Comic Strip Century.* 2 vols.
Englewood Cliffs, N.J.: O.G. Publishing Corp., 1995.

Blackbeard, Bill, and Martin Williams, eds. *The Smithsonian Collection of*
Newspaper Comics. Washington, D.C.: Smithsonian Institution Press and
Harry N. Abrams, 1977.

Brian, Denis. *Pulitzer: A Life.* New York: John Wiley & Sons, 2001.

Briggs, Clare. *How to Draw Cartoons.* New York: Harper & Brothers, 1926.

Carlin, John, and Sheena Wagstaff. *The Comic Art Show: Cartoons and Painting*
in Popular Culture. New York: Whitney Museum of American Art, 1983.

Carrier, David. *The Aesthetics of Comics.* University Park, Pa.: Pennsylvania
State University Press, 2000.

Castelli, Alfredo. *Waiting for the Yellow Kid.* Lucca, Italy: Museo Italiano del
Fumetto, 2003.

Caswell, Lucy. *See You in the Funny Papers.* Columbus: Ohio State University
Libraries, 1995.

———. *Historic Virtuoso Cartoonists.* Columbus: Ohio State University
Libraries, 2001.

Couperie, Pierre, and Maurice Horn. *A History of the Comic Strip.* New York:
Crown Publishers, 1968.

Crafton, Donald. *Before Mickey—The Animated Film: 1898–1928.* Chicago:
University of Chicago Press, 1993.

Craven, Thomas. *Cartoon Cavalcade.* New York: Simon and Schuster, 1943.

Dierick, Charles, and Pascal Lefevre, eds. *Forging a New Medium: The Comic*
Strip in the Nineteenth Century. Brussels: VUB University Press, 1998.

Duin, Steve, and Mike Richardson. *Comics Between the Panels.* Milwaukie,
Ore.: Dark Horse Comics, 1998.

Ellinport, Jeffrey M. *Collecting Original Comic Strip Art.* Norfolk, Va.: Antique
Trader Books, 1999.

Emery, Michael, Edwin Emery, and Nancy L. Roberts. *The Press in America.*
Boston: Allyn and Bacon, 2000.

Gordon, Ian. *Comic Strips and Consumer Culture.* Washington, D.C.:
Smithsonian Institution Press, 1998.

Goulart, Ron. *The Adventurous Decade.* New Rochelle, N.Y.: Arlington
House, 1975.

———. *The Encyclopedia of American Comics.* New York: Facts On File, 1990.

———. *The Funnies: 100 Years of American Comic Strips.* Holbrook, Mass.:
Adams Publishing, 1995.

Gowans, Alan. *The Unchanging Arts.* Philadelphia: Lippincott, 1971.

Hardy, Charles, and Gail F. Storm, eds. *Ethnic Images in the Comics.* Philadelphia: The Balch Institute for Ethnic Studies, 1986.

Harvey, Robert C. *The Art of the Funnies.* Jackson, Miss.: University Press of Mississippi, 1994.

————. *Children of the Yellow Kid.* Seattle: Frye Art Museum, 1998.

————. *A Gallery of Rogues: Cartoonists' Self-Caricatures.* Columbus: Ohio State University Cartoon Research Library, 1998.

————. *The Genius of Winsor McCay.* Columbus: Ohio State University Libraries, 1998.

Hess, Stephen, and Milton Kaplan. *The Ungentlemanly Art: A History of American Political Cartoons.* New York: Macmillan, 1975.

Hollis, Daniel W. *The Media in America.* Santa Barbara, Calif.: ABC-CLIO, 1995.

Horn, Maurice, ed. *75 Years of the Comics.* Boston: Boston Book and Art, Publisher, 1971.

————. *Comics of the American West.* South Hackensack, N.J.: Stoeger Publishing, 1977.

————. *Women in the Comics.* New York: Chelsea House Publishers, 1977.

————. *Sex in the Comics.* New York: Chelsea House Publishers, 1985.

————. *100 Years of American Newspaper Comics.* New York: Gramercy Books, 1996.

————. *The World Encyclopedia of Cartoons.* Philadelphia: Chelsea House Publishers, 1999.

————. *The World Encyclopedia of Comics.* Philadelphia: Chelsea House Publishers, 1999.

Hurd, Jud. *To Cartooning: 60 Years of Magic.* Fairfield, Conn.: PROfiles Press, 1993.

Inge, M. Thomas. *Comics as Culture.* Jackson, Miss.: University Press of Mississippi, 1990.

————. *Great American Comics.* Columbus: Ohio State University Libraries and Smithsonian Institution, 1990.

————. *Anything Can Happen in a Comic Strip.* Columbus: Ohio State University Libraries, 1995.

Janocha, Bill, ed. *The National Cartoonists Society Album 1996.* New York: National Cartoonists Society, 1996.

Katz, Harry L., and Sara W. Duke. *Featuring the Funnies: One Hundred Years of the Comic Strip.* Washington, D.C.: Library of Congress, 1995.

King Features Syndicate. *Famous Artists & Writers of King Features Syndicate.* New York: King Features Syndicate, 1949.

Koenigsberg, M. *King News: An Autobiography.* Philadelphia and New York: F. A. Stokes Company, 1941.

Kunzle, David. *The History of the Comic Strip: The Nineteenth Century.* Berkeley, Calif.: University of California Press, 1990.

Lent, John A. *Comic Books and Comic Strips in the United States: An International Bibliography.* Westport, Conn.: Greenwood Press, 1994.

Lesser, Robert. *A Celebration of Comic Art and Memorabilia.* New York: Hawthorne Books, 1975.

Lupoff, Dick, and Don Thompson. *All in Color for a Dime.* Iola, Wis.: Krause Publications, 1997.

Maltin, Leonard. *Of Mice and Magic: A History of American Animated Cartoons.* New York: Plume, 1987.

————. *The Great American Broadcast.* New York: Dutton, 1997.

Marschall, Richard. *The Sunday Funnies: 1896–1950.* New York: Chelsea House Publishers, 1978.

————. *What's So Funny: The Humor Comic Strip in America.* Salina, Kan.: Salina Art Center, 1988.

————. *America's Great Comic-Strip Artists.* New York: Abbeville Press, 1989.

————. *American Comic Classics.* Washington, D.C.: U.S. Postal Service, 1995.

Matthews, E. C. *How to Draw Funny Pictures.* Chicago: Frederick J. Drake & Co., 1944.

McGivena, Leo E. *The News: The First Fifty Years of New York's Picture Newspaper.* New York: News Syndicate Co., 1969.

Mott, Frank Luther. *American Journalism: A History, 1690–1960* (3rd ed.). New York: Macmillan, 1962.

Murrell, William. *A History of American Graphic Humor (1865–1938).* New York: Macmillan, 1938.

Nasaw, David. *The Chief: The Life of William Randolph Hearst.* Boston: Houghton Mifflin, 2000.

O'Sullivan, Judith. *The Great American Comic Strip.* Boston: Little, Brown and Company, 1990.

Overstreet, Robert M. *The Official Overstreet Comic Book Price Guide* (33rd ed.). Timonium, Md.: Gemstone Publishing, 2003.

Perry, George, and Alan Aldridge. *The Penguin Book of Comics.* Middlesex, England: Penguin Books, 1971.

Phelps, Donald. *Reading the Funnies.* Seattle: Fantagraphics Books, 2001.

Reitberger, Reinhold, and Wolfgang Fuchs. *Comics: Anatomy of a Mass Medium.* Boston: Little, Brown and Company, 1971.

Robbins, Trina. *Paper Dolls from the Comics.* Forestville, Calif.: Eclipse Comics, 1987.

————. *A Century of Women Cartoonists.* Northampton, Mass.: Kitchen Sink Press, 1993.

————. *The Great Women Cartoonists.* New York: Watson-Guptill Publications, 2001.

Robbins, Trina, and Catherine Yronwode. *Women and the Comics.* Forestville, Calif.: Eclipse Books, 1985.

Robinson, Jerry. *The Comics: An Illustrated History of Comic Strip Art.* New York: G. P. Putnam's Sons, 1974.

————. *Cartoon: A Celebration of American Comic Art.* Washington, D.C.: John F. Kennedy Center for the Performing Arts, 1975.

Seldes, Gilbert. *The Seven Lively Arts.* New York: Harper and Brothers, 1924.

Sheridan, Martin. *Comics and Their Creators.* Boston: Hale, Cushman & Flint, 1942.

Strickler, Dave. *Syndicated Comic Strips and Artists 1924–1995: The Complete Index.* Cambria, Calif.: Comics Access, 1995.

Stromberg, Fredrik. *Black Images in the Comics.* Seattle: Fantagraphics Books, 2003.

Thompson, Don, and Dick Lupoff. *The Comic Book Book.* New Rochelle, N.Y.: Arlington House, 1973.

Thorndike, Chuck. *The Business of Cartooning.* New York: The House of Little Books, 1939.

Turner, Hy B. *When Giants Ruled: The Story of Park Row, New York's Great Newspaper Street.* New York: Fordham University Press, 1999.

Varnum, Robin, and Christian Gibbons, eds. *The Language of Comics: Word and Image.* Jackson, Miss.: University Press of Mississippi, 2001.

Walker, Brian. *The Sunday Funnies: 100 Years of Comics in American Life.* Bridgeport, Conn.: The Barnum Museum, 1994.

Watson, Elmo Scott. *A History of Newspaper Syndicates.* Chicago: The Publishers' Auxiliary, 1936.

Waugh, Coulton. *The Comics.* New York: Macmillan, 1947.

Wheeler, John. *I've Got News for You.* New York: E. P. Dutton, 1961.

White, David Manning, and Robert H. Abel, eds. *The Funnies: An American Idiom.* New York: The Free Press of Glencoe/Macmillan, 1963.

Whyte, Malcolm. *Great Comic Cats.* San Francisco: Pomegranate, 2001.

Wood, Art. *Great Cartoonists and Their Art.* Gretna, La.: Pelican Publishing Company, 1987.

Yoe, Craig. *Weird But True Toon Factoids.* New York: Gramercy Books, 1999.

AUTOBIOGRAPHIES, BIOGRAPHIES, AND RETROSPECTIVE ANTHOLOGIES

Barrett, Robert R. *Tarzan of the Funnies.* Holt, Mich.: Mad Kings Publishing, 2002.

Becattini, Alberto, and Antonio Vianovi. *Profili Caniff—Milton Caniff: American Stars and Strips.* Lucca, Italy: Glamour International, 2001.

————. *Profili Raymond—Alex Raymond: The Power and the Grace.* Lucca, Italy: Glamour International, 2002.

Berger, Arthur Asa. *Li'l Abner: A Study in American Satire.* Jackson, Miss.: University Press of Mississippi, 1994.

Blackbeard, Bill. *Jiggs Is Back.* Berkeley, Calif.: Celtic Book Company, 1986.

Cahn, Joseph M. *The Teenie Weenies Book: The Life and Art of William Donahey*. La Jolla, Calif.: Green Tiger Press, 1986.

Canemaker, John. *Winsor McCay: His Life and Art*. New York: Abbeville Press, 1987.

Caplin, Elliott. *Al Capp Remembered*. Bowling Green, Ohio: Bowling Green State University Popular Press, 1994.

Capp, Al. *The Best of Li'l Abner*. New York: Holt, Rinehart and Winston, 1978.

———. *My Well Balanced Life on a Wooden Leg*. Santa Barbara, Calif.: John Daniel and Company, 1991.

Davidson, Harold G. *Jimmy Swinnerton: The Artist and His Work*. New York: Hearst Books, 1985.

Grandinetti, Fred M. *Popeye: An Illustrated History of E.C. Segar's Character in Print, Radio, Television and Film Appearances, 1929–1993*. Jefferson, N.C.: McFarland & Company, 1994.

Groensteen, Thierry. *Krazy Herriman*. Angoulême, France: Musée de la Band Dessinée, 1997.

———. *Popeye: Est C'Qu'il Est Voilà Tout C'Qu'il Est!*. Angoulême, France: Musée de la Band Dessinée, 2001.

Hall, Patricia. *Johnny Gruelle: Creator of Raggedy Ann and Andy*. Gretna, La.: Pelican, 1993.

Harvey, Robert C. *Accidental Ambassador Gordo*. Jackson, Miss.: University Press of Mississippi, 2000.

Higgs, Mike. *Popeye: The 60th Anniversary Collection*. London: Hawk Books, 1989.

Kane, Brian M. *Hal Foster: Prince of Illustrators—Father of the Adventure Strip*. Lebanon, N.J.: Vanguard Productions, 2001.

Maeder, Jay. *Dick Tracy: The Official Biography*. New York: Plume, 1990.

Marschall, Richard. *Screwball Comics*. Thousand Oaks, Calif.: Fantagraphics Books, 1985.

———. *Daydreams and Nightmares: The Fantastic Visions of Winsor McCay*. Westlake Village, Calif.: Fantagraphics Books, 1988.

———. *The Best of Little Nemo in Slumberland*. New York: Stewart, Tabori & Chang, 1997.

Marschall, Richard, and John Paul Adams. *Milt Caniff: Rembrandt of the Comic Strip*. Endicott, N.Y.: Flying Buttress Publications, 1981.

Marzio, Peter. *Rube Goldberg: His Life and Work*. New York: Harper and Row, 1973.

McDonnell, Patrick, Karen O'Connell, and Georgia Riley de Havenon. *Krazy Kat: The Comic Art of George Herriman*. New York: Harry N. Abrams, 1986.

Robbins, Trina. *Nell Brinkley and the New Woman in the Early 20th Century*. Jefferson, N.C.: McFarland & Company, 2001.

Roberts, Garyn G. *Dick Tracy and American Culture*. Jefferson, N.C.: McFarland & Company, 1993.

Robinson, Jerry. *Skippy and Percy Crosby*. New York: Holt, Rinehart and Winston, 1978.

Sagendorf, Bud. *Popeye: The First Fifty Years*. New York: Workman Publishing, 1979.

Smith, Bruce. *The History of Little Orphan Annie*. New York: Ballantine Books, 1982.

Theroux, Alexander. *The Enigma of Al Capp*. Seattle: Fantagraphics Books, 1999.

Walker, Brian. *The Best of Ernie Bushmiller's Nancy*. Wilton, Conn.: Comicana Books, 1988.

———. *Barney Google and Snuffy Smith: 75 Years of an American Legend*. Wilton, Conn.: Comicana Books/Ohio State University Libraries, 1994.

Walker, Mort. *Backstage at the Strips*. New York: Mason Charter, 1975.

Young, Dean, and Richard Marschall. *Blondie and Dagwood's America*. New York: Harper & Row, 1981.

Yronwode, Catherine. *The Art of Will Eisner*. Princeton, Wis.: Kitchen Sink Press, 1982.

REPRINTS

The publishers that have produced reprint collections of newspaper comic strips and panels are too numerous to list here. Among the more notable reprint series have been: *Alley Oop* (Kitchen Sink Press), *Dick Tracy* (IDW), *Flash Gordon* (Kitchen Sink, Nostalgia Press, and Checker), *Gasoline Alley* (Drawn & Quarterly), *Krazy Kat* (Remco/Kitchen Sink Press, Eclipse, and Fantagraphics), *Li'l Abner* (Kitchen Sink Press), *Little Nemo* (Checker), *Little Nemo in Slumberland* (Remco/Fantagraphics), *Little Orphan Annie* (Fantagraphics and IDW), *Polly and Her Pals* (Remco/Kitchen Sink), *Popeye* (Fantagraphics), *Prince Valiant* (Fantagraphics and Nostalgia Press), *Scorchy Smith* (IDW), *Tarzan* (NBM), *Terry and the Pirates* (Remco/Kitchen Sink, NBM, and IDW), and *Wash Tubbs and Captain Easy* (NBM). In 1977, Hyperion Press of Westport, Connecticut, published a series of twenty-two volumes entitled *Classic American Comic Strips*. The books in the series, which were edited by Bill Blackbeard, included collections of *A. Mutt, Abie the Agent, Barney Google, Baron Bean, Bobby Thatcher, Bobo Baxter, Bringing Up Father, The Bungle Family, Buster Brown, Connie, Dauntless Durham of the U.S.A., The Family Upstairs, Happy Hooligan, Jim Hardy, Minute Movies, Napoleon, Polly and Her Pals, School Days, Sherlocko the Monk, Skippy, Thimble Theatre,* and *Winsor McCay's Dream Days.*

DISSERTATIONS AND MANUSCRIPTS

Castelli, Alfredo. "Here We Are Again, 1895-1919: The First 25 Years of American Newspaper Comics." Milan, March 21, 2003.

Davidson, Sol. "Culture and Comic Strips." New York University, 1958.

Nystrom, Elsa. "A Rejection of Order: The Development of the Newspaper Comic Strip in America, 1830-1920." Loyola University of Chicago, 1989.

Young, William Henry. "Images of Order: American Comic Strips During the Depression, 1929-1938." Emory University, 1969.

PRINCE VALIANT by Hal Foster. © *1978 King Features Syndicate, Inc. Courtesy of The Ohio State University Cartoon Library and Museum*

BUZ SAWYER by Roy Crane. © 1978 King Features Syndicate, Inc. Courtesy of The Ohio State University Cartoon Library and Museum

LIMITED-EDITION COMIC ART

In 1978, Harry N. Abrams collaborated with the Newspaper Comics Council to produce a series of limited-edition comic art prints by twenty of America's top cartoonists. Each artist created a unique illustration that featured many of his most well-known characters. This project provided the cartoonists with the opportunity to showcase their talents in an unrestricted format. The resulting creations were then reproduced to the highest standards and printed on rag paper in a limited edition of one hundred sets, which were numbered and signed by the artist. The prints were initially offered for $250 per print or $6,000 for a set of twenty, but since that time individual prints have sold for considerably more. A selection of these prints is shown on this spread and on pages 670 and 671.

POPEYE by Bud Sagendorf. © 1978 King Features Syndicate, Inc. Courtesy of The Ohio State University Cartoon Library and Museum

The Picture Folk

MARGARET E. SANGSTER

They're of another world, perhaps,
  The little picture folk;
Just made to carry off a laugh,
  An epigram or joke.
They're of another world that lies
  Across a comic sheet,
And yet, beneath the fun of them,
  Is something real and sweet!

There's "*Polly*" and her many pals,
  There's "*Jerry*" and "*Us Boys*";
There's "*Jiggs*" and "*Maggie*" with their flood
  Of troubles and of joys.
There's "*Barney Google*" and his horse,
  There's "*Casper*" and his wife.
And "*Buttercup*," their infant child,
  And "*This is married life!*"

We read about them steadily,
  We know their tiny ways. . . .
Our hands reach out, in friendliness,
  Across the work-filled days.
They make us chuckle, for they bring
  A kindly sense of cheer;
We follow through their lives until
  We feel them very near!

There's "*Indoor Sports*" and "*Little Jim.*"
  There's "*Freddy*"—he works fast!
There's "*Tillie*" at the typewriter,
  Each moment seems her last. . . . .
The "*Piffles*," "*Happy Hooligan*,"
  "*Our Boss*" and "*Buster Brown*";
And "*Slim*" and "*Helpful Henry*," and
  Some others of renown.

They're of another world, perhaps,
  The little picture folk;
Just built to hang some laughter on,
  An epigram or joke,
But, oh, we love them for they're not
  Like books on musty shelves. . . . .
The reason? In their eyes, we see
  The image of ourselves!

In "*Krazy Kat*" we glimpse a heart
  That suffers and forgives;
In "*Father*"—stout and middle-aged,
  A vague romance still lives.
Ambition—it is "*Abie's*" text,
  They all strive toward some goal—
They may be only make-believes,
  But each one has a soul!

"THE PICTURE FOLK" by Margaret E. Sangster. *April 1923, Circulation magazine. Author's collection*

the comics
SINCE 1945

Speech bubbles in illustration:
WHAT A DISPOSITION TIGE

I'VE SOITNLY HAD AN EXCITING LIFE BUT I DIDN'T GET POIMANTLY HOIT

HULLY GEE!

R.F. Outcault AFTER F. OPPER

SUNDAY FUNNIES STARS—Buster Brown and Tige, Happy Hooligan, and The Yellow Kid. Illustration by R. F. Outcault from Circulation magazine, 1926

introduction

"THE SUNDAY FUNNIES" is a term that evokes nostalgic images. Family members arguing over who gets the comics first. Children on their hands and knees gazing at the colorful pages scattered across the living room floor. Father snoozing in his easy chair, the newspaper open in his lap.

It is hard to imagine a world without Little Orphan Annie, Popeye, Snoopy, and Garfield. Yet the comics as we know them today are a relatively recent invention. The roots of the art form can be traced to prehistoric cave paintings, Egyptian hieroglyphics, and Renaissance tapestries. The immediate antecedents of modern comics are the satirical prints, broadsheets, and illustrated magazines published in Europe during the eighteenth and nineteenth centuries. European artists pioneered the use of caricature, speech balloons, and sequential panels before graphic satire became popular in the colonies. It is in America, however, that the Sunday funnies were born.

American newspaper comics evolved during the latter half of the nineteenth century when powerful forces of social and technological change combined to revolutionize mass entertainment. All of the elements that gave birth to this new art form—the mechanization of printing and distribution, the concentration of population in urban centers, the acceptance of new forms of graphic expression—had been gaining momentum for decades. Critical mass was achieved in 1896, when the phenomenal popularity of Richard F. Outcault's Yellow Kid proved that a comic character could sell newspapers as effectively as blaring headlines and sensational gossip. The Yellow Kid is remembered today as a symbol of the fierce journalistic competition of that era and an icon of a new national institution, the Sunday funnies.

The birth of the comics was the direct result of three major developments in American newspaper publishing: Sunday editions, color printing, and national syndication. *The Katzenjammer Kids*, *Happy Hooligan*, *Buster Brown*, and the many other creations that followed in the wake of *The Yellow Kid*'s success appeared in color every Sunday and were distributed to newspapers throughout the country.

On March 20, 1825, the *New York Courier* published one of the first Sunday newspaper editions in America. James G. Edwards, the owner of the *Courier*, was immediately attacked by religious groups for violating "blue laws." "The Sunday paper, in its issue, its sale, and its reading," wrote one clergyman, "is antagonistic to the spirit of the Lord's day, and tends to subvert the institution." In spite of this opposition, Sunday newspapers gradually began to proliferate. In 1870 fewer than fifty papers put out Sunday editions, but by 1890 the number had risen to over 250.

The first syndicate was started by Ansel Kellogg in Wisconsin in the 1860s. At that time, small-town newspapers had modest resources and limited access to quality writers and national news. Country editors could save on production costs by buying preprinted pages from early syndicates such as Kellogg's. These sheets had generic columns and illustrations, known as "evergreen" features, printed on one side of the page. The other side was left blank, where client papers could print their own local news and advertising. This arrangement was particularly successful during the Civil War, when there was an acute shortage of newspaper workers.

In 1883 Joseph Pulitzer purchased the *New York World* from Jay Gould, and within months, as the result of Pulitzer's innovative changes, the circulation of the *World* rose from 22,000 to 100,000. Pulitzer outdid the competition by publishing a *Sunday World* that was bigger and better than anything on the street. It offered an entertaining mix of features for women, children, and sports fans, as well as humorous illustrations. In 1889 Pulitzer added cartoons to the *Sunday World*, and in 1893, when he obtained a color press, he launched one of the first Sunday color comics sections.

Richard F. Outcault, a freelance cartoonist who contributed regularly to *Truth* magazine as well as to the *New York World*, often depicted scenes of slum life in his drawings. On February 17, 1895, a small black-and-white cartoon by Outcault, featuring a bald-headed street urchin in a nightshirt, appeared in the *World*. A few months later, on May 5, the character that was to become the Yellow Kid made his first appearance in color, although his nightshirt was blue, not yellow. Outcault's kid was a slow developer. It took another six months before he donned his trademark yellow shift (November 24, 1895). In spite of this low profile, the Kid managed to attract the attention of newspaper readers. One of his admirers would change his destiny dramatically.

William Randolph Hearst took the town by storm in the fall of 1895, rejuvenating the *New York Journal* and stealing Joseph Pulitzer's thunder as well as his staff. Hearst dropped the price of his paper from two cents to a penny in December 1895, and in four months the circulation of the *Journal* soared from 20,000 to 150,000. In January 1896 Hearst dined with Morrill Goddard, editor of Pulitzer's *Sunday World*, at the Hoffman House in New York City and offered him a salary of $350 a week to edit his new *Sunday Journal*. When Goddard balked, Hearst presented him with $35,000 in cash as a guarantee. In the following months, Hearst lured away many more of Pulitzer's best people with lucrative salary offers, including S. S. Carvalho, the *World*'s vice-president and publisher, and its three top artists, Archie Gunn, Walt McDougall, and Richard F. Outcault. On October 18, 1896, Hearst launched his own Sunday color comic supplement, the *American Humorist*, with the Yellow Kid by Richard F. Outcault as the star attraction.

Pulitzer countered Hearst by dropping his price to a penny on February 10, 1896. When Outcault started working

THE YELLOW KID—"THE RACING SEASON OPENS IN HOGAN'S ALLEY," by R. F. Outcault. New York World, May 24, 1896. Courtesy of Richard Marschall

SPANNING THE GENERATIONS—FAMILY CIRCUS Sunday page by Bil Keane. © 6/1/80 King Features Syndicate, Inc.

for the *Journal* in October 1896, Pulitzer turned the *Hogan's Alley* feature over to George Luks. For the next year, the competing Yellow Kids ran simultaneously in both New York papers. Posters were plastered all over town, as each paper claimed to have the genuine article.

At the peak of his popularity in 1896 and 1897, the Yellow Kid's toothy grin showed up on hundreds of products, including buttons, crackers, cigars, and fans. The *Hogan's Alley* gang appeared on stage at Weber and Fields's Broadway Music Hall in 1896, numerous songs were published in sheet-music form, including "The Dugan Kid Who Lives in Hogan's Alley," and a *Yellow Kid* magazine was launched in 1897.

All of the characteristics now associated with comics— a continuing cast of characters, text in speech balloons, sequential panels, regular publication, color on Sundays— had been experimented with before the Yellow Kid made his first appearance. It was the commercial success of Outcault's creation, during the pivotal year of 1896, that was the crucial factor in establishing the new art form.

On January 5, 1896, the Yellow Kid took center stage in Outcault's Sunday comic for the first time. His bright yellow nightshirt attracted the attention of thousands of newspaper readers, who kept coming back, week after week, to see what this strange character would do next.

In the following months, more milestones were passed. On April 12, 1896, the Kid began talking directly to his audience, via crude writing on his nightshirt. On September 6 the supporting cast of *Hogan's Alley* was formally introduced, in an advertisement drawn by Outcault for a Broadway stage adaptation. On September 7 Outcault applied for a copyright to protect "The Yellow Dugan Kid" from infringement and to insure further profits from the Kid's merchandising success.

WERE THE COMICS INVENTED YET WHEN YOU WERE A GIRL, GRANDMA?

INDEED THEY WERE, JEFFY.

The episode on October 25 marked two firsts: the Kid spoke with the aid of a speech balloon, and Outcault utilized sequential comic strip panels. On November 14 the first of the "Yellow Kid Diaries" began appearing semiregularly in the daily edition of the *New York Journal*.

Richard Felton Outcault, the father of the funnies, had in one short year defined the form and content of the American newspaper comic feature. More significant, he proved that the art form had great commercial potential and the ability to build newspaper circulation. All of the developments that have taken place in the funnies business since 1896 rest upon Outcault's original foundation.

Soon after the debut of the Yellow Kid, large metropolitan papers in other cities, including the *San Francisco Examiner* and the *Philadelphia Inquirer*, began publishing their own Sunday comic sections. In New York City the competition between newspapers continued to rage. The *New York Herald*, some-

what less sensational than the *World* and the *Journal* but equally intrigued by the potential of the new medium, tried out sixty new comic features between 1899 and 1905. William Randolph Hearst sold and shipped the entire *New York Journal American Humorist* Sunday section to other cities across the country. As a result, the Yellow Kid became a national celebrity and his creator reaped huge profits from the hundreds of Yellow Kid licensed products.

Humorous drawings had appeared in daily newspapers since the mid-nineteenth century, but it was not until more than a decade after the success of the Yellow Kid that daily comic strips became a fixture in American newspapers.

In 1903 Clare Briggs created a comic strip, *A. Piker Clerk*, which ran on the daily sports page of the *Chicago American*. The star of the feature, a chinless racetrack gambler, placed bets, and readers had to wait until the next episode to learn the results. Briggs's promising formula failed to win the allegiance

COMIC KING—Bud Fisher discusses his annual earnings with his two stars, Mutt and Jeff. Self-caricature by Bud Fisher from The American Magazine, c. 1916

own syndicate operations within the next decade. There were also a number of independent distributors, such as the George Matthew Adams Syndicate and the McNaught Syndicate, which began selling comics in the first decade of the new century.

The Newspaper Feature Syndicate was incorporated in 1913. According to its founder Moses Koenigsberg, it was the "first independent syndicate organized to supply a complete budget of features to seven-day-a-week publications." At that time, the number of daily newspapers in America had reached a peak of 2,262, with a combined circulation of 28 million. These papers were serviced by about forty syndicates. Newspaper Feature Syndicate, an arm of the Hearst empire, was the largest of these distributors. It supplied its client newspapers with the papier-mâché matrices from which their comic features could be reproduced. Because the majority of papers could not afford the machinery to print their own color comics sections, N.F.S. could also arrange to have them preprinted at one of nine separate manufacturing stations, saving their clients one-third of labor and material costs. Today most of the nation's Sunday funnies are still prepared at a few large printing plants, such as American Color Graphics and Western Color.

On November 16, 1915, Koenigsberg launched King Features Syndicate. Named after its founder, it has been among the leading comics distributors ever since. The competition also continued to thrive. By 1935, 130 syndicates were offering over 1,600 features to almost 14,000 daily and Sunday newspapers throughout the world.

Syndication provided significant opportunities to cartoonists. In the early years cartoonists worked in their newspaper's art departments and were paid fixed salaries for drawing weekly comic features as well as sports, editorial, and filler cartoons. With the advent of syndication, artists were liberated from the regimentation of newspaper staff positions. Their creations were seen by a much larger audience and they received a cut (usually 50 percent) of the weekly fees paid by subscribing newspapers. The most successful ones, such as Bud Fisher and Sydney Smith, became wealthy and famous.

There was also a downside to the relationship. Syndicates spent a considerable amount of money developing, promoting, and marketing their features. To protect their investments, syndicates insisted on total control of their properties. Cartoonists were forced to sign "work-for-hire" contracts, relinquishing ownership of their creations. This situation has changed within the last two decades and now many cartoonists own the copyrights to their features and control the merchandising of their characters.

of readers, and William Randolph Hearst, who owned the *American*, canceled *A. Piker Clerk* after a few short months because he thought it was "vulgar."

Four years later Bud Fisher tried an almost identical formula in the *San Francisco Chronicle*, and the result, *A. Mutt*, went on to become the first successful daily comic strip. *Mutt and Jeff*, as Fisher's creation was later renamed, ran for seventy-five years and made Fisher the first millionaire cartoonist in the funnies business.

Daily comic strips appeared, in the early years, scattered throughout newspapers on editorial, sports, or classified pages. Gradually, small groupings of strips began to appear. One of the first daily comic-strip pages debuted in the *New York Evening Journal* on January 31, 1912.

National syndication of comic features began almost immediately after the commercial potential of the art form was realized. Hearst distributed a package of features to client newspapers as early as 1895, and Pulitzer followed his competitor's lead in 1897. Metropolitan papers in Philadelphia, Chicago, Boston, and St. Louis set up their

HOW HARD COULD IT BE?—THEY'LL DO IT EVERY TIME *daily panel by Al Scaduto, c. 1970.* © King Features Syndicate, Inc.

Syndicates are rarely given credit for their part in helping to establish the comics medium. By handling the distribution and financial headaches, syndicates enabled cartoonists to concentrate exclusively on what they did best: create. The goal of the syndicates was to offer the widest variety of features for their clients to choose from. As a result, they provided work for thousands of artists and writers over the years. There are, of course, many stories of unsavory syndicate dealings, but in general, it has always been in the best interests of the syndicates to preserve the delicate relationship with their most valuable resources, the cartoonists. Without their talents they have nothing to sell.

Two decades after the first appearance of the Yellow Kid in the *New York World*, the funnies business was a national institution. Comics appeared, both daily and on Sundays, in virtually every newspaper in the United States. Syndicates distributed the top comic features to over a thousand clients, and the most sought-after creators were well-known celebrities. Comic characters starred in stage adaptations and animated films, their praises were sung in hit songs, their adventures were collected in books and magazines, and their popular images were used to sell a wide variety of products, ranging from toys and dolls to cigars and whisky.

Since that time, the comics business has operated on the same basic principles. Syndicates are "content providers" to American newspapers. Cartoonists create content that the syndicates sell. Syndicates split the profits with the cartoonists. The process starts with the cartoonist, who develops an original concept for a new feature. The creator then submits a sampling of daily strips and Sunday pages to the comics editors of the syndicates.

The largest syndicates, King Features, United Media, Universal Press, Tribune Media Services, and Creators, each receive over 5,000 submissions annually and release approximately a dozen new features combined a year. If the comics editor sees promise in a submission, he or she might solicit the opinions of other syndicate executives and salespeople. If the consensus is positive, the comics editor will offer a contract to the cartoonist. A development period of six months to a year often follows, so that the cartoonist can work out the kinks in the original concept and hit the ground running when the strip begins.

Hopefully, by the date of the launch, a few dozen papers, preferably large metropolitan dailies, have agreed to carry the

WHERE IDEAS COME FROM—DOONESBURY Sunday page by Garry Trudeau. © 9/4/94 by G. B. Trudeau. Used by permission of Universal Press Syndicate. All rights reserved

feature. Salespeople work hard during these first months to build up momentum and convince other editors to sign on as well. The goal is to have more than 100 papers after the first year. Only about 40 percent of new features make it past their second year.

Newspaper editors have difficult choices to make. A feature often has to be eliminated to make room for a new one. Readership polls and telephone surveys are used to determine the most-liked and least-liked strips in a paper, but the results are rarely definitive. Editors will occasionally "test drop" a feature and wait to see if any readers protest. In the end, the decision about which comics to add and subtract is based on an editor's professional instincts.

While the feature is being marketed, the cartoonist is busy meeting deadlines. Every week or so, a batch of new material is sent to the syndicate. Dailies are typically completed six weeks before publication date and Sunday pages are done eight weeks ahead, although schedules vary from artist to artist. The basic steps involved in creating each daily installment are writing, editing, penciling, inking, and lettering. The majority of cartoonists do all of these chores themselves when they are first getting started. As a feature begins to generate additional income, the creator might choose to hire

assistants to perform one or more of these tasks. Most cartoonists have some form of help. Charles Schulz, who wrote, drew, lettered, and inked every *Peanuts* strip for almost fifty years, was an exception.

For many years the majority of cartoonists produced their camera-ready artwork with similar tools and materials. They would first draw their strips and panels in pencil on heavy-ply, plate-finish bristol board, at least twice the size it would appear in the newspaper, and then ink and letter over the pencil lines with a flexible nib pen or brush and India ink. Shading was sometimes added by applying a patterned adhesive overlay, commonly known as "Ben Day," over the desired areas. In more recent times, artists have employed a wider variety of supplies and methods, including vellum, chemically treated paper, graphite pencils, felt-tip pens, magic markers, and fountain pens, as well as digital drawing pads, software programs, and computer fonts.

Daily strips and Sunday pages are almost always done in black and white. The artist will often provide the syndicate with a color guide for the Sunday page, although since the mid-1990s, most of the coloring has been done by computer.

The production department at the syndicate photographs or scans the artwork and puts together weekly proof sheets, which are sent or transmitted to subscribing papers. Artwork for the Sunday pages takes a little longer to prepare, because the color needs to be added.

Some syndicates will pay a cartoonist a guaranteed minimum salary until there is enough additional income to divide. The split is usually fifty-fifty after the production costs are deducted. A cartoonist can hope to earn a modest living in the first year of syndication, although many keep their day jobs until the feature takes off.

Beyond that, the sky is the limit. The top strips in the business appear in over 2,000 newspapers (daily and Sunday clients are counted separately) and earn their creators million-dollar incomes. If a strip becomes a merchandising success, even greater profits are possible. The average cartoonist can hope to earn a six-figure salary for a strip that runs in a few hundred newspapers.

Of course, the process is never uniform or predictable. In the funnies business, exceptions are the rule. Each story is different.

There have been cartoonists who sell a strip on their first submission, and others who never succeed after developing dozens of ideas. A comics editor at one syndicate may pass on a submission that becomes a huge hit for another syndicate. Some cartoonists are rejected after going through the development period, whereas others go straight to the launch phase. A sales kit may be little more than a few pages of black-and-white samples, or it can be an elaborate, full-color masterpiece of graphic design. There have been strips that had over 500 clients at their launch date. Others were unable to sign up a single paper. New features may skyrocket and then drop off precipitously. Many grow gradually. A strip with a handful of large-circulation papers can earn more than a feature with over a hundred small-town subscribers. A cartoonist with a good lawyer might negotiate a huge guarantee, a more favorable split, and greater control of all merchandising. A cartoonist with no legal representation can get screwed.

The daily working methods of syndicated cartoonists also vary. Some manage to get months ahead of their deadlines and

can afford to pay assistants to do most of the work. Others are habitually behind schedule, sending in batches of a few strips at a time, their incomes depleted with late charges from the syndicates.

All cartoonists utilize the same basic building blocks. A cartoon is a picture that tells a story, or conveys an idea. A newspaper comic is a cartoon that appears in a newspaper. Speech balloons, sequential panels, a regular cast of characters, and a recurring title are only common characteristics, not the defining elements of the newspaper comic.

The two types of newspaper comic features are **strips** and **panels**. Daily comic strips can consist of either multiple panels or a single panel but are almost always horizontal in shape. Newspaper panels can be vertical, square, or circular in shape and usually consist of a single panel but also come in multipanel layouts.

Most syndicated comics appear in both **daily** and **Sunday** formats. Daily comics have traditionally been printed in black and white, but many newspapers are now featuring color comics seven days a week. Sunday pages are almost always printed in color and come in a variety of layouts: quarter-page, third-page, half-page, and full-page tabloid. Most cartoonists are required to construct their pages so that the panels can be rearranged to conform to all of these layouts. Others only use a rectangular configuration that cannot be reformatted.

Within these somewhat restricted boundaries of form, cartoonists explore a limitless world of content. In terms of writing there are two basic approaches. A **gag-a-day** strip delivers a complete joke or observation in each installment. A **continuity** strip has plotlines that can run for days or weeks. Many gag-a-day strips feature running themes and many continuity strips have punch lines—some cartoonists combine the two methods into what is called "narrative humor."

Drawing styles run the gamut from stick figures to anatomically correct illustrations, but three general descriptive terms are familiar to most cartoonists. The **big-foot** method, in which the characters have oversized feet, noses, and heads, is typical of most humor strips. The **five-finger** approach, found

FIVE FINGER MEETS BIG FOOT—SAM'S STRIP *daily strip by Mort Walker and Jerry Dumas.* © 5/9/62 King Features Syndicate, Inc.

A TRIBUTE TO PAST MASTERS—B.C. Sunday page by Johnny Hart. © 5/29/94 Creators Syndicate, Inc.

commonly in adventure and soap-opera strips, is a name for a realistic style of illustrating characters. The **semi-straight** school bridges the gap between big-foot and five-finger. Semi-straight characters can have large heads, with realistic bodies, and big feet, as in *Li'l Abner*, or a blend of characteristics, typified by *For Better or For Worse*. Many comics do not fit neatly into any of these traditional categories.

In terms of genres, newspaper comics cover the scope of human experience. Adventure, aviation, fantasy, science fiction, military, western, detective, sports, romance, soap opera, humor, screwball, pantomime, animals, pets, kids, teens, families, and babies are among the many popular themes and subjects for comics, but this list is hardly all-inclusive. Cartoonists have a talent for dreaming up ideas that are outside established genres. *Zippy the Pinhead* is a good example of a contemporary creation that defies categorization.

Every newspaper cartoonist working today is restricted by the rigid formats and demanding deadlines of the funnies business. They are also challenged by the infinite thematic possibilities of the art form. Fred Lasswell, who produced *Barney Google and Snuffy Smith* for 55 years, claimed, "The thing that drives you crazy in this business is that you should acquire two skills—both contradictory. One is having an

excellent memory so you can remember what you did in the past and not do the same thing today. The other is an ability to forget, so you can clear your head and think of something fresh."

Each syndicated cartoonist has complete control over a small patch of newsprint real estate. Some respond to the limitless possibilities of "filling in the boxes" with imagination and innovative solutions. Others experience "white paper fever" and are eventually worn down by the relentless deadlines of daily comics production. The sheer volume of output (365 installments a year) is staggering. The ways in which cartoonists have met this challenge have produced a fascinating spectrum of creative expression.

Although current events are reflected on the comics pages, social trends do not necessarily dictate the subject matter of comics features. Strips based on passing fads or changing lifestyles are usually short-lived. In the postwar era, technological advances such as television and computers and social changes brought about by the baby-boom generation have had a major influence on the comics business. Trends within the industry have had an even greater impact on cartoonists. The decline of story strips and the increasing dominance of humor features in the last fifty years have led to both terminated careers and new opportunities. The shrinking size that comics are printed in newspapers has posed an ongoing threat to creativity. Other issues—censorship, ownership, and merchandising—have presented additional challenges to creators.

Cultural elitists relegate comics to the status of "low art." Cartoon art should not be judged by the same criteria as fine art. Comics are a unique visual and narrative art form, and both elements should be considered when evaluating the work of an individual cartoonist. Comic creations are also products of the culture within which they are produced. All of these factors must be taken into account when developing an appreciation for cartoon art.

The achievements of the great pioneers and early masters of American newspaper comics have been well documented in previously published histories. The majority of these accounts trace the evolution of comics from the heady days of innovation at the turn of the century, through the widespread popularization of the funnies during the 1910s and 1920s, to the proliferation of adventure strips in the 1930s. The patriotic participation of characters in World War II is often depicted as the pinnacle of the glorious golden age of newspaper comics. The postwar period is then summed up in a few brief closing chapters.

Many comics historians believe that the funnies business has been in decline during the postwar era. In *America's Great Comic-Strip Artists* (1989), Richard Marschall stated: "There have been many new comic strips but few trends since the 1950s, a situation that falls somewhere between sad and frightening. Commerce, once such a benign partner, today smothers the newspaper comic strip in America. Licensing and merchandising considerations now often precede the creation of a strip, rather than the reverse. Printing quality has declined, and coloring is not as brilliant as it once was. Formats have shrunk, and Sunday comics are now crowded several to a page instead of each filling a whole sheet. New features seem imitative; the gag-a-day mode has degenerated into stale punch lines; and newspapers themselves no longer promote—or evidently, appreciate—comic strips as they once did."

In *The Comic Strip Century* (1995), Bill Blackbeard concluded that "by the late 1960s, the newspaper comic strip had largely self-destructed as a measurably competent narrative art form."

By writing off the last half-century of comic-strip history, some scholars overlook the contributions of great talents like Walt Kelly, Charles Schulz, Garry Trudeau, and Bill Watterson. They ignore the popularization of American comics around the world and the successful adaptation of comic creations to new media, such as television and computers.

The argument that comics have changed for the better has rarely been made. Yet today more minorities are represented on the funnies pages than ever before. Women cartoonists have established a voice, and old taboos have tumbled. Cartoons are read by far more people than in the "golden age" of the 1930s and 1940s.

Doomsayers underestimate the art form's ability to reinvent itself. "I've read articles that were about to put us all out of business," said Milt Caniff in 1984. "And the next year some new thing like *Hagar the Horrible* comes along and knocks all of the pins down." The same could be said in more recent years for *Mutts* and *Zits*.

The comics industry has changed dramatically during the past fifty years. Radio, television, and the internet have challenged newspapers for dominance. Cartoonists have been forced to adapt to shifting perceptions and economic realities.

A fuller appreciation of American newspaper comics can be gained by examining how this unique communicative medium has evolved from 1895 to the present. Documenting the second half of this story should provide a better understanding of the connections between recent creations and strips from the past. Throughout its more than 100-year history, the art form has, time and again, proved its popular appeal and commercial adaptability. From the newspaper wars at the end of the nineteenth century to the cutting-edge competition on the information superhighway at the beginning of the twenty-first century, comics have continued to thrive.

The funnies have endured primarily because comic characters have a universal, timeless appeal. Their daily appearances make them familiar to millions. Their triumphs make them heroic. Their struggles make them seem human. Cartoonists create friends for their readers. Pogo, Charlie Brown, Calvin and Hobbes, and Dilbert are part of a great cultural legacy that is being further enriched every day. The final panel has yet to be drawn.

WAR EFFORT—Superman rescues a Hollywood bond-selling tour from an Axis saboteur in this Sunday page by Wayne Boring.

the postwar years

LOWIZIE from BARNEY GOOGLE AND SNUFFY SMITH by Fred Lasswell. © King Features Syndicate, Inc.

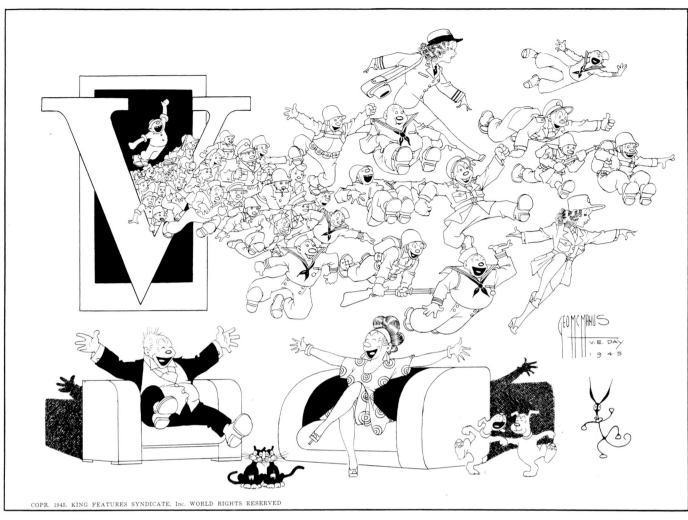

VICTORY—BRINGING UP FATHER by George McManus. © *1945 King Features Syndicate, Inc. Courtesy Howard Lowery Gallery*

ON A SUNNY AFTERNOON IN LATE JUNE 1945, THE *QUEEN MARY*, CARRYING 14,500 BATTLE-WEARY VETERANS, WAS WELCOMED INTO NEW YORK HARBOR WITH A CHORUS OF TUGBOAT WHISTLES. THE ALLIES HAD DECLARED VICTORY IN EUROPE ON MAY 8, 1945, AND THE JAPANESE SURRENDERED FOUR MONTHS LATER, AFTER ATOMIC BOMBS DEVASTATED HIROSHIMA AND NAGASAKI. ALTHOUGH 7 MILLION SOLDIERS REMAINED OVERSEAS, THE TROOPS WERE FINALLY COMING HOME.

The stars of America's funnies pages were also returning. They had served their country valiantly. "My people, the comic-strip characters, are in this war up to their inked-in eyebrows," wrote *Terry and the Pirates* creator Milton Caniff in 1943.

Snuffy Smith was one of the first to enlist, over a year before the Japanese attack on Pearl Harbor. He convinced Army recruiters to overlook his advanced age, flat feet, and toothlessness and was inducted on November 13, 1940. Snuffy's buddy, Barney Google, joined the Navy in September 1941. By the time America officially entered the war, many comic characters were doing their part, both in active duty and on the home front.

Skeezix said goodbye to the gang at *Gasoline Alley* and, after basic training, was shipped off to North Africa. Buz Sawyer was marooned on an island in the South Pacific.

Mickey Mouse went on a bombing mission over Germany. Little Orphan Annie organized the Junior Commandos to collect scrap metal for the war effort, and Dick Tracy helped sell government bonds.

"It's impossible to compute how many millions of dollars worth of War Bonds and Stamps have been sold through the constant plugging of the cartoonists in their daily releases," reported *Editor and Publisher* in 1942. "The cartoonists are up near the top among the various agencies now doing similar work throughout the country, if only for the fact that so many millions of persons read the comics daily and are influenced by them."

Not all cartoonists put their characters in uniform. On July 4, 1942, Al Capp explained to his readers why he had decided not to have his hillbilly star enlist. "Perhaps Li'l Abner and his friends, living through these terrible days in a peaceful,

COMING HOME—BARNEY GOOGLE AND SNUFFY SMITH *Sunday page by Joe Musial. © 10/28/45 King Features Syndicate, Inc.*

happy, free world, will do their part—by thus reminding us that this is what we are fighting for—to have that world again." Capp supported the war effort by doing special cartoons for the military, the Red Cross, and the Treasury Department, but his strip remained an oasis from the grim realities of the global conflict.

Front-line cartoon dispatches were provided by a handful of G.I. cartoonists. Sgt. George Baker (*The Sad Sack*), Lt. Dave Breger (*Private Breger*), Sgt. Dick Wingert (*Hubert*), and Sgt. Bill Mauldin (*Up Front*) chronicled the gritty aspects of training and combat in the pages of *Stars and Stripes*, *Yank*, and *Leatherneck*. When the fighting was over, Sad Sack, Hubert, and Mr. Breger became civilian stars of nationally syndicated features but never managed to recapture the popularity they had during the war.

Established comic characters adapted more successfully to life in peacetime. On October 28, 1945, Snuffy Smith's bride Loweezy doused herself in "odor coloney" to welcome him back to Hootin' Holler after almost five years of military service. Snuffy was reunited with his sidekick, Barney Google, the following February. When Skeezix returned home he proudly held his newborn son Chipper for the first time. The boy had been born nine months after Skeezix married his sweetheart Nina while on leave in 1944. After being discharged from the Navy, Buz Sawyer visited his family in Texas, traveled to New York, and was accused of murdering

his former girlfriend. After clearing himself of the charges, Buz was hired as a globe-trotting troubleshooter for an international airline.

Cartoonists also made adjustments. Alex Raymond, who served as a combat artist during the war, returned home in 1945 to find that his replacement on *Flash Gordon*, Austin Briggs, had been signed to a long-term contract with King Features. Raymond soon overcame his disappointment and helped King develop a detective strip to compete with *Dick Tracy*. *Rip Kirby* debuted on March 4, 1946, and starred a sophisticated private eye, who, like his creator, was a distinguished Marine veteran.

Discharged G.I.s faced rising unemployment and a shortage of available housing. Ten days after V-J Day, 1.8 million workers were unemployed; six months later 2.7 million were out of work. Although the U.S. economy was heading toward an unprecedented period of prosperity, the immediate postwar years were difficult for many veterans.

The economic future of the newspaper business was threatened by the escalating cost of newsprint in the late 1940s. The war cut off the supply of paper from overseas, which led to rationing in 1943. When the price controls ended in 1946, the cost of newsprint rose $35 a ton, and by 1948 it was at $100 a ton, double the prewar price. Newspapers experimented with ways to cut back on paper consumption. One solution was to reduce the size they printed the comics. Between 1937

A STAR IS BORN—STEVE CANYON introductory strip by Milton Caniff. © 1948 Milton Caniff Estate

and 1952, the average size of a daily comic strip shrank from 11½ to 7¼ inches in width.

In 1942 George McManus, creator of *Bringing Up Father*, complained about the effect this development was having on his work. "The space is so small today that I can show only the heads of the characters—or else must draw the complete figure very small—if I wish to have any room for the balloons at the top. While more and more space is being devoted to comics, the strips themselves are gradually being cut down in size." The shrinking of the comics would continue to restrict creativity in subsequent decades.

Newspaper circulation reached an all-time peak during the postwar period. In New York nine major papers boasted total daily sales of more than 6 million and the six papers that printed Sunday editions sold a total of 10.1 million copies per week. At the head of the pack was the *New York Daily News*, which distributed 2.4 million daily morning editions and 4.7 million papers wrapped in the funnies every Sunday.

Although an anticipated postwar sales boom never materialized, business was also good for the newspaper syndicates. In 1946 more than 125 new features were launched and fewer than 40 were dropped. Unsolicited submissions from returning G.I.s, anxious to break into the field, more than doubled at the fifteen major syndicates. King Features reported that with the return of its lucrative foreign markets, its sales were 75 percent above its 1938 total, the previous record year.

The most significant new comic strip of the postwar era was Milton Caniff's *Steve Canyon*. In 1944 Caniff was earning $70,000 a year producing *Terry and the Pirates* but was frustrated because he did not own the copyright to his creation. When publisher Marshall Field offered Caniff full ownership and a five-year contract worth $525,000 to develop a new adventure strip, he accepted the offer.

Caniff was not the first cartoonist to switch syndicates. As recently as 1943, Roy Crane had been lured away from the Newspaper Enterprise Association, which had distributed *Wash Tubbs* since 1924, to produce *Buz Sawyer* for King Features.

Caniff wanted the same opportunity to control his destiny.

In January 1945 columnist Walter Winchell broke the story that Caniff was jumping ship. *Time* magazine claimed the defection was equivalent to "Henry Ford quitting his motor company and setting up shop in competition across the street." Marshall Field, who signed a distribution agreement with King Features, sold the strip to 162 clients before Caniff had drawn a line.

In the meantime, Caniff was still under contract with the Chicago Tribune New York News Syndicate to continue *Terry and the Pirates* until the end of 1946. Not content to coast through his final two years, Caniff did some of the finest work of his career during this period.

By November 1946 Caniff had designed a character he described as "a modern-day Davy Crockett." "Steve Canyon's been around," Caniff continued. "I couldn't have Terry smoke, or even fall in love really without knowing

IN PROFILE—Steve Canyon's dramatic entrance. Panel from first Sunday page. © 1/19/47 Milton Caniff Estate

A NATIONAL CRAZE—Shmoo illustration by Al Capp from Life magazine, 1948

everything that led up to it. But this guy might have been in love a dozen times."

A war veteran, Steve Canyon ran an independent air-taxi service called "Horizons Unlimited." "He'll have lots of gals— one at every port," Caniff claimed. "With a big C-54 airplane they can move around very fast. Naturally one of the problems will be to keep him single."

Steve Canyon debuted on Monday, January 13, 1947, after a nationwide promotional blitz. It became the first comic strip introduced on television when NBC brought Caniff into the studio for a preview. Suspense built up throughout the opening week because Caniff had decided not to reveal his hero's handsome, square-jawed profile until halfway through the first Sunday page on January 19.

"It was very deliberate, of course," remembered Caniff years later. "Coming out like that after all the publicity and all the noise about it, I had to have something. It worked."

The other big newsmaker of the postwar era was Al Capp. Between 1946 and 1952, Li'l Abner's creator went on an unprecedented binge of artistic productivity and public notoriety. Capp's smiling mug appeared on the covers of both *Newsweek* (1947) and *Time* (1950), and his exploits were covered regularly in the national media.

In June 1946 Abner journeyed to Lower Slobbovia to meet Lena the Hyena, a girl so ugly Capp claimed he was

unable to draw her face. After asking his readers for help, he received 500,000 grisly portraits. The winning entry, by Basil Wolverton, was revealed in the October 28, 1946, issue of *Life* magazine.

The following year, after launching a $14 million lawsuit against his syndicate for underpayment of royalties, Capp created a thinly veiled satire of the dispute. In the *Li'l Abner* story, Rockwell P. Squeezeblood of the Squeezeblood Comic Strip Syndicate cheated two naive cartoonists out of the proceeds to their comic-strip creation, *Jack Jawbreaker.* "And the nicest part of it all is it's perfectly legal," boasted Squeezeblood.

In 1948 the National Cartoonists Society began investigating a long-running feud between Ham Fisher and Al Capp. Fisher had repeatedly accused his former assistant of stealing the hillbilly characters, Big Leviticus and his clan, from *Joe Palooka* and using them as the inspiration for *Li'l Abner.* The N.C.S. board of governors eventually told Fisher and Capp to settle their differences privately. This ugly dispute would erupt again in the 1950s.

At the end of August 1948, Capp introduced one of his most inspired creations. Shmoos were cute, ham-shaped creatures who could produce all of mankind's basic needs without any cost to the owner. They laid neatly packaged and bottled eggs and milk labeled "Grade A." When broiled, they tasted like steak. When fried, they resembled chicken. They multiplied at a rapid rate. They were the perfect solution to the shortages of the postwar economy. They were too good to be true.

Ignoring a warning that Shmoos pose the "greatest threat to humanity th' world has ever known," Abner let them loose in Dogpatch, and before long they were overrunning the countryside. "The U.S. Becomes Shmoo-Struck" announced a headline in *Life* magazine as Shmoo merchandise proliferated as rapidly as the Shmoos in *Li'l Abner.* There were Shmoo-shaped dolls, deodorizers, key chains, soap, and banks. By mid-1949, Capp Enterprises claimed that close to 100 different items were being produced by about seventy-five manufacturers creating an estimated $25 million in income. The Shmoo business was particularly lucrative for Al Capp, who had settled his dispute with United Feature Syndicate by setting up Capp Enterprises as his own licensing company.

Nogoodniks (bad Shmoos), Money Ha-Has (who laid money instead of eggs), Bald Iggles (whose gaze made everyone tell the truth), and Kigmies (who loved to be kicked) followed in the wake of the Shmoos. So did a colorful parade of Capp crazies, including J. Roaringham Fatback, One-Fault Jones, Evil Eye Fleegle, and Burping Buffalo.

Li'l Abner continued to be one of the most talked-about pop-culture institutions in America until Capp's surprising decision to have Abner marry Daisy Mae in 1952. In an era of increasing Cold War paranoia, Capp felt the mood of the nation had changed and was no longer receptive to his brand of social satire. "I was astounded to find it had become unpopular to laugh at any fellow Americans," he wrote in *Life* magazine. "I realized that a new kind of humorist had taken over, the humorist who kidded nothing but himself."

Capp took a long look at his characters. "I became reacquainted with Li'l Abner as a human being, with Daisy Mae as an agonizingly frustrated girl. I began to wonder myself what it would be like if they were ever married. The more I thought about it, the more complicated and disastrous and, therefore, irresistible the idea became."

It would be the most second-guessed decision in comics history. Capp's hillbilly hero had resisted his sweetheart's marriage proposals for years. Many readers felt that Abner lost some of his masculine appeal after he sacrificed his independence. *Li'l Abner* continued to be one of the top features in the business, reaching a circulation peak of 900 newspapers in the 1960s, but Capp's most daring and creatively productive period was behind him.

On April 25, 1944, George Herriman died quietly in his sleep. A week of unfinished *Krazy Kat* strips remained on his drawing board. Many of the art form's pioneers had passed away before the war, including Richard F. Outcault (*The Yellow Kid*), Frederick Opper (*Happy Hooligan*), Winsor McCay (*Little Nemo in Slumberland*), and E. C. Segar (*Popeye*). A hardy group of early innovators—Rudolph Dirks (*The*

Captain and the Kids), George McManus (*Bringing Up Father*), Cliff Sterrett (*Polly and Her Pals*), and Jimmy Swinnerton (*Little Jimmy*)—continued to produce their features well into the postwar years.

Many of the comic masters who began their careers in the 1920s and 1930s were the top cartoonists in the business in the late 1940s. In addition to Caniff, Raymond, Crane, and Capp, Harold Gray (*Little Orphan Annie*), Chester Gould (*Dick Tracy*), Hal Foster (*Prince Valiant*), and Ernie Bushmiller (*Nancy*) produced some of their best work during this period.

The most successful comic strip in postwar America was Chic Young's *Blondie*. The *Saturday Evening Post* reported in 1948 that *Blondie* appeared in a total of 1,136 daily and Sunday papers in the United States and abroad, earning its creator an annual salary of $300,000. Young had developed a strict set of rules for his comic strip. Most of the action in *Blondie* was limited to the Bumstead home and Dagwood's office. Dialogue was kept to a minimum. Certain taboos were followed, including avoidance of physical infirmities, politics, religion, liquor, and other subject matter that might offend or confuse readers.

"I think everybody is a little tired," observed Young in the *Post* article. He had discovered that *Blondie* readers experienced vicarious pleasure from observing Dagwood coping with his fatigue by eating, sleeping, or soaking in the bathtub. They saw their own lives reflected in the struggles of this common man. Strong reader identification with popular

NOW, In <u>1211</u> Newspapers, CHIC YOUNG'S "BLONDIE" HAS MORE READERS THAN ANY COMIC STRIP IN HISTORY!

Chic Young checks one of the daily "Blondie" panels in the studio of his Van Nuys, Cal., home

KING FEATURES SYNDICATE

235 EAST 45th STREET, NEW YORK 17, N. Y.

(Copyright, 1948, King Features Syndicate, Inc.)

BEST SELLER—BLONDIE sales advertisement. © 1948 King Features Syndicate, Inc. Courtesy of Richard Marschall

AMERICAN HERO—SUPERMAN by Jerry Siegel and Joe Shuster. c. 1930s. Panel from the first daily strip submission. © Superman™ and © DC Comics. All rights reserved. Used with permission

characters was the bedrock upon which all modern humor strips would be built.

In 1934 two teenagers from Cleveland, writer Jerry Siegel and artist Joe Shuster, began submitting an idea for a comic strip about a costumed superhero to all of the major newspaper syndicates. It was turned down by everyone. United Feature Syndicate called it "a rather immature piece of work" in a rejection letter. In 1937 Max Gaines of the McClure Syndicate showed the rejected strips to comic-book publisher Harry Donenfeld, who asked Siegel and Shuster to develop the strip idea into a thirteen-page comic-book story. *Superman* debuted in *Action Comics* no. 1, dated June 1938, and within a year Donenfeld's DC Comics was publishing 900,000 copies of its new hit comic book. The McClure Syndicate capitalized on this success by releasing a *Superman* daily comic strip on January 16, 1939, and two years later *Superman* was appearing in 300 daily and 90 Sunday newspapers. The first incarnation of the *Superman* strip survived for twenty-seven years until it was canceled due to lagging sales in 1966. McClure also adapted another DC property, *Batman and Robin*, to the comic-strip format in 1943, but that version lasted only until 1946.

The comic-book industry flourished during the war years with the most popular titles selling over a million copies each month. Newspapers and syndicates were becoming increasingly worried that competition from the new medium would adversely affect the sales of the Sunday funnies. Will Eisner, who ran an independent "shop" that produced art and stories for comic-book publishers, came up with a unique solution. In 1940 Eisner created a weekly, sixteen-page comic-book insert that was distributed to newspapers by the Register and Tribune Syndicate. The star of Eisner's creation was The Spirit, a masked detective, believed to be dead, who stalked the rain-drenched alleyways of Central City. A daily comic-strip version of *The Spirit* had a brief run, from 1941 to 1944, but his newspaper comic-book adventures lasted until 1952.

During the 1940s comic-book publishers faced increasing pressure from civic groups that objected to the violent and unwholesome content of certain titles. The newspaper syndicates were careful to distance themselves from this controversy. A representative from King Features, in a 1948 article in *Editor and Publisher*, described the strict taboos the syndicate applied to its comic features: "No blood, no torture, no horror, no controversial subjects such as religion, politics, and race. Above all, is the important matter of good taste. The comics must be clean."

The term "teenager" appeared in *Popular Science* magazine in 1941. Music, movies, clothing, and advertising were marketed to this emerging demographic group as teenage culture, from jalopies to jukeboxes, spread through middle-class America. In 1941 Bob Montana created a red-haired, freckle-faced teenager named Archie Andrews, who made his debut in *Pep Comics* no. 22. After the war, Archie, Jughead, Betty, and Veronica starred in their own newspaper comic strip, which was produced by Montana from 1946 to 1975. *Penny*, *Bobby Sox*, and *Teena* were among the numerous teen-oriented comic features that got their start during the decade.

After the war, aviation remained the most popular profession in the comics. Terry Lee, Steve Canyon, Johnny Hazard, and Buz Sawyer were among the flyboys who dominated the adventure-strip genre. Other occupations also began to emerge as inspiration for continuity features. Rip Kirby and Kerry Drake were private investigators. Brenda Starr and Steve Roper were newspaper reporters. Ozark Ike was a baseball player. Rex Morgan became the most famous medical doctor on the funnies pages.

The "soap-opera strip," patterned after the popular radio serials of the 1930s and 1940s, developed into a clearly defined genre when Apple Mary, who was created by Martha Orr in 1934, was transformed into Mary Worth by writer Allen Saunders and artist Ken Ernst in 1942. Mary abandoned her Depression-era, street-corner, social-worker persona and became a modern-day therapist who used grandmotherly wisdom to

TEEN TOON—ARCHIE Sunday page by Bob Montana. © 3/20/49 Creators Syndicate, Inc. Courtesy of International Museum of Cartoon Art.

solve the romantic problems of the rich and famous. During the postwar period she expanded her horizons and counseled combat veterans and newlywed couples. In the next decade, the soap-opera genre would continue to become increasingly sophisticated.

One of the most admired comic strips of the era was Crockett Johnson's *Barnaby*, which debuted in the liberal New York tabloid, *PM*, on April 20, 1942. Although his strip appeared in only fifty-two papers at its peak and lasted less than ten years, it was collected in book form and praised by writers, artists, and intellectuals. In the 1950s Johnson created a similar character, Harold, who drew an imaginary world with a purple crayon and starred in a series of seven classic children's stories.

Barnaby was a bright young boy who conversed freely with his bumbling fairy godfather, Mr. O'Malley. Barnaby's parents doubted the existence of this mysterious friend, who was invisible to everyone except Barnaby, his talking dog Gorgon, and the reader.

Johnson drew in a flat, economical style with a fixed perspective. The dialogue was set in type, to accommodate the extended conversations between Barnaby and O'Malley. Weary of daily deadlines, Johnson turned the production over to Ted Ferro and Jack Morley in 1946 but continued to be creatively involved until the strip ended on February 2, 1952.

In the final episode, O'Malley wished his friend a happy sixth birthday and then flew off into the starry heavens. Comic-strip continuities rarely had this type of closure.

Walt Kelly's Pogo, "a possum by trade," first appeared in *Animal Comics* in 1942 and, beginning in 1946, starred in his own comic book with his trusty sidekick Albert the Alligator. In June 1948 Kelly was hired as art director for the *New York Star*, a reincarnation of *PM*. In addition to drawing political cartoons, Kelly created a *Pogo* comic strip, which debuted in the *Star* on October 4, 1948. After the *Star* folded in 1949, *Pogo* was distributed by The Hall Syndicate.

By 1951 *Pogo* had evolved into a graphic tour de force that combined satire, caricature, slapstick, and whimsy. After only two years of syndication, the strip appeared in 100 newspapers and earned its creator an annual salary of $50,000. Kelly won the Reuben Award as the "outstanding cartoonist of the year" in 1951.

The accolades, particularly from the intelligentsia, were also piling up. Kelly never thought of himself as an intellectual. "If the high-brows find satire in my stuff, that's fine," he said in 1952. "The best I can say for myself is that I'm a high-brow low-brow. Kids and bartenders get as much bang out of *Pogo* as college professors."

Trained as an animation artist at the Walt Disney Studio,

SMART STRIP—BARNABY daily strip by Crockett Johnson. © 1945 The Newspaper PM, Inc.

Kelly filled *Pogo*'s Okefenokee Swamp with masterfully rendered flora and fauna. The colorful cast, which included Churchy LaFemme, Howland Owl, Porky Pine, Mam'selle Hepzibah, Beauregard, Pogo, and Albert, spoke in a unique blend of patois, puns, and prattle. Deacon Muskrat pontificated in Old English script and P. T. Bridgeport's balloons displayed circus-poster lettering. *Pogo* was brimming with inspired lunacy.

In 1952 Pogo ran for president against Dwight Eisenhower and Adlai Stevenson, and "I Go Pogo" rallies were held on college campuses across the country. Kelly gained national notoriety for his political satire and devastating caricatures of such public figures as Sen. Joseph McCarthy (Simple J. Malarky), Richard Nixon (Sam the Spider), and George Wallace (Prince Pompadoodle). He was also adept at social comment ("We have met the enemy and he is us") and cosmic musings ("God is not dead, He is merely unemployed").

Pogo strips were reprinted in thirty-two books, published by Simon & Schuster between 1951 and 1976, which sold an estimated 3 to 4 million copies. At its peak, *Pogo* ran in more than 600 newspapers. A modest amount of licensed adaptations were also produced, including a record album, *Songs of the Pogo* (1956), on which Kelly sang, and an animated cartoon, *The Pogo Birthday Special* (1969), directed by Chuck Jones.

Walt Kelly passed away in 1973 at the relatively tender age of sixty, but his legacy and influence live on. In 1989 Bill Watterson, the creator of *Calvin and Hobbes*, stated, "Although *Pogo* ended years before I ever had a drawing published, Kelly gave me a standard to apply to myself and cartooning as a whole."

Cartoonists are independent by nature, and sporadic attempts at forming a professional organization before the war met with failure. In 1927 Walt McDougall, Winsor McCay, Rube Goldberg, Clare Briggs, Harry Hershfield, and a host of other New York celebrities were among the guests at the first gathering of the Cartoonists of America. It was also the last. Another attempt to establish a cartoonist club in the early 1930s survived less than a year.

During World War II many of the top artists were called upon to travel around the country and entertain the troops. On one of these tours, a group that included Ernie Bushmiller, Gus Edson, Russell Patterson, Otto Soglow, and Rube Goldberg discussed the idea of forming a permanent organization after the war was over.

Goldberg was talked into taking a leadership role, and on February 20, 1946, he sent out a letter on behalf of the founders: "We got the idea it might be a very natural thing to have a cartoonists' club or society. Your name has been selected to join a group to sit down at dinner to make some

NEWSPAPER DEBUT—The first POGO strip by Walt Kelly. © 1949 Used by permission of Okefenokee Glee & Perloo, Inc. Courtesy of Craig Yoe

THE CLUB—Illustration for the 50th anniversary of the National Cartoonist Society, by Al Jaffee, 1996

The society faced its first major crisis in 1949 when Hilda Terry, creator of *Teena*, challenged the all-male status of the "club," as it was often called, and applied for membership. After many heated debates and two rounds of ballots, three women cartoonists, Hilda Terry, Barbara Shermund, and Edwina Dumm, were admitted to the N.C.S. in June 1950.

In 1949 Al Capp urged his fellow N.C.S. members to confront another issue that was vital to their existence. "Sooner or later," wrote Capp in the N.C.S. *Newsletter*, "the Society must justify its existence by being something more than it now is, by using its numbers and strength to do something affirmative for the cartoonist in the way that all associations of creative men, screenwriters, newspapermen, dramatists, and authors have made better and sounder the relationship between the artist and his business management."

Capp was proposing that the N.C.S. become a trade union and use its influence to challenge the archaic "work-for-hire" contracts the syndicates forced on eager cartoonists. Under the existing system, a newspaper syndicate owned the copyright to a cartoonist's feature. The creator could be fired at any time and replaced by another artist who would continue the strip, with the original characters, under the supervision of the syndicate.

The N.C.S. established a committee to investigate the feasibility of Capp's proposal. It eventually decided that the society could not realistically become a trade union because it did not have the clout to shut down the comics business by going on strike. Defeated, Capp curtailed his activities in the N.C.S.

Milton Caniff struck a blow for creative freedom when he secured the ownership of *Steve Canyon*. Al Capp and Walt Kelly also negotiated the copyrights to their features. But the majority of cartoonists had virtually no legal claim to what they created. This issue would continue to pose a challenge to cartoonists in the coming years.

plans—select a name, determine the dues, elect officers, and other such nonsense."

The inaugural meeting of the Cartoonists Society (the "National" was added later) was on Friday, March 1, 1946, in the Bayberry Room on East 52nd Street in Manhattan. The twenty-six cartoonists in attendance elected Goldberg president, Russell Patterson vice president, C. D. Russell secretary, and Milt Caniff treasurer.

When the N.C.S. gathered to celebrate its first anniversary in March 1947, it had 112 members. A few months later, the society presented its first award for "outstanding cartoonist of the year" to Milt Caniff. The trophy, a silver cigarette box engraved with the cast of *Barney Google and Snuffy Smith*, was named "The Billy DeBeck Memorial Award" after that strip's creator. Caniff had just quit smoking. The "Barney," as it came to be known, was replaced by the "Reuben," named after the society's first president, in 1953.

As the N.C.S. continued to grow, it became more than just a social organization. In 1948 members participated in the U.S. Treasury Bond Drive, a traveling exhibition of cartoon art, and a tour of veterans' hospitals. Milt Caniff served as president from 1948 to 1950 and was instrumental in guiding the N.C.S. during its formative years.

RING OUT THE OLD—The last TERRY AND THE PIRATES Sunday page by Milton Caniff. © 12/29/46 Tribune Media Services, Inc. All rights reserved. Reprinted with permission.
Courtesy of the Milton Caniff Collection, The Ohio State University Cartoon Research Library

milton caniff

THE "REMBRANDT of the comic strip," Milton Caniff created two masterpieces of graphic adventure, *Terry and the Pirates* in 1934 and *Steve Canyon* in 1947. Caniff's richly woven plots, memorable characters, distinctive dialogue, and exotic settings earned him the reputation as one of the greatest storytellers ever to work in the comics medium. His artistry influenced a generation of illustrators and revolutionized the adventure-strip genre. A founder of the National Cartoonists Society, Caniff was recognized as the "outstanding cartoonist of the year" in 1946 and 1971.

In the mid-1930s, Caniff shared a studio in Manhattan with Noel Sickles, a boyhood friend from Ohio. The young cartoonists collaborated closely on their two features, *Terry and the Pirates* and *Scorchy Smith*. Sickles began experimenting with a new technique, in which he rendered shadows and shapes with broad areas of black applied with a brush. Caniff borrowed Sickles's innovation and made it his own. He discovered he could maintain the realism in his adventure strip by indicating forms with impressionistic brush strokes, rather than inking in details with a pen. The method also saved time. An avid film buff, Caniff emulated the work of the movie directors he admired. He became a master at atmospheric lighting effects and dramatic perspective, using close-ups, long shots, and continuous tracking sequences.

When Caniff launched *Steve Canyon* in 1947, he was one of the most imitated artists in the comics business. He was also under tremendous pressure to do something

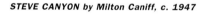

STEVE CANYON by Milton Caniff, c. 1947

different with his new feature, while not disappointing the fans who had been following *Terry and the Pirates* for twelve years. During the formative years of *Steve Canyon*, Caniff applied his creative talents to developing strong characters, fast-paced story lines, and realistically rendered scenes.

Dangerous and alluring women, such as the Dragon Lady, Burma, and April Kane, had been essential to the chemistry of *Terry and the Pirates*. Caniff continued to blend romance and adventure in *Steve Canyon*. Feeta-Feeta, Copper Calhoon, Delta, and Madame Lynx were among the seductive temptresses he introduced between 1947 and 1950.

When the Korean War escalated in 1951, Steve Canyon reenlisted in the Air Force and eventually rose to the rank of full colonel. The plots of Caniff's feature increasingly dealt with military intrigue, as Canyon was assigned to undercover operations around the world.

In 1953 Caniff hired Richard Rockwell, the nephew of Norman Rockwell, to pencil *Steve Canyon*. Penciling is regarded by most cartoonists as the crucial step in the production process and is therefore the last responsibility a creator is willing to relinquish to an assistant. Caniff felt that he could maintain his signature style more effectively by doing the final inking. Rockwell worked as Caniff's assistant until the strip ended in 1988.

The circulation of *Steve Canyon* reached a peak of 600 papers in the late 1950s but began declining in the 1960s and 1970s, a victim of size reduction and anti-military sentiment during the Vietnam War. Milton Caniff worked right up until his death in 1988, remaining a significant force in the cartoon business for more than half a century.

SELF-CARICATURE by Milton Caniff

STEVE CANYON Sunday page by Milton Caniff. © 1/26/47

All Steve Canyon comic strips © Milton Caniff Estate. Courtesy of the Milton Caniff Collection, The Ohio State University Cartoon Research Library

STEVE CANYON daily-strip sequence by Milton Caniff © 2/14–2/18/47

HIGH PRAISE Sylvan Byck, the comics editor of King Features Syndicate, wrote the following note to Caniff about the sequence above: "Frank Engli [Caniff's assistant at the time] just brought in the latest set of dailies. When I finished reading them, I felt that I had to write and tell you how wonderful they are. If this is not the best week of comic strips you have ever drawn, it certainly is a mighty strong challenger for the title." (Courtesy of R. C. Harvey)

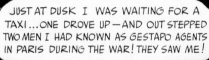

STEVE CANYON Sunday page by Milton Caniff © 8/17/47

STEVE CANYON daily-strip sequence by Milton Caniff © 8/18–8/21/47

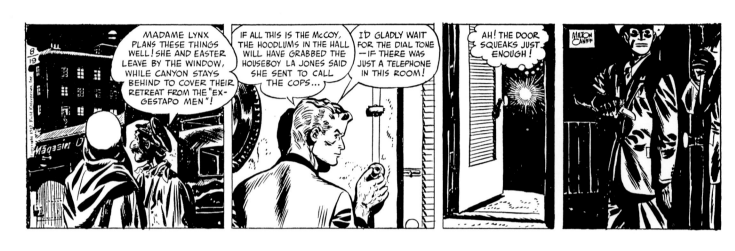

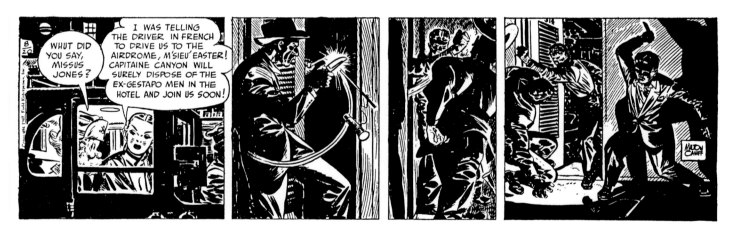

I'VE BEEN TRYING TO GET A STRAIGHT LINE ON YOU FOR A LONG TIME, BUT IT TOOK CONVOY TO REALLY NAIL YOU DOWN...

YOU WERE A WHIZ AT MATH IN SCHOOL! —YOU GOT INTO SUBMARINE SERVICE BECAUSE A GIRL COULD SHINE THERE! IT WAS TOUGH GOING, BUT YOU THOUGHT AND SLUGGED FAST ENOUGH TO RISE TO A COMMAND OF YOUR OWN!...

...YOU WERE SET TO BE THE FIRST REALLY BIG-SHOT WOMAN IN YOUR COUNTRY'S NAVY—THEN IT HAPPENED!

MAYBE IT WAS SOME NICE GUY FROM THE OUTSIDE WORLD WHO STARTED BELLS RINGING IN THE FEMININE SIDE OF YOUR BRAIN—WHICH YOU HAD KEPT DORMANT UP TO THEN BY SHEER FORCE OF WILL...

...MAYBE IT WAS AN AMERICAN MOVIE YOU SAW ON A TRIP...THE GALS IN THE PICTURE LOOKED GOOD IN THOSE NICE, FROTHY HOLLYWOOD CLOTHES!

—SO YOU MADE A GOWN IN SECRET, AND YOUR MIRROR SAID YOU COULD GIVE THEM CURVES ON EVERY PITCH...YOU COULD DO BETTER IN SILK THAN IN A SUBMARINE...

YOU'D BE A REAL SENSATION IN AMERICA, AND YOU KNOW IT! YOU BROUGHT HAPPY EASTER AND ME ALONG AS YOUR EXCUSE FOR TURNING THIS SCOW OVER TO THE U.S. NAVY AS IF WE HAD CAPTURED IT FROM YOU...

—AND WE'LL BE GLAD TO HELP YOU SWING THE DEAL!.. I EVEN HAVE SOME FRIENDS IN HOLLYWOOD WHO COULD TAKE IT FROM THAT END...

I---

OH — I DIDN'T SEE YOU! BUT SINCE YOU ARE HERE, DRAG CANYON BELOW! AFTER WHAT HE JUST SAID I HAVE NO ALTERNATIVE! HE MUST DIE!

Copyright 1948, SUN and TIMES Company 8-22

STEVE CANYON Sunday page by Milton Caniff. © 8/22/48

TERRY AND THE PIRATES daily strip by George Wunder. © 12/31/46 Tribune Media Services, Inc. All rights reserved. Reprinted with permission. Courtesy of William Crouch

THE CANIFF SCHOOL

The graphic techniques that Milton Caniff perfected in *Terry and the Pirates* and *Steve Canyon* influenced many of the story-strip artists of the post-war era. George Wunder was chosen as Caniff's successor on *Terry and the Pirates* (his second daily strip, from December 31, 1946, is shown above) and continued the feature until he retired in 1973. In the early years Wunder emulated Caniff's style closely, but he eventually developed a more distinctive look. Frank Robbins, who took over *Scorchy Smith* in 1939 and created his own adventure strip, *Johnny Hazard*, in 1944 (below), was a talented contemporary of Caniff's. Ray Bailey, who worked as Caniff's assistant on *Terry and the Pirates* in the early 1940s, launched another aviation adventure strip, *Bruce Gentry*, in 1945 (bottom).

JOHNNY HAZARD daily strip by Frank Robbins. © 9/2/47 King Features Syndicate, Inc. Courtesy of International Museum of Cartoon Art

BRUCE GENTRY daily strip by Ray Bailey. © 1/14/48 New York Post Corp. Courtesy of International Museum of Cartoon Art

JOE PALOOKA daily strip by Ham Fisher, c. 1940s. © McNaught Syndicate, Inc. Courtesy of International Museum of Cartoon Art

SPORTS

One of the most popular comics of the 1940s was Ham Fisher's *Joe Palooka*, which appeared in more than 1,000 newspapers at its peak. Fisher created the naive prizefighter in 1930 but employed numerous art assistants, including Phil Boyle, Al Capp, and Mo Leff, to illustrate the strip until his tragic suicide in 1955. Another sports-oriented feature of the era was Ray Gotto's *Ozark Ike*, which debuted in 1945 and dealt primarily with baseball stories, but switched to football and basketball continuities during the off-season.

OZARK IKE daily strip by Ray Gotto. © 6/6/49 King Features Syndicate, Inc. Courtesy of International Museum of Cartoon Art

SOUTH OF THE BORDER

Gus Arriola's *Gordo* debuted thirteen days before Pearl Harbor, was put on hold in 1942 when Arriola joined the Air Force, resumed daily distribution in 1946, and continued until 1985. R. C. Harvey, Arriola's biographer, wrote that "Gordo evolved into a cultural ambassador who represented life in Mexico to an American audience." In 1948 Arriola was deluged with thousands of letters when he offered his readers the secret recipe to Gordo's favorite dish, beans and cheese (referred to in the strip below).

GORDO daily strip by Gus Arriola. © 2/2/48 by United Feature Syndicate, Inc. Courtesy of International Museum of Cartoon Art

THE PHANTOM Sunday page by Lee Falk and Wilson McCoy. © 11/13/49 King Features Syndicate, Inc. Courtesy of International Museum of Cartoon Art

WORDSMITH Lee Falk created two long-running adventure strips in the 1930s and continued to write both features until he passed away in 1999. *Mandrake the Magician*, the mysterious crime-fighting illusionist, first appeared in 1934 and was illustrated by Phil Davis for thirty years, until Fred Fredericks took over in 1964. *The Phantom*, which starred one of the first costumed heroes, debuted in 1936 and was drawn in the 1940s by Wilson McCoy.

MANDRAKE THE MAGICIAN daily strip by Lee Falk and Phil Davis. © 5/9/1940s King Features Syndicate, Inc. Courtesy of International Museum of Cartoon Art

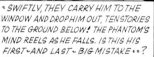

THE SPIRIT *splash page by Will Eisner.* © 10/19/49 by Will Eisner. Courtesy of International Museum of Cartoon Art

WILL EISNER   The Spirit, who starred in a sixteen-page newspaper comic-book insert beginning in 1940, was a gumshoe/flatfoot in the Sam Spade tradition. This dramatic splash page from 1949 recounts the background story of Eisner's masked crime fighter (a.k.a. Denny Colt).

DICK TRACY daily strip by Chester Gould. © 12/25/48

CHESTER GOULD

Dick Tracy, Chester Gould's classic plainclothes detective, started his battle against crime in 1931. Gould retired on Christmas Day, 1977, after forty-six years, two months, and twenty-one days of single-minded devotion to his creation. The postwar era was a significant transition period in Gould's artistic development. He introduced a lineup of unforgettable villains, showcased bold, black-and-white graphics in double-sized panels, and unraveled gripping stories filled with violence and pathos. In the 1950s Gould was forced to shrink the size of his art, and, graphically, the strip would never be the same as it was in the peak years of 1943 to 1950.

Shown on the next page are examples from two memorable sequences of Gould's postwar period. In the top two strips, from 1949, Dick Tracy and Tess are on their honeymoon and, after being stranded in a snowstorm, cross paths with Wormy Marron, a classic Gould villain (Wormy's demise is shown at the bottom of this page). In the bottom two strips, from 1950, Tracy valiantly tries to rescue his trusty sidekick, Junior, from his burning home.

DICK TRACY daily strip by Chester Gould. © 1/27/47

DICK TRACY daily strip by Chester Gould. © 3/25/50

DICK TRACY daily strip by Chester Gould. © 12/29/49

DICK TRACY daily strip by Chester Gould. © 12/30/49

DICK TRACY daily strip by Chester Gould. © 4/21/50

DICK TRACY daily strip by Chester Gould. © 4/22/50

CHAKA, POINTING TO THE SNAKE SYMBOL ABOUT TARZAN'S THROAT, SCREAMED THE DREAD CURSE OF THE DAGOMBAS AND COMMANDED THE SUPERSTITIOUS NATIVES TO ATTACK HIM.

CLEVELAND'S SHOUT OF TRIUMPH TOLD TARZAN THAT THE WARRIORS WERE IN NO MOOD FOR EXPLANATIONS. THEY ATTACKED WITH SAVAGE FEROCITY.

SNATCHING A CLAWING NATIVE OFF HIS BACK, HE USED THE MAN AS A FLAIL TO SWEEP A PATH TO THE WATER'S EDGE.

IN THE CLOSE-PACKED, TWISTING MASS, THE APE-MAN BEAT BACK HIS ATTACKERS WITH A FURY BORN OF JUNGLE DESPERATION.

SUDDENLY TARZAN SHOOK HIMSELF FREE. WITH A SINGLE BOUND, HE TOOK OFF IN A LONG FLAT DIVE.

3-19
HOGARTH

BURNE HOGARTH   This hand-colored Sunday page by Burne Hogarth is reportedly the last episode Tarzan's creator, Edgar Rice Burroughs, read before he passed away on March 19, 1950.

TARZAN Sunday page by Burne Hogarth. © 3/19/50 United Feature Syndicate, Inc. Courtesy of Ricardo Martinez

"YOU TWO GAMECOCKS CANNOT FINISH THIS BY SINGLE COMBAT, FOR YOUR FAMILIES WOULD ONLY CONTINUE THE FEUD FOR GENERATIONS TO COME."

"MAY I SUGGEST THAT WE LEAVE THE MATTER IN THE HANDS OF THESE YOUNG PEOPLE TO SETTLE?"

COPR. 1951, KING FEATURES SYNDICATE, Inc., WORLD RIGHTS RESERVED.   728. 1-21

MANY A VERSE WAS WRITTEN AND MANY A SONG SUNG TO THE YOUNG MAID WHO CHAINED HERSELF TO THE STAKE WITH HER LOVER.

THERE WERE ALSO SOME HUNDREDS OF WIDOWS AND ORPHANS WHO FAILED TO SEE ANYTHING ROMANTIC IN THE EVENT. BUT THEN, THEY HAD NO APPRECIATION OF POETRY!

NEXT WEEK— Unwanted Peace

HAL FOSTER   A spectacular page from 1951 in which Prince Valiant intercedes in a dramatic face-off. Foster created the epic illustrated Sunday-only feature in 1937 and continued working on it until he officially retired in 1979.

PRINCE VALIANT Sunday page by Hal Foster. © 1/21/51 King Features Syndicate, Inc. Courtesy of International Museum of Cartoon Art

ROY CRANE   A pioneer of the adventure-strip genre, Roy Crane created *Wash Tubbs* in 1924, which he abandoned to launch *Buz Sawyer* in 1943. In the late 1940s Buz Sawyer married his longtime sweetheart, Christy Jameson, and the two set off on a series of globe-trotting adventures to Europe, Africa, and Latin America. Exotic scenery and dramatic composition, masterfully rendered with the duo-shade technique, were typical of *Buz Sawyer* during this period. These sequences were illustrated by Crane's assistant, Hank Schlensker, and scripted by Ed Granberry.

BUZ SAWYER daily strip by Roy Crane. © 1/31/49

All Buz Sawyer strips © King Features Syndicate, Inc.

BUZ SAWYER daily strip by Roy Crane. © 4/13/49

BUZ SAWYER daily strip by Roy Crane. © 4/21/49

BUZ SAWYER daily strip by Roy Crane. © 5/12/49

BUZ SAWYER daily strip by Roy Crane. © 6/28/49

BUZ SAWYER daily strip by Roy Crane. © 9/23/49

BUZ SAWYER daily strip by Roy Crane. © 10/4/51

LITTLE ORPHAN ANNIE illustration by Harold Gray. © 10/20/46. Courtesy of Richard Marschall

LITTLE ORPHAN ANNIE daily strip by Harold Gray. © 9/17/45

LITTLE ORPHAN ANNIE daily strip by Harold Gray. © 11/11/48. Courtesy of The Harold Gray Collection, Boston University

HAROLD GRAY   *Little Orphan Annie* had been a fixture on the funnies pages for more than two decades when World War II ended in 1945. Throughout the Cold War era, the strip provided Gray with a platform to express his conservative views on politics, economics, and social injustice. Gray was

LITTLE ORPHAN ANNIE Sunday page by Harold Gray. © 12/16/56. Courtesy of The Harold Gray Collection, Boston University

also adept at sentimental digressions, as this seasonal Sunday page from 1956 demonstrates. Gray continued to produce his uniquely personal comic-strip fable until he died in 1968.

RIP KIRBY daily strip #8 by Alex Raymond. © 1946. Courtesy of Jack Gilbert

All Rip Kirby strips © King Features Syndicate, Inc.

ALEX RAYMOND

The illustrator of three classic adventure strips, *Secret Agent X-9*, *Flash Gordon*, and *Jungle Jim*, all of which made their debut in 1934, Alex Raymond distinguished himself in the postwar era as the creator of the cerebral detective feature *Rip Kirby*. From the beginning (the eighth episode from 1946 is shown above), the style of Raymond's new strip was influenced by the latest trends in magazine illustration. Glamorous women, realistically rendered settings, and understated action sequences complemented the scripts, which were written by Fred Dickenson. A decade after *Rip Kirby* was launched, Raymond was killed in an auto accident. His last signed strip, dated September 29, 1956, appears at the bottom of the next page.

SELF-CARICATURE by Alex Raymond

RIP KIRBY daily strip by Alex Raymond. (Note the self-caricature of Raymond in the right-hand corner of the first panel.) © 1/9/47. Courtesy of International Museum of Cartoon Art

RIP KIRBY daily strip by Alex Raymond. © 7/4/47. Courtesy of International Museum of Cartoon Art

RIP KIRBY daily strip by Alex Raymond. © 2/13/48. Courtesy of Art Wood Collection

RIP KIRBY daily strip by Alex Raymond. © 1/18/56. Courtesy of International Museum of Cartoon Art

RIP KIRBY daily strip by Alex Raymond. © 9/29/56. Courtesy of King Features Syndicate, Inc.

BRENDA STARR *Sunday page by Dale Messick.* © 12/30/45 Tribune Media Services, Inc. All rights reserved. Reprinted with permission. Courtesy of the Frye Art Museum, Seattle.

Photo credit: Susan Dirk/Under the Light

ROMANCE   Dale Messick, one of the first female cartoonists to succeed in the male-dominated story-strip genre, introduced the redheaded newspaper reporter Brenda Starr in 1940. For many years the romantic intrigue in Messick's strip revolved around the mysterious Basil St. John and his magical black orchids until Brenda and Basil were finally married in

1976. *Abbie an' Slats* (below), which was created by Al Capp in 1937 and written by his brother, Elliot Caplin, beginning in 1946, featured a blend of romance, adventure, and homespun humor. The long-running strip was ably illustrated by Raeburn Van Buren until 1971.

ABBIE AN' SLATS *daily strip by Raeburn Van Buren.* © 8/31/49 United Feature Syndicate, Inc. Courtesy of International Museum of Cartoon Art.

MARY WORTH Sunday page by Allen Saunders and Ken Ernst. © 3/25/45 King Features Syndicate, Inc. Courtesy of the Frye Art Museum, Seattle. Photo credit: Susan Dirk/Under the Light

SOAP OPERA

In 1939, when Allen Saunders took over the writing chores on Martha Orr's 1934 creation, *Apple Mary*, he decided to give the strip a contemporary makeover, as Mary became a counselor to the rich and famous. Ken Ernst came on board as the artist in 1942 and provided the perfect match to Saunders's sophisticated story lines. The strip was renamed *Mary Worth* in 1944 and established the definitive format for the emerging soap-opera genre. In 1948 Dr. Nicholas Dallis teamed up with artists Marvin Bradley and Frank Edginton to create *Rex Morgan M.D.* (below). The handsome, dark-haired medical doctor has been solving his patients' problems for more than half a century.

REX MORGAN M.D. daily strip by Dr. Nicholas Dallis, Marvin Bradley, and Frank Edginton. © 7/13/48 King Features Syndicate, Inc. Courtesy of International Museum of Cartoon Art

al capp

DOGPATCH U.S.A., Sadie Hawkins Day, Kickapoo Joy Juice, Shmoos, and Kigmies are among the lasting inspirations Al Capp contributed to American folklore. *Li'l Abner*, which debuted in 1934, was a direct reflection of Capp's colorful personality and provided him with a vehicle to lampoon the shortcomings of the human race. Social comment was only one of his tools, as he used suspense, slapstick, and characterization to establish *Li'l Abner* as one of the most consistently hilarious and wildly unpredictable strips in comics history.

Alfred Gerald Caplin was born in New Haven, Connecticut, in 1909 and lost his left leg when he was run over by a trolley car at the age of nine. This handicap was a source of ambition as well as insecurity for Capp throughout the rest of his life. "I wonder if it wasn't because of the wooden leg slowing me down, that I had patience to study art," he once said.

Capp first became interested in rural America during a trip he made to Tennessee when he was a teenager. In 1933, while working as the "ghost artist" on Ham Fisher's *Joe Palooka*, Capp introduced a hillbilly boxer named "Big Leviticus." Fisher later accused his former assistant of stealing the idea from him, but in truth, Capp had adapted his own creation when he came up with the idea for *Li'l Abner*.

In 1937 the first Sadie Hawkins Day took place in Dogpatch. The event, in which the unattached females chased the eligible bachelors, became an annual tradition at many college campuses across the country.

As Capp's style matured, he increasingly used a variety of visual techniques to maximize the strip's impact on the comics pages. Heavy black borders, bold lettering, and stylized speech balloons, as well as grotesque caricatures, exaggerated dialect, and voluptuous females, all served to grab the attention of newspaper readers.

SELF-CARICATURE by Al Capp

SHEET MUSIC 1946. *Courtesy of Kitchen Sink Press*

Capp hired his first assistant, Mo Leff, in 1935. Over the course of the next forty-two years, Capp employed many artists to help illustrate *Li'l Abner*, including Andy Amato, Harvey Curtis, Walter Johnson, Frank Frazetta, Lee Elias, Bob Lubbers, and Stan Drake. Although he remained creatively involved in the production of the strip, Capp kept up a busy schedule of extracurricular activities, pursuing stints as a columnist, lecturer, and television personality.

During the 1940s and 1950s, Capp ventured beyond Dogpatch and the adventures of the Yokum family, exploring a wide range of themes as his humor became more sardonic. Fearless Fosdick, a takeoff on Chester Gould's *Dick Tracy*, starred in a number of extended episodes. Creatures such as Shmoos, Kigmies, and the Bald Iggle exposed the selfishness and hypocrisy of human nature. Lower Slobbovia, a snowbound backwater populated with ignorant peasants, was an obvious Cold War dig at the Soviet Union. Capp's below-the-belt satire earned him the moniker of the "outhouse Voltaire" from one critic.

In the 1960s Capp began attacking liberals and college protesters with the same vehemence that he had directed toward conservatives in the previous decades. "My politics didn't change," he claimed. "I had always been for those who were despised, disgraced, and denounced by other people."

When *Li'l Abner* ended in 1977, the circulation of the strip had dropped from a peak of 900 papers to 300. Capp died two years later.

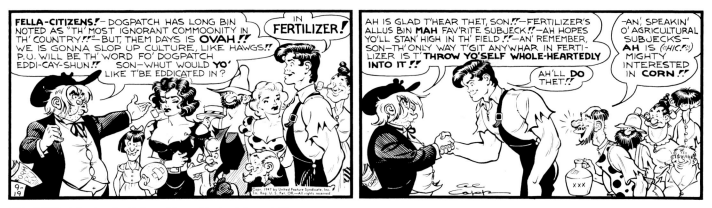

LI'L ABNER daily strip by Al Capp (the residents of Dogpatch). © 9/19/47. Courtesy of Howard Lowery Gallery

All Li'l Abner artwork © Capp Enterprises, Inc.

LI'L ABNER daily strip by Al Capp (Fearless Fosdick was a recurring spoof of Dick Tracy). © 3/18/48. Courtesy of Bruce Hamilton

LI'L ABNER daily strip by Al Capp (the legend of the Shmoo). © 9/1/48. Courtesy of Howard Lowery Gallery

LI'L ABNER daily strip by Al Capp (Daisy Mae and Li'l Gal Shmoo). © 10/27/48. Courtesy of Russ Cochran

LI'L ABNER Sunday page by Al Capp (takeoff on the popular TV show "This is Your Life"). © 3/21/54. Courtesy of Denis Kitchen.

LI'L ABNER daily strip by Al Capp (Capp self-caricature). © 7/20/49. Courtesy of Matt Masterson

LI'L ABNER daily strip by Al Capp (Cave Gal wins Sadie Hawkins race). © 11/27/51. Courtesy of William Crouch

LI'L ABNER daily strip by Al Capp (ghosted by Frank Frazetta). © 2/11/57. Courtesy of International Museum of Cartoon Art

LI'L ABNER daily strip by Al Capp (caricature of Beatle Ringo Starr). © 8/26/65. Courtesy of International Museum of Cartoon Art

LI'L ABNER Sunday page by Al Capp (poking fun at Peanuts and Charles Schulz). © 10/20/68. Courtesy of International Museum of Cartoon Art

LI'L ABNER Sunday page by Al Capp (attacking student protesters). © 9/21/69. Courtesy of International Museum of Cartoon Art

FRANK KING *Gasoline Alley*, which began as a daily feature in 1919, is unique in that it is one of the only strips in which the characters age at a natural rate. In 1921 a baby, later named Skeezix, was left on Walt Wallet's doorstep. In this hand-colored Sunday page by Frank King

from 1946, Skeezix, now a husband and a father, introduces Bix, a WWII Navy combat veteran, to his younger brother and sister, Corky and Judy.

BOBBY SOX Sunday page by Marty Links. © 10/16/49 United Feature Syndicate, Inc. Courtesy of International Museum of Cartoon Art.

HAPPY DAYS

Comics starring teenagers proliferated in the 1940s. Marty Links had just graduated from high school when her panel, *Bobby Sox*, was first published in the *San Francisco Chronicle*. It was nationally syndicated beginning in 1944 and was renamed *Emmy Lou* in the 1950s. America's most well-known pen-and-ink post-pubescents, Archie, Jughead, Betty, and Veronica, made their newspaper debut in 1946, five years after their initial appearance in a comic book. *Archie*'s creator, Bob Montana, continued the strip until 1975.

ARCHIE daily strip by Bob Montana. © 8/16/48 Creators Syndicate Courtesy of International Museum of Cartoon Art.

NANCY daily strip by Ernie Bushmiller. © 5/17/46

ERNIE BUSHMILLER

Nancy made her first appearance in Ernie Bushmiller's *Fritzi Ritz* in 1933. Fritzi's fuzzy-haired niece gradually usurped the starring role from her aunt, and in 1938 the name of the strip was officially changed. By the 1940s *Nancy* was among the top syndicated features, appearing in more than 450 newspapers. The years between 1944 and 1959 are considered to be the peak period of Bushmiller's long-running creation, as he refined his gag-a-day formula and introduced classic themes that would be endlessly recycled. The selection of *Nancy* strips shown here displays Bushmiller's graphic inventiveness and surreal sense of humor.

SELF-CARICATURE by Ernie Bushmiller

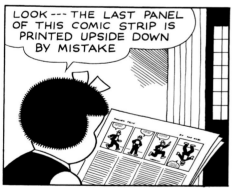

NANCY daily strip by Ernie Bushmiller. © 8/29/47

NANCY daily strip by Ernie Bushmiller. © 7/14/47

NANCY daily strip by Ernie Bushmiller. © 4/22/47

NANCY daily strip by Ernie Bushmiller. © 8/22/51

NANCY daily strip by Ernie Bushmiller. © 8/31/51

NANCY daily strip by Ernie Bushmiller. © 8/24/66

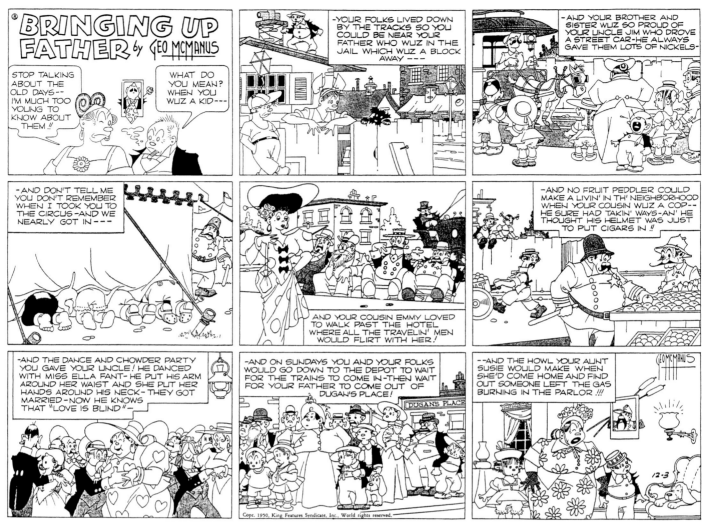

BRINGING UP FATHER Sunday page by George McManus. © 12/3/50 King Features Syndicate, Inc. Courtesy of International Museum of Cartoon Art

GEORGE MCMANUS

Bringing Up Father began in 1913, and George McManus's bickering costars, Maggie and Jiggs, were still popular with newspaper readers more than three decades later. By that time most of the artwork was being produced by McManus's talented assistant, Zeke

Zekley, who drew himself in the strip below. The Sunday page above represents a semiannual tradition in which Maggie and Jiggs would reminisce nostalgically about the good old days, growing up in the Irish neighborhood.

BRINGING UP FATHER daily strip by George McManus (Zeke Zekley in third panel). © 10/27/52 King Features Syndicate, Inc. Courtesy of Bill Janocha

BARNEY GOOGLE AND SNUFFY SMITH Sunday page by Fred Lasswell. © 9/8/46 King Features Syndicate, Inc.

FRED LASSWELL

In 1934 Billy DeBeck hired Fred Lasswell to assist him on *Barney Google and Snuffy Smith*, and after DeBeck died in 1942 Lasswell stepped in to continue the fading feature. In Lasswell's hands, Snuffy and his hillbilly clan took over the strip as the humor became more folksy and the circulation rose from 206 subscribers in 1946 to nearly 900 clients in 1989.

SMOKEY STOVER Sunday page by Bill Holman. © 2/18/51 Tribune Media Services, Inc. All rights reserved. Reprinted with permission. Courtesy of International Museum of Cartoon Art

BILL HOLMAN

A tour de force of screwball comedy, Bill Holman's *Smokey Stover* ran from 1935 to 1973. A Sunday-only feature for most of this time, Holman's creation starred a goofy fireman and was cluttered with cryptic references, such as "1506 Nix Nix," "Notary Sojac," and "Foo," and clever visual puns hanging in the backgrounds.

POGO painting for Newsweek magazine by Walt Kelly. © 1955. Courtesy of Carolyn Kelly

All Pogo artwork used by permission © Okefenokee Glee & Perloo, Inc.

Early POGO daily strip from the New York Star by Walt Kelly. © 11/1/48. Courtesy of Garry Trudeau

walt kelly

ONE OF THE MOST versatile talents ever to work in the comics medium, Walt Kelly mastered all of the art form's tools and techniques. He was adept at flights of fantasy as well as biting political satire. He loved clever wordplay and penned lines of nonsense and thought-provoking philosophy. Intellectuals praised *Pogo* for its literary content, and children delighted in the strip's visual slapstick and enchanting whimsy. With his facile brush, Kelly conjured up a world filled with talking animals and evocative scenery.

After graduating from high school in 1930, Kelly gained experience working as a reporter and cartoonist for his hometown newspaper in Bridgeport, Connecticut. In 1935 he traveled west to seek his fortune in the animation business. For the next five years, he honed his talents at the Walt Disney Studio and was credited as a storyboard artist and animator on *Pinocchio*, *Fantasia*, and *Dumbo*. The Disney influence was evident in the style of his later comics creations.

When he returned east Kelly worked on a number of comic-book titles for Western Printing, including *Fairy Tale Parade*, *Raggedy Ann and Andy*, *Our Gang*, *Santa Claus Funnies*, and *Walt Disney Comics and Stories*. Pogo made his first appearance in *Animal Comics* no. 1, which was published by Dell in 1942.

As Pogo evolved from a comic-book sidekick to the star of a nationally syndicated comic strip, he became increasingly subordinate to Kelly's expanding cast of colorful creatures. More than 150 characters, each with a distinct name and personality, eventually populated Pogo's Okefenokee Swamp. The many species represented included an alligator (Albert), an owl (Howland), a skunk (Mam'selle Hepzibah), a porcupine (Porky Pine), and a hound (Beauregard). There were bats, frogs, mice, ducks, rabbits, bears, birds and bugs, a jazz-playing pig (Solid Mac Hogany), and a boxing kangaroo (Basher).

In the early 1950s Kelly began introducing a new element into the fantasy world of *Pogo*—political satire. "I finally came to understand that if I were looking for comic material, I would never have to look long," he explained. "The news of the day would be enough. Perhaps the complexion of the strip changed a little in that direction after 1951. After all, it is pretty hard to walk past an unguarded gold mine and remain empty-handed."

To help combat the "growing peril" that threatened the swamp in 1953, Simple J. Malarky, a bobcat who was a dead ringer for Senator Joseph McCarthy, was called in to weed out the subversives. Although McCarthy never publicly complained about the portrayal, a number of newspapers dropped selected strips they considered objectionable.

POGO promotional piece for the Minneapolis Tribune by Walt Kelly.
© 1969. Courtesy of Art Wood Collection

Throughout the 1950s and 1960s Kelly continued to feature political satire. In 1962 when he depicted Soviet leader Khrushchev as a pig and Cuban dictator Castro as a goat, "inquiries" were made by the Russian embassy, forcing the cancellation of *Pogo* in a Japanese paper. During the 1960s the political humor in *Pogo* became more strident as Kelly's liberal leanings came to the surface. Overt commentary and unflattering caricatures of Richard Nixon, Lyndon Johnson, and Spiro Agnew alternated with surreal fantasy, as in the extended "Prehysterical *Pogo* (in Pandemonia)" sequence, which ran from July 1966 to April 1967. Eventually Kelly began offering replacement strips when he felt the political comment might be offensive to editors and readers. These innocuous episodes came to be known as his "bunny rabbit strips."

Walt Kelly died on October 18, 1973. Years earlier he challenged his readers with the following words of wisdom: "There is no need to sally forth, for it remains true that those things which make us human are, curiously enough, always close at hand. Resolve, then, that on this very ground, with small flags waving and tinny blasts on tiny trumpets, we may meet the enemy . . . and not only may he be ours, he may be us."

SELF-CARICATURE by Walt Kelly. © 1969

Unpublished illustration of Simple J. Malarky (Sen. Joseph McCarthy) from "King of Hearts" by Walt Kelly. © c. 1953. Courtesy of the Pogo Collection, The Ohio State University Cartoon Research Library

POGO daily strip by Walt Kelly (featuring Simple J. Malarky). © 9/23/54. Courtesy of Garry Trudeau

POGO daily strip by Walt Kelly (Little Orphan Annie takeoff). © 5/6/58. Courtesy of Scott Daley

POGO daily strip by Walt Kelly (caricatures of Khrushchev and Castro). © 6/22/62. Courtesy of Bruce Hamilton

POGO daily strip by Walt Kelly (caricature of Barry Goldwater). © 10/6/64. Courtesy of Garry Trudeau

POGO daily strip by Walt Kelly (comment on student protest movement). © 9/10/69. Courtesy of Scott Daley

POGO hand-colored Christmas Sunday page by Walt Kelly. © 12/24/67. Courtesy of Bruce Hamilton

POGO Sunday page by Walt Kelly (from the extended "prehysterical" sequence, a graphic homage to pen-and-ink artist T. S. Sullivant, one of Kelly's major influences). © 1/22/67. Courtesy of International Museum of Cartoon Art

POGO Sunday page by Walt Kelly (a romantic encounter between Churchy LaFemme and Mam'selle Hepzibah). © 5/10/70. Courtesy of Mark Evanier

POGO illustration from Ten Ever-Lovin' Blue-Eyed Years with Pogo *by Walt Kelly.* © 1959. Courtesy of Scott Daley

POGO daily strip by Walt Kelly (Christmas sentiment). © 12/23/67. Courtesy of International Museum of Cartoon Art

POGO daily strip by Walt Kelly (ecology statement). © 6/20/70. Courtesy of International Museum of Cartoon Art

BLONDIE Sunday page by Chic Young. © 3/9/52 King Features Syndicate, Inc.

CHIC YOUNG   At the end of the 1940s *Blondie* was the top strip in America and would remain so for many years to come. In 1950 Chic Young's longtime assistant, Jim Raymond (the brother of Alex Raymond), took over the sole artistic duties on the feature. The Sunday page above shows Dagwood Bumstead fixing his famous sandwich, and the daily strip below has an uncharacteristically gruesome ending.

BLONDIE daily strip by Chic Young. © 7/4/45 King Features Syndicate, Inc. Courtesy of Bruce Hamilton.

the fifties

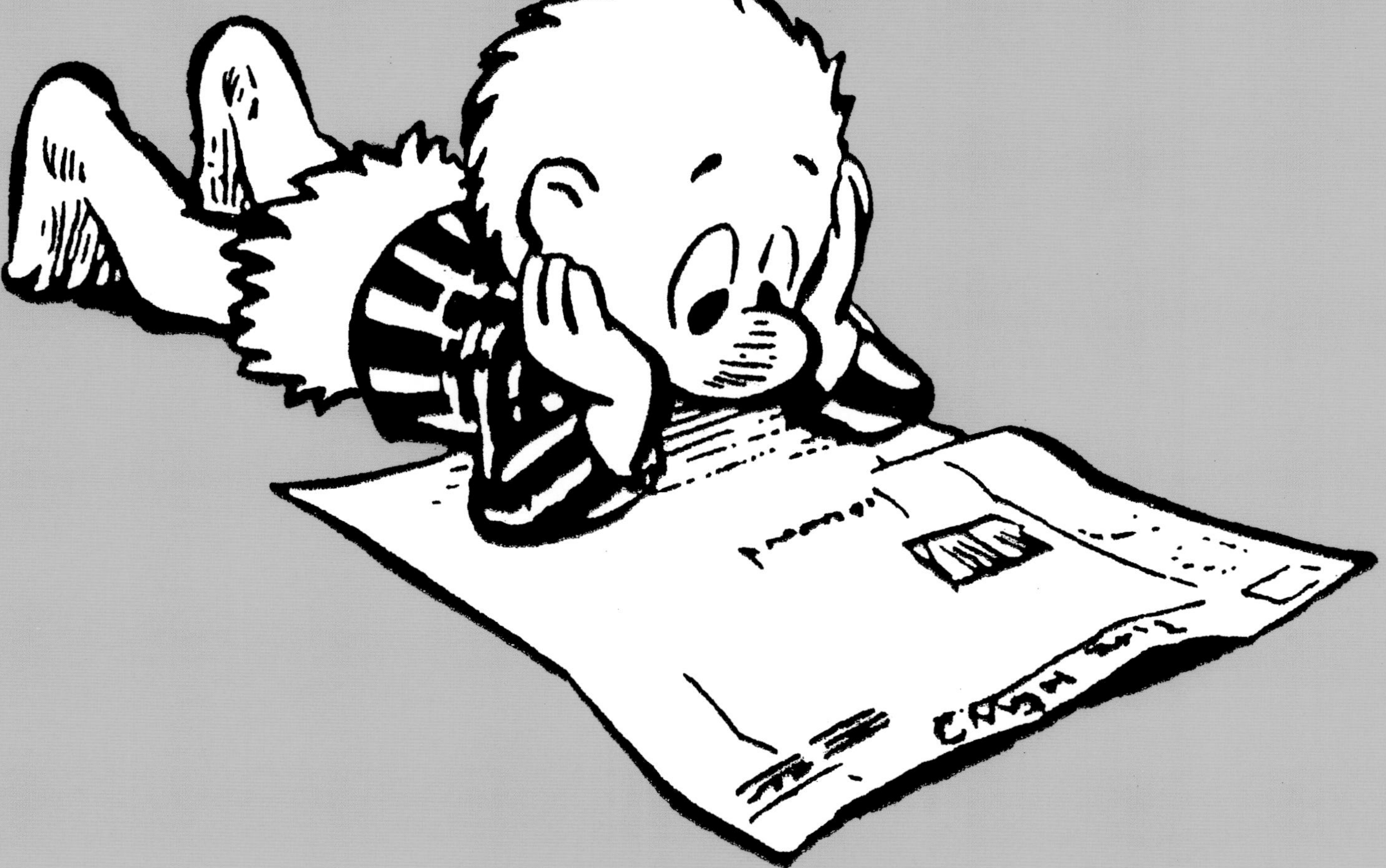

POGO by Walt Kelly.

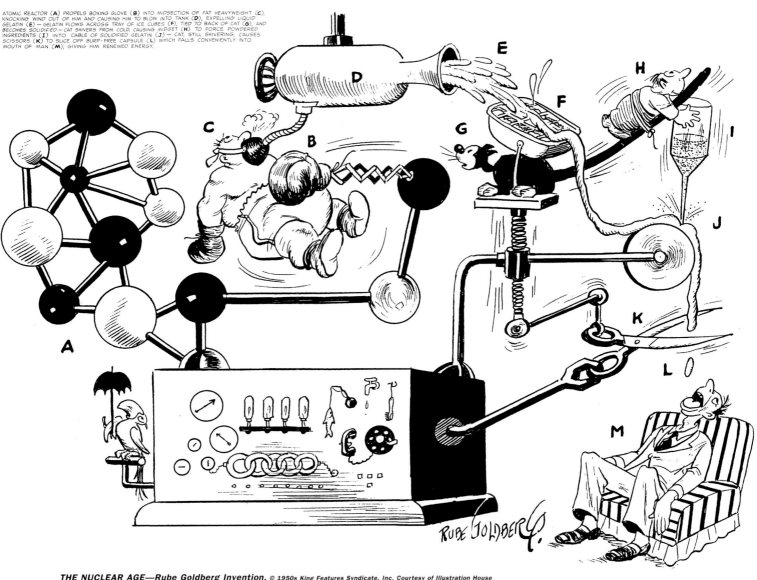

ATOMIC REACTOR (**A**) PROPELS BOXING GLOVE (**B**) INTO MIDSECTION OF FAT HEAVYWEIGHT (**C**), KNOCKING WIND OUT OF HIM AND CAUSING HIM TO BLOW INTO TANK (**D**), EXPELLING LIQUID GELATIN (**E**) — GELATIN FLOWS ACROSS TRAY OF ICE CUBES (**F**), TIED TO BACK OF CAT (**G**), AND BECOMES SOLIDIFIED — CAT SHIVERS FROM COLD, CAUSING MIDGET (**H**) TO FORCE POWDERED INGREDIENTS (**I**) INTO CABLE OF SOLIDIFIED GELATIN (**J**) — CAT, STILL SHIVERING, CAUSES SCISSORS (**K**) TO SLICE OFF BURP-FREE CAPSULE (**L**) WHICH FALLS CONVENIENTLY INTO MOUTH OF MAN (**M**), GIVING HIM RENEWED ENERGY.

THE NUCLEAR AGE—*Rube Goldberg Invention.* © 1950s King Features Syndicate, Inc. Courtesy of Illustration House

BY 1950 THE POSTWAR HOUSING CRISIS HAD BEEN SOLVED. IN THAT YEAR ALONE, 1.4 MILLION NEW HOMES WERE BUILT. AFFORDABLE SUBURBAN DEVELOPMENTS MADE THE AMERICAN DREAM OF MARRIAGE, HOME OWNERSHIP, AND PARENTHOOD POSSIBLE FOR THE VETERANS OF WORLD WAR II. BUILDERS AND DEVELOPERS STRUGGLED TO KEEP UP WITH THE DEMAND AS THE FLIGHT TO THE SUBURBS GREW AND THE BIRTH RATE SOARED. BETWEEN 1950 AND 1959, 30 MILLION BABIES WERE BORN.

The baby boom did not lead to a sudden proliferation of comics starring kids. Humorous features for "children of all ages" had been a staple of the medium since *The Yellow Kid* and *The Katzenjammer Kids* started the tradition in the 1890s. The only change was now Charlie Brown and Dennis the Menace competed for space with Henry and Nancy on the funnies pages.

Television would have a greater influence on the comics business than any other development of the decade. In 1950 TV sets were owned by only 3.1 million homes. Within five years the number jumped to 32 million. By 1959 the average family spent six hours a day, seven days a week, in front of the "boob tube."

Newspaper publishers were nervous. "The newspaper-TV battle is not merely a fight for the advertiser's dollar, as was the radio-newspaper fight," *Editor and Publisher* magazine warned in 1951. "This is a contest for the readers' time in which no holds are barred."

Artists were asked not to promote the new medium in their strips. One publisher in New Jersey actually billed United Feature Syndicate for advertising space when Al Capp "plugged" the Milton Berle show in *Li'l Abner.*

In spite of these objections, comics based on popular television shows were soon being offered. *Hopalong Cassidy* and *Howdy Doody* strips debuted in 1950, and *Dragnet* and *I Love Lucy* followed in 1952.

"Having a strip based on another medium is like getting a foot in the door," admitted comic-strip agent Toni Mendez in 1950. "It means immediate recognition for that particular strip. But once in, the strip will have to live on its own merits."

Most of the TV spin-off strips lasted only a few years. The syndicates were more successful with original ideas that provided an alternative to broadcast entertainment. Two distinct new genres of comic strips—soap opera and gag-a-day—began to emerge in the 1950s, at least partly in response to the growing popularity of television.

The success of *Mary Worth* in the 1940s convinced editors that they could lure women readers away from radio soap operas with romance and intrigue. A wave of "soap-opera strips," led by *The Heart of Juliet Jones* and *On Stage*, followed in the 1950s.

The difference between romance and adventure strips was debated among comics creators as the genres overlapped. Allen Saunders, writer of both *Mary Worth* and *Steve Roper*, pointed out that romance strips were built around emotional conflict whereas adventure strips emphasized physical confrontation. Editors believed that women readers preferred affairs of the heart, while the guys went for the guns. King Features made distinctions between "comic strips" (*Blondie*), "adventure strips" (*Rip Kirby*), and "romance and adventure strips" (*The Heart of Juliet Jones*) in its promotional material.

The illustrators of the new story strips were influenced by the work of two veterans of adventure comics, Milton Caniff (*Terry and the Pirates* and *Steve Canyon*) and Alex Raymond (*Flash Gordon* and *Rip Kirby*). They blended the cinematic composition of Caniff with the elegant line work of Raymond to create a modern hybrid.

Many of the story-strip illustrators were recruited from the ranks of comic-book artists after that industry fell on hard times in the 1950s. Jack Kirby, Wally Wood, and Lou Fine were among the comic-book legends who crossed over into the field of syndicated strips during the decade.

Other newcomers came from the ranks of commercial illustrators. One advertising art agency, Johnstone and Cushing, produced a crop of talented draftsmen that included Stan Drake (*Juliet Jones*), Leonard Starr (*On Stage*), Alex Kotzky (*Apartment 3-G*), and Neal Adams (*Ben Casey*).

Thematically, the new story strips featured a mix of violence and sex toned down for family newspaper readership. As the work of these creators became more polished, and western and science-fiction subgenres emerged, the term "soap opera" became outmoded. Cartoonists began using terms like "straight," "serious," or "illustrative" to

JULIET JONES

— an ideal girl for any man. Attractive, personable, intelligent but at 30 still unattached.

Everyone knows a Juliet Jones and wonders about the answer to her dilemma:

Should family responsibility deny a girl love and happiness?

EVE
Juliet's sister

She's young, beautiful, wild, used to getting away with anything— including Juliet's beaus.

You'll think about Eve and ask yourself if her unchecked abandon can lead anywhere but to tragedy.

SOAP OPERA STARS—Model sketches of Juliet and Eve Jones from THE HEART OF JULIET JONES sales brochure. © 1953 King Features Syndicate, Inc. Courtesy of Gill Fox

describe the modern trend in realistic rendering and story-telling.

There was nothing new about the gag-a-day formula. Chic Young had built *Blondie* into a circulation blockbuster with daily laughs. But a major shift was taking place. Humor strips were gradually replacing story strips as the dominant genre.

In 1950 *Time* magazine named as the top five newspaper comics *Little Orphan Annie, Dick Tracy, Joe Palooka, Li'l Abner*, and *Blondie*. Only *Blondie* was a gag-a-day strip.

A readership study by Boston University in 1962 listed as the top fifteen features *Blondie, Dick Tracy, Little Orphan Annie, Peanuts, Rex Morgan M.D., Dennis the Menace, Li'l Abner, Mary Worth, Nancy, Snuffy Smith, Beetle Bailey, Brenda Starr, Bringing Up Father, Steve Canyon*, and *Prince Valiant*. Humor and story strips were now split almost evenly in popularity.

Editors became increasingly convinced that newspaper readers no longer had the patience to follow plotlines that took weeks to develop when they could watch a complete episode on television in thirty minutes or an hour. Humor strips, they claimed, delivered a quick punch line and captured the shorter attention span of television viewers more effectively than continuity strips.

Story-strip artists objected to this assumption. "The best gag strip in the world in terms of just plain acceptance is *Blondie* and you can miss it any day," reasoned Milt Caniff. "But assuming you're hooked, you can't miss *Rex Morgan* because every day there's always a push forward of the story. If you miss it, you're penalized; you lack some significant bit of information about the story."

The argument fell on deaf ears. Newspaper editors continued to choose new humor strips over story strips, and the polls tended to reinforce the wisdom of their logic. As a result, the syndicates launched fewer and fewer continuity strips.

Between September 1950 and March 1951, a trio of comic features debuted that were to have a major influence on this shift in readership. All three started inauspiciously but eventually eclipsed *Steve Canyon, Li'l Abner*, and *Pogo* in popularity.

The creators of these features took similar paths to success. Mort Walker (*Beetle Bailey*), Charles Schulz (*Peanuts*), and Hank Ketcham (*Dennis the Menace*) grew up during the Depression, inspired by the fame and fortune of their cartoonist heroes. They all served in the military during World War II and started their professional careers selling single-panel "gag cartoons" to major magazines, such as the *Saturday Evening Post* and *Collier's*. Their comic creations would eventually pass the 1,000-paper plateau in circulation and endure for over fifty years.

Beetle Bailey was launched in twelve newspapers on September 4, 1950, and after six months had signed up only

FRAT BOY—This panel from an unpublished college-era strip is the only time Beetle Bailey ever exposed his eyes. © 1950 King Features Syndicate, Inc.

twenty-five clients. King Features considered dropping the college-themed strip after the first year's contract was over. The Korean War was heating up at the time, so Walker decided to have Beetle enlist in the army. He quickly picked up 100 papers. He redesigned the cast and a Sunday page was added in 1952.

After the Korean War was over, the army brass wanted to tighten up discipline and felt that *Beetle Bailey* encouraged disrespect for officers. The strip was banned in the Tokyo *Stars and Stripes*, and sympathetic publicity rocketed Beetle's circulation another 100 papers. When Walker won the National Cartoonists Society's Reuben Award as the "outstanding cartoonist of the year" in 1953, *Beetle Bailey* had become a certified success with a growing list of clients.

During that same year, Walker was concerned that the military theme of his strip would soon become irrelevant. He created a sister and brother-in-law, Lois and Hi Flagston, for Beetle and sent him home on a visit. After two weeks, readers demanded Beetle's return to the army. Walker enjoyed writing family gags, so he started a second comic strip and found the perfect partner in advertising artist Dik Browne.

Hi and Lois, which debuted on October 18, 1954, grew slowly and then took off around 1960 when the youngest of the Flagston children, Trixie, became the first "thinking baby" in the comics. Dik Browne won the Reuben Award as the "outstanding cartoonist of the year" in 1962, and in less than a decade, *Hi and Lois* had accumulated 400 subscribers.

From 1954 to 1968, the circulation of *Beetle Bailey* grew from 200 newspapers to 1,100, and many new characters were added to the cast. The lineup at that time included:

LOVABLE LOSER—Panel from the first PEANUTS daily strip. © 10/2/50
United Feature Syndicate, Inc.

Beetle, Sarge, Gen. Halftrack, Zero, Killer, Cookie, Capt. Scabbard, Lt. Fuzz, Major Greenbrass, Chaplain Staneglass, Rocky, Cosmo, Julius, Otto, Plato, Pvt. Blips, Martha, Dr. Bonkus, Bunny, Ozone, and Pop. (Lt. Flap, Miss Buxley, Sgt. Lugg, and Cpl. Yo came later.) A series of fifty animated television cartoons, produced by Paramount Studios, debuted in 1963 and led to a wave of licensed products, including books, toys, and dolls.

"As I zoomed past the 500-paper mark," Walker remembered, "I began to feel a tremendous responsibility to my readers, almost a stage fright. If I've done this good today I've got to do at least as good tomorrow, or better, if I can. If you're not moving forward in this business, you are moving backward." *Beetle Bailey* became the second feature in comics history, after *Blondie*, to appear in more than 1,000 newspapers when it passed that milestone in 1965.

Peanuts was initially marketed as a space-saving feature before its debut in seven newspapers on October 2, 1950. It was vertically shorter than other strips and could be reconfigured in square, vertical, and horizontal formats due to its four equal-sized panels, although most papers ran it horizontally. Charles Schulz's simple but expressive graphics stood out on the comics page, and his strip didn't suffer as much as other features when editors further reduced the size they printed the comics.

Thematically, *Peanuts* began as a conventional gag strip with stereotypical characters and stock juvenile situations. But Schulz was heading in a new direction. The *Peanuts* kids developed adultlike personalities, and the humor gradually became more introspective. In an age when television was drawing millions into its seductive universe, a comic strip that delivered wit and wisdom in daily doses and appealed to adults as well as kids was just what the newspapers needed.

During the 1960s, beginning with a series of television commercials for the Ford Motor Company, Schulz showed how comics could be adapted successfully to other media. In 1962 *Happiness Is a Warm Puppy* became a best-selling book, *A Charlie Brown Christmas Special* was the first prime-time animated television special in 1965, and *You're A Good Man Charlie Brown*, which opened off-Broadway in 1967, went on to become the most frequently produced musical in the history of American theater.

The *Peanuts* merchandising program became a licensing juggernaut in the 1970s as Snoopy rose to international superstar status. There were Snoopy telephones and toothbrushes, Cartier gold charms and designer dolls. Snoopy ran for president in 1972. The beagle took Japan by storm in the 1980s and appeared at major sporting events on the side of the MetLife blimp.

Schulz's creation was the perfect marriage of simple graphics, sophisticated humor, and commercial adaptability. *Peanuts* not only answered the challenges of size reduction and competition from television, it revolutionized the medium of newspaper comic strips. The next generation of creators, including Lynn Johnston (*For Better or For Worse*), Cathy Guisewite (*Cathy*), and Patrick McDonnell (*Mutts*), would all acknowledge the debt they owed to Schulz's innovations.

Hank Ketcham was inspired by his own four-year-old son, Dennis Lloyd Ketcham, when he created his famous panel. "One October afternoon in 1950," remembered Ketcham, " I was at work in my tiny studio, finishing a drawing for the *Saturday Evening Post*, when I was startled by a sudden outburst from the bedroom area of our new home in Carmel. 'Your son is a MENACE!' exclaimed my wife. 'Dennis . . . a menace?' I mused. 'Let's see, there's Tillie the Toiler and Felix

THE BABY BOOM—DENNIS THE MENACE promotional drawing from Editor and Publisher. © 1951 King Features Syndicate, Inc.

MAD SATIRE—"Pogum" (POGO spoof) by Wally Wood. © 1961 E. C. Publications, Inc. All rights reserved. Used with permission. Courtesy of David Applegate.

the Cat. Why couldn't there be—DENNIS THE MENACE?! Wow! Why not!'"

Dennis the Menace was released on March 12, 1951, in sixteen newspapers. Editors responded more favorably to Hank Ketcham's creation than they had to *Beetle Bailey* and *Peanuts*, and sales surged at a respectable pace. By the end of the first year, *Dennis* was appearing in 100 of the largest U.S. newspapers. In 1952 the syndicate launched a Sunday page, and Pines Publications came out with the first *Dennis the Menace* comic book.

In 1959 a live-action TV series, starring Jay North, debuted on CBS, and by the mid-1960s *Dennis* was at the top of many newspaper-readership polls. He also had his own line of successful comic books and trade paperback collections. Merchandise included Dennis dolls, hand puppets, children's clothes, and toys.

Ketcham earned respect among his peers for his single-minded devotion to the craft of cartooning. He approached each composition as a mini-masterpiece. "I seem to have trapped myself over the years into creating such realistic situations that I must resort to elaborate designs that penetrate

space and give the illusion of depth," Ketcham explained. "It's like peering through a window in the page. I try to draw so convincingly that the reader won't notice."

Ketcham's unique artistic perspective enabled readers to briefly recapture the innocence of childhood and imagine a life of white-picket fences, green grass, and golden sunsets. Although it reflected an idealized depiction of the Baby Boom era, *Dennis the Menace* endured because Ketcham's vision was timeless.

The 1950s, which is often dismissed as a placid period of conformity and consumerism, was in fact a time when rock and roll, Beat poetry, and abstract painting altered the cultural climate. A new brand of satiric humor also came into vogue. Lenny Bruce revolutionized the world of stand-up comedy with his controversial monologues. Sid Caesar and his troupe introduced an innovative style of live improvisation on *Your Show of Shows*. Billy Wilder's *Some Like It Hot* blended the sex appeal of Marilyn Monroe with the comedic talents of Tony Curtis and Jack Lemmon. Mike Nichols, Elaine May, Mort Sahl, and Shelly Berman were among the leading exponents of the new humor.

Cartoonists were also pushing the limits of creativity and convention. United Productions of America, which was founded by a group of Disney Studio dropouts, experimented with a fresh approach to cartoon animation. The design of U.P.A. films, such as *Gerald McBoing Boing*, written by Ted Geisel (Dr. Seuss), and *A Unicorn in the Garden*, based on the drawings of James Thurber, was influenced by the latest trends in modern art and magazine illustration.

MAD magazine, which was launched in 1952, pioneered a brand of humor that was aimed directly at the youth of America. Harvey Kurtzman, Jack Davis, Wally Wood, Bill Elder, and the rest of the "Gang of Idiots" at *MAD* turned out an endless stream of takeoffs on contemporary comic strips (*Gopo Gossum*), television programs (*Howdy Dooit!*), and movies (*Hah! Noon*). Many of the underground cartoonists of the 1960s were influenced by this irreverent publication while growing up in the 1950s.

The new humor was described by critics as "sick." Jules Feiffer, who had worked as an assistant to Will Eisner on *The Spirit* from 1946 to 1951, began drawing a multi-image cartoon for the *Village Voice* in 1956 that he sardonically titled *Sick, Sick, Sick*. Feiffer's sketchy style and probing dialogue earned him a following among New York intellectuals and influenced many cartoonists who were to follow. The weekly feature was renamed *Feiffer* and began national syndication in 1959.

The New York Herald Tribune Syndicate, which had failed to strike gold with a string of detective strips in the late 1940s and early 1950s (*Bodyguard*, *The Saint*, and *Sherlock Holmes*), saw the potential in the sophisticated humor being pioneered by Feiffer. Mell Lazarus's *Miss Peach*, which debuted in 1957, was touted by the syndicate as "different in that it has a four-column format, with almost every strip a single wide-screen panel." In *Miss Peach* the words took precedence over the art as the students of the Kelly School filled their speech balloons with thoughtful discussions about life, love, and other weighty matters. The drawing was appropriately childlike in its simplicity.

Johnny Hart presented his caveman creation, *B.C.*, to five other syndicates before he sold it to the Herald Tribune in 1958. The most successful of the new humor strips, *B.C.* combined a minimalist drawing style with dry wit, slapstick, puns, sound effects, and anachronisms to create a mood that was both modern and traditional. Hart started a second successful feature, *The Wizard of Id*, in 1964 and won the Reuben as the "outstanding cartoonist of the year" in 1968.

At the end of the decade, the Herald Tribune announced two other promising features. "Readers' heads today are too full of fact," stated a syndicate representative in 1958. "Poor

PUBLISHERS-HALL SYNDICATE
30 EAST 42nd STREET, NEW YORK, N.Y.

SOCIAL COMMENT—FEIFFER newspaper promotion by Jules Feiffer. © 1959 Jules Feiffer. Used by permission of Universal Press Syndicate. All rights reserved

Arnold's Almanac is designed to empty those heads and bring on a state of bliss. Each panel is a topnotch joke, but they are in sequence on one subject, giving the cumulative impact of 10 to 15 laughs in a row." *Poor Arnold* was Arnold Roth, a former writer, editor, and cartoonist for *Trump* and *Humbug*, two short-lived magazines launched by Harvey Kurtzman, the genius behind *MAD*.

The second creation was from another cartoonist with a *MAD* connection. Al Jaffee's *Tall Tales* was unusual in that it was exactly what it said it was: one column wide by 7½ inches tall. Similar to the famous *Fold-In* page Jaffee would later develop for *MAD*, *Tall Tales* attracted attention with clever visual compositions.

Apparently, newspapers readers weren't ready for these innovations. *Poor Arnold's Almanac* ended in 1960 and *Tall Tales* was gone by 1966.

The new humor strips made subtle observations about philosophy, politics, and religion but always maintained an air of playful unpretentiousness. When a cartoonist got up on his soapbox and expressed strong opinions, the editors howled in protest.

A 1950 column in the *Denver Post* set off a heated debate between newspaper editors and Al Capp, a frequent violator

KEEP IT CLEAN—LITTLE ORPHAN ANNIE promotional drawing from Editor and Publisher. © 1950s Tribune Media Services, Inc. All rights reserved. Reprinted with permission

of the unwritten "no comment" law in comics. The column writer expressed the widely held belief that politics belonged on the editorial page and whenever a cartoonist started preaching, the entertainment value of his feature went down.

"A cartoonist is a commentator," responded Capp. "Every line he draws, every word he writes IS a comment on the world he knows. When a newspaper editor asks a cartoonist to stop commenting, they ask him—in effect—to stop being a cartoonist."

James Pope, managing editor of the *Louisville* (Ky.) *Courier-Journal*, had his own ideas about the role a cartoonist was supposed to play. "They should think about human nature, about social foibles, about romance and adventure and laughter," wrote Pope. "I'm hanged if I see why any of them want to bother with the contentious artificial area of political and economic ideas, or any controversial issues whatever."

Harold Gray was another favorite target for critics in the Cold War era. After drawing a *Little Orphan Annie* sequence in which Daddy Warbucks thwarted a gang of Chinese Reds, Gray was accused of being both a right-wing warmonger and a Communist sympathizer. Another series on juvenile delinquency, which depicted violence, drug use, and anti-labor sentiment, set off a firestorm of protest and thirty newspapers canceled the strip.

Gray remained undaunted in defense of his beliefs. In response to a reader's complaint about his editorializing, he wrote: "I shall continue to pound on the idea that the old time way was the best for us—individual freedom, honest hard work, and a chance for any man with the proper drive and decency to gain and hold wealth and power."

In addition to Capp and Gray, Walt Kelly, Milt Caniff, and Chester Gould also spoke out for freedom of expression on the comics page. These influential creators were not as courageous when the comic-book industry came under attack in the 1950s.

A movement had been mounting to censor violence in comic books during the postwar years as concerned parents organized protests to put pressure on the publishers. In 1954 the psychologist Frederick Wertham charged, in his controversial book *Seduction of the Innocent*, that comic-book reading led directly to juvenile delinquency. A Senate committee was formed, which included Senators Kefauver (D-Tenn.), Hennings (D-Mo.), and Hendrickson (R-N.J.), to investigate the connection. A month after the McCarthy hearings got under way in Washington, D.C., Kefauver's committee questioned Wertham, William Gaines (the publisher of EC comic books), Walt Kelly, and Milt Caniff in a courthouse in lower Manhattan.

Kelly, the newly elected president of the National Cartoonists Society, defensively claimed that he had tried to help clean up the industry in the mid-1940s, when he was producing funny animal comic books. Caniff pointed out that newspaper strips were subjected to strict censorship rules by newspaper and syndicate editors as well as the good judgment of the artists. Both cartoonists implied that there was an important distinction to be made between the standards that governed the comic-strip business and the ethics of the comic-book industry.

Caniff and Kelly managed to take the spotlight off their branch of the profession, but William Gaines was not so fortunate. After the hearings were over, negative publicity and the threat of boycotts forced Gaines to shut down his entire line of horror comics. The comic-book publishers adopted a form of self-censorship, called the Comics Code Authority, which sent the industry into a creative and economic tailspin from which it took more than a decade to recover.

The National Cartoonists Society faced another crisis in 1955 when the feud between Al Capp and Ham Fisher escalated. Fisher continued to assert that Capp's lead character bore a striking resemblance to Big Leviticus, a supporting player in *Joe Palooka*. He argued that the theft was irrefutable because Capp had been working as his assistant the year before he created *Li'l Abner* in 1934. As Capp eclipsed Fisher in popularity during the late 1940s, the accusations became more vicious.

In April 1950 Capp wrote a piece for the *Atlantic Monthly* entitled "I Remember Monster," a thinly disguised account of his unpleasant experiences working as Fisher's assistant. In desperate retaliation, Fisher sent a batch of drawings to a New York state committee investigating comics, "proving" that Capp was sneaking pornography into the panels of *Li'l Abner*. Fisher denied having anything to do with the alleged forgeries, but in 1954 he staged the same stunt when Capp applied for a TV license from the Federal Communications Commission.

Capp was forced to withdraw his F.C.C. application and angrily demanded that the National Cartoonists Society Ethics Committee take action against Fisher. In 1955 Fisher was suspended from the N.C.S. for unprofessional conduct. Capp had won the feud. Rejected, depressed, and lonely, Fisher took an overdose of pills. Morris Weiss, a freelance comic-book artist and one of the last people Fisher considered a friend, found the disgraced cartoonist's body in his Madison Avenue studio on December 27, 1955.

Another tragic death occurred less than a year later. On September 6, 1956, Alex Raymond was killed when the

INSTEAD OF A SELF PORTRAIT I HAD PALOOKA DRAW ME! HAM FISHER.

EGO TRIP—Self-caricature of Ham Fisher from Comics and Their Creators by Martin Sheridan. © 1942 McNaught Syndicate

Corvette he was driving skidded on a rain-soaked road in Westport, Connecticut, and smashed into a tree. Stan Drake, illustrator of *The Heart of Juliet Jones*, was thrown clear of the overturned sports car but suffered a broken shoulder and other injuries. Raymond was a past president of the National Cartoonists Society and had won the award as the "outstanding cartoonist of the year" in 1949. John Prentice, who had been working as a magazine and comic-book illustrator, was selected to take over the production of Raymond's *Rip Kirby*, which appeared in 500 daily newspapers at the time.

Jack Cole, a veteran comic-book and magazine cartoonist, also suffered an untimely demise in the 1950s. Cole created the elastic superhero Plastic Man in 1941 but always yearned to return to his first love, gag cartooning. After *Playboy* was launched in 1953, Cole began submitting color cartoons to the new men's magazine and soon became a regular contributor. In 1958 he realized another dream when he sold a comic strip, *Betsy and Me*, about two doting parents and their genius son, to the Chicago Sun-Times Syndicate. After its launch, the strip was doing well and picking up papers. Three months later, Cole bought a .22 rifle, drove the family station wagon a few miles from his home, and shot himself. The next day, *Playboy* publisher Hugh Hefner and Cole's wife received letters from the cartoonist, but his motive remained a mystery. In a 1999

A CRY FOR HELP?—BETSY AND ME daily strip by Jack Cole. © 1958 Field Enterprises, Inc. Courtesy of Bill Janocha

COMICS PATRON—William Randolph Hearst, "The Wizard of Ooze," by William Rogers, 1906. *Harper's Weekly*

New Yorker article about Cole, the cartoonist and comics historian Art Spiegelman observed that *Betsy and Me* "reads like a suicide note delivered in daily installments. As he climbed the ladder of success, up from the primal mulch of the comic books, he finally arrived at air that was too thin to breathe: Jack Cole, a comics genius, died of growing up."

The comics industry lost its founding patron when William Randolph Hearst succumbed to a heart condition on August 14, 1951, at the age of eighty-eight. The Chief left behind sixteen daily and thirteen Sunday newspapers, eight monthly magazines, a sprawling real-estate empire, and a vast collection of art and antiques. The value of his estate was estimated at $200 million.

Hearst had remained personally involved in every detail of his publishing empire until his death, including the supervision of the comics. All new features had to be approved by The Chief before his syndicate, King Features, could sign them up. When Hearst saw a comic strip he liked that was not owned by King, he directed his people to hire the artist away from the current employer with a better offer. Many cartoonists, including Richard F. Outcault, Winsor McCay, and Roy Crane, came under Hearst's control in this way.

Ward Greene, who was the editor and general manager of King Features at the time of Hearst's death, made regular trips from the syndicate offices in New York to his boss's home in California. Hearst would pore over two bound volumes, containing all 300 of the syndicate's features, and make comments and suggestions. He frequently suggested plotlines for comic strips and objected to sequences that he disliked.

More than a half-century before his death, Hearst set the stage for the birth of the comics medium. On October 17, 1896, the day preceding the Yellow Kid's debut in Hearst's Sunday edition of the *New York Journal*, a full-page advertisement guaranteed "Eight pages of iridescent polychromous effulgence that makes the rainbow look like a lead pipe." Hearst didn't invent the comics, but his promotional bravado was what sold them to the American public.

A Hearst editor once said that his boss's goal was to make every reader exclaim "Gee whiz!" upon opening the newspaper. That phrase might have been a fitting epitaph for the greatest showman in the history of journalism.

THE OLDEST STRIP—MUTT AND JEFF's 45th anniversary. © 1952 McNaught Syndicate. Courtesy of International Museum of Cartoon Art

POPEYE Sunday page by Tom Sims and Bill Zaboly. © 1/21/51 King Features Syndicate, Inc. Courtesy of International Museum of Cartoon Art

SIMS & ZABOLY   Elzie Segar, the creator of *Popeye*, died in 1938, and after a short stint by King Features "bullpen" artist Doc Winner, Bill Zaboly (illustrator) and Tom Sims (writer) continued the classic comic strip. This outstanding *Popeye* Sunday page from 1951 is drawn in the classic 1930s "big-foot" style that Robert Crumb would revive in the 1960s.

BIG BEN BOLT *daily strip by John Cullen Murphy.* © 5/22/56

All Big Ben Bolt strips © King Features Syndicate, Inc. Courtesy of International Museum of Cartoon Art

JOHN CULLEN MURPHY

The first major story-strip debut of the decade was *Big Ben Bolt*, which began on February 20, 1950. This literate and stylish boxing feature was written by Elliot Caplin and illustrated by John Cullen Murphy. An accomplished artist who had painted covers for *Liberty*, *Sport*, *Holiday*, *Collier's*, and *Look* magazines, Murphy rendered the action scenes in *Big Ben Bolt* with drama and authenticity. The feature ended in 1978, eight years after Murphy started collaborating with Hal Foster on *Prince Valiant*.

BIG BEN BOLT *daily strip by John Cullen Murphy.* © 5/31/56

BIG BEN BOLT *daily strip by John Cullen Murphy.* © 6/25/56

BIG BEN BOLT *Sunday page by John Cullen Murphy.* © 3/4/62. *Courtesy of John Cullen Murphy*

THE HEART OF JULIET JONES *daily strip by Stan Drake.* © 3/29/54

STAN DRAKE In 1953 Elliot Caplin teamed up with another top illustrator, Stan Drake, to create the sexy soap-opera strip *The Heart of Juliet Jones.* Caplin's story lines revolved around the romantic exploits of two sisters. Juliet, the brunette, was older and more sensible than Eve, an impulsive and trouble-prone blonde. Drake, a veteran of the Johnstone and Cushing advertising art agency, brought a slick, commercial approach to the feature and pioneered the use of photorealistic backgrounds. On October 13, 1970 (in the Sunday-page episode on the next page), Juliet finally tied the knot with Owen Cantrell, but the attorney was later murdered, renewing the contrasting love interests between the Jones siblings.

THE HEART OF JULIET JONES *daily strip by Stan Drake.* © 2/22/57. Courtesy of International Museum of Cartoon Art

THE HEART OF JULIET JONES *daily strip by Stan Drake.* © 9/6/66

THE HEART OF JULIET JONES Sunday page by Stan Drake. © 10/18/70

ON STAGE daily-strip sequence by Leonard Starr. © 2/11–2/13/57

All On Stage strips © Tribune Media Services, Inc. All rights reserved. Used with permission. Courtesy of Leonard Starr and Jim Gauthier.

LEONARD STARR Mary Perkins, the raven-haired heroine of Leonard Starr's stylish story strip, *On Stage*, was a small-town girl who came to New York City to seek fame and fortune in the Broadway theater. Mary's arrival is shown in the strips on this page from February 1957, the first week of the feature. Over the years dishonest agents, unappreciative directors, and back-stabbing actors never dimmed her optimism, and in 1959 she married her longtime suitor, photographer Pete Fletcher. Starr was one of the most respected illustrators and writers of his generation, and he was recognized as the "outstanding cartoonist of the year" in 1965. *On Stage* ended in 1979, when Starr was hired to launch the revived *Annie* comic strip.

ON STAGE Sunday page by Leonard Starr. © 2/16/58

RIP KIRBY daily-strip sequence by John Prentice. © 11/12–11/14/56. King Features Syndicate, Inc.

JOHN PRENTICE

When Alex Raymond was killed in an automobile accident in 1956, John Prentice was selected by King Features Syndicate to take his place. The *Rip Kirby* strips shown here, unsigned by Prentice, are from the first story he illustrated. Prentice was the ideal choice because he had been an admirer of Raymond for many years. The transition was so seamless that many newspaper editors could not tell where Raymond's work ended and where Prentice's began. *Rip Kirby* by Prentice was recognized as Best Story Strip of the Year three times by the National Cartoonists Society and continued until Prentice's death in 1999.

CAPTAIN EASY hand-colored Sunday page by Leslie Turner. © 4/5/1950s by NEA Service, Inc. Courtesy of International Museum of Cartoon Art

LESLIE TURNER Historian Ron Goulart has described Leslie Turner as "the best strip successor in the long history of comics." Turner took over the humorous adventure feature *Wash Tubbs/Captain Easy* from Roy Crane in 1943 and continued it until 1970. Turner was responsible only for the daily strips until 1952, when he took over the Sunday page as well. This unusual autobiographical episode reveals the pressure Turner must have been under trying to keep up with his endless deadlines.

Among the many cowboy comic strips that were popular in the postwar era were *Red Ryder* (1938–64) by Fred Harmon, *Casey Ruggles* (1949–55) by Warren Tufts, *The Cisco Kid* (1951–68) by José-Luis Salinas, and *Rick O'Shay* (1958–81) by Stan Lynde.

RED RYDER Sunday page by Fred Harmon. © 12/4/1950s NEA Service, Inc. Courtesy of International Museum of Cartoon Art

CASEY RUGGLES Sunday page by Warren Tufts. © 12/2/51 United Feature Syndicate, Inc.

THE CISCO KID daily strip by José-Luis Salinas. © 11/3/1950s King Features Syndicate, Inc. Courtesy of Jack Gilbert

RICK O'SHAY daily strip by Stan Lynde. © 9/18/58 Tribune Media Services, Inc. All rights reserved. Reprinted with permission. Courtesy of David Applegate

TWIN EARTHS Sunday page by O. LeBeck and A. McWilliams. © 3/20/55 United Feature Syndicate, Inc. Courtesy of International Museum of Cartoon Art

SCIENCE FICTION

The space race helped launch a number of new strips, including *Twin Earths* (1952–63) by Oskar LeBeck and Alden McWilliams and *Sky Masters* (1958–60) by Jack Kirby and Wally Wood. An updated version of the *Flash Gordon* daily strip, which began as a Sunday page in 1934, was released by King Features in 1952, with Dan Barry as the artist.

SKY MASTERS daily strip by Jack Kirby and Wally Wood. © 9/8/58 by The George Matthew Adams Service, Inc. Courtesy of TRH Gallery/Tom Horvitz

FLASH GORDON daily strip by Dan Barry. © 4/16/62 King Features Syndicate, Inc. Courtesy of TRH Gallery/Tom Horvitz

ALLEY OOP Sunday page by V. T. Hamlin. © 4/25/54 NEA Service, Inc.

V. T. HAMLIN *Alley Oop*, V. T. Hamlin's classic caveman comic, debuted in 1933 and was still going strong in the 1950s. Originally set in the Mesozoic era, Hamlin introduced time travel to the plotlines in 1939, enabling his hero to range freely through a variety of periods and locations.

This Sunday page from 1954 demonstrates how Hamlin, a student of paleontology, rendered dinosaurs and scenery somewhat realistically, while Alley Oop and King Guzzle were drawn to look like prehistoric Popeyes.

LITTLE ANNIE ROONEY *daily strip by Darrell McClure.* © 10/7/50 King Features Syndicate, Inc. Courtesy of International Museum of Cartoon Art

KIDS AND DOGS

In the tradition of Little Orphan Annie and Sandy, comic-strip juveniles inevitably had canine companions. Shown here are Little Annie Rooney and Zero by Darrell McClure, Rusty Riley and Flip by Frank Godwin, and Cap Stubbs and Tippie by Edwina Dumm. In the *Dondi* Sunday episode by Gus Edson and Irwin Hasen on the next page, the recently adopted war orphan brings home a sick dog, who gives birth to puppies in the basement of his foster home.

RUSTY RILEY *daily strip by Frank Godwin.* © 11/22/52 King Features Syndicate, Inc. Courtesy of International Museum of Cartoon Art

CAP STUBBS AND TIPPIE *daily strip by Edwina Dumm, n.d.* © by The George Matthew Adams Service, Inc. Courtesy of International Museum of Cartoon Art

DONDI Sunday page by Gus Edson and Irwin Hasen. © 6/17/56 Tribune Media Services, Inc. All rights reserved. Used by permission. Courtesy of Richard Marschall

I'M **ONE** CAT WHO HATES JAZZ, MAN! ··· IT'S A DRAG!

GORDO

BY HIPALONG JAZZITY

LET'S SEE WHAT MENTAL IMAGES **JAZZ** CREATES FOR YOU, ONCLE GEE!

SHOOT!

THIS IS THELONIOUS MONK ON PIANO!

HOW DO YOU LIKE THAT GUITAR EH? ··· THAT'S BARNEY KESSEL!

HERE'S COUNT BASIE'S BAND! THAT'S FRANK WESS ON FLUTE!

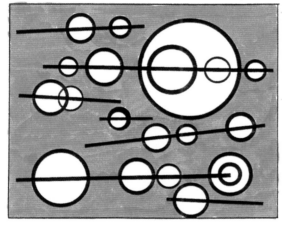

THIS IS THE COOL SOUND OF THE MODERN JAZZ QUARTET, WITH MILT JACKSON ON VIBES! ··

MAN! **THERE'S** A WILD ONE! WHO'S THAT?

THAT'S **YOU** ON **CAT!** GET UP!!

MODERN ART—In this abstract GORDO Sunday page from 1959, Gus Arriola provides a visual music appreciation lesson for his readers. GORDO hand-colored Sunday page by Gus Arriola. © 1959 United Feature Syndicate, Inc. Courtesy of R. C. Harvey

mort walker

A COMPULSIVELY creative cartoonist, Mort Walker has conceived and supervised the production of nine syndicated comic strips since 1950, including *Beetle Bailey*, *Hi and Lois*, *Boner's Ark*, and *Sam and Silo*. He founded the Museum of Cartoon Art and served as president of the National Cartoonists Society and vice-president of the Newspaper Comics Council.

"If there is such a thing as being born into a profession, it happened to me," claimed Walker in the introduction to his autobiography. "From my first breath, all I ever wanted to be was a cartoonist." He drew cartoons for his school newspaper, *The Scarritt Scout*, when he was ten. He sold his first cartoon to *Child Life* magazine at the age of eleven. His earliest comic strip, *The Limejuicers*, ran in the *Kansas City Journal* when he was thirteen. He submitted his first idea to a national syndicate at the age of fifteen. By the time he graduated from high school, his work was polished and professional.

Walker held down a full-time job as a greeting-card designer for Hallmark while he attended Kansas City Junior College. In 1942 he was drafted into the army and served in Italy during the war. He kept an illustrated diary, and some of the G.I.s he met along the way later became inspirations for *Beetle Bailey* characters. When he returned home, he attended journalism school at the University of Missouri and was editor of the campus humor magazine, the *Showme*.

After graduation Walker was working as a magazine cartoonist in New York when John Bailey, the cartoon editor of the *Saturday Evening Post*, encouraged him to do some cartoons based on his college experiences. One character, a goof-off with a hat over his eyes named "Spider," emerged from these efforts. After selling a few college cartoons to the *Post*, Walker decided to submit a comic strip to King Features Syndicate starring Spider and his fraternity brothers. When King bought the strip, Mort changed Spider's first name to "Beetle" (another King strip, *Big Ben Bolt*, had a character named Spider) and added "Bailey" in honor of John Bailey.

Beetle Bailey debuted inauspiciously in twelve newspapers on September 4, 1950. The strip got a boost in circulation when Beetle enlisted in 1951, and again in 1954 when it was censored by the army brass for encouraging disrespect for officers. It continued to gain momentum, and by the mid-1960s only *Blondie* had more newspaper clients.

Beetle Bailey wasn't just about the army. The military pecking order of Camp Swampy represented all organizations in which incompetent bosses imposed pointless rules on those below them. Beetle was the classic low man on the totem pole who resisted authority. He became a hero to millions of readers.

Walker enjoyed working with other cartoonists, and his staff expanded as he continued to come up with ideas for new features. Eventually the studio became known as "King Features East," and the classic big-foot house style was dubbed "the Connecticut school." In 1975 Walker wrote *Backstage at the Strips*, a behind-the-scenes look at the workings of his laugh factory. He followed that in 1980 with *The Lexicon of Comicana*, a compendium of visual devices used by cartoonists, such as "plewds" (sweat drops), "hites" (speed lines), and "briffits" (dust clouds).

Over the years *Beetle Bailey* has been criticized for political incorrectness and challenged by newcomers to the comics field. Walker's creation endured and was still among the most popular features in the business when its fiftieth anniversary was celebrated in 2000.

"Someone said a diamond is just a piece of coal that stuck with the job," Walker mused. "To me the strip is a diamond. I never knew where that first step would take me and there were many rocky times, but a certain amount of fame and fortune were my reward for keeping at it."

It is ironic that Beetle Bailey, the laziest character in the history of comics, was created by Mort Walker, one of the hardest-working and most prolific cartoonists of all time.

SELF-CARICATURE by Mort Walker

BEETLE BAILEY daily strip by Mort Walker. © 10/22/63

All Beetle Bailey and Hi and Lois Strips © King Features Syndicate, Inc. Courtesy of Comicana, Inc.

BEETLE BAILEY daily strip by Mort Walker. © 5/5/65

BEETLE BAILEY daily strip by Mort Walker. © 3/29/67

BEETLE BAILEY daily strip by Mort Walker. © 1/6/70

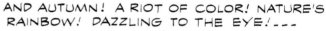

BEETLE BAILEY hand-colored Sunday page by Mort Walker. © 1/1/60

BEETLE BAILEY daily strip by Mort Walker. © 5/22/70

BEETLE BAILEY daily strip by Mort Walker (first appearance of Lt. Flap). © 10/5/70

BEETLE BAILEY daily strip by Mort Walker (first appearance of Miss Buxley). © 11/17/71

BEETLE BAILEY daily strip by Mort Walker. © 3/23/72

BEETLE BAILEY Sunday page by Mort Walker. © 10/23/66

HI and LOIS

HI AND LOIS daily strip by Mort Walker and Dik Browne. © 12/19/1960s

WALKER AND BROWNE

The co-creators of *Hi and Lois* were the odd couple of cartooning. Mort Walker was as neat and orderly as Dik Browne was messy and disorganized. The two were friends and partners for thirty-five years. The Flagston family consisted of Hi, a decent, hardworking father, Lois, a pretty baby-boom mother, Chip, a mildly rebellious teenager, twins Dot (precocious) and Ditto (a cookie thief), and Trixie, the sunbeam kid. The cast was rounded out by Thirsty and Irma, the childless next-door neighbors, Abercrombie and Fitch, the garbagemen, Mr. Foofram, Hi's boss, and Dawg, the family pet. A reader once wrote to Walker and Browne about a favorite strip that struck a familiar chord. "You must have been looking through my window, because the same thing happened to me," she speculated. This family-friendly coziness was the secret to the success of *Hi and Lois.*

HI AND LOIS daily strip by Mort Walker and Dik Browne. © 5/16/62

HI AND LOIS daily strip by Mort Walker and Dik Browne. © 6/20/62

HI AND LOIS Sunday page by Mort Walker and Dik Browne. © 9/6/64

HI AND LOIS daily strip by Mort Walker and Dik Browne. © 6/28/65

HI AND LOIS daily strip by Mort Walker and Dik Browne. © 12/10/65

HI AND LOIS daily strip by Mort Walker and Dik Browne. © 12/23/67

HI AND LOIS daily strip by Mort Walker and Dik Browne. © 6/21/71

HI AND LOIS hand-colored Sunday page by Mort Walker and Dik Browne. © 11/28/65

charles schulz

SELF-CARICATURE by Charles Schulz

ON OCTOBER 2, 1950, an unassuming four-panel comic strip, with the curiously generic title *Peanuts*, debuted in seven newspapers. The strip's creator, Charles Monroe Schulz, kept his day job at the Art Instruction Schools in Minneapolis.

Peanuts grew slowly. In 1951 it was in thirty-five papers; a year later, forty-one; fifty-seven the next. A Sunday page was added in 1952, and by 1956 it finally passed the 100-paper mark in circulation.

During this time Schulz was refining his formula. The original cast—Charlie Brown, Shermy, Patty, and Snoopy—expanded to include Schroeder (1951), Violet (1951), Lucy and Linus (1952), and Pigpen (1954). As the decade progressed, Snoopy became more anthropomorphic. He began communicating with thought balloons in 1952 and started walking on two legs in 1956.

Each of the characters developed distinctive personalities and had a defined role in the ensemble. Charlie Brown, who started out as an obsessive perfectionist, became the quintessential loser. Lucy was the fussbudget, Linus the philosopher, Schroeder the artist, Pigpen the slob, and Snoopy the dreamer.

Schulz would place these pen-and-ink performers in different situations and let the sparks fly. Unlike the predictable pattern of most traditional gag strips, the humor in *Peanuts* was derived from the characters rather than the situations. "I introduced the slight incident," Schulz proudly explained. The dilemma of the day could be as insignificant as taking out the dog dish or kicking a football. It was how Schulz's kids responded to these minor events that produced the laughs.

Some of the slight incidents gradually evolved into running gags. The "twelve devices" that Schulz identified as crucial to the success of *Peanuts* were: 1. the kite-eating tree; 2. Schroeder's music; 3. Linus's security blanket; 4. Lucy's psychiatry booth; 5. Snoopy's doghouse; 6. Snoopy himself; 7. the Red Baron;

8. Woodstock; 9. the baseball games; 10. kicking the football; 11. the Great Pumpkin; 12. the little red-haired girl. These themes were repeated regularly, like the changing of the seasons, and gave readers a comforting sense of familiarity.

Adults rarely appeared in *Peanuts*. The children were left on their own to figure out the world they inhabited. The resulting conversations blended childlike innocence with grown-up concerns. In a very subtle way, Schulz was revealing the universality of human emotions. Readers of all ages saw their insecurities, frustrations, and fears reflected in the struggles of the *Peanuts* gang.

Graphically, Schulz was a master of minimalism. Charlie Brown could convey a wide range of emotions with the simple lines that floated within his large, round face. Schulz delighted in rendering Woodstock's scratchy dialogue or rain cascading down on the pitcher's mound. Backgrounds were indicated with a squiggle, lettering was customized to fit the mood of a situation, and comic sound effects were used effectively. Late in his career, Schulz's hand became unsteady. His lines, although shaky, were just as expressive as they had always been.

Schulz was the most influential cartoonist of his generation. "A comic strip like mine would never have existed if Charles Schulz hadn't paved the way," claimed Cathy Guisewite, creator of *Cathy*. "He broke new ground, doing a comic strip that dealt with real emotions, and characters people identified with."

Peanuts was an intimately autobiographical creation. "If you read the strip for just a few months, you will know me,"

PEANUTS daily strip by Charles Schulz. © 8/23/89

said Schulz, "because everything that I am goes into the strip. That is me." Charles Schulz could be as philosophical as Linus, as insecure as Charlie Brown, or as crabby as Lucy. He was a shy and sensitive man who was easily wounded. He was also deeply religious and had an abiding faith in human resilience and eternal hope. His comic strip read like a daily letter to millions of his closest friends.

PEANUTS daily strip by Charles Schulz. © 9/27/56

PEANUTS daily strip by Charles Schulz © 10/29/59

PEANUTS daily strip by Charles Schulz © 11/25/59

PEANUTS daily strip by Charles Schulz © 4/25/60

PEANUTS daily strip by Charles Schulz © 8/22/60

PEANUTS *daily strip by Charles Schulz* © 7/18/63

PEANUTS *daily strip by Charles Schulz* © 11/15/63

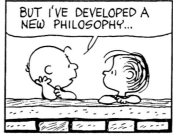

PEANUTS *daily strip by Charles Schulz* © 8/8/66

PEANUTS *daily strip by Charles Schulz* © 1/27/68

PEANUTS *daily strip by Charles Schulz* © 6/22/70

PEANUTS Sunday page by Charles Schulz © 1/10/60

PEANUTS Sunday page by Charles Schulz © 8/14/60

PEANUTS *daily strip by Charles Schulz* © 4/9/73

PEANUTS *daily strip by Charles Schulz* © 6/30/73

PEANUTS *daily strip by Charles Schulz* © 5/24/79

PEANUTS *daily strip by Charles Schulz* © 7/21/79

PEANUTS *daily strip by Charles Schulz* © 3/11/80

the fifties 443

PEANUTS Sunday page by Charles Schulz. © 12/24/67

I HIT A HOME RUN IN THE NINTH INNING, AND WE WON! I WAS THE HERO!!

YOU?!

PEANUTS daily strip by Charles Schulz. © 3/30/93

SOMETIMES I LIE AWAKE AT NIGHT, AND I ASK MYSELF, "IS THIS ALL THERE IS?"

THEN I HEAR A VOICE THAT SAYS..

"WHAT KIND OF A QUESTION IS THAT?"

PEANUTS daily strip by Charles Schulz. © 8/4/93

Dear Mom, Just a note to tell you I am well. They say we will be home by Christmas. I hope so.

PEANUTS daily strip by Charles Schulz. © 6/10/94

PEANUTS daily strip by Charles Schulz. © 6/1/98

hank ketcham

DENNIS THE MENACE made his first appearance in sixteen newspapers on March 12, 1951. Fifty years and more than 18,000 daily installments later, Dennis was still a frisky "five-ana-half"-year-old bundle of fun.

When asked to explain Dennis's enduring appeal, his creator, Hank Ketcham, said with paternal pride, "He makes people smile and laugh when they read his words and see his actions, which expresses an innocence shared universally by five-year-olds. Some things fortunately never change."

Like Walt Kelly, Ketcham received his early art training at the Walt Disney Studio between 1939 and 1942. After serving in the navy during the war, he started selling gag cartoons to the major magazines in New York. In 1948 he moved to California, where he created his classic newspaper feature.

Putting his magazine experience to good use, Ketcham became a master of single-panel composition. "I'm like a director," he explained. "I set up the thing with the camera and spot the actors in a certain area. If I don't like it, I move the camera to the left or right or bring one of the people up close and balance it that way. When I have that figured out I go in and draw. I become the actor for every character. So it becomes an acting situation after you've done the staging."

Ketcham was a stickler for details. Objects such as bicycles, automobiles, and appliances had to be rendered accurately. His drawings never looked mechanical, however. Each composition was a perfect blend of graphic elements, creating the illusion of gazing through a window at a realistic setting. He was also a skilled draftsman. His lines were smooth and clean,

SELF-CARICATURE by Hank Ketcham

and he experimented endlessly with shading, silhouetting, and perspective.

Almost from the beginning, the central cast of *Dennis the Menace* was limited to Dennis, his parents Alice and Henry Mitchell, his dog Ruff, the next-door neighbors George and Martha Wilson, and friends Joey, Margaret, and Gina. They lived in a small Midwestern town with a main street, barbershop, soda fountain, schoolhouse, library, movie theater, restaurant, grocery store, and doctor's office. The houses were close together and had small backyards and white-picket fences.

Thematically, Ketcham adhered to a simple philosophy. "I make a point of staying away from the ugly side of life," he stated. "It's just my nature. I'd rather have upbeat things around me. Lord knows, there are enough things dragging you down."

Dennis tended to be insatiably curious rather than mischievous. When he did get in trouble, his parents made him sit in the corner in a rocking chair. At night Dennis would try to make amends with his bedtime prayers. Repeated situations like these reinforced Dennis's basically wholesome nature.

Ketcham employed many art assistants and gag writers over the years. In the early 1980s Ron Ferdinand took over the Sunday page, and in the mid-1990s Marcus Hamilton began producing the daily panel. Ketcham continued to closely supervise his creation until his death in 2001.

Dennis the Menace has had remarkable staying power. The King Features syndicated panel appears in over 1,000 newspapers around the world. Fifty million Dennis books have been sold since the first collection was published in 1952. The 1959–63 Jay North television series, as well as ninety-six animated programs and two live-action feature films, are being aired to a new generation of viewers. Dennis has transcended pen-and-ink to become an international cultural icon. Hank Ketcham raised him right.

(N°1. DRAWN OCT., 1950)

"GO AHEAD, DADDY—— SQUIRT IT RIGHT IN HIS EYE!"

DENNIS NO. 1 drawn in October 1950, five months before the debut of the feature.

The Perfect Day

"A BOY'S WILL IS THE WIND'S

WILL, AND THE THOUGHTS OF YOUTH ARE LONG,

LONG THOUGHTS." Henry Wadsworth Longfellow

DENNIS THE MENACE Sunday page by Hank Ketcham. © 6/7/81

"THIS IS MY MOTHER, TOMMY. ISN'T SHE PRETTY?"

DENNIS THE MENACE *daily panel by Hank Ketcham.* © 11/9/51

"DENNIS!"

DENNIS THE MENACE *daily panel by Hank Ketcham.* © 2/18/53

DENNIS THE MENACE *daily panel by Hank Ketcham.* © 12/25/67

"YOU BETTER HURRY HOME, MARGARET! IT WOULD BE *TERRIBLE* IF YOU GOT STUCK HERE IN A BLIZZARD!"

DENNIS THE MENACE *daily panel by Hank Ketcham.* © 1/28/80

"I DON'T KNOW WHETHER TO BE A CARTOONIST WHEN I GROW UP, OR WORK FOR A LIVING."

DENNIS THE MENACE daily panel by Hank Ketcham. © 12/12/86

"YUP, FIVE YEARS OLD IS A VERY GOOD AGE FOR BOYS!"

DENNIS THE MENACE daily panel by Hank Ketcham. © 11/24/86

"I DON'T LIKE THE WAY THIS YEAR'S STARTIN' OUT!"

DENNIS THE MENACE daily panel by Hank Ketcham. © 1/1/81

"FIRST, THE GOOD NEWS..."

DENNIS THE MENACE daily panel by Hank Ketcham. © 9/9/89

POOR ARNOLD'S ALMANAC Sunday page by Arnold Roth. © 9/4/60 New York Herald Tribune, Inc. Courtesy of Arnold Roth.

THE NEW HUMOR A pair of innovative but short-lived humor features were introduced by the *New York Herald Tribune* in 1959. *Poor Arnold's Almanac* by Arnold Roth offered a clever visual digression on a different subject each Sunday, and *Tall Tales* by Al Jaffee was done daily in pantomime.

TALL TALES Sunday page by Al Jaffee. © 3/13/60 New York Herald Tribune, Inc. Courtesy of International Museum of Cartoon Art

the sixties

I LOVE READING THE COMICS

THE BEAGLE HAS LANDED—"Snoopy on the Moon," panel from PEANUTS strip by Charles Schulz. © 3/14/69 United Feature Syndicate, Inc.

T HE MAJOR EVENTS AND SOCIAL CHANGES OF THE 1960S—THE KENNEDY ASSASSINATION, THE MOON LANDING, THE WAR IN VIETNAM, THE CIVIL RIGHTS MOVEMENT, THE CULTURAL REVOLUTION—WERE REFLECTED IN THE COMICS BUT DID NOT DIRECTLY INSPIRE ANY ENDURING CREATIONS. THE STARS OF THE FUNNIES PAGES WERE NOT ASTRO-NAUTS, HIPPIES, PROTESTERS, OR ROCK MUSICIANS. A LAZY ARMY PRIVATE, A FLYING BEAGLE, A MISCHIEVOUS TOWHEAD, AND AN ACERBIC CAVEMAN WERE AMONG THE MOST POPULAR PEN-AND-INK PERSONALITIES OF THE ERA.

It was a period of transition for the print media. During the decade at least 163 magazines ceased publication, including the 148-year-old *Saturday Evening Post*. The *Boston Traveler*, the *Houston Press*, the *Portland Reporter*, and the *Indianapolis Times* were among 160 daily newspapers that folded. The most dramatic failure was the 1967 demise of New York's *World Journal Tribune*. "The *Wijit*," which barely lasted for nine months, was the last chapter in a journalistic legacy that stretched back to the Park Row moguls of the nine-teenth century. Thirteen New York dailies could be found in the *W.J.T.*'s long ancestry of mergers, including Joseph Pulitzer's *World*, William Randolph Hearst's *Journal*, and James Gordon Bennett's *Herald*.

Newspaper strikes, rising production costs, and the loss of advertising revenue to television were all blamed for the crisis, but another force was also at work. During the decade, 176 new daily papers were launched. The large metropolitan newspapers were gradually being replaced by publishing ventures outside the cities. New York, the nation's largest urban market, lost more than half of its daily newspapers (from seven to three). At the same time the Gannett Company, which began publishing medium-size newspapers in New York, New Jersey, and Connecticut in the 1920s, expanded its holdings dramatically, from sixteen newspapers in 1957 to seventy-three dailies in 1977.

Summing up this trend, Stanford Smith, general manag-er of the American Newspaper Publishers Association, stated in 1963: "Where some newspapers have suspended, merged, or consolidated in some metropolitan cities since the end of World War II, new daily newspapers have been established

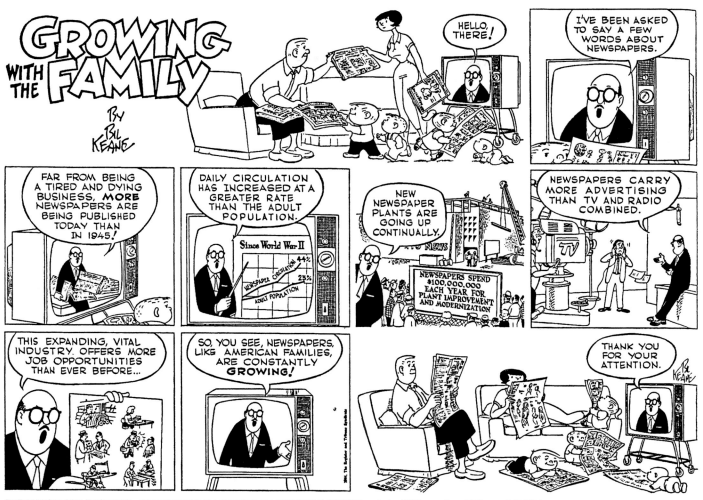

THE NEWSPAPER BUSINESS—"Growing with the Family," special FAMILY CIRCUS page by Bil Keane from Editor and Publisher. © 1964 The Register and Tribune Syndicate

in surrounding suburban communities so that the total number of newspapers has remained virtually constant while the total circulation has steadily increased."

This change had a major impact on the comics business. Syndicate salespeople had less leverage with editors in the growing number of cities that had only one newspaper. They could no longer threaten to take their strips "across town" when rate hikes were refused. At the same time, the number of cities with one or more daily newspapers also increased. This created new opportunities for the syndicates. Exclusive territories were being carved up into smaller portions, and the circulation figures for the top strips reached unprecedented highs. The immediate beneficiaries of this trend were the new humor strips. *Beetle Bailey*, *Peanuts*, *Dennis the Menace*, and *B.C.* were winning readership polls by the mid-1960s as their subscriber lists continued to grow.

The uneasy relationship between the comics business and television also began to change as syndicates discovered additional sources of revenue in the growing broadcast medium. In 1959 a successful live adaptation of Hank Ketcham's *Dennis the Menace*, starring Jay North, debuted on CBS. That same year the Ford Motor Company signed a licensing agreement with United Feature Syndicate for the advertising

rights to *Peanuts*. Charles Schulz's characters were animated in a series of television commercials for the Ford Falcon in the early 1960s. Newspaper editors argued that comic-strip characters, which had been promoted and popularized in their pages, should not be sold to the competition. Syndicates claimed that television and advertising increased the exposure of their features, which benefited both newspapers and creators. *A Charlie Brown Christmas*, which was originally broadcast on December 9, 1965, proved that comic-strip properties could be successfully adapted to television, without compromising the integrity of the newspaper feature.

The syndicates also turned television stars into comics characters. Yogi Bear, who made his first appearance on *The Huckleberry Hound Show* in 1958, received his own strip in 1961. *The Flintstones*, which debuted in 1960 as the first prime-time animated series, also became a newspaper feature in 1961. Although credited to Hanna Barbera Studios, both strips were drawn by animation artist Gene Hazelton. *Rocky and His Friends*, which premiered on ABC in 1959, was retitled *The Bullwinkle Show* in 1961 after its charismatic costar. A year later, a *Bullwinkle* comic strip, drawn by Al Kilgore, was released by the McClure Syndicate. "For some time now television has been cashing in on newspaper-built features,"

TV SPIN-OFF STRIP—THE FLINTSTONES daily strip by Hanna Barbera Productions. © 10/2/61 McNaught Syndicate

explained a syndicate spokesman. "*Bullwinkle* gives editors and publishers a turn-about opportunity to exploit a ready-made, enthusiastic audience."

Medical dramas were also popular on television in the early 1960s. *Dr. Kildare*, who was created by writer Max Brand in 1938, starred in a successful television series beginning in 1960. Ken Bald, a veteran comic-book artist, was selected to illustrate the *Dr. Kildare* comic strip, which was launched by King Features in 1962 and continued until 1983. Neal Adams, a twenty-four-year-old comic-book and advertising artist, took on the challenge of adapting *Ben Casey* to pen and ink later that same year. "The amazing thing about this young man," explained Ernest Lynn of the N.E.A. syndicate, "is the extraordinary likeness he bears to Vincent Edwards, the actor who plays Ben Casey on television." Adams was also a talented artist and, after the *Ben Casey* strip was discontinued in 1966, helped to revitalize such classic comic-book heroes as Batman, Green Lantern, and Green Arrow.

In 1962 William Steven, the editor of the *Houston Chronicle*, conducted an "unscientific and highly opinionated" poll of a dozen syndicate editors and salespeople. The twelve strips the voters regarded as "essential" to any comics page were (in alphabetical order): *Beetle Bailey, Blondie, Dennis the Menace, Dick Tracy, Family Circus, Grin & Bear It, Li'l Abner,*

Mary Worth, Peanuts, Pogo, Rex Morgan, and *Steve Canyon.* The old story-strip standbys seemed to be holding their ground against the new humor upstarts. But debuts of new romance and adventure strips were few and far between in the 1960s. The syndicates seemed convinced that the genre was dying, and editors claimed that readers no longer had the patience for continuity strips.

A few notable exceptions existed. *Apartment 3-G*, which debuted in 1961, revolved around the romantic adventures of three career girls. This stylish soap-opera strip was written by Nick Dallis, a former psychiatrist who also scripted *Rex Morgan* and *Judge Parker*, and illustrated by the veteran comic-book and commercial artist Alex Kotzky.

Al Williamson, a gifted draftsman who emulated the style of Alex Raymond, took over King Feature's *Secret Agent X-9* (renamed *Secret Agent Corrigan*) in 1967. In spite of the waning interest in adventure strips, Williamson maintained *Corrigan* as one of the best illustrated features in the business until he quit in 1980.

Other attempts at launching adventure strips in the 1960s suffered from bad timing. *Dan Flagg*, which debuted in 1963, starred a Marine Corps major and was illustrated by ex-Marine Don Sherwood, a former assistant to George Wunder on *Terry and the Pirates. Tales of the Green Beret*, which began two years later, was produced by Joe Kubert,

ILL-TIMED ADVENTURE—TALES OF THE GREEN BERET daily strip by Joe Kubert. © 4/4/66 Tribune Media Services, Inc. All rights reserved. Reprinted with permission

an accomplished comic-book artist, and Robin Moore, the author of the best-selling novel *The Green Berets*. With the Vietnam War escalating, the American public was not in the mood for military-themed adventure strips, and both features were short-lived.

A live-action *Batman* television series debuted on January 12, 1966. The campy comic-book spoof, starring Adam West as Batman, set off a wave of merchandising that included, not surprisingly, a new comic-strip adaptation. "The kids will love it for its deeds of derring-do, and adult newspaper readers are going to see the tongue-in-cheek camp and humor of it all," promised *Batman* creator Bob Kane. "To bring this across, I have developed a new art style that is pop, hard, clean, and flexible, and best suited to express both the action and humor contained in the script." *Batman & Robin* was produced by a competent string of DC comic-book artists, including Sheldon Moldoff, Carmine Infantino, Joe Giella, and Al Plastino, until it ended in 1974.

After the wave of political assassinations in the 1960s, editors became increasingly critical of violence on the funnies pages. On June 11, 1968, the *Greensboro* (N.C.) *Daily News* canceled *Dick Tracy* and *Little Orphan Annie* due to their "constant exploitation and advocacy of violence." Editor Charles Hauser added that "the June 7th *Tracy* strip summed it up in a panel that said 'Violence is golden when it's used to put down evil.'"

On September 26, 1968, the Newspaper Comics Council held a symposium on "Violence in the Comics." Dr. Joyce Brothers reported that, at a meeting of the American Psychiatric Association, doctors were asked if they thought fictional violence, as portrayed in comics, TV shows, and movies, promoted violent behavior. Thirty percent said yes; 24 percent said fictional violence actually helped to dissipate aggression. Dr. Brothers concluded that although the psychiatrists disagreed about the effects of graphic violence, there was a consensus that comic strips influenced the behavior of readers.

Milt Caniff, who also attended the conference, pointed out that violence existed in human society long before cartoons and that blaming the medium for the spread of aggressive behavior was illogical. "It's a schluffing off of responsibility on long-suffering comic artists," argued Caniff.

Adventure-strip creators struggled to keep their features relevant in the rapidly changing times. *Dick Tracy* entered the space age when Junior Tracy married Moon Maid in 1964. Terry and the Pirates fought the Viet Cong in Southeast Asia. Winnie Winkle joined the Peace Corps. Newspaper editors complained that the comics were becoming too serious. "Many comic-strip cartoonists are, with increasing frequency,

JUNIOR TRACY WEDS MOON MAID—Panel from DICK TRACY by Chester Gould. © 10/4/64 Tribune Media Services, Inc. All rights reserved

taking the pedestal to expound a wide range of cold war views without even a pretense of mockery or ridicule," complained newspaper reporter Dennis Blank in 1966. "Cartoonists can do a much better job of easing world tensions through humor."

Other journalists looked at this trend in a different way. On April 9, 1965, *Time* magazine featured a cover story on "Comment in the Comics." Bernard M. Auer wrote in his "Letter from the Publisher" that "the comics have gone through a slump as well as a renaissance" since Milton Caniff and Al Capp had appeared on the cover of *Time* in 1947 and 1950, respectively. After studying contemporary creations, Auer concluded that "more and more strips are offering political satire, psychology, and comments of varying subtlety on the rages and outrages of everyday life."

The majority of the *Time* piece, as well as the cover, was devoted to *Peanuts*, although other features, including *Li'l Abner*, *Pogo*, *B.C.*, *Miss Peach*, and *Beetle Bailey*, were cited as examples of increasing sophistication in modern humor strips.

Another group of cartoonists was taking social and political comment in new directions. Jules Feiffer started the movement with his weekly feature, which began national syndication in 1959. Feiffer attacked Nixon and Kennedy, segregationists and pseudoliberals with equal fervor. Editors had the option to reject his cartoon if they disagreed with the political sentiment or if they felt their readers might be offended. Feiffer argued that he was a satirist, not an editorial cartoonist. "The editorial cartoonist should look angry," he explained. "But the satirist is defeating himself when he reveals his true feelings."

BERRY'S WORLD

© 1969 by NEA, Inc. Jim Berry

"Oh, nothing—it's just that this is the first time I've ever seen you without your bell bottoms!"

SOCIAL COMMENT—BERRY'S WORLD by Jim Berry. © 1969 by NEA, Inc.

In 1963 N.E.A. released *Berry's World*, a single-panel cartoon that came out initially in triweekly installments. The creator, Jim Berry, was described as one of the "young moderns" of editorial cartooning who eschewed the labels and symbols of traditional political cartoons in favor of humorous social commentary. Newspaper editors were given the choice of running *Berry's World* on the editorial page or in any other part of the paper.

A handful of other syndicated features released in the 1960s also bridged the gap between humor strips and political cartoons. In Jerry Robinson's *Still Life*, inanimate objects made pithy observations about current events. Morrie Brickman's *the small society* was a single-panel strip that typically featured citizens and elected officials discussing the affairs of the day. Editors did not object to commentary in the comics as long as they knew beforehand what they were buying and were given the option to place the feature wherever they wanted in their newspapers. These creations blazed the path upon which Garry Trudeau's *Doonesbury* would soon follow.

The National Cartoonists Society held a roundtable discussion on "New Directions" in comics on April 20, 1964. One of the participants was Sylvan Byck, comics editor of King Features Syndicate. Byck stressed that successful features were built around strong characters. "Characterization is not new," he explained. "It started years ago in humor strips when cartoonists began to abandon the joke-book type of gag." Byck cited *Blondie* and *Beetle Bailey* as two outstanding comics that had well-developed characters.

Johnny Hart's two successful strips, *B.C.* and *The Wizard of Id*, added another element to the formula—situation comedy. Many new humor strips of the 1960s featured clearly defined characters who inhabited colorful locales, ranging from a desert island to an Indian reservation. As in *B.C.* and *The Wizard of Id*, none of these settings were historically accurate or realistic. They existed only in the imaginations of their creators and served as the stage upon which their pen-and-ink actors could perform.

The most surreal of the new humor strips was Mort Walker and Jerry Dumas's *Sam's Strip*, which debuted in 1961. Sam and his cartoonist assistant owned and operated the comic strip they inhabited. Famous cartoon characters, including The Yellow Kid, Jiggs, Dagwood, and Charlie Brown, would make walk-on appearances. Sam and his sidekick discussed the inner workings and hidden secrets of life within the panel borders. "Sam is in and of the world of drawing and comics and journalism," explained Dumas. "He exists in that abstract world where Krazy Kat still lives, though rarely seen today. It's a spiritual world of ideas, where Daumier and Happy Hooligan mix with Humpty Dumpty and Bing, Bang, Pow." The concept was too esoteric for most readers and *Sam's Strip*, which never appeared in more than sixty papers, was canceled in 1963.

Another offbeat creation was Howie Schneider's *Eek and Meek*, which made its first appearance on September 5, 1965. The two mouselike lead characters strolled through a minimally abstract world pondering the great mysteries of life. Schneider, who was often associated with the current intellectual movement in cartooning, saw his creation as an outlet for personal expression. In 1982 *Eek and Meek* miraculously transformed into human beings.

Two mid-decade offerings featured western locales. Tom K. Ryan's *Tumbleweeds* (1965) was set in the remote outpost of Grimy Gulch and starred a motley assortment of cowboys, Indians, lawmen, outlaws, and townspeople. When Gordon Bess's *Redeye* debuted in 1967, a King Features publicist claimed, "The gags and style of *Redeye* are on the 'wild' side. Although the characters are Indians and the setting is a reservation, the whole approach to humor is

WHIMSY—KING AROO daily strip by Jack Kent. (This intellectual fantasy strip debuted in 1950 and ended in 1965.) © 6/12/64 McClure Syndicate. Courtesy of Bill Janocha

as modern as mini-skirts. The strip is designed to appeal to those who are attracted to 'New Wave' comics, but it is not so far out it will miss the mark with the great mass of comic strip readers."

In 1968 Mort Walker's laugh factory produced another successful humor strip. *Boner's Ark* starred an inept sea captain who made the monumental mistake of bringing only one animal of each species on board his ark. Among the passengers were Arnie Aardvark, Priscilla Pig, Sandy Ostrich, Dum Dum the gorilla, Duke the penguin, and Rex the dinosaur. All of these creatures had distinctive personalities and interacted intimately on the aimlessly drifting vessel. *Boner's Ark* was continued by Frank Johnson until 2000.

Alf and Sandy, the lead players in Howie Post's 1968 creation, *The Dropouts*, were also stranded at sea. The "desert island gag" had always been a popular cliché for magazine cartoonists, and Post borrowed it as the setting for his new feature. After running out of fresh ideas in this limited locale, Post shipped *The Dropouts* to another island in 1969, which was inhabited by a colorful cast of misfits and outcasts.

Months before Beatlemania swept America, a British cartoon star invaded the nation's comics pages. Andy Capp, the diminutive Yorkshire limey with the oversized checkered cap, made his debut stateside on September 16, 1963. This popular anti-hero was created in 1957 by Reg Smythe

and appeared in twenty-eight countries before he was introduced to American newspaper readers. Although he never held down a job and spent his days sipping ale in a pub, Andy won the hearts of blue-collar readers around the world. In his early days, Andy was known to knock his poor wife Flossie to the ground and spend the night with a young barmaid, but Smythe eventually toned down the spousal abuse and adultery. "He's a horrible little man, really, and I'm always a little ashamed of the things he gets up to," Smythe admitted in a 1968 interview. "Oh I know he's a good giggle in the morning when the world gets up; but sometimes I worry about his behavior, the example he's setting."

Reg Smythe was not the only British cartoonist to cross the pond in the hopes of striking it rich in America. Harry Hanan relocated to New Jersey after his long-suffering nebbish, *Louie*, started appearing in American papers in 1947. Alex Graham's droll hound, *Fred Bassett*, made his U.S. debut in 1965. *Modesty Blaise*, a sophisticated spy thriller created by Peter O'Donnell and illustrated by Jim Holdaway, was imported from London in 1966.

Family-friendly comic strips continued to be the most popular genre during the 1960s. *Blondie* still had the largest list of subscribers, and *Peanuts*, *Dennis the Menace*, and *Hi and Lois* appeared regularly at the top of readership polls. One of the most successful new domestic features was Bil Keane's *Family Circus*, which debuted on February 29, 1960. Keane

COMICS ON COMICS—SAM'S STRIP daily strip by Mort Walker and Jerry Dumas. © 10/30/62 King Features Syndicate, Inc.

THE FAMILY CIRCUS Sunday page by Bil Keane. © 5/8/66
King Features Syndicate, Inc. Courtesy of Bil and Jeff Keane

had been producing *Channel Chuckles*, a TV-themed panel, for the Register and Tribune Syndicate since 1954. "The funniest things happen around the house," remarked Keane in an interview just before the launch of his new circular-shaped comic. "For the last year I have been loafing around our new desert home in Scottsdale, Arizona, just drawing what I see. And if my wife and our five little comic characters will forgive me, family life is just one cartoon after another."

The original cast of kids, Billy, Dolly, and Jeffy, was based on Keane's own children. *The Family Circus* was appearing in 125 newspapers in 1961, when readers were invited to guess the sex, birthdate, and name of a new arrival to the nation's comic pages. The baby boy, christened "Peter John," was called "PJ" by his siblings as soon as he came home from the hospital.

The public responded favorably to Keane's autobiographical feature. A poll taken in 1966 by the *Des Moines Register* revealed that *The Family Circus* was the favorite comic among all age groups, ahead of *Blondie*, *Peanuts*, and *Pogo*. Keane was voted Best Syndicated Panel creator by the National Cartoonists Society in 1967 as *The Family Circus* continued to grow in popularity.

Bud Blake's *Tiger* moved into the funnies neighborhood in 1965. The cast of the new strip—docile Tiger and his spotted dog Stripe, kid brother Punkinhead, dimwitted Hugo, brainy Julian, and precocious Suzy—was a throwback to clas-

sic comic kids like *Skippy* and *Reg'lar Fellers*. *Tiger* was drawn in a distinctive style, an elegant blend of flowing line and balanced composition, that earned Blake praise from his peers. It was voted Best Humor Comic Strip by the N.C.S. twice in the 1970s, again in 2000, and built a healthy list of 400 clients.

The feel-good domestic features were complemented on the comics pages by a group of new dysfunctional family comics. Art Sansom's *Born Loser*, which debuted in 1965, starred a bumbling breadwinner, Brutus T. Thornapple, who faced rejection and ridicule at home and at the office. King Features' answer to Andy Capp was Bob Weber's *Moose*, a lazy lowbrow who barely supported his family of five. The battle of the sexes was waged in daily installments by Leroy and Loretta Lockhorn, the childless couple in Bill Hoest's 1968 single-panel creation, *The Lockhorns*.

Among the other offerings in the gag-a-day genre in the 1960s were features that focused on individual family members. Lee Holley's *Ponytail* (1960) and Bernard Lansky's *Seventeen* (1956) were

A PIONEER—Self-caricature by
Morrie Turner

INTEGRATION—PEANUTS daily strip (early appearance of Franklin) by Charles Schulz. © 11/12/69 United Feature Syndicate, Inc.

typical teenage fare. Jerry Marcus's *Trudy* (1963) was a hard-working housewife from the suburbs. Brad Anderson's *Marmaduke* (1954) was an ungainly house pet. *Amy*, a panel Jack Tippit inherited from Harry Mace in 1964, starred a female Dennis the Menace. In 1969 Ted Key's busybody maid, *Hazel*, made the transition from magazine and television stardom to the funnies pages.

Racial integration came late to the comics. Ethnic caricatures were a staple of the medium in its formative years but had fallen out of favor in the postwar period. It wasn't until the changes brought about by the civil rights movement in the 1960s that black cartoonists finally broke into the syndication business, and realistic black characters began appearing in major strips.

Immediately after the war, African Americans found work primarily in the black press. The *Chicago Defender*, the *Pittsburgh Courier*, and the *Baltimore Afro-American* were among the leading newspapers to publish comic strips by black cartoonists. One of the longest-running features was *Bungleton Green*, which debuted in 1920 and was continued by five different artists until 1968. Ollie Harrington (*Bootsie*) and Jackie Ormes (*Torchy Brown*) were also outstanding black cartoonists, who might have had a greater impact if they had been allowed to break into national syndication.

E. Simms Campbell was one of the first black artists to cross the color barrier. His cartoons of voluptuous white women in the pages of *Esquire* attracted the attention of King Features, which released the Sunday feature *Hoiman* in 1937 and the daily panel *Cuties* in 1943. *Cuties* lasted until Campbell's death in 1971. Very few readers were aware that Campbell was black, however.

Morrie Turner began submitting ideas to the syndicates in the 1950s, but it was not until 1965 that he finally sold a feature. *Wee Pals* was the first comic strip by a black artist to be syndicated to the mainstream press. It started in only five papers, but after the assassination of Martin Luther King, Jr., in 1968, Turner's list began to build. Other strips by black artists, starring black characters, soon followed. *Luther*, by Brumsic Brandon, Jr., debuted in 1968, and Ted Shearer's *Quincy* began in 1970.

All three creations starred children. "Black kids are much less threatening than black adults (to white editors and readers)," observed Brandon. "It's a shame that it's that way."

Creators of the leading humor features also experimented with adding black characters to their casts. Hank Ketcham made the fatal mistake of drawing his new *Dennis the Menace* character, Jackson, with racially stereotyped features. After protests erupted at a number of newspapers, Jackson went back into the ink bottle. Charles Schulz had better results with the inoffensive Franklin, who joined the *Peanuts* gang in 1969 but never became a major player in the strip. Lt. Flap, the first black character in *Beetle Bailey*, was initially controversial, but Mort Walker managed to diffuse criticism by making Flap a confident officer who was proud of his heritage.

A new adventure strip, *Dateline Danger*, was launched in 1968 with a black character in the leading role. Danny Raven was a news reporter and a former gridiron star who traveled the world in search of romance and adventure. Alden

SOUL BROTHER—Self-caricature by Ted Shearer

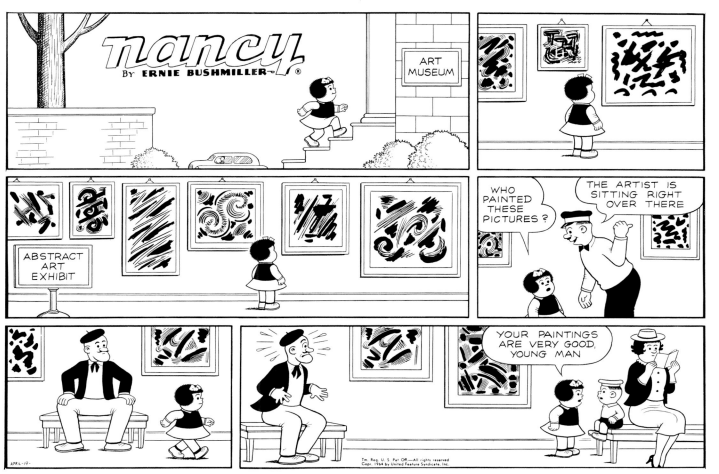

ABSTRACT ART—NANCY Sunday page by Ernie Bushmiller. © 4/19/64 United Feature Syndicate, Inc. Courtesy of James T. Carlsson

McWilliams, the illustrator of *Dateline Danger*, struggled at first with rendering black characters until he realized that "there is no such thing as a typical black face any more than there is a typical white one."

In 1969 Arthur Laro, the president of the Chicago Tribune New York News Syndicate, lamented that "for years America's 'invisible people'—the black people who make up ten percent of our newspaper readership—were unable to see themselves or to be seen in any but the most humble fictional roles." His solution to this inequity was a new comic strip, *Friday Foster*, which starred a black female fashion photographer.

By 1973 both *Dateline Danger* and *Friday Foster* were gone from the comics pages. Both strips, which were produced by white artists, had failed to attract a black audience. Although progress had been made toward integrating the comics, many barriers remained to be overcome.

Newspaper comic strips, like jazz, are an indigenous American art form. Yet they have often not been regarded highly in their country of origin. Americans appreciate the entertainment value of their popular arts but rarely take them seriously. The Europeans were the first to recognize both jazz and comics as forms of self-expression with a status equal to painting, sculpture, and classical music.

In 1967 the Decorative Arts Department of the Louvre in Paris featured an exhibition entitled *The Comic Strip and Narrative Figurative Art*. The main section of the display was devoted to American newspaper comics. In the 256-page book that accompanied the exhibition, a group of European scholars, the Société d'Etudes et de Recherches des Littératures Dessinées (Organization for the Study and Research of Pictorial Literatures), concluded that "the comic strip has created original works of which it can no longer be said that they are not art."

American cartoonists were unaccustomed to such high praise. "How did we ever make it to the Louvre?" marveled Milt Caniff. The National Cartoonists Society and the Newspaper Comics Council had held exhibitions at galleries and museums. They wondered if something more permanent could be established in the birthplace of the comics.

"It's wonderful to see that there's currently a renaissance of comics going on," remarked N.C.S. president Jerry Robinson in 1968. "We've had comics exhibitions all over the world and have many more planned. What we really do need, however, is a permanent home for both cartoonists and their work. Cartoons are housed in various museums all over the world and what we'd really like to get is a permanent National Museum for them." That dream would be realized in the next decade.

JACKYS DIARY Sunday page by Jack Mendelsohn. © 2/19/61 King Features Syndicate, Inc. Courtesy of International Museum of Cartoon Art

GRAPHIC MINIMALISM

The "new look" in sophisticated modern humor strips was pioneered by Jules Feiffer, Johnny Hart, Mell Lazarus, and Jack Mendelsohn in the late 1950s and early 1960s.

FEIFFER weekly page by Jules Feiffer © 1/12/64 Jules Feiffer. Used by permission of Universal Press Syndicate. All rights reserved. Courtesy of International Museum of Cartoon Art

DR. KILDARE daily strip by Ken Bald. © 11/5/62 King Features Syndicate, Inc.

STORYTELLING   Among the relatively few new
continuity features introduced during the 1960s were medical
dramas and soap operas. *Dr. Kildare* (above) was based on
the television program starring Richard Chamberlain that
debuted in 1960. It was competently illustrated by Ken Bald
and lasted for more than twenty years (1962–84). *Ben Casey*

(below), which was inspired by the TV show starring
Vincent Edwards and was illustrated by Neal Adams, had
a shorter run (1962–66). *Apartment 3-G* (bottom) revolved
around the romantic adventures of three career girls and was
written by Nicholas Dallis and illustrated by Alex Kotzky. It
debuted in 1961 and is currently syndicated by King Features.

BEN CASEY daily strip by Neal Adams. © 10/22/64 NEA Inc. Courtesy of Jim Gauthier

APARTMENT 3-G daily strip by Alex Kotzky. © 12/4/64 King Features Syndicate, Inc.

BATMAN Sunday page Batman™ and © DC Comics. All rights reserved. Used with permission.

THE THRILL IS GONE

Debuts of new adventure comics were even rarer in the 1960s. The *Batman* strip (above) was revived after the success of the television program starring Adam West and lasted for eight years (1966–74). Many of the adventure features that had been around since the 1930s got a new lease on life when they were taken over by younger artists. Sy Barry was hired to illustrate Lee Falk's long-running classic, *The Phantom* (below), in 1962 after Wilson McCoy passed away. The strip frequently focused on the relationship between the "ghost who walks" and Lady Diana, until their inevitable marriage in 1977.

THE PHANTOM daily strip by Lee Falk and Sy Barry. © 6/13/62 King Features Syndicate, Inc. Courtesy of International Museum of Cartoon Art

"I don't ask that you agree with what I say, boys, but in a democracy you must defend to the death my right to deny having said it!"

GRIN AND BEAR IT daily panel by Lichty. © 8/19/64 Publishers Newspaper Syndicate. Courtesy of Art Wood Collection

"WHAT ARE WE DOING ON THE MOON, WHEN WE HAVEN'T EVEN DEVELOPED AN INDUSTRIAL COMPLEX BIG ENOUGH TO ENDANGER OUR ENVIRONMENT?"

BERRY'S WORLD daily panel by Jim Berry. © 1970 NEA, Inc. Courtesy of International Museum of Cartoon Art

SOCIAL COMMENT

A number of artists explored the boundaries between editorial cartoons and gag panels in the 1960s. George Lichtenstein had been mining the fertile fields of political satire in *Grin and Bear It* since 1932. "Lichty," who drew in a loose, free-flowing style, is best remembered as the creator of the pompous Senator Snort (above). Jim Berry, whose innovative panel *Berry's World* (above right) debuted in 1963, used pencils and felt-tip pens to create a spontaneous, contemporary look. Jerry Robinson employed inanimate objects to voice his opinions in *Still Life* (right), which began in 1963 and was followed by the self-syndicated *Life with Robinson* in 1970. These features paved the way for more direct political and social comment on the funnies pages.

STILL LIFE daily panel by Jerry Robinson. © 1965 Tribune Media Services. All rights reserved. Reprinted with permission

POPEYE *daily strip by Bud Sagendorf.* © 3/14/66 King Features Syndicate, Inc.

LAUGH-IN *daily strip by Roy Doty.* © 8/5/70 Tribune Media Services, Inc. All rights reserved. Reprinted with permission. Courtesy of International Museum of Cartoon Art

BIG-FOOT BOOM   Humor strips of all types dominated the comics pages during the decade. Elzie Segar's former assistant, Bud Sagendorf, took over *Popeye* (top) in 1959 and continued to produce the daily and Sunday feature until 1986.

Roy Doty was hired to develop a comic strip (above) based on the *Laugh-In* television show in 1969. *Animal Crackers* (below) by Rog Bollen, which began in 1967, starred a cast of African game animals.

ANIMAL CRACKERS *daily strip by Rog Bollen.* © 9/14/76 Tribune Media Services, Inc. All rights reserved. Reprinted with permission. Courtesy of International Museum of Cartoon Art

MISS PEACH daily strip by Mell Lazarus. © 7/12/62 Courtesy of International Museum of Cartoon Art

All Miss Peach strips © Creators Syndicate, Inc.

MISS PEACH daily strip by Mell Lazarus. © 10/14/64

MELL LAZARUS

Miss Peach, Mell Lazarus's 1957 creation, was initially inspired by the success of Charles Schulz's *Peanuts*. It combined simple graphics with sophisticated humor, pioneering a new "minimal" style that would influence a later generation of cartoonists. The star of Lazarus's single-panel daily strip was a well-meaning teacher who struggled to manage a classroom of big-headed, tiny tots. The students of the Kelly School, named after the creator of *Pogo*, included

the brilliant Freddy, bossy Marcia, timid Ira, gullible Arthur, sickly Lester, and wily Francine. These kids mirrored the grown-up world by analyzing each other's problems, forming useless committees, and mimicking professional occupations. Lazarus created a second successful comic strip, *Momma*, in 1970 and was recognized by the National Cartoonists Society for his career achievements, winning the Reuben Award in 1981.

MISS PEACH Sunday page by Mell Lazarus. © 6/15/69 Courtesy of International Museum of Cartoon Art

MISS PEACH Sunday page by Mell Lazarus. © 2/21/60 New York Herald Tribune Inc. Courtesy of Richard Marschall.

johnny hart

SELF-CARICATURE by Johnny Hart

THE CREATOR of two classic humor strips, *B.C.* and *The Wizard of Id*, Johnny Hart was serious about being funny. "The comic field is an exciting one," he said. "It is made up principally of people who have refused to grow up and who offer their marvelous fantasies to those who wish they hadn't."

Born in Endicott, New York, in 1931, Hart was the oldest of three children. He began drawing cartoons as far back as he can remember. His formal education ended after he graduated from high school. At the age of nineteen, Hart met a young cartoonist from California who would become a major influence in his life. Brant Parker had worked at the Walt Disney Studio as an "in-betweener" and encouraged Hart to pursue a career in cartooning. Years later the two would collaborate on the *The Wizard of Id*.

After a tour in the Air Force, Hart began submitting cartoons to the national magazines. He made his first sale to the *Saturday Evening Post* for $65 in 1954. Realizing he couldn't support a family on such a meager income, he took a job in the art department at General Electric in Endicott. He also continued to sell cartoons to the *Saturday Evening Post*, *Collier's*, and *Redbook*.

"Caveman gags, for reasons which I still cannot explain, were an obsession in those days," remembered Hart, "although I must reluctantly confess, I have not sold a caveman gag to a magazine, to this date." Inspired by the success of Charles Schulz, he decided to create a comic strip. "Why don't you make it a caveman strip?" joked one of his coworkers. "You can't seem to sell them anywhere else."

Hart took on the challenge. After being rejected by five other syndicates, he finally sold his concept to the Herald Tribune. *B.C.* first appeared in thirty newspapers on February 17, 1958, just before Hart's twenty-seventh birthday. Six years later, on November 9, 1964, his second creation, *The Wizard of Id*, debuted.

B.C. was voted Best Humor Strip in 1967 and *The Wizard of Id* earned that distinction five times (1971, 1976, 1980, 1982, and 1983). Hart won the Reuben Award in 1968, and in 1973 *B.C. The First Thanksgiving* was chosen as the best animated film of the year by the National Cartoonists Society.

The central cast of *B.C.*, which was based on many of Hart's friends and family, included B.C. the innocent everyman, Curls the wise guy, Wiley the poet, Peter the genius, Thor the inventor, Clumsy Carp the ichthyologist, Grog the proto-caveman, and two females, Fat Broad and Cute Chick.

At first the humor in *B.C.* was essentially derived from the contrast between the prehistoric setting and the modern proclivities of its characters. Eventually Hart branched out into clever wordplay, slapstick, and cosmological musings.

The original lineup in *The Wizard of Id* consisted of the diminutive King, Bung the drunken court jester, Rodney the cowardly knight, Spook the prisoner, Gwen the fair maiden, the inept Wizard, and his nagging wife, Blanch.

Set in the medieval kingdom of Id, *Wizard* also relied on the interplay between its historical setting and contemporary references. Hart, along with his team of Jack Caprio, Dick Boland, and Dick Cavalli, supplied gags for both strips, while Parker was responsible for the artwork on *Wizard*.

Beginning in 1984 Hart had a gradual religious conversion and eventually began expressing his new-found Christian faith in *B.C.* Not wanting to be perceived as "a whacked-out religious-zealous fanatic," Hart maintained a playfully philosophical attitude about his beliefs. "Entertaining isn't always funny," he argued. "We entertain thoughts." Hart, who passed away on April 7, 2007, believed that humor was a form of salvation.

THE B.C. CAST—illustration by Johnny Hart

B.C. Sunday page by Johnny Hart. © 6/19/66

All B.C. and The Wizard of Id comic strips © Creators Syndicate, Inc. Courtesy of John Hart Studio

B.C. daily strip by Johnny Hart. © 10/12/66

B.C. daily strip by Johnny Hart. © 10/25/67

B.C. daily strip by Johnny Hart. © 2/6/70

B.C. daily strip by Johnny Hart. © 2/9/70

B.C. daily strip by Johnny Hart. © 1/19/72

B.C. daily strip by Johnny Hart. © 10/24/72

B.C. daily strip by Johnny Hart. © 7/30/79

B.C. daily strip by Johnny Hart. © 3/28/88

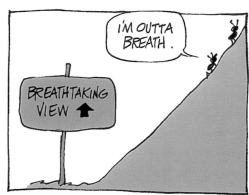

B.C. Sunday page by Johnny Hart. © 7/29/90

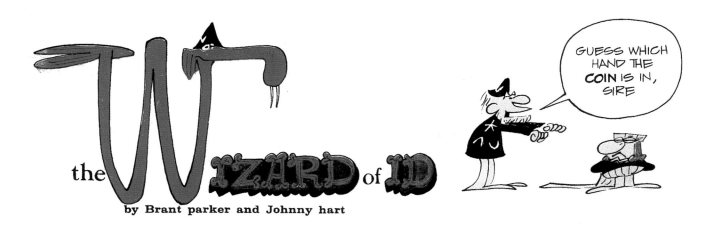

the WIZARD of ID

by Brant parker and Johnny hart

THE WIZARD OF ID Sunday page by **Brant Parker** and **Johnny Hart.** © 11/2/75

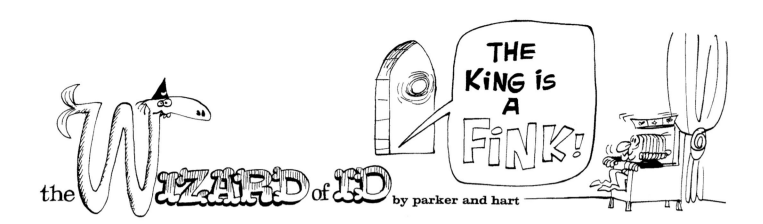

THE WIZARD OF ID Sunday page by Brant Parker and Johnny Hart. © 5/1/65

THE WIZARD OF ID daily strip by Brant Parker and Johnny Hart. © 5/3/65

THE WIZARD OF ID daily strip by Brant Parker and Johnny Hart. © 1/7/66

THE WIZARD OF ID daily strip by Brant Parker and Johnny Hart. © 6/10/66

THE WIZARD OF ID daily strip by Brant Parker and Johnny Hart. © 10/20/88

SAM'S STRIP daily strip by Mort Walker and Jerry Dumas. © 11/9/61

WALKER AND DUMAS

Sam's Strip was ahead of its time when it debuted in 1961. Mort Walker and Jerry Dumas's offbeat creation took the inside joke to a new level, playing with the basic elements of the cartoon form, experimenting with different art styles, and featuring guest appearances by famous characters from other strips. This type of self-referential humor, called "metacomics" by scholar Thomas Inge, had been explored previously by Al Capp, Ernie Bushmiller, and Walt Kelly and has been used on a more regular basis by such contemporary cartoonists as Garry Trudeau, Berke Breathed, and Bill Griffith. *Sam's Strip* had a brief life (twenty months), but it is considered a cult classic among comic-strip aficionados today.

SAM'S STRIP daily strip by Mort Walker and Jerry Dumas. © 3/2/62

SAM'S STRIP daily strip by Mort Walker and Jerry Dumas. © 10/3/62

SAM'S STRIP *daily strip by Mort Walker and Jerry Dumas.* © 5/3/62

SAM'S STRIP *daily strip by Mort Walker and Jerry Dumas.* © 10/31/61

SAM'S STRIP *daily strip by Mort Walker and Jerry Dumas.* © 8/16/62

SAM'S STRIP *daily strip by Mort Walker and Jerry Dumas.* © 9/5/62

EEK AND MEEK daily strip by Howie Schneider. © 10/11/71 NEA, Inc.

THE NEW WAVE Colorful characters, unusual set-tings, and a distinctive graphic style were the defining charac-teristics of the new humor strips that proliferated in the 1960s. Among the many outstanding features that debuted were *Eek and Meek* (1965) by Howie Schneider, about a pair of philosophizing rodents (above); *The Dropouts* (1968) by Howard Post, two shipwrecked castaways on a desert island who observed contemporary civilization from afar (below); *The Born Loser* (1965) by Art Sansom, otherwise known as Brutus P. Thornapple, the Rodney Dangerfield of the comics (bottom); and *Boner's Ark* (1968) by Addison (Mort Walker), helmed by a bungling sea captain who brought along only one animal of each species on his leaky vessel (next page).

THE DROPOUTS daily strip by Howard Post. © 3/14/74 United Feature Syndicate, Inc. Courtesy of International Museum of Cartoon Art

THE BORN LOSER daily strip by Art Sansom. © 4/30/73 NEA, Inc. Courtesy of International Museum of Cartoon Art

BONER'S ARK Sunday page by Addison. © 7/21/68 King Features Syndicate, Inc. Courtesy of Comicana, Inc

TUMBLEWEEDS *daily strip by T. K. Ryan.* © 7/16/66 North America Syndicate, Inc.

THE NEW WAVE (CONTINUED)

Western locales were also popular during the decade. Tom K. Ryan's *Tumbleweeds* (1965) featured an eccentric cast of cowboys, Indians, and townsfolk, a quirky big-foot style, and a dry sense of humor that was appropriate to the setting. *Redeye* (1967), which starred an equally inept tribe of Native Americans, was created by Gordon Bess, who lived in Utah and Idaho for most of his life. This firsthand knowledge brought a touch of authenticity to the strip. Morrie Brickman's *the small society* (1966) took place in a more contemporary milieu as generic civilians, businessmen, and politicians debated current events, often with the U.S. Capitol dome or an urban skyline in the background.

TUMBLEWEEDS *Sunday page by T. K. Ryan.* © 2/17/74 North America Syndicate, Inc. Courtesy of International Museum of Cartoon Art

TUMBLEWEEDS *daily strip by T. K. Ryan.* © 2/22/79 North America Syndicate, Inc.

REDEYE hand-colored Sunday page by Gordon Bess. © 10/12/1960s King Features Syndicate, Inc. Courtesy of International Museum of Cartoon Art

THE SMALL SOCIETY hand-colored Sunday page by Morrie Brickman. © 7/28/68 Washington Star Syndicate, Inc. Courtesy of International Museum of Cartoon Art

ANDY CAPP daily strip by Reg Smythe. © 8/4/64 Creators Syndicate, Inc.

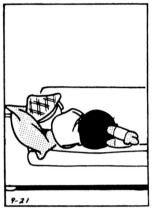

ANDY CAPP daily strip by Reg Smythe. © 9/21/64 Creators Syndicate, Inc.

ANDY CAPP daily strip by Reg Smythe © 8/14/69 Creators Syndicate, Inc.

ANDY CAPP daily strip by Reg Smythe © 9/18/69 Creators Syndicate, Inc.

THE LOCKHORNS *daily panel by Bill Hoest.* © 9/9/68 *King Features Syndicate, Inc.*

"HI! I BROUGHT HOME A FEW LEFTOVERS FROM THE OFFICE PARTY!"

THE LOCKHORNS *daily panel by Bill Hoest.* © 12/31/68 *King Features Syndicate, Inc.*

"NOTHING'S WRONG, OFFICER. WE'RE JUST HAVING OUR TWO-O'CLOCK BOTTLE."

THE LOCKHORNS *daily panel by Bill Hoest.* © 9/20/69 *King Features Syndicate, Inc.*

"SORRY····HE'S PART OF A SET."

THE LOCKHORNS *daily panel by Bill Hoest.* © 4/21/70 *King Features Syndicate, Inc.*

DOMESTIC DYSFUNCTION

The battle of the sexes was waged with renewed vigor in two 1960s comic features. Reg Smythe's *Andy Capp* (previous page), who made his British debut in 1957 and was imported to America in 1963, became a hero to readers around the world for his antisocial behavior. Leroy and Loretta Lockhorn, who first appeared on September 9, 1968 (upper left), in Bill Hoest's daily panel, *The Lockhorns*, were a throwback to the storm and strife of Maggie and Jiggs in their prime. These features must have provided some comic relief to readers who might have experienced increasing marital tension during the early years of the feminist movement.

THE LOCKHORNS *first Sunday page by Bill Hoest.* © 4/9/72 *King Features Syndicate, Inc.*

BIG GEORGE Sunday page by Virgil Partch. © 1960s King Features Syndicate, Inc. Courtesy of International Museum of Cartoon Art

"IT SCARES ME. MARILYN MONROE'S BODY AND MINE HAVE THE EXACT SAME CHEMICAL CONTENT!"

PONYTAIL daily panel by Lee Holley. © 11/17/60 King Features Syndicate, Inc.

FAMILY FARE   Many of the second-tier humor strips of the decade were domestic comedies produced by former magazine gag cartoonists. *Big George* (1960), the harried husband in Virgil Partch's offbeat feature, was a city-bred office worker struggling with life in the suburbs (above). *Ponytail* (1960) by Lee Holley, a former assistant to Hank Ketcham on *Dennis the Menace*, starred a perky teenager (left). Next page (top to bottom): Harry Haenigsen's *Penny* (1943), a stylishly designed family strip, was ghosted by Bill Hoest in the late 1960s. *Professor Phumble* (1960), by Bill Yates, involved an absent-minded inventor who, when not tinkering in his basement, would hit the golf links; Dick Cavalli's *Morty Meekle* (1955) morphed into the durable kid strip *Winthrop* in 1966; Bob Weber's *Moose* (1965) was an American Andy Capp who avoided gainful employment and mooched off his neighbors.

PENNY daily strip by Harry Haenigsen. © 4/26/65 King Features Syndicate, Inc. Courtesy of Bill Janocha

PROFESSOR PHUMBLE daily strip by Bill Yates. © 7/21/60 King Features Syndicate, Inc.

MORTY MEEKLE daily strip by Dick Cavalli. © 3/9/60 NEA, Inc.

MOOSE daily strip by Bob Weber. © 2/28/72 King Features Syndicate, Inc.

TIGER'S NEIGHBORHOOD—Special illustration by Bud Blake. © 1976 King Features Syndicate, Inc. Courtesy of Richard Marschall

BUD BLAKE Among the most admired cartoonists in the comics business, Bud Blake was frequently praised by his peers for the deceptively simple elegance of his linework and the understated honesty of his writing. The children in *Tiger*, which has maintained a solid list of clients for more than three decades, are not precocious mini-adults. They talk and act like real kids. As a testament to Blake's dedication to his craft, *Tiger* was voted Best Comic Strip of the Year by the National Cartoonists Society in 2000 (it was also honored twice in the 1970s), thirty-five years after its debut.

TIGER daily strip by Bud Blake. © 8/25/65 King Features Syndicate, Inc.

TIGER Sunday page by Bud Blake. © 8/8/65 King Features Syndicate, Inc. Courtesy of Richard Marschall

bil keane

FAMILY AFFAIR—Self-caricature by Bil Keane

A NATIVE OF PHILADELPHIA, Bil Keane claimed that when he was a boy, his father knocked the "L" out of him for drawing on the wall. The characters in his successful humor panel, *The Family Circus*, are based on himself, his wife Thel, and his five children, Gayle, Neal, Glen, Chris, and Jeff.

"I dream about them (*The Family Circus* characters) as real kids," Keane claimed. "I've had dreams where they are intermingled with our own children. I can have Jeffy and Dolly and Billy running around with Neal and Gayle and Chris."

Keane, who never had any formal art training, learned the craft by imitating his favorite cartoonists, George Price (a cartoonist for *The New Yorker*), Al Capp (*Li'l Abner*), and George Lichtenstein (*Grin and Bear It*). After three years in the army, he joined the art staff of the *Philadelphia Bulletin*, and in 1954 started the feature *Channel Chuckles* to capitalize on the growing popularity of television. He also sold gag cartoons to the *Saturday Evening Post* and other major magazines.

"Most of the stuff I was selling had to do with family and little children," Keane remembered, "so I decided to try another feature dealing with those subjects." The round panel was originally called *The Family Circle* when it debuted on February 29, 1960, but Keane had to change the name six

months later because there was a magazine with the same title. "Taking advantage of the leap year date," said Keane in 1968, "I have determined that the characters are growing older at the rate of one year in every four." This policy was soon abandoned and the children's ages were fixed at seven (Billy), five (Dolly), three (Jeffy), and one and a half years (PJ).

Keane discovered that a low-key approach worked best. "As I developed a warm feeling for the characters," he explained, "I would take a chance on something that wasn't really funny but was a commentary on today's society or life with a child or memories." Keane stated, "I would rather have a reader feel a warm, knowing glow—even a heart tug or shed a nostalgic tear—than roar with laughter."

The Family Circus Sunday pages often featured a large, detailed drawing. The kids would be shown commenting on a single subject in a multiballoon format or having elaborate fantasies that were revealed in a single dream balloon. Keane drew aerial views of the neighborhood and traced Billy's wanderings with a dotted line. This idea has been recycled many times and is a favorite with readers. Other popular recurring themes are the "not me" gremlin, appearances by Granddad's ghost, and the summer vacation sequences.

Keane designed *The Family Circus* to be easy to read and understand. "There's a general tendency among people who want to be funny to exaggerate," he explained. "I do just the opposite. I tone down every idea I get. I also keep my drawing style simple, using only the lines that are necessary."

Bud Warner began assisting Keane on *The Family Circus* in 1964. Warner would "clean up" Keane's pencil drawings, ink the panels, and do the coloring for the Sunday page. He retired in the mid-1990s, after contributing to the feature more than thirty years.

The Family Circus has always scored high in readership polls and passed the 1,000-paper mark in circulation in the 1980s. It was voted Best Syndicated Panel by the membership of the National Cartoonists Society four times (1967, 1971, 1973, and 1974) and Keane won the Reuben Award in 1982. In addition to more than forty book collections, three animated television specials were based on the feature.

Now that Keane's children are adults, he relies on his grandchildren for inspiration. Jeff Keane collaborates with his father on the feature, so *The Family Circus* is guaranteed to continue for another generation.

THE FAMILY CIRCUS daily panel by Bil Keane. © 1961

"I've only had time to read two pages."

THE FAMILY CIRCUS daily panel by Bil Keane. © 7/17/62

"Mommy, can you find our swimsuits and take us down to the beach?"

THE FAMILY CIRCUS daily panel by Bil Keane. © 8/11/66

"Mommy, why do you always wave your arms and say 'abracadabra' before you start to iron?"

THE FAMILY CIRCUS daily panel by Bil Keane. © 1/7/69

THE FAMILY CIRCUS hand-colored Sunday page by Bil Keane. © 6/11/89

THE FAMILY CIRCUS hand-colored Sunday page by Bil Keane. © 5/16/82

THE FAMILY CIRCUS hand-colored Sunday page by Bil Keane. © 8/14/77

THE FAMILY CIRCUS hand-colored Sunday page by Bil Keane. © 10/21/79

"Hooray! We're here! Let's make a fire, Daddy, and put up the tent!"

THE FAMILY CIRCUS daily panel by Bil Keane. © 8/1/70

"This air smells funny -- I guess it doesn't have enough PLUTION in it."

THE FAMILY CIRCUS daily panel by Bil Keane. © 8/24/70

''This is the bestest time of day. Dinners are cookin', kids are bathed and daddys come home.''

THE FAMILY CIRCUS daily panel by Bil Keane. © 10/15/85

"Grandma says we don't hear back from Granddad 'cause he's havin' too much fun with those angels."

THE FAMILY CIRCUS daily panel by Jeff and Bil Keane. © 7/19/2001

WEE PALS daily strip by Morrie Turner. © 1995 Creators Syndicate, Inc.

WEE PALS daily strip by Morrie Turner. © 8/13/80 Creators Syndicate, Inc.

INTEGRATION   Morrie Turner, the first black cartoonist to sell a comic strip to a major syndicate, has been actively promoting racial tolerance and education for more than forty years. The cast of his 1965 creation, *Wee Pals*, was from a variety of backgrounds and provided graphic proof of Turner's belief in "Rainbow Power." "I decided that just by exposing readers to the sight of Negroes and whites playing together in harmony," Turner wrote, "rather than pointing up aggravations, a useful,

if subliminal, purpose would be served, and ultimately would have as great effect for good as all the freedom marchers in Mississippi." Among the African-American cartoonists who followed Turner's trailblazing path were Brumsic Brandon, Jr., who sold the mildly militant kid strip *Luther* in 1968, and Ted Shearer, who began drawing the evocative, Harlem-based *Quincy* in 1970.

LUTHER daily strip by Brumsic Brandon, Jr. © 4/24/81 Los Angeles Times Syndicate. Courtesy of International Museum of Cartoon Art

QUINCY debut strip by Ted Shearer. © 7/13/70 King Features Syndicate, Inc.

QUINCY daily strip by Ted Shearer. © 8/18/70 King Features Syndicate, Inc.

QUINCY daily strip by Ted Shearer. © 4/7/71 King Features Syndicate, Inc.

QUINCY daily strip by Ted Shearer. © 12/20/79 King Features Syndicate, Inc.

the seventies

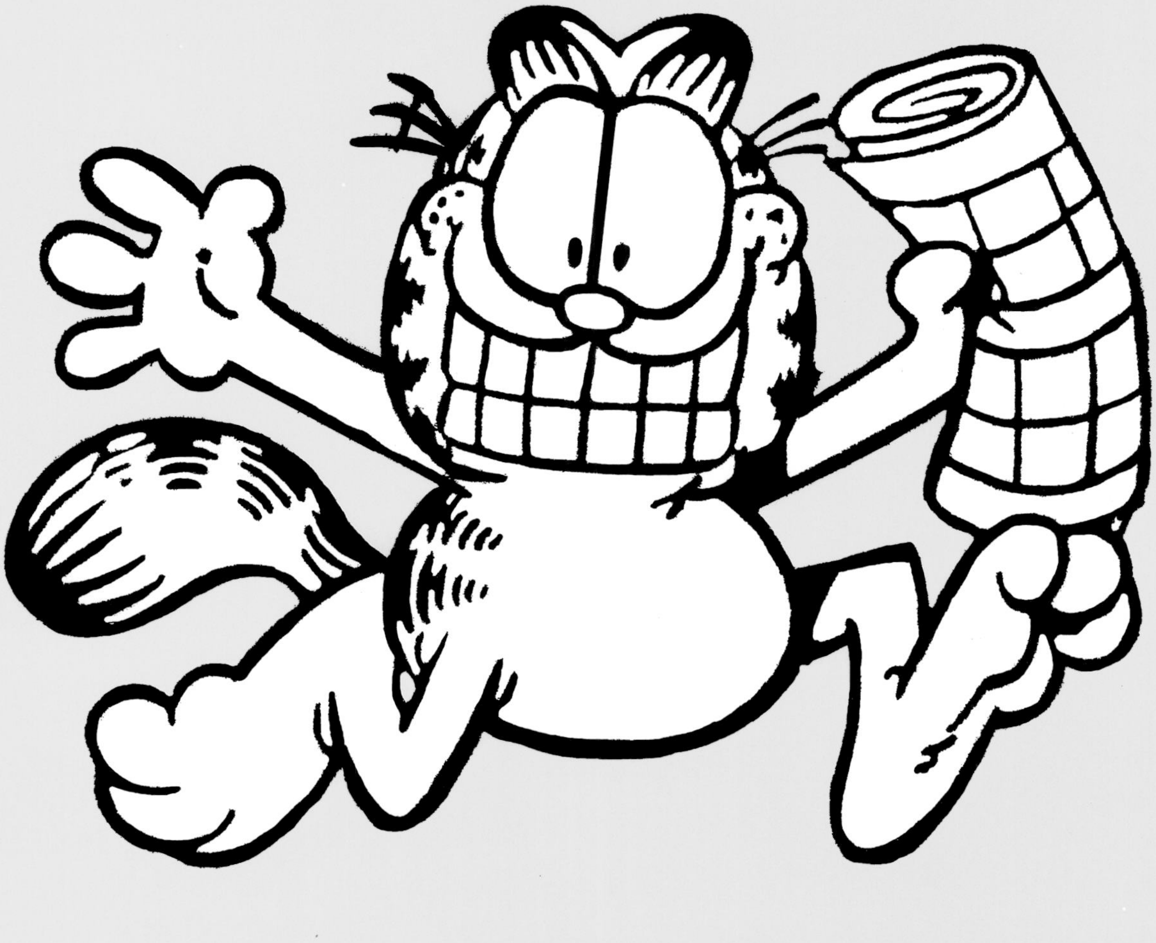

GARFIELD by Jim Davis. © Paws, Inc.

ECOLOGY—POGO Earth Day strip by Walt Kelly. © 1971 Used by permission © Okefenokee Glee & Perloo, Inc.
Courtesy of the Pogo Collection, The Ohio State University Cartoon Research Library

TOM WOLFE OFFICIALLY CHRISTENED IT "THE ME DECADE " IN THE AUGUST 23, 1976, ISSUE OF *NEW YORK* MAGAZINE. A GENERATION OF SELF-INDULGENT BABY BOOMERS WAS COMING OF AGE. THEY EXPERIMENTED WITH NEW APPROACHES TO SELF-IMPROVEMENT (EST, GESTALT, PRIMAL SCREAM), PHYSICAL FITNESS (JOGGING, DIETING, HEALTH CLUBS), SEX (SINGLES BARS, PORNO MOVIES, BIRTH CONTROL), AND RELIGION (HARE KRISHNA, MOONIES, CULTS). THEY DONNED HOT PANTS, LEISURE SUITS, AND PLATFORM SHOES. THEY DANCED TO DISCO AND STOOD IN LINE TO SEE *STAR WARS*. THEY BOUGHT PET ROCKS, MOOD RINGS, AND LAVA LAMPS.

Beneath the superficial parade of fads and fashions, major changes were taking place during the 1970s. The Watergate scandal further alienated an electorate disillusioned by the war in Vietnam. Crime, divorce, drug abuse, and teenage pregnancy frayed the social fabric. The women's movement made significant gains, and by the end of the decade more than half of adult females had jobs. Native Americans, blacks, senior citizens, and homosexuals fought for equal rights. Weakened by oil shortages and a slumping auto industry, the U.S. economy went into a downward spiral, and by 1979 inflation was at an alarming 13.3 percent. The first Earth Day on April 22, 1970, marked the dawn of a new global awareness.

The comics business was also in transition. In 1976 *Time* magazine reported, "Rising prices and chronic shortages of

newsprint have driven editors to drop marginally popular panels and shrink survivors to the size of chewing-gum wrappers." But *Time* also offered hope: "*Doonesbury* seems likely to be the strip of the '70s, if any strips survive," concluded the article.

Garry Trudeau, the creator of *Doonesbury*, was the first baby boomer to succeed with a nationally syndicated comic strip. His crudely drawn college cartoon, *Bull Tales*, which clearly showed the influence of Jules Feiffer, debuted in the *Yale Daily News* on September 30, 1968. At the time, James Andrews and John McMeel were launching a new syndicate and were searching for young talent. They saw potential in Trudeau's lampoon of college life and talked him into signing a contract. *Doonesbury*, which was loosely adapted from *Bull Tales*, was released to twenty-eight newspapers by Universal Press Syndicate on October 26, 1970. Trudeau was twenty-two years old.

By 1976 *Doonesbury* was appearing in 449 newspapers and had earned its creator the Pulitzer Prize. President Gerald Ford summed up the strip's impact when he remarked: "There are only three major vehicles to keep us informed as to what is going on in Washington—the electronic media, the print media, and *Doonesbury*, and not necessarily in that order."

The original cast—Michael J. Doonesbury, Zonker Harris, Mark Slackmeyer, B.D., Boopsie, and Joanie Caucus—were joined by an ever-expanding troupe of supporting players that included such characters as Phred, a Viet Cong terrorist, and Duke, a thinly veiled takeoff on Gonzo journalist Hunter S. Thompson. Trudeau viewed American life through the half-lidded eyes of these pen-and-ink personalities and delivered his observations with deadpan accuracy and biting satire.

Al Capp and Walt Kelly had paved the way for political comment on the funnies pages, but Trudeau took it a step further. He had his semifictional characters refer to public figures by name, without the protective layer of caricature and pseudonym that Capp and Kelly had employed. In 1973, when Trudeau showed Mark Slackmeyer announcing on his radio show that Watergate conspirator and former U.S. Attorney General John Mitchell was "Guilty, guilty, guilty!!" dozens of newspapers refused to print the strip. Trudeau continued to be censored on a regular basis for such offenses as introducing a gay character, showing an unmarried couple in bed, and calling the president's son a "pothead."

The upstart cartoonist earned reluctant praise from his peers. "Anybody who can draw bad pictures of the White House four times in a row and succeed knows something I don't know," grumbled Al Capp. Although nominated numerous times, Trudeau did not win the Reuben Award from the National Cartoonists Society until 1995.

On May 25, 1971, Trudeau was a guest on *To Tell the Truth*. Three out of four panelists failed to guess his identity. Preferring anonymity, he would make only one more television appearance in the next thirty years. An intensely private person, Trudeau eventually refused to do interviews of any kind. "I don't like celebrification," he explained. "Everything I have to share I share in the strip."

Trudeau also broke an age-old industry tradition when he announced in 1982 that he was taking a twenty-month leave of absence beginning on January 2, 1983. Syndicated cartoonists had always been reluctant to take vacations, fearing the loss of their coveted space on the comics pages. During his time off, Trudeau produced *The Doonesbury Musical*, in which his characters escaped from their "time warp" and finally graduated from college.

STUDENT MOVEMENT—Early DOONESBURY cast (left to right: Mark, Mike, and B.D.).

When he returned to work in 1984, Trudeau defended the historic hiatus in a speech to the Associated Press Managing Editors convention by saying, "Daily comic strips continue to be regarded as a kind of public utility; they are viewed as providing a routine service, a dependable day-in, day-out source of light entertainment. This attitude goes a long way toward explaining some of the widespread resentment in the industry when I took a leave of absence."

Doonesbury not only recovered virtually all of its 723 clients, Trudeau actually gained papers after his "sabbatical." In the late 1980s, many cartoonists followed his lead and began taking well-deserved time off.

Trudeau continued to speak out for his principles. In 1984 he told newspaper editors they had to run *Doonesbury* at 44 picas in width (7 5/16 inches), instead of a new industry standard of 38.6 picas (6 7/16 inches), or not run it at all. "It is self-defeating—and not a little ironic—that in an era when newspapers face their gravest threat from television and other visual media," stated Trudeau, "they have continued to reduce the comics page, the one area of genuine pictorial interest in their papers (and one of proven popularity)."

The editors were threatened by this affront to their authority and howled in protest, but only a handful canceled the strip. Although all cartoonists were affected by the shrinking size of comics, not many of Trudeau's professional peers supported his courageous stand. Approximately one-quarter

WOMEN'S RIGHTS—CATHY illustration © 1986 Cathy Guisewite. Used by
permission of Universal Press Syndicate. All
rights reserved

of the newspapers elected to print the 44-pica *Doonesbury* on the editorial page rather than upset the symmetry of their comics pages.

In 1990, after seventeen years of public silence, Trudeau granted an interview to *Newsweek* magazine. In the article, Jonathan Alter wrote that the creator of *Doonesbury* was "as much journalist as artist—an investigative cartoonist. Zeitgeist megaphone, flight attendant for his generation. . . ." *Doonesbury* was unlike any comic strip that had come before it, and reporters often struggled to describe exactly what it was that made Trudeau unique.

Trudeau preferred to call himself a "satirist." In 1995, in the introduction to his silver-anniversary anthology, he wrote, "Twenty-five years into it, I'm still trying to get it right. The strip remains a work in progress, an imperfect chronicle of human imperfection." A youth movement followed Trudeau's trailblazing path in the 1970s. These newcomers, all born in the postwar years, brought fresh insights to the comics pages. The funnies would never be the same.

In 1976 Cathy Guisewite was a vice president at an advertising agency in Detroit and coming off a "disaster" in her love life. She discovered that doodling helped relieve some of her anxieties. "I started seeing myself with a sense of humor," she remembered. "It became a big release for me to draw pictures of myself and my friends." Guisewite's mother convinced her to send a batch of her cartoons to Universal Press. "The syndicate that *Doonesbury* built" had been looking for a feature that reflected the experiences of a modern working woman. They offered the twenty-six-year-old cartoonist a contract and, on November 22, 1976, the *Cathy* comic strip debuted.

In Guisewite's autobiographical creation, her namesake shared the cartoonist's intimate fears and dreams with millions of readers. The supporting players in the feature—Cathy's doting parents, her on-again, off-again boyfriend, Irving, her exploitive boss, Mr. Pinkley, and her feminist coworker, Andrea—were inspired by Guisewite's friends and family. The humor in the strip focused on what she called the "four basic guilt groups—food, love, mother, and career."

Cathy became the poster girl for a generation of single women who juggled the demands of a career with the hope of eventually settling down and starting a family. "Helping women to laugh at themselves when they fall a bit short of the new liberated woman is what this strip is all about," claimed Guisewite in a 1977 interview. *Cathy* was their voice on the comics pages.

Jeff MacNelly was the youngest political cartoonist to win the Pulitzer Prize when he received the coveted honor in 1972 at the age of twenty-five. He was awarded two more Pulitzers (1978, 1985) as well as the National Cartoonists Society's Reuben in 1978 for editorial cartooning. In 1979 he won the Reuben for his comic strip, *Shoe*.

When MacNelly created *Shoe* in 1977 he became the first of the "double dippers"—cartoonists who produced both a daily comic strip and a weekly batch of editorial cartoons. In a remarkably short period of time, *Shoe* became a fixture on the funnies pages, and in 1989 its circulation passed the 1,000-paper mark.

The bird-brained stars of MacNelly's creation were the tough-talking editor in chief of the *Treetops Tattler Tribune*, J. Martin Shoemaker, and his disheveled reporter, Perfessor Cosmo Fishhawk. The cast also included Skylar, the Perfessor's nerdy nephew; Roz, the proprietress of the local greasy spoon; and Loon, a high-flying delivery boy.

MacNelly saved most of the topical humor for his political cartoons, but he couldn't help sneaking comments into his strip. Senator Battson D. Belfry, a corrupt Southern politician,

MODERN MOTHER—Illustration from David, We're Pregnant! by Lynn
Johnston. © 1974 Lynn Johnston Productions, Inc. All rights reserved

became a regular vehicle for jabs at government fat cats. Most of the gags in *Shoe*, however, revolved around eating, drinking, smoking, and the accumulation of clutter.

MacNelly's droll wit and graphic genius garnered almost universal praise from his fellow cartoonists and newspaper columnists. In the introduction to *The Very First Shoe Book*, published in 1978, Art Buchwald wrote: "MacNelly, with one stroke of his brush, has seared our conscience, and has grabbed us by the throat and made us sit up in our chairs, and admit that it is we, not he, who are marching to a different drummer."

In the early 1970s Lynn Johnston was a divorced mother pursuing a career as a freelance artist, designing posters, billboards, TV graphics, and medical illustrations. She had tried sending a batch of cartoons to *Ms.* magazine, but they had been rejected. When she was pregnant with her first child, she had created some drawings for her obstetrician while sitting in his waiting room. By the time she gave birth, she had finished eighty cartoons, which her doctor hung in the examining room to entertain his other patients. A few years later Dr. Murray Enkin convinced Johnston to do a book collection of her cartoons, and in 1974 *David We're Pregnant!* was published. With the success of this book, she published two more collections, *Hi Mom!, Hi Dad!* (about newborns) and *Do They Ever Grow Up?* (about toddlers).

In the summer of 1977, Jim Andrews from Universal Press Syndicate was looking for a cartoonist to do a strip about family life from a woman's perspective and saw one of Johnston's books. He asked her to submit twenty samples for a syndicated comic strip. A few months later she got a letter from U.P.S. comics editor Lee Salem with a critique of the strip and a twenty-year contract. He urged the thirty-year-old cartoonist to fly to Kansas City from her home in Manitoba right away. Racked with self-doubt about making such a long-term commitment, Johnston signed anyway. She got sick to her stomach immediately after.

For Better or For Worse debuted on September 9, 1979. The strip, which starred Elly Patterson, her husband, John, her two children, Michael and Elizabeth, and Farley the dog, was a chronicle of Johnston's own family life. A third child, April, was born in 1991. Similar to the characters in *Gasoline Alley*, the Pattersons aged at a relatively normal rate.

The feminine point of view of *For Better or For Worse* made it stand out from other family strips. "There are so many men in the business who are good at the comedy part," explained Johnston in a 1994 interview. "But the subtle, gentle, nuance part, you don't see that much."

Sensitive topics, such as teenage drinking, child abuse, and homosexuality, were dealt with honestly in the strip, earning Johnston supporters and detractors. The 1995 sequence in which Farley died after saving April from drowning was one of the most moving episodes in the history of modern newspaper comics.

Johnston was the first woman to win the Reuben Award when she was honored as the "outstanding cartoonist of the year" in 1985. *For Better or For Worse* consistently topped readership polls throughout the 1980s and 1990s and built a circulation list of over 2,000 papers.

"I GOT MINE"—HAGAR illustration by Dik Browne. © King Features Syndicate, Inc.

Not all of the successful new features of the 1970s were produced by baby boomers. Dik Browne, who had illustrated *Hi and Lois* since 1954, was fifty-five years old when he created *Hagar the Horrible* in 1973. Browne was having trouble with his eyesight and worried about the financial future of his family. Sitting in his cluttered laundry-room studio, he remembered some old Norse legends his Swedish aunt had told him when he was a child. His hand sketched out a horned Viking helmet sitting on top of a big round nose. The rest of the figure seemed to draw itself. The cartoon barbarian's portly frame was draped with a rumpled bearskin, his shield was hacked and worn, and the crowning touch was a snarled beard encircling his bewildered face. The answer to the cartoonist's dilemma was staring him in the face.

Browne named his new comic-strip hero "Hagar the Horrible" and provided him with a strong-willed wife, Helga, a neat, studious son, Hamlet, a protofeminist daughter, Honi, and a loyal dog, Snert. He drew up some samples and took them to King Features Syndicate. It signed him up and quickly sold the strip to 200 newspapers. After its debut on February 4, 1973, *Hagar the Horrible* became

FAT CAT—GARFIELD illustration by Jim Davis. © Paws, Inc. Used by permission of
Universal Press Syndicate. All rights reserved. Courtesy of Editor and Publisher

the fastest-growing feature in comics history, passing the 1,000-paper mark in five years.

In the 1985 anthology collection *The Best of Hagar the Horrible*, Dik Browne described the philosophy behind his remarkable creation: "A great historian once said that history is like a bloody flaming river cutting its way through the centuries. But on the banks families are doing the ordinary things—raising kids, paying bills, making love, shooting craps, whatever. . . . That's sorta the way I feel about Hagar the Horrible. He is a Viking and God knows he is a barbarian, but he is also a family man, a loving husband, and a devoted father."

One of the most successful comic strips of the modern era was created by another veteran in the 1970s. Jim Davis had worked as an assistant to Tom Ryan on *Tumbleweeds* for nine years before he launched *Garfield* in 1978. Cats had always been popular in the comics, but the success of

Davis's feature set off a feline frenzy that would reach its peak in the 1980s.

The lasagna-eating fat cat was not an overnight sensation. In 1980 *Garfield* was appearing in only 180 newspapers when Davis's marketing genius finally began to pay off. He came up with a clever horizontal shape (now known as the "*Garfield* format") for his first paperback collection, designed a special display rack, and went on a twenty-city book tour. At the beginning of the tour *Garfield*'s circulation was growing at the rate of seven newspapers per month. Two months later the strip was being picked up at the rate of one a day. *Garfield At Large* hit number one on the *New York Times* best-seller list, and by 1982 seven *Garfield* titles appeared on the best-seller list simultaneously. By 1988 the strip was appearing in over 2,000 newspapers and more than 3,000 licensed products had been designed and approved by Davis's multimillion-dollar cottage industry, Paws Incorporated. One hundred million *Garfield* books were eventually sold.

The 1970s was a particularly fertile period for new humor strips of all types. Although the copycat mentality still prevailed at the syndicates, it was no longer a reliable road to success. Editors were looking for fresh voices and unique perspectives to compete with the established features.

Russ Myers wrote and designed greeting cards at Hallmark for ten years before co-creating *Broom-Hilda* with Elliot Caplin in 1970. The strip starred a cigar-chomping, sex-starved, 1,500-year-old witch who traveled freely through time and space. *Broom-Hilda* and her two sidekicks, Gaylord the buzzard and Irwin the troll, lived in an enchanted forest that was graphically reminiscent of Krazy Kat's Coconino County. Myers's bold style and surreal imagination won over readers, and *Broom-Hilda* was appearing in 300 newspapers by the end of the decade.

Tom Wilson was also an artist in the sentiment industry when he created Ziggy in 1966. His employer, American Greetings, published a best-selling book collection of cartoons starring the round-headed nebbish in 1968, and the *Ziggy* syndicated panel was launched by Universal Press in 1971. Wilson consciously designed a character with minimal identity—

HIPPIES AND BUMS—BENJY daily strip by Jim Berry and Bill Yates. © 1973 NEA Inc.

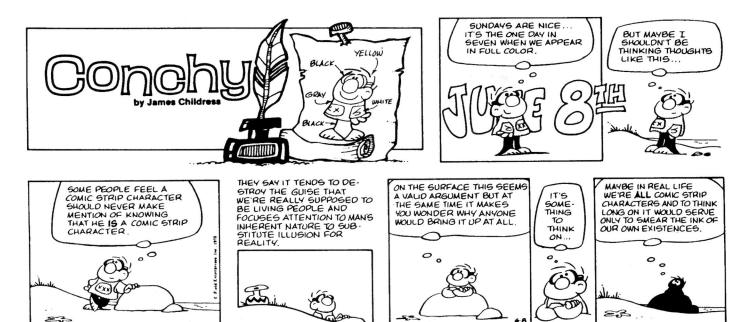

SELF-REFLECTION—CONCHY Sunday page by James Childress. © 6/8/75 Field Enterprises Inc. Courtesy of Thomas Inge

Ziggy had no discernible class, race, or character—so that he would be appealing to all readers. "Ziggy is a lot of things we don't talk about," explained Wilson in a 1973 interview. "There's a kind of loneliness about him none of us can ever shake, even in a room full of friends." The formula worked, as Ziggy's placid features appeared on millions of greeting cards, coffee mugs, and calendars, as well as in over 400 newspapers.

The "Everyman" theme was popular during the decade. *Frank and Ernest*, the Mutt and Jeff–like duo in Bob Thaves's 1972 single-panel strip creation, changed identities daily to fit the gag but were often depicted as tramps sitting on a park bench. *Benjy*, the star of a short-lived feature produced by Jim Berry and Bill Yates between 1973 and 1975, was a bum who was frequently mistaken for a hippie. *Herman*, the middle-aged slouch in Jim Unger's 1974 panel, took abuse from everyone with whom he came in contact.

In 1977 Mort Walker and Jerry Dumas were approached by the N.E.A. syndicate with an offer to revive their offbeat 1960s creation, *Sam's Strip*. The cartoonists asked King Features for permission, and King decided it wanted to do a strip utilizing the same characters but in a different setting. Sam and his assistant became Sam and Silo, a sheriff and his deputy from the town of Upper Duckwater (pop. 437). Shortly after its debut on April 18, 1977, Dumas took over the sole artistic duties on *Sam and Silo*.

A handful of established creators also launched second features during the decade. Mell Lazarus (*Miss Peach*) started *Momma*, a doodle about a doting mom, on October 26, 1970. Brant Parker (*The Wizard of Id*) helped Don Wilder (writer) and Bill Rechin (artist) develop a French Foreign Legion farce, *Crock*, in 1975. Bill Hoest (*The Lockhorns*) added *Agatha Crumm*, about a seventy-seven-year-old, penny-pinching tycoon, in 1977.

Many new humor features reflected contemporary lifestyles in an effort to be relevant to readers. *Funky Winkerbean* (1972), by twenty-five-year-old Tom Batiuk, was set in a high school, and *Drabble* (1979), by twenty-two-year-old Kevin Fagan, took place on a college campus. *Mixed Singles* (1972), by Mel Casson and Bill Brown, dealt with the dating scene, and *Splitsville* (1978), by Frank Baginski and Reynolds Dodson, looked at the lighter side of divorce. The central character in *Tank McNamara* (1974), by Jeff Miller and Bill Hinds, was a former gridiron great trying to make it as a television sportscaster. *Motley's Crew* (1976), by Tom Forman and Ben Templeton, starred two blue-collar workers from the "Silent Majority."

It often took extraordinary perseverance to break into the comics business. In 1970 James Childress took out a full-page advertisement in *Editor and Publisher* announcing the debut of a new comic strip entitled *Conchy*. His home address and phone number appeared at the bottom of the page for the benefit of editors. "We will admit that signing newspapers before establishing syndicate sponsorship may be a method of the unorthodoxed," wrote Childress in the ad. "But there are times that if any measure of success is to be realized, stepping from the norm is essential. This is the story of *Conchy*."

The saga started in October 1960 when a young G.I. submitted an idea for a caveman strip to the major syndicates. It didn't sell. After being discharged a year later, Childress tried again with a strip about a hobo, but, once again, the syndicates weren't interested. In 1962 he created a strip about a beach-comber his wife named after a conch shell. "With *Conchy* I got stubborn," Childress remembered. "I saw in this strip a bright future and each time it was rejected I'd improve on it and resubmit it." After seven years of futility he finally decided to market his cherished creation directly to newspaper editors without syndicate representation.

THE END IS NEAR—LI'L ABNER daily strip by Al Capp (caricatured in second panel). © 10/7/71 Capp Enterprises, Inc. Courtesy of International Museum of Cartoon Art

By 1973 *Conchy* was appearing in thirteen newspapers, and Childress had a book deal with Grosset and Dunlap. After *Conchy on the Half-Shell* was published, Childress finally got the break he had been waiting for. In 1974 Field Enterprises Syndicate took over the distribution of *Conchy* and claimed that it had 157 daily and Sunday clients lined up. After sales of the strip stalled, Field suggested to Childress that he abandon the philosophical bent of his creation and try a more conventional gag-a-day approach. In May 1976, disagreeing with his syndicate over the direction the strip was taking, Childress asked to be released from his contract and his wish was granted. A year later, in deep financial and marital trouble, Childress committed suicide.

The decade also saw the demise of two long-running classics. After Walt Kelly passed away in 1973, his widow, Selby Kelly, tried valiantly to continue *Pogo*. When the strip was finally canceled in 1975, the blame was laid directly on the reduced size that it was printed in the newspapers. Selby Kelly, who had worked as an animator at many of the major Hollywood studios, felt that it was no longer possible to do justice to her husband's creation in such cramped quarters.

Al Capp was also struggling with his allotted space. "I have enlarged my lettering so that a reader can simply NOT overlook it," Capp complained in 1975. "I long for the days when I was able to draw twice as much, write twice as much,

and give newspapers what I was able to give them in the days of the Shmoo." In 1977 Capp turned to an assistant in his Boston studio and casually remarked, "You can stop cutting the paper. I'm not going to draw any more." Capp had tried out a few artists as potential successors, but in the end, he knew that no one else could continue his creation. The last episode of *Li'l Abner* appeared on November 13, 1977. Two years later Capp was dead.

Only a handful of illustrative features survived. John Cullen Murphy (*Big Ben Bolt*) took over as the artist on Hal Foster's *Prince Valiant* in 1970. Dick Moores won the Reuben Award for his work on *Gasoline Alley* in 1974. After a number of attempts to revive *Little Orphan Annie*, Leonard Starr introduced a redesigned version with the shortened title *Annie* in 1979. Chester Gould, who had produced *Dick Tracy* for forty-seven years, retired in 1977 and handed over the chores to Rick Fletcher (artist) and Max Collins (writer). Losing papers and readers, Milt Caniff managed to keep *Steve Canyon* going until his death in 1988.

Story-strip casualties continued to mount. The last episode of *Terry and the Pirates* by George Wunder appeared on February 25, 1973. The demise of *Smilin' Jack, Johnny Hazard, On Stage*, and *Dateline Danger* followed. Although many of the soap-opera strips, such as *Mary Worth, Rex Morgan M.D.*, and *Apartment 3-G* still appeared, the future for new adventure strips looked bleak.

THE GREAT OUTDOORS—MARK TRAIL by Ed Dodd. (Dodd created his long-running adventure strip in 1946 and retired in 1978.) © 5/16/74 King Features Syndicate, Inc.
Courtesy of International Museum of Cartoon Art

SCI-FI REVIVAL—STAR HAWKS by Gil Kane and Ron Goulart. © 12/25/78 United Feature Syndicate, Inc.

The success of George Lucas's *Star Wars* film in 1977 launched a mini-revival of science-fiction features. *Star Wars* (1979) and *Star Trek* (1980) comic strips soon followed, and *Buck Rogers in the 25th Century* (1979) was brought back to life after a live-action movie was produced. One original new outer-space creation, *Star Hawks* (1977), by Gil Kane (artist) and Ron Goulart (writer), was offered in an innovative two-tiered daily strip format.

Costumed superheroes also made a comeback in the late 1970s. Marvel jumped on the bandwagon with comic-strip adaptations of *The Amazing Spider-Man* (1977), *Conan the Barbarian* (1977), and *The Incredible Hulk* (1979). DC joined in with *The World's Greatest Superheroes* (1978), which teamed up Batman, Superman, Wonder Woman, and Flash.

The comics gained new respectability during the decade. In 1974 the Museum of Cartoon Art, the first institution in the world devoted to the collection, preservation, and exhibition of cartoon art, opened to the public. It was the realization of a dream for the founder, Mort Walker.

More than a decade before that historic occasion, Mort Walker and Dik Browne were attending a cartoonists outing in Jamaica. Relaxing after a round of golf, they slipped into a philosophical mood. "Why aren't cartoons considered art?" wondered Browne. "We don't have a museum," answered Walker. In that moment, an idea was hatched that would take years of perseverance to turn into reality.

A committee was formed, including Milt Caniff, Walt Kelly, Rube Goldberg, and Hal Foster as well as Walker and Browne, to investigate the establishment of a permanent museum devoted to cartoon art. They met with corporations, foundations, and government agencies and considered sites in Washington, D.C., Manhattan, Syracuse, and New Haven. Walker secured a promise from the Hearst Corporation for funding. A proposed budget was put together, a board of

UNDER CONSTRUCTION—A sketch by MAD cartoonist Sergio Aragonés, made while visiting the Museum of Cartoon Art in 1978

CARTOON MUSEUM—KERRY DRAKE Sunday page by Al Andriola. (The conclusion of a story based on the 1977 opening of the Museum of Cartoon Art in Ward's Castle. A caricature of the author, in a tuxedo, appears in the lower left panel.) © 11/19/78 Field Enterprises, Inc.

directors was formed, and a promotional brochure was printed. But the project never seemed to get off the ground.

In 1973 Walker heard that an old mansion, around the corner from his home in Greenwich, Connecticut, was for rent. The building was ideally suited for a museum and was located in an affluent suburb of New York City where many professional cartoonists lived. Walker knew that this was the opportunity for which he had been waiting. He put up some of his own money, signed a lease, and hired a staff. His personal collection of cartoons became part of the first exhibition. When the Museum of Cartoon Art opened on August 11, 1974, the event was national news.

In the first year of operation more than $200,000 was raised and 25,000 original cartoons were donated. In 1975 the museum displayed *A Retrospective of Walt Kelly and Pogo* and *The Hal Foster Exhibit*, and fourteen cartoon pioneers were elected to the museum's Hall of Fame by a distinguished panel of writers and scholars.

By 1976 the museum had outgrown its original home. John Mead, the owner of the mansion, was concerned that the thousands of visitors were putting too much wear and tear on his family estate and declined to renew the lease. After a year of searching, another location was found just a few miles away. The Ward Castle, in Rye Brook, New York, was the first residence in the world built entirely of reinforced concrete. Completed in 1875, the castle had been a private home until the early 1970s, when it was vacated due to maintenance problems. The task of renovating the building and converting it into a museum presented a daunting challenge. A crew of struggling artists, college dropouts, friends, and volunteers pulled off the impossible. Within months after the takeover of the castle, a gala opening reception was held on November 12, 1977.

Walker often wondered if it had been worth all the time and money he had put into the effort. Standing in the lobby of the museum one Sunday afternoon, he saw an elderly woman coming out of one of the galleries. "I feel like I've just spent an hour with some old friends," she said. The museum's founder was reassured that the positive public response more than justified the sacrifices.

Before the Museum of Cartoon Art opened, original cartoons were often thrown away, lost, or destroyed by artists, syndicates, publishers, and studios. The finest examples of the art form were traded at comic conventions, among a small group of collectors, for a few hundred dollars each.

The museum led the way in elevating the appreciation of cartoon art. Ohio State University established the Cartoon Research Library in 1977 and held the first Festival of Cartoon Art in 1983. The Cartoon Art Museum opened in San Francisco in 1987. By the 1990s cartoon museums could be found in France, Belgium, England, Switzerland, Bulgaria, Poland, Germany, Sweden, and Japan. Prestigious auction houses sold original cartoons to wealthy clients for prices that reached as high as a quarter of a million dollars. Cartoonists now had more respect for their own work.

"I don't think of comics as just entertainment," wrote Bill Watterson, creator of *Calvin and Hobbes*, in 1995. "To attract and keep an audience, art must entertain, but the significance of any art lies in its ability to express truths—to reveal and help us understand our world. Comic strips, in their own humble way, are capable of doing this."

Many of Watterson's contemporaries were equally enlightened about the importance of cartoon art. After all, their creations were now hanging in museums.

garry trudeau

TIME **MAGAZINE** **WROTE** of Garry Trudeau in 1976, "an indifferent draftsman, the artist is usually just good enough to strike an attitude or sink a platitude. But at his best, Trudeau manages to be a Hogarth in a hurry, a satirist who brings political comment back to the comics pages."

This assessment was typical of the pre-sabbatical *Doonesbury* era (1970 to 1982). Trudeau's static graphics were widely criticized while his biting social satire was universally praised. A typical strip from the early years would feature three nearly identical panels of a character watching television, followed by a subtle reaction in the final panel. The repetitious pictures tended to amplify the narrative, setting up a visually understated but powerful conclusion.

When Trudeau broke into national syndication, his experience was limited to the cartoons he had done for the *Yale Daily News*. The learning curve was evident in the early years of *Doonesbury*, as Trudeau went through a period of on-the-job training.

In November 1976 Trudeau drew a weeklong series in which Joanie Caucus and Rick Redfern, both unmarried, spent the night together. More than thirty newspapers dropped the controversial final strip in which the couple were shown in bed. More important, the brilliantly orchestrated "zoom," from Joanie's bedroom to Rick's, was completely wordless. Trudeau had come a long way from the stiff, posed look of his Jules Feiffer–influenced college cartoons.

During his twenty-month sabbatical, from January 1983 to September 1984, Trudeau made a conscious decision to overhaul the look of the strip. A talented graphic designer, Trudeau had served as his own art director on many special projects, including posters, book covers, and calendars. In the mid-1980s he applied these skills to a series of visually innovative *Doonesbury* episodes featuring J.J.'s performance art, Duke's flashbacks, "The Return to Reagan's Brain," and Boopsie's harmonic convergence.

In 1990 *Newsweek* described how Trudeau penciled the strip at his studio in New York and faxed it to his inker in Kansas City. Don Carlton began working as Trudeau's assistant in September 1971. "The first weeks he sent me (he penciled very tightly and still does) were inked and lettered by me," remembered Carlton in 1993. The two collaborated closely as the graphic look of the strip matured. This arrangement had changed very little in two decades.

A year after the *Newsweek* article appeared, *Entertainment Weekly* described Carlton as Trudeau's "ghost artist." After a call from Universal Press Syndicate, *EW* ran a retraction admitting that it had misrepresented Carlton's role. The conservative *Wall Street Journal*, looking for an excuse to attack the liberal-leaning Trudeau, ran an editorial on November 21, 1991, comparing him to Milli Vanilli, the duo who had been exposed for using other musicians to sing on their Grammy Award–winning album. Trudeau's syndicate threatened legal action, and on December 18, 1991, the *Journal* reluctantly admitted that "if our 'Garry Vanilli' headline and reference to Cartoon Syncing suggested that we consider Mr. Trudeau a complete fraud, we somewhat overstated the case."

This episode revealed the persistent ignorance among the general public about the demands of producing a daily comic feature. The majority of top-selling cartoonists have assistants. Garry Trudeau works closer to his deadline (often less than two weeks) than any other artist. After scripting his dailies on Wednesday and Thursday each week, the final strips are produced in a flurry of faxes between Trudeau and Carlton on Friday. This collaboration is essential to maintaining the topical content of *Doonesbury* and meeting the deadlines of its subscribers.

Doonesbury earned a reputation for being poorly drawn during its formative years. By the mid-1980s Trudeau's creation was among the most graphically adventurous strips on the comics (and editorial) pages. It has continued to provide a consistently high level of satire and entertainment for more than thirty years.

DOONESBURY *daily strip penciled by Garry Trudeau.* © 9/27/2002

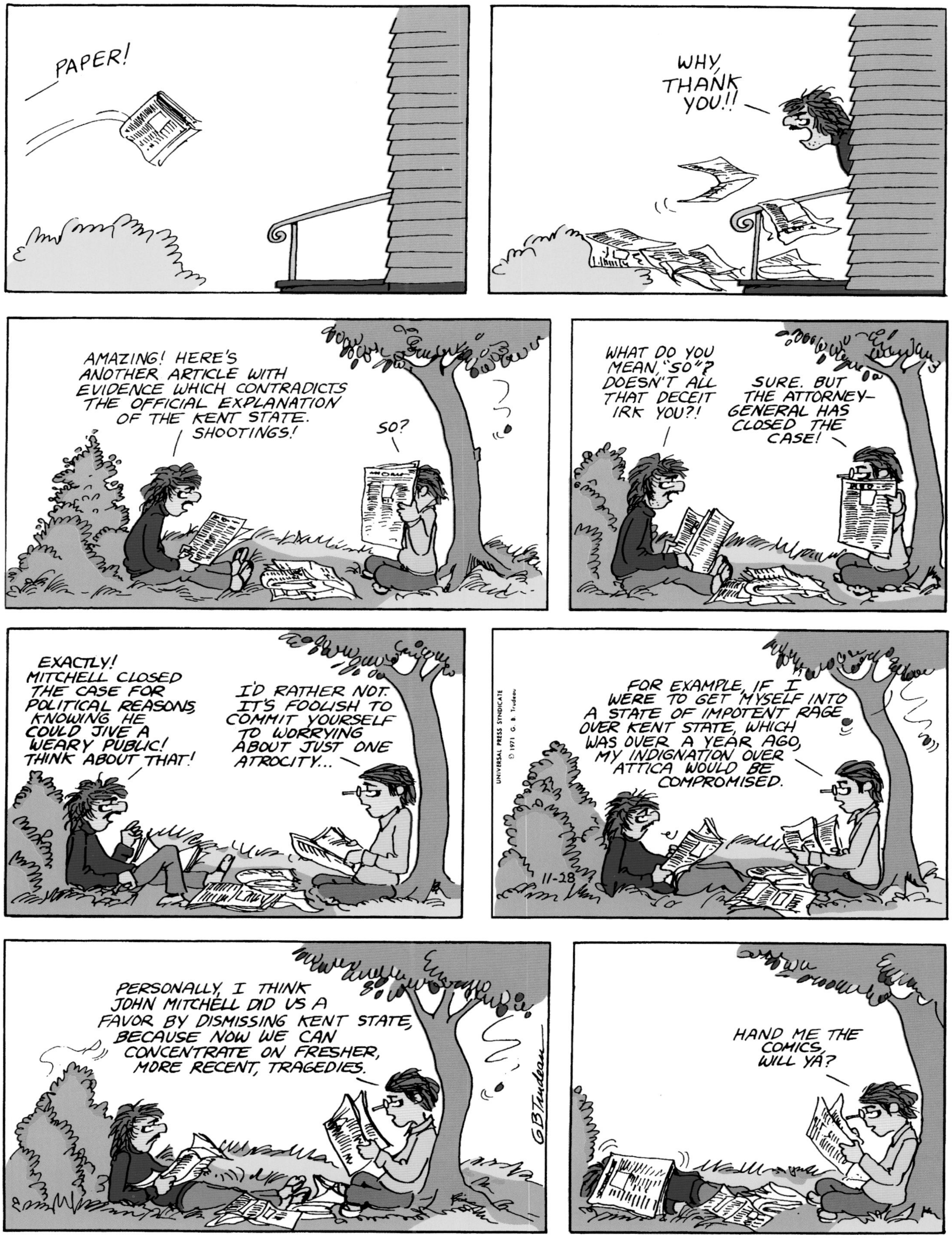
PAPER!
WHY, THANK YOU!!
AMAZING! HERE'S ANOTHER ARTICLE WITH EVIDENCE WHICH CONTRADICTS THE OFFICIAL EXPLANATION OF THE KENT STATE SHOOTINGS!
SO?
WHAT DO YOU MEAN, "SO"? DOESN'T ALL THAT DECEIT IRK YOU?!
SURE. BUT THE ATTORNEY-GENERAL HAS CLOSED THE CASE!
EXACTLY! MITCHELL CLOSED THE CASE FOR POLITICAL REASONS, KNOWING HE COULD JIVE A WEARY PUBLIC! THINK ABOUT THAT!
I'D RATHER NOT. IT'S FOOLISH TO COMMIT YOURSELF TO WORRYING ABOUT JUST ONE ATROCITY...
UNIVERSAL PRESS SYNDICATE © 1971 G. B. Trudeau
FOR EXAMPLE, IF I WERE TO GET MYSELF INTO A STATE OF IMPOTENT RAGE OVER KENT STATE, WHICH WAS OVER A YEAR AGO, MY INDIGNATION OVER ATTICA WOULD BE COMPROMISED.
11-28
PERSONALLY, I THINK JOHN MITCHELL DID US A FAVOR BY DISMISSING KENT STATE, BECAUSE NOW WE CAN CONCENTRATE ON FRESHER, MORE RECENT, TRAGEDIES.
GBTrudeau
HAND ME THE COMICS, WILL YA?

DOONESBURY Sunday page by Garry Trudeau.

DOONESBURY *daily strip by Garry Trudeau.* © 5/29/73

DOONESBURY *daily strip by Garry Trudeau.* © 12/13/73

DOONESBURY *daily strip by Garry Trudeau.* © 5/31/75

DOONESBURY *daily strip by Garry Trudeau.* © 2/10/76

DOONESBURY daily-strip sequence by Garry Trudeau. © 11/10–11/13/76

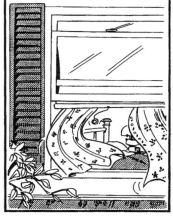

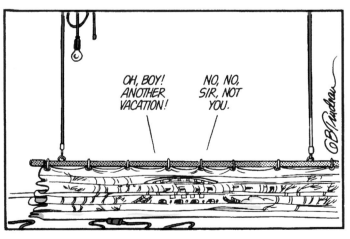

DOONESBURY Sunday page by Garry Trudeau (the last episode before Trudeau went on sabbatical). © 1/2/83

DOONESBURY daily strip by Garry Trudeau. © 9/11/86

DOONESBURY daily strip by Garry Trudeau. © 10/23/86

DOONESBURY daily strip by Garry Trudeau. © 3/23/87

DOONESBURY daily strip by Garry Trudeau. © 8/12/87

DOONESBURY daily strip by Garry Trudeau. © 6/14/88

DOONESBURY daily strip by Garry Trudeau. © 4/4/89

DOONESBURY daily strip by Garry Trudeau. © 4/21/89

DOONESBURY daily strip by Garry Trudeau. © 5/6/91

DOONESBURY Sunday page by Garry Trudeau. © 5/26/96

DOONESBURY *daily strip by Garry Trudeau.* © 9/9/93

DOONESBURY *daily strip by Garry Trudeau.* © 8/18/94

DOONESBURY *daily strip by Garry Trudeau.* © 11/20/99

DOONESBURY *daily strip by Garry Trudeau.* © 3/23/2000

cathy guisewite

CATHY REPRESENTS the foremost example of what comics historian Ron Goulart calls the "Grandma Moses School of Comic Strips." The success of Cathy Guisewite's creation inspired a wave of contemporary features that derived their humor from autobiographical experience and were rendered with minimal graphic flair.

honesty of Guisewite's voice. There is no question of authorship. She does all the writing and drawing herself and inks the final strips directly onto bristol board without penciling, to create a look of spontaneity.

Cathy still wishes she hadn't used her own name for the title. "I feel comfortable with the character; she's my creation,"

CATHY daily strip by Cathy Guisewite. © 8/13/82

Guisewite admitted, "I quit taking art class when I was seven years old because I was planning a career as a cowboy and felt it would be a waste of time to learn how to draw." She has been insecure about her abilities since *Cathy* debuted in 1976.

"Except for the basic things, like trying to connect the heads to the bodies, I've never consciously changed the way the characters looked, but have always just drawn them the only way I could," wrote Guisewite in her fifteenth-anniversary collection.

After she signed her contract with Universal Press Syndicate, Guisewite frantically tried to improve her drawing skills and told no one, other than her immediate family, that she was working on a comic strip. She studied how Charles Schulz communicated emotions with a few simple lines, and Mort Walker's *Backstage at the Strips* became her bible.

"The first day *Cathy* ran in the paper, I hid in my office in the advertising agency where I worked as a writer, praying that no one would read the comics that day," she recounted in her twentieth-anniversary collection.

Guisewite majored in English at the University of Michigan, was a copywriter at Campbell-Ewald advertising in Detroit, and had considerable experience in other types of creative writing. She frequently describes "writing" the strip rather than drawing it, and that is clearly her strength.

The artistic style of *Cathy*, which Universal Press once described as "primitively energetic," helped establish the

Guisewite explains. "She's not *me*, but she is *of* me—a large part of me." Many of her personal feelings are expressed through the character, but all of the experiences chronicled in the strip are not necessarily autobiographical. When Cathy used a computer dating service in one sequence, for example, Guisewite did extensive research but did not try out the service herself. Readers have always been convinced that everything that goes on in the strip actually happened to its creator, and Guisewite gave up dissuading them years ago.

"My syndicate says the worst thing that could happen to me would be if I fell in love and became content," said the cartoonist in an early interview. During the 1990s Guisewite won the Reuben Award, adopted a baby girl, and got married. Universal Press is no longer concerned. Cathy, the comic-strip character, is still single, frustrated, and unfulfilled. Fortunately for Cathy Guisewite, life doesn't always imitate art.

CATHY by Cathy Guisewite

CATHY daily strip by **Cathy Guisewite**, n.d.

CATHY daily strip by **Cathy Guisewite**. © 9/7/78

CATHY daily strip by **Cathy Guisewite**, n.d.

CATHY daily strip by **Cathy Guisewite**. © 4/30/84

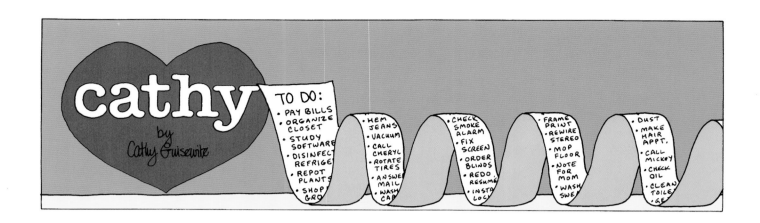

CATHY Sunday page by Cathy Guisewite. © 11/8/87

IN PARIS: PATTERNED TIGHTS, OVERSIZED TOP.

IN MILAN: PATTERNED TIGHTS, OVERSIZED TOP.

IN LONDON: PATTERNED TIGHTS, OVERSIZED TOP.

IN MY BATHROOM: PATTERNED TIGHTS, OVERSIZED TOP.

CATHY daily strip by Cathy Guisewite. © 9/10/90

WHAT A WOMAN SAYS:

I KNOW YOU THINK I'M TOO JEALOUS, BUT WHY SHOULD CHARLENE GET GIFTS ALL VALENTINE'S WEEK WHEN YOU AND I GO BACK SO MUCH FURTHER? CAN'T YOU PLAY ALONG WITH ROMANCE A LITTLE?? IS YOUR WHOLE HEART USED UP BY YOUR STUPID GOLF GAME??

WHAT A MAN HEARS:

I KNOW YOU THINK I'M TOO JEALOUS, BUT WHY SHOULD CHARLENE GET GIFTS ALL VALENTINE'S WEEK WHEN YOU AND I GO BACK SO MUCH FURTHER? CAN'T YOU PLAY ALONG WITH ROMANCE A LITTLE?? IS YOUR WHOLE HEART USED UP BY YOUR STUPID GOLF GAME??

OK.

CATHY daily strip by Cathy Guisewite. © 2/9/93

EVERY TIME I TURN AROUND ANOTHER MEMBER OF THE BABY BOOM GENERATION IS PREGNANT. THIS WAS **NOT** SUPPOSED TO HAPPEN TO US.

I KNOW. WE GREW UP, WE GOT INDEPENDENT, WE THREW OUT THE NOTION OF MOTHERHOOD...

...AND NOW MOTHERHOOD HAS COME FLYING RIGHT BACK AT US.

WHAT'S GOING **ON** WITH EVERY-ONE, CATHY?!

THE BABY BOOMERANG.

CATHY daily strip by Cathy Guisewite, n.d.

TO DO, 1955:

1. MARRY WELL.

TO DO, 1975:

1. TRANSFORM ROLE OF WOMEN IN SOCIETY.

TO DO, 1995:

1. EARN LIVING.
2. BUY, FURNISH AND MAINTAIN HOME.
3. PAY ALL BILLS.
4. DO ALL LAUNDRY.
5. BUY ALL GROCERIES.
6. COOK ALL MEALS.
7. LOCATE AND MARRY HUSBAND.
8. HAVE AND RAISE CHILDREN.
9. TONE ALL MUSCLES.
10. REBEL AGAINST AGING.
11. SAVE PLANET.
12. BUY AND MAINTAIN AUTOMOBILE.
13. FIGHT AGAINST EVIL.
14. TAKE CHARGE OF LIFE.
15. GO INTO THERAPY TO REGAIN VULNERABILITY.

I AM WOMAN. HEAR ME SNORE.

TO PAY   TO ANSWER

TO DEAL WITH

CATHY daily strip by Cathy Guisewite. © 11/6/95

SHOE *daily strip by Jeff MacNelly.* © 9/16/77

SELF-CARICATURE *by Jeff MacNelly*

JEFF MACNELLY   P. Martin Shoemaker, the star of Jeff MacNelly's 1977 comic strip creation, *Shoe*, was named after Jim Shumaker, a cigar-smoking journalism professor at the University of North Carolina who was also MacNelly's former editor at the *Chapel Hill Weekly*. The Walt Kelly influence was evident in the first few years of the feature, as MacNelly drew his birds and trees with fluid brush strokes and detailed crosshatching. The style of *Shoe* eventually became more simplified, and in the 1990s MacNelly began using computers to aid with the production of the strip. Amazingly prolific, he also launched a cartoon panel, *Pluggers*, in 1993, illustrated Dave Barry's weekly humor column, and continued to turn out political cartoons until his death in 2000. *Shoe* is carried on today by the team of Gary Brookins and Chris Cassatt.

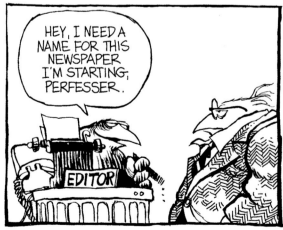

SHOE *daily strip by Jeff MacNelly.* © 10/22/77

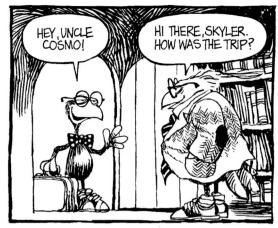

SHOE daily strip by Jeff MacNelly. © 11/1/77

SHOE daily strip by Jeff MacNelly. © 1/11/78

SHOE daily strip by Jeff MacNelly. © 4/26/78

SHOE daily strip by Jeff MacNelly. © 7/20/78

SHOE Sunday page by Jeff MacNelly. © 11/27/77

SHOE Sunday page by Jeff MacNelly. © 8/27/78

lynn johnston

FOR BETTER OR FOR WORSE daily strip by Lynn Johnston. © 11/7/79

FOR BETTER OR FOR WORSE is the quintessential modern family strip. Lynn Johnston has portrayed domestic life from a distinctly feminine point of view in her autobiographical creation for more than two decades. The stars of the feature, Elly and John Patterson and their children, Michael, Elizabeth, and April, as well as a large supporting cast, have confronted the challenges of interpersonal relationships with courage and compassion. Millions of readers feel like members of this extended family by following the unfolding drama in daily installments as the characters age gracefully.

Johnston attended the Vancouver School of Art and worked in illustration, animation, and graphic design before launching her comic strip in 1979. Although her art has matured, Johnston's talent was evident from the start. *For Better or For Worse* was rendered in a semirealistic style with elegant, fluid linework and balanced compositions. Johnston was adept at conveying subtle emotions, as well as the more animated antics of her characters. The backgrounds were filled with convincing details, and her interiors captured the cozy intimacy of the Patterson home.

At first Johnston fretted over the demands of producing punch lines on a daily basis. She eventually took a different approach. "I segued into the little vignettes that have moralistic and motherly values, like little parables," Johnston explained. "I might not be able to have a joke every day, but I could have a thought every day."

The stories in *For Better or For Worse* are fictional, but as Johnston admits, the strip "is a fiction where I can undo wrongs that have been inflicted on me or others." Johnston added a new member to the cast in 1991 when, at age forty-five, she longed for another child. The Patterson's new baby, April, brought fresh energy to the strip as Johnston nurtured her with motherly devotion.

"What sets Lynn's strip apart from the others," claimed Elizabeth Anderson, Johnston's former editor at Universal Press Syndicate, "is that her characters and readers are not spared midlife crises, financial hardships, or confrontations with prejudice, child abuse, and death."

In 1995 Johnston made a daring move. She killed off one of her major characters. The four-week sequence was reminiscent of the death of Raven Sherman in Milton Caniff's *Terry and the Pirates*. Farley, the Patterson's fourteen-year-old sheepdog, suffered a heart attack after saving April from drowning. Many readers were upset, while others expressed their condolences in heartfelt letters. One man sent Johnston a granite tombstone carved with the inscription, "Farley, Our Hero 1981–1995." Farley's son, Edgar, who had also played a role in April's rescue, took over as the top dog in the Patterson family.

Lynn Johnston is the most successful female cartoonist in the history of comics. In addition to being the first woman to win the Reuben Award, in 1985, she was also the first to serve as president of the National Cartoonists Society, in 1988, and the first to be inducted in the International Museum of Cartoon Art's Hall of Fame, in 1997. *For Better or For Worse* consistently wins readership polls and appears in more than 2,000 newspapers.

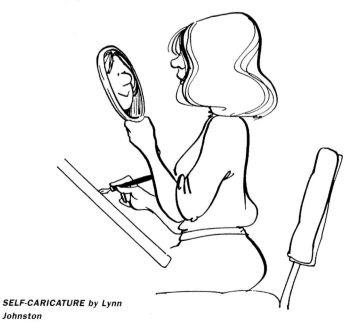

SELF-CARICATURE by Lynn Johnston

FOR BETTER OR FOR WORSE daily strip by Lynn Johnston. © 11/17/80

All For Better or For Worse strips © Lynn Johnston Productions, Inc. Distributed by Universal Press Syndicate. All rights reserved

FOR BETTER OR FOR WORSE daily strip by Lynn Johnston. © 10/31/81

FOR BETTER OR FOR WORSE daily strip by Lynn Johnston. © 6/23/89

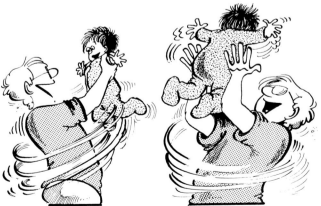

FOR BETTER OR FOR WORSE daily strip by Lynn Johnston. © 10/5/91

FOR BETTER OR FOR WORSE daily strip by Lynn Johnston. © 2/22/90

FOR BETTER OR FOR WORSE daily strip by Lynn Johnston. © 3/6/92

FOR BETTER OR FOR WORSE daily strip by Lynn Johnston. © 3/18/95

FOR BETTER OR FOR WORSE daily strip by Lynn Johnston. © 6/12/99

FOR BETTER OR FOR WORSE Sunday page (the birth of April) by Lynn Johnston. © 3/31/91

FOR BETTER OR FOR WORSE daily-strip sequence (the death of Farley) by Lynn Johnston. © 4/11–4/21/95 (4/12, 4/16, 4/19 not included)

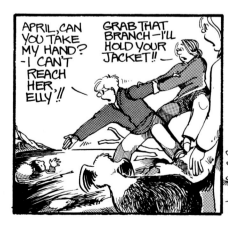

I'VE GOT HER!

I'VE GOT FARLEY BY THE COLLAR!

IS EVERYBODY SAFE? YES, GRANDMA. EVERYONE'S OK!

4-17

OH, GOOD.... NOW I CAN CRY!!

GOOD BOY, FARLEY. YOU'RE A GOOD BOY!

WHEN APRIL FELL INTO THE RIVER, HE WENT IN AFTER HER. I DON'T KNOW HOW HE MANAGED TO KEEP HER HEAD OUT OF THE WATER FOR SO LONG... BUT HE DID IT!!

4-18

HE'S AMAZING! HE'S A HERO!

.... HE'S EXHAUSTED.

ELLY, WHY DON'T YOU AND MOM TAKE APRIL UP TO THE HOUSE AND GET WARM... I'LL BE THERE IN A MINUTE.

DADDY....

4-20

HEY, FARLEY! WHAT'S THE MATTER, OLD BOY? WHAT'S THE MATTER?!!

DADDY..... HE ISN'T BREATHING!!

I WENT BACK DOWN TO THE RIVER, AND I WRAPPED HIM IN A BLANKET.

ELIZABETH AND I PUT HIM IN THE CAR, AND DROVE INTO TOWN.

THE VETERINARIAN SAID IT WAS HIS HEART. HE SAID THAT THE COLD AND THE STRESS WERE TOO MUCH FOR HIM. FARLEY WAS AN OLD DOG, JOHN. I KNOW.

4-21

... BUT I DIDN'T THINK THAT A HEART SO BIG WOULD EVER STOP BEATING.

FOR BETTER OR FOR WORSE daily strip by Lynn Johnston. © 3/30/93

FOR BETTER OR FOR WORSE daily strip by Lynn Johnston. © 1/30/97

FOR BETTER OR FOR WORSE daily strip by Lynn Johnston. © 7/11/98

FOR BETTER OR FOR WORSE daily strip by Lynn Johnston. © 3/4/99

For Better or For Worse

By Lynn Johnston

MMMMM

FOR ME, JOHN ... THIS TIME OF YEAR IS PURE HEAVEN!

THE SMELL, THE COLORS, THE MARKETS, THE COOL, FRESH WINDS.

OF ALL THE SEASONS—I THINK I LIKE THIS THE BEST.

10-19

WE'VE SEEN A LOT OF AUTUMNS TOGETHER, HAVEN'T WE, EL.

MORE THAN 20!

I GUESS YOU COULD SAY WE'RE IN THE "AUTUMN OF OUR LIVES!"

THAT'S A NICE ANALOGY, JOHN – COMPARING A LONG-LASTING RELATIONSHIP TO THIS TIME OF YEAR.

YEAH...

FOR ONE THING, THERE'S FEWER BUGS.

©1997 Lynn Johnston Productions Inc./Dist. by United Feature Syndicate

FOR BETTER OR FOR WORSE Sunday page by Lynn Johnston. © 10/19/97

DIK BROWNE Affectionately known by his peers in the profession as the "cartoonists' cartoonist," Dik Browne was universally loved by his family, friends, and fans as a gentle, wise, and generous soul. After gaining experience in the 1940s and 1950s as a magazine and advertising illustrator, Browne broke into the comics field when he teamed up with Mort Walker on *Hi and Lois* in 1954. Almost twenty years later he launched his own creation, *Hagar the Horrible*, which skyrocketed in sales to become one of the top features in the business within a few short years. Browne drew *Hagar* in a rough-hewn manner, quite different from the clean style he had perfected on *Hi and Lois*. "Your lines should not be too slick," the talented draftsman advised. "They should look like a human being drew them." Browne won the Reuben Award for *Hi and Lois* in 1962 and again for *Hagar* in 1973.

SELF-CARICATURE by Dik Browne

HAGAR THE HORRIBLE Sunday page by Dik Browne. © 7/15/73

HAGAR THE HORRIBLE daily strip by Dik Browne. © 11/29/73

HAGAR THE HORRIBLE daily strip by Dik Browne. © 2/5/75

HAGAR THE HORRIBLE daily strip by Dik Browne. © 10/15/75

HAGAR THE HORRIBLE daily strip by Dik Browne. © 12/29/75

HAGAR THE HORRIBLE Sunday page by Dik Browne. © 6/2/74

HAGAR THE HORRIBLE daily strip by Dik Browne. © 12/12/73

HAGAR THE HORRIBLE daily strip by Dik Browne. © 6/6/74

HAGAR THE HORRIBLE daily strip by Dik Browne. © 9/23/82

HAGAR THE HORRIBLE daily strip by Dik Browne. © 3/6/84

HAGAR THE HORRIBLE Sunday page by Dik Browne. © 12/26/82

THE FIRST GARFIELD daily strip by Jim Davis. © 6/19/78

JIM DAVIS *Garfield*, the second most successful comic strip of all time after *Peanuts*, appeals to both cat-lovers and cat-haters. "People relate to him because he is them," explained creator Jim Davis. "After all, he's really a human in a cat suit." Garfield's owner, Jon Arbuckle, was introduced as a cartoonist when the strip debuted on June 19, 1978 (above). The limited supporting cast included Odie, a witless pooch, Nermal, a cutesy kitty, Arlene, his love interest, and Pooky, a stuffed teddy bear, but there was never any question who the real star of the strip was. Davis designed the feature to be reader-friendly, with heavy outlines and a minimum of dialogue, and concentrated on basic themes, like eating and sleeping. A number of talented artists, including Brett Koth, Gary Barker, Valette Green, Lori Barker, Larry Fentz, and Eric Reaves, have assisted with the production of the strip over the years, although Davis continues to be involved in generating scenarios for his famous fat cat.

GARFIELD Sunday page by Jim Davis. © 3/18/79

GARFIELD daily strip by Jim Davis. © 9/18/78

GARFIELD daily strip by Jim Davis. © 11/13/80

GARFIELD daily strip by Jim Davis. © 10/18/83

GARFIELD daily strip by Jim Davis. © 12/27/85

GARFIELD *daily strip by Jim Davis.* © 9/21/87

GARFIELD *daily strip by Jim Davis.* © 11/14/88

GARFIELD *daily strip by Jim Davis.* © 4/27/89

GARFIELD *daily strip by Jim Davis.* © 5/30/89

GARFIELD Sunday page by Jim Davis. © 4/30/95

GARFIELD Sunday page by Jim Davis. © 9/10/95

BROOM-HILDA *daily strip by Russ Myers, n.d.*

RUSSELL MYERS Broom-Hilda was once described by her creator, Russell Myers, as "a dirty old man in a dress." The eternally horny witch has been searching for a mate since her breakup with Attila the Hun in the fifth century and entertaining newspaper readers for more than thirty years. Myers, who once claimed Johnny Hart and Brant Parker's *The*

Wizard of Id as a major inspiration, introduced a distinctively energetic art style, blending surreal scenery with classic, big-nosed characters. Broom-Hilda and her two companions, Gaylord the buzzard and Irwin the troll, exist in a world that could only be conjured up by the fertile imagination and free-flowing pen of this gifted cartoonist.

BROOM-HILDA *daily strip by Russ Myers.* © 7/14/73

BROOM-HILDA *daily strip by Russ Myers.* © 6/23/75

ZIGGY daily panel by Tom Wilson. © 8/28/71

ZIGGY daily panel by Tom Wilson. © 8/12/75

TOM WILSON   Ziggy, the quintessential loser, has been a big winner in the merchandising business. Hundreds of items, from dolls and games to ashtrays and soup bowls, have been decorated with the character's placid features, earning millions for his creator. Cartoonist Tom Wilson dreamed up the lovable character, with the big head and the generous

heart, when he was a card designer for American Greetings in the late 1960s. The syndicated panel debuted in 1971 and appears in more than 600 newspapers. "Ziggy must be part of me because he feels as if he's been with me all my life," states Wilson. "It feels like I acknowledged him rather than invented him."

ZIGGY daily panel by Tom Wilson, n.d.

ZIGGY daily panel by Tom Wilson, n.d.

HERMAN daily panel by Jim Unger. © 12/15/84, Universal Press Syndicate 1974–1992,
Reprinted with permission by LaughingStock Licensing Inc.

"HE'S PRACTICING HIS SLAM DUNK!"

HEATHCLIFF daily panel by George Gately. © 1980 Creators Syndicate, Inc.
Courtesy of International Museum of Cartoon Art

LAUGHTER RULES

Gag-a-day comics continued to dominate the industry in the 1970s, as the story-strip genre faded. Among the dozens of new humor creations that debuted were wacky single panels (*Herman, Heathcliff,* and *Frank and Ernest*), strips by established pros (*Sam and Silo,*

Half Hitch, Momma, Crock, and *Catfish*), comics by young cartoonists (*Funky Winkerbean* and *Drabble*), and offerings that focused on changing lifestyles and social trends (*Mixed Singles, Splitsville,* and *Motley's Crew*). More than half of the features shown on these pages are still syndicated today.

FRANK AND ERNEST Sunday page by Bob Thaves © 4/1/90 NEA, Inc.

SAM AND SILO Sunday page by Mort Walker and Jerry Dumas. © 5/8/1970s King Features Syndicate, Inc.

HALF HITCH Sunday page by Hank Ketcham, Bob Saylor (writer), and Dick Hodgins, Jr. (artist). © 3/3/74 King Features Syndicate, Inc.

Courtesy of International Museum of Cartoon Art

FUNKY WINKERBEAN daily strip by Tom Batiuk. © 6/12/72 North America Syndicate, Inc

MIXED SINGLES daily strip by Mel Casson and Bill Brown. © 7/16/73 United Feature Syndicate, Inc. Courtesy of Richard Marschall

SPLITSVILLE daily strip by Frank Baginski and Reynolds Dodson. © 12/18/78 Los Angeles Times Syndicate, Inc.

DRABBLE daily strip by Kevin Fagan. © 3/27/79 United Feature Syndicate, Inc.

MOMMA daily strip by Mell Lazarus. © 3/15/71 Creators Syndicate, Inc. Courtesy of International Museum of Cartoon Art

CROCK daily strip by Don Wilder and Bill Rechin. © 11/15/75 North America Syndicate, Inc.

CATFISH daily strip by Rog Bollen. © 4/22/76 Tribune Media Services, Inc. All rights reserved. Reprinted with permission

MOTLEY'S CREW daily strip by Ben Templeton and Tom Forman. © 11/17/77 Tribune Media Services, Inc. All rights reserved. Reprinted with permission

DUNAGIN'S PEOPLE Sunday page by Ralph Dunagin. © 10/5/75 Tribune Media Services, Inc. All rights reserved. Reprinted with permission. Courtesy of International Museum of Cartoon Art

CURRENT EVENTS Topical humor was the primary focus of many new features introduced during the decade. *Dunagin's People* (1970) by Ralph Dunagin followed in the tradition of *Berry's World* and *the small society*, providing timely observations about the latest developments. *Tank McNamara* (1974) by Jeff Miller (writer) and Bill Hinds (artist) featured a retired football jock trying to make it as a sports broadcaster. *Travels with Farley* by Phil Frank, which was self-syndicated beginning in 1975 and picked up by Chronicle Features in 1978, starred a wandering backpacker in search of America.

TANK MCNAMARA daily strip by Jeff Millar and Bill Hinds. © 1974 Miller/Hinds. Used by permission of Universal Press Syndicate, Inc. All rights reserved

TRAVELS WITH FARLEY daily strip by Phil Frank. © 5/18/79 Chronicle Features Syndicate, Inc.

GASOLINE ALLEY daily strip by Dick Moores. © 10/4/74 Tribune Media Services, Inc. Courtesy of David Applegate

RICK O'SHAY daily strip by Stan Lynde. © 6/8/77 Tribune Media Services, Inc. Courtesy of David Applegate

TO BE CONTINUED . . .

A few story strips survived the gag-a-day onslaught. During the 1960s *Gasoline Alley* was taken over by Frank King's former assistant, Dick Moores, who won the Reuben Award in 1974 for his outstanding efforts. *Rick O'Shay*, which debuted in 1958 as a humorous western, evolved into a realistically rendered story strip in 1964. Its creator, Stan Lynde, left the feature in 1977 after a dispute with his syndicate, and it was continued by other artists until 1981. The newspaper adaptation of *The Amazing Spider-Man*, which was written by Stan Lee and illustrated initially by John Romita, made its debut in 1977 and was one of the few successful adventure-strip launches of the decade.

THE AMAZING SPIDER-MAN Sunday page by Stan Lee and John Romita. © 2/5/78 King Features Syndicate, Inc.

STAR WARS Sunday page by Archie Goodwin and Al Williamson. © 2/26/84 Lucasfilm LTD. Courtesy of the Frye Art Museum, Seattle. Photo credit: Susan Dirk/Under the Light

THE ART OF ILLUSTRATION   The classic spy strip *Secret Agent X-9* was written by Dashiell Hammett and illustrated by Alex Raymond when it debuted in 1934. The daily-only feature was continued by a long string of artists until Al Williamson, a devotee of Alex Raymond and a former assistant to John Prentice, took over the renamed *Secret Agent Corrigan* in 1967. After he quit *Corrigan* in 1980,

Williamson illustrated the short-lived *Star Wars* adaptation. Leonard Starr terminated his long-running feature, *On Stage*, in 1979 to produce the new *Annie* strip, which was reintroduced after the success of the Broadway stage adaptation of Harold Gray's classic creation. John Cullen Murphy, who began assisting Hal Foster on *Prince Valiant* in 1970, assumed control entirely after Foster's retirement in 1979.

SECRET AGENT CORRIGAN daily strip by Al Williamson. © 2/22/73 King Features Syndicate, Inc. Courtesy of the Frye Art Museum, Seattle. Photo credit: Susan Dirk/Under the Light

ANNIE Sunday page by Leonard Starr. © 6/8/80 Tribune Media Services, Inc. Courtesy of International Museum of Cartoon Art

Our Story: SPRING GLIDES INTO SUMMER AND ARN IS IN DESPAIR. THE COUNTLESS DELAYS TO HIS HOMEWARD JOURNEY, THE UNCERTAINTY OF HIS RECEPTION THERE, AND THE PAIN OF HIS BROKEN ARM ADD TO HIS MISERY.

HE LEAVES THE GRIM FORTRESS TO STAY WITH HIS CREW AND SPEED THE REPAIRS TO THE SHIP. AT LAST IT IS SEAWORTHY AND IS LAUNCHED FOR THE LONG JOURNEY NORTH.

AT LAST! THE COAST OF THULE RISES IN ALL ITS AWESOME GRANDEUR. THE SKALD TAKES UP HIS HARP AND THE OARSMEN SING AS THEY ROW. ARN REMOVES THE SPLINTS AND PAINFULLY, BUT CHEERFULLY, BEGINS TO EXERCISE HIS ARM.

NEXT WEEK— *Midsummer's Eve*   2-18

PRINCE VALIANT Sunday page by Hal Foster and John Cullen Murphy. *© 8/18/74 King Features Syndicate, Inc. Courtesy of International Museum of Cartoon Art*

the eighties

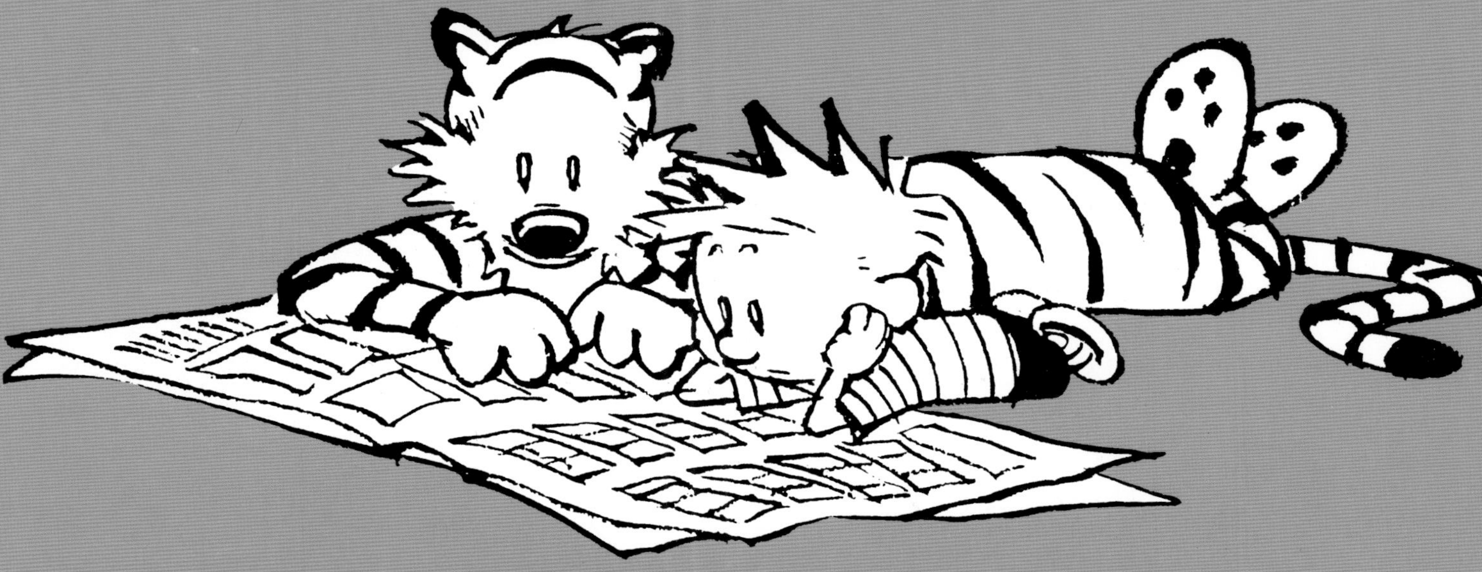

CALVIN AND HOBBES by Bill Watterson.

ARE WE HAVING FUN YET?—*Griffy* and *Zippy* by Bill Griffith. © 1990 Bill Griffith. Courtesy Cartoonist PROfiles

T

HE REAGAN YEARS WERE GOOD FOR BUSINESS. AMERICA ENJOYED ITS LONGEST PEACETIME ECONOMIC EXPANSION TO DATE BETWEEN 1982 AND 1988. SEVENTEEN MILLION NEW JOBS WERE CREATED, INFLATION DROPPED TO SINGLE DIGITS, AND THE GROSS NATIONAL PRODUCT SHOWED THE LARGEST INCREASE IN THIRTY-THREE YEARS.

The baby boomers had grown into yuppies, and these young urban professionals had discovered a new thrill–investing in the stock market. The prevailing mood of the era was summed up by the master of high-risk arbitrage, Ivan Boesky, when he brazenly justified his profit motives by claiming, "Greed is all right. . . . You can be greedy and still feel good about yourself."

The moneymaking spree ended on "Black Monday," October 19, 1987, when the stock market lost 22 percent of its value. An estimated $870 billion in equity vanished, double the loss of the 1929 crash that marked the start of the Great Depression. The economy eventually stabilized in the early 1990s, but the party was over.

The accelerated pace of progress during the decade created changes in all areas of American life. Consumers were confronted by a dizzying array of technological gadgets and entertainment options. Fax machines, cellular telephones, microwave ovens, and compact discs became commonplace, seemingly overnight. More than 60 percent of homes had cable television by 1989, and eleven million videocassette recorders were sold during the decade. In 1981 I.B.M. sold 25,000 units of its first personal computer. Three years later there were three million I.B.M. PCs in American offices and homes. Video games, big-budget movies, and televised sports all competed for the public's increasingly divided attention.

Newspaper comics, which were still produced the old-fashioned way—by hand—somehow managed to thrive in this intensely competitive environment. A fresh crop of new talent, an audience receptive to irreverent humor, and a boom in character licensing were among the many factors that led to a modern renaissance in the fun-nies business.

Three of the top comics creators of the 1980s had careers as precipitous as the stock market. Gary Larson, Berke Breathed, and Bill Watterson rose quickly to the top of their profession, reached creative peaks by the end of the decade, and eventually succumbed to "burnout" in the 1990s. Unable to meet the daily demands of syndication and unwilling to compromise the quality of their work, all three retired from the business in 1995.

In the late 1970s Gary Larson was working at a music store in Seattle. He hated his job and decided to take a few days off to think about what he wanted to do with his life. While sitting in his kitchen, he started doodling on a sheet of paper and drew six cartoons. The next day he took them to a local magazine, *Pacific Search*, and the editor bought the batch for $90. Larson immediately quit his job and started selling cartoons. His first regular single-panel creation, *Nature's Way*, appeared in a small weekly paper, the *Sumner News Review*. Larson was paid $3 a drawing. In 1979 a friend showed *Nature's Way* to the editor of the *Seattle Times*, which began running Larson's panel in its Saturday edition.

During his summer vacation in 1979, Larson drove to San Francisco to seek his fortune as a cartoonist. He showed his portfolio to Stan Arnold at the *San Francisco Chronicle*, who liked Larson's work and asked if he could hold on to the sam-ples for a few days. When Larson returned home, he found a letter from the *Seattle Times* notifying him that *Nature's Way* was going to be canceled. The next day he got a call from Stan Arnold telling him that Chronicle Features, the syndicate affil-iated with the *San Francisco Chronicle*, wanted to distribute his panel and rename it *The Far Side*. Larson agreed, signed a con-tract with Chronicle Features, and *The Far Side* debuted on January 1, 1980.

Two years later, Andrews and McMeel, the publishing division of Universal Press Syndicate, released a book collection of Larson's panels and it became a best-seller. In 1984, when his contract expired with Chronicle Features, Larson signed with Universal.

The Far Side was one of the most successful syndicated cartoons of the 1980s and inspired a wave of "way out" panels and strips. Among the best of these were *The Quigmans* (1984) by Buddy Hickerson, *Caldwell* (1985) by John Caldwell, *Bizarro* (1985) by Dan Piraro, and *Mr. Boffo* (1986) by Joe Martin. When asked about the sudden proliferation of offbeat creations, one syndicate editor explained, "There is a general cynicism in the public and a tendency to question traditional values. This is particularly true of the new generation of baby boomers and yuppies. They look for comics that reflect a disenchantment with the conventional."

Larson's dark humor, which often featured bizarre role reversals between humans and animals, explored previously taboo subjects such as cannibalism, suicide, and extinction. By 1987 more than six million book collections of *The Far Side* had been sold, and an exhibition of Larson's cartoons, organized by the California Academy of Sciences, traveled to the Smithsonian in Washington, D.C. Larson won the Reuben Award in 1990 and 1994 and retired after the last panel of *The Far Side* appeared, on January 1, 1995, to pursue an interest in music.

Berke Breathed, who claimed he was never interested in comics as a youth, created a strip entitled *Academia Waltz* while majoring in photojournalism at the University of Texas in 1978 and 1979. During that time, Breathed turned out an estimated 658 episodes of *Academia Waltz*, which were published in two book collections. One store on the Austin campus sold 10,000 copies. Encouraged by his local success, he sent some samples to the national syndicates but got no takers. A year later, the Washington Post Writers Group called Breathed to see if he wanted to create a syndicated feature.

Bloom County debuted on December 8, 1980. Initially set in a boardinghouse run by Ma Bloom in "the center of the deepest, darkest, middlest America," Breathed's strip was drawn in a crude style without the use of speech balloons. The simi-larities to *Doonesbury* were evident in the beginning. "Obviously

SYNDICATED SERVITUDE—BLOOM COUNTY daily strip by Berke Breathed (written during Garry Trudeau's sabbatical). © 8/17/83 Rosebud Productions, Inc.

A WELL-DESERVED REST—CALVIN AND HOBBES illustration by Bill Watterson. © 1991 Watterson. Used by permission of Universal Press Syndicate. All rights reserved. Courtesy of Editor and Publisher

I've been influenced by Garry Trudeau," Breathed admitted. "But people seem to overlook the fact that, really, in concept and in style of humor, you could trace my roots back to more irreverent forms of humor, even back to Dr. Seuss."

When Trudeau went on sabbatical in 1983, many editors picked up *Bloom County* as a replacement, although the strip lost very few of its 550 clients when *Doonesbury* returned in 1984. Breathed used this opportunity to take his strip in bold new directions. The original human cast—Cutter John, a paraplegic Vietnam vet; Steve Dallas, a self-centered lawyer; Lola Granola, a former flower child; Milo Bloom, reporter for the *Bloom Beacon*; Mike Binkley, with his closet full of insecurities; and Oliver Wendall Jones, a computer hacker—was eventually eclipsed by Opus the penguin and Bill the Cat. Breathed's art style blossomed as his satire became more adventurous. *Bloom County* was now a comic strip that defied comparison.

Loose Tales, the first *Bloom County* book collection, was on the *New York Times* best-seller list for thirty-two weeks in 1983. Breathed won the Pulitzer Prize in 1987 and, at its peak, the strip appeared in more than 1,000 newspapers.

By 1989 Breathed was tapped out. "A good comic strip is no more eternal than a ripe melon," he explained. "The ugly truth is that, in most cases, comics age less gracefully than their creators. *Bloom County* is retiring before the stretch marks show."

Between 1990 and 1995 Breathed produced a Sunday-only feature, entitled *Outland*. This follow-up creation,

although showcasing some inspired fantasy and appearances by many of the original *Bloom County* gang, never captured a large audience. After retiring from the comics business for good, Breathed released a series of children's books and produced a pair of animated specials starring Opus and Bill.

In 1980 Bill Watterson graduated from Kenyon College in Ohio, hoping to follow in the footsteps of another Kenyon alumnus, Jim Borgman, who was then working as the editorial cartoonist for the *Cincinnati Enquirer*. Watterson landed a job with the *Cincinnati Post* as its political cartoonist but was fired six months later.

After trying unsuccessfully to get a position at another paper, Watterson realized that he didn't have the zeal it took to be a political cartoonist. He then started submitting ideas for comic strips. His first proposal was an outer-space parody. He drew up several weeks of strips and mailed them to five syndicates simultaneously. It was rejected at all five. Over the next few years he continued to come up with ideas he thought the syndicates would buy and tried a number of topical "'80s-oriented" strips, with no success.

Finally, United Feature Syndicate suggested that he take two characters from one of his submissions and build a strip around them. Calvin was the little brother of the main character in the original proposal, and Hobbes was Calvin's stuffed tiger. United Feature gave Watterson a development contract to work on this idea, but in the end the syndicate rejected it.

STAYING ON SCHEDULE—*Opening panel from "Daily Strip" story by Bill Griffith.* © 1988 Bill Griffith

One U.F.S. employee suggested to Watterson that he incorporate another established character, Robotman, into his strip. Robotman was the star of a toy product line in England, and the syndicate thought he had great merchandising potential in America. Watterson declined the offer, and United eventually hired another cartoonist, Jim Meddick, to draw the *Robotman* comic strip, which debuted in 1984. The Robotman merchandising program never took off, but the comic strip survived.

After being rejected by United, Watterson started shopping *Calvin and Hobbes* around to the other syndicates, and after five years of perseverance, he finally sold his idea to Universal Press Syndicate. *Calvin and Hobbes* debuted on November 18, 1985.

In an interview at the time Watterson cautiously remarked, "Of course, launching a comic strip does not guarantee me a lifetime of steady income. Universal Press is gambling on the strip, and if it bombs, I'll be back to robbing the elderly of their welfare checks before the year is out."

Watterson's creation, which borrowed a bit of smart-aleck wisdom from *Skippy*, a dose of fantasy from *Barnaby*, and a touch of graphic flair from *Pogo*, was both traditional and innovative. The central concept of the strip—that Hobbes, a stuffed tiger, was real to Calvin but to no one else—became more than just a gimmick in Watterson's

gifted hands. It was the launching pad into a brilliantly conceived world of childhood imagination.

Watterson set his own standards of artistic integrity by refusing to merchandise his feature in any form other than books and, later, by demanding that his Sunday page run in a half-page format that could not be reduced or rearranged to fit any other configurations.

Calvin and Hobbes appeared in over 1,800 newspapers at its peak, and book collections of the strip continued to shatter sales records well into the 1990s. Watterson won the Reuben Award twice, in 1986 and 1988. He retired from the profession in 1995, citing fatigue and frustration with the demands and limitations of the comics business.

The accomplishments of these three creators inspired other cartoonists with unconventional ideas to take a plunge into national syndication. The saga of how Bill Griffith's *Zippy the Pinhead* made its way from underground comix to the mainstream press was one of the more remarkable success stories of the era. "It was a ten-year process that was completely unplanned by me," claimed Griffith. "And in each case, the way it happened was, I was asked in."

Zippy the Pinhead was first conceived in 1970 and made his debut in the underground comic book *Real Pulp* a year later. Griffith's non sequitur–spouting, polka-dot-suited, existential

PHYSICIST TURNED CARTOONIST—Self-caricature by Bud Grace

clown evolved over the next few years in the pages of a variety of alternative comics and magazines. In 1976 Griffith started doing a weekly *Zippy* comic strip for the *Berkeley Barb* and eventually self-syndicated his feature to about forty clients.

In 1985 Griffith was invited by Will Hearst III and his editor, Dave Burgin, to do a daily strip for the *San Francisco Examiner*. After a difficult year of adjusting to the demands of producing a daily version of *Zippy*, Griffith was offered a contract by King Features Syndicate. Fearful of making the commitment, Griffith drew up a list of about twenty demands that he hoped would be unacceptable. To his surprise, Alan Priaulx, an executive at King, agreed to all of them. Griffith found out later that Priaulx was about to quit his job and wanted to leave a "ticking time bomb" behind when he left.

Within a few months after its release in 1986, the daily *Zippy* strip was running in many of the nation's largest papers, including the *Washington Post*, *Baltimore Sun*, *L.A. Times*, and *Dallas Times-Herald*. "Seeing *Zippy* in the mainstream press," commented Griffith, "is like seeing some gaudily painted

motorboat weaving in and out of these slow-moving yachts and sailboats."

Griffith admitted that he felt like the "house weirdo of King Features" but was told by one syndicate employee that "they really enjoy the fact that, although King has always been accused of being the most conservative, stuck-in-the-mud syndicate, the fact that they have *Zippy* gives them a little kick." Griffith claimed that "there is a parallel with the way King Features supported me and stayed with me and the way they treated George Herriman. The original Hearst indulged in what amounted to personal taste. He was kind of a patron, and maybe Will Hearst is a little bit of that to me."

Another King Features discovery of the 1980s was Bud Grace, who graduated from Florida State University in 1971 with a Ph.D. in physics. After two years as a professor at the University of Georgia, he returned to teach at his alma mater. Grace began doodling in his spare time and developed an interest in cartooning. His first published work was a strip called *Nuclear Funnies* for the university paper.

In 1980 Grace had a "midlife crisis" and changed careers for good. He sold freelance cartoons successfully to national magazines for the next six years until, with a new baby on the way, he decided he needed more financial security. He worked up an idea for a strip and sent it to Bill Yates, the comics editor of King Features. Yates took it home and handed the strips to his wife, Skippy, before retiring to bed. Skippy woke Bill up at two o'clock in the morning and said she thought the strip was hilarious. Yates invited Grace to come to New York City and told him that, although he liked the characters, his writing needed some work. After some changes were made, *Ernie* was released on February 1, 1988.

In the first sequence, Ernie Floyd, the star of the strip, worked as the assistant manager of a "Mr. Squid" fast-food franchise. Ernie's uncle, Sid Fernwilter, a founding member and eternal treasurer of the Piranha Club, supported himself by conning people out of their money. Other characters in the strip included the homely Doris Husselmeyer, landlady Effie

WHAT READERS WANT—SHOE daily strip by Jeff MacNelly. © 3/14/85 Tribune Media Services, Inc. All rights reserved. Reprinted with permission

DADDY... CONRAD AND I ARE GETTING MARRIED...

BUT, DEAR... WHAT CAN A WEDDING BETWEEN A FROG AND A ROYAL PRINCESS POSSIBLY LEAD TO?

THE COVER OF THE NATIONAL ENQUIRER...

DOUBLE DIPPER—CONRAD daily strip by Bill Schorr. © 1982 Tribune Media Services, Inc. All rights reserved. Reprinted with permission

Munyon, doctor Enos Pork, the crooked Wurlitzer Brothers, and the lecherous Arnold Arnoldski. Grace described the humor in *Ernie* as "a comedy of low manners."

In 1994 Grace won the award for Best Humor Strip from the National Cartoonists Society and gradually built a respectable list of clients. In 1998 the name of the strip was changed to *The Piranha Club*.

Newsweek magazine, in a 1980 cover story on "The Art of Politics," observed, "There have never been so many good cartoonists—or more incompetence, folly and hypocrisy for them to lampoon." Many of the political cartoonists profiled in the article, including Mike Peters, Doug Marlette, and Tony Auth, would eventually follow Jeff MacNelly's lead and explore the greener pastures of comic-strip syndication.

Artists with an established reputation had an advantage when a syndicate looked at a submission. David Hendin, a former United Feature executive, explained, "They are not going to send you a comic strip that sucks wind. They may send you one that doesn't work, for one reason or another, but they're not going to send you something drawn on tissue paper that's the wrong size, that's drawn in magic marker and bleeding all over the place with a little note that says, 'I need somebody to edit these.'"

Experience didn't guarantee success, however. Bill Schorr, a political cartoonist for the Tribune Syndicate, created *Conrad*, a strip starring a cigar-chomping frog, in 1982. It only survived for two years. Wayne Stayskal's *Balderdash* (1983) had an even shorter run. Two Pulitzer Prize winners had better results. Doug Marlette's *Kudzu* (1981) and Mike Peters's *Mother Goose and Grimm* (1984) had large client lists by the end of the decade. All of these features were originally signed by Tribune, a syndicate that specialized in double-dipper strips.

In contrast to the meteoric rise of *The Far Side*, *Bloom County*, and *Calvin and Hobbes*, a number of new creations built momentum gradually throughout the decade. Among these solid family-oriented features were: *Marvin* (1982) by Tom Armstrong, *Sally Forth* (1982) by Greg Howard, *Rose Is Rose* (1984) by Pat Brady, *Luann* (1985) by Greg Evans, *Fox Trot* (1988) by Bill Amend, *Curtis* (1988) by Ray Billingsley, *One Big Happy* (1989) by Rick Detorie, and *Jumpstart* (1989) by Robb Armstrong. All of these strips went through a period of evolution, built respectable lists of clients, and achieved their full potential in the 1990s.

On September 21, 1981, *Jim Henson's Muppets*, drawn by Guy and Brad Gilchrist, debuted in 550 newspapers and soon reached a peak of 660 subscribers. It was the most successful start-up of all time, but a pattern familiar to many spin-off strips soon set in. The talented young cartoonists struggled to adapt the live-action puppet stars to the two-dimensional comic-strip medium. Although disappointed editors began canceling the feature, the Gilchrists managed to maintain a list of 300 papers until moving on to other challenges in 1986.

A number of period creations showcased caricatures of famous personalities. *John Darling* (1979), by Tom Armstrong and Tom Batiuk, starred a television talk-show host. *Rock Channel* (1984), by the Gilchrist brothers and Greg Walker, was inspired by MTV. *Betty Boop and Felix* (1984), by the Walker Brothers, placed the two vintage animation stars in a modern Hollywood setting. *Benchley* (1984), by Mort Drucker and Jerry Dumas, revolved around the day-to-day activities of the Reagan White House. None of these strips survived the decade.

Ernie Bushmiller, the creator of *Nancy*, died of a heart attack on August 15, 1982. The strip was taken over by Mark Lasky, a staff cartoonist for United Feature, who emulated the original Bushmiller style. On July 31, 1983, Lasky succumbed to cancer at

MISS PIGGY AND KERMIT by Guy and Brad Gilchrist. © 1981 Henson Associates, Inc.

MILESTONE—DICK TRACY 50TH ANNIVERSARY Sunday page by Chester Gould, Rick Fletcher, and Max Collins. © 10/4/81 Tribune Media Services, Inc. All rights reserved. Reprinted with permission

the age of twenty-nine. Jerry Scott, who had been producing *Gumdrop* since 1981, was selected as Lasky's successor.

Scott, who admitted that he had hated *Nancy* when he was growing up, agreed to continue Bushmiller's creation on the condition that he could update the feature. Although criticized by traditionalists, Scott introduced a new, improved Nancy and built the list of subscribers to 500 newspapers by 1988.

A number of other legendary creators also died during the decade. Hal Foster (1982), Chester Gould (1985), Dick Moores (1986), and Milton Caniff (1988) had all been active in the comics business for over fifty years when they passed away. Bill Hoest (1988) and Dik Browne (1989) were among the most successful cartoonists in the business when they

died. In all but one case (Caniff's *Steve Canyon* ended upon his death), their features were left in able hands.

Although adventure strips had all but disappeared by the 1980s, readers of the remaining continuity strips were intensely loyal to their favorites. When two Lexington, Kentucky, newspapers, the *Herald* and the *Leader*, merged in 1983, *Apartment 3-G* was dropped. "There was tremendous public reaction," reported the editor. "We got at least five times as many calls and letters protesting the loss of *3-G* than for any of the other comics we dropped." It was promptly put back in the paper. A similar response occurred in Rochester when the *Times-Union* canceled *Rex Morgan*. The paper received 237 letters demanding its return.

BUNNY'S FUNNIES—Bunny Hoest and John Reiner continued Bill Hoest's comic creations after his death in 1988. Left to right: The Lockhorns, Agatha Crumm, Laugh Parade, Howard Huge, Bumper Snickers, and What a Guy. © King Features Syndicate, Inc. and Hoest Enterprises, Inc.

SELLING OUT—CALVIN AND HOBBES *daily strip by Bill Watterson.* ©

In 1985 *Rex Morgan* was in 350 papers, *Judge Parker* ran in 250, and *Apartment 3-G* had 200 clients. Dr. Nicholas Dallis, the writer of all three features, believed his strips continued to be relevant because they "address the problems that are occurring today." During the decade, Dr. Dallis tackled cocaine addiction, fetal alcohol syndrome, and spousal abuse.

Forbes magazine estimated, in a 1989 survey, that the combined annual income generated by the major syndicates from newspapers, excluding licensing revenue, was about $100 million, and that comic strips accounted for 70 percent of that amount. According to their research, when licensing revenue was added, United Media earned $140 million annually, King Features $120 million, Tribune Media $40 million, Universal Press $40 million, and Creators $8 million.

The *Forbes* article concluded, "The big syndicates, in any case, had been declining for decades—victims of stagnating newspaper readership, fewer dailies and more homegrown feature material. The syndicates responded by mining the gold in beloved characters like Snoopy, Garfield and Popeye, who are adapted and repackaged for animated TV shows, movies and books, and licensed to manufacturers of just about everything."

Charles Schulz and Jim Davis were listed in *Forbes* as among the highest-paid entertainers in the 1980s. The magazine estimated that Schulz earned $55 million in 1986 and 1987 combined, and Davis was not far behind with a two-year total of $31 million. Davis, who preferred not to discuss his salary, claimed, "Those figures are inflated. I don't make the kind of money *Forbes* suggested, although I'm not complaining. *Forbes* must have been confusing sales of *Garfield* products with my actual royalty, which is far less than they estimated."

According to *The Licensing Letter*, between 1978 and 1982 annual retail revenues from all licensed products rose from $6.5 billion to $20.6 billion, and comic properties accounted for approximately 20 percent of this business. In 1982 *People* magazine estimated that there were 1,500 Garfield products on the market that had earned between $14 million and $20 million. Davis's phenomenal success also made him a target of criticism.

In 1989 Bill Watterson gave a speech at Ohio State University, entitled "The Cheapening of Comics." Watterson lamented that "with the kind of money in licensing nowadays, it's not surprising many cartoonists are as eager as the syndicates for easy millions, and are willing to sacrifice the heart and soul of their strip to get it."

In Watterson's feature, Hobbes was a product of Calvin's imagination. He didn't want a toy designer determining how his tiger would look and act. It was his belief that merchandise would alter the delicate chemistry of his creation.

Most cartoonists didn't agree with Watterson. Some thought their syndicates were not doing enough to generate business. "Universal is a brilliant syndicate," said Cathy Guisewite in 1989, "but there are licensing companies out there that are more expert at it." The majority of cartoonists earned very little additional income beyond the fees paid by the newspapers for their strips.

The artists wanted more control of their merchandising programs, and this brought up the ownership issue. In the 1980s and 1990s a number of cartoonists fought for and successfully obtained the copyrights to their features, as well as increased licensing control and a more favorable split of the income. Bil Keane (*Family Circus*), Lynn Johnston (*For Better or For Worse*), Tom Wilson (*Ziggy*), and Cathy Guisewite (*Cathy*) were among the artists who renegotiated their contracts.

Corporate mergers also dramatically altered the funnies business. In March 1986 the second-most-profitable syndicate, King Features, under the leadership of Joe D'Angelo, absorbed the seventh-largest, Cowles (formerly known as the Register and Tribune Syndicate). The following February, King purchased News America Syndicate, the third-largest comics distributor, from Rupert Murdoch for a reported $23 million. King, which incorporated the renamed North America Syndicate into its group of companies, now controlled 225 syndicated features, including nine strips and panels with over 1,000 clients.

Jay Kennedy, a former cartoon editor and consultant to *Esquire, People, National Lampoon,* and *Lear's* magazines, took over as comics editor at King Features in 1989. Kennedy, who

COMIC RELIEF—DOONESBURY daily strip (from the first Thanksgiving Day Hunger Project) by Garry Trudeau. © 11/28/85 G.B. Trudeau. Used by permission of
Universal Press Syndicate

had represented a number of "alternative" comics artists, promised to complement King's mainstream features with edgier creations. One of the first ideas the young editor developed was *The New Breed*, a syndicated panel that presented, on a rotating basis, the work of about thirty emerging talents, a dozen of whom became regular contributors. Kennedy would have a major hand in bringing fresh ideas to the syndicate in the 1990s.

Richard Newcombe, the former C.E.O. of News America Syndicate, responded to the King/N.A.S. merger by founding Creators Syndicate in 1987. To attract established talent, Newcombe promised cartoonists and writers full legal ownership of their creations, shorter contracts, and a larger percentage of the income generated by their features. On February 21, 1987, he announced the signing of superstar advice columnist Ann Landers. Johnny Hart (*B.C.* and *The Wizard of Id*) and Mell Lazarus (*Miss Peach* and *Momma*) were among the first cartoonists to join the new syndicate.

Lazarus, who was on the syndicate relations committee of the National Cartoonists Society before taking over as president in 1989, was a strong advocate for creator ownership. "There are still guys who sign standard syndication agreements," Lazarus stated. "But the next five to eight years are

going to see syndicate ownership of features as an occasional thing. More people will be owning their own work."

The 1980s weren't all about business. A number of highly publicized charity events during the decade provided concerned individuals with an opportunity to show that they were interested in more than just personal gain. In 1985 the Live Aid concert was broadcast to a global audience of 1.8 billion people and raised more than $50 million for famine relief in Africa. A year later, 6 million people linked up in Hands Across America, focusing attention on the domestic problem of homelessness.

In the summer of 1985 Milton Caniff, Charles Schulz, and Garry Trudeau sent letters to 250 syndicated cartoonists inviting them to dedicate their features to the topic of world hunger on November 28, 1985. Initially worried about the response, Trudeau was surprised to discover, when he opened his newspaper on Thanksgiving Day, that "175 artists, inspired by the potential impact of a concerted effort among their ranks, did something they had never attempted before—they worked together."

For that one day, America's cartoonists had raised awareness about a crisis of global proportions. The next day it was back to business as usual—helping the world to laugh at itself.

HELPING HANDS—ANNIE daily strip (from the second year of the cartoon charity effort) by Leonard Starr. © 11/27/86 Tribune Media Services, Inc. All rights reserved.
Reprinted with permission. Courtesy of International Museum of Cartoon Art

ANNIVERSARY PRESENT—*Dagwood finally gets a day off, after a half-century of creating hilarity, in this* BLONDIE *Sunday page by Dean Young and Jim Raymond.* © 9/7/80 King Features Syndicate, Inc.

gary larson

IN 1990 KEN TUCKER of *Entertainment Weekly* rated the top daily comics in the nation's newspapers. He gave *The Far Side* an "A" and offered the following words of praise: "Gary Larson has brought laugh-out-loud humor back to the funny pages with one-panel drawings that combine surrealism with an amateur's interest in science to create a comic tone that's at once eccentric and aggressive." Less than five years later, on January 1, 1995, *The Far Side* ended.

In his final book, *Last Chapter and Worse*, published in 1996, Larson promised, "The Call of the Vial (of ink) still speaks to me, and the thought of creating more mischief—somewhere, sometime—rumbles in the reptilian complex of my brain." His post-retirement output has been limited to thirteen panels of *The Far Side* (to fill out the last book collection), a sequel to his first animated special, *Tales from the Far Side II*, and one illustrated "children's" book, *There's A Hair in My Dirt! A Worm's Story*. A deluxe, two-volume, slipcased collection of every single *Far Side* cartoon (4,081 to be exact), with a comprehensive introduction by Gary Larson, was published by Andrews McMeel in the fall of 2003.

Terms such as "bizarre," "absurd," "demented," and "weird" were frequently used to describe Larson's creation. He found humor in all forms of organic life, and among his favorite subjects were cows, dogs, chickens, insects, amoebas, and cavemen.

In the early 1980s Larson's ghoulish scribblings attracted a cult following. As his cartoons became more sophisticated, the audience grew, and by the 1990s *The Far Side* was appearing in more than 1,800 newspapers and book collections of the popular panel were selling in the millions. The general mood of Larson's world was one of impending doom. Disaster, death, and even extinction were always lurking in the shadows. This playfully apocalyptic vision tapped a deeply cynical vein in the youth of America.

Readers often wonder where cartoonists get their ideas. Gary Larson was asked this question even more frequently than his professional peers. "Every time I hear it," he said, "I'm struck by this mental image where I see myself rummaging through my grandparents' attic and coming across some old, musty trunk. Inside I find this equally old and elegant-looking book. I take it in my hands, blow away the dust, and embossed on the front cover in large, gold script is the title, *Five Thousand and One Weird Cartoon Ideas*."

In truth, Larson developed some of his best material by doodling in his sketchbook. "The act of drawing is a continuous learning process for me," he admitted, "and I greatly envy a number of cartoonists who have truly mastered their 'instrument.' I haven't—but I'm working on it." A talented draftsman, Larson mastered the subtle nuances of timing, delivery, and visual humor in his cartoons. *The Far Side* was one of the most consistently funny features in the newspapers during its relatively brief fifteen-year run.

Gary Larson was only forty-five years old when he retired. His loyal fans cling to the hope that some day this brilliant cartoonist may return to his drawing board and pick up where he left off. The world needs a tour guide to *The Far Side*.

THE FAR SIDE® BY GARY LARSON

The real reason dinosaurs became extinct

HIGH ON HUMOR

The success of *The Far Side* inspired a proliferation of offbeat creations in the 1980s. Among the notable single-panel debuts were *Bizarro* (1985) by Dan Piraro, *The Neighborhood* (1981) by Jerry Van Amerongen, *Caldwell* (1985) by John Caldwell, *The New Breed* (1989) by various artists, *The Quigmans* (1984) by Buddy Hickerson, and *Mr. Boffo* (1986) by Joe Martin. These, and other far-out features that started in the following decade, helped to fill the void on the funnies pages when Gary Larson retired in 1995.

How the brain works.

THE NEIGHBORHOOD **Sunday page by Jerry Van Amerongen.** © *King Features Syndicate, Inc.*

Bobby Tanner proves to be the weak link.

THE NEIGHBORHOOD **Sunday page by Jerry Van Amerongen.** © *5/4/86 King Features Syndicate, Inc.*

CALDWELL *Sunday page by John Caldwell.* © 1/4/87 King Features Syndicate, Inc.

THE NEW BREED *daily panel by Oliver (Revilo) Christianson.* © 1/5/90 by Revilo. Distributed by King Features Syndicate, Inc.

THE QUIGMANS *daily panel by Buddy Hickerson.* © Tribune Media Services, Inc. All rights reserved. Reprinted with permission

MR. BOFFO *daily strip by Joe Martin* © Joe Martin. Used by permission of Universal Press Syndicate. All rights reserved

berke breathed

BLOOM COUNTY daily strip by Berke Breathed, n.d. All Bloom County and Outland strips © Rosebud Productions, Inc. Courtesy of Washington Post Writers Group

IN 1987, AFTER Berke Breathed won the Pulitzer Prize for *Bloom County*, Pat Oliphant delivered an impassioned speech to the Association of American Editorial Cartoonists. "The work makes no pretense of being an editorial cartoon," protested Oliphant. "It's on the funny pages. It does, however, make the pretense of passing off shrill potty jokes, crotch jokes, and grade-school sight gags as social commentary. The Pulitzer Board was wrong, dead wrong, to overrule the nominating committee in selecting this year's winner."

Breathed, in response to this attack, pointed out that the official requirements for submitting work to the Pulitzer Prize committee did not specify that they had to be political cartoons. He described Oliphant's outburst as "the most magnificent display of sour grapes ever to be recorded within the known universe."

The thirtysomething cartoonist continued to court controversy in his rowdy feature. Li'l Ollie Funt, an obvious spoof of Oliphant's Punk the penguin, shouted "Reagan Sucks!" during a brief cameo appearance. The drug-addled Bill the Cat had a love affair with ex-U.N. ambassador Jeane Kirkpatrick. Opus discovered to his dismay that his mother was being used to test Mary Kay Cosmetics. Steve Dallas appeared nude in *Dog World* magazine.

Breathed also took shots at liposuction, home-shopping networks, and heavy-metal bands. Donald Trump, Madonna, Carl Sagan, Prince William, Tammy Faye Baker, and Lee Ioacocca were among the media personalities skewered in *Bloom County*.

OPUS THE PENGUIN by Berke Breathed

Breathed's most costly faux pas was when he attempted to respond humorously to feminist critics who had accused him of sexism. In the last panel of an *Outland* Sunday page, Opus and Bill were shown gazing down into their underwear, looking for the one thing that brought the most meaning to their lives. Breathed lost about $14,000 in income when half a dozen papers canceled the strip permanently after this episode ran.

As Breathed's art matured during the mid-1980s, *Bloom County* relied more on visual humor than on traditional gags. Strips often ended with a dumbstruck expression and a surprising twist of dialogue. Breathed became increasingly frustrated with the small size his daily strips were printed and by the late 1980s was devoting most of his creative energy to the Sunday page.

Opus, a refugee from the Falkland Islands, was the cartoonist's most cherished creation. Breathed once confessed a desire to be as innocent, naive, and unworldly as his favorite bow-tied waterfowl. To him, Opus was an ideal to which to aspire.

In 1989 Breathed stated, "I have grown stubbornly affectionate toward my characters, and I have little desire to see Opus, Bill the Cat, and others disappear from my life." But he had made his decision. "After ten years of squeezing Bloom Countians into smudgy, postage stamp–sized stories, I thought it might be more comfortable for all concerned if we took a powder from the daily pages."

Breathed continued *Outland*, a Sunday-only spin-off of *Bloom County*, until 1995 and, eight years later, returned with the weekly *Opus*. When asked to assess his contributions, the pen-and-ink prankster answered in typical fashion, "I want to be remembered for taking a ninety-two percent cut in my income for the sake of my cartoons. I figure attaining immortality as an artist is a long shot. But I'm a shoo-in as a martyr."

BLOOM COUNTY *daily strip by Berke Breathed.* © 5/25/81

BLOOM COUNTY *daily strip (first appearance by Opus) by Berke Breathed.* © 6/26/81

BLOOM COUNTY *daily strip by Berke Breathed.* © 11/9/81

BLOOM COUNTY *daily strip by Berke Breathed.* © 11/7/84

IT WAS A DARK AND STORMY NIGHT... A HUDDLED, SHIVERING FIGURE MOVES ACROSS THE HORIZON TOWARD THE BLOOM COUNTY BOARDING HOUSE...

HE WALKS WEARILY.. HEAVILY... AS IF EXHAUSTED FROM A LONG JOURNEY.. AS IF SQUID HAD BEEN NIBBLING HIS TOES RECENTLY...

BUT WITH HIM COME OUR QUESTIONS... WHERE IS HE FROM? WHAT DOES HE WANT?... AND, FOR CRYING OUT LOUD...

..JUST WHO IS THIS DARK, WET MYSTERY FIGURE?!

CLUE

SIGH..

BLOOM COUNTY daily strip by Berke Breathed. ©8/12/85

QUICHE...SHOOGUMS... TRUST ME...THIS MEDICAL CRISIS IS GONNA STRENGTHEN US...

NOW, I'LL NEED A SPONGE BATH DAILY, MY INCISION AND STITCHES WILL NEED SCRUBBING TWICE A WEEK...AND NATURALLY MY PERSONAL BODILY FUNCTIONS WILL NEED TENDING CONSTANTLY.

THINK YOU CAN HANDLE ALL THAT?

WHY OF COURSE YOU CAN!

STEVE, I CAN'T EVEN WASH YOUR SOCKS WITHOUT TOSSING MY COOKIES.

BLOOM COUNTY daily strip by Berke Breathed. © 5/5/86

UNO... DOS...

OOF! UH OH...

BANG BANG BANG BANG BANG! BANG!!

HOLY MACKEREL... RUN!!

THIS UNFORTUNATE AFFAIR WAS TO END SUDDENLY DOWN IN 'MILLER'S MUD FLATS WITH SOME INJURY. AND WHILE EVENTS WERE MARKED WITH GENERAL CHAOS, IT WAS, NEVERTHELESS, APPARENT TO ALL THAT THE "SCHWARTZENEGGERIZATION" OF OPUS WAS SIMPLY NOT TO BE.

BANG!

BLOOM COUNTY daily strip by Berke Breathed. © 1/30/87

...I PRONOUNCE YOU WATERFOWL AND WIFE. YOU MAY KISS THE BRIDE.

KISS? BUT I'VE NEVER KISSED ANYONE BEFORE! I WAS SAVING MYSELF FOR MARRIAGE.

THIS IS IT, BUCKAROO. JUMP UP HERE AND PLANT 'EM.

—WHICH, GENTLE READERS, OUR HERO **DID**. WHAT HAPPENED NEXT WOULD NOT ONLY AFFECT FUTURE EVENTS IN WAYS UNIMAGINED, BUT WOULD ALSO HIGHLIGHT A MARITAL PROBLEM HERETOFORE UNDISCOVERED...

...INCOMPATIBLE NOSES. LOLA WAS UNDAMAGED. THE GROOM, HOWEVER, WAS OUT COLD.

OW.

CONTINUED—

BLOOM COUNTY daily strip by Berke Breathed. © 5/23/87

BLOOM COUNTY Sunday page by Berke Breathed, n.d.

BLOOM COUNTY Sunday page by Berke Breathed, n.d.

BLOOM COUNTY Sunday page by Berke Breathed, n.d.

BLOOM COUNTY daily strip by Berke Breathed. © 9/26/87

BLOOM COUNTY daily strip by Berke Breathed. © 11/6/87

BLOOM COUNTY daily strip by Berke Breathed. © 12/28/88

BLOOM COUNTY daily strip by Berke Breathed. © 8/4/89

OUTLAND *The infamous Sunday page by Berke Breathed.* © 1993

OUTLAND *Sunday page by Berke Breathed.* © 1995

SALLY FORTH *daily strip by Greg Howard.* © 2/9/82 *King Features Syndicate, Inc.*

GREG HOWARD *Sally Forth*, a strip that appealed primarily to working women, was created by Greg Howard, a former attorney, in 1982. Howard recognized that his strength was writing and admitted that his drawing was "crude" in the beginning (above) and eventually improved to "mediocre" (below). In 1991, when he hired a replacement artist, Craig MacIntosh, to redesign *Sally Forth*, more than a thousand loyal fans called King Features Syndicate to protest the changes. Apparently, readers had become accustomed to Howard's awkward art. MacIntosh quickly developed a more acceptable blend between the old and new styles, and the circulation of the popular domestic feature grew to more than 600 newspapers.

SALLY FORTH *daily strip by Greg Howard.* © 5/23/84 *King Features Syndicate, Inc.*

SALLY FORTH *daily strip by Greg Howard and Craig MacIntosh.* © 10/31/92 *King Features Syndicate, Inc.*

LUANN *daily strip by Greg Evans.* © 1988 United Feature Syndicate, Inc.

LUANN *daily strip by Greg Evans.* © 3/19/85 United Feature Syndicate, Inc.

GREG EVANS An updated version of the classic teenager strip, Greg Evans's 1985 creation, *Luann*, focused on the contemporary world of video games and shopping malls as well as the eternal themes of homework and dating. In addition to thirteen-year-old Luann DeGroot, the cast included Brad, her seventeen-year-old brother; Aaron, the boy of her dreams; Bernice, her best friend; Delta, her fashion consultant; and her understanding Mom and Dad. In 1991 Evans made comics history by introducing a story line in which Luann had her first menstrual period (bottom). The sequence was presented with humor and sensitivity, and the response from readers was overwhelmingly positive.

LUANN *daily strip by Greg Evans.* © 5/10/91 United Feature Syndicate, Inc.

MIKE PETERS Often introduced as the "Peter Pan of Cartooning," the eternally youthful Mike Peters won the Reuben Award in 1991 for his achievements in both the comics field and political cartooning. Peters launched *Mother Goose and Grimm* on October 1, 1984, three years after receiving the Pulitzer Prize for his editorial work at the *Dayton Daily News.* The clever comic strip was initially a spoof of fairy tales and popular culture, but its canine star, Grimmy, eventually stole the spotlight. Peters's pooch is a dog's dog, who chases cars, pees on fire hydrants, and drinks out of toilet bowls. The strip is drawn in a bold, visual style, and the humor is wildly entertaining and laden with puns. In the 1990s Grimmy was the star of an animated television series as well as a modestly successful line of licensed products.

SELF-CARICATURE by Mike Peters

MOTHER GOOSE & GRIMM *Sunday page by Mike Peters.* © 1992 Tribune Media Services, Inc. All rights reserved. Reprinted with permission

MOTHER GOOSE & GRIMM *daily strip by Mike Peters.* © 10/23/87 Tribune Media Services, Inc. All rights reserved. Reprinted with permission

MOTHER GOOSE & GRIMM *daily strip by Mike Peters.* © 1/22/97 Tribune Media Services, Inc. All rights reserved. Reprinted with permission

KUDZU daily strip by Doug Marlette. © 6/15/81 Tribune Media Services, Inc. All rights reserved. Reprinted with permission

DOUBLE DIPPERS

The success of Jeff MacNelly's *Shoe* encouraged other political cartoonists to try their hand at comic-strip syndication in the 1980s. Among the artists who took on double duty were Pulitzer Prize winner Doug Marlette, who launched the Southern-flavored *Kudzu* in 1981; Brian Basset, who created the stay-at-home dad *Adam* in 1984; and Bill Schorr, who tried a comic strip starring a frog, *Conrad*, in 1982 but had more success with bears in *The Grizzwells*, which began in 1987.

ADAM daily strip by Brian Basset. © 9/26/84 Brian Bassett. Used by permission of Universal Press Syndicate. All rights reserved

THE GRIZZWELLS daily strip by Bill Schorr. © 7/4/88 NEA Inc. Courtesy of International Museum of Cartoon Art

FRESH PERSPECTIVES

Two solid new creations of the 1980s (next page) were based on contemporary lifestyles. Bill Holbrook's *On The Fastrack* (1984) was set in the high-tech corporate world, and Rick Detorie's *One Big Happy* (1989) featured a multi-generation, extended family.

ON THE FASTRACK Sunday page by Bill Holbrook. © 1984 by King Features Syndicate, Inc. Courtesy of Richard Marschall

ONE BIG HAPPY Sunday page by Rick Detorie, n.d. © Creators Syndicate, Inc.

ROSE IS ROSE daily strip by Pat Brady. © 5/15/84

All Rose is Rose strips © United Feature Syndicate, Inc.

PAT BRADY   For the first seven years after Pat Brady's *Rose is Rose* debuted in 1984, the strip's juvenile star, Pasquale Gumbo, spoke in a phonetic baby talk the cartoonist dubbed "Pasqualian" (above). Concerned that the gimmick was getting tedious for his readers, on August 9, 1991, Brady decided to have Pasquale suddenly start speaking coherently (below). The *Rose is Rose* cast also included Rose and Jimbo Gumbo, Peekaboo the cat, cousin Clem, and neighbor Mimi. Brady did not shy away from sentiment in his warm, loving family strip and often suggested a strong physical attraction between Rose and Jimbo. He also explored his characters' daydreams in ambitiously designed episodes that featured innovative use of perspective, background, and color. Rose's transformation into Vicki the Biker has become one the most popular of these graphic fantasies. Brady was nominated four times for the Reuben Award in the 1990s and finally won in 2004.

SELF-CARICATURE by Pat Brady

ROSE IS ROSE daily strip by Pat Brady. © 8/9/91

ROSE IS ROSE daily strip by Pat Brady. © 6/10/96

ROSE IS ROSE daily strip by Pat Brady. © 7/4/96

ROSE IS ROSE daily strip by Pat Brady. © 9/6/96

ROSE IS ROSE daily strip by Pat Brady. © 6/9/97

ROSE IS ROSE daily strip by Pat Brady. © 8/3/98

ROSE IS ROSE daily strip by Pat Brady. © 9/1/98

ROSE IS ROSE daily strip by Pat Brady. © 4/20/99

ROSE IS ROSE daily strip by Pat Brady. © 10/11/99

ROSE IS ROSE Sunday page by Pat Brady. © 9/22/96

BETTY BOOP AND FELIX Sunday page by the Walker Brothers. © 6/16/85 King Features Syndicate, Inc.

THE MUPPETS daily strip by Guy and Brad Gilchrist. © 5/8/84 King Features Syndicate, Inc.

McCALL OF THE WILD daily strip by Jerry Dumas and Mel Crawford © 1987 Creators Syndicate, Inc.

BENCHLEY Sunday page by Jerry Dumas and Mort Drucker. © 1986 Cowles Syndicate, Inc.

FAMILIAR FACES

A mini-wave of comics starring personalities from entertainment and politics swept through the funnies business in the 1980s. *Betty Boop and Felix* (1984) by the Walker Brothers revived two classic characters from the golden age of cartoon animation. *The Muppets* (1981) by Guy and Brad Gilchrist brought Kermit and Miss Piggy and the rest of Jim Henson's television puppets to the comics pages. *Rock Channel* (1984) by the Gilchrists and Greg Walker capitalized on the rising popularity of MTV. *Benchley* (1984) by Mort Drucker and Jerry Dumas provided a vehicle for poking fun at political figures. *McCall of the Wild* (1987), a team effort by Jerry Dumas and illustrator Mel Crawford, featured visits with fairy-tale creatures and old comic-strip characters.

ROCK CHANNEL Sunday page by the Gilchrists and Greg Walker. © 3/17/85 Cowles Syndicate, Inc.

bill watterson

PROFESSIONAL CARTOONISTS recognized the brilliance of Bill Watterson's *Calvin and Hobbes* soon after it debuted on November 19, 1985. In the foreword to the first book collection, Garry Trudeau wrote: "Watterson is the reporter who has gotten it right; childhood as it actually *is*, with its constantly shifting frames of reference." Watterson won the Reuben Award from the National Cartoonists Society in 1986, after only a year in syndication, and again in 1988.

The stars of the strip were a hyperactive six-year-old and a stuffed tiger who came alive in the boy's imagination. They were named after John Calvin and Thomas Hobbes, two philosophers Watterson studied while majoring in political science in college. Calvin was surrounded by a small circle of supporting players, which included his bewildered Mom and Dad, Susie the girl next door, Rosalyn the babysitter, Miss Wormwood the teacher, and Moe the bully. But his constant companion was Hobbes. The duo delighted in reckless wagon and sled rides, playing pranks on Susie, and inventing the ever-changing rules to "Calvinball." Their relationship alternated between intense competition and cooperative camaraderie. In one early sequence, during which Hobbes was temporarily lost, Calvin's close emotional attachment to his pretend friend was touchingly revealed.

Calvin also took off on solo flights of fantasy, escaping from the real world of parental discipline and tedious schoolwork. He traveled through the galaxy as Spaceman Spiff and hacked his way through jungles as Safari Al. He vanquished authority as Stupendous Man or battled petty crime as Tracer Bullet, private detective. He defied

SELF-CARICATURE by Bill Watterson

the laws of physics with his "transmogrifier" and "duplicator" inventions.

Dialogue was an important element of the strip. Calvin's running commentary railed against the injustices of childhood and voiced his views on the way things should be. The boy had no qualms about expressing selfish indignation, undisguised greed, or downright mean-spiritedness. He was devilish but lovable.

Watterson was a versatile draftsman and designer who could seemingly render anything that Calvin would dream up. Anatomically correct dinosaurs, bug-eyed aliens, and oozing gunk flowed from his pen. He expertly captured the shifting perspectives of Calvin's aerial adventures. He depicted the changing seasons with the balanced hues of his Sunday pages. His characters moved with grace and energy.

He also expanded the visual vocabulary of the art form. Cartoonists had previously used the comics medium to communicate the internal thoughts and emotions of their characters, but Watterson developed this technique into an established graphic language. Readers of *Calvin and Hobbes* became accustomed to interpreting images that shifted back and forth between the "real" world and Calvin's daydreams. This visualization method is now used commonly in the comics, and certain artists, most notably Pat Brady (*Rose is Rose*) and Jim Borgman (*Zits*), have refined it even further.

Watterson's ambitious agenda eventually took its toll. He went on two sabbaticals, in 1992 and 1994, during which newspapers offered *Calvin and Hobbes* reruns. He talked openly about battles with Universal Press Syndicate over his refusal to merchandise the characters. In a rare public appearance at Ohio State University, he criticized editors for shrinking the size of the comics and his fellow cartoonists for selling out for licensing dollars. Watterson's frustrations also became evident in the strip as Calvin frequently went off into tirades about the shallowness of consumer culture.

In 1995 Watterson ended *Calvin and Hobbes*. "Professionally, I had accomplished far more than I'd ever set out to do and there were no more mountains I wanted to climb," he remembered five years later. "I had given the strip all my time and energy for a decade (and was happy to do so), but now I was that much older and I wanted to work at a more thoughtful pace, out of the limelight, and without the pressures and restrictions of newspapers."

Bill Watterson pushed the limits of his abilities to explore the potential of the art form. In a relatively brief period of time, he dramatically demonstrated how a comic strip could challenge the imagination and tickle the funny bone. The void he left behind has yet to be filled.

CALVIN AND HOBBES daily strip by Bill Watterson. © 7/4/86

CALVIN AND HOBBES daily strip by Bill Watterson. © 3/28/87

CALVIN AND HOBBES daily strip by Bill Watterson. © 9/8/n.d.

CALVIN AND HOBBES daily strip by Bill Watterson. © 4/12/93

UH-OH, HERE COMES MOE, THE CLASS BULLY!

Okay twinky, let's have that ball.

SURE, MOE. ALL YOURS

NEVER ARGUE WITH A SIX-YEAR-OLD WHO SHAVES.

CALVIN AND HOBBES *daily strip by Bill Watterson.* © 1/30/86

ISN'T IT GREAT TO GET OUT OF THE HOUSE ALONE TOGETHER FOR A CHANGE?

IT'S SO NICE AND QUIET. WE SHOULD DO THIS MORE OFTEN.

CALVIN, YOU'VE GOT FIVE SECONDS TO OPEN THE DOOR BEFORE I BREAK A WINDOW!

I'M TELLING YOU CHUCK, YOUR GIRLFRIEND IS A PSYCHO! I HOPE YOU'RE NOT MAKING ANY LONG-RANGE PLANS AROUND HER.

CALVIN AND HOBBES *daily strip by Bill Watterson.* © 10/4/89

IT'S NO SURPRISE TO *ME* THAT NOBODY'S SOLD A HOUSE ON THIS STREET FOR SIX YEARS.

CALVIN AND HOBBES *daily strip by Bill Watterson.* © 2/4/92

..AND SO, IN 1654...

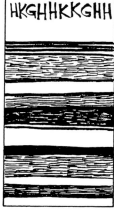
HKGHHKKGHH

MYSTERIOUS PLANET ZARTOK-3 APPEARS FROM...

KHGHHKGGH

PAY ATTENTION!

WHEN YOU CHANGE THE CHANNEL, I DON'T THINK THE ORIGINAL PROGRAM SHOULD BE ABLE TO CHANGE IT BACK.

CALVIN AND HOBBES *daily strip by Bill Watterson.* © 11/12/93

CALVIN AND HOBBES Sunday page by Bill Watterson. © 1987

CALVIN AND HOBBES daily strip by Bill Watterson. © 5/16/87

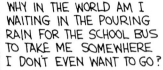

CALVIN AND HOBBES daily strip by Bill Watterson. © 11/13/88

CALVIN AND HOBBES daily strip by Bill Watterson. © 11/24/89

CALVIN AND HOBBES daily strip by Bill Watterson. © 12/2/95

THE DREADED SCUM BEINGS FIRE! SPACEMAN SPIFF IS *HIT!*

IT NEVER FAILS. I JUST WASHED AND WAXED THIS THING.

OUR HERO, THE INTREPID SPACEMAN SPIFF, STRUGGLES WITH THE CONTROLS OF HIS DAMAGED SPACECRAFT!

THE FREEM PROPULSION BLASTERS ARE USELESS! SPIFF CRASHES ONTO THE SURFACE OF AN ALIEN PLANET!

UNSCATHED, THE FEARLESS SPACE EXPLORER EMERGES FROM THE SMOLDERING WRECKAGE! HE IS MAROONED ON A HOSTILE WORLD!

SCORCHED BY TWIN SUNS, THE PLANET IS NOTHING BUT BARREN ROCK AND METHANE! THERE'S NO HOPE OF FINDING FOOD OR WATER!

SPIFF COLLAPSES! OH NO, A HIDEOUS ALIEN SPOTS HIM! IN HIS WEAKENED STATE, SPIFF IS NO MATCH FOR THE MONSTER! *THIS COULD BE THE END.!!*

7-5 WATTERSON

LUNCHTIME! I BROUGHT YOU A SANDWICH AND SOME LEMONADE.

© 1987 Universal Press Syndicate

BRING THE DISHES BACK WHEN YOU'RE DONE, OK?

...OH WELL.

THANKS, MOM.

CALVIN AND HOBBES Sunday page by Bill Watterson. © 7/5/87

Panel 1: GRANDPA SAYS THE COMICS WERE A LOT BETTER YEARS AGO WHEN NEWSPAPERS PRINTED THEM BIGGER.

Panel 2: HE SAYS COMICS NOW ARE JUST A BUNCH OF XEROXED TALKING HEADS BECAUSE THERE'S NO SPACE TO TELL A DECENT STORY OR TO SHOW ANY ACTION.

Panel 3: HE THINKS PEOPLE SHOULD WRITE TO THEIR NEWSPAPERS AND COMPLAIN.

Panel 4: YOUR GRANDPA TAKES THE FUNNIES PRETTY SERIOUSLY. — YEAH, MOM'S LOOKING INTO NURSING HOMES.

CALVIN AND HOBBES daily strip by Bill Watterson. © 11/11/87

Panel 1: OH GREATEST OF THE MASS MEDIA, THANK YOU FOR ELEVATING EMOTION, REDUCING THOUGHT, AND STIFLING IMAGINATION.

Panel 2: THANK YOU FOR THE ARTIFICIALITY OF QUICK SOLUTIONS AND FOR THE INSIDIOUS MANIPULATION OF HUMAN DESIRES FOR COMMERCIAL PURPOSES.

Panel 3: THIS BOWL OF LUKEWARM TAPIOCA REPRESENTS MY BRAIN. I OFFER IT IN HUMBLE SACRIFICE. BESTOW THY FLICKERING LIGHT FOREVER.

Panel 4: ?

CALVIN AND HOBBES daily strip by Bill Watterson. © 8/7/92

Panel 1: OH LOOK, YET ANOTHER CHRISTMAS TV SPECIAL!

Panel 2: HOW TOUCHING TO HAVE THE MEANING OF CHRISTMAS BROUGHT TO US BY COLA, FAST FOOD, AND BEER CONGLOMERATES.

Panel 3: WHO'D HAVE EVER GUESSED PRODUCT CONSUMPTION, POPULAR ENTERTAINMENT, AND SPIRITUALITY WOULD MIX SO HARMONIOUSLY. IT'S A BEAUTIFUL WORLD, ALL RIGHT.

Panel 4: DAD DOESN'T HANDLE THE SEASON'S STRESS VERY GRACEFULLY.

CALVIN AND HOBBES daily strip by Bill Watterson. © 12/14/92

Panel 1: A PAINTING. MOVING. SPIRITUALLY ENRICHING. SUBLIME. ..."HIGH" ART!

Panel 2: THE COMIC STRIP. VAPID. JUVENILE. COMMERCIAL HACK WORK. ..."LOW" ART.

Panel 3: A PAINTING OF A COMIC STRIP PANEL. SOPHISTICATED IRONY. PHILOSOPHICALLY CHALLENGING. ..."HIGH" ART.

Panel 4: SUPPOSE I DRAW A CARTOON OF A PAINTING OF A COMIC STRIP? — SOPHOMORIC. INTELLECTUALLY STERILE. ..."LOW" ART.

CALVIN AND HOBBES daily strip by Bill Watterson. © 7/20/93

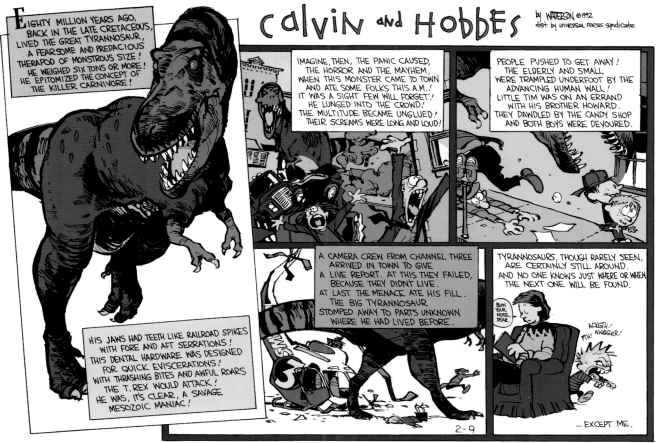

CALVIN AND HOBBES Sunday page by Bill Watterson. © 2/9/92

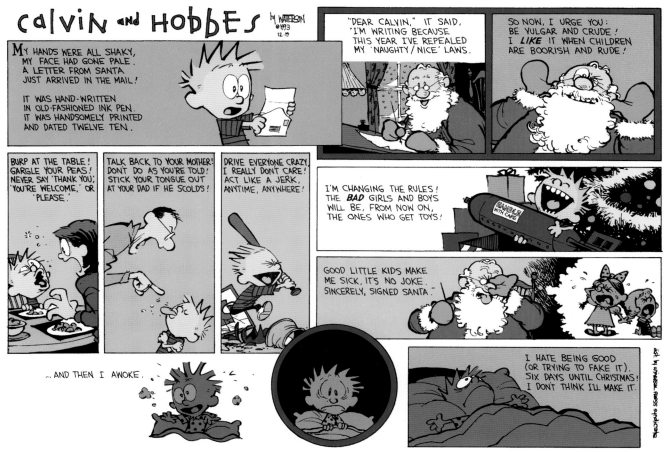

CALVIN AND HOBBES Sunday page by Bill Watterson, © 12/19/93

BILL GRIFFITH The only cartoonist from the alternative comix scene to cross over into mainstream syndication, Bill Griffith has carved out a unique niche for his unconventional creation, *Zippy*, on the nation's comics pages. The daily strip, which has been distributed by King Features since 1986, stars Zippy the Pinhead, a compulsive consumer of pop culture, and Griffy, a cranky social critic. "What Griffy and Zippy represent," explains Griffith, "is the dialogue between those two parts of myself, the critic and the fool." The autobiographical nature of the strip was fully explored in an ambitious continuity, entitled "The Pin Within," which ran from

December 30, 1991, to February 8, 1992. In this six-week sequence Griffy traveled back and forth in time, from Griffith's Brooklyn birthplace to other significant moments in the cartoonist's life, to reconcile his troubled relationship with his father, who died in 1972. A selection of episodes from this story are reproduced on the following pages. The *Zippy* Sunday strip, which was launched in 1990, provided Griffith with an opportunity to experiment with color, special effects, different artistic styles, and, as in the daily version, self-referential humor.

ZIPPY daily strip by Bill Griffith. © 6/30/86. Courtesy of Bill Janocha

All Zippy strips © Bill Griffith. Distributed by King Features Syndicate, Inc.

ZIPPY daily strip by Bill Griffith. © 5/19/95

ZIPPY first Sunday strip by Bill Griffith. © 1990

ZIPPY Sunday strip by Bill Griffith. © 11/3/91

ZIPPY Sunday strip by Bill Griffith. © 4/11/93

ZIPPY Sunday strip by Bill Griffith. © 9/5/93

ZIPPY daily strip by Bill Griffith (selections from "The Pin Within" sequence on these two pages). © 1/16/92

ZIPPY daily strip by Bill Griffith. © 1/22/92

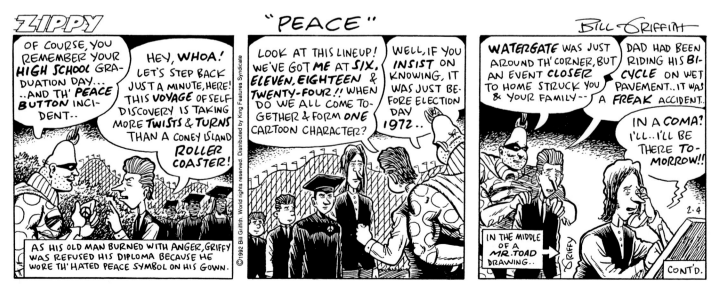

ZIPPY daily strip by Bill Griffith. © 2/4/92

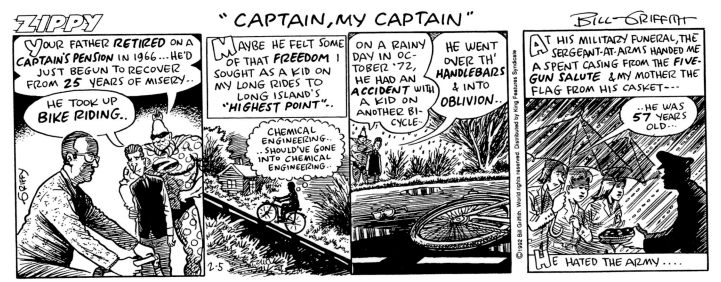

ZIPPY daily strip by Bill Griffith. © 2/5/92

ZIPPY daily strip by Bill Griffith. © 2/7/92

ZIPPY daily strip by Bill Griffith. © 2/8/92

Panel 1: I JUST GOT A PROMOTION— I'M AN ASSISTANT MANAGER / DO NOT TALK TO DRIVER

Panel 2: FRANCHISES IS WHERE IT'S AT! AND I'M IN ON THE GROUND FLOOR / DO NOT TALK TO DRIVER / TAP TAP

Panel 3: SOME DAY WE'LL BE AS BIG AS BONGO BURGER, OR POPEYE'S OR MAYBE EVEN McDONALD'S! / DO NOT TALK TO DRIVER

Panel 4: MR. SQUID / OF COURSE IT MAY TAKE A WHILE FOR SQUID BURGERS TO CATCH ON / ERNIE

ERNIE daily strip by Bud Grace. © 1988

All Ernie strips © King Features Syndicate, Inc.

BUD GRACE

Influenced by underground cartoonists Robert Crumb and Kim Deitch, Bud Grace developed a drawing style that provided the perfect vehicle for the lowbrow humor in his 1988 comic creation, *Ernie.* Grace researched the strip's offbeat subject matter with his scientifically trained powers of observation, and many of the quirky cast members were inspired by either real-life acquaintances or people Grace encountered in his travels. The cartoonist also made frequent guest appearances in the strip to kvetch about his home life or disagreements with his editor. His repeated forays into tastelessness led to numerous cancellations, although *Ernie* continued to build a sizable list of clients and is popular in Scandinavia, where political correctness is not as much of a concern as it is in America. In 1999 the name of the feature was changed to *The Piranha Club.* "I think they were trying to slip it by editors as a brand new strip," mused Grace. "I even considered changing my name as well. From now on I'm Bill Watterson."

Panel 1: JUST LIKE THE LIONS CLUB HAS AN EYE BANK AND THE SHRINERS HAVE A HOSPITAL, THE PIRANHA CLUB HELPS DISADVANTAGED YOUNG PEOPLE! / THAT'S NICE

Panel 2: EVERY YEAR WE RAISE MONEY TO HELP SOME POOR, DEPRIVED YOUNG PEOPLE EARN A LIVING! / HOW POOR ARE THEY?

Panel 3: ERNIE! THEY HARDLY HAVE ENOUGH CLOTHES TO WEAR! / HOW MUCH?

ERNIE daily strip by Bud Grace. © 9/2/88

Panel 1: AREN'T YOU GOING TO TAKE OFF YOUR BEACH ROBE?

Panel 3: I'M NOT USED TO A STRING BIKINI. IT'S THE FIRST TIME I EVER WORE ONE

Panel 4: THE TOP SEEMED SO MUCH BIGGER WHEN I PUT IT ON AT THE STORE / MAYBE AT THE STORE YOU DIDN'T PUT IT ON BACKWARDS

ERNIE daily strip by Bud Grace. © 9/6/88

ERNIE daily strip by Bud Grace. © 3/29/99

ERNIE daily strip by Bud Grace. © 7/13/99

ERNIE daily strip by Bud Grace. © 4/19/2000

ERNIE daily strip by Bud Grace. © 6/15/2001

ERNIE Sunday page by Bud Grace. © 12/8/96

THE PIRANHA CLUB Sunday page by Bud Grace. © 5/7/2000

ROBOTMAN daily strip by Jim Meddick. © 2/15/86 NEA, Inc.

JIM MEDDICK

In 1985 Robotman was a successful licensing property in England when United Feature Syndicate hired Jim Meddick to develop a comic strip based on the character. As the merchandising program for Robotman failed to take off in the United States, Meddick was given more freedom with the newspaper feature. In the beginning, the character was an alien who was adopted by the Milde family. Eventually Robotman moved into an apartment of his own and Meddick experimented with parodies and bizarre plot twists. In 1993 a nerdy inventor, Monty Montahue, was added to the cast, and eight years later the strip was renamed *Monty* and Robotman bid a final farewell. The end result of this gradual evolution is a quirky comic strip, which frequently scores high in readers' polls, that is a direct reflection of Meddick's unique comedic vision.

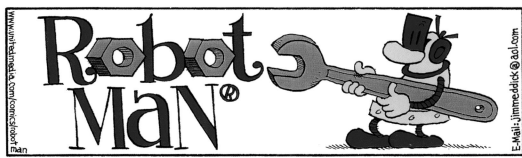
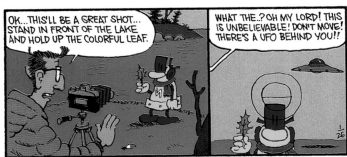

ROBOTMAN AND MONTY Sunday page by Jim Meddick. © 1/26/97 NEA, Inc.

FOX TROT daily strip by Bill Amend. © 2/12/90

FOX TROT cast by Bill Amend. © 1998 Courtesy of Cartoonist PROfiles

BILL AMEND

Fox Trot, which debuted in 1988, shortly after *The Simpsons* first appeared on television, starred a modern family with a similarly acerbic edge. "I think the strong part of the strip," creator Amend stated in 1988, "was that it has a very contemporary setting—it contains a lot of the trappings of our times." Story lines revolved around current television programs (*Star Trek*), music stars (Bruce Springsteen), and consumer electronics (video games and computers).

Amend's style, described by R. C. Harvey as having an "abstract cubistic quality," was initially limited to a static fixed perspective but improved with the introduction of more varied "camera angles." The strength of the strip was the writing, presented from the perspective of the Fox kids. Peter's rock-and-roll aspirations, Paige's romantic fantasies, and Jason's budding cartoon career struck a chord with youthful readers. *Fox Trot* became a Sunday-only feature at the end of 2006 and, five months later, Amend won the Reuben Award.

FOX TROT daily strip by Bill Amend. © 2/19/91

There, in the shadows of the forest, Galahunk and the princess fell madly in love.

As the sun set, they kissed. It was for each their first kiss. That magic kiss. The kiss that feels like...

feels like...

YOU REALLY DON'T **KNOW**?

SCREAM IT, WHY DON'T YOU?!

QUINCY'LL SHOW YOU...

FOX TROT daily strip by Bill Amend. © 7/17/91

PETER, PASS THE SUNSCREEN.

I GAVE IT TO PAIGE.

I GAVE IT TO JASON.

I GAVE IT TO DAD.

ARE YOU SURE?

FOX TROT daily strip by Bill Amend. © 8/10/91

DAD, I THINK YOU NEED MORE CLUB.

SON, PLEASE. I THINK I KNOW WHAT I'M DOING.

DON'T FORGET, **I'M** THE ONE WHO'S BEEN PLAYING THIS GAME FOR 26 YEARS. **I'M** THE ONE WHO SPENDS TWO HOURS A WEEK AT THE DRIVING RANGE. **I'M** THE ONE WHO TAUGHT YOU HOW TO EVEN **SWING** A GOLF CLUB.

.........°.SPLASH!

DON'T FORGET **I'M** THE ONE STUCK LOOKING FOR YOUR BALL.

MAYBE IT BOUNCED OUT...

FOX TROT daily strip by Bill Amend. © 6/9/92

What **really** killed Superman

He saw me in a bathing suit.

© 1993 Bill Amend/Dist. by Universal Press Syndicate

FOX TROT daily strip by Bill Amend. © 9/7/93

FOX TROT daily strip by Bill Amend. © 4/5/94

FOX TROT daily strip by Bill Amend. © 10/9/95

FOX TROT daily strip by Bill Amend. © 11/21/95

FOX TROT daily strip by Bill Amend. © 8/13/97

FoxTrot
BILL AMEND

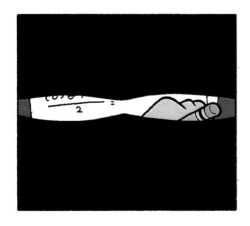

FOX TROT Sunday page by Bill Amend. © 9/14/97

NANCY daily strip by Jerry Scott. © 9/17/85 United Feature Syndicate, Inc.

CARRYING ON A number of long-running features were taken over by new artists in the 1980s. Jerry Scott introduced a redesigned *Nancy* in 1983 and continued Ernie Bushmiller's creation until 1995. Stan Drake, who had been illustrating the soap-opera strip *The Heart of Juliet Jones* since 1953, was hired as the artist for *Blondie* in 1985. Bobby

London, the creator of the underground comic strip *Dirty Duck*, began producing *Popeye* in 1986. Six years later, after doing a controversial story line in which a priest mistakenly thinks Olive Oyl is in a "family way" and Popeye wants her to have an abortion, King Features Syndicate declined to renew London's contract.

BLONDIE daily strip by Dean Young and Stan Drake. © 4/2/86 King Features Syndicate, Inc.

POPEYE daily strip by Bobby London. © 2/19/87 King Features Syndicate, Inc. Courtesy of International Museum of Cartoon Art

CURTIS daily-strip sequence by Ray Billingsley. © 7/8–7/11/91 King Features Syndicate, Inc.

RAY BILLINGSLEY   The setting of *Curtis* was a realistic inner city based on creator Ray Billingsley's own hometown Harlem neighborhood. Eleven-year-old Curtis and his eight-year-old brother, Barry, faced the challenges of city life with resourcefulness and optimism, as the examples from Billingsley's acclaimed 1991 crack-baby episode, shown here, demonstrate. The cartoonist has also been praised for his sequences on African folklore and the dangers of gangs, drugs, and smoking. On a more lighthearted note, Curtis is a devoted rap-music fan and interacts humorously with his idiosyncratic schoolmates Chutney, Michelle, Sheila, Verbena, Derrick, and Gunk as well as his teacher, Mrs. Nelson, Gunther the barber, and his parents, Greg and Diana. *Curtis* has been distributed by King Features Syndicate since 1988.

MARVIN Sunday page by Tom Armstrong. © 8/16/92 King Features Syndicate, Inc.

TOM ARMSTRONG   *Marvin* was created by Tom Armstrong in 1982. Drawn in a clean, well-defined style, this popular modern kid strip starred the one-year-old toddler, his doting parents, Jeff and Jenny, the family dog, Bitsy, and his protofeminist cousin, Megan. Marvin's fantasies inspired many graphically innovative episodes, as in the Sunday funnies dream above. Armstrong also collaborated on *John Darling*, a feature starring a television talk show host, with Tom Batiuk, beginning in 1979. When the strip ended in 1990, the creators decided to kill off their character in a shockingly violent conclusion (below).

JOHN DARLING daily strip by Tom Armstrong and Tom Batiuk. © 8/3/90 North America Syndicate, Inc.

the nineties

MARCY AND JOE from JUMP START by Robb Armstrong. © United Feature Syndicate, Inc.

HOMAGE TO A HERO—Mooch, Earl, and Snoopy illustration by Patrick McDonnell. © Patrick McDonnell. Reprinted with special permission of King Features Syndicate, Inc.

WILLIAM JEFFERSON CLINTON WAS THE FIRST AMERICAN PRESIDENT BORN AFTER WORLD WAR II. CLINTON'S TRIUMPHS AND FAILURES IN THE DECADE OF THE 1990S WERE EMBLEMATIC OF THE STRUGGLES MANY BABY BOOMERS WERE EXPERIENCING AS THEY APPROACHED MIDDLE AGE.

David Brooks, in his best-selling book about the decade, *Bobos in Paradise*, identified a new class of "bourgeois bohemians" who had reconciled the idealism of the 1960s with the pragmatism of the 1980s. "Bobos" had pioneered a new lifestyle that blended hippie ethics with the realities of personal affluence and political power.

Brooks argued that "the Clinton-Gore administration embodied the spirit of compromise that is at the heart of Bobo enterprise. In the first place, the Clintons were both 1960s antiwar protesters and 1980s futures traders. They came to the White House well stocked with bohemian ideals and bourgeois ambitions."

The leader of the free world played the saxophone and admitted to experimenting with marijuana during his college years. He was also a Rhodes scholar and a skilled orator. Clinton combined the common sense of the World War II generation with the social concerns of the baby boomers. The new hybrid was labeled "compassionate conservatism" or "practical idealism" as political persuasions became less polarized.

This same reconciliation process was also at work in the comics business during the 1990s. Three of the most successful new features of the decade—*Baby Blues*, *Mutts*, and *Zits*—blended traditional themes with fresh perspectives. Jerry Scott, Rick Kirkman, Patrick McDonnell, and Jim Borgman, the creators of these King Features–distributed comic strips, were all born during the postwar years. They helped to revive classic, family-oriented genres and brought quality draftsmanship back to the funnies pages.

IN THE BEGINNING . . . —BABY BLUES DAY 1 by Rick Kirkman and Jerry Scott. © 1990 Baby Blues Partnership. Reprinted with special permission of King Features Syndicate, Inc.

In the early 1970s Rick Kirkman and Jerry Scott worked together at an art agency in Phoenix, Arizona. During their lunch hour they often talked about a shared dream of creating a syndicated comic strip. They developed some ideas, including a strip called *Hide and Zeke*, about two miners in the Arizona desert, and *Copps and Robberts*, which starred a pair of inept policemen. Their boss, Audrey Keyes, liked the latter concept so much that she started a new syndicate, Southwestern Features, solely to distribute it. *Copps and Robberts* ran from 1978 to 1980 and appeared in about thirty papers at its peak.

During this time, Jerry Scott moved to California and started his own ad agency. He was introduced to cartoonist Foster Moore, the creator of the syndicated panel *Gumdrop*. When Moore retired in 1981, Scott took over *Gumdrop*, which was syndicated by United Feature. Two years later he also started producing the *Nancy* comic strip.

Rick Kirkman had stayed at the agency in Arizona and was now a successful art director. During this ten-year period the two had never given up their ambition of collaborating on a syndicated feature. In 1984 Kirkman had a baby daughter, which gave him the idea of doing a strip about a newborn. When Scott moved back to Phoenix in 1987, the two developed the concept and started sending samples of the strip, originally titled *Oh Baby*, to the syndicates. They got rejection letters back. One syndicate suggested trying the idea as a panel. Renamed *Baby Blues*, it was turned down because the same syndicate said panels were too hard to sell. Kirkman and Scott tried it as a strip again, and three syndicates showed interest. One wanted to see an older child in the family. Another wanted to see a continuing story line. There were still no offers.

Then one afternoon Anita Medeiros, comics editor of Creators Syndicate, called to tell the cartoonists that she loved the proposal and wanted to discuss a contract. *Baby Blues* began syndication in January 1990.

The strip starred a thirtysomething, college-educated couple, Wanda and Daryl MacPherson, and their newborn baby, Zoe. Kirkman and Scott's creation struck a chord with the millions of Americans who were just starting families after pursuing careers during the 1980s. Zoe aged slowly and was joined by baby brother Hamish in 1995 and sister Wren in 2002.

By 1994 *Baby Blues* was appearing in over 200 newspapers, when the contract with Creators Syndicate expired. Kirkman and Scott entertained offers from other syndicates and eventually signed with King Features. *Baby Blues* won the award for Best Humor Strip from the National Cartoonists Society in 1996, debuted as a weekly animated series on the Warner Brothers television network in 2000, and increased its circulation to over 800 papers.

After graduating from the School of Visual Arts in 1978, Patrick McDonnell thought briefly about doing a comic strip. A friend set up an appointment with Bobby Miller, comics editor at United Feature Syndicate, but the meeting was so discouraging that McDonnell decided to put his first ambition on hold and embark on a career in freelance cartoon illustration. He put together a portfolio and started showing his work around to second-rate publications, hoping they might give a newcomer a chance. After repeated rejections, he decided that if he was going to be turned down, it might as well be by the top magazines.

McDonnell's first big break came when Ruth Ansel, art director of the *New York Times Magazine*, hired him to illustrate

Russell Baker's "Sunday Observer" column, which he did every week for the next ten years, until the feature was retired. This job gave him the exposure and the experience to sell to all the top magazines, including *Forbes*, *Time*, *Life*, and *Self*. He also did regular features for *Parents Magazine*, *Sports Illustrated*, *Parade*, and *Reader's Digest*.

Although his illustration career temporarily kept McDonnell from pursuing his dream of creating a comic strip, he still managed to incorporate many comic-strip elements into his illustration work. He frequently used the same small cast of characters and played with multipanel layouts and speech balloons. He drew a regular strip, *Bad Baby*, which ran for ten years in *Parents Magazine* and was collected in a book published by Fawcett.

In the 1980s McDonnell also spent four years researching and writing, with his wife Karen O'Connell and Graham Gallery director Georgia Riley DeHavenon, a book devoted to one of his major influences. *Krazy Kat: The Comic Art of George Herriman*, published by Harry N. Abrams, Inc., in 1986, was a landmark work of comics scholarship.

In 1990 Carolyn and Arnold Roth invited McDonnell to join the National Cartoonists Society. "As soon as I went to my first N.C.S. event," he remembered, "it hit home that these were my type of people who were doing the thing I would love to do." In 1992 McDonnell won two awards from the N.C.S. for magazine illustration and greeting cards. This gave him the impetus to finally begin work on a comic strip.

MAGIC INK—MUTTS logo. © 1995 Patrick McDonnell. Reprinted with special permission of King Features Syndicate, Inc.

Jay Kennedy, the comics editor at King Features Syndicate, had been a classmate of McDonnell's at the School of Visual Arts during the 1970s. In 1990 the two had lunch together, and McDonnell showed Kennedy some idea sketches for a strip about a stray dog. For the next two years, McDonnell continued to be occupied with his illustration career but kept thinking about his comic-strip concept. Finally, in late 1992, he drew up four weeks of finished strips and two Sunday pages and mailed them to King Features, Universal Press, and Creators Syndicate. The feature was named *Zero Zero*, and it starred a dog and his mustached owner. It was also populated with frogs, rabbits, elephants, and a menagerie of other creatures that the dog (Zero Zero) encountered in his wanderings.

Universal Press Syndicate, which had a policy against "talking animal strips," passed on the proposal, but King decided to sign McDonnell up. During a yearlong development period, he honed his cast down to six characters in two family groups. In one house lived Ozzie and his dog, Earl (named after McDonnell's own dog). The other household consisted of Frank and Millie, their cat, Mooch, and their fish, Sid. The title *Mutts* was finally chosen from a dwindling list of names at the eleventh hour.

During the development period McDonnell also made a pilgrimage to visit Charles Schulz at his studio in California. His boyhood hero offered some sage advice on avoiding self-referential humor and concentrating on establishing believable characters. Schulz's praise and support eventually helped to sell *Mutts* to the *Los Angeles Times*, one of the first major papers to buy the strip before it debuted on September 5, 1994. When Bill Watterson retired at the end of 1995, McDonnell picked up many of the spaces vacated by *Calvin and Hobbes*. *Mutts* was appearing in close to 500 newspapers when McDonnell won the Reuben Award in 1999.

He had realized his dream. "What I really love about comics is that magic, that these little ink things are alive," McDonnell said. "That's what I love and hopefully that's what comes across."

In 1996 Jerry Scott was enjoying the success of *Baby Blues* but felt he needed a new challenge. A friend suggested that he try doing a strip with a teenager as the central character. It sounded like a good idea. The only problem was that all the characters Scott drew looked like Nancy and Sluggo, the stars of the strip he had drawn for twelve years. Scott mentioned this dilemma to his good friend Jim Borgman, the Pulitzer Prize–winning political cartoonist for the *Cincinnati Enquirer*. Borgman, who had a teenage son at home, offered to collaborate with Scott as the artist on the strip.

Zits, which Charles Schulz claimed was the worst name for a comic strip since *Peanuts*, debuted in July 1997. In six

TEEN ANGST—Jeremy from ZITS by Jerry Scott and Jim Borgman. © 1997 Zits Partnership. Reprinted with permission of King Features Syndicate, Inc.

months it had a list of 425 clients. The reputation of the two established creators was only part of the reason *Zits* took off so quickly.

"The artwork is the best I've seen in years," said Carl Crothers, editor of the *Winston-Salem Journal* in North Carolina. "The strip has movement that you don't get in a lot of comics. So many are so static."

Jeremy Duncan, the star of *Zits*, was a typical hormone-addled, insecure fifteen-year-old, who played in a rock band and fumbled through a relationship with his girlfriend, Sara Toomey. Although Jeremy was in constant conflict with his parents, Walt and Connie Duncan, there was a tender side to the family relationships. "Jerry and I never have to remind each other, 'Remember these folks like each other,'" claimed Borgman.

Zits was named the Best Comic Strip of the Year by the National Cartoonists Society in 1998 and 1999 and doubled its list of papers in less than four years. Scott and Borgman's creation managed to be cutting-edge and traditional at the same time. The strip was not dependent on clever gimmicks or a niche marketing concept. Scott's perceptive writing and Borgman's brilliant artwork provided a strong foundation upon which the successful collaboration was built.

The emergence of the internet as a global communications network in the 1990s had parallels to the rise of television in the 1950s. The new electronic medium presented both a challenge and an opportunity to the comics business. Syndicates, initially concerned about competing with their newspaper subscribers, eventually set up websites and marketed features directly to internet clients. Aspiring cartoonists showcased their work on the web and benefited from the increased exposure. Publishers, manufacturers, and creators earned additional income from on-line sales of books and licensed products. In spite of these digital-age developments, comic strips continued to generate most of their profits from newspaper fees.

Scott Adams was one cartoonist who used modern technology to build a modestly successful feature, *Dilbert*, into a mega-hit in the 1990s. Adams had an M.B.A. from the University of California at Berkeley and was earning about $70,000 a year as an applications engineer for Pacific Bell when he created *Dilbert* in 1989. The strip grew slowly, so he continued to produce it during his off-hours while working in the corporate world.

In 1993 Adams decided it might be useful to get some input from his readers, so he printed his e-mail address within the strip. The response he received revealed that the office-oriented episodes in *Dilbert* were the ones his fans were hanging up on the walls of their cubicles. He switched the emphasis of the feature almost entirely to business and technology, and it took off. Adams began receiving 300 to 800 e-mail messages a day from all over the world, and he used these ideas and suggestions in the strip. His fans also actively petitioned newspaper editors to buy *Dilbert*, which helped build the list of subscribers. Adams finally left PacBell when he was downsized on June 30, 1995.

POTSHOT—DILBERT daily strip by Scott Adams (in retaliation for criticism by Bill Griffith). © 5/18/98 United Feature Syndicate, Inc.

The following year Adams attained superstar status. His comic strip passed the 1,000-client mark. The Dilbert Zone website was receiving an estimated 75,000 visitors a day. Adams was profiled in a *Newsweek* cover story. The *Dilbert Principle* stayed perched atop the *New York Times* best-seller list for months. *Dilbert* calendars, coffee mugs, ties, dolls, and mouse pads sold at a record pace. To top it off, Adams made more money that year giving speeches to corporations (at $7,500 an appearance) than he earned from the strip.

"I was a total failure in corporate America in terms of my career," Adams admitted in 1996. But he still wondered what might have happened had he not scored with *Dilbert*. "I truly think by now I would have been a fairly high-level manager and made more money than I do now," he speculated. "But I started doing cartooning just when I was most promotable, and the more I cartooned, the less promotable I became. I'll never know. It's a great mystery to me."

Adams won the Reuben Award in 1997, and a *Dilbert* animated television series debuted in 1999. *Dilbert* was the fifth strip, after *Peanuts*, *Garfield*, *For Better or For Worse*, and *Blondie*, to pass the 2,000-paper mark, in 2001.

As the new generation of cartoonists matured, they tackled more provocative issues. Among the sensitive subjects broached during the 1990s were crack babies (*Curtis*), menstruation (*Luann*), Alzheimer's disease (*Crankshaft*), and breast cancer (*Funky Winkerbean*). Some readers questioned whether the funnies were becoming too serious. Socially relevant story lines seemed more tragic than comic.

Lynn Johnston set off a storm of controversy in 1993 when Lawrence, a regular character in *For Better or For Worse*, admitted to his longtime friend, Michael Patterson, that he was gay. Johnston had sent letters of warning to all 1,400 newspapers that carried her strip before the four-week sequence was scheduled to appear. Although the subject was handled with sensitivity, a handful of editors and thousands of readers objected vehemently. When the dust settled, nineteen

papers had canceled *For Better or For Worse* permanently, and Johnston's phone rang off the hook for weeks.

A new term entered the national vocabulary in the 1990s: "political correctness." Americans became increasingly sensitive to the way certain groups were portrayed in the media. Initially the term was employed by conservatives to derisively label progressive causes. Eventually "politically correct" was used to describe socially acceptable references to gays, women, racial and ethnic minorities, and disabled persons. This uptight atmosphere made life difficult for many in the humor business.

"It's a new label," remarked Jeff MacNelly. "Every complaint we've ever had has been lumped into this huge monster. I'm politically incorrect. That's what I do for a living."

Mort Walker, who had deflected criticism for years about alleged sexism in *Beetle Bailey*, finally capitulated in 1997. General Halftrack, who had been ogling his curvaceous secretary, Miss Buxley, since she joined the cast in 1971, apologized for his behavior and attended a sensitivity training seminar. "I read my mail," said Walker. "I want to entertain my readers and when I find that certain subjects are not funny, I'm willing to change."

Beginning in 1989 Johnny Hart, a born-again Christian, began introducing overt religious commentary into his *B.C.* comic strip on certain holidays, such as Christmas and Easter. Many newspapers, including the *Washington Post* and *Los Angeles Times*, refused to run some of these episodes, claiming they were objectionable to their non-Christian readers. On Easter Sunday, 2001, the *B.C.* cartoon depicted a Jewish symbol, the Menorah, gradually transforming into a Christian symbol, the cross. The Anti-Defamation League, the American Jewish Committee, and other groups denounced the cartoon as a religious slur and many newspapers pulled the strip. Rick Newcombe, president of Creators Syndicate, Hart's distributor, issued a statement saying, "I interpreted it the same way as Johnny intended for it to be interpreted—that Christianity is rooted in Judaism."

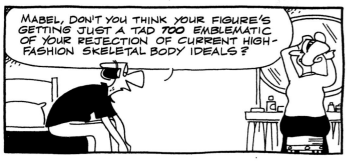

POLITICAL CORRECTNESS—MOTLEY'S CREW Sunday page by Ben Templeton and Tom Forman. © 6/15/97 Tribune Media Services, Inc. All rights reserved. Used by permission

Cartoonists were finding it dangerous to poke fun at anyone. Berke Breathed, who was frequently censored for politically incorrect humor in *Bloom County* and *Outland*, claimed that if a woman did anything objectionable in his strip she became a "symbol for her gender," and if a black character did anything controversial he was regarded as a "minority icon."

"I am not free to portray minorities in the way they portray themselves. I have to be careful in dealing with drug issues and with minorities," Breathed stated. "The effect of political correctness is very powerful on the page."

Minority cartoonists also felt the heat. Aaron McGruder's comic strip, *The Boondocks*, which starred two black kids from inner-city Chicago who had just moved to the white suburbs, generated controversy from the day of its debut on April 19, 1999. Black readers complained that the strip perpetuated racial stereotypes. White readers felt they were being ridiculed. Others objected to the way McGruder portrayed an interracial married couple.

The twenty-five-year-old black cartoonist seemed unfazed by the criticism. "The focus of the strip is race," argued

McGruder. "Just like the focus of *Dilbert* is cubicles."

Although *The Boondocks* was canceled by a handful of small-town newspapers, it had 195 clients within two months of its launch. Many editors rallied to McGruder's defense. Kristin Tillotson of the *Minneapolis Star-Tribune* wrote that readers who didn't appreciate the humor of the strip suffered from "irony deficiency." It was time for America to lighten up.

The centennial anniversary of the funnies was celebrated in 1995. The first color appearance of Richard F. Outcault's Yellow Kid in the *New York World* on May 5, 1895, was widely recognized as the birth of the art form. Many cartoonists did special tributes in their strips on the day of the milestone. A retrospective exhibition, "Featuring the Funnies: 100 Years of the Comic Strip," was held at the Library of Congress. The U.S. Postal Service released a series of twenty commemorative comic-strip stamps on October 1. Writers, columnists, and reporters across the nation featured stories on this major cultural event. Even the *New York Times*, one of the few newspapers in the country that does not publish comics, saluted the funnies.

RELIGIOUS MESSAGE—B.C. daily strip by Johnny Hart. © 4/13/2001 Creators Syndicate, Inc.

COMICS CENTENNIAL—THATCH daily strip by Jeff Shesol. Many cartoonists created tributes on the day of the anniversary. © 5/5/95 Creators Syndicate, Inc.

The comics were basking in a warm glow of public acceptance. A study by Metropolitan Sunday Newspapers in 1993 reported that 113 million Americans read the comics regularly. In 1995 four strips were each appearing in more than 2,000 newspapers. The renamed International Museum of Cartoon Art opened a new, expanded facility in Boca Raton, Florida, in 1996. Other institutions devoted to the art form opened in San Francisco, Northampton, Massachusetts, and Washington, D.C. Membership in the National Cartoonists Society was at an all-time high. On April Fools' Day, 1997, forty-six syndicated artists swapped features in "The Great Comics Switcheroonie." Mike Peters ghosted *For Better or For Worse*, and Garfield and Jon moved in with Blondie and Dagwood in the crossover spoof.

A few prophets of gloom tried to spoil the fun. Bill Griffith, the creator of *Zippy the Pinhead*, wrote the following assessment in the *Boston Globe* on November 10, 1996: "The newspaper comic strip is 100 years old—and looks it. Shrunken. Pale. Shaky. One foot in the grave. Diagnosis: in desperate need of new blood. Instead, it gets *Dilbert*."

Anthony Lejeune, in a *National Review* article entitled "Eek! Sob! It's the Death of Comics," lamented, "Nobody fights over the breakfast table for a first glimpse of *Calvin and Hobbes* or hurries to the street corner for the latest episode of *Cathy*."

"Too many newspapers are running too many cartoons done by dead guys," claimed *Non Sequitur* cartoonist Wiley

Miller. "The guys who created *Blondie* and *Dick Tracy* have been dead for years and so are the strips." Miller urged editors to get rid of the "deadwood" and open up their pages to artists with cutting-edge creations.

The competitive nature of the comics business intensified in the 1990s as the number of papers dwindled and editors feared the wrath of loyal readers when they tried to cancel long-running features. Young cartoonists found it increasingly difficult to break in and resented the old standby strips that had been around since before they were born.

"Most new comics die," claimed David Seidman, a former comics editor of the *Los Angeles Times*. "After accounting for the big important strips, the average editor might have one or two spots to play around with for new strips." Most newspapers gave a strip six months to a year to establish a readership. Syndicates canceled the majority of features after a year if they didn't catch on. The odds of survival beyond that point were less than 40 percent.

When Bill Watterson, Gary Larson, and Berke Breathed retired in 1995, approximately 4,700 spaces opened up on the nation's comic pages. A handful of established features got an immediate boost in circulation. The rest of the talent found themselves scrambling for the remaining spots.

During the 1990s each of the major syndicates reported receiving more than 5,000 submissions from aspiring cartoonists every year. Many of these concepts tried to emulate the

APRIL FOOLS—GARFIELD daily strip by Jim Davis. Cartoonists swap features for a day. © 4/1/97 Paws, Inc. Used by permission of Universal Press Syndicate. All rights reserved

BREAKING IN—NINA'S ADVENTURES weekly page by Nina Paley. © 2/13/92 Nina Paley

proven formula of an existing feature. In 1997 Lee Salem, comics editor of Universal Press Syndicate, remarked, "I just got one in my 'In' box that was called 'The Other Side.'"

Syndicate editors searched through these proposals for the next promising creation. Any envelope that crossed their desk could contain a unique idea whose time had come. Only a few blockbusters surface each decade.

"Comics are still one of the few Cinderella businesses," claimed King Features comics editor Jay Kennedy in 1996. "You don't need an agent and you don't need to know anyone—if you're good enough you can send it in and have a shot at seeing a dream come true."

The greatest success story in the history of comics came to an end in December 1999 when Charles Schulz announced that he was retiring after more than forty-nine years of producing the *Peanuts* comic strip. "Good Grief!"; "Aaugh!"; and "Nuts! No *Peanuts*" appeared as headlines in *Newsweek*, *People*, and the *New York Daily News*. "Aack! I can't stand it!!" shrieked the comic character Cathy, facing a future on the funnies pages without Charlie Brown and Lucy.

Schulz, who had been diagnosed with colon cancer after hospitalization on November 16, 1999, appeared emotionally drained in a *Today* show interview with Al Roker the following January. Although he had been contemplating retirement for many years, his health problems forced him

to make the decision prematurely. In his last daily strip, dated January 3, 2000, Schulz regretfully admitted to his readers, "Unfortunately, I am no longer able to maintain the schedule demanded by a daily comic strip, therefore I am announcing my retirement." The last *Peanuts* Sunday page was scheduled to appear on February 13, 2000.

Doonesbury creator Garry Trudeau wrote an elegant appreciation of Schulz's legacy in the *Washington Post* on December 19, 1999. "While the public at large regards *Peanuts* as a cherished part of our shared popular culture, cartoonists also see it as an irreplaceable source of purpose and pride, our gold standard for work that is both illuminating and aesthetically sublime. We can hardly imagine its absence."

United Media made plans to fill the void on the funnies pages with classic *Peanuts* strips from 1974. Only 140 of the strip's subscribers opted not to pay for the reruns. The licensing program continued. In fact, after the retirement announcement, interest in Schulz's creation increased.

A second shock wave hit on February 12, 2000, when Schulz died in his sleep less than three hours before the final *Peanuts* episode appeared in the Sunday newspapers. "The timing was prophetic and magical," said Lynn Johnston, a close friend of Schulz. "He made one last deadline. There's romance in that."

"Sparky," as his friends and fellow cartoonists called him, single-handedly conceived, drew, inked, and lettered over 17,500

PEANUTS PATIENT—JUMP START by Robb Armstrong. (Schulz was in the hospital.) © 1/5/2000 United Feature Syndicate, Inc.

individual *Peanuts* comic strips and Sunday pages. The feature appeared in 2,600 newspapers and consistently placed its creator on the *Forbes* magazine list of highest-paid entertainers.

Schulz's accomplishments cannot be measured solely by numbers, however. The *Peanuts* gang—Charlie Brown, Lucy, Linus, Schroeder, Pigpen, Sally, Marcie, Peppermint Patty, and Snoopy—were among the most recognized and beloved personalities on the planet. Schulz's strokes of genius—Linus's security blanket, Snoopy's flights of fantasy, Charlie Brown's travails on the baseball mound—became as much a part of American folklore as Tom Sawyer and Huck Finn's adventures.

"I have been asked many times if I ever dreamed that *Peanuts* would become so successful," wrote Schulz in the introduction to his fiftieth-anniversary anthology, *Peanuts: A Golden Celebration.* "Obviously I did not know that Snoopy

was going to go to the moon and I did not know that the term 'happiness is a warm puppy' would prompt hundreds of other such definitions and I did not know that the term 'security blanket' would become part of the American language; but I did have the hope that I would be able to contribute something to a profession that I have loved all my life."

Although his genius was universally recognized during his lifetime, Schulz did not regard what he produced as "Great Art." "Having a large audience does not, of course, prove that something is necessarily good," he modestly stated. "I subscribe to the theory that only a creation that speaks to succeeding generations can truly be labeled art."

Charles Schulz's impressive body of work, as well as the imaginative creations of his contemporaries in the comics field, will have their day of reckoning in the twenty-first century.

A SAD FAREWELL—Charlie Brown by Charles Schulz. © United Feature Syndicate, Inc.

DENNIS THE MENACE Sunday page by Ron Ferdinand. © 5/28/2000 North America Syndicate. Used by permission of Hank Ketcham Enterprises

COMIC LEGACIES

A number of classic features, whose creators or successors died or left to pursue other opportunities in the 1980s and 1990s, were continued by former assistants, experienced pros, or family members. Ron Ferdinand began illustrating the *Dennis the Menace* Sunday page (above) in the early 1980s, and Marcus Hamilton took over the *Dennis* daily panel (right) in the mid-1990s. Hank Ketcham worked closely with both artists until his death in 2001. Jim Scancarelli took over *Gasoline Alley* (following page) after Dick Moores passed away in 1986. He won the Best Story-Strip Award from the National Cartoonists Society in 1989 for his distinguished work. Guy and Brad Gilchrist succeeded Jerry Scott on *Nancy* (following page) in 1995, restoring it to the original Bushmiller style, while exploring more contemporary themes.

"BOY, GRAMPA! NATURE'S SO MUCH *BIGGER* IN PERSON, THAN IT IS ON TV."

DENNIS THE MENACE daily panel by Marcus Hamilton. © 8/15/2001 North America Syndicate. Used by permission of Hank Ketcham Enterprises

GASOLINE ALLEY Sunday page by Jim Scancarelli (to mark the comics centennial). © 4/16/95 Tribune Media Services, Inc. All rights reserved. Used by permission

NANCY Sunday page by Guy & Brad Gilchrist. © 11/19/95 United Feature Syndicate, Inc.

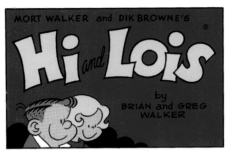

HI AND LOIS Sunday page by Brian and Greg Walker and Chance Browne. © 8/29/93 King Features Syndicate, Inc.

COMIC LEGACIES (CONTINUED)

When Dik Browne died on June 4, 1989, his two strips were left in able hands. The art production of *Hi and Lois*, which had been scripted by Mort Walker's sons, Brian and Greg, since the mid-1980s, was officially assumed by Chance Browne, who had been working with his father for many years. Frank Johnson, who had been inking *Hi and Lois* since the early 1970s, also continued. Dik's other son, Chris, who had been involved with *Hagar the Horrible* since its inception in 1973, took over the production of that strip with the help of Bud Jones (writing) and Dick Hodgins, Jr. (artwork).

HAGAR THE HORRIBLE daily strip by Chris Browne. © 6/11/90 King Features Syndicate, Inc. Courtesy of Bill Janocha.

JUMP START Sunday page by Robb Armstrong. © 6/19/94 United Feature Syndicate, Inc.

ROBB ARMSTRONG   When *Jump Start* began in 1989, the characters spoke in modern street slang. "I was trying to be blacker," admitted Armstrong, the African-American creator of the strip. "Then a black woman wrote me, and she was just irate. I said, 'You know, she's right—I don't use this slang.' I was feeding into all those stereotypes." Armstrong decided to develop a more mainstream family feature that "flies in the face of racial stereotypes." The loving relationship between his two main characters, Joe, a policeman, and Marcy, a nurse, culminated in the dramatic 1994 episode, shown here, in which Marcy gives birth to a baby girl, Sunny, in the back of the family car. *Jump Start* was inspired by Armstrong's own happy home life with wife Sherry, daughter Tess, and son Rex, and millions of newspapers readers have responded to his positive outlook on contemporary marriage and parenthood.

JUMP START daily strip by Robb Armstrong. © 6/20/94 United Feature Syndicate, Inc.

Panel 1: I CAN REMEMBER WHEN THESE WERE ONLY FIFTEEN CENTS.

Panel 2: BUT I'M REALLY DATING MYSELF NOW...

Panel 3: WELL, IT'S NOT AS IF ANYBODY ELSE WOULD DATE YOU.

DILBERT daily strip by Scott Adams. © 4/17/89

All Dilbert strips © United Feature Syndicate, Inc.

SCOTT ADAMS   The most successful comic strip of the last decade, Scott Adams's 1989 creation *Dilbert*, gained a large following among cubicle-dwelling office workers before expanding its appeal to a broader audience by the mid-1990s. The star of the strip is a hapless techno-nerd who lives with a cynical canine named Dogbert and is victimized by his pointy-haired boss and befuddled by his neurotic coworkers, Alice, Tina, Wally, Albert, and Asok. *Dilbert* was produced, until 1995, during Adams's off-hours from his job at a high-tech company that inspired the environment in the strip. His graphically minimal doodles manage to convey the bleak futility of Dilbert's pathetic existence. The character's appeal is similar to Charles Schulz's lovable loser, Charlie Brown. Readers identify with Dilbert because he puts up with the petty insults of the corporate world and comes back each day for more abuse.

SELF-CARICATURE by Scott Adams

Panel 1: OH GOOD, THE LAST STOP OF THE DAY.

Panel 2: FREEZE, MORTAL! LET ME SEE THE EXPIRATION DATE ON THAT MILK!

Panel 3: I CAN GO TO HELL FOR DRINKING OLD MILK?! NAH. I'M FROM "HECK." WE HANDLE THE LITTLE STUFF.

DILBERT daily strip by Scott Adams. © 5/1/89

DILBERT daily strip by Scott Adams. © 9/25/89

DILBERT daily strip by Scott Adams. © 4/2/90

DILBERT daily strip by Scott Adams. © 9/21/90

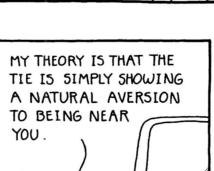

DILBERT daily strip by Scott Adams. © 8/7/91

DILBERT daily strip by Scott Adams. © 5/3/93

DILBERT daily strip by Scott Adams. © 8/21/93

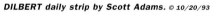

DILBERT daily strip by Scott Adams. © 10/20/93

DILBERT daily strip by Scott Adams. © 7/25/94
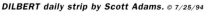

YOU HAVE TO GO, CAT. YOU HAVE NO VALUE TO US.

9-16

ACTUALLY, MY MERE EXISTENCE WILL WIDEN YOUR DEMO-GRAPHIC APPEAL AND MAKE YOU IMMORTAL.

OH... A CAT. THAT'S ORIGINAL.

GIVE IT A REST, "MICKEY."

PURR

E-Mail: SCOTTADAMS@AOL.COM
© 1994 United Feature Syndicate, Inc.

DILBERT daily strip by Scott Adams. © 9/16/94

THIS CARTOON SEEMS TO BE SAYING THAT MANAGEMENT DECISIONS ARE A JOKE.

CARTOONS ARE NOT ALLOWED ON CUBICLES. IT HURTS MORALE. I DON'T WANT TO SEE THIS WHEN I RETURN.

9-28

I'VE NOTICED A REAL IMPROVEMENT IN MORALE SINCE YOU REMOVED THE CARTOON.

E-Mail: SCOTTADAMS@AOL.COM
© 1994 United Feature Syndicate, Inc.

DILBERT daily strip by Scott Adams. © 9/28/94

DILBERT IS TRAPPED IN THE BOWELS OF ACCOUNTING

I UNDERSTAND YOU HAVE DILBERT IN THERE. FREE HIM, OR ELSE...

ELSE WHAT?

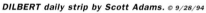

OR ELSE I WILL PUT THIS CAP ON MY HEAD BACKWARDS! YOUR LITTLE HARDWIRED ACCOUNTING BRAIN WILL EXPLODE JUST LOOKING AT IT.

E-Mail: SCOTTADAMS@AOL.COM

WHAT WAS THAT POPPING SOUND?

A PARADIGM SHIFTING WITHOUT A CLUTCH.

8/25 © 1995 United Feature Syndicate, Inc. (NYC)

DILBERT daily strip by Scott Adams. © 8/25/95

HEY, EVERYBODY. MEET OUR NEW INTERN, ASOK.

E-mail: SCOTTADAMS@AOL.COM

I HOPE THIS ONE'S STURDIER THAN THE LAST ONE.

MY STAPLE REMOVER IS BROKEN. SOMEBODY TOSS THAT INTERN TO ME!

© 1996 United Feature Syndicate, Inc. (NYC)

DILBERT daily strip by Scott Adams. © 3/18/96

DILBERT Sunday page by Scott Adams. © 5/7/95

DILBERT Sunday page by Scott Adams. © 4/7/96

rick kirkman & jerry scott

SUCCESSFUL COLLABORATIONS are rare in the comics. Most features are produced by a single creator, often with the help of assistants. Even when gag writers and ghost artists are used, there is almost always one individual who guides the direction of a strip. During the last fifty years, very few features have begun as collaborations. Mort Walker and Dik Browne teamed up to produce *Hi and Lois* in 1954. Johnny Hart and Brant Parker, who created *The Wizard of Id* in 1964, were another successful partnership.

A more recent collaborative effort is Rick Kirkman and Jerry Scott's *Baby Blues*. When this family feature was launched in 1990, Scott, the writer, did not have children of his own. He depended on Kirkman, the artist, who had two young daughters at home, to provide inspiration for gags.

In a 1990 article in *Cartoonist PROfiles*, Scott described their working methods: "While I generate all of the actual gags, it's conversations with Rick about the strip that get the ideas started. After I give Rick the gags I've written (between seven and twelve a week), he goes through them and chooses the ones he feels are the strongest and makes suggestions on improving the rest. This is really where the fun starts for me because some of our best material has come out of these sessions. Tearing ideas apart and rearranging them into totally different gags not only improves the existing gags that we're working on, it also results in the creation of new material. Often the new stuff is more insightful or just plain sillier than what we started with. When we agree on seven cartoons for the week, Rick does roughs of each gag, and we do the same critique, with me making comments and suggestions on the art. We push each other toward constant improvement, and the result is a better product than either of us could produce alone."

The finished strips are then drawn on two-ply bristol board with black colored pencils. Kirkman's pencil line gives *Baby Blues* a relaxed, friendly look.

Despite the title, the focus of the strip is on parenting, not babies. In the beginning, Zoe, who was drawn smaller than most comic-strip infants, did not speak or "think" in balloons. As she grew (she was one year old after two years on the comics pages), Zoe began to babble like a baby, and before long she was talking like a toddler. Her parents, Wanda and Darryl, confronted many of the same child-rearing issues that contemporary parents face, including disposable diapers vs. cloth diapers, breast-feeding in public, unisex toys, potty-training, preschool, and husband-coached natural childbirth (when Hamish and Wren arrived in 1993 and 2001).

In 1996 the National Cartoonists Society presented the award for Best Comic Strip of the Year to Rick Kirkman for *Baby Blues*. Jerry Scott, the co-creator of the feature, was not given an equal share of the honor. This situation set off a heated debate within the organization. The existing bylaws of the N.C.S. restricted full membership to individuals who earned more than 50 percent of their income as cartoonists (defined as a "graphic storyteller"). Writers could only be associate members and were not eligible for awards. The rule was particularly hard to justify in the case of collaborators whose duties often overlapped. In 1998, when *Zits* was nominated for best comic strip, Scott, who was also the co-creator of that feature, was left off the ballot again. Scott's partner, Jim Borgman, protested, and the N.C.S. was finally forced to amend the rules to recognize collaborators equally.

Scott no longer depends on Kirkman as the main source of his gag material. "The strip was originally based on Rick's second daughter," he remembers. "But in 1993 Kim (Scott's wife) and I welcomed Abbey into our lives to love, educate, and help produce gags." A second child, Cady, was born on October 26, 2001. Scott now writes from firsthand experience.

BABY BLUES daily strip by Rick Kirkman and Jerry Scott, © 11/5/97

All Baby Blues strips © Baby Blues Partnership. Reprinted with special permission of King Features Syndicate, Inc.

BABY BLUES daily strip by Rick Kirkman and Jerry Scott. © 6/19/90

BABY BLUES daily strip by Rick Kirkman and Jerry Scott. © 10/6/90

BABY BLUES daily strip by Rick Kirkman and Jerry Scott. © 7/23/91

BABY BLUES daily strip by Rick Kirkman and Jerry Scott. © 12/27/96

BABY BLUES daily strip by Rick Kirkman and Jerry Scott. © 2/21/94

BABY BLUES daily strip by Rick Kirkman and Jerry Scott. © 9/21/94

BABY BLUES daily strip by Rick Kirkman and Jerry Scott. © 4/29/95

BABY BLUES daily strip by Rick Kirkman and Jerry Scott. © 8/25/97

BABY BLUES Sunday page by Rick Kirkman and Jerry Scott. © 9/6/92

BABY BLUES Sunday page by Rick Kirkman and Jerry Scott. © 7/28/96

BABY BLUES Sunday page by Rick Kirkman and Jerry Scott. © 1/25/98

BABY BLUES *daily strip by Rick Kirkman and Jerry Scott.* © 3/27/2000

BABY BLUES *daily strip by Rick Kirkman and Jerry Scott.* © 4/14/2000

BABY BLUES *daily strip by Rick Kirkman and Jerry Scott.* © 6/20/2001

BABY BLUES *daily strip by Rick Kirkman and Jerry Scott.* © 6/22/2001

HERE COMES THE SON

SUNG TO THE TUNE OF THE BEATLES' "HERE COMES THE SUN"

HERE COMES A SON (doo'n doo-doo)
HERE COMES A SON,
AND I SAY, "IT'S A FRIGHT!"

LITTLE DARLIN', IT WAS A
SHOCK TO SEE YOUR GENDER!
LITTLE DARLIN', WE THOUGHT
A GIRL WAS TO APPEAR!

HERE COMES A SON (doo'n doo-doo)
WE'RE BOTH SO STUNNED,
AND I SAY, "YOU'RE A SIGHT!"

LITTLE DARLIN', THE BLOOD'S
RETURNING TO OUR FACES.
LITTLE DARLIN', WE SEE THE YEARS
THAT YOU'LL BE HERE.

HE IS OUR SON.
LOOK WHAT WE'VE DONE,
AND I SAY, "HE'S JUST RIGHT."

SON, SON, SON, HERE WE COME!
SON, SON, SON - OF-A-GUN!
SON, SON, SON, HERE WE COME!
SON, SON, SON-OF-A-GUN!
SON, SON, SON, HERE WE COME!

LITTLE DARLIN', YOUR VERY
FIRST SUNRISE IS DAWNING.
LITTLE DARLIN', IT'S JUST AN
HOUR SINCE YOU GOT HERE.

HERE COMES THE SUN (doo'n doo-doo)
WE HAVE A SON,
AND I SAY, "IT'S SO RIGHT!"

HERE COMES THE SUN (doo'n doo-doo)
WE HAVE A SON.
IT'S SO RIGHT!
IT'S SO RIGHT!

(WITH APOLOGIES TO
GEORGE HARRISON)

BABY BLUES Sunday page by Rick Kirkman and Jerry Scott. © 4/30/95

HAPPY FATHER'S DAY!

WOW! WHAT'S ALL THIS?

WELL, WE MADE YOU SOME COLD TOAST AND WEAK COFFEE.

OH, GOODIE.

AND AFTER YOU OPEN YOUR PRESENTS, WE'RE GOING TO DISAPPEAR FOR A WHILE, LEAVING YOU TO CLEAN UP THE INCREDIBLE MESS WE LEFT IN THE KITCHEN.

HUH?

THEN WE'RE GOING TO PIN A HUGE UGLY FLOWER ON YOUR SHIRT AND TAKE YOU OUT TO BRUNCH AT A BIG, IMPERSONAL HOTEL RESTAURANT WHERE THEY SERVE VATS OF RUNNY SCRAMBLED EGGS AND UNDERCOOKED BACON THAT TASTE LIKE THEY WERE PREPARED IN A PRISON KITCHEN, AND, OF COURSE, THEY'LL HAVE CHAMPAGNE BY THE PITCHER.

THIS IS BEGINNING TO SOUND A LOT LIKE WHAT WE DID FOR MOTHER'S DAY...

♪ TURNABOUT IS FAIR PLAY! ♪

GET DRESSED! LET'S GO!

YAY!

BABY BLUES Sunday page by Rick Kirkman and Jerry Scott. © 6/18/2000

Hammie and Me

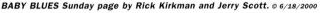

WHEREVER I AM, THERE'S ALWAYS HAM, BUT WE ALL JUST CALL HIM "HAMMIE." WHATEVER I DO, HE WANTS TO, TOO. EVEN WHEN I TELL HIM TO "SCRAMMIE!"

"WHERE ARE YOU GOING? WHAT SHOULD WE DO?" HE WANTS TO KNOW ONE OR THE OTHER. "LEAVE ME ALONE," I WEARILY GROAN. IT AIN'T EASY HAVING A BROTHER.

HE WANTS TO PLAY TRUCKS OR CARS OR TRAINS (IT IS CONSTANTLY SOMETHING WITH WHEELS). HE WON'T DRESS-UP WITH ME ANYMORE EVEN THOUGH HE LOOKS GREAT IN HIGH HEELS.

ONE TIME GRAPE JUICE GOT SPILLED ON THE COUCH, WHEN MOM SAW IT I KNEW SHE WOULD SNAP. I HAD NO DOUBT I'D GET A TIME-OUT, BUT HEROICALLY, HAM TOOK THE RAP.

SO WHEREVER I AM, THERE'S ALWAYS HAM, AND SOMETIMES I THINK I MIGHT SMOTHER. BUT ORNERY, STINKY AND CLINGY ASIDE, THER'RE WORSE THINGS THAN HAVING A BROTHER.

© 2001, BABY BLUES PARTNERSHIP. DIST. BY KING FEATURES SYNDICATE

www.babyblues.com

BABY BLUES Sunday page by Rick Kirkman and Jerry Scott. © 2/18/2001

GRAPHIC OPINION   The tradition of social and political humor on the funnies pages was continued in the 1990s by a number of talented artists. Wiley Miller's innovative 1992 creation, *Non Sequitur* (above and below), was designed to run in both the strip and panel format. Wiley's favorite targets were lawyers, businessmen, doctors, and entertainers. Jim Borgman, whose political cartoons had been distributed by King Features since 1980, launched a short-lived weekly strip in 1994 entitled *Wonk City* (next page, top), which tackled "inside the beltway satire." Barbara Brandon, daughter of *Luther* creator Brumsic Brandon, Jr., became the first black woman with a syndicated feature, when her weekly autobiographical strip, *Where I'm Coming From* (next page, bottom), debuted in 1991.

WONK CITY weekly page by Jim Borgman. © 1994 King Features Syndicate, Inc.

MALLARD FILLMORE Sunday page by Bruce Tinsley. © 1994 King Features Syndicate, Inc.

THE NORM Sunday page by Michael Jantze. © 1996 King Features Syndicate, Inc.

RHYMES WITH ORANGE Sunday page by Hillary Price. © 1995 King Features Syndicate, Inc.

STAYING POWER

A small group of new humor features, introduced in the first half of the decade, held on in the competitive comics market. *Mallard Fillmore* (1994) by Bruce Tinsley provided a conservative alternative to *Doonesbury* on many of the nation's editorial pages. Michael Jantze's *The Norm*, which began as a college strip in the 1980s, was developed at United Media in 1992, and finally sold to King Features in 1996, focused on "Life, Love, Work, and Technology." Hillary Price's *Rhymes With Orange* (1995) was a free-form, gag-based strip without recurring characters. *Pickles* (1991) by Brian Crane starred two senior citizens, Earl and Opal Pickles. Jim Toomey's undersea fantasy, *Sherman's Lagoon*, was launched by Creators Syndicate in 1991 and switched to King Features in 1998.

PICKLES Sunday page by Brian Crane. © 1991 Washington Post Writers Group

SHERMAN'S LAGOON Sunday page by Jim Toomey. © 1998 King Features Syndicate, Inc.

patrick mcdonnell

THE LAUNCHING OF MUTTS in 1994 was the culmination of a life-long ambition for Patrick McDonnell. "When I actually started doing the comic strip it was like a semireligious experience," he recalled. "I realized it was what I was meant to do."

The first episodes of *Mutts* were in a traditional gag-a-day format with occasional running themes. McDonnell soon began featuring two-week stories and found he enjoyed the challenge of extended continuity. He has done stories that have lasted for as long as four weeks. "I think one of the exciting things about comics is not just to tell jokes but to have stories that people can get involved in," he says.

McDonnell initially would do five weeks of strips in four weeks, and then take a week off. The pressure of meeting daily deadlines eventually forced him to change this routine. He now produces a week of strips at a time, often working seven days a week with infrequent breaks.

After outlining his stories at the beginning of each sequence, he continues to add and refine the material while he is drawing the individual strips. "I'm writing and drawing and doing concepts all at the same time," McDonnell explains. "Every day is a surprise." He does the inking and lettering last, as well as the coloring of the Sunday page, which is the final chore in completing each week of work.

Accustomed to using half-tones in his magazine cartoons, McDonnell experimented with "Duo-Shade," a commercial paper that revealed tonal patterns when a clear liquid chemical was applied. This gave the *Mutts* dailies a black-and-white-and-gray "painted" quality. He eventually abandoned this technique when he became concerned about exposure to the chemicals and discovered he preferred a cleaner black-and-white look.

Like most syndicated cartoonists, McDonnell works at home and has very few opportunities to bask in his newfound fame and fortune. "I'm not looking for celebrity," he claims. He receives regular feedback in the form of fan mail, but he produces his strip primarily to amuse himself. He hopes that his readers will enjoy it too, but realizes he has no control over the public's taste.

McDonnell often creates *Mutts* Sunday pages that pay homage to George Herriman's *Krazy Kat*, his primary source of inspiration. Subtle color palettes, delicate line work, and distinctive dialogue convey a mood that is more lyrical than laughable. McDonnell transforms his Sunday logo panels (which many newspapers don't use, for space reasons) into re-creations of famous masterpieces of art and cartooning. He has done graphic tributes to Degas, Dalí, Warhol, McCay, Crumb, and Kurtzman. Readers delight in trying to match the subject referenced in the title panel to the theme of that day's strip.

McDonnell has no specific policy against licensing, but because he devotes all of his energy toward producing *Mutts*, he has little time to think about other projects. He has approved a few items, including dolls of Earl and Mooch made in Japan, but has apprehensions about adapting his characters to animation. He does not relish the idea of battling with Hollywood producers for creative control.

His opinions about the current state of newspaper comics come from a highly personal perspective. "I'm doing the exact comic strip I want to do and it's getting printed and people are reading it and writing me letters saying they like it," he explains. His experiences convince him that "the potential of the art form is always there for it to be anything it wants to be. I wouldn't close the patent office yet. There are still people who love cartoons."

McDonnell is as much a fan of the art form as his readers. "I love comic strips—words and pictures, pen and ink, black and white," he explains. "I love the music in the line, the rhythm of a gag, the variation on a theme. I love repetition. I love repetition."

MUTTS daily strip by Patrick McDonnell. © 3/17/95

MUTTS daily strip by Patrick McDonnell. © 9/13/94

MUTTS daily strip by Patrick McDonnell. © 9/19/94

MUTTS daily strip by Patrick McDonnell. © 9/20/94

MUTTS daily strip by Patrick McDonnell. © 5/20/95

MUTTS daily strip by Patrick McDonnell. © 8/30/95

MUTTS daily strip by Patrick McDonnell. © 4/6/96

MUTTS daily strip by Patrick McDonnell. © 5/21/96

MUTTS daily strip by Patrick McDonnell. © 1/19/98

MUTTS Sunday page by Patrick McDonnell (logo panel after Edgar Degas). © 10/19/97

MUTTS Sunday page by Patrick McDonnell (logo panel after Bob Kane). © 10/26/97

MUTTS Sunday page by Patrick McDonnell (logo panel after Maxfield Parrish). © 11/9/97

MUTTS Sunday page by Patrick McDonnell (logo panel after Hiroshige). © 1/4/98

MUTTS daily strip by Patrick McDonnell. © 1/9/97

MUTTS daily strip by Patrick McDonnell. © 1/13/97

MUTTS daily strip by Patrick McDonnell. © 1/15/97

MUTTS daily strip by Patrick McDonnell. © 1/17/97

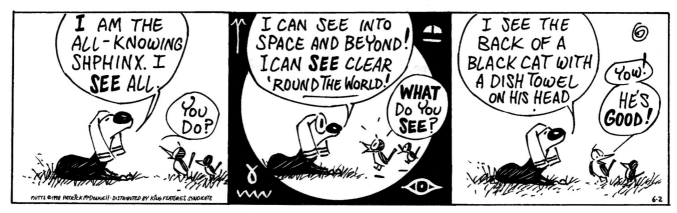

MUTTS daily strip by Patrick McDonnell. © 6/2/98

MUTTS daily strip by Patrick McDonnell. © 4/23/99

MUTTS daily strip by Patrick McDonnell. © 9/18/99

MUTTS daily strip by Patrick McDonnell. © 11/13/2000

MUTTS Sunday page by Patrick McDonnell. © 10/13/96

MUTTS Sunday page by Patrick McDonnell. © 4/14/96

MUTTS Sunday page by Patrick McDonnell. © 11/1/98

MUTTS Sunday page by Patrick McDonnell (logo panel after Jack Kirby). © 8/8/99

MUTTS Sunday page by Patrick McDonnell (logo panel inspired by a silent movie poster). © 9/12/99

MUTTS Sunday page by Patrick McDonnell (logo panel inspired by an African cloth design). © 10/22/2000

MUTTS Sunday page by Patrick McDonnell (logo panel after Gustav Klimt). © 2/18/2001

IN THE BLEACHERS daily panel by Steve Moore. © 8/4/95 Tribune Media Services, Inc. All rights reserved. Used by permission

It all made sense later that evening.

BALLARD STREET daily panel by Jerry Van Amerongen. © 1996 Creators Syndicate, Inc.

BEYOND THE FAR SIDE

Among the single-panel features that helped fill the void when Gary Larson retired in 1995 were *In the Bleachers*, a sports-oriented panel created by Steve Moore in 1986; *Ballard Street* by Jerry Van Amerongen, which started as a strip in 1990 and evolved into a panel in 1994; *Pluggers* (1993) by Jeff MacNelly, which starred Andy Bear and all the folks from Pluggerville and accepted gag ideas from real "pluggers"; and *Speed Bump* (1994) by Dave Coverly, which was recognized as Best Panel of the Year by the National Cartoonists Society in 1995.

THANKS, SON... GRAB A SEAT, THE FIGHT'S STARTING.

THANKS TO
Hardy Davis
WRITE TO PLUGGERS,
P.O. BOX 66, FLINT HILL VA 22627
(E-MAIL: JEFF@PLUGGERS.COM)

To a plugger, love means never having to get your own beer.

PLUGGERS daily panel by Jeff MacNelly. © 12/26/94 Tribune Media Services, Inc. All rights reserved. Used by permission

HOW'S MY DRAWING?
1-800-894-1616

SPEED BUMP daily panel by Dave Coverly. © 1995 Creators Syndicate, Inc.

FUNKY WINKERBEAN *daily strip by Tom Batiuk.* © 12/2/86 King Features Syndicate, Inc.

FUNKY WINKERBEAN *daily strip by Tom Batiuk.* © 1/30/99 King Features Syndicate, Inc.

THE "TRAGICS"   During the 1980s and 1990s a number of cartoonists tackled serious subjects in their strips. In addition to Lynn Johnston (homosexuality) and Ray Billingsley (drug abuse), Tom Batiuk courageously examined such issues as teenage suicide, violence, and smoking in *Funky Winkerbean*. A 1986 series provided a sympathetic view of teen pregnancy (top), and in 1999 Batiuk did a moving story on breast cancer (above) that was reprinted in the acclaimed book *Lisa's Story*. *Crankshaft*, a second feature Batiuk co-created with Chuck Ayers in 1987, focused on another contemporary crisis in 1996, when one of the main characters, Lucy McKenzie, was diagnosed with Alzheimer's disease (below).

CRANKSHAFT *daily strip by Tom Batiuk & Chuck Ayers.* © 1/29/96 Media Graphics. Used by permission of Universal Press Syndicate. All rights reserved

LIBERTY MEADOWS -
aNimal saNctuary for
creatures who have
lost their natural
habitats - or their minds.

FRANK - resident
aNimal doctor.
Neurotic, iNsecure,
Pessimistic and
siNgle.

DEAN - a male chauvinistic
pig and ex-college fraternity
mascot. The epitome of manhood
from yesteryear. Resides at
Liberty Meadows for detox.

BRANDY - animal
Psychologist.
iNtelligeNt,
idealistic and
beautiful. constantly
worries about her
weight.

LESLIE -
hypochondriac
bullfrog and
ralph's best
friend. once
almost named
the village
idiot but scored
poorly in the
compulsory
swimsuit
round.

RALPH - a midget
circus bear who was
rescued from an
abusive trainer.
special talent: can
eat pudding through
a straw.

TRUMAN -
a duckling. childlike
and innocent. openly
cries whenever he
hears "puff the
magic dragon"

LIBERTY MEADOWS cast © 1997

All Liberty Meadows strips © Creators Syndicate, Inc. Courtesy of Insight Studios Group

FRANK CHO   One of the most original comic-strip creations of the 1990s was Frank Cho's *Liberty Meadows*. Cho, a young Korean-born cartoonist, was signed to a contract with Creators Syndicate in 1995 but wanted to finish college before launching his strip in 1997. A gifted draftsman and designer, Cho blended fluid penmanship with innovative layouts and clever self-referential humor. The *Liberty Meadows* Sunday pages provided showcases for his impressive graphic technique, which was influenced by great pen-and-ink artists of the past, such as Franklin Booth, Howard Pyle, and Joseph Clement Coll. Set in a wildlife preserve and animal shelter, the plots revolved around the romantic tension between Brandy, an animal psychologist, and Frank, a veterinarian. A favorite among loyal readers of *Liberty Meadows*, the buxom Brandy turned off some editors, limiting the strip's chances for success. Cho decided to terminate *Liberty Meadows* at the end of 2001, with a cliff-hanger about Brandy's wedding. This story reached its conclusion in a special publication sold only in comic-book shops in 2002. Cho plans to continue *Liberty Meadows* in a comic-book format and pursue projects in other fields of cartooning.

SELF-CARICATURE by Frank Cho

LIBERTY MEADOWS daily strip by Frank Cho. © 8/21/97

LIBERTY MEADOWS Sunday pages by Frank Cho. © 1997–1999

jerry scott & jim borgman

JERRY SCOTT'S SECOND co-creation is produced differently from his first. The ideas for *Baby Blues* are scripted on paper whereas the gags for *Zits* are drawn as rough sketches. Scott, who lives in California, talks with his partner, Jim Borgman, in Cincinnati almost every day on the phone to discuss ideas. He then draws up the gags and faxes them to Borgman, who refines the layouts by changing the expressions or adjusting the perspective. The drawings are often faxed back and forth until both artists are satisfied.

"It's a real, kind of, sloppy arrangement where we both do about three-fourths of the work," explained Scott in an interview. "Both Jerry and I originate and write strip ideas, and we both draw, compose, and design the strip," added Borgman.

The product of this unique collaboration is one of the most visually innovative comic strips to come along in years. Scott and Borgman experiment constantly with the artwork. Daily strips often consist of multilayered, overlapping images and panels-within-panels. The Sunday pages can be conventional six- or eight-panel sequences or wildly creative compositions with fractured borders, spectacular special effects, and vivid coloring. Borgman's graphic pyrotechnics are the perfect complement to Scott's carefully designed layouts.

Scott and Borgman also make liberal use of the visualization techniques Bill Watterson introduced in *Calvin and Hobbes*. The perceptions and fantasies of fifteen-year-old Jeremy Duncan, the star of *Zits*, are shared with the readers. Jeremy's reaction to his mother's new haircut (clownish) or his take on his father's limited computing skills (gorilla-like) are hilariously depicted rather than merely implied. The strip provides a refreshing contrast to the talking-head graphics that dominate contemporary comics pages.

Zits accurately captures the awkwardness of the teenage years. Although Borgman's son Dylan, who was born in 1983, provides inspiration, he is not the model for Jeremy. Scott develops most of the material by observation and reflection.

"My sisters both have teenagers and I also pick up ideas from newspapers," Scott explains. "A lot is from memory too."

The majority of gags revolve around Jeremy, who self-reflectively describes himself as "a high school freshman with, thank God, four good friends but other than that a seriously boring life in a seriously boring town made livable only by the knowledge that someday in the far-off future at least this will all be over and you'll turn sixteen and get a driver's license which you so richly deserve and then life will finally be good. Oh, and your parents are seriously ruining your life."

In addition to Jeremy and his parents, Walt and Connie Duncan, the cast has expanded since the strip's debut in July 1997. Hector Garcia is Jeremy's best "amigo" and plays in "Goat Cheese Pizza," one of the ever-changing names for a rock band that also includes Tim and Pierce. Sara Toomey is Jeremy's sometimes girlfriend, and among the other high school classmates are know-it-all Brittany, the inseparable RichandAmy, and Zuma, Redondo, and LaJolla, members of "The Posse." Jeremy's overachieving older brother, Chad, occasionally returns home from college.

Both cartoonists carry a heavy workload. Borgman continues to produce editorial cartoons for the *Cincinnati Enquirer* and King Features Syndicate. "The strip lets me get away from political thoughts, which refreshes that part of my brain," says Borgman. He is also less tempted to compromise his more serious work with unnecessary humor.

Scott works ten hours a day on *Zits* and *Baby Blues*. "I'm certainly busier than I've ever been in my life," he says. "But I'm having a lot of fun."

Zits was voted the Best Comic Strip of the Year in 1999 and 2000 and, in 2002, it passed the 1,000-newspaper mark in circulation and Jerry Scott won the Reuben Award. The unappealing name of the feature, originally suggested as a joke by Scott, hasn't hurt its success. *Zits* just keeps on growing and growing.

ZITS daily strip by Jerry Scott and Jim Borgman. © *1/26/98*

All Zits strips © Zits Partnership. Reprinted with special permissions of King Features Syndicate, Inc.

ZITS daily strip by Jerry Scott and Jim Borgman. © 7/8/97

ZITS daily strip by Jerry Scott and Jim Borgman. © 7/10/97

ZITS daily strip by Jerry Scott and Jim Borgman. © 7/18/97

ZITS daily strip by Jerry Scott and Jim Borgman. © 7/22/97

ZITS daily strip by Jerry Scott and Jim Borgman. © 8/27/97

ZITS daily strip by Jerry Scott and Jim Borgman. © 3/24/98

ZITS daily strip by Jerry Scott and Jim Borgman. © 8/28/98

ZITS daily strip by Jerry Scott and Jim Borgman. © 12/4/98

ZITS Sunday page by Jerry Scott and Jim Borgman. © 4/26/98

ZITS Sunday page by Jerry Scott and Jim Borgman. © 6/28/98

ZITS Sunday page by Jerry Scott and Jim Borgman. © 10/26/98

ZITS daily strip by Jerry Scott and Jim Borgman. © 4/1/99

ZITS daily strip by Jerry Scott and Jim Borgman. © 4/19/99

ZITS daily strip by Jerry Scott and Jim Borgman. © 8/4/99

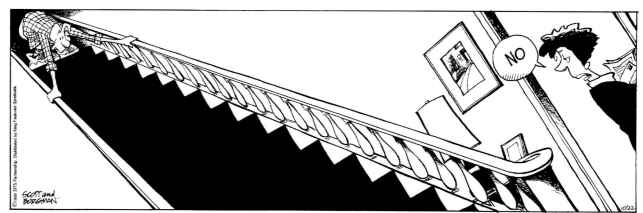

ZITS daily strip by Jerry Scott and Jim Borgman. © 10/22/99

ZITS Sunday page by Jerry Scott and Jim Borgman. © 3/21/99

ZITS Sunday page by Jerry Scott and Jim Borgman. © 7/22/2001

ZITS Sunday page by Jerry Scott and Jim Borgman. © 9/9/2001

COMPETITION AND SURVIVAL

Breaking into the comics business has never been easy, but in recent years the opportunities for success have become even more limited. The five major syndicates release only about a dozen new features each year combined, and these must compete for the remaining slots not taken up by established strips and panels. There are fewer newspapers, devoting less space to the comics, which makes the prospects even more daunting. Only about 40 percent of new comics survive beyond the second year of syndication.

On the following pages is a selection of features that were introduced between 1990 and 2002. Some have managed to build up a respectable list of subscribers and could last well into the next decade and beyond. Others might not survive much past the publication of this book. All are promising creations by talented cartoonists who worked hard to develop their ideas just to be selected from the thousands of submissions received annually by the syndicates. Editors cannot predict what will catch on with readers, so they must remain open-minded to new offerings. The potential rewards for those who succeed are great. It is still a business in which the dreams of an aspiring artist can be transformed into fulfilling reality.

PEARLS BEFORE SWINE *daily strip by Stephan Pastis.* © *1/31/2002 Stephan Pastis. Distributed by United Feature Syndicate, Inc.*

THE DUPLEX *daily strip by Glenn McCoy.* © *4/26/93 Glenn McCoy. Used by permission of Universal Press Syndicate. All rights reserved*

SOUP TO NUTZ *daily strip by Rick Stromoski.* © *4/19/2005 by Rick Stromoski. Distributed by NEA, Inc*

CUL DE SAC *daily strip by Richard Thompson.* © *10/17/07 by Richard Thompson. Distributed by Universal Press Syndicate.*

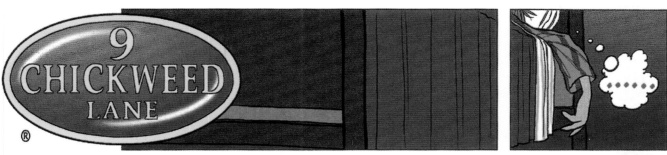

9 CHICKWEED LANE Sunday page by Brooke McEldowney. © 10/6/97 United Feature Syndicate, Inc.

OVER THE HEDGE Sunday page by Michael Fry and T. Lewis. © 9/17/95 United Feature Syndicate, Inc.

STONE SOUP Sunday page by Jan Eliot. © 1/28/95 Jan Eliot. Used by permission of Universal Press Syndicate. All rights reserved

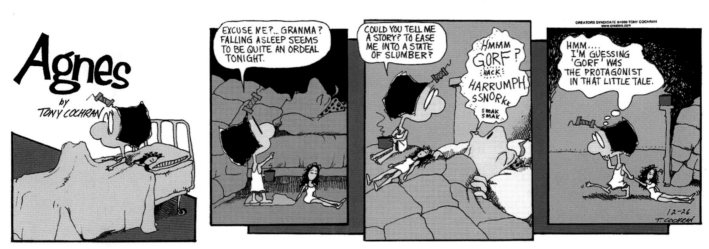

AGNES Sunday page by Tony Cochran. © 12/26/99 Creators Syndicate, Inc.

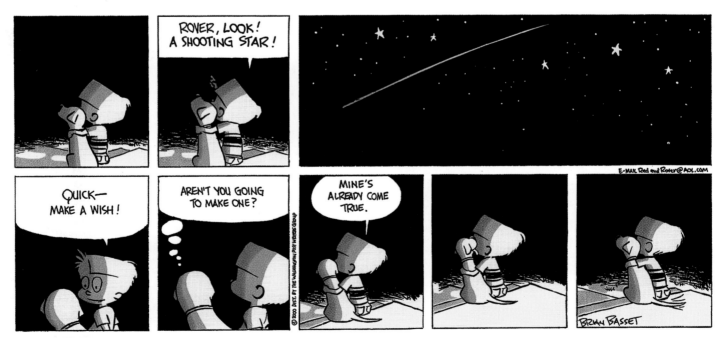

RED AND ROVER Sunday page by Brian Basset. © 2000 Brian Bassett. Distributed by the Washington Post Writers Group

BLONDIE *Sunday page by Dean Young and Denis Lebrun (a pre-Thanksgiving salute).* © 10/28/2001 King Features Syndicate, Inc.

A TRIBUTE TO HEROES

In response to the September 11 terrorist attacks on America, National Cartoonists Society president Steve McGarry, at the suggestion of Patrick McDonnell, invited each of its members to create a special cartoon for Thanksgiving Day, November 22, 2001. More than 125 cartoonists participated in the event by providing graphic tributes to rescue workers, survivors, and those who lost their lives in the senseless acts of violence. The Network for Good website address was included in many of the strips and panels, which helped direct potential donors to relief organizations of their choice. The original artwork was also auctioned off on-line, raising close to $50,000 for the September 11th Fund. Once again, the nation's cartoonists had used the power of their pens to focus attention on an issue of serious concern to their readers.

"Don't worry, PJ, we'll rebuild! It's the 'Merican way."

THE FAMILY CIRCUS *daily panel by Jeff and Bil Keane.* © 11/22/2001 King Features Syndicate, Inc.

HI AND LOIS *daily strip by Brian and Greg Walker and Chance Browne.* © 11/22/2001 King Features Syndicate, Inc.

658   *the comics*

DOONESBURY Sunday page by Garry Trudeau. © 2/13/94 G.B. Trudeau. Used by permission of Universal Press Syndicate. All rights reserved

the twenty-first century

ARE NEWSPAPERS a dying medium? Is the future of the funnies in cyberspace? Will there be a new technology that will revolutionize graphic entertainment? These questions will be answered in the coming years.

Newspapers and syndicates now have websites on the internet where readers can create their own personal comics pages and view a selection of features that are updated each day. Although this a convenient way to get a daily dose of comics, the graphics don't look the same on a computer screen as they do in the newspapers. There is something pleasing and permanent about the clean, black-and-white lines of a daily comic strip and the bold, primary colors of a Sunday page when they are printed on paper.

Perhaps someday, in the not-too-distant future, an enterprising newspaper editor will experiment with enlarging the comics and printing them on higher-quality paper. Readers would welcome seeing their favorite features in a more luxurious format. The newspaper's circulation might take off. Competing papers would be forced to print their comics the same way. Publishers would discover, as Joseph Pulitzer and William Randolph Hearst did in 1896, that the funnies will sell newspapers when they are displayed prominently and promoted aggressively.

As long as there is money to be made in the comics business, cartoonists will continue to come up with new ideas. The possibilities are limitless. Every decade or so, a fresh creation leaps off the funnies pages and captures the public's attention. This will not change.

Cartoonists will adapt to new technologies. Cartoons can be drawn on anything from cave walls to digital tablets. The future of the art form is not limited by the fate of the print medium.

Humans have a basic need to communicate, and cartoons are one of the most effective means of self-expression. When words and pictures are blended together successfully, they can tell stories, state opinions, or convey feelings in a simple, direct way. A well-crafted cartoon may elicit a gasp of surprise, a howl of laughter, a sigh of recognition, or a mixture of emotions.

In the past half-century, thousands of cartoonists have created millions of images that have been enjoyed by billions of readers. In the history of human communication, this is but a brief flash of our creative potential. The words and pictures will continue to captivate us for as long as we have the desire to be entertained and enlightened.

ACKNOWLEDGMENTS

The author would like to thank the following individuals and organizations for their invaluable assistance in producing this book:

Artists: Jim Borgman, Pat Brady, Chance Browne, Frank Cho, Brian Crane, Rick Detorie, Jerry Dumas, Will Eisner, Ron Ferdinand, Guy Gilchrist, Bud Grace, Marcus Hamilton, Johnny Hart, Michael Jantze, Lynn Johnston, Bil and Jeff Keane, Gary Larson, Mell Lazarus, Patrick McDonnell, John Cullen Murphy, Nina Paley, Dan Piraro, Arnold Roth, Jim Scancarelli, Jerry Scott, Leonard Starr, Garry Trudeau, and Mort Walker.

Other individuals: Rafaella Allesandrio, David Applegate, David Astor, Helen W. Bertholet, Bill Blackbeard, Katie Burke, Mark Burstein, Jim Carlsson, Russ Cochran, Nikki Columbus, Bill Crouch, Scott Daley, Mark Evanier, Gill Fox, Jim Gauthier, Steve Geppi, Jack Gilbert, Ed Glisson, Carole Goodman, Ron Goulart, Bruce Hamilton, R. C. Harvey, Eric Himmel, Tom Horvitz, Jud Hurd, Bill Janocha, Harry Katz, Carolyn Kelly, Pete Kelly, Denis Kitchen, Judith Kliban, Howard Lowery, Ricardo Martinez, Richard Marschall, Matt Masterson, Toni Mendez, Richard Olson, Trina Robbins, Mike Seeley, Richard Slovak, David Stanford, Catherine Walker, Malcolm Whyte, Art Wood, and Craig Yoe.

Syndicates: King Features—Jim Cavett, Mark Johnson, Jay Kennedy, Karen Moy, and Claudia Smith. United Media—Amy Lago and Maura Peters. Universal Press—Lee Salem and Mary Suggett. Tribune Media Services—Jan Bunch and Lee Hall. Creators—Christina Lee, Rick Newcombe, Lori Sheehey, and Mary Ann Sugawara. Washington Post Writers Group—Bethany Cain and Suzanne Whelton. Copley News Service—Glenda Winders.

Organizations and institutions: American Color—Andy Olsen. Boston University—Sean Noel. Cartoon Art Museum—Jenny Robb Dietzen. Cartoon Research Library, Ohio State University—Lucy Shelton Caswell. FarWorks—Melissa Irons. Frye Art Museum—Richard West. Johnny Hart Studios—Perri Hart. Illustration House—Kim Deitz, Roger Reed, and Walt Reed. International Museum of Cartoon Art—Stephen Charla, Alexis Faro, and Jeanne Greever. Lynn Johnston Productions—Laura Pische. Hank Ketcham Enterprises—Dottie Roberson. Rosebud Productions—Jody Boyman. Storyopolis—Fonda Snyder.

ARTICLES

The following comics-related periodicals are currently being published regularly:

Comic Buyer's Guide. Published monthly by F + W Publications, Inc., 700 E. State St., Iola, WI 54990.

The Comics Journal. Published monthly by Fantagraphics Books, Inc., 7563 Lake City Way N.E., Seattle, WA 98115.

Editor & Publisher. Published monthly by BPI Communications, Inc. 770 Broadway, New York, NY 10003.

Hogan's Alley. Published semi-annually by Bull Moose Publishing Corp., P.O. Box 4784, Atlanta, GA 30362.

The following comics-related periodicals are no longer being published:

Cartoonist PROfiles. 146 issues were published quarterly between March 1969 and June 2005 by Cartoonist PROfiles Inc., 281 Bayberry Lane, Westport, CT 06430.

Inks. Twelve issues were published tri-annually between February 1994 and November 1997 by the Ohio State University Press, 1070 Carmack Road, Columbus, OH 43110.

Nemo. Thirty-two issues were published semi-annually between June 1983 and January 1992 by Fantagraphic Books, Inc. 7563 Lake City Way N.E., Seattle, WA 98115.

NOTES

The following articles and books were quoted directly or referred to for specific facts. The listings are by chapter and subject, in order of appearance.

INTRODUCTION

Sunday papers: Bevona, Donald E. "First Sunday Editions Had No Place in Home." *Editor & Publisher,* June 27, 1959.

Early syndicates: Emery, Michael, Edwin Emery, and Nancy L. Roberts. *The Press in America.* Boston: Allyn and Bacon, 2000, pp. 248–49.

Pulitzer and Hearst: Turner, Hy. "This Was Park Row!" *Editor & Publisher,* June 27, 1959.

Richard F. Outcault: Olson, Richard D. "Richard Fenton Outcault's Yellow Kid." *Inks: Cartoon and Comic Art Studies,* vol. 2, no. 3, November 1995.

The Yellow Kid: Blackbeard, Bill. *The Yellow Kid.* Northampton, Mass.: Kitchen Sink Press, 1995.

Daily comic strips: Harvey, R. C. "Bud Fisher and the Daily Comic Strip." *Inks: Cartoon and Comic Art Studies,* vol. 1, no. 1, February 1994.

First comics page: Blackbeard, Bill, and Dale Crain, eds. *The Comic Strip Century.* 2 vols. Englewood Cliffs, N.J.: O.G. Publishing Corp., 1995.

National syndication: Collings, James L. "Personalities and Piracy in Early Syndicate Days." *Editor & Publisher,* June 27, 1959.

King Features: Koenigsberg, M. *King News: An Autobiography.* Philadelphia and New York: F. A. Stokes Company, 1941.

Syndication and circulation: "The Funny Papers." *Fortune,* April 1933.

Syndication process: Interviews with syndicate comics editors in *Cartoonist PROfiles:* Sarah Gillespie (UFS) 3/86, 12/87, 9/89. David Hendin (UFS) 6/85, 6/93. Jay Kennedy (KFS) 9/89, 3/90, 9/91, 9/94. Lee Salem (UPS) 3/82, 12/88, 9/89, 6/95. David Seidman 3/89, 6/89, 9/89, 12/89, 6/90. Evelyn Smith (TMS) 9/89, 9/90. Bill Yates (KFS) 3/89.

Contemporary cartooning: Nordling, Lee. *Your Career in the Comics.* Kansas City: Andrews and McMeel, 1995.

Creative challenges: Thomas, Keith L. "Comic Relief." *Atlanta Constitution,* May 5, 1991.

Rivenburg, Roy. "Sunset Strips." *Los Angeles Times,* Dec. 31, 1995.

Comics decline: Marschall, Richard. *America's Great Comic-Strip Artists.* New York: Abbeville Press, 1989.

Blackbeard, Bill, and Dale Crain, eds. *The Comic Strip Century.* 2 vols. Englewood Cliffs, N.J.: O.G. Publishing Corp., 1995.

THE POSTWAR YEARS

World War II: Monchak, S. J. "Cartoonists Important Factor in Keeping Nation's Morale." *Editor & Publisher,* Sept. 12, 1942.

Caniff, Milton. "Comic Strips at War." *Vogue,* July 15, 1943.

Marschall, Rick. "The World War II Cartoonist Corps." *Nemo,* June 1985.

Vaughn, Don. "War-Toons." *The Retired Officer Magazine,* June 1998.

Newsprint: Hollis, Daniel W. *The Media in America.* Santa Barbara, Calif.: ABC-CLIO, 1995, pp. 192–94.

Size reduction: Goulart, Ron. *The Funnies: 100 Years of American Comic Strips.* Holbrook, Mass.: Adams Publishing, 1995, p. 229.

Ivey, Jim, and Allan Holtz. "Stripper's Guide Q&A." *Hogan's Alley,* no. 5, 1998, pp. 35–36.

George McManus: Sheridan, Martin. *Comics and Their Creators.* Boston: Hale, Cushman & Flint, 1942, p. 46.

Postwar circulation: Emery, Michael, Edwin Emery, and Nancy L. Roberts. *The Press in America.* Boston: Allyn and Bacon, 2000, p. 352.

Syndicate business: Staunton, Helen M. "Syndicates Enjoyed Good Year in 1946." *Editor & Publisher,* Dec. 28, 1946.

Milton Caniff: Staunton, Helen M. "Steve Canyon—Milton Caniff Unveils His New Strip." *Editor & Publisher,* Nov. 23, 1946.

Jenson, Chris. "Setting the Stage." *Steve Canyon Magazine,* no. 1, 1983.

Saba, Arn. "Milton Caniff—An Interview with One of the Masters of Comic Art." *The Comics Journal,* no. 108, May 1986.

Al Capp: Staunton, Helen M. "Capp Sues Syndicate on $14,000,000 Claim." *Editor & Publisher,* July 19, 1947.

"Li'l Abner's Mad Capp." *Newsweek,* Nov. 24, 1947.

McMaster, Jane. "Li'l Abner Sideline is Shmoopendous." *Editor & Publisher,* July 16, 1949.

"Die Monstersinger." *Time,* Nov. 6, 1950.

Capp, Al. "Why I Let Abner Marry." *Life,* March 31, 1952.

Ellison, Harlan, and Dave Schreiner. Introduction to *Li'l Abner Meets the Shmoo.* Northampton, Mass.: Kitchen Sink Press, 1992.

Chic Young: Alexander, Jack. "The Dagwood and Blondie Man." *Saturday Evening Post,* April 10, 1948.

Superman: Hill, Roger. "Comic Books and Comic Art." *Sotheby's.* Auction catalog, Sale 6588. June 18, 1994.

Will Eisner: Yronwode, Catherine. *The Art of Will Eisner*. Princeton, Wis.: Kitchen Sink Press, 1982.

Censorship: Rochelle, Ogden J. "Syndicates Tighten Up Taboos in Comic Strips." *Editor & Publisher*, Dec. 11, 1948.

Teenagers: Hine, Robert. *The Rise and Fall of the American Teenager*. New York: Avon Books, 1999, pp. 8–9.

Soap-opera strips: Andriola, Alfred. "The Story Strips." *Cartoonist PROfiles* #15, September 1972.

Crockett Johnson: Harvey, R. C. "Cushlamochree! Their Creators Abandoned Them!" *Comic Buyer's Guide* #1225, May 9, 1997.

Walt Kelly: "Our Archives of Culture: Enter the Comics and Pogo." *Newsweek*, June 21, 1954.

Maley, Don. "Walt Kelly Muses on his 20 Years of Playing Possum." *Editor & Publisher*, April 19, 1969.

Mastrangelo, Joseph. "Unforgettable Walt Kelly." *Reader's Digest*, July 1974.

Thompson, Steve. "Highlights of Pogo" from *A Retrospective Exhibit of Walt Kelly*. Ohio State University Libraries, 1988.

Watterson, Bill. "Some Thoughts on Pogo," adapted from a speech at Ohio State University. *The Comics Journal* #140, February 1991.

National Cartoonists Society: Becker, Stephen. *Comic Art in America*. New York: Simon and Schuster, 1959, pp. 285–87.

Harvey, R. C. "Tales of the Founding of the National Cartoonists Society." *Cartoonist PROfiles* #109, March 1996, and #110, June 1996.

THE FIFTIES

Television: "Comics and TV" editorial. *Editor & Publisher*, June 2, 1951.

McMaster, Jane. "51 to Test 'Other Media' Comics Trend." *Editor & Publisher*, Dec. 23, 1950.

Romance vs. adventure: Brandenburg, George A. "Soap Opera in Comics?" *Editor & Publisher*, April 22, 1950.

Top strips (1950 and 1962): "Die Monstersinger." *Time*, Nov. 6, 1950.

White, David Manning, and Robert H. Abel, eds. *The Funnies: An American Idiom*. New York: The Free Press of Glencoe/Macmillan, 1963.

Story strips vs. humor strips: Harvey, R. C. Caniff quote from unpublished biography.

Mort Walker: Walker, Mort. *The Best of Beetle Bailey*. Bedford, N.Y.: Comicana Books, 1984.

———. *Mort Walker's Private Scrapbook*. Kansas City: Andrews McMeel Publishing, 2000.

Charles Schulz: Johnson, Rheta Grimsley. *Good Grief: The Story of Charles Schulz*. New York: Pharos Books, 1989.

Schulz, Charles. *Peanuts: A Golden Celebration*. New York: HarperCollins Publishers, 1999.

Harvey, R. C. "The Age of Schulz." *Hogan's Alley* #8, 2000.

Hank Ketcham: Ketcham, Hank. *The Merchant of Dennis*. New York: Abbeville Press, 1990.

Herald Tribune Syndicate: Collings, James L. "Miss Peach Peachy Strip for Herald Trib." *Editor & Publisher*, Jan. 26, 1957.

"He Was Going to be a Cartoonist, By Gosh," profile of Johnny Hart. *Editor & Publisher*, Dec. 28, 1957.

"Roth's 'Almanac.'" *Editor & Publisher*, April 11, 1958.

"Jaffees 'Tall Tales' Good for Tall Laughs." *Editor & Publisher*, Sept. 6, 1958.

Capp comments: McMaster, Jane. "Editor, Capp Disagree on Opinions in Strips" and "Capp's Position on Strip Opinion Draws Dissent." *Editor & Publisher*, June 10 and 24, 1950.

Harold Gray: Smith, Bruce. *The History of Little Orphan Annie*. New York: Ballantine Books, 1982, p. 67.

Comics investigation: Scholz, Carter. "Seduction of the Ignorant." *The Comics Journal* #80, March 1983.

Capp-Fisher feud: Maeder, Jay. "Spitting on Pictures." *New York Daily News*, Sept. 18, 1998.

"Fisher's End." *Hogan's Alley* #8, 2000.

Raymond death: "Alex Raymond 'Kirby' Artist Dies in Crash." *Editor & Publisher*, Sept. 15, 1956.

Schumer, Arlen. "Alex Raymond's Last Ride." *Hogan's Alley* #3, 1996.

Jack Cole suicide: Goulart, Ron. "Betsy and Me and Jack Cole." *Hogan's Alley* #6, 1999.

Spiegelman, Art. "Forms Stretched to Their Limits." *The New Yorker*, April 19, 1999.

Hearst passing: Knoll, Erwin. "Chief had Direct Control of Syndicate Operation." *Editor & Publisher*, Aug. 18, 1951.

"The King is Dead." *Time*, Aug. 20, 1951.

THE SIXTIES

Newspaper business: "ANPA Statement on the Newspaper Business." *Editor & Publisher*, March 16, 1963.

Advertising: Erwin, Ray. "Editors Slash at Comics Sale to Advertising Agencies." *Editor & Publisher*, Feb. 13, 1960.

Licensing: Maley, Don. "Super Roads to Riches are Paved with Daily Comics." *Editor & Publisher*, Nov. 30, 1968.

Spin-off strips: "TV's 'Flintstones' Join Papers, Too." *Editor & Publisher*, Sept. 23, 1961.

Erwin, Ray. "'Bullwinkle' Moose Becomes Comic Strip." *Editor & Publisher*, Feb. 10, 1962.

"Ken Bald Will Draw 'Dr. Kildare.'" *Editor & Publisher*, June 30, 1962.

Erwin, Ray. "'Ben Casey' Joins Comic Pages Soon." *Editor & Publisher*, Oct. 6, 1962.

Top strips: "Essential Features in Salesman's Poll." *Editor & Publisher*, June 30, 1962.

Soap-opera strips: Erwin, Ray. "Physician Writes 'Rex Morgan, M.D.'" *Editor & Publisher*, Jan. 26, 1963.

Adventure strips: Erwin, Ray. "Don Sherwood Draws 'Dan Flagg' Marine." *Editor & Publisher*, March 9, 1963.

"The Green Berets Land on Comics Page." *Editor & Publisher*, Feb. 12, 1966.

"Pow! Bam! Zap! 'Batman' Returns." *Editor & Publisher*, March 5, 1966.

Violence: "Editors Displeased with Violent Strips." *Editor & Publisher*, June 22, 1968.

Maley, Don. "Violence in Comics Discussed by NCC." *Editor & Publisher*, Oct. 5, 1968.

Brothers, Dr. Joyce. "Violence in Comics." *Cartoonist PROfiles* #7, January 1969.

Social comment: Blank, Dennis. "Comics Aren't Funny Telling Off the World." *Editor & Publisher*, June 25, 1966.

"Comment in the Comics." *Time*, April 9, 1965.

Friedman, Rick. "Feiffer—Cartoonist with a Point of View." *Editor & Publisher*, June 10, 1961.

"Jim Berry Begins Gag Panel Comment." *Editor & Publisher*, Feb. 16, 1963.

"Berry's World." *Cartoonists PROfiles* #7, September 1970.

Erwin, Ray. "Inanimate Objects Converse in Panel." *Editor & Publisher*, April 6, 1963.

"Still Life by Jerry Robinson." *Cartoonist PROfiles* #13, March 1972.

"New Strip Satirizes 'the small society.'" *Editor & Publisher*, April 16, 1966.

New directions: "It's Characterization and Sophistication." *Editor & Publisher*, April 25, 1964.

Humor features: Erwin, Ray. "2 Cartoonists Create New 'Sam's Strip.'" *Editor & Publisher*, July 29, 1961.

"Eek and Meek are Mouse-Like Comics." *Editor & Publisher*, July 31, 1965.

"Of Mice and Howie Schneider." *Cartoonist PROfiles* #2, June 1969.

"Tom Ryan's Cartoon Old West Lampoon" (on *Tumbleweeds*). *Editor & Publisher*, Nov. 13, 1965.

"Wackiest Warriors Follow Chief Redeye." *Editor & Publisher*, June 3, 1967.

"Mort Walker Begins Third Comic Strip" (on *Boner's Ark*). *Editor & Publisher*, Jan. 20, 1968.

Maley, Don. "Beachcomber Strip Hit with Editors" (on *The Dropouts*). *Editor & Publisher*, Aug. 3, 1968.

"'The Dropouts' by Howard Post." *Cartoonist PROfiles* #9, March 1971.

"'Andy Capp' Comic Strip is Imported." *Editor & Publisher*, Aug. 24, 1963.

Dean, Paul. "Reggie Smythe Draws 'Andy Capp' for Belly Laughs and Profit." *Editor & Publisher*, Nov. 16, 1968.

Johnny Hart: "He Was Going to be a Cartoonist, By Gosh." *Editor & Publisher*, Dec. 28, 1957.

"Prehistoric Account of Current Success." *Editor & Publisher*, March 16, 1968.

"'B.C.' by Johnny Hart." *Cartoonist PROfiles* #9, March 1971; #26, June 1975; #48, December 1980; #49, March 1981; and #78, June 1988.

Marschall, Richard. "The Johnny Hart Interview." *Hogan's Alley* #2, 1995.

Bil Keane: "'Family Circle' Round & Round." *Editor & Publisher*, Feb. 27, 1960.

"'Family Circus' has New Baby." *Editor & Publisher*, Aug. 4, 1962.

"Cartoonist Studies to be Arizona Cactus." *Editor & Publisher*, Sept. 28, 1968.

"Report from Paradise Valley." *Cartoonist PROfiles* #5, March 1970.

The Family Circus Treasury. Kansas City: Sheed Andrews and McMeel, 1977.

Ropp, Thomas. "Bil Keane's Illustrated Circus. *Arizona Republic*, Sept. 4, 1983.

Bud Blake: "Bud Blake's 'Tiger' Leads Comic Kids." *Editor & Publisher*, Jan. 30, 1965.

"'Tiger' by Bud Blake." *Cartoonist PROfiles* #29, March 1976.

Family dysfunction: "New Cartoon Hero: 'The Born Loser.'" *Editor & Publisher*, March 20, 1965.

"'The Born Loser' featuring Brutus Thornapple." *Cartoonist PROfiles* #9, March 1971.

"Loafer and Family Generate Laughs" (on *Moose*). *Editor & Publisher*, June 12, 1965.

"'The Lockhorns' Unlock the Fun in Marital Woes." *Editor & Publisher*, May 31, 1969.

Racial integration: Jones, Steven Loring. "From 'Under Cork' to Overcoming: Black Images in the Comics." In *Ethnic Images in the Comics*, ed. Charles Hardy and Gail F. Storm. Philadelphia: The Balch Institute for Ethnic Studies, 1986.

"Comic Strip Plugs Racial Integration" (on *Wee Pals*). *Editor & Publisher*, Jan. 23, 1965.

Carter, Tom. "Cartoonist Morrie Turner." *Essence*, July 1974.

"Morrie Turner." *Cartoonist PROfiles* #6, June 1970.

"'Luther' by Brumsic Brandon, Jr." *Cartoonist PROfiles* #69, March 1986.

"'Quincy' Will Deliver Gags of Inner City." *Editor & Publisher*, June 13, 1970.

"'Quincy' by Ted Shearer." *Cartoonist PROfiles* #11, November 1971.

Maley, Don. "Cartoonist Finds Integrated Strip Poses New Art Problem" (on *Dateline Danger*). *Editor & Publisher*, Aug. 16, 1969.

"Adventure Strip and Column Feature Blacks" (on *Friday Foster*). *Editor & Publisher*, Dec. 6, 1969.

"Lieut. Flap's Friends Break Through Army Censorship." *Editor & Publisher*, Jan. 23, 1971.

Cartoon art: Couperie, Pierre, and Maurice Horn. *A History of the Comic Strip*. New York: Crown Publishers, 1968 (Caniff "Louvre quote" from preface, p. 3. SOCERLID quote, p. 219).

Maley, Don. "'Batman' Made Him a Dropout from J-School" (Jerry Robinson quote). *Editor & Publisher*, Nov. 9, 1968.

THE SEVENTIES

Garry Trudeau: Williamson, Lenora. "Fresh Air from the Campus in Trudeau's 'Doonesbury.'" *Editor & Publisher*, Jan. 16, 1971.

"'Doonesbury': Drawing and Quartering for Fun and Profit." *Time*, Feb. 9, 1976.

"Speech Before Associated Press Managing Editors." Nov. 27, 1984.

Alter, Jonathan. "Real Life with Garry Trudeau." *Newsweek*, Oct. 15, 1990.

Astor, David. "The Wall Street Journal vs. 'Doonesbury.'" *Editor & Publisher*, Dec. 28, 1991.

Carlton, Don. Letter to Bill Janocha. June 28, 1993.

Trudeau, G. B. *Flashbacks: Twenty-Five Years of Doonesbury.* Kansas City: Andrews and McMeel, 1995.

Cathy Guisewite: "'Cathy' by Cathy Guisewite." *Cartoonist PROfiles* #34, June 1977, and #101, March 1994.

Astor, David. "Guisewite Works Overtime on 'Cathy.'" *Editor & Publisher*, June 25, 1983.

Guisewite, Cathy. *Reflections.* Kansas City: Andrews and McMeel, 1991.

———. *Twentieth Anniversary Collection.* Kansas City: Andrews and McMeel, 1996.

Jeff MacNelly: "MacNelly: The Richmond News Leader." *Cartoonist PROfiles* #20, December 1973.

Buchwald, Art. "MacNelly as Seen by Another Artist." In *The Very First Shoe Book.* New York: Avon Books, 1978.

"Jeff MacNelly: An Interview with the Creator of 'Shoe.'" *Clockwatch Review*, 1985.

Daley, Steve. "Poison Pen and A Pink Desoto." *The Washingtonian*, November 1999.

Lynn Johnston: "Best Selling Author Creates Comic Strip." *Editor & Publisher*, Sept. 8, 1979.

Astor, David. "Finding Universality in One Family's Life." *Editor & Publisher*, July 14, 1984.

"'For Better or For Worse' by Lynn Johnston." *Cartoonist PROfiles* #71, September 1986, and #118, June 1998.

Heintjes, Tom. "The Lynn Johnston Interview." *Hogan's Alley* #1, 1994.

Johnston, Lynn. *Remembering Farley: A Tribute to the Life of Our Favorite Cartoon Dog.* Kansas City: Andrews and McMeel, 1996.

———. *The Lives Behind the Lines: 20 Years of For Better or For Worse.* Kansas City: Andrews McMeel Publishing, 1999.

"Comic Relief." *Chatelaine*, March 1997.

Dik Browne: Williamson, Lenora. "Dik Browne Presents 'Hagar the Horrible.'" *Editor & Publisher*, Jan. 20, 1973.

Marschall, Rick. "Browne the Magnificent: On Comics, Commentary and Contentment." *Nemo*, June 1983.

Walker, Brian. *The Best of Hagar the Horrible.* Bedford, N.Y.: Comicana Books, 1985.

Jim Davis: "Fat Cat is Hero of Comic Strip." *Editor & Publisher*, April 22, 1978.

"'Garfield' by Jim Davis." *Cartoonist PROfiles* #40, December 1978; #55, September 1982; #71, September 1986; and #118, June 1998.

Pauer, Frank. "From Gnorm the Gnat to 'Garfield.'" *WittyWorld*, Autumn 1988.

Davis, Jim. *20 Years and Still Kicking: Garfield's Twentieth Anniversary Collection.* New York: Ballantine Books, 1998.

Walker, Brian. "'Garfield' Turns 20." *Collectors Showcase*, May/June 1998.

Humor strips: "Broom-Hilda's Potion of Fun Dispels Gloom." *Editor & Publisher*, April 11, 1970.

"Consistency is Key for New Cartoon Hero" (on *Ziggy*). *Editor & Publisher*, May 5, 1973.

Williamson, Lenora. "Walker and Dumas Producing New Strip" (on *Sam & Silo*). *Editor & Publisher*, April 23, 1977.

James Childress: Maley, Don. "Undaunted Cartoonist Tries for Big Time." *Editor & Publisher*, Feb. 7, 1970.

Williamson, Lenora. "Staff Cartoonist's Strip Makes it to Paperback." *Editor & Publisher*, March 10, 1973.

"Self-Syndicated 'Conchy' Strip Goes National." Oct. 12, 1974.

Ivey, Jim. "Jim Childress . . . Self-Made Man." *Cartoonews* #13, 1976.

Ivey, Jim, and Allan Holtz. "Stripper's Guide—'Conchy.'" *Hogan's Alley* #5, 1998.

Passings: Williamson, Leonora. "Reduced Size of Comics Gets Blamed in 'Pogo' Demise. *Editor & Publisher*, June 21, 1975.

"Cartoonist Al Capp Writes a Letter to the Editor." *Editor & Publisher*, July 19, 1975.

"Dogpatch is Ready for Freddie: After 43 Years, Al Capp Decides to Hang Up His Pen." *Time*, Oct. 17, 1977.

Story-strip survivors: Williamson, Lenora. "'Gasoline Alley' Cartoonist Wins Reuben." *Editor & Publisher*, April 26, 1975.

"Orphan Annie Being Re-Born December." *Editor & Publisher*, Nov. 10, 1979.

"By-Line for 'Prince Valiant' to Change." *Editor & Publisher*, Dec. 8, 1979.

Sci-fi revival: "'Spider-Man' Debuts." *Editor & Publisher*, Nov. 6, 1976.

"'Star Hawks' Debut. *Editor & Publisher*, Aug. 13, 1977.

"'Buck Rogers' Being Re-Launched This Fall." *Editor & Publisher*, June 9, 1979.

Cartoon Museum: Walker, Mort. *Backstage at the Strips.* New York: Mason Charter, 1975.

Williamson, Lenora. "Comics Museum and Hall of Fame Will Open." *Editor & Publisher*, Aug. 10, 1974.

"Museum of Cartoon Art." *Cartoonist PROfiles* #23, September 1974; #30, June 1976; and #38, June 1978.

Museum of Cartoon Art Inklings #s 1–12, fall 1975 to summer 1978.

Cartoon art: Watterson, Bill. *The Calvin and Hobbes Tenth Anniversary Book.* Kansas City: Andrews and McMeel, 1995 (quote from p. 207).

THE EIGHTIES

Gary Larson: Astor, David. "Larson Explores 'The Far Side' of Life." *Editor & Publisher*, July 2, 1983.

Larson, Gary. *The PreHistory of The Far Side.* Kansas City: Andrews and McMeel, 1989.

———. *Last Chapter and Worse.* Kansas City: Andrews and McMeel, 1996.

Tucker, Ken. "Black and White . . . and Read All Over." *Entertainment Weekly*, Oct. 5, 1990.

Far-out humor: Astor, David. "Soaring Popularity for 'Way Out' Comics." *Editor & Publisher*, July 26, 1986.

"How Dan Piraro Came to Draw 'Bizarro.'" *Editor & Publisher*, Aug. 9, 1986.

Berke Breathed: Astor, David. "Off the Wall Strip Blooms in Popularity." *Editor & Publisher*, June 18, 1983.

"'Bloom County' by Berke Breathed." *Cartoonist PROfiles* #76, December 1987.

Oliphant, Pat. AAEC speech, reprinted in *The Comics Journal* #119, January 1988.

Breathed, Berke. AAEC response speech, reprinted in *The Comics Journal* #124, August 1988.

Jannot, Mark. "Can Berke Breathed Be Taken Seriously?" *The Comics Journal* #125, October 1988.

"Berke Breathed Ends 'Bloom County.'" *The Comics Journal* #130, July 1989.

Levy, Daniel S. "A Hooligan Who Wields a Pen." *Time*, Dec. 25, 1989.

Bill Watterson: "'Calvin and Hobbes' by Bill Watterson." *Cartoonist PROfiles* #68, December 1985.

Christie, Andrew. "Bill Watterson" interview. *Honk!* #2, 1986.

Marschall, Richard. "Oh You Kid: A Strip of Leviathan Quality." *The Comics Journal* #127, March 1989.

West, Richard Samuel. "Interview: Bill Watterson." *The Comics Journal* #127, March 1989.

Watterson, Bill. *The Calvin and Hobbes Tenth Anniversary Book*. Kansas City: Andrews and McMeel, 1995.

———. *Calvin and Hobbes Sunday Pages 1985–1995*. Kansas City: Andrews McMeel Publishing, 2001.

Bill Griffith: Groth, Gary. "Bill Griffith Interview." *The Comics Journal* #157, March 1993.

Harvey, R. C. "Zippy and Griffy." *Cartoonist PROfiles* #101, March 1994.

Bud Grace: Drevets, Tricia. "Bud Grace: Physicist Turned Cartoonist." *Editor & Publisher*, April 9, 1988.

"'Ernie' by Bud Grace." *Cartoonist PROfiles* #80, December 1988.

Double dippers: "The Finer Art of Politics." *Newsweek*, Oct. 13, 1980.

Williamson, Lenora. "Editorial Cartoonist Introduces Comic Strip" (on *Kudzu*). *Editor & Publisher*, May 16, 1981.

Astor, David. "Double-Duty Cartoonists." *Editor & Publisher*, Oct. 29, 1983.

Huisking, Charlie. "The Peter Pan of Cartooning." *Sarasota Herald-Tribune*, Oct. 15, 1989.

Humor features: "'Marvin' by Tom Armstrong." *Cartoonist PROfiles* #55, September 1982, and #75, September 1987.

"'Sally Forth' by Greg Howard." *Cartoonist PROfiles* #55, September 1982, and #94, June 1992.

"'Rose is Rose' by Pat Brady." *Cartoonist PROfiles* #63, September 1984.

"'Luann' by Greg Evans." *Cartoonist PROfiles* #65, March 1985, #103, September 1994, and #115, September 1997.

"'Robotman' by Jim Meddick." *Cartoonist PROfiles* #65, March 1985.

Heinjtes, Tom. "Toy Story: The Jim Meddick Interview." *Hogan's Alley* #9, 2001.

"'Fox Trot' by Bill Amend." *Cartoonist PROfiles* #84, December 1989.

Harvey, R. C. "Foxtrotting at Ten." *Cartoonist PROfiles* #119, September 1998.

"'Curtis' by Ray Billingsley." *Cartoonist PROfiles* #101, March 1994.

"'Jumpstart' by Robb Armstrong." *Cartoonist PROfiles* #88, December 1990.

Spin-off strips: Williamson, Lenora. "Miss Piggy to Meet Newspaper Readers." *Editor & Publisher*, Aug. 8, 1981.

Condon, Garret. "Drawing Upon the 'Muppets' Success." *Hartford Courant*, Jan. 23, 1983.

The new Nancy: "New 'Nancy' Cartoonist." *Editor & Publisher*, Sept. 17, 1983.

"'Nancy!' by Jerry Scott." *Cartoonist PROfiles* #69, March 1986.

Webb, Dewey. "What's It All About Nancy?" *New Times*, Nov. 30, 1988.

Story strips: Astor, David. "Editors: Comics Readership Holding Up." *Editor & Publisher*, June 11, 1983.

"Creator of Three Enduring Serial Strips." *Editor & Publisher*, June 29, 1985.

Licensing: Schmuckler, Eric. "Free 'Peanuts!' Free 'Beetle Bailey!'" *Forbes*, Oct. 30, 1989.

"The Forbes Top 40 Highest-Paid Entertainers." *Forbes*, September 1987.

Vespa, Mary. "'Garfield' Goes Hollywood." *People*, Nov. 1, 1982.

Astor, David. "Comics Characters Spawn Licensed Products Boom." *Editor & Publisher*, March 12, 1983.

Power, William. "Some People May Still Call Them Funnies, But Comics Have Become Serious Business." *Wall Street Journal*, Aug. 6, 1986.

Watterson, Bill. "The Cheapening of the Comics." Speech at OSU Festival of Cartoon Art, reprinted in *The Comics Journal* #137, September 1990.

Astor, David. "Watterson and Walker Differ on Comics." *Editor & Publisher*, Nov. 4, 1989.

Ownership: Cleaveland, Carol. "Comics Business Not All Funny." *Allentown Morning Call*, Dec. 28, 1989.

Astor, David. "Contracts are a Hot Topic of Discussion." *Editor & Publisher*, April 4, 1987.

"NFC to Discuss Ownership Rights Issue." *Editor & Publisher*, Aug. 29, 1987.

"Three Get New Pacts as Suit is Dropped." *Editor & Publisher*, Oct. 20, 1990.

Mergers: Astor, David. "King Buying Cowles Syndicate." *Editor & Publisher*, March 8, 1986.

"The Syndicate World Reacts to NAS Deal." *Editor & Publisher*, Jan. 10, 1987.

"King-News America Deal Finalized." *Editor & Publisher*, Feb. 14, 1987.

Syndicates: Alexander, Katina. "A Superhero for Cartoonists?" *New York Times*, June 14, 1987.

Astor, David. "Strong Opinions About a New Syndicate." *Editor & Publisher*, March 7, 1987.

"'B.C.' Comic Joining Ann Landers at CS." *Editor & Publisher*, March 21, 1987.

"Mell Lazarus Moves to Creators." *Editor & Publisher*, March 12, 1988.

"King Appoints New Comics Editor." *Editor & Publisher*, Feb. 18, 1989.

"New Comics Editor in Time of Transition." *Editor & Publisher*, July 15, 1989.

Comic relief: Orwen, Pat. "Cartoonists Take Up Pen to Aid Hungry." *Toronto Star*, July 29, 1985.

"More Than Just Comic Relief." *Time*, Dec. 9, 1985.

Comic Relief: Drawings from the Cartoonists Thanksgiving Day Hunger Project. New York: Henry Holt and Company, 1986.

THE NINETIES

Kirkman and Scott: "'Baby Blues' Comic Will Make Its Debut Next Month." *Editor & Publisher*, Dec. 16, 1989.

"Baby Blues." *Cartoonist PROfiles* #85, March 1990.

Beiswinger, George L. "'Baby Blues' Has a Successful Formula." *Editor & Publisher*, Dec. 1, 1990.

Kirkman, Rick, and Jerry Scott. *Baby Blues: Ten Years and Still in Diapers*. Kansas City: Andrews McMeel Publishing, 1999.

Patrick McDonnell: "'Mutts' by Patrick McDonnell." *Cartoonist PROfiles* #104, December 1994.

Walker, Brian. Interview with Patrick McDonnell. Nov. 5, 1996.

Folkman, David. "The Inspired 'Mutts.'" *Hogan's Alley* #7, 1999.

Scott and Borgman: Astor, David. "Why 'Zits' Zoomed Up the Sales Charts." *Editor & Publisher*, Feb. 28, 1998.

Stepp, Laura Sesssions. "Drawn from Life." *Washington Post*, Dec. 1, 2000.

Carter, Kellye. "The Line." *Raising Teens*, 2000.

Scott Adams: "'Dilbert' by Scott Adams." *Cartoonist PROfiles* #84, December 1989, and #106, June 1995.

Dolan, Carrie. "People at Pacific Bell See One Another in the Funny Paper." *Wall Street Journal*, Sept. 6, 1994.

Meisler, Andy. "Yes, Dilbert's Dad Has A Cubicle of His Own." *New York Times*, Jan. 25, 1995.

Van Biema, David. "Layoffs for Laughs." *Time*, March 18, 1996.

Levy, Steven. "Working in Dilbert's World." *Newsweek*, Aug. 12, 1996.

Heintjes, Tom. "Interviewing with Dilbert's Boss." *Hogan's Alley* #3, 1996.

Serious issues: Myers, Greg. "'Funky Winkerbean' Deals With Teen Pregnancy." *Comic Buyer's Guide*, Nov. 14, 1986.

Kiernan, Laura A. "Comic Strip's Storyline on Gay Teen Stirs Controversy." *Boston Globe*, March 1993.

Astor, David. "Comic With Gay Character is Dropped by Some Papers." *Editor & Publisher*, April 3, 1993.

"More Papers Cancel Controversial Comic." *Editor & Publisher*, April 10, 1993.

Teegarden, Carol. "Are Gloom and Doom Invading the Comics?" *Free Press*, April 1995.

Political correctness: Astor, David. "A Session on 'Political Correctness.'" *Editor & Publisher*, June 20, 1992.

"Frank Language in Comics: OK or #*&+%!<@>#?" *Editor & Publisher*, Aug. 15, 1998.

Lang, Tony. "That's Not Funny! P.C. War Flared on the Comics Page." *Cincinnati Enquirer*, Oct. 31, 1993.

Mullen, Rodger. "Rank Humor: 'Beetle' Artist Changes Tactics With Time." *Fayetteville Observer-Times*, Jan. 19, 1997.

Fazio, Debbie. "'Beetle Bailey's' General Halftrack Ordered to Sensitivity Training." Tryon Communications, July 1997.

"'B.C.' Strips Pulled from L.A. Times." *The Comics Journal* #186, April 1996.

Van Biema, David. "Preach It Caveman!" *Time*, April 19, 1998.

Neven, Tom. "Lessons from the Hart." *Focus on the Family*, April 1999.

Chafets, Zev. "It's No Joke When Papers Cut Comics." *New York Daily News*, April 16, 2001.

"'B.C.' Pulled, Impugned, and Praised." *Editor & Publisher*, April 23, 2001.

Kiska, Tim. "Movin' Out to 'The Boondocks.'" *Detroit News*, April 17, 1999.

Hornblower, Margot. "Comics N the Hood." *Time*, July 5, 1999.

Croal, N'Gai. "What's the Color of Funny?" *Newsweek*, July 5, 1999.

Comics centennial: "A Century of the 'Funnies.'" *New York Times*, April 9, 1995 (editorial page).

Precker, Michael. "Comic Relief." *Dallas Morning News*, April 9, 1995.

Adler, Eric. "100 Years of Laughter." *Charlotte Observer*, May 5, 1995.

DeLeon, Clark. "A Century of Comics." *Philadelphia Inquirer*, April 30, 1995.

Hinckley, David. "Comic-Strip Stamp Draws on the Heart of American Culture." *New York Daily News*, May 5, 1995.

Astor, David. "Study Finds Comics Read by 113 Million." *Editor & Publisher*, Jan. 30, 1993.

"International Museum of Cartoon Art Opens." *The Comics Journal* #185, March 1996.

Frankenhoff, Brent. "Comics Creators Switch Strips for April 1." *Comic Buyer's Guide* #1225, May 9, 1997.

State of the art: Griffith, Bill. "Comics at 100 . . . Fading to Gray and Little to Smile About." *Boston Sunday Globe*, Nov. 10, 1996.

LeJeune, Anthony. "Eek! Sob! It's the Death of Comics!" *National Review*, Aug. 29, 1994.

Falk, William B. "Serious Business on the Funny Pages." *Newsday*, Feb. 10, 1997.

Kamp, David. "That Joke Isn't Funnies Anymore." *GQ*, April 2000.

Thomas, Jack. "Let's Face It: The Comics Aren't Funny." *Boston Globe*, Nov. 13, 2000.

Breaking in: Asimov, Eric. "Fledgling Cartoonists Pin Hopes on an Increasingly Unlikely Break." *New York Times*, 1991.

Astor, David. "Speakers Feel Comics Pages are Too Safe." *Editor & Publisher*, Oct. 19, 1991.

Peterson, Iver. "The Search for the Next 'Doonesbury.'" *New York Times*, Oct. 28, 1996.

Charles Schulz: Hinckley, David. "Nuts! No 'Peanuts.'" *New York Daily News*, Dec. 15, 1999.

Trudeau, Garry. "For 'Peanuts,' Americans Got a New Form of Comics." *Washington Post*, Dec. 19, 1999.

Poniewozik, James. "The Good and the Grief." *Time*, Dec. 27, 1999.

Begley, Sharon. "So Long, Snoopy & Co." *Newsweek*, Jan. 1, 2000.

Astor, David. "For United Media, Hapiness is a Warm Response to Reruns." *Editor & Publisher*, Jan. 10, 2000.

Boxer, Sarah. "Charles M. Schulz, 'Peanuts' Creator, Dies at 77." *New York Times*, Feb. 14, 2000.

Astor, David. "Sunday Will Never be the Same." *Editor & Publisher*, Feb. 21, 2000.

"Gentle Genius." *People*, Feb. 28, 2000.

Astor, David. "'Peanuts' Still Holding on to 2,460 Clients." *Editor & Publisher*, Oct. 30, 2000.

Schulz, Charles. *Peanuts: A Golden Celebration*. New York: HarperCollins Publishers, 1999.

The next generation: Astor, David. "The Cartoon Dilema." *Editor & Publisher*, May 8, 2000.

For further listings of articles on contemporary cartoonists, see: Harvey, R. C. "Complete 30-Year Index." *Cartoonist PROfiles* #123, September 1999.

BOOKS

GENERAL HISTORIES

Appel, John J. *Cartoons and Ethnicity*. Columbus: Ohio State University Libraries, 1992.

Becker, Stephen. *Comic Art in America*. New York: Simon and Schuster, 1959.

Berger, Arthur Asa. *The Comic-Stripped American*. Baltimore: Penguin Books, 1973.

Blackbeard, Bill. *The Yellow Kid*. Northampton, Mass.: Kitchen Sink Press, 1995.

Blackbeard, Bill, and Dale Crain, eds. *The Comic Strip Century*. 2 vols. Englewood Cliffs, N.J.: O.G. Publishing Corp., 1995.

Blackbeard, Bill, and Martin Williams, eds. *The Smithsonian Collection of Newspaper Comics*. Washington, D.C.: Smithsonian Institution Press and Harry N. Abrams, 1977.

Carlin, John, and Sheena Wagstaff. *The Comic Art Show: Cartoons and Painting in Popular Culture*. New York: Whitney Museum of American Art, 1983.

Carrier, David. *The Aesthetics of Comics*. University Park, Pa.: The Pennsylvania State University Press, 2000.

Caswell, Lucy. *See You in the Funny Papers*. Columbus: Ohio State University Libraries, 1995.

——— . *Historic Virtuoso Cartoonists*. Columbus: Ohio State University Libraries, 2001.

Couperie, Pierre, and Maurice Horn. *A History of the Comic Strip*. New York: Crown Publishers, 1968.

Ellinport, Jeffrey M. *Collecting Original Comic Strip Art*. Norfolk, Va.: Antique Trader Books, 1999.

Emery, Michael, Edwin Emery, and Nancy L. Roberts. *The Press in America*. Boston: Allyn and Bacon, 2000.

Goulart, Ron. *The Encyclopedia of American Comics*. New York: Facts On File, Inc., 1990.

——— . *The Funnies: 100 Years of American Comic Strips*. Holbrook, Mass.: Adams Publishing, 1995.

Hardy, Charles, and Gail F. Storm, eds. *Ethnic Images in the Comics*. Philadelphia: The Balch Institute for Ethnic Studies, 1986.

Harvey, Robert C. *The Art of the Funnies*. Jackson, Miss.: University Press of Mississippi, 1994.

——— . *Children of the Yellow Kid*. Seattle: Frye Art Museum, 1998.

——— . *A Gallery of Rogues: Cartoonists' Self-Caricatures*. Columbus: Ohio State University Cartoon Research Library, 1998.

Hollis, Daniel W. *The Media in America*. Santa Barbara, Calif.: ABC-CLIO, 1995.

Horn, Maurice, ed. *75 Years of the Comics*. Boston: Boston Book and Art, Publisher, 1971.

——— . *Comics of the American West*. South Hackensack, N.J.: Stoeger Publishing, 1977.

——— . *Women in the Comics*. New York: Chelsea House Publishers, 1977.

——— . *Sex in the Comics*. New York: Chelsea House Publishers, 1985.

——— . *100 Years of American Newspaper Comics*. New York: Gramercy Books, 1996.

——— . *The World Encyclopedia of Cartoons*. Philadelphia: Chelsea House Publishers, 1999.

——— . *The World Encyclopedia of Comics*. Philadelphia: Chelsea House Publishers, 1999.

Hurd, Jud. *To Cartooning: 60 Years of Magic*. Fairfield, Conn.: PROfiles Press, 1993.

Inge, M. Thomas. *Comics as Culture*. Jackson, Miss.: University Press of Mississippi, 1990.

——— . *Great American Comics*. Columbus: Ohio State University Libraries and Smithsonian Institution, 1990.

——— . *Anything Can Happen in a Comic Strip*. Columbus: Ohio State University Libraries, 1995.

Janocha, Bill, ed. *The National Cartoonists Society Album 1996*. New York: National Cartoonists Society, 1996.

Katz, Harry L., and Sara W. Duke. *Featuring the Funnies: One Hundred Years of the Comic Strip*. Washington, D.C.: Library of Congress, 1995.

King Features Syndicate. *Famous Artists & Writers of King Features Syndicate*. New York: King Features Syndicate, Inc., 1949.

Koenigsberg, M. *King News: An Autobiography*. Philadelphia and New York: F. A. Stokes Company, 1941.

Lent, John A. *Comic Books and Comic Strips in the United States: An International Bibliography*. Westport, Conn.: Greenwood Press, 1994.

Marschall, Richard. *The Sunday Funnies: 1896–1950*. New York: Chelsea House Publishers, 1978.

——— . *What's So Funny: The Humor Comic Strip in America*. Salina, Kan.: The Salina Art Center, 1988.

——— . *America's Great Comic-Strip Artists*. New York: Abbeville Press, 1989.

Nordling, Lee. *Your Career in the Comics*. Kansas City: Andrews and McMeel, 1995.

O'Sullivan, Judith. *The Great American Comic Strip*. Boston: Little, Brown and Company, 1990.

Phelps, Donald. *Reading the Funnies*. Seattle: Fantagraphics Books, 2001.

Robbins, Trina. *The Great Women Cartoonists*. New York: Watson-Guptill Publications, 2001.

Robinson, Jerry. *The Comics: An Illustrated History of Comic Strip Art*. New York: G. P. Putnam's Sons, 1974.

——— . *Cartoon: A Celebration of American Comic Art*. Washington, D.C.: John F. Kennedy Center for the Performing Arts, 1975.

Sheridan, Martin. *Comics and Their Creators*. Boston: Hale, Cushman & Flint, 1942.

Strickler, Dave. *Syndicated Comic Strips and Artists 1924–1995: The Complete Index*. Cambria, Calif.: Comics Access, 1995.

Thorndike, Chuck. *The Business of Cartooning*. New York: The House of Little Books, 1939.

Turner, Hy B. *When Giants Ruled: The Story of Park Row, New York's Great Newspaper Street*. New York: Fordham University Press, 1999.

Van Hise, James. *Calvin and Hobbes, Garfield, Bloom County, Doonesbury and All That Funny Stuff*. Las Vegas: Pioneer Books, 1991.

Walker, Brian. *The Sunday Funnies: 100 Years of Comics in American Life*. Bridgeport, Conn.: The Barnum Museum, 1994.

Waugh, Coulton. *The Comics*. New York: Macmillan, 1947.

White, David Manning, and Robert H. Abel, eds. *The Funnies: An American Idiom*. New York: The Free Press of Glencoe/Macmillan, 1963.

Whyte, Malcolm. *Great Comic Cats*. San Francisco: Pomegranate, 2001.

Wood, Art. *Great Cartoonists and Their Art*. Gretna, La.: Pelican Publishing Company, 1987.

Yoe, Craig. *Weird But True Toon Factoids*. New York: Gramercy Books, 1999.

AUTOBIOGRAPHIES, BIOGRAPHIES, AND RETROSPECTIVE ANTHOLOGIES

Adams, Scott. *Seven Years of Highly Defective People*. Kansas City: Andrews McMeel Publishing, 1997.

Bang, Derrick. *50 Years of Happiness: A Tribute to Charles M. Schulz*. Peanuts Collectors Club, 1999.

Berger, Arthur Asa. *Li'l Abner: A Study in American Satire*. Jackson, Miss.: University Press of Mississippi, 1994.

Breathed, Berkeley. *One Last Little Peek, 1980–1995*. Boston: Little Brown and Company, 1995.

Burstein, Mark. *Much Ado: The Pogofenokee Trivia Book*. Forestville, Calif.: Eclipse Books, 1988.

Caplin, Elliott. *Al Capp Remembered*. Bowling Green, Ohio: Bowling Green State University Popular Press, 1994.

Capp, Al. *The Best of Li'l Abner*. New York: Holt, Rinehart and Winston, 1978.

———. *My Well Balanced Life on a Wooden Leg*. Santa Barbara, Calif.: John Daniel and Company, 1991.

Davis, Jim. *20 Years and Still Kicking: Garfield's Twentieth Anniversary Collection*. New York: Ballantine Books, 1998.

Feiffer, Jules. *Jules Feiffer's America*. New York: Alfred A. Knopf, 1982.

Grandinetti, Fred M. *Popeye: An Illustrated History of E.C. Segar's Character in Print, Radio, Television and Film Appearances, 1929–1993*. Jefferson, N.C.: McFarland & Company, 1994.

Guisewite, Cathy. *Reflections*. Kansas City: Andrews and McMeel, 1991.

———. *Twentieth Anniversary Collection*. Kansas City: Andrews and McMeel, 1996.

Harvey, Robert C. *Accidental Ambassador Gordo*. Jackson, Miss.: University Press of Mississippi, 2000.

Inge, Thomas M., ed. *Charles M. Schulz Conversations*. Jackson, Miss.: University Press of Mississippi, 2000.

Johnson, Rheta Grimsley. *Good Grief: The Story of Charles Schulz*. New York: Pharos Books, 1989.

Johnston, Lynn. *A Look Inside . . . For Better or For Worse: The 10th Anniversary Collection*. Kansas City: Andrews and McMeel, 1989.

———. *It's the Thought that Counts . . . For Better or For Worse Fifteenth Anniversary Collection*. Kansas City: Andrews and McMeel, 1994.

———. *Remembering Farley: A Tribute to the Life of Our Favorite Cartoon Dog*. Kansas City: Andrews and McMeel, 1996.

———. *The Lives Behind the Lines: 20 Years of For Better or For Worse*. Kansas City: Andrews McMeel Publishing, 1999.

Kane, Brian M. *Hal Foster: Prince of Illustrators—Father of the Adventure Strip*. Lebanon, N.J.: Vanguard Productions, 2001.

Keane, Bil. *The Family Circus Treasury*. Kansas City: Sheed Andrews and McMeel, 1977.

Kelly, Selby, and Bill Crouch, Jr., eds. *The Best of Pogo*. New York: Simon and Schuster, 1982.

———. *Pogo Even Better*. New York: Simon and Schuster, 1984.

———. *Outrageously Pogo*. New York: Simon and Schuster, 1985.

———. *Pluperfect Pogo*. New York: Simon and Schuster, 1987.

———. *Phi Beta Pogo*. New York: Simon and Schuster, 1989.

Kelly, Selby, and Steve Thompson. *Pogo Files for Pogofiles*. Richfield, Minn.: Spring Hollow Books, 1992.

Kelly, Walt. *Ten Ever-Lovin' Blue-Eyed Years with Pogo*. New York: Simon and Schuster, 1959.

Ketcham, Hank. *The Merchant of Dennis*. New York: Abbeville Press, 1990.

———. *Dennis the Menace: His First 40 Years*. New York: Abbeville Press, 1991.

Kidd, Chip, ed. *The Art of Charles M. Schulz*. New York: Pantheon Books, 2001.

Kirkman, Rick, and Jerry Scott. *Baby Blues: Ten Years and Still in Diapers*. Kansas City: Andrews McMeel Publishing, 1999.

Larson, Gary. *The PreHistory of The Far Side*. Kansas City: Andrews and McMeel, 1989.

Lazarus, Mell. *The Momma Treasury*. Kansas City: Sheed Andrews and McMeel, 1978.

Maeder, Jay. *Dick Tracy: The Official Biography*. New York: Plume, 1990.

Marschall, Rick, and John Paul Adams. *Milt Caniff: Rembrandt of the Comic Strip*. Endicott, N.Y.: Flying Buttress Publications, 1981.

Roberts, Garyn G. *Dick Tracy and American Culture*. Jefferson, N.C.: McFarland & Company, 1993.

Sagendorf, Bud. *Popeye: The First Fifty Years*. New York: Workman Publishing, 1979.

Schulz, Charles. *Peanuts Jubilee*. New York: Holt, Rinehart and Winston, 1975.

———. *You Don't Look 35, Charlie Brown!* New York: Holt, Rinehart and Winston, 1985.

———. *Around the World in 45 Years*. Kansas City: Andrews and McMeel, 1994.

———. *Peanuts: A Golden Celebration*. New York: HarperCollins Publishers, 1999.

Smith, Bruce. *The History of Little Orphan Annie*. New York: Ballantine Books, 1982.

Theroux, Alexander. *The Enigma of Al Capp*. Seattle: Fantagraphics Books, 1999.

Trimboli, Giovanni. *Charles M. Schulz: 40 Years Life and Art*. New York: Pharos Books, 1990.

Trudeau, G. B. *Flashbacks: Twenty-Five Years of Doonesbury*. Kansas City: Andrews and McMeel, 1995.

Walker, Brian. *The Best of Hagar the Horrible*. Bedford, N.Y.: Comicana Books, 1985.

———. *The Best of Hi and Lois*. Bedford, N.Y.: Comicana Books, 1986.

———. *The Best of Ernie Bushmiller's Nancy*. Wilton, Conn.: Comicana Books, 1988.

———. *Barney Google and Snuffy Smith: 75 Years of an American Legend*. Wilton, Conn.: Comicana Books/Ohio State University Libraries, 1994.

Walker, Mort. *Backstage at the Strips*. New York: Mason Charter, 1975.

———. *The Best of Beetle Bailey*. Bedford, N.Y.: Comicana Books, 1984.

———. *Mort Walker's Private Scrapbook*. Kansas City: Andrews McMeel Publishing, 2000.

Watterson, Bill. *The Calvin and Hobbes Tenth Anniversary Book*. Kansas City: Andrews and McMeel, 1995.

———. *Calvin and Hobbes Sunday Pages 1985–1995*. Kansas City: Andrews McMeel Publishing, 2001.

Young, Dean, and Richard Marschall. *Blondie and Dagwood's America*. New York: Harper & Row, 1981.

Yronwode, Catherine. *The Art of Will Eisner*. Princeton, Wis.: Kitchen Sink Press, 1982.

REPRINTS

Thousands of book collections of newspaper comic strips and panels have been published since 1945 and are too numerous to list here. Andrews McMeel Publishing in Kansas City currently offers annual reprint collections of many of the major contemporary features, including *Baby Blues, Cathy, Dilbert, Doonesbury, For Better or For Worse, Foxtrot, Mutts,* and *Zits*. Classic Comics Press of Chicago is reprinting *Dondi, On Stage,* and *The Heart of Juliet Jones* and Checker Book Publishing has published collections of *B.C.* and *Beetle Bailey*. Fantagraphics Books of Seattle has published collections of *Betsy and Me, Dennis the Menace, Peanuts, Pogo, Prince Valiant, Sam's Strip,* and *Zippy*.

INDEX

Page numbers in italics refer to illustrations.

Abbie an' Slats, 276, 380, *380*
Abie the Agent, 75, 85, 117, 188, *266*
Adam, 576, *576*
Adams, Neal, 405, 454, 462, *462*
Adams, Scott, 611–612, *612*, 621, *621–25*
Adventures of Mr. Obadiah Oldbuck, The, 9–10, *9*
Adventures of Patsy, 207, 314
Adventures of Prudence Primm, The, 294
Advice fo' Chillun, 257, *259*
Afonsky, Nicholas, *219*, 282
Agatha Crumm, 501, *558*
Agnes, 657
Ahearn, Gene, *84, 158, 159,* 264, *267*
Ain't It a Grand and Glorious Feeling, 76, *116*
Alexander, Franklin Osborne, 25
Alley Oop, 192, *260–62,* 425, *425,* 671
Ally Sloper, 9
Alphonse and Gaston, 42, 121
Amato, Andy, 382
Amazing Spider-Man, The, 503, 547, *547*
Amend, Bill, 557, 600, *600–603*
Among Us Mortals, 160
Amos and Andy, 116
A. Mutt, 29, 78
Anderson, Brad, 459
Anderson, Carl, 192, *281*
And Her Name was Maud, 42, *45*
Andriola, Al, *236, 504,* 671
Andy Capp, 457, *482,* 483
Angel Child, The, 293
Animal Crackers, 465, *465*
Annie, 502, 548, *549,* 560
Apartment 3-G, 405, 454, 462, *462,* 502, 558, 559
A. Piker Clerk, 341–342
Apple Mary, 276, 294, 315; *See also Mary Worth*
Aragonés, Sergio, *503*
Archie, 355, *356,* 389, *389*
Armstrong, Robb, 557, *607,* 616, 620, *620*
Armstrong, Roger, *317*
Armstrong, Stanley, *109*

Armstrong, Tom, 557, 606, *606*
Arriola, Gus, 290, *317,* 367, *367, 428*
Associated Newspapers, 69, 186
Associated Press, 186, 190, 191, 207, 208, 254
Auto Otto, 84
Ayers, Chuck, 645, *645*

Baby Blues, 608, *609,* 610, 626, *626–631*
Baginski, Frank, 501, *544*
Bailey, Ray, *300,* 366, *366*
Baker, George, *290,* 291, 296, *304*
Bald, Ken, 454, 462, *462*
Baldwin, Summerfield, 76
Ballard Street, 644, *644*
Barnaby, 316, 356, *357,* 555
Barney Baxter, 298
Barney Google (later *Barney Google and Snuffy Smith*), 54, 119–21, *120,* 148, *149–53,* 154, 188, 269, 288, 289, 292, 297, 319
Barney Google and Snuffy Smith, 346, *349,* 351, *351,* 358, 393, *393*
Baron Bean, 92, 97
Baron Mooch, 25, 92, *93*
Barry, Dan, 424, *424*
Barry, Sy, 463, *463*
Basset, Brian, 576, *576,* 657
Batiuk, Tom, 501, *544,* 557, 606, *606,* 645, *645*

Batman, 355, 455, 463, *463*
Batman and Robin, 306, *308*
B.C., 346, 409, 453, 455, 456, 468, *468–72,* 612, *613,* 671
Beetle Bailey, 406–407, *406,* 408, 429, *429–433,* 453, 454, 455, 456, 459, 612, *671*
Bell Syndicate, 116, 186, 244, 290
Ben Casey, 405, 454, 462, *462*
Benchley, 557, 583
Benjy, 500, 501
Bennett, James Gordon, 10, 26, 30
Berndt, Walter, *119, 166, 169*
Beroth, Leon, *237*
Berry, Jim, 456, *456, 464, 500,* 501
Berry's World, 456, *456, 464, 464,* 546
Bess, Gordon, 456, 480, *481*
Betsy and Me, 411, *411,* 412
Betty, 145
Betty Boop, 187, *269*
Betty Boop and Felix, 557, *582,* 583
Big Ben Bolt, 414, *414,* 415, 429, 502
Big Chief Wahoo, 276
Big George, 484, *484*
Bill, 265
Billingsley, Ray, 557, 605, *605*
Billy Bounce, 25, *52*
Bishop, Wally, *281*
Bizarro, 553, 563, *563*
Blackbeard, Bill, 13, 14, 121
Blake, Bud, 458, 486, *486,* 487
Block, Rudolph, 36, 39, 71
Blondie, 144, 189, 190, 191–92, *191,* 200, 244, *245–49,* 289, 291, 292, 295, 354, *354,* 402, *402,* 405, 406, 407, 429, 454, 456, 457, 458, *561,* 604, *604,* 612, *658*
Bloom County, 553–554, *553,* 557, 566, *556–560,* 613
Blosser, Merrill, 73, 75, *84,* 159
Bobby Make-Believe, 28, 75, *112,* 130, 293
Bobby Sox, 355, 389, *389*
Bobby Thatcher, 121, *176*
Bobo Baxter, 72
Bollen, Rog, 465, *465,* 545
Boner's Ark, 429, 457, *479*
Boob McNutt, 72, *89,* 265
Boob McNutt's Ark, 265
Boondocks, The, 613, *654*
Boots and Her Buddies, 142, 159
Borgman, Jim, 584, 608, 610, *611,* 626, *633,* 648, *648–63*
Boring, Wayne, *192,* 307, 348
Born Loser, The, 458, 478, *478*
Bourjaily, Monte, 186
Boyle, Phil, 367
Bradley, Marvin, 381, *381*
Brady, Pat, 557, 578, *578–581,* 584
Brandon, Barbara, 633
Brandon, Brumsic, Jr., 459, 493, *493*
Branner, Martin, 73, 119, *140, 141*
Breathed, Berke, 553, *553,* 566, *556–71,* 613, 614
Breger, Dave, *291,* 296, *305*
Brenda Starr, 293, *294,* 315, *380,* 406
Brick Bradford, 215, *224*
Brickman, Morrie, 456, 480, *481*
Briggs, Austin, 200, 290, *310,* 351
Briggs, Claire, 28, *65,* 73, 76, *113, 116, 162,* 188, 341, 357
Bringing Up Father, 54, 73–74, *100, 102–5,* 117, 188, 189, 289, 292, *350,* 352, 354, 392, *392,* 406
Brinkley, Neil, *147,* 294
Brisbane, Arthur, 56, 72, 238
Broncho Bill, 313
Broom-Hilda, 500, 540, *540*
Brown, Bill, 501, *544*
Browne, Chance, 619, *619*
Browne, Chris, 619, *619*

Browne, Dik, 406, 434, *434–437,* 499–500, *499,* 503, 530, *530–535,* 558, 626
Brownies, 9, 10, *53*
Bruce Gentry, 366, *366*
Brutus, 273
Buck Nix, 108
Buck Rogers, 116, 122, 190, 200, *214,* 215
Bugs Bunny, 317
Bullwinkle, 453–54
Bungle Family, The, 75, 120, 124, *127, 129,* 188
Bunky, 153, *319*
Burnley, Jack, 306
Burroughs, Edgar Rice, 372, *372*
Busch, Wilhelm, *10,* 36
Bush, Charles Green, *10*
Bushmiller, Ernie, 144, 192, *284, 285,* 289, 354, 390, *390,* 391, *460,* 557–58, 604, 617, 671
Buster Brown, 21, 22, 23, 25–26, *25,* 30, *33–35,* 69, 73, *338*
Buz Sawyer, 178, *292, 299, 335,* 350, 351, 352, 355, 374, *374,* 375
Byrnes, Gene, 73, *166, 167,* 281

Cady, Harrison, *110*
Caldwell, 553, 563, *565*
Caldwell, John, 553, 563, *565*
Calkins, Dick, 122, *214, 215,* 237
Calvin and Hobbes, 357, 504, 551, 554–555, *554,* 557, *559,* 584, *585–89,* 610, 614, 648
Campbell, E. Simms, 459
Camp Newspaper Service, 291
Canemaker, John, 56
Caniff, Milton, 73, 122, 190–91, *190,* 207, *208–13, 218,* 236, 253, 289, 291, 292–93, 294–95, *295,* 301, *303,* 314, 347, 350, 352–53, *352,* 354, 358, *359,* 360, *360–65,* 366, 405, 406, 410–12, 455, 502, 522, 558, *560,* 671
Caplin, Elliot, 380, 416, 500
Capp, Al, 192, 222, *254–59,* 276, 289, 296, 350–51, 353–54, *353,* 358, 367, 380, 382, *382–87,* 404, 410, *411,* 455, 497, 502, *502,* 671
Cap Stubbs and Tippie, 73, 75, *277, 281,* 293, 426, *426*
Captain and the Kids, The, 36, 71, 186, 354
Captain Easy, 122, 180, *182,* 289, 292, 421, *422*
Carew, Kate, 293
Carlson, W.A., *127*
Carr, Gene, 144
Casey Ruggles, 423, *424*
Casson, Mel, 501, 544
Catfish, 542, *545*
Cathy, 407, 438, 498, *498,* 514, *514–17,* 559, 614
Cavalli, Dick, 484, *485*
Central Press Association, 69, 186
Chaffin, Glenn, 122, *224*
Charlie Chan, 191, *236,* 314
Charlie Chaplin's Comic Capers, 238
Charteris, Leslie, 200
Chicago Inter-Ocean, 7
Chicago Tribune, 63, 65, 75, 76, 111, 112, 115, 118, 130, 131, 162, 170, 293
Chicago Tribune–New York Syndicate (originally *Chicago Tribune Syndicate*), 69, 75, 84, 116, 118, 120, 128, 160, 188, 190–91, 193, 208, 226, 292, 293, 294
Childress, James, 501–2, *501*
Cho, Frank, *646,* 647
Christianson, Oliver, 555
Christman, Bert, *237,* 290
Cigarette Sadie, 128
Cisco Kid, The, 422, *423*
Clarence the Cop, 24, 25

Clark, George, *287*
Clark, Virginia, 293
Cochran, Tony, *657*
Cole, Jack, *323,* 411–412, *411*
Coll, Charles, *237*
Collins, Max, 502, *558*
Conchy, 501–2, *501*
Condo, A.D., *83*
Connie, 220
Conley, Darby, *654*
Conrad, 557, *557,* 576
Conselman, Bill, *142, 143*
Consolidated News Features, 290
Cory, J. Campbell, *11*
Counihan, Bud, 187, *269*
Count Screwloose of the Nut House, 268
Coverly, Dave, 644, *644*
Cox, Palmer, 9, 10, *53*
Crane, Brian, 634, *635*
Crane, Roy, 73, 121–22, *122,* 159, 176, *178–82,* 289, *292, 299, 335,* 352, 354, 374, *374, 375,* 412, 421
Crankshaft, 612, 645, *645*
Crawford, Arthur, 188, 193
Crawford, Mel, *582*
Crock, 5001, *542, 545*
Crosby, Percy, *280*
Cruikshank, George, 9
cummings, e.e., 76
Curley Harper, 234
Curtis, 557, 605, *605,* 612
Curtis, Harvey, 382
Cuties, 459

Daily Strip, 555
Dallis, Nicholas, 381, *381,* 454, 462, 559
Dan Dunn, 189, 191, *234*
Dan Flagg, 454
Danny Dreamer, 28, 65
Dart, Harry Grant, 28, 64
Dateline Danger, 459–60, 502
Dave's Delicatessen, 268
Davis, Jim, 500, *500,* 536, *536–39,* 559, 614
Davis, Phil, *217,* 368, *368*
Days of Real Sport, The, 76, *113*
Dean, Allen, *312*
DeBeck, Billy, 119–21, *120,* 128, *148–53, 288,* 289, 292, 294, *297, 319,* 393
Dennis the Menace, 406, 407–8, *407,* 446, *446–49,* 453, 454, 457, 459, 484, 590, *590*
Desperate Desmond, 82, 85, *85*
Detorie, Rick, 557, 576, *577*
Dickie Dare, 190, 191, 208, 209, *218,* 293
Dick Tracy, 73, 116, 189, 190, 191, 200, *226–31,* 232, 234, 259, 289, 295, 350, 351, 354, 370, *370,* 371, *371,* 382, 406, 454, *455,* 455, 502, *558,* 671
Dierick, Charles, 13
Difficult Decisions, 163
Dilbert, 611–12, *612,* 613, 621, *621–25*
Dimples, 107, 293
Dingbat Family, The, 25, 76, *82,* 92
Dinny's Family Album, 261
Dirks, Gus, *50*
Dirks, John, 70
Dirks, Rudolph, 10, 12, 21, 25, *36–39,* 50, 70–71, *70,* 94, 354
Disney, Walt, 271
Doc Wright, 72
Dodd, Ed, 502
Dodson, Reynolds, 501, 544
Dolly Dingle, 107
Donahey, William, *111*
Dondi, 426, 427
Don Winslow of the Navy, 237, 289
Doonesbury, 344, 456, 496–98, *497,* 505, *505–13,* 553–54, 560, 615, 659

Dorgan, Thomas Aloysius, "TAD", 28, 71–72, *72*, *86*, *87*, *92*, 162
Dot and Dash, 128
Doty, Roy, 456, *465*
Drabble, 501, 542, *544*
Draftie, 301
Drake, Stan, 382, 405, 411, 416, *416*, 417,604, *604*
Dream of the Rarebit Fiend, 28, 56, *57*, *58*, 73
Dr. Kildare, 462, *462*
Dropouts, The, 457, 478, *478*
Dr. Seuss (Geisel, Theodor), 187
Drucker, Mort, *486*, 557
Dumas, Jerry, 345, 456, *457*, 476, *476*, *477*, 501, *543*, 557, 582, *583*
Dumb Dora, 144, 244, *253*
Dumm, Edwina, 73, 75, *277*, *281*, 293, 358, *426*, *426*
Dunagin, Ralph, 546, *546*
Dunagin's People, 546, *546*
Dunn, Bob, 78
Duplex, The, *655*
Duval, Marie, 9
Dwiggins, Clare, 76, 162, *163*, *165*
Dwyer Bill, *253*

Ed, Carl, 75, *84*, *119*, *168*
Edginton, Frank, 381, *381*
Editor & Publisher (originally *The Fourth Estate*), 11, 21, 22, 25, 69, 71, 116, 119, 123, 186, 187, 188, 289, 293, 294
Edson, Gus, 188, 289, 357, 426, *427*
Eek and Meek, 456, 478, *478*, 671
Eisner, Will, *293*, *320–23*, 355, 369, *369*
Elias, Lee, 382
Eliot, Jan, 657
Ella Cinders, 120, *142*, *143*, 186
Embarrassing Moments, 92
Emmy Lou, 389
Ernie, 557, 596, *596–98*
Ernst, Ken, 276, *315*, 355, 381, *381*
Etta Kett, 120, *142*, 252
Evans, Greg, 557, 573, *573*
Ewer, Raymond Crawford, 109
Explorigator, The, 28, *64*

Fagan, Kevin, 501, *544*
Falk, Lee, 192, *216*, *217*, 368, 368, 463, *463*, 671
Family Circus, The, 340, *453*, 454, 457–58, *458*, 488, *488–92*, 559, *658*
Family Upstairs, The, 76, *93*
Far Side, The, 553, 557, *562*, 563
Fearless Fosdick, 259
Feiffer, Jules, 409, *409*, 455, 461, *461*, 496
Feininger, Lyonel, 28, *63*
Felix the Cat, 73, *269*
Fera, A. C., 75
Ferdinand, Ron, 446, 617, *617*
Ferguson, Fred, 292
Fillum Fables, 226
Fine, Lu, 320, *323*
Fineheimer Twins, The, 36
Fisher, Bud, *28–29*, 70, *71*, *73*, *78–81*, *92*, 116, 121, 188, 342, *342*
Fisher, Dudley, *274*, *275*
Fisher, Ham, 189, 192, *193*, *222*, *223*, 254, 289, *297*, 353, 367, *367*, 382, 411, *411*
Fisher's Foolish History, 223
Five Fifteen, The, *239*
Flagg, James Montgomery, *23*, *68*
Flanders, Charles, 200
Flapper Fanny, 251, 294
Flash Gordon, 190, 200, *203–6*, 215, 290, *310*, 351, 378, 405, 424, *424*
Fletcher, Rick, 502, *558*
Flintstones, The, 453, *454*
Flop Family, The, *319*

Flowers, Don, *252*
Flying Jenny, *314*
Fogarty, Paul, *301*
Foolish Questions, 72, 88
For Better or For Worse, 72, 346, 407, 499, 522, *522–529*, 559, 612
Foreign Correspondent, *314*
Forman, Tom, 501, *545*, *613*
Forrest, Hal, 122, *224*
For This We Have Daughters? 136
Foster, Hal, 122, *122*, 189–90, 191, *194–99*, 200, *224*, *334*, 354, 375, *375*, 502, 503, 548, *550*, *558*
Forsythe, Vic, *154*
Fox, Fontaine, 69, 73, 76, 116, 162, *163*, *164*
Fox Feature Syndicate, 293
Foxy Grandpa, *21*, 22, 25, *51*, 73
Fox Trot, 557, 600, *600–3*
Frank, Phil, 546, *546*
Frank and Earnest, 501, 542, *542*
Frazetta, Frank, 382
Freckles and His Friends, 73, 75, *84*, *159*, 188, 289
Fred Basset, 457
Friday Foster, 460
Frink, George, 109
Fritzi Ritz, *144*, 186, *284*, *285*
Frost, A. B., 10
Fry, Michael, *656*
Fuller R. B., 192, 260, *263*
Fung, Paul, 136, *142*, 253
Fun in the Zoo, 25
Funky Winkerbean, 501, 542, *544*, 612, 645, *645*

Gags and Gals, *253*
Gallup, George, 186
Garfield, 455, 500, *500*, 536, *536–39*, 559, 612, 614, *614*
Gary, Jim, *312*
Gasoline Alley, 54, 112, *118*, 119, 120, 124, *130–35*, 188, 189, 289, 291, 350, 351, 388, *388*, 499, 502, 457, *457*, 617, *618*, *670*
Gately, George, 542, *542*
Geisel, Theodor (Dr. Seuss), 187
George Matthew Adams Syndicate, 69
Get Fuzzy, 654
G.I. Joe, 291, *305*
Gilchrist, Guy and Brad, 557, *582*, 583, *583*, 617, *618*
Gillray, James, *8*
Gizmo & Eightball, 290, 291
Goddard, Morrill, 8, 11
Godwin, Frank, *220*, 426, *426*
Goldberg, Rube, 28, 70, 72, 73, 78, *88*, *89*, 162, 264, *265*, 289, 294, 357–58, *404*, 503
Goodwin, Archie, 548
Gooseberry Sprig, 92
Gordo, 290, *317*, 367, *367*, *428*
Gordon, Ian, 26
Gottfredson, Floyd, 192, *270*, 271
Gotto, Ray, 367, *367*
Goulart, Ron, 120, 254, 503, *503*
Gould, Chester, 73, 128, 191, *226–31*, 232, 259, 295, 314, 354, 370, *370*, 371, *371*, 382, 410, 455, 502, 558, *558*, 671
Gould, Will, *233*
Grace, Bud, 556, *556*, 596, *596–598*
Graff, Mel, *207*
Graham, Alex, 457
Granberry, Ed, 374
Gray, Clarence, *224*
Gray, Harold, 120, 121, *123*, 128, *170–75*, *185*, 289, 295, 354, *374*, 375, *375*, 410, 548
Greene, Vernon, *310*
Grey, Zane, *312*

Griffith, Bill, *552*, 555–56, *555*, 592, *592–95*, 612, *614*
Grin and Bear It, 454, 464, *464*
Grizwells, The, 576, *576*
Gross, Milt, 264, *268*
Gruelle, Johnny, 28, *66*, *273*
Guisewite, Cathy, 407, 438, 498, *498*, 514, *514–517*, 559
Gumdrop, 558, 609
Gumps, The, 69, 75, 108, 116, 118–19, *118*, 120, 121, *124–26*, 127, 170, 176, 188, 189, 282, 289
Gus and Gussie, *142*

Haenigsen, Harry, 484, 485
Hagar the Horrible, 457, 499–500, *499*, 530, *530–35*, 619, *619*
Hairbreadth Harry, 22, 25, 85, 121, *176*, *177*, 188
Half Hitch, 542, *543*
Hall Room Boys The, 28, *83*
Hamilton, Marcus, 446, 617, *285*
Hamlin, V.T., 192, *260–62*, 425, *425*, 671
Hammett, Dashiell, 200, *201*
Hanan, Harry, 457
Hanna Barbera Studios, 453, *454*
Hans und Fritz, 71
Hap Hooper, Washington Correspondent, *314*
Happy Hooligan, 12, *21*, *22*, 42, *43*, *44*, 69, 72–73, 188, *338*, 354
Harmon, Fred, 192, *224*, 225, 422, *422*
Harold Teen, 75, *84*, *118*, 119, 120, *168*, 188
Harry N. Abrams, 335, 671
Hart, Johnny, 346, 409, 456, 461, 468, *468–72*, *473–475*, 612, *613*, 626, 671
Harvey, Robert C., 13, 28, 122, 178, 189
Hasen, Irwin, 426, *427*
Hashmark, 291
Hatlo, Jimmy, *183*, *318*
Hays, Ethel, *251*, 294
Hayward, A. E., 119, *140*
Hazel, 459
Hazelton, Gene, 453
Hearst, William Randolph, 10, *11*, 13, 14, *20*, 21, 22, 25–26, 28, 29, 30, 35, 36, 37, 39, 42, 46, 56, 70, 71, 73, 76, 78, 82, 83, 90, 92, 97, 99, 115, 120, 148, *186*, 187, 189, 238, 244, 266, 339, 341, 342, 412, *412*, 452, 556
Heart of Juliet Jones, The, 405, *405*, 411,416, *416*, *417*, 604
Heathcliff, 542, *542*
Hejji, 187
Held, John, Jr., *114*, 120, *146*, 250
Henry, 189, 192, 269, *281*
Herman, 501, 542, 542
Herriman, George, 25, 28, *76–77*, 82, *92–99*, 188, 238, 354, 556, 636
Hershfield, Harry, 72, 75, *82*, 85, 92, 117, 264, *266*, 294
Hess, Sol, *127*
Hi and Lois, 406, 429, 434, *434–37*, 457, 499, 619, *619*, 626, 658
Hickerson, Buddy, 553, 563, *565*
Hill, W. E., *160*
Hinds, Bill, 501, 546, *546*
Hoban, Walter, 75, *84*
Hodgins, Dick, Jr., *543*, 619
Hoest, Bill, 458, 483, *483*, 484. 501, 558
Hoest, Bunny, *558*
Hogan's Alley, *7*, 8, 11, 13, *15*, *18*, 25, *31–32*, 339, 340–41
Hogarth, Burne, 311, 372, *372*
Hogarth, William, 9
Holbrook, Bill, 576, *577*
Holdaway, Jim, 457
Holley, Lee, 458, 484, *484*
Holman, Bill, 192, *264*, 393, *393*
Howard, Greg, 557, 572, *572*

Howarth, F. M., *50*
Howson Lott, 42
Hubert, 291
Hungry Henrietta, 28

I'm the Guy, 72, 88
Indoor Sports, 72, *87*
Inge, Thomas, 92
In the Bleachers, 644, *644*
Inventions of Professor Lucifer G. Butts, The, 72, *88*
Invisible Scarlett O'Neil, *314*
Ireland, Billy, 208
It's Papa Who Pays, 128, *250*
Iwerks, Ub, 271

Jaffee, Al, *358*, 409, 450
Jane Arden, 291
Jantze, Michael, 634, *63*
Jerry on the Job, 73, 75, *84*, 120
Jim Hardy, 232
Joe and Asbestos, 154
Joe Jinks, 154
Joe Palooka, , 189, 192, *193*, *222*, *223*, 254, 289, 291, *297*, 353, 367, *367*, 382, 406, 411
John Darling, 557, 606, *606*
Johnny Hazard, *310*
Johnson, Crockett, *316*, 356, *357*
Johnson, Ferd, 293, 671
Johnson, Walter, 382
Johnston, Lynn, 407, 498, 522, *522–29*, 559, 612, 615
Johnstone, Thomas, 187
Journal Tigers, The, 46, *47*
Judge, 9, 10, 25, 30, 36, 253, 276
Judge, Parker, 454, 615
Judge Rummy's Court, 72, *86*
Juhre, William, *301*
Jump Start, 613, 607, 616, 620, *620*
Jungle Jim, 190, 200, *202*, *204*, 205, 292, 378
Just Boy, 75

Kahles, Charles William, *24*, 25, *52*, 85, 121, *176*, *177*
Kane, Bob, *306*, *308*, 320
Kane, Gil, 503, *503*
Katzenjammer Kids, The, 10, 12, *21*, 25, 36, *37–39*, 40, *41*, 69–71, 73, 188, 269
Keane, Bil, *340*, *453*, 457–58, *458*, 488, *488–492*, 615, *658*
Keaton, Russell, *237*, *314*
Keeping Up with the Joneses, 124, *127*
Kelly, Selby, 502, 671
Kelly, Walt, 347, 356–57, *357*, 358, *394–401*, 395, 410–11, *496*, 497, 502, 503, 671
Kemble, E. W., 10
Kent, Jack, *457*
Kerry Drake, 504, 671
Ketcham, Hank, 406, 407–408, 446, *446–49*, 453, 459, 484, *543*, 617
Ketten, Maurice, 72
Kewpies, The, 187, *279*, 293
Key, Ted, 459
Kilgore, Al, 446
Kin-der-Kids, The, 28, *63*
King Aroo, 457
King, Frank, 28, 73, 75, *112*, 119, 128, *130–35*, 289, 293, 388, *388*, 547
King Features Syndicate, 38, 69, 71, 76, 92, 119, 120, 128, 178, 186, 187, 188, 190, 200, 238, 244, 254, 267, 268, 291, 292, 295
King of the Royal Mounted, *312*
King, Ken, *117*, *154*
Kirby, Jack, 405, 424, *424*
Kirkman, Rick, 608, 609, *609*, 626, *626–31*
Knerr, Harold, 36, *40*, *41*, 71, 294

Knight, "Tack", *281*
Koenigsberg, Moses, 69
Kotzky, Alex, 405, 454, 462, *462*
Krazy Kat, 25, 73, 76–77, *77*, 92, *93–96*, 97, *98*, *99*, 188, 269, 636
Kubert, Joe, 454–55, *454*
Kudzu, 557, 576, *576*

Laas, William, *314*
Lady Bountiful, 144
Lady Luck, 293, 320
LaGuardia, Fiorello, 295
Lait, Jack, *142*
Lala Palooza, 72
Larson, Gary, 553, 562, *562*, 563, 614
Lasky, Mark, 557–58
Lasswell, Fred, 148, 291, *319*, 346, *349*, 393, *393*, 671
Latest News from Bugville, 50
Laugh-In, 465, *465*
Lawler, Will, 69–70
Lazarus, Mell, 409, 461, 466, *466*, 467, 501, 545, 671
LeBeck, Oskar, 424, *424*
Lebrun, Denis, *658*
Ledger Syndicate, 69, 176
Lee, Stan, 547, *547*
Lefevre, Pascal, 13
Leff, Mo, 367, 382
Leonard, Lank, *224*, 235
Lewis, T., *656*
Liberty Meadows, *614*, 615
Lichtenstein, George "Lichty", 464, *464*
Life, 9, 25, 30, 36, 280, 290
Life's Darkest Moments, 76
Life Sketches, 160
Li'l Abner, 189, 192, 254, *255–59*, 291, *296*, 346, 350, 353–54, 382, *382–87*, 404, 406, 411, 454, 455, 502, 671
Links, Marty, 389, *389*
Link, Stanley, 121, *126*, 188, *219*
Little Alby, *187*
Little Annie Rooney, 120, 219, *282*, 426, *426*
Little Bears, 9, 46, 47
Little Folks, *281*
Little Iodine, *318*
Little Jimmy, 23, 46, *48*, *49*, 73, 188, 269, 354
Little King, The, 192, *272*
Little Nemo in Slumberland, 22, *26*, 28, 56, 60, *61*, 62, 66, 73, 354
Little Orphan Annie, 116, *118*, 120, 121, *123*, *170–75*, 176, 185, 189, 280, 282, 289, 295, 350, 354, 376, *377*, 377, 406, 410, *410*, 426, *426*, 455, 502
Little Sammy Sneeze, 21, 26, 28, *59*
Lockhorns, The, 458, 483, *483*, 501, 558
London, Bobby, 604, *604*
Louie, 457
Luann, 557, 573, *573*, 612
Lubbers, Bob, 382
Luks, George B., 11, 14, *18*
Lulu and Leander, 21, *50*
Luther, 459, 493, *493*
Lynde, Stan, 422, *423*, 547, *547*

McBride, Clifford, *278*
McCall of the Wild, 582, *583*
McCardell, Roy, 7, 11, 13–14, 24
McCay, Winsor, 26–28, *26*, *35*, *56–61*, 62, 73, 354, 357, 412
McClure, Darrell, *282*, 426, *426*
McClure Syndicate, 22, 25, 55, 192
McCormick, Robert, 118, 130
McCoy, Glenn, *655*
McCoy, Wilson, 368, *368*, 463
McCutcheon, John, 76, 162
McDonnell, Patrick, 407, 608, *608*, 610, 636, *636–43*, 668

McDougall, Walt, 7, *115*
McEldowney, Brooke, *656*
McGill, Harold, Arthur, *83*
McGruder, Aaron, 613, *654*
McManus, George, 28, *54*, *62*, 70, 73–74, *74*, 78, *100–105*, 117, 128, 188, *350*, 352, 354, 392, *392*
McNamara, Tom, 72, 75, *82*, 92, *166*
McNaught Syndicate, 88, 89
McWilliams, Alden, 424, *424*, 459–60
Machamer, Jefferson, *253*
MacIntosh, Craig, 572, *572*
Mack, Ed, 78, 80
MacNelly, Jeff, 498–99, 518, *518–21*, *556*, 557, 576, 612, 644, *644*
Maeder, Jay, 226
Mager, Gus, 28, 72, *82*, *90*, *91*, 92
Maitland, Lester, 122, 237
Major Ozone, 25, *93*
Male Call, 291, *303*
Mallard Fillmore, 634, *634*
Mama's Angel Child, 106
Mandrake the Magician, 192, *217*, 368, *368*, 671
Marcus, Jerry, 459
Mark Trail, 502
Marlette, Doug, 576, *576*
Marmaduke, 459
Married Life, 148
Marriner, Billy, *55*
Marschall, Richard, 36, 77, 170
Marsh, Norman, *234*
Marsten, William Moulton, *306*
Martin, Edgar (Abe), *142*, *159*
Martin, Joe, 553, 563, *565*
Martinek, Frank V., *237*
Marvin, 557, 606, *606*
Mary Worth, 276, 291, *315*, 355–56, 381, *381*, 405, 406, 454, 502, 671
Matthews, E. C., 54
Mauldin, Bill, 290, 291, 296, *302*, 351
Maw Green, 128, *185*
Max and Mortiz, 10, 36
Maxon, Rex, 189
Meddick, Jim, 555, 699
Mendelsohn, Jack, *461*
Merely Margy, *114*, 120, *146*
Messick, Dale (Dalia), 293, *294*, *315*, 380, *380*
Messmer, Otto, 269
Metropolitan Movies, 184
Metropolitan Newspaper Service, 186, 189
Mickey Finn, 224, 235
Mickey Mouse, 73, 192, 269, *270*, *271*, 292
Midget Movies, 121, 238; See also Minute Movies
Mike and Ike–They Look Alike, 72, *88*
Miller, Frank, *298*
Miller, Jeff, 501, 546, *546*
Miller, Wiley, 614, 632, *632*
Mills, Tarpe, 293, *309*
Ming Foo, 219
Minute Movies, 121, *176*; See also Midget Movies
Miss Fury, 293, *309*
Miss Peach, 409, 455, 466, *466*, 467, 501, 671
Mixed Singles, 501, 542, *544*
Modest Maidens, 252
Modesty Blaise, 457
Momand, Pop, *127*
Momma, 466, 501, 542, *545*
Monk Family, 90
Montana, Bob, 355, *356*, 389, *389*
Moon Mullins, 54, *118*, 119–20, *154–57*, 189, 671
Moore, Don, 200
Moore, Ray, *216*
Moore, Steve, 644, *644*

Moores, Dick, 130, *232*, 502, 547, *547*, 558, 617, 670
Moose, 458, 484, *485*
Morty Meekle, 484, *485*
Mosley, Zack, 192, *221*, 290, 310
Mother Goose and Grimm, 557, 574, *574*, 575
Motley's Crew, 501, 542, *545*, 613
Mr. Boffo, 553, 563, *565*
Mr. Ex, 293
Mr. Jack, 23, 28, 46, *48*
Mr. Mystic, 293, 320
Mr. Twee Deedle, 28, *66*
Muggs and Skeeter, *281*
Muppets, The, 557, *557*, 582, 583
Murphy, John Cullen, 414, *414*, 415, 502, 548, 550
Murphy, Jimmy, 70, 75, *127*, *128*, 250
Musial, Joe, *351*
Mutt and Jeff, 28–29, 69, 70, *71*, 73, 78, 79–81, 116, 121, 154, 188, 342, *342*, 412, 671
Mutts, 347, 407, 608, 610, *610*, 636, *636–43*, 668
Myers, Russell, 500, 540, *540*
Myra North, Special Nurse, 237
Myrtle, 274

Nancy, 192, *284*, *285*, 289, 291, 354, 390, *390*, *391*, 406, 460, 557–58, 604, *604*, 609, 617, *618*, 671
Napoleon, 278
Nebbs, The, 120, 124, *127*
Neighborhood, The, 563, *564*
Neighbors, The, 287
New Breed, The, 560, 563, *565*
Newlyweds, The, 22, 70, 73, 74, 100, *101*
Newspaper Comics Council, 335, 671
Newspaper Enterprise Association, 69, 84, 158, 159, 178, 244, 251, 260, 267, 292
Newspaper Feature Syndicate, 69
New York American, 26, 29, 42, 71, 78, 83, 92, 244, 320
New York Daily News, 115, 118, 119, 294
New York Herald, 22, 25–26, 28, 30, 35, 66, 83, 136
New York Journal, 11, *14*, 21, 25–26, 30, 36, 42, 46, 70–71, 72, 84, 85, 86, 92, 119, 136, 144, 162
New York World, 7, 8, 10, 11, 13, 14, 21, 22, 24, 25, 30, 54, 62, 64, 70–71, 74, 100, 119, 178, 186, 187, 268
Nina's Adventures, 615
9 Chickweed Lane, 656
Nipper, 163, *165*
Nippie, 235
Nisby, the Newsboy, in Funny Fairyland, 28, 62, 74, 100
Non Sequitor, 614, 632, *632*
Norm, The, 634, *634*
North American Newspaper Alliance, 186
Nowlan, Phil, *214*, 215
Now Listen Mabel, 92

Oaky Doaks, 192, 260, *263*
Oh, Diana, 252, 293
Old Doc Yak, 108
Old Judge Rumhauser, 86
One Big Happy, 557, 576, *577*
O'Neill, Harry, *313*
O'Neill, Rose, 187, *279*, 293
On Stage, 405, 418, *418*, 419, 502, 548
On the Fast Track, 576, 577
Opper, Frederick, 9, 10, 12, *19*, 21, *22*, *42–45*, 50, 72–73, 121, 188, 354
Orr, Martha, 276, 294
Our Antediluvian Ancestors, *19*, 42
Our Boarding House, 84, *158*, *159*, 267
Our Secret Ambitions, 162

Outbursts of Everett True, The, 28, *83*
Outcault, Richard Felton, 6, 7–8, *7*, 9, 11–12, *12*, 13–15, *14*, *15–18*, 23, 25–26, *25*, 30–34, 35, 50, 73, 106, 238, 338–41, *338*, *339*, 354, 412, 613
Outdoor Sports, 72, *87*
Out Our Way, *158*, *159*, *163*, 180, *189*
Over the Hedge, 656
Ozark Ike, 367, *367*

Paine, Robert F., 158
Paley, Nina, *615*
Panhandle Pete, 74, 100
Parker, Brant, *473–75*, 501, 626
Parlor, Bedroom and Sink, 128, *153*
Partch, Virgil, 484, *484*
Pa's Son in Law, 75
Pastis, Stephan, *655*
Patterson, Joseph Medill, 75, 84, 115, 118–20, 188, 190, 208, 226, 294
Patton, George, 290
Paw, 144
Peanuts, 344, 406, 407, *407*, 408, 438, *438–45*, 452, 453, 454, 455, 457, 458, *459*, 612, 615–16, *616*
Pearls Before Swine, 655
Penny, 355, 484, *485*
Perry, Bill, 130
Peter, H. G., *306*
Peter Rabbit, 69, *110*
Peters, Mike, 574, *574*, 614
Pete the Tramp, 276
Petey, 144
Phantom, The, 192, *216*, 368, *368*, 463, *463*
Phil Fumble, 285
Phil Hardy, 121, 176
Pickles, 634, *635*
Piranha Club, 557, 596, *598*
Piraro, Dan, 553, 563, *563*
Plub, Charlie, *142*, *143*
Pluggers, 644, *644*
Pogo, 356–57, *357*, *394–401*, 395, *403*, 408, 454, 455, 458, 466, *496*, 502, 555, 671
Polly and Her Pals, 75, 124, 136, *137–39*, 188
Ponytail, 458, 484, *484*
Poor Arnold's Almanac, 409–10, 450, *450*
Popeye, 335, 354, 413, *413*, 465, *465*, 604, *604*; See also Thimble Theatre Starring Popeye
Pore Li'l Mose, 25
Positive Polly, 136
Post, Howie, 457, 478, *478*
Powers, T. E., *42*, 72
Prentice, John, 411, 420, *420*, 548
Press Publishing Company, 39, 187
Price, Hillary, 634, *634*
Prince Valiant, 13, 189–90, *194*, *195*, *198*, *199*, *334*, 354, 373, *373*, 406, 502, 548, *550*
Private Breger, 291, *305*
Professor Otto, 25
Professor Phumble, 384, *385*
Pulitzer, Joseph, 10, 11, 13, 14, 18, 21, 24, 30, 31, 36, 69, 70, 339–40, 342, 452

Quigmans, The, 553, 563, *565*
Quincy, 459, 493, *492*

Raab, Charles, 236, *314*
Radio Bugs, The, 115
Radio Patrol, 191, *232*
Raggedy Ann and Andy, 66, 273
Raymond, Alex, 190, 191, 192, *200–206*, 244, 290, 294, 310, 351, 354, 378, *378*, *379*, 405, 411, 420, 454, 548
Raymond, Jim, 402, *561*
Rechin, Bill, 501, *545*

Rectangle, The, 119, 130, 131
Red and Rover, 657
Red Barry, 191, 233
Redeye, 456, 480, 489
Red Ryder, 192, 224, 225, 422, 422
Register and Tribune Syndicate, 293, 320
Reg'lar Fellers, 73, 166, 167, 281
Reiner, John, 558
Rex Morgan M.D., 381, 381, 406, 454, 502, 558, 559
Rhoades, Fred, 290, 291
Rhymes With Orange, 634, 634
Rick O'Shay, 422, 423, 547, 547
Right Around Home, 274, 275
Rip Kirby, 200, 351, 355, 378, 378, 379, 405, 411, 420, 420
Ripley, Robert, 161
Ripley's Believe It or Not, 161
Robbins, Frank, 310, 366, 366
Robinson, Jerry, 456, 464, 464
Robinson, Paul, 142, 252
Robotman, 555, 599, 599
Rock Channel, 557, 583, 583
Rockwell, Richard, 360
Rogers, Gordon "Boody", 310
Rogers, William, 412
Romita, John, 547, 547
Room and Board, 267
Rose is Rose, 557, 578, 578–81, 584
Rosie's Beau, 105, 128
Ross, Charles, 9
Ross, Penny, 106
Roth, Arnold, 409, 450, 450
Rowlandson, Thomas, 9
Rube Goldberg's Slideshow, 72
Russell, C. D., 276
Rusty Riley, 426, 426
Ryan, Jack, 293
Ryan, Tom K., 456, 480, 480, 500

Saalburg, Charles, 7
Sad Sack, The, 290, 291, 304
Sagendorf, Bud, 238, 335, 465, 465
Salesman Sam, 158, 159, 319
Salinas, José-Luis, 432, 433
Sally Forth, 557, 572, 572
Sam and Silo, 429, 501, 542, 543
Sambo and His Funny Noises, 55
Sam's Strip, 345, 456, 457, 476, 476, 477, 501
San Francisco Chronicle, 28–29, 71, 78
San Francisco Examiner, 9, 11, 29, 46, 78
Sansom, Art, 458, 478, 478
Sansone, Leonard, 291
Sappo, 240
Saunders, Allen, 276, 315, 455, 381, 381, 405, 671
Saylor, Bob, 543
Scaduto, Al, 343
Scancarelli, Jim, 130, 617, 618
Schlensker, Hank, 374
Schmidt, Charlie, 232
Schneider, Howie, 556, 478, 478, 671
Schoenfeld, Amram, 117, 294
School Days, 76, 163, 165
Schorr, Bill, 657, 657, 476, 476
Schultze, Carl "Bunny", 25, 51
Schulz, Charles, 344, 347, 406, 407, 438, 438–45, 451, 452, 453, 459, 559, 560, 610, 615–16, 616
Scorchy Smith, 191, 207, 237, 290, 360, 366
Scott, Jerry, 558, 604, 604, 608, 609, 609, 610, 611, 617, 626, 626–31, 648, 648–53
Secret Agent Corrigan, 200, 554, 648, 648
Secret Agent X-9, 190, 191, 200, 201, 289, 378, 554, 648
Segar, Elzie Crisler, 73, 188, 191, 238,

239–43, 269, 354, 465
Seldes, Gilbert, 77, 118, 154
Sentinel Louie, 272
Shadow, The, 310
Shearer, Ted, 459, 459, 463, 464
Shenanigan Kids, The, 36, 40
Sherlocko the Monk, 82, 90, 91
Sherman's Lagoon, 634, 635
Sherwood, Don, 454
Shesol, Jeff, 614
Shoe, 498–99, 508, 518–21, 556, 576
Shuster, Joe, 306, 355, 355
Sickles, Noel, 191, 207, 208, 237, 290, 360
Siegel, Jerry, 306, 355, 355
Silk Hat Harry's Divorce Suit, 72, 73, 86
Silly Symphony, 270, 271
Sims, Tom, 188, 413, 413
Skeets, 283
Skippy, 280
Sky Masters, 424, 424
Skyroads, 122, 237
Slim Jim and the Force, 22, 109, 188
Slott, Mollie, 208, 292, 294
Small Fry (later Small Change), 289
small society, the, 456, 480, 481, 546
Smilin' Jack, 192, 221, 290, 291, 294, 310, 502
Smith, Al, 78, 671
Smith Sidney, 73, 75, 108, 116, 118–19, 120, 124–26, 127, 170, 188
Smitty, 118, 119, 120, 166, 169
Smokey Stover, 192, 264, 294, 493, 493
Smolderen, Thierry, 13
Smythe, Reg, 457, 482, 483
Snuffy Smith, 406, 671
Soglow, Otto, 192, 272
Somebody's Stenog, 119, 140
Soup to Nutz, 655
Spare Ribs and Gravy, 54, 74, 100
Sparky Watts, 310
Sparling, Jack, 314
Speed Bump, 644, 644
Spiegelman, Art, 136
Spirit, The, 293, 320–23
Splitsville, 501, 542, 544
Sporting Decision, A, 251
Sprang, Dick, 306
Squirrel Cage, The, 267
Stamm, Russell, 314
Star Company, 26, 39, 71
Starr, Leonard, 505, 418, 418, 419, 502, 548, 549, 560
Steinbeck, John, 254
Sterrett, Cliff, 56, 75, 128, 136–39, 144, 354
Steve Canyon, 208, 292–93, 352–53, 352, 355, 358, 360, 360–65, 366, 405, 406, 454, 502, 558, 671
Steve Roper, 405
Still Life, 456, 464, 464
Stone Soup, 657
Storm, George, 121, 176
Stromoski, Rick, 655
Stumble Inn, 92
Sullivan, Eddie, 232
Sullivan Pat, 269
Sunny Sue, 147
Superman, 122, 192, 193, 292, 295, 306, 307, 348, 355, 355
Swanson, George, 158, 159, 264, 319
Swinnerton, Jimmy, 9, 28, 46–49, 50, 72, 354

Tailspin Tommy, 122, 224
Tales of the Green Beret, 454–55, 454
Taliaferro, Al, 270
Tall Tales, 409–10, 450, 450
Tank McNamara, 501, 546, 546
Tarzan of the Apes, 13, 122, 186, 189, 190, 194, 196, 197, 200, 311, 372
Teena, 293, 355, 358

Teenie Weenies, 69, 111
Templeton, Ben, 501, 545, 613
Terry and the Pirates, 350, 352, 355, 359, 360, 366, 366, 405, 454, 455, 502, 522
Terry, Hilda, 293
Terry and the Pirates, 73, 116, 122, 190–91, 190, 208, 209–13, 289, 291, 292, 294–95, 295, 301, 303, 314
Texas Slim, 293
Thatch, 614
That Phoney Nickel, 128
Thaves, Bob, 501, 642, 642
Their Only Child, 74
They'll Do It Every Time, 183, 318, 343
Thimble Theatre Starring Popeye, 73, 188, 189, 191, 238, 239–43, 269, 289, 292; See also Popeye
Thompson, Ray, 237
Thrill That Comes Once in a Lifetime, The, 67, 76, 286
Thwaites, Ted, 271
Tiger, 458, 486, 486, 487
Tillie the Toiler, 29, 42, 120, 140, 189, 200, 250, 289, 300
Timid Soul, The, 76, 162
Tim Tyler's Luck, 122, 190, 200, 218, 234, 292, 301
Ting Ling Kids, The, 7
Tinsley, Bruce, 634, 634
Tiny Tim, 219
Tippie, 277
Tom Sawyer and Huck Finn, 163
Toomey, Jim, 634, 635
Toonerville Folks, 69, 76, 116, 163, 164, 188, 269
Toots and Casper, 70, 75, 124, 127, 128, 188, 250
Töpffer, Rodolphe, 9–10, 13
Travels with Farley, 546, 546
Trudeau, Garry, 344, 347, 456, 496–97, 505, 505–13, 554, 560, 560, 615, 659
Truth, 7, 8, 11, 30
Tufts, Warren, 422, 423
Tumbleweeds, 456, 480, 480, 500
Turner, Leslie, 292, 421, 421
Turner, Morrie, 458, 459, 493, 493
Tuthill, Harry, 75, 127, 129
Twin Earths, 424, 424

Uncle Wiggily's Adventures, 69
Unger, Jim, 501, 642, 642
United Feature Syndicate, 71, 186, 189, 254, 290, 291
Up Front, 290, 291, 302, 351
Upside Downs, 51
Us Boys, 75, 82, 166
Us Husbands, 92, 97

Van Amerongen, Jerry, 563, 564, 644, 644
Van Buren, Raeburn, 276, 380, 380
Van Swaggers, The, 250
Verbeck, Gustave, 51
Vesta West, 300
Voight, C. A., 144, 145

Wailing, Dow, 283
Walker, Brian, 619, 619, 644
Walker, Greg, 557, 583, 583, 619, 619, 658
Walker, Mort, 345, 406, 407, 429, 429–33, 434, 434–37, 456, 457, 457, 459, 501, 503–4, 543, 612, 626, 671
Walker Brothers, 557, 582, 583
Walsh, Brandon, 121, 126, 219, 282
Wash Tubbs, 121–22, 122, 159, 176, 178, 179–81, 292, 352, 374, 421
Watterson, Bill, 347, 504, 551, 553, 554–55, 554, 559, 559, 584, 584–91, 610, 614, 648

Waugh, Coulton, 7, 8
Waugh, Odin, 293
Weber, Bob, 458, 484, 485
Webster, H. T., 67, 76, 162, 178, 286
Weekly Meeting of the Tuesday's Ladies Club, 88
Wee Pals, 459, 493, 493
Wee Willie Winkie's World, 28, 63
Wellington, Charles, 75
Westover, Russ, 29, 42, 140, 200, 250, 289, 300
Wheelan, Ed, 121, 176, 238
Wheeler, Doug, 12–13
Wheeler Syndicate, 69, 71, 78, 163
When a Feller Needs a Friend, 76, 162
Where I'm Coming From, 633
Whitman, Bert, 293
Whittington, Larry, 144
Wilder, Don, 501, 545
Willard, Frank, 119–20, 154–57
Williams, Garr, 162
Williams, Gluyas, 163
Williams, Jay Jerome, 121
Williams, J. R., 158, 159, 162, 163, 180, 189
Williamson, Al, 454, 548, 548
Wilson, Tom, 500–1, 541, 541, 559
Windy Riley, 117
Wingert, Dick, 291
Winner, Doc, 188
Winnie Winkle the Breadwinner, 73, 118, 119, 120, 140, 141
Winthrop, 484
Wizard of Id, The, 409, 456, 473–75, 501, 626
Woggon, Elmer, 276
Wolf, The, 291
Wonder Woman, 306
Wonk City, 633
Wood, Wally, 405, 408, 424, 424
World Color Printing Company, 22, 109
World Feature Service, 186
Worman, Denys, 184
Wunder, George, 366, 454, 502

Yates, Bill, 484, 485, 500, 501
Yellow Kid, The, 6, 7–8, 7, 9, 11–12, 11, 12, 13–15, 14–18, 21, 30, 31–32, 34, 121, 295, 338, 338, 339, 339, 340–41, 343, 354, 412, 613
Young, Chic, 144, 191, 192, 200, 244–49, 253, 295, 354, 354, 402, 402, 406
Young, Dean, 561, 604, 658
Young, Lyman, 122, 190, 200, 218, 234, 301
Yronwode, Catherine, 320

Zaboly, Bela "Bill", 188, 413, 413
Zekley, Zeke, 74, 100, 392, 392
Zero Zero, 610
Ziggy, 500–501, 541, 541, 559
Zimmerman, Eugene, 9
Zippy the Pinhead, 346, 552, 555–56, 592–95, 612
Zits, 347, 584, 608, 610–11, 611, 626, 648, 648–53

GASOLINE ALLEY by Dick Moores. © 1978 Tribune Media Services. Courtesy of The Ohio State University Cartoon Library and Museum

POGO by Walt Kelly. © 1978 Okefenokee Glee & Perloo, Inc. Courtesy of The Ohio State University Cartoon Library and Museum

LIMITED-EDITION COMIC ART

In 1978, Harry N. Abrams collaborated with the Newspaper Comics Council to produce a series of limited-edition comic art prints by twenty of America's top cartoonists. A selection of these prints is shown on this spread and on pages 334 and 335. Also participating in the series were Al Capp (*Li'l Abner*), Howie Schneider (*Eek and Meek*), Lee Falk (*Mandrake the Magician*), Allen Saunders (*Mary Worth*), Ernie Bushmiller (*Nancy*), Johnny Hart (*B.C.*), V.T. Hamlin (*Alley Oop*), Milton Caniff (*Steve Canyon*), Mell Lazarus (*Miss Peach*), Chester Gould (*Dick Tracy*), Ferd Johnson (*Moon Mullins*), Al Smith (*Mutt & Jeff*), Fred Lasswell (*Snuffy Smith*), and Al Andriola (*Kerry Drake*).

BEETLE BAILEY by Mort Walker. © 1978 King Features Syndicate, Inc. Courtesy of The Ohio State University Cartoon Library and Museum

THE BASIC ELEMENTS—Special *MUTTS* page by Patrick McDonnell created for the anniversary of *The Comics Journal.* © 1997 Patrick McDonnell

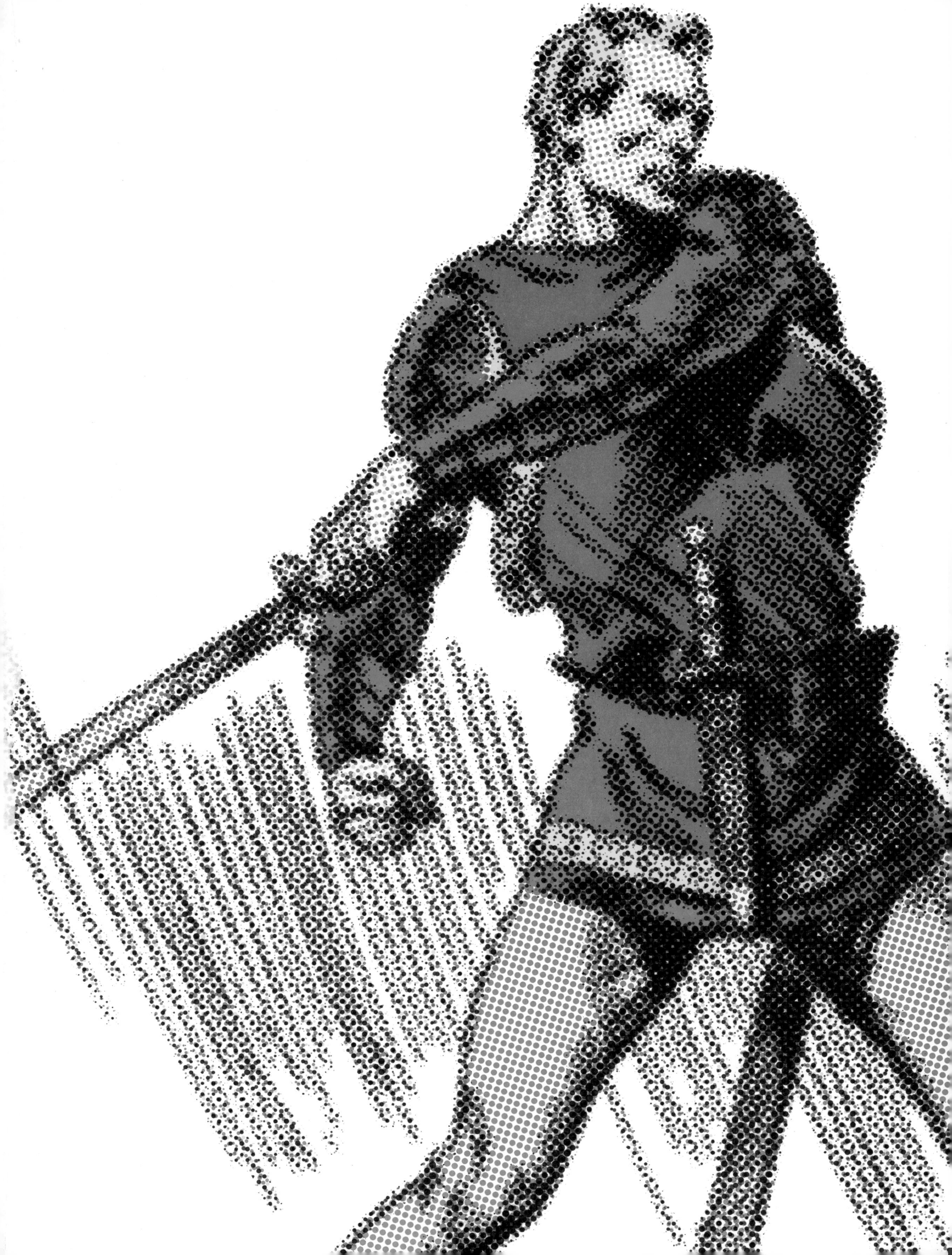

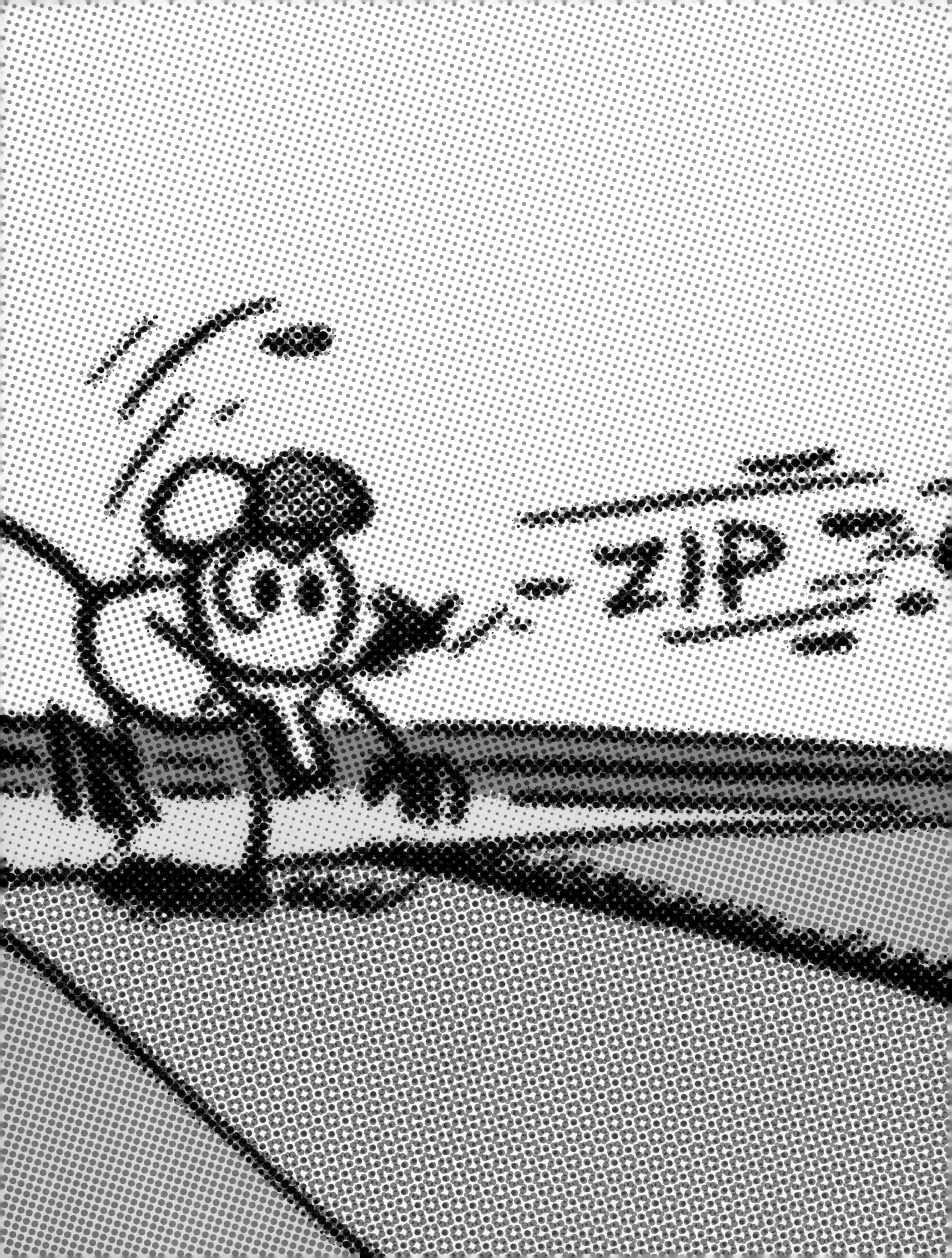
ZIP